# Medical Image Recognition, Segmentation and Parsing

## Machine Learning and Multiple Object Approaches

# The Elsevier and MICCAI Society Book Series

## Advisory board

# Medical Image Recognition, Segmentation and Parsing

## Machine Learning and Multiple Object Approaches

Edited by

**S. Kevin Zhou**

AMSTERDAM • BOSTON • HEIDELBERG • LONDON
NEW YORK • OXFORD • PARIS • SAN DIEGO
SAN FRANCISCO • SINGAPORE • SYDNEY • TOKYO

Academic Press is an imprint of Elsevier

Academic Press is an imprint of Elsevier
125 London Wall, London, EC2Y 5AS, UK
525 B Street, Suite 1800, San Diego, CA 92101-4495, USA
225 Wyman Street, Waltham, MA 02451, USA
The Boulevard, Langford Lane, Kidlington, Oxford OX5 1GB, UK

**Notices**

Knowledge and best practice in this field are constantly changing. As new research and experience broaden our understanding, changes in research methods, professional practices, or medical treatment may become necessary.

Practitioners and researchers must always rely on their own experience and knowledge in evaluating and using any information, methods, compounds, or experiments described herein. In using such information or methods they should be mindful of their own safety and the safety of others, including parties for whom they have a professional responsibility.

To the fullest extent of the law, neither the Publisher nor the authors, contributors, or editors, assume any liability for any injury and/or damage to persons or property as a matter of products liability, negligence or otherwise, or from any use or operation of any methods, products, instructions, or ideas contained in the material herein.

**British Library Cataloguing in Publication Data**
A catalogue record for this book is available from the British Library

**Library of Congress Cataloging-in-Publication Data**
A catalog record for this book is available from the Library of Congress

ISBN: 978-0-12-802581-9

For information on all Academic Press publications
visit our website at http://store.elsevier.com/

*Publisher*: Joe Hayton
*Acquisition Editor*: Tim Pitts
*Editorial Project Manager*: Charlotte Kent
*Production Project Manager*: Melissa Read
*Designer*: Matthew Limbert

Printed and bound in the USA

# Contents

# Foreword

Solving the problems of medical image segmentation, along with image registration, have long been thought of as the two basic touchstones of research in medical image analysis. The early work in these areas that began several decades ago often adapted techniques and strategies developed in the computer vision and pattern recognition communities to problems in medical imaging. However, over the past 20 years or so, researchers dedicated to working specifically in the area of medical image analysis have been able to articulate and identify many of the issues unique to this field in general, and medical image segmentation in particular. These ideas include noting the deformable nature of the underlying structures or regions to be segmented, the natural statistical variation of these structures/regions themselves and any parameters that might be derived from them (perhaps for use as biomarkers) and the notion that the typical medical image segmentation problem often involves knowledge of multiple structures/regions (sometimes thought of as objects) and/or the contextual information surrounding the segmentation problem at hand.

From an application's standpoint, the need for robust and accurate medical image segmentation runs through a significant range of problems that include the identification of multiple organs in the body for use in the development of patient atlases for rapid labeling of CT or MRI-derived information; finding brain neuroanatomy for guiding interventional procedures; parsing out the lungs and surrounding airways to monitor and treat lung disease; and isolating vessels, valves and chambers in the cardiovascular system for quantifying the extent of disease and polyp segmentation from CT colonoscopies to guide treatment procedures. This list is obviously much longer, and includes problems over a variety of imaging scales all the way to visualizing and capturing the signature of individual cells.

In *Medical Image Recognition, Segmentation and Parsing: Machine Learning and Multiple Objects Perspectives*, Dr. S. Kevin Zhou from Siemens Healthcare Technology Center has nicely captured the state-of-the-art in terms of current thinking in the medical image segmentation arena in 2015 that addresses many of the problems noted in the last paragraph. The book is logically divided into three sections, each capturing a current line of thinking in the field: (I) Automatic Recognition and Detection Algorithms, (II) Automatic Segmentation and Parsing Algorithms, and (III) Recognition, Segmentation and Parsing of Specific Objects. Within these general areas, a set of 21 chapters, written by many of the top researchers in this field, discuss strategies that nicely capture the key issues that are common either to a single application/problem or a set of medical image analysis problems and then develop modeling and decision-making approaches that capitalize on the latest thinking in the areas of machine learning to address them. The need for original thinking with regard to the computational strategies used to address these problems becomes clear as one reads through the text. Some of the most current state-of-the-art ideas in the field are reported and offer sometimes immediate and often very promising solutions, incorporating work based on discriminative learning, information theoretic scheduling, random forests, unsupervised deep learning, graph-based strategies, sparse representation/dictionary learning, marginal space learning and the latest thinking on deformable model representations. For practitioners and researchers working in this exciting field, which continues to be challenging, this text will become a "go-to" standard reference in the years ahead that can serve as a roadmap and a guide for further efforts.

**James S. Duncan, Ph.D.**
Yale University

# Acknowledgments

I am indebted to numerous people who made this book possible.

First, I thank all chapter authors who diligently finished their chapters and provided reviews on time and with quality, and Dr. Mingqing Chen of Siemens who reviewed a chapter.

My special thanks go to Prof. James Duncan from Yale University, who wrote the foreword for the book.

Further, I extend my gratitude to the best-ever Elsevier publisher team, especially my editor, Tim Pitts, editorial project manager, Charlotte Kent, and production project manager, Melissa Read who provided every help when needed and kept the book production on schedule.

I am grateful to all my past and current colleagues at Siemens Corporate Technology, including Dr. Dorin Comaniciu, Dr. Bogdan Georgescu, Dr. Zhuowen Tu, Dr. Jingdan Zhang, Dr. Yefeng Zheng, Dr. Michal Sofka, Dr. Shaolei Feng, Dr. Haibin Ling, Dr. Neil Birkbeck, Dr. Timo Kohlberger, Dr. Dirk Breitenreicher, Dr. David Liu, Dr. Jin-Hyeong Park, Dr. Dijia Wu, Dr. Nathan Lay, Dr. Le Lu, Dr. Adrian Barbu, Dr. Daguang Xu, etc., for the great teamwork and stimulating brainstorming. I also thanks many Siemens colleagues and clinical collaborators for their support.

Finally, I thank my wife, son, and parents for their endless love!

S. Kevin Zhou

# Contributors

**M.D. Abràmoff**
Iowa Institute for Biomedical Imaging, University of Iowa, Iowa City, IA, USA

**M.A. González Ballester**
Department of Information and Communication Technologies, Pompeu Fabra University, and Catalan Institution for Research and Advanced Studies, Barcelona, Spain

**A. Barbu**
Department of Statistics, Florida State University, Tallahassee, FL, USA

**N. Birkbeck**
Google, Mountain View, CA, USA

**H. Bogunović**
Iowa Institute for Biomedical Imaging, University of Iowa, Iowa City, IA, USA

**A. Carass**
Department of Electrical and Computer Engineering, The Johns Hopkins University, Baltimore, MD, USA

**M. Chen**
Computer Engineering Department, State University of New York, Albany, NY, USA

**D.J. Collins**
Cancer Research UK Cancer Imaging Centre, Institute of Cancer Research and Royal Marsden Hospital, London, United Kingdom

**D. Comaniciu**
Imaging and Computer Vision, Siemens Corporate Technology, Princeton, NJ, USA

**S. Doran**
Cancer Research UK Cancer Imaging Centre, Institute of Cancer Research and Royal Marsden Hospital, London, United Kingdom

**B. Georgescu**
Imaging and Computer Vision, Siemens Corporate Technology, Princeton, NJ, USA

**B. Glocker**
Biomedical Image Analysis Group, Imperial College London, London, United Kingdom

**S. Grbic**
Imaging and Computer Vision, Siemens Corporate Technology, Princeton, NJ, USA

**J. Feulner**
Giesecke & Devrient GmbH, Munich, Germany

**D.R. Haynor**
Department of Radiology, University of Washington, Seattle, WA, USA

**G. Hermosillo**
Siemens Medical Solutions USA, Inc., Malvern, PA, USA

**R. Ionasec**
Siemens Healthcare, Forchheim, Germany

**T. Kanade**
Robotics Institute, Carnegie Mellon University, Pittsburgh, PA, USA

**S. Kashyap**
Iowa Institute for Biomedical Imaging, University of Iowa, Iowa City, IA, USA

**B.M. Kelm**
Siemens Healthcare GmbH, Forchheim/Erlangen, Germany

**M. Kim**
Department of Radiology and BRIC, University of North Carolina at Chapel Hill, Chapel Hill, NC, USA

**A.P. Kiraly**
Siemens Corporate Technology, Princeton, NJ, USA

**E. Konukoglu**
Martinos Center for Biomedical Imaging, MGH, Harvard Medical School, Boston, MA, USA

**N. Lay**
Siemens Corporate Technology, Princeton, NJ, USA

**M.O. Leach**
Cancer Research UK Cancer Imaging Centre, Institute of Cancer Research and Royal Marsden Hospital, London, United Kingdom

**C. Ledig**
Department of Computing, Biomedical Image Analysis Group, Imperial College London, London, United Kingdom

**D. Liu**
Siemens Corporate Technology, Princeton, NJ, USA

**T. Mansi**
Imaging and Computer Vision, Siemens Corporate Technology, Princeton, NJ, USA

**D.N. Metaxas**
Department of Computer Science, Rutgers University, Piscataway, NJ, USA

**C.L. Novak**
Siemens Corporate Technology, Princeton, NJ, USA

**B.L. Odry**
Siemens Corporate Technology, Princeton, NJ, USA

**I. Oguz**
Iowa Institute for Biomedical Imaging, University of Iowa, Iowa City, IA, USA

**M. Orton**
Cancer Research UK Cancer Imaging Centre, Institute of Cancer Research and Royal Marsden Hospital, London, United Kingdom

**Z. Peng**
Siemens Medical Solutions USA, Inc., Malvern, PA, USA

**J.L. Prince**
Department of Electrical and Computer Engineering, The Johns Hopkins University, Baltimore, MD, USA

**D. Rueckert**
Department of Computing, Biomedical Image Analysis Group, Imperial College London, London, United Kingdom

**G. Sanroma**
Department of Radiology and BRIC, University of North Carolina at Chapel Hill, Chapel Hill, NC, USA, and Department of Information and Communication Technologies, Pompeu Fabra University, Barcelona, Spain

**D. Shen**
Department of Radiology and BRIC, University of North Carolina at Chapel Hill, Chapel Hill, NC, USA

**H.-C. Shin**
National Institutes of Health, Bethesda, MD, USA

**M. Sofka**
Security Business Group, Cisco Systems, and Department of Computer Science, Czech Technical University, Prague, Czech Republic

**M. Sonka**
Iowa Institute for Biomedical Imaging, University of Iowa, Iowa City, IA, USA

**R.M. Summers**
Imaging Biomarkers and Computer-Aided Diagnosis Laboratory and Clinical Image Processing Service, Radiology and Imaging Sciences Department, Clinical Center, National Institutes of Health, Bethesda, MD, USA

**I. Voigt**
Imaging and Computer Vision, Siemens Corporate Technology, Princeton, NJ, USA

**A. Wimmer**
Siemens Healthcare GmbH, Forchheim/Erlangen, Germany

**G. Wu**
Department of Radiology and BRIC, University of North Carolina at Chapel Hill, Chapel Hill, NC, USA

**X. Wu**
Iowa Institute for Biomedical Imaging, University of Iowa, Iowa City, IA, USA

**D. Xu**
Medical Imaging Technologies, Siemens Healthcare Technology Center, Princeton, NJ, USA

**D. Yang**
Rutgers, New Brunswick, NJ, USA

**J. Yao**
Imaging Biomarkers and Computer-Aided Diagnosis Laboratory and Clinical Image Processing Service, Radiology and Imaging Sciences Department, Clinical Center, National Institutes of Health, Bethesda, MD, USA

**Y. Zhan**
Computer-Aided Diagnosis and Therapy Research and Development, Siemens Healthcare, and Siemens Medical Solutions USA, Inc., Malvern, PA, USA

**S. Zhang**
Department of Computer Science, University of North Carolina at Charlotte, Charlotte, NC, USA

**Y. Zheng**
Imaging and Computer Vision, Siemens Corporate Technology, Princeton, NJ, USA

**S. Kevin Zhou**
Medical Imaging Technologies, Siemens Healthcare Technology Center, and Siemens Corporate Technology, Princeton, NJ, USA

**X.S. Zhou**
Siemens Medical Solutions USA, Inc., Malvern, PA, USA

# INTRODUCTION TO MEDICAL IMAGE RECOGNITION, SEGMENTATION, AND PARSING

# 1

### S. Kevin Zhou
*Medical Imaging Technologies, Siemens Healthcare Technology Center, Princeton, NJ, USA*

## CHAPTER OUTLINE

## 1.1 INTRODUCTION

Medical image recognition, segmentation, and parsing are essential topics of medical image analysis. Medical image recognition is about recognizing which objects are inside a medical image. In principle, it is not necessary to detect or localize the objects for object recognition; but in practice, often it is beneficial to associate object recognition with object detection or localization. Once the object is recognized or detected using, say, a bounding box, medical image segmentation further concerns finding the exact boundary of the object in a medical image. When there are multiple objects in the images, segmentation of multiple objects becomes medical image parsing that, in the most general form, assigns semantic labels to pixels in a 2D image or voxels in a 3D volume. By grouping the pixels or voxels with the same label, segmentation is realized.

Effective and efficient methods for medical image recognition, segmentation, and parsing bring a multitude of important clinical benefits. Below, we highlight the benefits to imaging scanner, image reading, and advanced quantification and modeling.

- *Scanner.* Because the computer tomography (CT) or magnetic resonance imaging (MRI) scanner is equipped with many configuration possibilities or imaging protocols, it is challenging to produce consistent and reproducible images of high quality across patients and this is only possible if the scanning is personalized with respect to a patient. High scanning throughput is also of interest for cost saving. Protecting patients from unnecessary radiation from the CT scanner is of major concern. An ideal diagnostic CT scan should be personalized to image only the target region of a given patient, no more (to reduce dose) or no less (to avoid missing information). Therefore, efficient detection of organs from a scout image enables personalized scanning at a reduced dose, saves exam time and cost, and increases consistency and reproducibility of the exam.
- *Image reading for diagnosis, therapy, and surgery planning.* During image reading, when searching for disease in a specific organ or body region, a radiologist needs to navigate the volume to the right location. Further, after certain disease is found, he or she needs to report the finding. Medical image parsing enables structured reading and reporting for a streamlined work flow, thereby improving image reading outcome in terms of accuracy, reproducibility, and efficiency. Finally, in radiation therapy, intervention procedures, and orthopedic surgery, medical image parsing is prerequisite in the planning phase.
- *Advanced quantification and modeling.* Clinical measurements such as organ volumes are important for quantitative disease diagnosis. But it is time-consuming for a physician to identify the target object especially in 3D and perform quantitative measurements without the aid of an intelligent postprocessing software system. Automatic image parsing also overcomes the difficulty in reproducing the measurement even when reading the same image for the second time. Finally, with 3D objects segmented as boundary conditions, more advanced modeling that simulates biomechanical or hemodynamical processes is feasible.

The holy grail of a medical image parsing system is that its parsing complexity matches that of Foundational Model of Anatomy (FMA) ontology,[a] which is concerned with the representation of classes or types and relationships necessary for the symbolic representation of the phenotypic structure of the human body in a form that is understandable to humans and is also navigable, parsable, and interpretable by machine-based systems. As one of the largest computer-based knowledge sources in the biomedical sciences, it contains approximately 75,000 classes and over 120,000 terms, and over 2.1 million relationship instances from over 168 relationship types that link the FMA classes into a coherent symbolic model. A less complex representation is Terminologica Anatomica,[b] which is the international standard of human anatomic terminology for about 7500 human gross (macroscopic) anatomical structures.

Current medical image recognition, segmentation, and parsing methods are far behind the holy grail, concerning mostly the following semantic objects:

- *Anatomical landmarks.* An anatomical landmark is a distinct point in a body scan that coincides with anatomical structures, such as liver top, aortic arch, pubis symphysis, to name a few.
- *Major organs.* Examples of major organs include liver, lungs, kidneys, spleen, prostate, bladder, rectum, etc.
- *Major bones.* Examples of major bones include ribs, vertebrae, pelvis, femur, tibia, fibula, skull, mandible, hand and foot bones, etc.
- *Lesions, nodules, and nodes.* Examples include liver and kidney lesions, lung nodules, lymph nodes, etc.

## 1.2 CHALLENGES AND OPPORTUNITIES

Medical image recognition, segmentation, and parsing confront a lot of challenges to obtain results that can be used in clinical applications. The main challenge is that anatomical objects exhibit *significant shape and appearance variations* caused by a multitude of factors:

- *Sensor noise/artifact.* As in any sensor, medical equipment generates noise/artifact inherent to its own physical sensor and image formation process. The extent of the artifact depends on image modality and imaging configuration. For example, while high-dose CT produces images with fewer artifacts, low-dose CT is quite noisy. Also, metal objects (such as implants) can generate a lot of artifacts in CT. In MRI scans, artifacts are generated due to inhomogeneous magnetic field, gradient nonlinearity, etc.
- *Patient difference and motion.* Different patients exhibit different build forms: fat or slim, tall or short, adult or child, etc. As a result, the anatomical structures also exhibit different shapes. Also, patients undergo motions from respiration, cardiac cycle, blood and cerebrospinal fluid flow, peristalsis and swallowing, and voluntary movement, all contributing to the creation of different images, causing anatomical shape deformation.
- *Pathology, surgery, and contrast agents.* Pathology can give rise to highly deformed anatomical structures or even missing ones with varying appearances and shapes. This makes statistical modeling very difficult. To better understand the pathological conditions, contrast agents are utilized to better visualize the anatomical morphology. Image appearances under different contrast phases are different. Finally, a surgical resection completely changes the shape and image appearance of anatomical object(s) in an unexpected manner.
- *Partial scan and field of view.* Dose radiation is a major concern in CT. In an effort to minimize the dose radiation, only the necessary part of the human is imaged. This creates partial scans and narrow field of view, in which the anatomical context is highly weakened or totally gone. As a result, the landmarks or organs are missing or partially visible. In MRI, the scan range is often minimized for fast acquisition.
- *Soft tissue.* Anatomical structures such as internal organs are soft tissues with similar properties. They (such as liver and kidney) might even touch each other, forming a very weak boundary between them. But, it is a must that the segmented organs be nonoverlapping.

Figure 1.1(a) shows 3D CT scans with different sources of appearance variation and Figure 1.1(b) displays CT examples of various pathologies and conditions associated with a knee joint.

Another challenge lies in stringent *accuracy, robustness, and speed* requirements arising from real clinical applications. Image reading and diagnosis allow almost no room for mistakes. Despite the high accuracy and robustness requirements, the demand for speedy processing does not diminish. A speedy work flow is crucial to any radiology lab that strives for high throughput. Few radiologists or physicians can wait for hours or even minutes to obtain the analysis results.

To build effective and efficient algorithms to tackle these challenges, one has to exploit the opportunities with leverage. There are two main opportunities:

- *Large database.* There is a deluge of medical scans. Take CT scans, for example. In 2005, approximately 57 million individuals in the USA received CT exams. By 2012, the number of annual CT exams rose to over 85 million.[c] The hypothesis that a large database exhibits the appearance variations commonly found in patients is statistically significant.
- *Anatomical context.* Unlike natural scene images, medical images manifest strong contextual information, such as a limited number of anatomical objects (say only one left ventricle), constrained and structured background, the relationship between different anatomies, strong prior information about the pose parameter, etc.

In light of these opportunities, statistical machine learning methods that exploit such contextual information exemplified by a large number of data sets are highly desired. This whole book is dedicated to approaches based on machine learning. It also covers approaches that cope with multiple objects.

## 1.3 ROUGH-TO-EXACT OBJECT REPRESENTATION

Any intelligent system starts from a sensible knowledge representation (KR). The most fundamental role that a KR plays (Davis et al., 1993) is that "it is a surrogate, a substitute for the thing itself. This leads to the so-called fidelity question: how close is the surrogate to the real thing? The only completely accurate representation of an object is the object itself. All other representations are inaccurate; they inevitably contain simplifying assumptions and possibly artifacts."

In the literature, there are many representations that approximate a medical object or anatomical structure using different simplifying assumptions. Figure 1.2 shows a variety of shape representations commonly used in the literature.[d]

- *Rigid representation.* The simplest representation is to translate a template to the object center $\mathbf{t} = [t_x, t_y, t_z]$ as shown in Figure 1.2(a). In other words, only the object center is considered. A complete rigid representation in Figure 1.2(b) consists of translation, rotation, and scale parameters $\theta = [\mathbf{t}, \mathbf{r}, \mathbf{s}]$. When the scale parameter is isotropic, this reduces to a similarity transformation. An extension of rigid representation is affine representation.
- *Free-form representation.* Common free-form representations, shown in Figure 1.2(c-e), include point-based presentation (2D curve $\mathcal{S}$ or 3D mesh $\mathcal{M}$), mask function $\phi(x, y, z)$, level set function $\phi(x, y, z)$, etc.

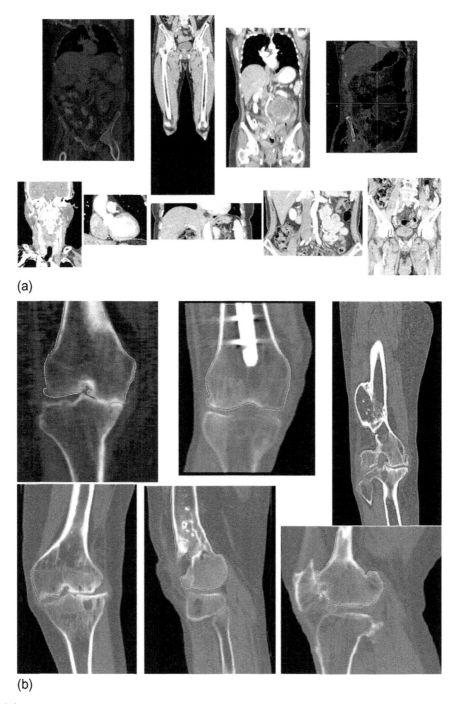

(a)

(b)

**FIGURE 1.1**

(a) Example of CT images with different body regions, severe pathologies, contrast agents, weak contrast, etc. (b) Example of CT images with various knee pathologies and conditions. From left to right, top to bottom: Touch between femur and tibia, metallic implant inside femur, femur with major defects, osteoporosis, osteoporosis with minor femur defects, and touch between femur and patella.

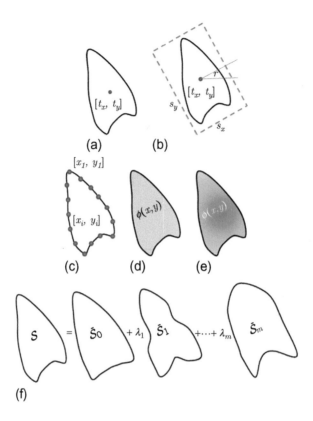

**FIGURE 1.2**

A graphical illustration of different shape representations using 2D shape as an example. (a) Rigid representation: translation only $\mathbf{t} = [t_x, t_y]$. (b) Rigid representation: $\theta = [t_x, t_y, r, s_x, s_y]$. (c) Free-form representation: $\mathcal{S} = [x_1, y_1, \ldots, x_n, y_n]$. (d) Free-form representation: a 2D binary mask function $\phi(x, y)$. (e) Free-form representation: a 2D real-valued level set function $\phi(x, y)$ (only the interior part is displayed). (f) Low-dimensional parametric representation: PCA projection $\mathcal{S} = \bar{\mathcal{S}}_0 + \sum_{m=1}^{M} \lambda_m \bar{\mathcal{S}}_m$.

- *Low-dimensional parametric representation.* The so-called statistical shape model (SSM) (Heimann and Meinzer, 2009) shown in Figure 1.2(f) is a common low-dimensional parametric representation based on principal component analysis (PCA) of a point-based free-form shape. Other low-dimensional parametric representations include M-rep (Pizer et al., 2003), spherical harmonics (SPHARM) (Shen et al., 2009), spherical wavelets (Nain et al., 2006), etc.

A KR also is a medium for pragmatically efficient computation (Davis et al., 1993). Therefore, it is beneficial to adopt a hierarchical, *rough-to-exact* representation that gradually approximates the object itself with increasing precision, which also makes computational reasoning more amenable and efficient as shown later.

A common rough-to-exact 3D object representation (Zheng et al., 2008; Zhou, 2010; Kohlberger et al., 2011; Wu et al., 2014) consists of a rigid part fully specified by translation, rotation, and scale parameters $\theta = [\mathbf{t}, \mathbf{r}, \mathbf{s}]$, a low-dimensional parametric part such as from the PCA shape space specified by the top PCA coefficients $\lambda = [\lambda_{1:m}]$ and a free-form nonrigid part such as a 3D shape $\mathcal{S}$, a 3D mesh $\mathcal{M}$, or a 3D mask or level set function $\phi$.

$$\mathbf{O} = [\mathbf{t}, \mathbf{r}, \mathbf{s}; \lambda_{1:m}; \mathcal{S}] = [\theta; \lambda; \mathcal{S}]; \quad \mathbf{O} = [\theta; \lambda; \mathcal{M}]; \quad \mathbf{O} = [\theta; \lambda; \phi] \tag{1.1}$$

The PCA shape space characterizes a shape by a linear projection:

$$\mathcal{S} = \bar{\mathcal{S}}_0 + \sum_{m=1}^{M} \lambda_m \bar{\mathcal{S}}_m \tag{1.2}$$

where $\bar{\mathcal{S}}_0$ is the mean shape and $\bar{\mathcal{S}}_m$ is the $m$th top eigen shape. This PCA shape modeling forms the basis of the famous active shape model (ASM) (Cootes et al., 1995). In this hierarchical representation, the free-form part can be rough-to-exact too. For a 3D mesh, the mesh vertex density can be a control parameter, from sparse to dense. For a level set function, it depends on the image resolution, from coarse to fine.

## 1.4 SIMPLE-TO-COMPLEX PROBABILISTIC MODELING

To handle a single object $\mathbf{O}$ from a 3D volume $\mathbf{V}$, the posterior distribution $P(\mathbf{O}|\mathbf{V})$ offers the complete characterization of the object $\mathbf{O}$ given the volume $\mathbf{V}$. Once $P(\mathbf{O}|\mathbf{V})$ is known, inferring the object can be done by taking the conditional mean, which is the minimum mean square error estimator, or conditional mode, which is the maximum a posteriori estimator, or a function of the posterior. By the same token, the posterior distribution $P(\mathbf{O}_{1:n}|\mathbf{V})$ completely characterizes the multiple objects $\mathbf{O}_{1:n}$ in a statistical sense.

### 1.4.1 CHAIN RULE

When the rough-to-exact representation for a single object $\mathbf{O}$ is used, joint modeling of the full object is challenging and often less effective. To tackle this challenge, a common strategy is to perform simple-to-complex modeling by breaking a complex task into a few simple tasks. For each simple task, effective modeling is more feasible.

One way is to utilize the chain rule that permits the calculation of a joint probability using conditional probabilities.

$$P(\mathbf{O}|\mathbf{V}) = P(\theta, \lambda, \mathcal{S}|\mathbf{V}) = P(\theta|\mathbf{V})P(\lambda|\mathbf{V}, \theta)P(\mathcal{S}|\mathbf{V}, \theta, \lambda) \tag{1.3}$$

This breaks the overall task into three simpler tasks. The first task is to infer the rigid object, also known as object detection or recognition, using $P(\theta|\mathbf{V})$; the second task is to infer both the rigid and low-dimensional shape model parameters using $P(\lambda|\mathbf{V}, \theta)$; and the last is full object inference using $P(\mathcal{S}|\mathbf{V}, \theta, \lambda)$, solving the segmentation problem.

In fact, for a single object $\mathbf{O}$, effective modeling of its 3D pose part alone $\theta = [\mathbf{t}, \mathbf{r}, \mathbf{s}]$ is difficult. The simple-to-complex modeling is applied here too.

$$P(\theta|\mathbf{V}) = P(\mathbf{t}|\mathbf{V})P(\mathbf{r}|\mathbf{V}, \mathbf{t})P(\mathbf{s}|\mathbf{V}, \mathbf{t}, \mathbf{r}) \tag{1.4}$$

Marginal space learning (MSL) (Zheng et al., 2008) leverages such a strategy.

When dealing with multiple objects $\mathbf{O}_{1:n}$, the chain rule also applies.

$$P(\mathbf{O}_{1:n}|\mathbf{V}) = P(\mathbf{O}_1|\mathbf{V})P(\mathbf{O}_2|\mathbf{V}, \mathbf{O}_1), \dots, P(\mathbf{O}_n|\mathbf{V}, \mathbf{O}_{1:n-1}) \qquad (1.5)$$

In Eq. (1.5), each conditional probability spells a simpler task, which can be further decomposed using Eqs. (1.3) and (1.4). Integrating Eqs. (1.3)–(1.5) endows a general-purpose computational pipeline as shown in Figure 1.3(a), in which a series of simple tasks are connected.

## 1.4.2 BAYES' RULE AND THE EQUIVALENCE OF PROBABILISTIC MODELING AND ENERGY-BASED METHOD

According to the Bayes' rule, the posterior probability $P(\mathbf{O}|\mathbf{V})$ is proportional to the product of the likelihood $P(\mathbf{V}|\mathbf{O})$ and the prior $P(\mathbf{O})$,

$$P(\mathbf{O}|\mathbf{V}) \propto P(\mathbf{V}|\mathbf{O})P(\mathbf{O}) \qquad (1.6)$$

Energy-based methods (Mumford and Shah, 1989; Chan and Vese, 2001) often minimize an energy function $\mathcal{E}(\mathbf{O}; \mathbf{V})$, consisting of two parts. The first energy function $\mathcal{E}_1(\mathbf{O}; \mathbf{V})$ relates the image $\mathbf{V}$ with the object $\mathbf{O}$ and the second energy function $\mathcal{E}_2(\mathbf{O})$ represents the prior belief about the object.

$$\mathcal{E}(\mathbf{O}; \mathbf{V}) = \mathcal{E}_1(\mathbf{O}; \mathbf{V}) + \mathcal{E}_2(\mathbf{O}) \qquad (1.7)$$

By letting

$$\mathcal{E}(\mathbf{O}; \mathbf{V}) = -\log P(\mathbf{O}|\mathbf{V}); \quad \mathcal{E}_1(\mathbf{O}; \mathbf{V}) = -\log P(\mathbf{V}|\mathbf{O}); \quad \mathcal{E}_2(\mathbf{O}) = -\log P(\mathbf{O})$$

then the probabilistic model is equivalent to the energy-based method. In the previous discussion, we use the whole object $\mathbf{O}$ for illustration, but the derivations hold even when a partial object representation is used.

When this Bayes' rule is integrated into the chain rule, complete modeling of object appearances and prior beliefs about the object at different representation levels and using different models is provided.

## 1.4.3 PRACTICAL MEDICAL IMAGE RECOGNITION, SEGMENTATION, AND PARSING ALGORITHMS

In general, practical algorithms for medical image recognition, segmentation, and parsing are special examples of this computational pipeline. They, however, differ depending on their specialization in the following two aspects:

- *The changes to the computational architecture.* Depending on independence assumptions they make or the representation they choose, practical algorithms modify or simplify the architecture accordingly. For example, if detecting only one object is concerned, the pipeline reduces to the one shown in Figure 1.3(b). Figure 1.3(c) shows the MSL pipeline (Zheng et al., 2008) for 3D rigid object detection. In Figure 1.3(d), a complete pipeline for segmenting a single object is presented, going from detecting or recognizing the rigid part, to deformable shape segmentation, to the freeform shape segmentation. Figure 1.3(e) presents an architecture that deals with multiple

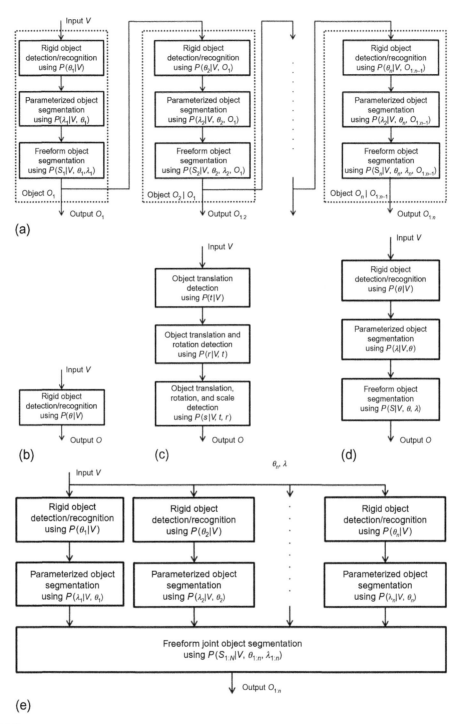

**FIGURE 1.3**

(a) A general-purpose computational pipeline for medical image recognition, segmentation, and parsing based on rough-to-exact object representation and simple-to-complex modeling. (b-e) Special realizations of the computational pipeline.

objects, which is used in Kohlberger et al. (2011), Lu et al. (2012), and Wu et al. (2014). Here, the conditional dependency among different objects is assumed for the rigid and low-dimensional parametric parts; hence each object is processed independently. Finally, the joint freeform segmentation is applied for segmenting multiple shapes together.

- *The modeling choices of the conditional probabilities.* Good algorithm performance needs effective modeling of the conditional probabilities. For medical image recognition or detection, machine learning methods are prevalent to leverage anatomic context embedded in the medical images. Section 1.5 defines the concept of anatomic context and briefly reviews several machine learning methods that model the anatomic context. After object detection, object segmentation follows. Section 1.6 lists a few classical image segmentation methods, each having its own modeling choice based on its particular object representation. Throughout the whole book, each book chapter will discuss its own choices of modeling, either from a general theoretic perspective or in a particular application setting.

## 1.5 MEDICAL IMAGE RECOGNITION USING MACHINE LEARNING METHODS
### 1.5.1 OBJECT DETECTION AND CONTEXT

Consider the task of detecting human eyes from the three images in Figure 1.4. To detect the human eye(s) in Figure 1.4(a) in which all different objects are juxtaposed randomly, one is likely to scrutinize the image pixels row by row, column by column till the eye is located. However, to detect the eye(s) in Figure 1.4(c) in which a perfect human face is presented, it is effortless because the image is so structured or full of context. A medical image is the kind of image with contextual information with respect to anatomies. Such context is referred to as *anatomical context*. To detect the two eyes in Figure 1.4(b), the relationship between them can be useful. Once, say, the left eye is detected, the detection of the right eye becomes less complicated.

As shown in Figure 1.4, the context can be roughly categorized into three types, namely *unitary or local*, *pairwise or higher-order*, and *holistic or global* context.

- The *unitary or local context* refers to the local regularity surrounding a single object.
- The *pairwise or higher-order context* refers to the joint regularities between two objects or among multiple objects.
- The *holistic or global context* goes beyond the relationships among a cohort of objects and refers to the whole relationship between all pixels/voxels and the objects: in other words, regarding the image as a whole.

Different detection methods basically operate with different trade-offs between offline model learning complexity and online computational complexity, depending on *how to leverage which context(s)*. For example, a binary classifier that separates the object instances from nonobject instances is learned to model the local context. Given a test image like Figure 1.4(a), exhaustive scanning of the image using the learned classifier is needed to localize the object (eye). To leverage the global context, a regression function can be learned to predict the object location directly from any pixel. Given a test image like Figure 1.4(c), the regression function is used for a few sparsely sampled pixel locations to reach a consensus prediction decision about the object location. Learning a binary classifier is easier

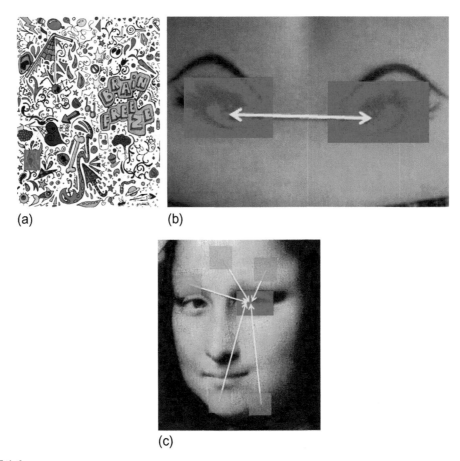

(a)    (b)

(c)

**FIGURE 1.4**

Three types of context: (a) unitary or local context; (b) pairwise or higher-order context; and (c) holistic or global context.

than a regression function, but exhaustive scanning is more computationally intensive than testing a few locations. Below, we review several modern machine learning methods for binary classification, multi-class classification, and regression. The subsequent book chapters present different recognition methods that employ machine learning.

## 1.5.2 MACHINE LEARNING METHODS

Statistical machine learning models the statistical dependence of an unobserved variable $y$ on an observed variable $x$ via the posterior probability distribution $P(y|x)$. Such a distribution can be used to predict the unobserved variable $y$. Modeling $P(y|x)$ can be done in two ways, namely discriminative learning and generative learning. While generative learning models $P(y|x)$ indirectly via the joint distribution $P(x, y)$, discriminative learning instead directly models the posterior. Discriminative models are effective for supervised learning tasks such as classification and regression that do not necessarily require the joint distribution.

### 1.5.2.1 Classification

The goal of binary classification is to learn a function $F(x)$ that minimizes the misclassification probability $P\{yF(x) < 0\}$, where $y$ is the class label with $+1$ for positive and $-1$ for negative. There are many influential binary classification methods such as kernel methods (Hofmann et al., 2008), ensemble methods (Polikar, 2006), and deep learning methods (Bengio, 2009). Support vector machine (SVM) (Vapnik, 1999) is a classical kernel method. Ensemble methods include boosting (Freund and Schapire, 1997; Friedman et al., 2000) and random forest (RF) (Breiman, 2001). Deep learning methods are based on artificial neural networks (ANNs) (Bishop and et al., 1995).

SVM seeks a separating hyperplane with a maximum margin. As shown in Figure 1.5(a), the hyperplane is defined as $w \cdot x + b$, where $x$ is the input vector, $w$ is the slope vector, "$\cdot$" means the dot product, and $b$ is the intercept. The max-margin plane is obtained by solving the following task:

$$\arg\min_{w,b} \max_{\alpha_i} \left\{ \frac{1}{2}\|w\|^2 - \sum_i \alpha_i[y_i(w \cdot x_i + b) - 1] \right\} \tag{1.8}$$

The solution is $F(x) = \sum_j \alpha_j y_j(x_j \cdot x) + b$, where $x_j$s are support vectors. Often the number of support vectors is much smaller than that of input training data. The kernel trick $K(x_j, x) = \phi(x_i) \cdot \phi(x)$ is widely used to model data nonlinearity, hence the name *kernel method*.

An ensemble method combines multiple learners into a committee for final decision. In boosting (Freund and Schapire, 1997; Friedman et al., 2000), instead of minimizing the misclassification probability, it minimizes its upper bound $E\{\exp(yF(x))\}$ as

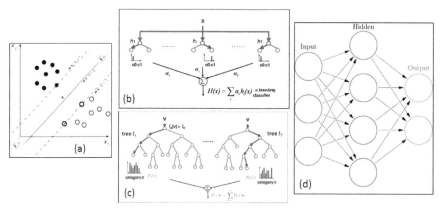

**FIGURE 1.5**

Binary classification methods: (a) support vector machine, (b) AdaBoosting, (c) random forest, and (d) neural network. Image courtesy of Wiki for (a, d) and of ICCV 2009 tutorial entitled "Boosting and random forest" for (b, c).

$$P\{yF(x) < 0\} \le E\{\exp(yF(x))\} \tag{1.9}$$

The classification function $F(x)$ in boosting takes an additive form as in Figure 1.5(b):

$$F_n(x) = F_{n-1}(x) + f_n(x) = \sum_{m=1}^{n} \alpha_m h_m(x) \tag{1.10}$$

where $F_n(x)$ is a strong learner that is well correlated with the true classification and $h_m(x)$ is a weak learner that is only slightly correlated with the true classification (better than random guessing). This minimization is done iteratively. At the $n$th iteration, it selects the minimizing weak learner $h_n(x)$ and then adjusts the weights for training examples, weighing more on misclassified examples. The posterior $P(+1|x)$ is approximated as

$$P(+1|x) = \frac{1}{1 + \exp(-2F(x))} \tag{1.11}$$

The RF (Breiman, 2001) classifier consists of a collection of binary classifiers as in Figure 1.5(c), each being a decision tree casting a unit vote for the most popular class label. To learn a "random" decision tree, either the training examples for each decision tree are independent, identically distributed (i.i.d.) sampled from the full training set or the features used in the tree nodes are i.i.d. sampled from the full feature set or both. It is shown in Breiman (2001) that the RF accuracy is comparable to boosting with the added benefits of being relatively robust to outliers and noise and amenable to parallel implementation.

When these ensemble methods are applied to image applications, the weak learners in boosting are associated with image features (Viola and Jones, 2001; Tu, 2005) and the decision tree in RF (Criminisi et al., 2009) uses an image feature in a tree node. Often a highly redundant feature pool is formed to cover large appearance variation in the object. Learning the weak learner or the decision tree hence becomes a *feature selection* process.

An ANN consists of an interconnected group of nodes as shown in Figure 1.5(d), each circular node representing a neuron and an arrow representing a connection from the output of one neuron to the input of another. A deep learning method concerns an ANN with multiple hidden layers. Often a neuron takes the following form $\sigma(w \cdot x + b)$, where $x$ is the input vector to the neuron, $y$ is the output of the neuron, $w$ is the weight vector, $b$ is the bias term, and $\sigma$ is a nonlinear function such as a sigmoid function. The final output from the ANN (say with one hidden layer and one node in the output layer) is

$$F(x) = \sigma\left(\sum_h \alpha_h \sigma(w_h \cdot x + b) + c\right) \tag{1.12}$$

where $w_h$ is the weight vector for the input vector to the node $h$ in the hidden layer, $\alpha_h$ is the weight coefficient from the hidden node $h$ to the output node. Typically, the weights for all neurons are learned using stochastic gradient descent. Since combining the input using weighted linear coefficients amounts to feature computation, ANN training performs feature learning.

The goal of multi-class classification is to classify an input $x$ into one of $J > 2$ class labels. The LogitBoost algorithm (Friedman et al., 2000) fits an additive symmetric logistic model via the maximum-likelihood principle. This fitting proceeds iteratively by selecting weak learners and combining them into a strong classifier. The output of the LogitBoost algorithm is a set of $J$ response functions $\{F^j(x); j = 1, \ldots, J\}$, where each $F^j(x)$ is a linear combination of a subset of weak learners:

$$F_n^j(x) = F_{n-1}^j(x) + f_n^j(x) = \sum_{m=1}^{n} f_m^j(x) \tag{1.13}$$

where $f_m^j(x)$ is a weak learner and $n$ is the number of weak learners. "LogitBoost" provides a natural way to calculate the posterior distribution of class label:

$$P(j|x) = \frac{\exp(F^j(x))}{\sum_{k=1}^{J} \exp(F^k(x))} \tag{1.14}$$

To use the LogitBoost for image classification, the weak classifiers are associated with image features. Refer to Zhou et al. (2006) for more details.

### 1.5.2.2 Regression

Regression (Hastie et al., 2001) finds the solution to the following minimizing problem:

$$\hat{g}(x) = \arg\min_{g} \frac{1}{N} \sum_{n=1}^{N} L(y_n, g(x_n)) + \lambda K(g) \tag{1.15}$$

where $\{(x_n, y_n)\}_{n=1}^{N}$ are training examples, $L(\circ, \circ)$ is the loss function that penalizes the deviation of the regressor output $g(x)$ from the true output $y$, $\lambda > 0$ is the *regularization coefficient* that controls the degree of regularization, and $K(g)$ is the regularization term that combats overfitting. Regularization often imposes a certain smoothness constraint on the output function or reflects some prior belief about the output. There are many regression approaches (Hastie et al., 2001) in the literature; here we briefly review boosting regression and regression forest, which are often used for object detection.

As in any boosting procedure (Freund and Schapire, 1997; Friedman et al., 2000), boosting regression assumes that the regression output function $g(x)$ takes an additive form: $g_t(x) = g_{t-1}(x) + h_t(x)$. Boosting is an iterative algorithm that leverages the additive nature of $g(x)$. At the $t$th iteration, one more weak function $h_t(x)$ is added to the target function $g(x)$ to maximally reduce the cost function as follows:

$$J_t(h_t) = \sum_{n=1}^{N} \|r_t(x_n) - h_t(x_n)\|^2 + \lambda K_t(h_t) \tag{1.16}$$

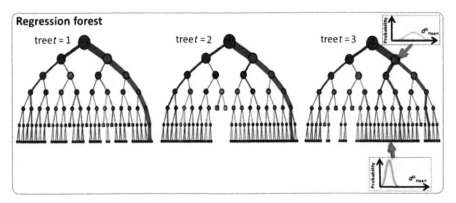

**FIGURE 1.6**

Graphical illustrations of regression forest proposed in Criminisi et al. (2013). Reprinted with permission, ©2013 Elsevier.

where $r_t(x_n) = y_n - g_{t-1}(x_n)$ is the residual and the $L^2$ loss function is used. To derive Eq. (1.16), the regularization term $K(g)$ is chosen to take an additive form: $K(g_t) = K(\sum_{i=1}^{t} h_i) = \sum_{i=1}^{t} K_i(h_i)$. In Zhou (2010), the ridge regression principle (also known as Tikhonov regularization) is incorporated into a boosting framework to penalize overly complex models and the image features are connected with weak learners. This leads to the image-based boosting ridge regression framework.

Similar to RF for classification, regression forest (Breiman, 2001; Criminisi et al., 2013) is a collection of regression trees that jointly predict continuous output(s). To learn a "random" regression tree, either the training examples for each regression tree are i.i.d. sampled from the full training set or the features used in the tree nodes are i.i.d. sampled from the full feature set or both. Training the node of a regression tree is typically done by maximizing an information gain measure, variance reduction, or optimizing other splitting criteria. Unlike the boosting regression that is a black box to predict the output, the regression forest carries a probabilistic nature that provides a confidence measure with the predicted output. Figure 1.6 shows a graphical illustration of regression forest.

# 1.6 MEDICAL IMAGE SEGMENTATION METHODS

Assuming the object is recognized or localized, the next step is to perform precise image segmentation again using the local context between the shape and appearance. Medical image segmentation is about partitioning a medical image into multiple segments or regions, each segmentation or region composed of a set of pixels or voxels. Often, segments correspond to semantically meaningful anatomical objects. Here we review a few image segmentation methods for segmenting a single object. The remaining book chapters will cover methods that handle multiple objects (*aka* medical image parsing) and/or utilize machine learning for more effective modeling of appearance and shape.

## 1.6.1 SIMPLE IMAGE SEGMENTATION METHODS

Thresholding is the simplest segmentation method by converting a gray-scale image into a binary image based on clip levels (or thresholds). The key is to utilize a proper threshold value.

Clustering often invokes the $K$-means algorithm to assign a pixel or voxel into one of the $K$ cluster labels to which its distance is the minimal. The cluster centers are then computed again using all current pixels belonging to the cluster. This iteration goes on until convergence.

Region growing assumes that the neighboring pixels (voxels) within one region share similar values. Starting from a set of seed pixel (voxel), the regions are iteratively grown, merging new unallocated neighboring pixels (voxels) into the region if the unallocated pixel (voxel) is close enough to those in the region.

For all the previously mentioned methods, the computation can happen on a feature image rather the original image or the distance or similarity can be computed based on image feature values. With a proper feature choice, segmentation becomes more robust.

## 1.6.2 ACTIVE CONTOUR METHOD

The active contour model or snake (Kass et al., 1988) seeks a parameterized curve $\mathcal{S}(s)$ that minimizes the cost function $\mathcal{E}_{\text{snake}}(\mathcal{S})$:

$$\mathcal{E}_{\text{snake}}(\mathcal{S}) = \int_0^1 \{-\mu|\nabla\mathbf{I}(\mathcal{S}(s))|^2 + w_1(s)|\mathcal{S}'(s)|^2 + w_2(s)|\mathcal{S}''(s)|^2\}\,ds \tag{1.17}$$

where $\mu$ controls the magnitude of the potential, $\nabla$ is the gradient operator, $\mathbf{I}$ is the image, $w_1(s)$ controls the tension of the curve, and $w_2(s)$ controls the rigidity of the curve. The implicit assumption of the snake model is that edge defines the curve due to the use of the gradient operator. The gradient descent minimization computes the force on the snake, defined as the negative of the gradient of the energy field, which evolves the curve. Important variants of the active contour model include the gradient vector flow snake model (Xu and Prince, 1998), geodesic active contour (Caselles et al., 1997), etc.

## 1.6.3 VARIATIONAL METHODS

In the Mumford-Shah variational method (Mumford and Shah, 1989), the minimal partition problem is studied, where a curve $\mathcal{S}$, together with two constants $u_i$ and $u_o$, is sought to minimize the cost function $\mathcal{E}_{\text{ms}}(\mathcal{S})$:

$$\mathcal{E}_{\text{ms}}(\mathcal{S}) = \int_{\Omega_i} |\mathbf{I}(x,y) - u_i|^2\,dx\,dy + \int_{\Omega_o} |\mathbf{I}(x,y) - u_o|^2\,dx\,dy + \mu\mathcal{L}(\mathcal{S}) \tag{1.18}$$

where $\Omega_i$ and $\Omega_o$ denote the inside and outside regions, respectively, with respect to the curve $S$, $u_i$ and $u_o$ are piecewise constants for the two regions, and $\mathcal{L}(S)$ is the length of the curve. The region homogeneity is assumed here.

### 1.6.4 LEVEL SET METHODS

A level set function $\phi$ is an implicit shape representation with the boundary of the shape being the zero level set of $\phi$. The advantage of the level set model (Osher and Sethian, 1988) is that it allows tractable numerical computations involving curves and surfaces on a fixed Cartesian grid and it is easy to follow shapes with changed topology. In Chan and Vese (2001), the authors propose a model that unifies level set and variational method into one framework. This results in an active contour evolution that does not explicitly depend on image edges.

### 1.6.5 ACTIVE SHAPE MODELS AND ACTIVE APPEARANCE MODELS

ASMs (Cootes et al., 1995) and active appearance models (AAMs) (Cootes et al., 2001) are two of the most popular model-based segmentation methods, in which a model is learned offline and fitted online to an unseen image. In ASM, based on a point-based representation, a shape model is learned via PCA as depicted in Eq. (1.2) in Section 1.3. To fit the model, typically a line search is first performed for every point to deform the shape to best match the image evidence, and then the deformed shape is constrained to conform to the learned statistical shape model.

An AAM further includes the image appearance, in addition to the shape, into the statistical model. It jointly characterizes the appearance $\mathbf{I}$ and shape $S$ using a linear generative model:

$$S = \bar{S}_0 + \mathbf{Q}_c\lambda; \quad \mathbf{I} = \bar{\mathbf{I}}_0 + \mathbf{Q}_i\lambda \tag{1.19}$$

where $\bar{S}_0$ is the mean shape, $\bar{\mathbf{I}}_0$ is the mean appearance in a normalized patch, and $\lambda$ is the blending coefficient vector shared by both the shape and appearance. To fit the AAM parameters, it takes an analysis-by-synthesis approach by minimizing the deviation from the estimated appearance as parameterized by AAM and the target image. This optimization is driven by the difference between the current estimate of appearance and the target image; often it can match to new images efficiently.

### 1.6.6 GRAPH CUT METHOD

A graph $G = (V, E)$ comprises a set $V$ of vertices or nodes together with a set $E$ of edges or links, each edge linking two vertices. In graph-based methods, the image grid points are often regarded as nodes in a graph and the neighboring pixels (voxels) are connected with edges. This is equivalent to a Markov random field formulation. With this, image segmentation becomes a graph cut problem that labels the nodes with different labels and hence splits the graph into subgraphs. Define $L = \{L_p | p \in \mathbf{I}\}$ as the binary labeling function that labels all pixels in the image $\mathbf{I}$ as 0 or 1. Mathematically, the graph cut problem (Boykov et al., 2001; Boykov and Funka-Lea, 2006) seeks the optimal binary function that minimizes the following energy function:

$$\mathcal{E}_{\text{gc}}(L) = \sum_{p \in \mathcal{P}} D_p(L_p) + \sum_{(p,q) \in \mathcal{N}} V_{p,q}(L_p, L_q) \tag{1.20}$$

where $D_p(L_p)$ is the unary data term that determines the cost of assigning the pixel $p$ to a label $L_p$, $\mathcal{N}$ is the set of all pairs of neighboring pixels, and $V_{p,q}$ is the pairwise interaction function that encourages the neighboring pixels with similar properties (such as intensity) to be assigned the same label.

## 1.7 CONCLUSIONS

In this chapter, we have introduced a probabilistic formulation that unifies medical image recognition, segmentation, and parsing into one framework. This is due to the use of a rough-to-exact representation and simple-to-complex modeling. A general-purpose computational pipeline then results. We have demonstrated that practical algorithms are a special instance of such a computational pipeline with customized architecture and/or modeling choices. Then we have defined the concept of anatomical context and discussed the use of discriminative learning methods for recognition. We have also reviewed modern classification and regression methods. Finally we have offered a brief review of classical image segmentation methods for segmenting a single object.

The rest of the book provides a comprehensive review of medical image recognition and parsing, assembling a collection of generic theories for recognizing or detecting and parsing or segmenting a cohort of anatomical structures from medical images and a variety of specific solutions for known anatomical structures. The underlying basis of these new approaches is that, unlike conventional algorithms, they exploit the inherent anatomical context embedded in the medical images and best exemplified by annotated datasets and modern machine learning paradigms, thus offering automatic, accurate, and robust algorithms for recognition and parsing of multiple anatomical structures from medical images. The latest theories related to multiple object segmentation and parsing are sufficiently addressed.

## RECOMMENDED NOTATIONS

Throughout the whole book, we utilize the following notations as in Table 1.1 unless otherwise specified. If necessary, each chapter might introduce its own set of notations.

**Table 1.1  A List of Notations**

| 2D image | $I$ | 3D volume | $V$ |
|---|---|---|---|
| 2D or 3D object | $O$ | $n$ objects | $O_{1:n}$ |
| 2D landmark | $l = [l_x, l_y]$ | 3D landmark | $l = [l_x, l_y, l_z]$ |
| 2D point | $x = [x, y]$ | 3D point | $x = [x, y, z]$ |
| 2D point | $v = [v_x, v_y]$ | 3D vertex | $v = [v_x, v_y, v_z]$ |
| 2D object translation | $t = [t_x, t_y]$ | 3D object translation | $t = [t_x, t_y, t_z]$ |
| 2D object rotation | $r = r$ | 3D object rotation | $r = [r_x, r_y, r_z]$ |
| 2D object scale | $s = [s_x, s_y]$ | 3D object scale | $s = [s_x, s_y, s_z]$ |
| 2D object pose | $\theta = [\mathbf{t}, \mathbf{r}, \mathbf{s}]$ | 3D object pose | $\theta = [\mathbf{t}, \mathbf{r}, \mathbf{s}]$ |
| 2D or 3D shape | $S$ | 2D or 3D shape in point-based model | $S = [\mathbf{x}_1, \ldots, \mathbf{x}_n]$ |
| 2D or 3D mean shape | $\bar{S}_0$ | 2D or 3D shape PCA eigen-pairs | $\left\{\langle \lambda_m, \bar{S}_m \rangle\right\}_{m=1}^{M}$ |
| 3D mesh | $\mathcal{M} = (\mathcal{P}, \mathcal{T})$ with the vertex set $\mathcal{P} = \{\mathbf{v}_i \in \mathbb{R}^3\}_{i=1}^{I}$ and the triangle set $\mathcal{T} = \{\Delta_j \in \mathbb{Z}^3\}_{j=1}^{J}$ | | |
| 2D mask function (2- or $n$-label) | $\phi(x, y)$ | 3D mask function (2- or $n$-label) | $\phi(x, y, z)$ |
| 2D level set function | $\phi(x, y)$ | 3D level set function | $\phi(x, y, z)$ |
| 2D patch or ROI | $I[\mathbf{x}]$, $I[l]$, $I[\mathbf{p}]$, $I[\mathbf{t}]$, $I[\mathbf{t}, \mathbf{r}]$, $I[\mathbf{t}, \mathbf{r}, \mathbf{s}]$, $I[\theta]$, $I[S]$ | 3D patch or ROI | $V[\mathbf{x}]$, $V[l]$, $V[\mathbf{p}]$, $V[\mathbf{t}]$, $V[\mathbf{t}, \mathbf{r}]$, $V[\mathbf{t}, \mathbf{r}, \mathbf{s}]$, $V[\theta]$, $V[S]$, $V[\mathcal{M}]$, $V[\phi]$ |
| Probability | $P(.)$ or $P(.\|.)$ | | |

## NOTES

a. http://sig.biostr.washington.edu/projects/fm/AboutFM.html.
b. http://en.wikipedia.org/wiki/Terminologia_Anatomica.
c. http://www.oecd-ilibrary.org/social-issues-migration-health/computed-tomography-ct-exams-total_ct-exams-tot-table-en.
d. In texts or equations, we always use 3D as an example unless otherwise noted; in principle, applying 3D to 2D is an easy task. However, in Figure 1.2, we use 2D as an example for graphical illustration.

## REFERENCES

Bengio, Y., 2009. Learning deep architectures for AI. Found. Trends Mach. Learn. 2 (1), 1–127.

Bishop, C.M., et al., 1995. Neural Networks for Pattern Recognition. Clarendon Press, Oxford.

Boykov, Y., Funka-Lea, G., 2006. Graph cuts and efficient ND image segmentation. Int. J. Comput. Vis. 70 (2), 109–131.

Boykov, Y., Veksler, O., Zabih, R., 2001. Fast approximate energy minimization via graph cuts. IEEE Trans. Pattern Anal. Mach. Intell. 23 (11), 1222–1239.

Breiman, L., 2001. Random forests. Mach. Learn. 45 (1), 5–32.

Caselles, V., Kimmel, R., Sapiro, G., 1997. Geodesic active contours. Int. J. Comput. Vis. 22 (1), 61–79.

Chan, T.F., Vese, L.A., 2001. Active contours without edges. IEEE Trans. Image Process. 10 (2), 266–277.

Cootes, T.F., Taylor, C.J., Cooper, D.H., Graham, J., 1995. Active shape models—their training and application. Comput. Vis. Image Underst. 61 (1), 38–59.

Cootes, T.F., Edwards, G.J., Taylor, C.J., 2001. Active appearance models. IEEE Trans. Pattern Anal. Mach. Intell. 23 (6), 681–685.

Criminisi, A., Shotton, J., Bucciarelli, S., 2009. Decision forests with long-range spatial context for organ localization in CT volumes. In: MICCAI Workshop on Prob. Models for MIA.

Criminisi, A., Robertson, D., Konukoglu, E., Shotton, J., Pathak, S., White, S., Siddiqui, K., 2013. Regression forests for efficient anatomy detection and localization in computed tomography scans. Med. Image Anal. 17, 1293–1303.

Davis, R., Shrobe, H., Szolovits, P., 1993. What is a knowledge representation? AI Magazine 14 (1), 17.

Freund, Y., Schapire, R.E., 1997. A decision-theoretic generalization of on-line learning and an application to boosting. J. Comput. Syst. Sci. 55 (1), 119–139.

Friedman, J., Hastie, T., Tibbshirani, R., 2000. Additive logistic regression: a statistical view of boosting. Ann. Stat. 28 (2), 337–407.

Hastie, T., Tibshirani, R., Friedman, J., 2001. The Elements of Statistical Learning. Springer, New York.

Heimann, T., Meinzer, H.P., 2009. Statistical shape models for 3D medical image segmentation: a review. Med. Image Anal. 13 (4), 543–563.

Hofmann, T., Schölkopf, B., Smola, A.J., 2008. Kernel methods in machine learning. Ann. Stat. 36 (3), 1171–1220.

Kass, M., Witkin, A., Terzopoulos, D., 1988. Snakes: active contour models. Int. J. Comput. Vis. 1 (4), 321–331.

Kohlberger, T., Sofka, M., Zhang, J., Birkbeck, N., Wetzl, J., Kaftan, J., Declerck, J., Zhou, S.K., 2011. Automatic multi-organ segmentation using learning-based segmentation and level set optimization. In: Medical Image Computing and Computer-Assisted Intervention—MICCAI 2011. Springer, Heidelberg, pp. 338–345.

Lu, C., Zheng, Y., Birkbeck, N., Zhang, J., Kohlberger, T., Tietjen, C., Boettger, T., Duncan, J.S., Zhou, S.K., 2012. Precise segmentation of multiple organs in CT volumes using learning-based approach and information theory. In: Medical Image Computing and Computer-Assisted Intervention—MICCAI 2012. Springer, Heidelberg, pp. 462–469.

Mumford, D., Shah, J., 1989. Optimal approximations by piecewise smooth functions and associated variational problems. Commun. Pure Appl. Math. 42 (5), 577–685.

Nain, D., Haker, S., Bobick, A., Tannenbaum, A., 2006. Shape-driven 3D segmentation using spherical wavelets. In: Medical Image Computing and Computer-Assisted Intervention—MICCAI 2006. Springer, Heidelberg, pp. 66–74.

Osher, S., Sethian, J.A., 1988. Fronts propagating with curvature-dependent speed: algorithms based on Hamilton-Jacobi formulations. J. Comput. Phys. 79 (1), 12–49.

Pizer, S.M., Fletcher, P.T., Joshi, S., Thall, A., Chen, J.Z., Fridman, Y., Fritsch, D.S., Gash, A.G., Glotzer, J.M., Jiroutek, M.R., et al., 2003. Deformable M-Reps for 3D medical image segmentation. Int. J. Comput. Vis. 55 (2/3), 85–106.

Polikar, R., 2006. Ensemble based systems in decision making. IEEE Circuits Syst. Mag. 6 (3), 21–45.

Shen, L., Farid, H., McPeek, M.A., 2009. Modeling three-dimensional morphological structures using spherical harmonics. Evolution 63 (4), 1003–1016.

Tu, Z., 2005. Probabilistic boosting-tree: learning discriminative methods for classification, recognition, and clustering. In: Proc. Int. Conf. Computer Vision, vol. 2, pp. 1589–1596.

Vapnik, V., 1999. The Nature of Statistical Learning Theory. Springer, New York.

Viola, P., Jones, M., 2001. Rapid object detection using a boosted cascade of simple features. In: Proc. IEEE Conf. Computer Vision and Pattern Recognition, pp. 511–518.

Wu, D., Sofka, M., Birkbeck, N., Zhou, S.K., 2014. Segmentation of multiple knee bones from CT for orthopedic knee surgery planning. In: Medical Image Computing and Computer-Assisted Intervention—MICCAI 2014. Springer, Heidelberg, pp. 372–380.

Xu, C., Prince, J.L., 1998. Snakes, shapes, and gradient vector flow. IEEE Trans. Image Process. 7 (3), 359–369.

Zheng, Y., Barbu, A., Georgescu, B., Scheuering, M., Comaniciu, D., 2008. Four-chamber heart modeling and automatic segmentation for 3D cardiac CT volumes using marginal space learning and steerable features. IEEE Trans. Med. Imaging 27 (11), 1668–1681.

Zhou, S.K., 2010. Shape regression machine and efficient segmentation of left ventricle endocardium from 2D B-mode echocardiogram. Med. Image Anal. 14, 563–581.

Zhou, S.K., Park, J.H., Georgescu, B., Simopoulos, C., Otsuki, J., Comaniciu, D., 2006. Image-based multiclass boosting and echocardiographic view classification. In: Proc. IEEE Conf. Computer Vision and Pattern Recognition, vol. 2, pp. 1559–1565.

# AUTOMATIC RECOGNITION AND DETECTION ALGORITHMS

# A SURVEY OF ANATOMY DETECTION

S. Kevin Zhou

*Medical Imaging Technologies, Siemens Healthcare Technology Center, Princeton, NJ, USA*

## CHAPTER OUTLINE

S. Kevin Zhou (Ed): Medical Image Recognition, Segmentation and Parsing. http://dx.doi.org/10.1016/B978-0-12-802581-9.00002-0

## 2.1 INTRODUCTION

Detecting a single anatomy or a plurality of anatomical objects, such as landmarks or organs, in a medical image is an important but challenging task. Here we define an anatomical landmark as a distinct point in a body scan that coincides with anatomical structures, such as liver top, aortic arch, pubis symphysis, to name a few. From anatomical object detection, body regions can be determined (Liu and Zhou, 2012) to trigger subsequent, computationally intensive applications such as computer-assisted diagnosis. Anatomy detection also provides initialization to image segmentation (Rangayyan et al., 2009) and registration (Johnson and Christensen, 2002; Crum et al., 2004) and enables applications such as semantic reporting (Seifert et al., 2010), optimal organ display (Pauly et al., 2011), etc. It is challenging as it has to deal with *significant appearance variations* due to sensor noise, patient difference and motion, pathology, contrast agent, partial scan and narrow field of view, weak contrast between soft tissues, etc.

General object detection is well studied in computer vision. Discriminative modeling is prevalent for modeling general object appearance. Unlike natural scene images, medical images manifest additional contextual information, such as a limited number of anatomical objects (e.g. only one left ventricle [LV]), constrained and structured background, strong prior information about the pose parameter, etc.; hence discriminative learning methods should exploit such contextual information to reduce *model learning complexity*. This survey will focus on such discriminative learning methods for anatomical object detection. In particular, we will discuss two major detection approaches, *classification-based* and *regression-based*, and their corresponding learning complexities. Note that this survey is not meant for detecting general objects such as faces, cars, and pedestrians in natural scenes. For surveys of general object detection, refer to Hjelmås and Low (2001), Yang et al. (2002), Enzweiler and Gavrila (2009), and Geronimo et al. (2010).

Another important aspect for object detection is *search strategy* and its *computational complexity*. The discriminative models are often not differentiable, thereby leading to an exhaustive search scheme that is not computationally scalable to a high-dimensional pose parameterization (e.g., a nine-dimensional box for a 3D object). The search for multiple objects further exacerbates the computational burden. We will survey various search strategies, along with an analysis of their computational complexities, that leverage the anatomical context embedded in the medical image for more efficient detection.

As mentioned in Chapter 1, the anatomical context can be roughly categorized into three types, namely *unitary or local*, *pairwise or higher-order*, and *holistic or global* context. The *unitary or local context* refers to the local regularity surrounding a single object. The *pairwise or higher-order context* refers to the joint regularities between two objects or among multiple objects. The *holistic or global context* goes beyond the relationships among a cohort of objects and refers to the whole relationship between all pixels/voxels and the objects: in other words, regarding the image as a whole.

Different methods presented in this survey basically operate with different trade-offs between offline model learning complexity and online computational complexity, depending on *how to leverage which context(s)*. It will be shown that, however, there is no absolute relationship between these two different complexities. In other words, low learning complexity does not necessarily mean high computational complexity or vice versa. There are methods with low learning complexity and low computational complexity.

Section 2.2 surveys methods for detecting a single anatomical object, including marginal space learning (MSL) (Zheng et al., 2008), probabilistic boosting network (PBN) (Zhang et al., 2007), shape regression machine (SRM) (Zhou, 2010), etc., and Section 2.3 briefly mentions a few approaches for detecting a plurality of anatomical objects, including active scheduling (Zhan et al., 2008), submodular optimization (Liu et al., 2010), regression forest (Criminisi et al., 2013), integrated detection network (IDN) (Sofka et al., 2010), context integration (Lay et al., 2013), etc. These approaches are also covered in detail in subsequent book chapters: Chapter 3 for active scheduling, Chapter 4 for submodular detection, Chapter 5 for regression forest, Chapter 6 for IDN, and Chapter 10 for context integration. Section 2.4 concludes the chapter and points out some future research directions.

## 2.2 METHODS FOR DETECTING AN ANATOMY

In this section, we present in detail classification-based and regression-based methods for detecting a single anatomy, along with analysis of their offline model learning and online computational complexities. The classification-based method leverages the local context while the regression-based method leverages the global context.

### 2.2.1 CLASSIFICATION-BASED DETECTION METHODS

The classification-based detection method aims to separate the object as foreground from background using discriminative classifiers. It leverages only the local context for such discrimination and uses an exhaustive search scheme that is not computationally scalable when dealing with pose variation in an anatomy. Here we present various methods attempting to address such a computational challenge.

#### 2.2.1.1 Boosting detection cascade

The classical classification-based object detection method proposed in Viola and Jones (2001) reaches real-time detection of a frontal-view 2D face by exhaustively searching all possible translations and a sparse set of isotropic scales. It has three contributions: invoking the AdaBoost algorithm to do feature selection, using the so-called integral image to enable fast evaluation of features, and training a boosting cascade to quickly eliminate negatives. Note that in Viola and Jones (2001) no orientation is searched; that is, the parameters of interest are $\alpha = [\mathtt{t}, \mathtt{s}]$, and the scale is isotropic, that is, $\mathtt{s} = s$.

Figure 2.1(a) shows the detection cascade structure, which is introduced to deal with severely unbalanced sample size, that is, the number of negatives is much larger than that of positives. The dominance of negatives poses a significant challenge for learning an effective classifier of good separability between positives and negatives. Suppose that the cascade has $N$ stages, then the discriminative detector $\mathbf{D}(+1|\mathtt{I}[\mathtt{t}, \mathtt{s}])$ is computed as

$$\mathbf{D}(+1|\mathtt{I}[\mathtt{t}, \mathtt{s}]) = \prod_{n=1}^{N} \mathbf{D}_n(+1|\mathtt{I}[\mathtt{t}, \mathtt{s}]) \qquad (2.1)$$

where $\mathbf{D}_n(+1|\mathtt{I}[\mathtt{t}, \mathtt{s}])$ is the binary classifier for the $n$th cascade. Typically, the complexity of the classifier $\mathbf{D}_n(+1|\mathtt{I}[\mathtt{t}, \mathtt{s}])$ increases as the number of stages increases, as only increasingly difficult negatives can survive the early cascades.

Because only the *local context* is leveraged in training the binary detectors offline, exhaustive scanning is needed for online inference to search for a local object instance from the whole image. Assuming that the detector consists of $N$ cascades and the unit time needed to evaluate up to the $n$th cascades is $\tau(\mathbf{D}_{1:n})$, the exhaustive scanning carries a computation of $|t| \times |s| \times \{\sum_{n=1}^{N} \lambda_n \tau(\mathbf{D}_{1:n})\}$, where $|t|$ is the number of all translation candidates (i.e., $|t| = |\mathbf{I}|$, the image size), $|s|$ is the number of all isotropic scales being searched (i.e., $|s| = |s|$), and $\lambda_n$ is the fraction of all candidates that pass up to the $n$th cascades. Further if we define $\tau(\mathbf{D}) = \sum_{n=1}^{N} \lambda_n \tau(\mathbf{D}_{1:n})$, which is the average unit time needed to evaluate one candidate, then the total computation is $|t| \times |s| \times \tau(\mathbf{D})$. If anisotropic scales are searched, then $|s| = |s_x s_y|$.

### 2.2.1.2 Probabilistic boosting tree

Boosting cascade learns a sequential cascade of boosted classifiers. While each cascade classifier rejects more negatives, it also loses a few positives. Tu (2005) proposes a probabilistic boosting tree (PBT) to address this limitation by combining a binary decision tree with boosting, letting each tree node be an AdaBoost classifier. This way the misclassified positive or negative examples can have further chances to be correctly classified. The PBT shown in Figure 2.1(b) calculates the posterior probability as

$$\mathbf{D}(y|\mathbf{I}[\alpha]) = \sum_{l_1, l_2, \dots, l_n} \mathbf{D}(y|l_n, \dots, l_1, \mathbf{I}[\alpha]) \dots \mathbf{D}(l_2|l_1, \mathbf{I}[\alpha])\mathbf{D}(l_1|\mathbf{I}[\alpha]) \tag{2.2}$$

where $n$ is the total number of tree nodes and $l \in \{+1, -1\}$. Empirically, the learning and computational complexities of PBT are similar to those of the boosting cascade.

### 2.2.1.3 Randomized decision forest

Criminisi et al. (2009) use randomized decision forests to automatically detect and localize the anatomical structures. In particular, visual features that capture long-range spatial context are proposed to integrate information coming from multiple regions in different signal channels which are offset by a given quantity in a given direction. The examples of signal channel include the computed tomography

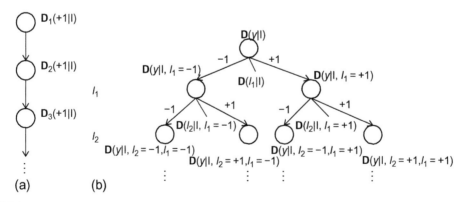

**FIGURE 2.1**

Graphical illustrations of (a) detection cascade proposed in Viola and Jones (2001) and (b) PBT proposed in Tu (2005).

(CT) intensity, the magnitude of the 3D gradient, etc. Because of the parallelism of the forest and the use of integral volumes, its graphics processing unit implementation runs in about 2 s for an approximately $512^3$ volume and it achieves a mean detection error of 28.2 mm when applied to detect nine organs from a CT scan.

### 2.2.1.4 Exhaustive search to handle pose variation

It is challenging to build a real-time detector that incorporates accurate pose estimation using a scheme such as Viola and Jones (2001), that is, exhaustively scanning the space of all possible combinations of translation and pose.

Consider detecting the LV in a 3D echocardiogram, an ultrasound volume of the human heart. Discovering the LV configuration is helpful—from a known LV configuration, one can automatically display canonical 2D slices for diagnosis. Because the LV can occur at an arbitrary location and orientation, one needs to search over nine parameters to fully align the LV. When extending the method of Viola and Jones (2001), the total computation $|\mathtt{I}| \times |r_x r_y r_z| \times |s_x s_y s_z| \times \tau(\mathbf{D})$, where $| \circ |$ is the number of possible hypotheses for $\circ$, increases exponentially with the cardinality of the parameter space. Similarly, for detecting a 2D object (Georgescu et al., 2005), the total computation is $|\mathtt{I}| \times |r| \times |s_x s_y| \times \tau(\mathbf{D})$. Furthermore, volume rotation and integral volume calculation with additional computation of $|r_x r_y r_z| \times [\tau(\mathbf{ROT}) + \tau(\mathbf{INT})]$ are time consuming because their computation is proportional to the number of voxels. To aggravate the problem, learning one monolithic detector to handle all possible variations is challenging and such a learned detector carries a high complexity, resulting in a high value of $\tau(\mathbf{D})$.

### 2.2.1.5 Parallel, pyramid, and tree structures

An alternative solution that requires only one integral volume/image is to train a collection of binary classifiers to handle different poses. A variety of structures is proposed to combine these classifiers. The most straightforward way is a parallel structure (Figure 2.2) that trains a classifier for each discretized pose (Wu et al., 2004). In detection, all classifiers are tested for every scanning window. The total computation, linearly depending on the number of poses, amounts to $|\mathtt{I}| \times |s_x s_y| \times \sum_r \tau(\mathbf{D}_r)$, where $\mathbf{D}_r$ is the specific detector corresponding to the orientation $r$. If say $\tau(\mathbf{D}_r) \equiv \tau(\mathbf{D})$ for simplicity, then the total computation is the same as above $|\mathtt{I}| \times |s_x s_y| \times |r| \times \tau(\mathbf{D})$, but without the overhead of rotating images and computing multiple integral images. The cons are that, for the parallel structure, several classifiers might fire up at the same place when the actual pose is in-between the discretized poses and that estimating the accurate pose needs additional work due to the difficulty in comparing responses among these classifiers.

To reduce the computational complexity in parallel structure-based multiview object detection, Torralba et al. (2007) propose to share visual features among different detectors learned for different views. As the majority of $\tau(\mathbf{D}_r)$ is spent to compute the image features in the detector $\mathbf{D}_r$, sharing features among different detectors saves the overall time $\sum_r \tau(\mathbf{D}_r)$. This feature sharing approach is also used for multiclass object detection.

To accelerate the parallel structure, Li and Zhang (2004) propose a pyramid structure in a coarse-to-fine fashion shown in Figure 2.2 for multipose detection. It consists of several levels from the coarsest view partition at the top to the finest partition at the bottom. At each level of the pyramid, the full range of out-of-plane rotation is partitioned into a number of sub-ranges and a separate detector is trained for

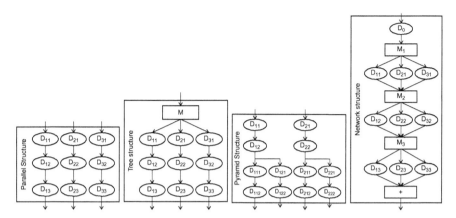

**FIGURE 2.2**

Different structures for detecting objects with pose variation. The circle represents a binary foreground/background classifier. The rectangle represents a multiclass pose classifier.

*Reprinted from Zhou (2014) with permission, ©2014 Elsevier.*

each sub-range. This way the linear dependency on the number of poses is broken down and there is no need to evaluate all detectors.

To discriminate different poses explicitly, a tree structure as in Figure 2.2 that uses the multiclass classifier as a differentiator is applied. In Jones and Viola (2003), a multiclass classifier is used to determine the pose of an object, followed by the binary classifier trained for that pose only. Here the computation is $|\mathtt{I}| \times |s_x s_y| \times [\tau(\mathbf{M}) + \tau(\mathbf{D})]$, where $\mathbf{M}$ is the multiclass classifier. This also breaks down the linear dependency on the number of poses, with additional computation of multiclass classifier. The tree-structure poses a computational dilemma: a multiclass classifier is used to select proper binary classifiers to reject background, but determining the pose of these background patches wastes computation. For the tree structure, only one branch is evaluated based on the multiclass classifier in Jones and Viola (2003) and, hence, the error made by the multiclass classifier has great influence on the detection result.

### 2.2.1.6 Network structure: Probabilistic boosting network

Assuming that the pose parameter $\beta = [\mathtt{r}, \mathtt{s}]$ is discretized into $\{\beta_1, \beta_2, \ldots, \beta_J\}$, a probabilistic boosting network (PBN) leverages the fundamental total probability law to compute the probability of being an object:

$$\mathbf{D}(+1|\mathtt{I}[\alpha]) = \sum_{j=1}^{J} \mathbf{D}(+1|\mathtt{I}[\mathtt{t}, \beta_j]) \mathbf{M}(\beta_j|\mathtt{I}) = \sum_{j=1}^{J} \prod_{n=1}^{N_j} \mathbf{D}_n(+1|\mathtt{I}[\mathtt{t}, \beta_j]) \mathbf{M}(\beta_j|\mathtt{I}) \qquad (2.3)$$

where $\mathbf{D}(+1|\mathtt{I}[\mathtt{t}, \beta_j])$ is the binary detector specific to the parameter $\beta_j$. The detector $\mathbf{D}(+1|\mathtt{I}[\mathtt{t}, \beta_j])$ is implemented using the cascade of boosted binary classifiers, which has $N_j$ stages. The probability $\mathbf{M}(\beta_j|\mathtt{I})$ is implemented using, say, the multiclass LogitBoost algorithm. PBN estimates the pose parameter $\beta$ by using the minimum mean square error (MMSE) estimator: $\hat{\beta} = \sum_j \beta_j \mathbf{M}(\beta_j|\mathtt{I})$. This gives a better estimate than the maximum a posterior (MAP) estimate from a discrete set of possible values of $\beta$ because of its interpolation capability.

The total probability law in Eq. (2.3) can be implemented in a tree-structured network, which has the computational dilemma as mentioned previously. PBN uses two strategies to address this dilemma. The first is to discard as many background windows as possible via a focus-of-attention mechanism, that is, training a prefilter that has a 100% detection rate, regardless of the pose, while rejecting a large percentage of the background candidates. The second trick follows the idea of the cascade structure for binary detector, which breaks its computation into several stages with increasing complexity. It also decomposes the computation of $\mathbf{M}(\beta|\mathbf{I})$ into several stages by taking the advantage of the additive model arising from the LogitBoost algorithm. This endows a network structure as shown in Figure 2.2, which alternates the two tasks of pose estimation and background rejection by hierarchically distributing the overhead of computing $\mathbf{M}(\beta|\mathbf{I})$.

The computational complexity of the network structure of PBN is difficult to quantify exactly, but it is definitely more efficient than parallel or tree structure. In Zhang et al. (2007), PBN was applied for real-time detection of the LV from 3D ultrasound volumes and the left atrium from 2D images.

### 2.2.1.7 Marginal space learning

The approaches reviewed so far mostly focus on computational structures for efficient detection. MSL (Zheng et al., 2008) instead harnesses both learning and computational complexities by decomposing the complicated learning and inference tasks into a series of simple ones. Simple mathematical derivation tells us that

$$\mathbf{D}(+1|\mathbf{I}[t, r, s]) = \mathbf{D}(+1|\mathbf{I}[t]) \frac{\mathbf{D}(+1|\mathbf{I}[t, r])}{\mathbf{D}(+1|\mathbf{I}[t])} \frac{\mathbf{D}(+1|\mathbf{I}[t, r, s])}{\mathbf{D}(+1|\mathbf{I}[t, r])} \tag{2.4}$$

So, instead of learning one single-shot detector, MSL learns three detectors for a series of marginal spaces with increasing dimensionality, specifically the T-detector $\mathbf{D}(+1|\mathbf{I}[t])$ for translation, the TR-detector $\mathbf{D}(+1|\mathbf{I}[t, r])$ for translation-rotation, and the TRS-detector $\mathbf{D}(+1|\mathbf{I}[t, r, s])$ for translation-rotation-scale. The three detectors are learned using PBT.

Figure 2.3 graphically illustrates the MSL scheme for detection, which applies the three detectors sequentially. When comparing MSL with the cascade scheme, the main difference lies in that MSL learns the different detectors with a subspace of the full parameter space while the cascade scheme learns the detectors with a subset of the full training set.

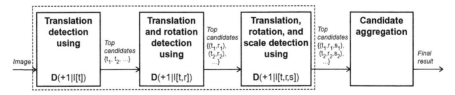

**FIGURE 2.3**

Diagram for anatomical object detection using MSL.

When compared with the full space exhaustive search, the computational complexity of MSL in inference is significantly reduced. The MSL computation amounts to $|\mathbf{I}| \times \tau(\mathbf{D_T}) + n_T |r_x r_y r_z| \times \tau(\mathbf{D_{TR}}) + n_{TR} |s_x s_y s_z| \times \tau(\mathbf{D_{TRS}})$, where $n_T$ and $n_{TR}$ are the number of top candidates kept from the T-detector $\mathbf{D_T}$ and the TR-detector $\mathbf{D_{TR}}$, respectively. Typically $n_T \ll |\mathbf{I}|$ and $n_{TR} \ll |\mathbf{I}| \times |r_x r_y r_z|$.

In Zheng et al. (2008), the computational efficiency of MSL is reported using the experiment of heart chamber detection from 3D cardiac CT. At the 3 mm resolution, a typical cardiac CT volume has roughly $64 \times 64 \times 64$ voxels, corresponding to around 260,000 translation candidates. The orientation space is discretized under a resolution of 0.2 radians, resulting in a total of about 1000 rotation candidates. Under two-voxel searching step size, there are about 1000 scale candidates. If the parameter space is searched uniformly and exhaustively, there are about $2.6 \times 10^{11}$ candidates to be tested! However, using MSL, only about $260,000 + 100 \times 1000 + 50 \times 1000 = 4.1 \times 10^5$ candidates are tested, reducing the computation by almost six orders of magnitude.

MSL significantly reduces the learning complexity too. For example, when learning the TR-detector, only those joint hypotheses whose translation passes the T-detector are used. This bootstrapping procedure significantly reduces the number of negatives and hence makes the learning of binary classifiers more tractable; otherwise it is simply too hard to learn a classifier due to the dominance of negatives. The efficacy of the MSL models is shown in Zheng et al. (2009b). For LV detection from 2D magnetic resonance imaging (MRI) images, both MSL and full space learning (FSL) methods are thoroughly compared. Experiment shows that MSL significantly outperforms FSL in terms of both accuracy and speed.

Another contribution of MSL is the use of steerable features to capture the rotation and scale of the object while being computationally efficient. This is done by sampling a few points from the volume under a sampling pattern and then extracting a few local features for each sampling point (e.g., voxel intensity and gradient) from the original volume. This way the rotation and scale information is embedded into the distribution of sampling points, while each individual feature is locally defined.

In MSL, each of the three subspaces (the translation, rotation, and scale spaces) are uniformly sampled without considering the correlation among parameters in the same marginal space. The constrained MSL (Zheng et al., 2009a) further decreases the computational complexity by another order of magnitude by exploiting the correlation among subspaces. Other MSL extensions include 2D MSL (Zheng et al., 2009b), augmenting the MSL with leading PCA components of deformable shape (Ling et al., 2008) for liver segmentation, clustered MSL (Chen et al., 2009) used for detecting follicles from 3D ultrasound volumes, iterated MSL (Kelm et al., 2011) for spine disk detection, etc.

### 2.2.1.8 Probabilistic, hierarchical, and discriminant framework

MSL is originally designed for detecting rigid objects. The probabilistic, hierarchical, and discriminant (PHD) framework (Zhou et al., 2007a) is similar to MSL but more amenable to deformable objects. It probabilistically integrates distinctive primitives manifested by the anatomic structure at global, segmental, and landmark levels to give an accurate account of the object. Because the configuration of the anatomic structures lies in a high-dimensional parameter space, the PHD framework seeks the best configuration via a hierarchical evaluation of the detection probability that quickly prunes the search space. Inspired by the argument that "visual processing in cortex is classically modeled as a hierarchy of increasingly sophisticated representations" (Riesenhuber et al., 1999), it builds up the hierarchy to support fast evaluation in a simple-to-complex fashion, that is to start with simple models and progressively move to complex ones in terms of computation. Each model implemented using the discriminative boosting learning separates the primitives from the background.

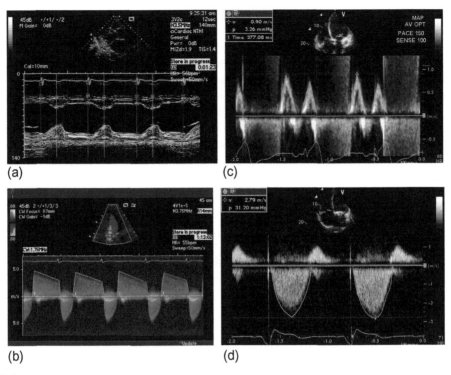

**FIGURE 2.4**

(a) M-mode echocardiogram and (b–d) Doppler echocardiogram: (b) mitral inflow, (c) aortic regurgitation, (d) tricuspid regurgitation.

*Reprinted with permission from Zhou et al. (2007a) ©2007 IEEE.*

The PHD framework is applied for detecting various deformable anatomic structures such as a cohort of landmarks, triangles, quadrilaterals, and curves from M-mode and Doppler echocardiograms as shown in Figure 2.4, taking about a second per structure.

### 2.2.1.9 Multiple instance boosting to handle inaccurate annotation

In order to train a high-performing object detector, often a big number of exact annotations is needed, which is tedious and expensive to obtain. Multiple instance learning (MIL) (Keeler et al., 1990; Maron and Lozano-Pérez, 1998) is often used to alleviate the manual annotation burden and to accommodate imprecise annotations.

MIL uses instance bags as inputs for training. A positive instance bag contains at least one positive and a negative bag contains all negatives. In anatomical object detection, we construct a positive bag by placing a bounding box big enough to guarantee that a true positive exists inside it. This construction yields a positive bag with only one or very few positive instances.

In Viola et al. (2006), multiple instance boosting (MILBoost) is proposed to leverage the AnyBoost framework (Mason et al., 1999) and to combine boosting with cost functions from the MIL literature, specifically the integrated segmentation and recognition (ISR) rule (Keeler et al., 1990) and the

"Noisy-OR" rule (Maron and Lozano-Pérez, 1998). The MILBoost achieves improved performance for object detection.

In Swoboda et al. (2013), a spatially regularized MILBoost algorithm is presented. It introduces the soft max cost function for better handling of the practical situation in object detection that most positive bags only contain very few true positives while including the ISR rule and AdaBoost as special examples. In addition, in contrast with conventional methods that treat instances in a bag independently, the approach in Swoboda et al. (2013) exploits for better detection the spatial context embedded in a medical image, specifically the grid arrangement of the training instances with strong correlation, and encourages a concentrated detection response map so that the final detection result can be derived with more confidence. This is realized using total variation regularization. Experimentally the proposed approach achieves significantly better detection performance than MILBoost and other state-of-the-art detection methods in detecting anatomical landmarks with few or even no annotations.

## 2.2.2 REGRESSION-BASED DETECTION METHODS

The regression-based detection method formulates the detection problem into a regression setting in order to better leverage the global context in anatomies. This avoids the need for exhaustive scanning, leading to a more efficient solution.

### 2.2.2.1 Shape regression machine

The idea of SRM (Zhou and Comaniciu, 2007; Zhou et al., 2007b; Zhou, 2010) is to learn a regression function $\mathbf{R}$ that predicts the different vector between any arbitrary parameter $\theta$ and the target parameter $\theta_0$. This way theoretically the detection is achieved using *just one scan*.

$$d\theta = \mathbf{R}(\mathbf{I}[\theta]), \quad \theta_0 = \theta + d\theta = \theta + \mathbf{R}(\mathbf{I}[\theta]) \tag{2.5}$$

In practice, a sparse set of random scans (Zhou, 2010) or a sparse set of exhaustive scans (Lay et al., 2013) is tested for a robust solution. Suppose that $M \ll |I|$ random samples $\{\theta^{\langle 1 \rangle}, \theta^{\langle 2 \rangle}, \ldots, \theta^{\langle M \rangle}\}$ are scanned. For each $\theta^{\langle m \rangle}$, the regressor is invoked to predict the difference parameter $d\theta^{\langle m \rangle}$ and, subsequently, the target parameter $\theta_0^{\langle m \rangle}$ as follows:

$$\theta_0^{\langle m \rangle} = \theta^{\langle m \rangle} + d\theta^{\langle m \rangle} = \theta^{\langle m \rangle} + \mathbf{R}(\mathbf{I}[\theta^{\langle m \rangle}]), \quad m = 1, 2, \ldots, M \tag{2.6}$$

A simple fusion strategy is to take the sample mean,

$$\theta_0 = \frac{1}{M} \sum_{m=1}^{M} \theta_0^{\langle m \rangle} \tag{2.7}$$

Figure 2.5 demonstrates the idea using LV detection from the 2D B-mode echocardiogram in an apical four chamber view, which is a 2D image slice of the heart acquired by an ultrasonic imaging device. It contains all four heart chambers, namely LV, right ventricle, left atrium, and right atrium. For illustrative purposes, only the translation parameter is shown in Figure 2.5.

While taking the sample mean is quite effective, some of the predicted difference parameters far away from the ground truth could compromise the final estimation. To this end, a binary detector $\mathbf{D}$ is

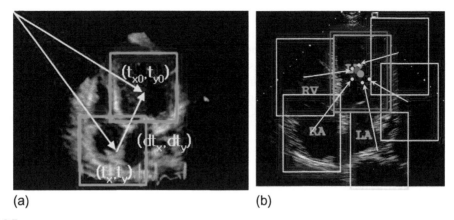

(a)                              (b)

**FIGURE 2.5**

(a) A graphical illustration of regression-based detection using a 2D translation parameterization: the learned regressor predicts the difference vector. (b) A robust fusion algorithm for regression-based object detection. The yellow denotes scanning boxes and predicted difference vectors, the green is the fused box, and the red is the ground truth box.

*Reprinted with permission from Zhou (2010) ©2010 Elsevier.*

used to provide a confidence score. After finding the $m$th prediction $\theta_0^{\langle m\rangle}$, the detector $\mathbf{D}$ is applied to the image patch $\mathtt{I}[\theta_0^{\langle m\rangle}]$. If the detector $\mathbf{D}$ fails, this $m$th sample is discarded; otherwise, the sample is kept with its confidence score $\mathbf{D}(+1|\mathtt{I}[\theta_0^{\langle m\rangle}])$. The weighted mean is calculated as the final estimate:

$$\theta_0 = \frac{\sum_{j=1}^{J} \mathbf{D}(+1|\mathtt{I}[\theta_0^{\langle j\rangle}])\,\theta_0^{\langle j\rangle}}{\sum_{j=1}^{J} \mathbf{D}(+1|\mathtt{I}[\theta_0^{\langle j\rangle}])} \qquad (2.8)$$

where $J < M$ as the samples might be rejected.

Combining the regressor and binary detector yields an effective tool for medical anatomy detection. When compared with the method using only the regressor, it needs only a smaller number of scans to reach a better precision. The total computation amounts to $J \times (\tau(\mathbf{R}) + \tau(\mathbf{D}))$, which is much more efficient than the classification-based detection method that uses exhaustive scanning. Experiments in Zhou et al. (2007b) show that the "weighted"-regression approach runs the fastest, about 7 times faster than the "unweighted"-regression method and more than 50 times faster than classification-based exhaustive search.

SRM confronts a multiple regression setting with a multidimensional output. In other words, the regression function $\mathbf{R}$ takes an image patch, depicted by a multidimensional vector, as input and outputs a multidimensional displacement vector. The image-based boosting ridge regression algorithm (Zhou, 2010) is specifically proposed for this purpose.

### 2.2.2.2 Hough forest

Gall and Lempitsky (2009) proposed the so-called Hough forest for object detection. Each tree in a Hough forest is learned, using a set of patches $\{\mathtt{I}_i, c_i, d_i\}$, where $\mathtt{I}_i$ is the appearance of the patch,

$c_i$ is the class label of the patch, and $d_i$ is the offset vector of the patch, to cast probabilistic Hough votes about the existence of the object at different positions. To split the tree node, the entropy is used as class-label uncertainty measuring the impurity of the class labels and the total square distance to the mean vector as the offset uncertainty measuring the impurity of the offset vectors. A randomized decision is made whether the node should minimize the class-label uncertainty or the offset uncertainty. The Hough forest essentially does regression and classification at the same time, performing regression only when the scanned patch passes the classifier. The final detection is derived by aggregating the Hough votes.

## 2.2.3 CLASSIFICATION-BASED VS REGRESSION-BASED OBJECT DETECTION

A successful object detection approach based on machine learning must harness the learning complexity in its offline learning and the computational complexity in its online inference from a test image.

- *Learning complexity.* In the classification-based approach, the main challenge lies in handling the number of negatives—anything other than positive is negative, apart from the large image appearance variations in positives and negatives. In theory, one image contributes one positive (assuming the single presence of the anatomy) but innumerable negatives. The dominance of negatives poses a significant challenge for learning an effective classifier of good separability between positives and negatives. In the regression-based approach, the challenge is aggravated because we have to associate a real-valued output or vector for each sample, rather than a binary variable in the classification-based approach.
- *Computational complexity in inference.* This is related to the running-time detection speed. In the classification-based approach, brute force exhaustive search is time-consuming as its computation is exponential in the dimensionality of the parameter space. In the regression-based approach, the exponential nature of the computation in inference no longer exists. Also, the learned model complexity affects the inference complexity: the more sophisticated the model is, the slower is the inference. Though the learned regressor is more complex than the binary detector, its overall computational complexity in inference is much less than that of the binary detector because of the avoidance of exhaustive search.

Clearly, there is a *trade-off* between the learning complexity and computational complexity in inference. The classification-based approach learns a less complex model and runs slower; the regression-based approach learns a more complex model and runs faster. However, for the regression-based detection to work, the image has to possess the anatomically global context (or some kind of geometric context). Table 2.1 presents a summary of comparison between the classification-based and regression-based object detection approaches.

Given the computational advantage and increased modeling capability of regression, recently the literature witnesses an emerging trend of using regression to solve computer vision problems, including age estimation (Guo et al., 2008; Fu et al., 2010), object detection (Gall and Lempitsky, 2009), anatomy localization and segmentation (Zhou, 2010; Criminisi et al., 2011), face alignment (Cao et al., 2012), human pose estimation (Bissacco et al., 2007; Sun et al., 2012), etc.

**Table 2.1 Comparison of the Classification- and Regression-Based Approaches for Detecting a Single Object**

| Detection Approach | Regression-Based | Classification-Based |
|---|---|---|
| Where applicable | Medical anatomy detection | Generic object detection |
| Use of context | Global and local context | Local context only |
| Number of target objects | Known | Unknown |
| Learning method | Regression | Binary classification |
| Learning complexity | High | Low |
| Inference method | Sparse scanning and sample averaging | Exhaustive scanning and *ad hoc* grouping |
| Detection speed | Extremely fast | Fast |

## 2.3 METHODS FOR DETECTING MULTIPLE ANATOMIES

In this section, we first review three types of approach for detecting a plurality of anatomies: detection network, sequential detection, and one-shot regression. The former two types of methods, both classification-based, aim to leverage pairwise context but with different search strategies, while the regression method leverages the global context. Figure 2.6 schematically illustrates these methods. In general, the approach leveraging the pairwise context speeds up the computation when compared with those without using the pairwise context as it computationally breaks down the linear dependency on the number of anatomies. The proper use of global context brings further computational benefit when compared with the classification-based method, though maybe less accurate in the anatomy localization as it is challenging to learn an effective regressor. Finally, we present an approach that integrates both local and global contexts, which is empirically shown to be both efficient and effective.

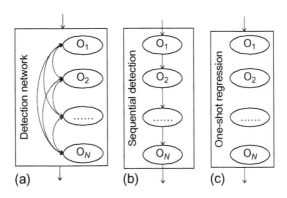

**FIGURE 2.6**

Three types of approaches for multiple anatomy detection.

## 2.3.1 CLASSIFICATION-BASED METHODS

One naive approach (Criminisi et al., 2009) for detecting $N$ objects is to run an independent, exhaustive detection for each object, resulting in a linear dependency on the number of objects in addition to the dependency on volume size, the number of rotation and scale candidates. This approach cannot scale up well and is slow to evaluate when $N$ is large. To speed up the detection, the pairwise context is leveraged in the literature.

### 2.3.1.1 Discriminative anatomical network

In discriminative anatomical network (DAN) (Seifert et al., 2009), the landmarks are connected in a network as shown in Figure 2.6(a). Information regarding the location of each landmark is propagated across the edges of the graph, which not only speeds up detection, but also increases detection accuracy. This is because the edges encode geometric relationships such as "to the right of," "close to," etc., and thus constrain the search problem into a smaller domain.

Denote the detector for landmark $i$ by $D_i(t_i|I)$. The landmark detectors are incorporated into the DAN through a Markov random field as follows:

$$P(t_1, \ldots, t_N|I) = \frac{1}{Z} \prod_i D_i(t_i|I) \prod_{(i,j) \in E} \psi_{ij}(t_i, t_j) \tag{2.9}$$

where $E$ denotes the set of edges in the network between landmarks and $\psi_{ij}(t_i, t_j)$ expresses the pairwise geometric relationship between landmarks.

In DAN, the pairwise context information is explicitly incorporated into the formulation. The belief propagation algorithm is used to provide the final solution for all objects from the object candidates passing the detectors.

The experiment at the landmark level shows that, in each of 80 evaluated volumes, all landmarks were detected in all volumes, without false positive detections. The average landmark error is 7 mm and the 95% error is less than 18.5 mm.

### 2.3.1.2 Active scheduling

In Zhan et al. (2008), the authors present a sequential multiple landmark detection approach that schedules the detection tasks in such an order that the expected information gain is maximized in each scheduling step.

Consider a volume with $N$ landmarks $\{t_1, t_2, \ldots, t_N\}$. Assume that the distribution of $y$ is $\Psi$ before measurement and becomes $\Phi$ after measurement. The information gain after a measurement of $y$ is defined as

$$IG_y = \sum_n \left\{ H(t_n|y \in \Psi) - \int_{y \in \Psi} H(t_n|y \in \Phi)P(y) \, dy \right\} \tag{2.10}$$

where $H(t_n|y \in \Psi)$ is the conditional entropy. The consequences of maximizing the information gain are twofold. First, it more likely schedules earlier a task with higher confidence. Second, it more likely schedules earlier a task with higher predictive power for other tasks.

The pairwise context is used. A multivariant Gaussian distribution is learned offline from 40 training samples to model the joint spatial distribution of one pair of landmarks. This is done for all possible pairs of landmarks. These distributions are incorporated into a Monte-Carlo simulation method to compute the information gain online. Chapter 3 describes this information theoretic approach in detail.

The experiment of detecting carina of trachea, L1 vertebra, left kidney, right kidney, left femoral head, right femoral head from 18 whole-body CT scans reports the average error ranging from 1.97 to 8.97 mm, with a speed of about 4 s.

### 2.3.1.3 Submodular detection

In Liu et al. (2010, 2011) and Liu and Zhou (2012), the authors present a submodular approach for triggering the landmark detectors sequentially. Once a landmark position is refined by a detector, the local search ranges for the other landmarks are reduced by using the pairwise spatial statistics that embody the *pairwise context.*

Denote by $T_{(1):(n)} = \{t_{(1)} \prec t_{(2)} \prec \cdots \prec t_{(n)}\}, n \leq N$ the ordered set of landmarks that have been refined by detectors and by U the unordered set of landmarks that remains to be refined. For each landmark $t_i \in U$, its search range $\Omega[t_i|T_{(1):(n)}]$ is defined as the intersection of the search ranges predicted by the already detected landmarks:

$$\Omega[t_i|T_{(1):(n)}] = \bigcap_{t_{(j)} \in T_{(1):(n)}} \Omega[t_i|\{t_{(j)}\}] \tag{2.11}$$

where $\Omega[t_i|\{t_{(j)}\}]$ denotes the local search neighborhood for landmark $t_i$ conditioned on the position of a detected landmark $t_{(j)}$. The goal is then to find the ordered set $T_{(1):(N)}$ that minimizes the *total computation,*

$$T'_{(1):(N)} = \underset{T_{(1):(N)}}{\operatorname{argmin}} \left\{ \lambda[t_{(1)}] \, V(\Omega[t_{(1)}]) + \sum_{i=2}^{N} \lambda[t_{(i)}] V(\Omega[t_{(i)}|T_{(1):(i-1)}]) \right\} \tag{2.12}$$

where $V(\Omega[t_i|T])$ is the volume of search range $\Omega[t_i|T]$ and $\lambda[t_j]$ is the unit computation cost for evaluating the landmark detector $t_j$.

A *greedy algorithm* that triggers the detector with the smallest computation for each round is proposed in Liu et al. (2010).

Initialize $T = \phi$.
**for** *j=1,...,N* **do**
$\quad$ $t_{(j)} = \arg\min_{t_{(k)}} \lambda[t_{(k)}]V(\Omega[t_{(k)}|T]);$
$\quad$ Append $t_{(j)}$ to the ordered set T to form the new set $T = t_{(1)}, \ldots, t_{(j)}.$
**end**

It is guaranteed to find an ordered set $\Lambda$ such that the invoked cost is at least 63% of its optimal value (Liu et al., 2010). Chapter 4 explains why and elaborates this submodular detection algorithm.

### 2.3.1.4 Integrated detection network

The IDN approach in Sofka et al. (2010, 2011) is motivated by sequential estimation techniques (Doucet et al., 2001), frequently applied in visual tracking. The state of the modeled object $t$ is denoted by $\theta_t$ and the sequence of multiple objects by $\theta_{0:t} = \{\theta_0, \theta_1, \ldots, \theta_t\}$. The observations for object $t$ are obtained from the image neighborhood $I_t$. The sequence of observations is denoted as $I_{0:t} = \{I_0, I_1, \ldots, I_t\}$. This is possible since prior knowledge exists for determining these image neighborhoods. The image neighborhoods in the sequence $I_{0:t}$ might overlap and can have different sizes. An image neighborhood $I_i$ might even be the entire volume I. The observations $I_t$ with the likelihood $P(I_t|\theta_t)$ are assumed conditionally independent given the state $\theta_t$. In Sofka et al. (2010), the observation model is set as discriminative PBT classifier in order to leverage the power of large annotated datasets, that is $P(\mathbf{I}_t|\theta_t) = \mathbf{D}(+1|\mathbf{I}_t[\theta_t])$. The state dynamics, that is, relationships between object poses, are modeled with an initial distribution $P(\theta_0)$ and a transition distribution $P(\theta_t|\theta_{0:t-1})$. Note that here the Markov transition $P(\theta_t|\theta_{t-1})$ often used in visual tracking is not used. Instead, IDN uses a transition kernel with a pairwise dependency to better leverage the *pairwise context*,

$$P(\theta_t|\theta_{0:t-1}) = P(\theta_t|\theta_j), \quad j \in \{0, 1, \ldots, t-1\} \tag{2.13}$$

where the best precursor $j$ is selected such that the posterior probability $\theta_{0:t}|\mathbf{I}_{0:t})$ is maximized. Refer to Chapter 6 for more details.

In Sofka et al. (2011), IDN is further introduced as a conceptual framework for designing large-scale detection systems. The candidates are propagated and refined throughout the detection network. It implements a flexible interface for rearranging modules such that this rearrangement is correctly handled for both training and detection. In one experiment of MRI-based liver segmentation, it achieves a mean symmetric surface-to-surface distance of 2.53 mm.

## 2.3.2 REGRESSION-BASED METHOD: REGRESSION FOREST

Detecting one single structure using regression to leverage the global context is reported in Zhou (2010). Criminisi et al. (2013) extend it to multiple structures including abdomen, left and right adrenal glands, left and right clavicles, left and right femoral necks, gallbladder, heads of left and right femurs, femur, heart, left and right atria, left and right ventricles, left and right kidneys, liver, left and right lungs, left and right scapulae, spleen, stomach, thorax, and thyroid gland, with each structure parameterized by an axis-aligned bounding box with $d = 6$ degrees of freedom, that is, skipping the $\theta$ component in the 3D pose. Instead of learning different regressors for different structures, one single regression function is learned, thus breaking the computational dependency on the number of structures. Refer to Criminisi et al. (2013) and Chapter 5 for more information about regression forest.

In the experiment of localizing 26 structures from CT scans, the regression forest records the mean bounding box localization errors for 26 structures ranging from 9.7 to 19.1 mm, with a detection speed of about 4 s. In comparison, it outperforms the template matching and multiatlas registration methods.

## 2.3.3 COMBINING CLASSIFICATION AND REGRESSION: CONTEXT INTEGRATION

The classification-based method leverages the local context and achieves high detection accuracy but with relatively slow speed. The regression-based method, on the other hand, uses global context and achieves fast speed but with relatively low accuracy. The context integration method proposed by Lay et al. (2013) combines the local and global context into one framework and achieves both good accuracy and fast speed. This general framework is used to detect multiple landmarks for the purpose of initializing anatomy segmentation.

Leveraging global context, a regression function is learned to simultaneously predict the offset vectors for all landmarks, given a test image patch I[y], following Zhou (2010) and Criminisi et al. (2013). The regression function is applied on a sparse set of y locations, predicting multiple candidate locations for all landmarks. Further, these candidate locations are verified by specific landmark detectors based on local context. Figure 2.7 graphically shows how the approach works. It also gives an example of detection candidates derived by using only local, only global, and joint context. Even though

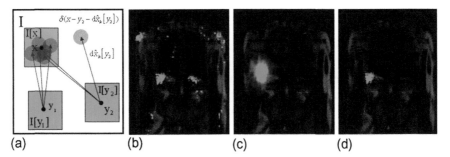

**FIGURE 2.7**

(a) An illustration of how image patches (green) predict the landmark location using global context and then these predictions are combined with local context at (blue). (b) Detection scores for a landmark on the top left of the liver in a low resolution MR FastView 3D volume, where local context gives spurious responses. (c) Global context gives a coarse localization. (d) The integration of local and global detection gives a fine scale density.

*Reprinted from Lay et al. (2013).*

the local detector may be inaccurate, it is only being applied at locations predicted from the global context, meaning it is possible to get a highly peaked posterior when integrating evidence from local and global contexts. Refer to Chapter 10 for more information about the context integration approach.

## 2.4 CONCLUSIONS

We have surveyed state-of-the-art discriminative methods for detecting a single anatomy or a cohort of anatomies. The classification-based detection method utilizes the local context and entails an exhaustive search scheme. When dealing with the pose variation of a single anatomy, various efficient detection structures have been proposed to reduce the computational complexity. When addressing multiple objects, effective search strategies have been designed to leverage the pairwise context for reduced computation. The regression-based detection method employs the global context, leading to fast detection but sometimes with outliers. Combining the regressors with classifiers integrates both global and local context, yielding the best of both worlds.

We anticipate the following future research directions that could lead to even more efficient and effective anatomy detection methods.

- *More effective discriminative learning approaches.* This is mostly driven by the machine learning community. When more powerful learning methods are invented, these methods such as boosting and random forest can offer immediate benefits. Recently, deep learning shows a lot of promise (Hinton and Salakhutdinov, 2006). The use of deep learning for anatomy detection (Shin et al., 2013) is yet to be fully explored. Refer to Chapter 7 for more detail.
- *More informative and fast-to-compute features.* Features play an essential role for final detection performance. There is a constant desire for more informative features that are fast to compute.
- *More efficient detection structures and search strategies.* Detection structures and search strategies have direct impact on the learning and computational complexities. The key is how to design

detection structures and search strategies to better leverage the anatomical context. Feature sharing among different detectors is one way to speed up the processing time.

- *Novel combinations of regression and classification.* Combining regressors and classifiers clearly shows promise. Currently only a simple product rule has been used for this combination. There is lots of room for researching novel ways of combining regressors and classifiers.
- *Using larger database and fewer annotations.* A large number of medical images are acquired and more will be acquired. To create user annotations needed for supervised learning is costly. Semi-supervised or unsupervised learning (Le et al., 2011) methods are needed to better tap the full potential of larger databases with fewer annotations.

# REFERENCES

Bissacco, A., Yang, M.H., Soatto, S., 2007. Fast human pose estimation using appearance and motion via multi-dimensional boosting regression. In: Proc. IEEE Conf. Computer Vision and Pattern Recognition, pp. 1–8.

Cao, X., Wei, Y., Wen, F., Sun, J., 2012. Face alignment by explicit shape regression. In: Proc. IEEE Conf. Computer Vision and Pattern Recognition, pp. 2887–2894.

Chen, T., Zhang, W., Good, S., Zhou, S.K., Comaniciu, D., 2009. Automatic ovarian follicle quantification from 3D ultrasound data using global/local context with database guided segmentation. In: Proc. Int. Conf. Computer Vision, pp. 795–802.

Criminisi, A., Shotton, J., Bucciarelli, S., 2009. Decision forests with long-range spatial context for organ localization in CT volumes. In: MICCAI Workshop on Prob. Models for MIA.

Criminisi, A., Shotton, J., Robertson, D., Konukoglu, E., 2011. Regression forests for efficient anatomy detection and localization in CT studies. In: MICCAI Workshop on Medical Computer Vision, pp. 106–117.

Criminisi, A., Robertson, D., Konukoglu, E., Shotton, J., Pathak, S., White, S., Siddiqui, K., 2013. Regression forests for efficient anatomy detection and localization in computed tomography scans. Med. Image Anal. 17 (8), 1293–1303.

Crum, W.R., Phil, D., Hartkens, T., Hill, D.L.G., 2004. Non-rigid image registration: theory and practice. Br. J. Radiol. 77, 140–153.

Doucet, A., De Freitas, N., Gordon, N., et al., 2001. Sequential Monte-Carlo Methods in Practice, vol. 1. Springer, New York.

Enzweiler, M., Gavrila, D.M., 2009. Monocular pedestrian detection: survey and experiments. IEEE Trans. Pattern Anal. Mach. Intell. 31 (12), 2179–2195.

Fu, Y., Guo, G., Huang, T.S., 2010. Age synthesis and estimation via faces: a survey. IEEE Trans. Pattern Anal. Mach. Intell. 32 (11), 1955–1976.

Gall, J., Lempitsky, V., 2009. Class-specific Hough forests for object detection. In: Proc. IEEE Conf. Computer Vision and Pattern Recognition, pp. 1022–1029.

Georgescu, B., Zhou, X.S., Comaniciu, D., Gupta, A., 2005. Database-guided segmentation of anatomical structures with complex appearance. In: Proc. IEEE Conf. Computer Vision and Pattern Recognition, vol. 2, pp. 429–436.

Geronimo, D., Lopez, A.M., Sappa, A.D., Graf, T., 2010. Survey of pedestrian detection for advanced driver assistance systems. IEEE Trans. Pattern Anal. Mach. Intell. 32 (7), 1239–1258.

Guo, G., Fu, Y., Dyer, C.R., Huang, T.S., 2008. Image-based human age estimation by manifold learning and locally adjusted robust regression. IEEE Trans. Image Process. 17 (7), 1178–1188.

Hinton, G.E., Salakhutdinov, R.R., 2006. Reducing the dimensionality of data with neural networks. Science 313 (5786), 504–507.

Hjelmås, E., Low, B.K., 2001. Face detection: a survey. Comput. Vis. Image Underst. 83 (3), 236–274.

Johnson, H.J., Christensen, G.E., 2002. Consistent landmark and intensity-based image registration. IEEE Trans. Med. Imaging 21, 450–461.

Jones, M., Viola, P., 2003. Fast multi-view face detection. MERL-TR2003-96.

Keeler, J.D., Rumelhart, D.E., Leow, W.K., 1990. Integrated segmentation and recognition of hand-printed numerals. In: Advances in Neural Information Processing Systems, vol. 3, pp. 557–563.

Kelm, B., Zhou, S.K., Suehling, M., Zheng, Y., Wels, M., Comaniciu, D., 2011. Detection of 3D spinal geometry using iterated marginal space learning. In: MICCAI Workshop on Medical Computer Vision, pp. 96–105.

Lay, N., Birkbeck, N., Zhang, J., Zhou, S.K., 2013. Rapid multi-organ segmentation using context integration and discriminative models. In: Information Processing in Medical Imaging, pp. 450–462.

Le, Q.V., Monga, R., Devin, M., Corrado, G., Chen, K., Ranzato, M., Dean, J., Ng, A.Y., 2011. Building high-level features using large scale unsupervised learning. arXiv preprint arXiv:1112.6209.

Li, S., Zhang, Z., 2004. FloatBoost learning and statistical face detection. IEEE Trans. Pattern Anal. Mach. Intell. 26, 1112–1123.

Ling, H., Zhou, S.K., Zheng, Y., Georgescu, B., Suehling, M., Comaniciu, D., 2008. Hierarchical, learning-based automatic liver segmentation. In: Proc. IEEE Conf. Computer Vision and Pattern Recognition.

Liu, D., Zhou, S.K., 2012. Anatomical landmark detection using nearest neighbor matching and submodular optimization. In: Proc. Int. Conf. Medical Image Computing and Computer Assisted Intervention. Springer, pp. 393–401.

Liu, D., Zhou, S.K., Bernhardt, D., Comaniciu, D., 2010. Search strategies for multiple landmark detection by submodular maximization. In: Proc. IEEE Conf. Computer Vision and Pattern Recognition, pp. 2831–2838.

Liu, D., Zhou, S.K., Bernhardt, D., Comaniciu, D., 2011. Vascular landmark detection in 3D CT. In: SPIE Medical Imaging.

Maron, O., Lozano-Pérez, T., 1998. A framework for multiple-instance learning. Adv. Neural Inform. Process. Syst. 10, 570–576.

Mason, L., Baxter, J., Bartlett, P., Frean, M., 1999. Boosting algorithms as gradient descent in function space. In: Advances in Neural Information Processing Systems.

Pauly, O., Glocker, B., Criminisi, A., Mateus, D., Möller, A., Nekolla, S., Navab, N., 2011. Fast multiple organ detection and localization in whole-body Mr Dixon sequences. In: Proc. Int. Conf. Medical Image Computing and Computer Assisted Intervention. Springer, pp. 239–247.

Rangayyan, R., Banik, S., Rangayyan, R., Boag, G.S., 2009. Landmarking and segmentation of 3D CT images. Morgan & Claypool Publishers, Los Altos.

Riesenhuber, M., Poggio, T., et al., 1999. Hierarchical models of object recognition in cortex. Nat. Neurosci. 2, 1019–1025.

Seifert, S., Barbu, A., Zhou, S.K., Liu, D., Huber, M., Suehling, M., Cavallaro, A., Comaniciu, D., 2009. Hierarchical parsing and semantic navigation of full body CT data. In: SPIE Medical Imaging, p. 725902.

Seifert, S., Kelm, M., Moeller, M., Mukherjee, S., Cavallaro, A., Huber, M., Comaniciu, D., 2010. Semantic annotation of medical images. In: SPIE Medical Imaging, p. 762808.

Shin, H.C., Orton, M.R., Collins, D.J., Doran, S.J., Leach, M.O., 2013. Stacked autoencoders for unsupervised feature learning and multiple organ detection in a pilot study using 4D patient data. IEEE Trans. Pattern Anal. Mach. Intell. 35 (8), 1930–1943.

Sofka, M., Zhang, J., Zhou, S.K., Comaniciu, D., 2010. Multiple object detection by sequential Monte Carlo and hierarchical detection network. In: Proc. IEEE Conf. Computer Vision and Pattern Recognition, pp. 1735–1742.

Sofka, M., Ralovich, K., Birkbeck, N., Zhang, J., Zhou, S.K., 2011. Integrated detection network (IDN) for pose and boundary estimation in medical images. In: Proc. IEEE Int. Symp. Biomedical Imaging, pp. 294–299.

Sun, M., Kohli, P., Shotton, J., 2012. Conditional regression forests for human pose estimation. In: Proc. IEEE Conf. Computer Vision and Pattern Recognition, pp. 3394–3401.

Swoboda, P., Liu, D., Zhou, S.K., 2013. Anatomical landmark detection using multiple instance boosting with spatial regularization. In: Proc. IEEE Int. Symp. Biomedical Imaging.

Torralba, A., Murphy, K.P., Freeman, W.T., 2007. Sharing visual features for multiclass and multiview object detection. IEEE Trans. Pattern Anal. Mach. Intell. 29 (5), 854–869.

Tu, Z., 2005. Probabilistic boosting-tree: learning discriminative methods for classification, recognition, and clustering. In: Proc. Int. Conf. Computer Vision, vol. 2, pp. 1589–1596.

Viola, P., Jones, M., 2001. Rapid object detection using a boosted cascade of simple features. In: Proc. IEEE Conf. Computer Vision and Pattern Recognition, pp. 511–518.

Viola, P.A., Platt, J.C., Zhang, C., 2006. Multiple instance boosting for object detection. In: Advances in Neural Information Processing Systems, pp. 1417–1424.

Wu, B., Ai, H., Huang, C., Lao, S., 2004. Fast rotation invariant multi-view face detection based on real AdaBoost. In: Proc. Auto. Face Gesture Recognition, pp. 79–84.

Yang, M.H., Kriegman, D.J., Ahuja, N., 2002. Detecting faces in images: a survey. IEEE Trans. Pattern Anal. Mach. Intell. 24 (1), 34–58.

Zhan, Y., Zhou, X., Peng, Z., Krishnan, A., 2008. Active scheduling of organ detection and segmentation in whole-body medical images. In: Proc. Int. Conf. Medical Image Computing and Computer Assisted Intervention. Springer, pp. 313–321.

Zhang, J., Zhou, S.K., McMillan, L., Comaniciu, D., 2007. Joint real-time object detection and pose estimation using probabilistic boosting network. In: Proc. IEEE Conf. Computer Vision and Pattern Recognition.

Zheng, Y., Barbu, A., Georgescu, B., Scheuering, M., Comaniciu, D., 2008. Four-chamber heart modeling and automatic segmentation for 3D cardiac CT volumes using marginal space learning and steerable features. IEEE Trans. Med. Imaging 27 (11), 1668–1681.

Zheng, Y., Georgescu, B., Ling, H., Zhou, S.K., Scheuering, M., Comaniciu, D., 2009a, Constrained marginal space learning for efficient 3D anatomical structure detection in medical images. In: Proc. IEEE Conf. Computer Vision and Pattern Recognition, pp. 194–201.

Zheng, Y., Lu, X., Georgescu, B., Littmann, A., Mueller, E., Comaniciu, D., 2009b, Robust object detection using marginal space learning and ranking-based multi-detector aggregation: application to automatic left ventricle detection in 2D MRI images. In: Proc. IEEE Conf. Computer Vision and Pattern Recognition, pp. 1343–1350.

Zhou, S.K., 2010. Shape regression machine and efficient segmentation of left ventricle endocardium from 2D B-mode echocardiogram. Med Image Anal. 14, 563–581.

Zhou, S.K., 2014. Discriminative anatomy detection: classification vs regression. Pattern Recogn. Lett. 43, 25–38.

Zhou, S.K., Comaniciu, D., 2007. Shape regression machine. In: Information Processing in Medical Imaging, pp. 13–25.

Zhou, S.K., Guo, F., Park, J.H., Carneiro, G., Jackson, J., Brendel, M., Simopoulos, C., Otsuki, J., Comaniciu, D., 2007a, A probabilistic, hierarchical, and discriminant framework for rapid and accurate detection of deformable anatomic structure. In: Proc. Int. Conf. Computer Vision.

Zhou, S.K., Zhou, J., Comaniciu, D., 2007b, A boosting regression approach to medical anatomy detection. In: Proc. IEEE Conf. Computer Vision and Pattern Recognition.

CHAPTER

# ROBUST MULTI-LANDMARK DETECTION BASED ON INFORMATION THEORETIC SCHEDULING

3

**Y. Zhan, Z. Peng, G. Hermosillo and X.S. Zhou**

*Siemens Medical Solutions USA, Inc., Malvern, PA, USA*

## CHAPTER OUTLINE

## 3.1 INTRODUCTION

Anatomical landmarks are biologically meaningful points existing in various organ systems. Historically, anatomical landmarks are defined to describe the morphological characteristics of anatomical structures and facilitate communication between scientists in the fields of biology and medicine, etc. In the medical imaging community, while most anatomical landmarks become *in vivo* visible, they play important roles in the interpretation of medical images. In analogy to geographic landmarks that guide travelers in exploring the earth, anatomical landmarks provide guidance to navigate medical images. For

S. Kevin Zhou (Ed): Medical Image Recognition, Segmentation and Parsing. http://dx.doi.org/10.1016/B978-0-12-802581-9.00003-2

example, anatomical contents within a medical image can be determined by the locations of anatomical landmarks. In addition, some anatomical landmarks also provide critical clues to diagnose diseases. For example, the posterior junction point of a lumbar vertebra and the spinal cord can be used to diagnose spondylolisthesis and evaluate the disease stage. Hence, algorithms that can automatically detect anatomical landmarks can directly benefit various clinical use cases. Besides the direct impact on clinical use cases, automatic detection of anatomical landmarks also paves the way for other medical image analysis tasks. For example, automatically detected landmarks can be used to initialize the deformable model for organ segmentation (Zhan et al., 2009; Zhang et al., 2012). They can also provide an initial transformation for image registration (Zhan et al., 2011).

In most of the aforementioned applications, more than one landmark need to be detected. In addition, as landmark detection is often the first step of a medical image analysis system, the detection of multiple landmarks is required to be fast and robust. To satisfy these two requirements, the spatial correlation across multiple landmarks should be exploited. Specifically, due to the strong anatomical context information existing in the human body, the locations of different landmarks are highly dependent. Therefore, instead of treating each landmark as an independent entity, the spatial configuration between them should be leveraged to increase both the speed and the robustness of a system. A more specific example related to whole-body CAD is shown in Figure 3.1. Here, a CAD system aims to detect the abdominal lymph node clusters. To achieve this goal, it is important to localize the iliac bifurcation of the aorta, which defines the local search region of the abdominal lymph node clusters. However, due to the uncertainty of the location and appearance of the iliac bifurcation, some other landmarks, for example, femoral heads and kidney centers, can also be detected to provide additional information. Specifically, the dependency (spatial correlation) between these "auxiliary"

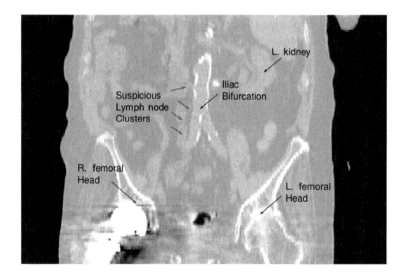

**FIGURE 3.1**

A representative CT image. The blue arrow points to an artificial metal "femoral head." The red arrows point to suspicious abdominal lymph node clusters, which are often close to the iliac bifurcation of the aorta.

landmarks and the iliac bifurcation should be exploited to increase the robustness and speed of the system. The remaining question is, What is the optimal order to detect these "auxiliary" landmarks? Intuitively, since the femoral head has the most distinctive appearances in computed tomography (CT) (bone is very bright in CT), it may be detected first, which in turn helps the detection of other landmarks and abdominal lymph node clusters. However, a more principled way is desired to determine the detection order of multiple landmarks and, hence, maximally increase the robustness and speed of the system. How to schedule the detection of multiple landmarks will be the major focus of this chapter.

If a complex medical image analysis algorithm consisting of multiple landmark detection can be considered as a system, the detection of each individual landmark becomes a "vision task" or "vision operation." Therefore, one way to principally exploit the dependency among different landmarks is to model the ordering of landmark detection as a *scheduling problem*. Due to the unique nature of human anatomy, the scheduling problem of multi-landmark detection has the following characteristics:

1. The same vision task in the system can be executed either independently or depending on the outcome of other tasks. Thus, the scheduling problem has a high level of flexibility, which might be exploited to substantially increase the speed and performance of the entire medical image analysis system.
2. Due to missing data, artifacts, or diseases, the scheduler of multi-landmark detection must be an *active* one. In other words, the scheduling must be adaptive to the specific patient data at the *runtime*.[a] Referring to the previous example, in general cases, the detector of iliac bifurcation should be invoked next to the "femoral head localization." However, as shown in Figure 3.1, for a patient who has an *artificial* metal femoral head, the femoral head's detector might not detect it correctly and usually returns a very low confidence. In this situation, instead of invoking the "iliac bifurcation detector," the scheduler should trigger the detectors of other organs, which can be localized accurately without the inference of femoral heads.
3. Similar to many vision problems, the probabilistic factors influence multi-landmark detection systems in two aspects. First, tasks in a multi-landmark detection system are often statistically dependent. Referring to the previous example, "iliac bifurcation localization" is statistically dependent on "femoral head localization," as the relative locations of the iliac bifurcation with respect to the femoral heads are not deterministic. Second, the outcome of vision tasks usually embeds uncertainties. Since tasks are mutually dependent, uncertainties in one task might influence the speed and performance of other tasks.

Although scheduling problems have been extensively studied in different research areas (a brief review will be presented in Section 3.2), the existing methods cannot be directly borrowed for the scheduling problem in multi-landmark detection, due to the aforementioned unique characteristics. In this chapter, we propose to study the scheduling problem of multi-landmark detection from an information theoretic view. In this way, vision tasks (individual landmark detections) of the system are modeled as a set of *measurements* that aim to extract the anatomical information from medical images. The principle of our method is to schedule vision tasks in an order that is optimal in an information-theoretic sense. More specifically, we explore the gauge of *information gain* to define the scheduling criterion. Based on this criterion, a sequential decision-making process is employed to schedule vision tasks in a multi-landmark detection system. There are two major advantages of our method. First, various probabilistic factors that influence the performance and speed of landmark detection are incorporated in the scheduling criterion. Therefore, the scheduled system is able to achieve more efficient and accurate detection results. Second, in our scheduling method, the *next* task is always determined based on current system status. In this way, the multi-landmark detection system is scheduled in an *active* way and thus adaptive to different patient images. It is also worth noting that, although we will focus on the scheduling of multi-landmark detection in this chapter, the information theory-based scheduling can be extended to other vision tasks, for example, multi-organ segmentation and multi-step disease identification, etc.

The rest of this chapter is organized as follows. We start from Section 3.2 by reviewing some related works. The problem is stated in Section 3.3.1 and the formulation of our scheduling criterion is carried out in Section 3.3.2. In Section 3.3.3, we describe the Monte-Carlo simulation method, which aims to efficiently evaluate the information gain. The specific implementation of our landmark detectors and the modeling of the spatial correlation across landmarks are introduced in Section 3.3.4. In Section 3.4, very diverse applications that use multi-landmark detection are presented to demonstrate the effectiveness of our method. This chapter concludes in Section 3.5.

## 3.2 LITERATURE REVIEW

Thanks to the requirements from various clinical use cases, automatic landmark detection has gained significant interest in the medical imaging research community. Most of these studies focus on the detection of individual landmarks. The most recent advances include the employment of machine learning technologies to capture the appearance characteristics of anatomical landmarks (Criminisi et al., 2011; Liu and Zhou, 2012). As the main focus of this chapter is the scheduling of the multi-landmark detection, we will review the papers relevant to task scheduling in the remainder of this section.

In the last several decades, the topics of scheduling have been extensively studied in the areas of operation research (Brucker, 2004) and theoretical computer science (Pruhs et al., 2003). Many scheduling rules/methods were proposed to deal with scheduling problems in various applications, including manufacturing, service industries, transportation and practical computer systems, etc. While earlier studies mainly focus on deterministic systems, more researchers have moved to flexible and stochastic systems recently. In Nam (2001), the scheduling policies for flexible systems are investigated. That paper analyzes an open processing network model with discretionary routing and shows, in general, unbalanced workload routing with priority sequencing gives better performance than a balanced one. Chou et al. (2006) studied a stochastic single machine problem, where the actual processing time of tasks is not known until processing is completed. They proved that when the task weights and processing times are bounded and task processing times are mutually independent random variables, the weighted shortest expected processing time among available jobs (WSEPTA) heuristic is asymptotically optimal for the single-machine problem. Although these scheduling problems share one or several features with those of multi-landmark detection, neither of them account for all the aforementioned characteristics of multi-landmark detection.

The scheduling problem of multi-landmark detection is akin to an extensively studied topic in computer vision, *active object recognition*, in the sense of information gain. Recall in the previous example, the system aims to gain diagnostic *information* (Do the abdominal lymph node clusters exist? Where are they?) through a set of *measurements* (femoral heads localization, iliac bifurcation localization, and lymph node clusters detection). From an information theoretic view, it is analogous to active object recognition, which aims to identify objects (*information*) by collecting images with different sensor parameters (*measurements*). Indeed, information theory has been successfully employed in active object recognition. In Denzler et al.'s (2002) pioneering work, a formalism is proposed for optimal sensor parameter selection for iterative state estimation. They used Shannon's information theory to select information-gathering actions that maximize mutual information. The benefits of the method were demonstrated in an object recognition application using an active camera. An extension of Denzler and Brown (2002) to the multi sensor active recognition problem is carried out by Farshidi et al. (2005). A recursive Bayesian state estimation problem is formulated to employ the mutual information. This idea is also applied on a tracking problem in Kreuchera et al. (2005), where the active sensing approach is adopted to schedule sensors for target tracking applications that combine particle filtering, predictive density estimation, and relative entropy maximization. These methods are not off-the-shelf methods for the multi-landmark detection scheduling problem due to two reasons: (1) The tasks (operations) in multi-landmark detection systems are usually more closely dependent. More specifically, outcome of pre-executed tasks are often used as the input of subsequent tasks. Referring to the previous example, the location of the femoral head (outcome of a task) is used as the input of "iliac birufcation detection" to dramatically narrow down the search range. This situation is significantly different from the sequential sensor positioning problem in active recognition. (2) While all the measurements of active recognition focus on the identification of one objective, that is, object identification, multiple measurements in the multi-landmark detection may focus on different objectives.

## 3.3 METHODS
### 3.3.1 PROBLEM STATEMENT

Inspired by the ideas of active object recognition, we observe the scheduling problem of multi-landmark detection from an information theoretic view. From this perspective, a multi-landmark detection system aims to obtain anatomical information, by executing a set of vision tasks. (In the remainder of this chapter, the words "task," "operation," and "examination" share the same meaning.)

Mathematically, the anatomical information is presented by a set of variables $\{x_i\}$, for example, the locations of the landmarks under study. In a multi-landmark detection system, each vision task, that is, detection of an individual landmark, delivers a measurement $y$ to decrease the ambiguity of $\{x_i\}$. In most cases, $y$ is the measurement of one interested variable $x_i$, that is, detection of an individual landmark. However, in a more general sense, $y$ can be out of $\{x_i\}$. For example, $y$ can be a variable representing the center of a template with multiple landmarks, which is not of interest to clinical use cases but is helpful to landmark detection.

The dependency between different tasks is modeled by conditional probability. Therefore, prior to the execution of a task, its outcome $y$ has the prior distribution $p(y|y_o)$, where $y_o$ is the outcome of *historically executed* tasks. (For simplicity, in the remainder of this chapter, $p(y|y_o)$ is denoted by $\Psi$.) In the context of landmark detection, $p(y|y_o)$ describes the conditional probability of the landmark locations given the previously detected ones. It is determined by the spatial correlation across different landmarks. It is worth noting that, in a multi-landmark detection system, the prior distribution can be effectively used to increase the efficiency and the accuracy of the measurement $y$. Therefore, we propose to model *the dependency between tasks* (measurements), which is not explicitly modeled in the formulations of Denzler and Brown (2002) and Farshidi et al. (2005).

After the execution of a task (detection of a specific landmark), the distribution of its measurement $y$ shrinks, or *changes* in general, to $\Phi$. The shrink/change of $y$ in turn reduces/changes the uncertainty of $\{x_i\}$. Importantly, the uncertainties in the outcome of tasks are incorporated in this way.

Overall, we model the scheduling problem as a sequential decision-making process. At each step, the decision is: "Given the current measurements $y_0$, what is the next task, which, upon execution, gains most anatomical information?" From an information theoretic view, the information gain is equivalent to the reduction of uncertainty of $\{x_i\}$.

## 3.3.2 SCHEDULING CRITERION BASED ON INFORMATION GAIN

According to information theory (Cover and Thomas, 1991), the information gain is defined by the reduction of entropy. In particular, the conditional entropy has been successfully employed as the gauge of information gain in the areas of feature selection (Peng et al., 2005) and active recognition (Zhou et al., 2003). Accordingly, we use conditional entropy to define our scheduling criterion.

Based on the previous definition, the information gain, IG, after this particular measurement of $y$ is:

$$\mathrm{IG}_y = \sum_i \left( H(x_i | y \in \Psi) - \int_{y \in \Psi} H(x_i | y \in \Phi) p(y) \, \mathrm{d}y \right) \tag{3.1}$$

Here, we use the expression $y \in \Psi$ to mean "$y$ has the support $\Psi$" or "$y$ has the distribution $\Psi$." And $H(x_i | y \in \Psi)$ and $H(x_i | y \in \Phi)$ are conditional entropies defined in the following form:

$$H(x_i | y \in \Phi) = -\int_{y \in \Phi} p(y) \int_{x_i \in X_i} H(x_i | y) \, \mathrm{d}x_i \, \mathrm{d}y \tag{3.2}$$

$$= -\int_{y \in \Phi} p(y) \int_{x_i \in X_i} p(x_i | y) \log p(x_i | y) \, \mathrm{d}x_i \, \mathrm{d}y \tag{3.3}$$

In a straightforward implementation, $y$ is the spatial coordinates of one of the anatomical landmarks. In this scenario, $y$ is taken from the set $\{x_i\}$, so the first term in Eq. (3.1) goes away because it becomes constant for all $y$. In general, however, we can have $y$s outside of $\{x_i\}$. Then, Eq. (3.1) is meaningful in its complete form.

The basic principle of our IG-based scheduling rule is that a particular measurement operation $y^*$ will be preferred over others if it delivers a maximal value for IG. The justification behind this principle is described as follows. According to Eq. (3.1), information gain is determined by three factors: (1) the support of $y$ before measurement, $\Psi$ (the spatial probability of landmark $y$ predicted by the detected ones). (2) The measurement uncertainty of $y$, $\Phi$ (the uncertainty of the detection of $y$) and (3) the dependency between $y$ and $\{x_i\}$, $p(x_i | y)$ (the spatial probabilities of all other landmarks after the detection of $y$). Indeed, it is the interplay of all these three factors that determine the speed and performance of scheduled multi-landmark detection systems according to our previous analysis. In this way, the definition of IG intrinsically incorporates all the probabilistic factors that influence the speed and performance of a scheduled system. Therefore, the IG-based scheduling method is expected to provide better scheduled systems than *ad hoc* strategies, such as "prefer the task that has the less support before measurement," "prefer the task with less uncertain outcome," or "prefer the task that is more correlated with other tasks," which is shown next.

In Figure 3.2, we present a rather simplified but intuitive example to show the effectiveness of the IG-based scheduling criterion. In this example, the system aims to localize four anatomical landmarks: carina of trachea, left femoral head, right femoral head, and L1 vertebra. Each operation/examination in this system is the invocation of a detector to localize a specific landmark. The dependency between different tasks is modeled by the relative spatial locations between different organs. More specifically, the positions of the localized landmarks are used to estimate the positions of the remaining ones to reduce the search range of other landmark detectors. Let us assume the carina of trachea has been detected. As shown in Figure 3.2(a), the estimated position of the L1 vertebra has the minimum support (denoted by the red-dashed ellipses). If we use an *ad hoc* schedule strategy that prefers the task having the minimum support, the next organ to be localized should be the L1 vertebra. However, since the neighboring anatomical structures, for example, the L2 and the T12 vertebra, usually have similar appearance as L1, the L1 detector is easily confused in the vertical direction (Gaussian-fitted uncertainty is denoted by the blue-dashed ellipses in Figure 3.2(a)) and get the wrong result (denoted by the red point in Figure 3.2(a)). In other words, the measurement of L1 has large uncertainty, which is not expected to deliver large information gain. According to our IG-based scheduling criterion, instead, the two femoral heads that have stronger "shrink" from $\Psi$ to $\Phi$ are preferred as the next organs to be localized. (In this example, $\Psi$ and $\Phi$ in Eq. (3.1) are defined by the red-dashed lines and the blue-dashed ellipses in Figure 3.2(a), respectively.) After localizing the two femoral heads, the support of the "un-measured" L1 vertebra is significantly reduced (denoted by the red-dashed ellipses in Figure 3.2(b)) and the detector is able to successfully localize it (denoted by the green point in Figure 3.2(b)) without being confused by L2 or T12 vertebra.

In summary, the proposed scheduling rule incorporates all probabilistic factors that are critical to the speed and performance of a system into a unified framework. Two intuitive principles are embodied in the formulation: (1) an examination (task) with higher confidence, that is, a stronger "shrink" from $\Psi$ to $\Phi$, tends to be scheduled earlier and (2) an examination with higher dependency (predictive power) to all tasks, that is, a strong influence of $y^*$ over other variables (Eq. 3.3), tends to be scheduled earlier.

### 3.3.3 MONTE-CARLO SIMULATION METHOD FOR THE EVALUATION OF INFORMATION GAIN

Given the definition of IG, we use a forward sequential algorithm to schedule multi-landmark detection. At each step, we evaluate the IG of each remaining task and pick the task that delivers the maximal IG as the next one to be executed. A Monte-Carlo simulation method is employed to evaluate IG.

Recalling the definition of information gain (Eq. 3.1), the key point of IG evaluation lies in the calculation of the conditional entropy. Actually, it is trivial to calculate the conditional entropy $H(x|y)$, given the conditional probability density function $p(x|y)$. However, in most practical systems, it is very difficult, if not impossible, to estimate the conditional probability density function which describes the dependency between different tasks. Instead, the dependency between multiple landmarks is usually provided as a predictive function with uncertainty:

$$x = f(y) + \varepsilon, \quad \epsilon \sim \gamma(\epsilon) \tag{3.4}$$

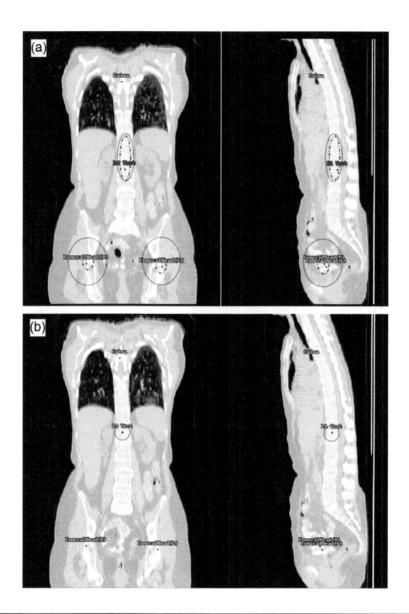

**FIGURE 3.2**

An example to show the effectiveness of the proposed scheduling method in multi-landmark detection. (a) Uncertainty of landmark positions after the trachea carina is localized. The red-dashed ellipses denote the uncertainty of the landmark locations estimated by the trachea carina, that is, $\Psi$ in Eq. (3.1). The blue-dashed ellipses denote the expected uncertainty of the landmark detectors, that is, $\Phi$ in Eq. (3.1). The red point denotes the falsely detected L1 vertebra. (b) Uncertainty of landmark positions after the trachea carina and the femoral heads are localized. The red-dashed ellipse denotes the uncertainty of landmark locations estimated by the trachea carina and femoral heads.

where $f(.)$ is the predictive function, $\epsilon$ is a random variable with the probability density function $\gamma(\epsilon)$. In a multi-landmark detection system where $x$ and $y$ represent the positions of two landmarks, $f(.)$ becomes a position predictor of $x$ based on its relative location to $y$, and $\gamma(\epsilon)$ reflects the uncertainty of this predictor.

Since $f(.)$, $\gamma(\epsilon)$, as well as the measurement uncertainty, $\Psi(y)$, can be learned from a set of training data, we employ a Monte-Carlo simulation method to calculate the conditional entropy as Algorithm 1. In this method, the conditional entropy is directly calculated, without estimating the conditional probability density function $p(x|y)$.

---

**ALGORITHM 1 MONTE-CARLO SIMULATION METHOD TO CALCULATE $H(x|y \in \Psi)$**

**Require:** $\Psi(y), f(y), \gamma(\epsilon)$
  **for** $m = 1$ to $M$ **do**
  Sample $y_m$ i.i.d from $\Psi(y)$
  **for** $n = 1$ to $N$ **do**
    Sample $\epsilon_n$ i.i.d from $\gamma(\epsilon)$
  **end for**
  $x_{m,n} = f(y_m) + \epsilon_n$
  **end for**
  Calculate $H(x|y \in \Psi)$ upon the sampled set $\{x_{m,n} | m = 1, \ldots, N, n = 1, \ldots, N\}$

---

Following the similar idea, the second term of Eq. (3.1) is calculated using Algorithm 2.

---

**ALGORITHM 2 MONTE-CARLO SIMULATION METHOD TO CALCULATE $\int_{y \in \Psi} H(x|y \in \Phi)p(y)\,dy$**

**Require:** $\Phi(y), \Psi(y), f(y), \gamma(\epsilon)$
  $E = 0$
  **for** $l = 1$ to $L$ **do**
  Sample $y_l$ i.i.d from $\Psi(y)$
    **for** $m = 1$ to $M$ **do**
    Sample $y_m$ i.i.d from $\Phi(y)$
      **for** $n = 1$ to $N$ **do**
      Sample $\epsilon_n$ i.i.d from $\gamma(\epsilon)$
    **end for**
    $x_{l,m,n} = f(y_m + y_l) + \epsilon_n$
    **end for**
  Calculate $H(x|y_l \in \Phi)$ upon the sampled set $\{x_{l,m,n} | m = 1, \ldots, N, n = 1, \ldots, N\}$
  $E = E + H(x|y_l \in \Phi)p(y_l)$
  **end for**
  $\int_{y \in \Psi} H(x|y \in \Phi)p(y)dy = E/L$

---

## 3.3.4 IMPLEMENTATION

In this section, we will briefly introduce the implementation of our individual landmark detection algorithm and the modeling of spatial correlation across landmarks. It is worth noting that these implementations are just one possible selection. In the proposed scheduling framework, alternative algorithms for landmark detection and spatial correlation modeling can be employed.

## Learning-based landmark detection

Due to the complex appearance of different anatomical landmarks, we resort to a learning-based approach for individual landmark detection. Thanks to its data-driven nature, learning-based approaches also make our method highly scalable to different imaging modalities, for example, CT, magnetic resonance (MR), positron emission tomography (PET), ultrasound. We formulate landmark detection as a voxel-wise classification problem. Specifically, voxels close to the landmark are considered as positive samples and voxels away from the landmark are regarded as negative ones. To learn a specific landmark detector, we first annotate the landmark in a set of training images. The positive and negative samples/voxels are determined based on their distances to the annotated landmark. For each training sample (voxel), a set of elementary features are extracted in its neighborhood. Our elementary features are generated by a set of mother functions, $\{H_l(\mathbf{x})\}$ extended from Haar wavelet basis. As shown in Eq. (3.5) and Figure 3.3, each mother function consists of one or more three-dimensional (3D) rectangle functions with different polarities.

$$H(\mathbf{x}) = \sum_{i=1}^{N} p_i R(\mathbf{x} - \mathbf{a_i}) \tag{3.5}$$

where polarities $p_i = \{-1, 1\}$, $R(\mathbf{x}) = \begin{cases} 1, & \|\mathbf{x}\|_\infty \leq 1 \\ 0, & \|\mathbf{x}\|_\infty > 1 \end{cases}$ denotes rectangle functions and $\mathbf{a_i}$ is the translation.

By scaling the mother functions and convoluting them with the original image, a set of spatial-frequency spaces are constructed as Eq. (3.6).

$$F_l(\mathbf{x}, s) = H_l(s\mathbf{x}) \times I(\mathbf{x}) \tag{3.6}$$

where $s$ and $l$ denote the scaling factor and index of mother functions, respectively.

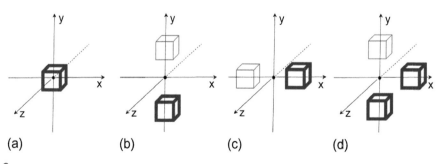

(a)          (b)          (c)          (d)

**FIGURE 3.3**

Some examples of Haar-based mother functions.

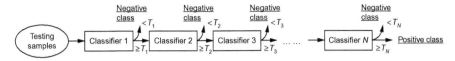

**FIGURE 3.4**

Schematic explanation of cascade AdaBoost classifiers.

Finally, for any voxel $\mathbf{x_0} \in \mathfrak{R}^3$, its feature vector $\mathfrak{F}(\mathbf{x_0})$ is obtained by sampling these spatial-frequency spaces in the neighborhood of $\mathbf{x_0}$ (Eq. 3.7). It provides cross-scale appearance descriptions of voxel $\mathbf{x_0}$.

$$\mathfrak{F}(\mathbf{x_0}) = \bigcup_{l=1,\dots,L} \{F_l(\mathbf{x_i}, s_j) | \mathbf{x_i} \in \mathbb{N}(\mathbf{x_0}), s_{min} < s_j < s_{max}\} \qquad (3.7)$$

Compared to standard Haar wavelet, the mother functions we employed are not orthogonal. However, they provide more comprehensive image features to characterize different anatomy primitives. For example, as shown in Figure 3.3, mother function (a) potentially works as a smoothing filter, which is able to extract regional features. Mother functions (b) and (c) can generate horizontal or vertical "edgeness" responses, which are robust to local noises. More complicated mother function like (d) is able to detect "L-shape" patterns, which might be useful to distinguish some anatomy primitives. In addition, our features can be quickly calculated through integral image (Crow, 1984). It paves the way to an efficient landmark detection system.

All elementary features are then fed into a cascade classification framework (Viola and Jones, 2004) as shown in Figure 3.4. The cascade framework is designed to address the highly unbalanced positive and negative samples. In fact, since only voxels around landmarks under study are positives and all other voxels are negatives, the ratio of positives to negatives is often less than $1:10^5$. In the training stage, all positives but a small proportion of negatives are used at every cascade level. The training algorithm is "biased" to positives, such that each positive has to be correctly classified but the negatives are allowed to be misclassified. These misclassified negatives, that is, false positives, will be further used to train the following cascades. At run-time, while positives are expected to go through all cascades, most negatives can be rejected in the first several cascades and do not need further evaluation. In this way, the run-time speed can be dramatically increased. In our study, we use *AdaBoost* (Freund and Schapire, 1997) as the basic classifier in the cascade framework. The output of the learned classifier $\mathcal{A}(\mathfrak{F}(\mathbf{x}))$ indicates the likelihood of the specific landmark appearing at $\mathbf{x}$.

At run-time, a sliding window approach is employed to apply the learned classifiers on each voxel in the image. The voxel that has the highest response of $\mathcal{A}(\mathfrak{F}(\mathbf{x}))$ can be considered as the detected landmark. In addition, the response map describes the probability distribution of a specific landmark in the spatial domain, which will be used to estimate $\Phi$ in the scheduling framework.

### Spatial correlation across landmarks

Different from the active shape model that learns global shape statistics, we propose to learn distributed anatomy models, that is, for each anatomy $p_i$, we aim to learn its spatial relations with other anatomies in a group-wise fashion. Assume $p_i$ is the anatomy under study, and $U(\mathbf{p} \backslash p_i)$ is a subset of anatomy primitives which does not contain $p_i$, that is, $U(\mathbf{p}\backslash p_i) \subset \{\mathbf{p}\backslash p_i\}$. The group-wise spatial configuration between $p_i$ and $U(\mathbf{p}\backslash p_i)$ is modeled as a conditional probability following multi-variant Gaussian distribution:

$$s(p_i|U(\mathbf{p}\backslash p_i)) = \frac{1}{(2\pi)^{(3/2)}|\Sigma|^{1/2}} \exp\left(-\frac{1}{2}(p_i - \mu)^T \Sigma^{-1}(p_i - \mu)\right) \tag{3.8}$$

where $\mu$ and $\Sigma$ are two statistical coefficients that are learned as follows.

We employ a linear model to capture the spatial correlation between $p_i$ and $U(\mathbf{p}\backslash p_i)$ as Eq. (3.9):

$$p_i = \mathfrak{C} \cdot \mathbb{U} \qquad \cdot \tag{3.9}$$

where $\mathbb{U}$ is a vector concatenated by $\{p_j|p_j \in U(\mathbf{p}\backslash p_i)\}$ and $\mathfrak{C}$ denotes the linear correlation matrix. Given a set of training samples, $\mathfrak{C}$ can be learned by solving a least squares problem. Furthermore, $\mu$ and $\Sigma$ are calculated as:

$$\mu = E[\mathfrak{C} \cdot \mathbb{U}]$$
$$\Sigma = E[(\mathfrak{C} \cdot \mathbb{U} - \mu)(\mathfrak{C} \cdot \mathbb{U} - \mu)^T] \tag{3.10}$$

Recall Eq. (3.4); $\mathfrak{C}$ and $\Sigma$ become the coefficients of $f(.)$ and $\gamma(.)$, respectively.

## 3.4 APPLICATIONS

In this section, we will demonstrate the performance of our method on applications that relate to different imaging modalities (CT, MR, PET, and radiograph) and clinical fields (neurology, oncology, and orthopedics).

### 3.4.1 AUTOMATIC VIEW IDENTIFICATION OF RADIOGRAPHS

Based on the projection view, radiographs can be categorized as posteroanterior/anteroposterior (PA-AP) and lateral (LAT) views. Although the DICOM header may contain the projection and orientation of a radiograph, the information may be wrong or missing in about 30% to 40% of cases. Hence, we developed an image-based algorithm to automatically annotate the chest radiographs. In this work, multi-landmark detection in 2D radiographs is used to provide local appearance cues. Followed by a sparse spatial configuration model, which aggregates these appearance cues for high-level image interpretation, our algorithm can achieve very high accuracy (99.97%) for radiograph view identification. It is worth noting that the high accuracy of view identification is very important, because even "occasional" mistakes can shatter users' confidence in the system, thus reducing its usability in the clinical settings. Figure 3.5 shows some examples of the detected landmarks. Please refer to Tao et al. (2011) for more details of the method.

The algorithm framework is highly scalable to tackle other radiograph parsing problems. For example, by simply reusing the detected/filtered landmarks, we can successfully address two other image parsing problems, anatomy/organ ROI prediction (Figure 3.6) and optimized image visualization (Figure 3.7).

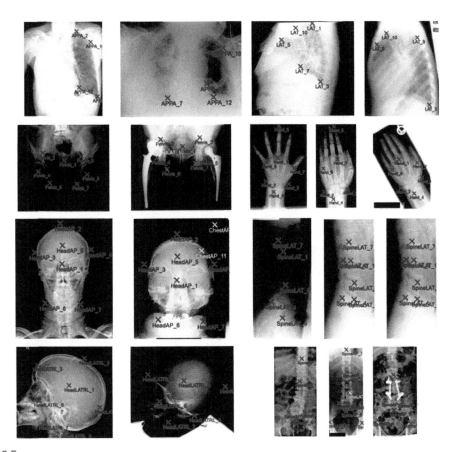

**FIGURE 3.5**

Examples of the detected landmarks on different images.

## 3.4.2 AUTO-ALIGNMENT FOR MR KNEE SCAN PLANNING

Magnetic resonance imaging (MRI) has been successfully used to diagnose various knee diseases ranging from acute knee injuries to chronic knee dysfunction, for example, ligament tears, patella dislocation, meniscal pathology, and arthropathies (Ostlere, 2007). The inherent imaging physics and speed limitations of MR typically constrain the diagnostic MR images to have isotropic high resolution in 3D. Instead, diagnostic MR image is a 2.5D modality with high in-slice resolution and low through-slice resolution (Figure 3.8(c)). Hence, their diagnostic quality is highly dependent upon the positioning accuracy of the slice groups (imaging planes). Good centering and orientation ensures that the anatomy of interest is optimally captured within the high-resolution (high-res) imaging plane.

Traditionally, this is achieved by acquiring 2D scout images (called "localizers"): technicians can then plan out high-res slice groups based on relevant anatomies visible in these scouts. Recently, a 3D knee scout scan has been introduced to improve the quality of the workflow. A 3D knee scout scan has

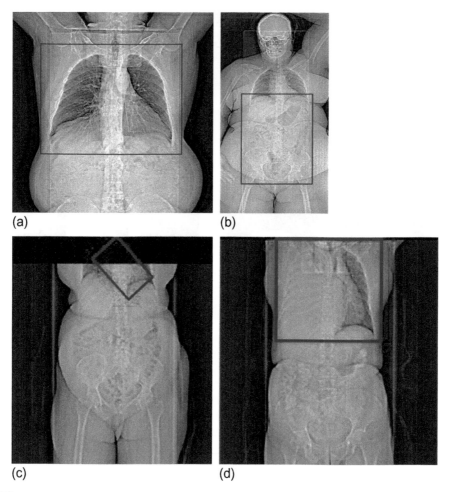

(a)    (b)

(c)    (d)

**FIGURE 3.6**

Anatomy ROI prediction in the topogram for CT scan automation. The blue rectangle bounded regions in (a)–(d) correspond to ROIs of lung, abdomen, heart, and lung. It can be seen that the ROI prediction algorithm is robust under the FoV variation and disease influences.

low but isotropic resolution. Although it might not be of diagnostic quality, it provides complete 3D context which enables a human operator, or a computer, to plan out all required high-res slice groups without any additional scout scans. Figure 3.8 shows an example of how to plan a high-res slice group using the 3D scout in a reproducible way: to image the menisci, the transversal slice group should be parallel to the meniscus plane, and the in-plane rotation is determined by aligning to the line connecting the two lower edges of the femoral condyle (the yellow-dashed line).

Technically, the slice positioning problem is equivalent to align a 3D scout scan based on several anatomical landmarks. Therefore, we incorporate our multi-landmark detection algorithm into the automatic slice positioning system. (Besides the aforementioned algorithms, additional strategies, e.g.,

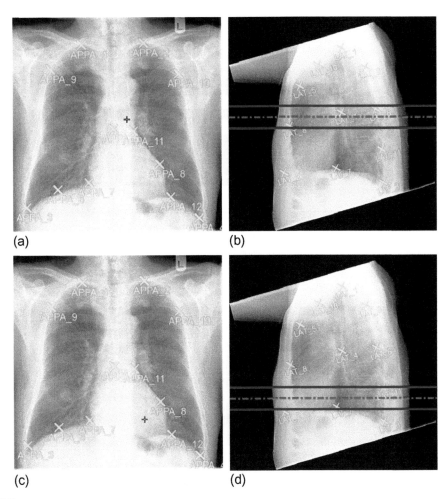

(a)   (b)

(c)   (d)

**FIGURE 3.7**

Optimized image visualization: (a) the PA-AP chest image with pinpointed position shown as cross and (b) the orientation corrected LAT chest image with the estimated corresponding position/range shown within the blue band. (c) and (d) show that when the pinpointed position on the PA-AP chest image moves, the corresponding position on the LAT chest image moves accordingly.

hierarchal learning, redundant detection (Zhou et al., 2010), are added to the system. Please refer to Zhan et al. (2011) for more details.)

We evaluated our method on 744 knee scout scans. The alignment results are visually checked and evaluated by two experienced professionals as "accurate (AC)": accurate positioning that is acceptable by technicians; "reasonable (RE)": reasonable good positioning but still has the space to improve; and "gross failure (GF)." Our method can achieve "AC" in 736 (98.9%) cases and has only 1 (0.1%) "GF." As shown in Figure 3.9, our system is able to achieve robust knee alignment even on challenging cases, for example, severe bone diseases, metal implants, etc.

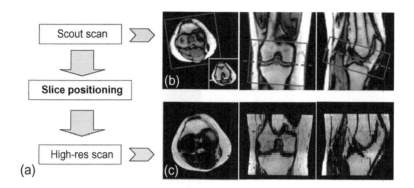

**FIGURE 3.8**

MR slice positioning using scout scans. (a) Workflow of knee MR scans. (b) An MR knee scout scan. Rectangle boxes: coverage of MR slice group. Circles: imaging centers. Yellow-dashed line (in the small thumbnail) defines the in-plane rotation. (c) A typical high-resolution diagnostic MR knee transversal scan.

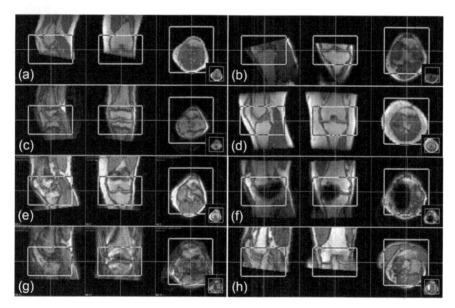

**FIGURE 3.9**

Robust slice positioning of our algorithm on "stress testing" cases. Each subfigure shows the three orthogonal MPRs of the aligned volume at the center of the knee meniscus slice box: (a) tibia out of FoV, (b) femur out of FoV, (c) a pediatric patient, (d) an old patient, (e) a patient with bone disease, (f) a patient with metal implant, (g) motion artifacts, and (h) folding artifacts.

**Table 3.1 Quantitative Errors (Average and Standard Deviation) of Our Alignment Method Compared to Manual Alignment**

|  | Knee Meniscus | Femur Cartilage | Patella Cartilage |
|---|---|---|---|
| Trans. (mm) | $0.93 \pm 0.27$ | $1.53 \pm 0.42$ | $1.53 \pm 0.38$ |
| Rot. tra≫cor (°) | $0.83 \pm 0.31$ | $1.99 \pm 0.60$ | $2.01 \pm 0.77$ |
| Rot. sag≫tra (°) | $0.54 \pm 0.28$ | $0.72 \pm 0.25$ | $3.14 \pm 1.16$ |
| Rot. sag≫cor (°) | $0.63 \pm 0.27$ | $0.82 \pm 0.35$ | $1.35 \pm 0.52$ |

Note: *Rot. tra≫cor, sag≫tra, and sag≫cor denote the rotation angles from transversal to coronal, from sagittal to transversal, and from sagittal to coronal, respectively.*

We also quantitatively evaluate the accuracy of the alignment using the detected landmarks on 50 cases with manual alignment. As shown in Table 3.1, the errors are very limited and our system can satisfy clinical requirements.

### 3.4.3 AUTO-NAVIGATION FOR ANATOMICAL MEASUREMENT IN CT

Tibiofemoral joint space width (JSW) measurement is one important quantification in musculoskeletal radiology studies. JSW is one of the measures for longitudinal studies on progression of knee osteoarthritis, because JSW reduction can serve as a surrogate for the thinning of articular cartilage. Traditionally, this measurement is performed on weight-bearing radiographs. However, the joint flexion and imaging parameters need to be carefully controlled by an experienced radiographer. Three-dimensional imaging modalities, such as MRI or CT, although not weight-bearing, record all anatomical information without occlusion. Therefore, the measurement of JSW in 3D carries some intrinsic advantages and can be more reproducible. However, it is a very tedious task for the clinician to navigate to the correct 3D viewing-plane to perform these measurements. Here, our method is employed to detect multiple anatomical landmarks. As shown in Figure 3.10, based on these landmarks, viewing-planes can be automatically corrected in a consistent manner.

The prototype algorithm was evaluated on 30 randomly selected CT scans of the knee (mean age 51 years, range 12-76 years), all performed on 64-slice scanners, and reconstructed at 0.75-3.00 mm slice thickness. Results were reviewed by an experienced musculoskeletal radiologist who measured joint space in the medial (Figure 3.11(a)), lateral, and patella-femoral (Figure 3.11(b)) compartments of the knee using manual aligned conventional CT views. The same measurements were then performed on computer auto-aligned CT images (ACT) obtained by the above prototype system which reorients the images for optimal display of the knee joint space. Differences in joint space measurements and time for evaluation were recorded.

The study shows that computer auto-alignment of CT image reconstructions (ACT) allows significantly faster evaluation time without statistically significant impact on the results of joint space measurements. It can save radiologists' time and potentially lead to cost savings. Please refer to Chhabra et al. (2014) for more detailed information on the study.

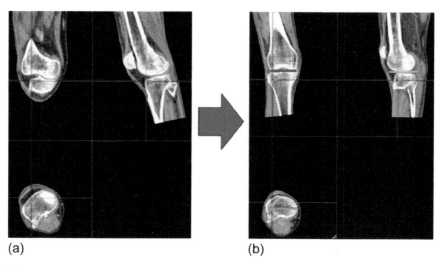

**FIGURE 3.10**

Computer auto-alignment of knee in CT. (a) Original volume before alignment and (b) after alignment.

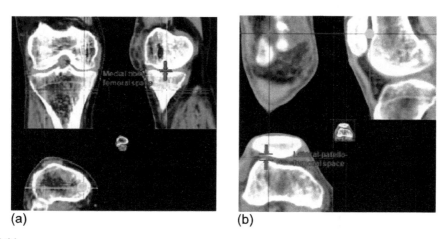

**FIGURE 3.11**

Joint space measurements in the knee. (a) Medial-tibio-femoral space: widest distance between cortices of medial femoral condyle and opposing medial tibial condyle and (b) lateral-patello-femoral space: widest distance between cortices of lateral facets of patella and trochelea.

### 3.4.4 AUTOMATIC VERTEBRAE LABELING

The spine is one of the major organs in the human body. It includes the vertebral column and spinal cord. A human vertebral column typically consists of 33 vertebrae; 24 of them are articulating (7 cervical, 12 thoracic, and 5 lumbar vertebrae) and 9 of them are fused vertebrae in the sacrum and the coccyx. As the spine strongly correlates to both neural and skeletal systems, various neurological, orthopedic, and oncological studies involve the investigations of spine anatomies. In addition, due to the strong spatial correlations between specific vertebrae and their surrounding organs, the spine may also be used as a vertical reference framework to describe the locations of other organs in the trunk, for example, transpyloric plane. In spine image analysis, localization and labeling of vertebrae is often the first step, which is tedious and time consuming for manual operators. Accordingly, we employ the multi-landmark detection algorithm to automatically localize and label vertebrae. (Besides the algorithms introduced in this section, we also treat different vertebrae as "anchor" and "bundle" and train vertebrae detectors in a hierarchical way. In addition, an articulated model is used to model the spine geometry. Please refer to Zhan et al. (2012) for more details.)

Our method is evaluated on both CT and MR datasets. The CT dataset includes 189 randomly selected CT cases with partial or whole spine coverage. A wide range of imaging parameters are used for these datasets, including different reconstruction kernels and slice thickness. Our MR dataset includes 300 T1-weighted 3D MR scout scans. These scout scans have relatively low but isotropic resolution of 1.7 mm and large fields of view. These datasets come from different clinical sites and were generated by different types of Siemens MR Scanners (Avanto 1.5T, Verio 3T, Skyra 3T, etc.). Both MR and CT datasets include partial or whole spines.

The automatic vertebrae labeling results were shown to experienced radiologists and rated as "perfect" (no manual editing required), "acceptable" (minor manual editing required), and "rejected" (major manual editing required).

As shown in Table 3.2, our method reaches "perfect" detection in 95+% cases. It is worth noting that our testing set includes CT/MR scans with severe diseases or imaging artifacts. However, our method can still detect vertebrae and discs robustly. Figures 3.12 and 3.13 show the results of our method on challenging CT and MR scans. As shown in these cases, our method is robust to different kinds of imaging artifacts (Figures 3.12(a, b) and 3.13(c, g)), large imaging noises (Figure 3.12(f)), metal implants (Figures 3.12(d, e) and 3.13(d, f)), severe scoliosis (Figure 3.13(a)), pathologies (Figures 3.12(c) and 3.13(e)), congenital abnormality (Figure 3.13(b)), and scans that have anchor vertebrae out of field of view (Figure 3.13(h)).

**Table 3.2 Evaluations of Spine Detections in CT and MR Scans**

|  | Number of Cases | Perfect | Acceptable | Reject |
|---|---|---|---|---|
| CT | 189 | 180 (95.2%) | 6 (3.2%) | 3 (1.6%) |
| MR | 300 | 293 (97.7%) | 4 (1.3%) | 3 (1.0%) |

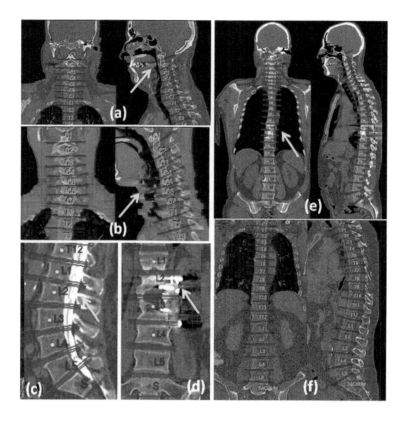

**FIGURE 3.12**

Examples of vertebrae labeling results in challenging CT scans. (a) C-spine scan with metal artifacts.
(b) C-spine scan with motion artifacts. (c) L-spine scan with spinal cord disease. (d) L-spine scan with metal
implant. (e) Whole spine scan with metal artifacts. (f) Whole spine scan with large imaging noises.

## 3.4.5 VIRTUAL ATTENUATION CORRECTION OF BRAIN PET IMAGES

Dementia/epilepsy-related neuro degenerative disorders are on the rise mainly due to increasing life
expectancy (35 million people worldwide are affected by dementia, with 5 million new cases added
every year). In recent years, $^{18}$F-FDG PET imaging has become an effective tool in the clinician's
arsenal for dementia patients and increasing their diagnostic confidence (Mehta and Thomas, 2012).
The PET imaging workflow involves attenuation correction (AC) with CT to correct nonuniform
absorption patterns within the body, which adds to the radiation dose exposure, especially for follow-
up and monitoring applications. If one could do this step of AC without having to do a CT, this would
be a huge benefit in preventing additional radiation exposure. Therefore, we develop a prototype for
"virtual" AC of brain PET scans (see Figure 3.14(a)).

The essential goal of virtual attenuation correction (VAC) is to recover the structural information from a functional imaging modality (PET). To tackle this challenging problem, we resort to
"borrowing" structural information from nonattenuation corrected (NAC) PET-CT pairs—namely

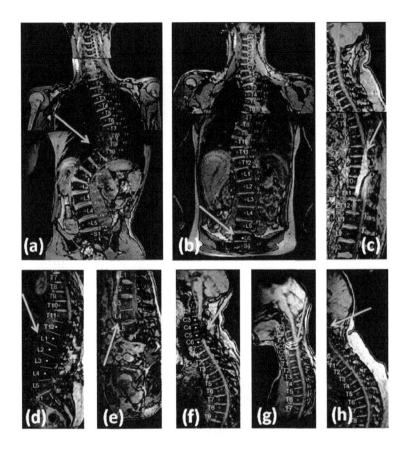

**FIGURE 3.13**

Examples of vertebrae labeling results in challenging MR scans. (a) Whole-spine scan with strong scoliosis. (b) Whole-spine scan with congenital abnormality (six lumbar vertebra). (c) Whole-spine scan with folding artifact. (d) L-spine scan with metal implant. (e) L-spine scan with vertebral pathology. (f) C-spine scan with metal artifact. (g) C-spine scan with ring artifact. (h) C-spine scan where anchor vertebra is out of field of view.

"model scan." More specifically, the current patient PET image is registered with a selected model PET image scan. The structural information can then be "borrowed" from the model scan by warping the model CT image scan to the patient space (see Figure 3.15 for the algorithm workflow). Our multi-landmark detection algorithm is employed in this prototype as a key step. The detected landmarks (see Figure 3.14(b)) are utilized in twofold: (1) based on the spatial configurations of the detected landmarks, the model scan that is the most similar to the subject under study is selected and (2) the detected landmarks are used to initialize the deformable registration of PETs.

To evaluate the influence of the VAC errors on the diagnostic results, we use a diagnostic statistical tool that provides voxel-wise statistical scores ($z$-score compared to a normal template). Based on the $z$-score value, a voxel is classified as normal ($-3 \leq z_{voxel} \leq 3$), hyponormal ($z_{voxel} < -3$), or hypernormal ($z_{voxel} > 3$). For dementia-related disorders, hyponormal areas with reduced metabolism

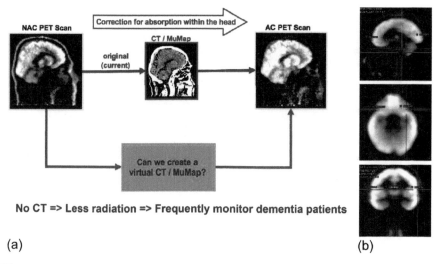

**FIGURE 3.14**

(a) Problem definition. (b) Representative landmarks defined in PET.

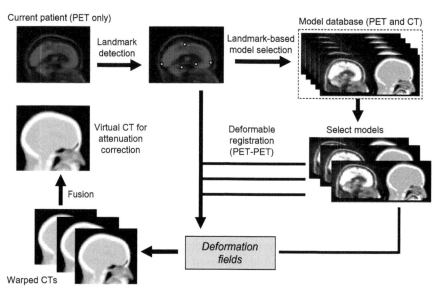

**FIGURE 3.15**

Workflow of the brain PET virtual attenuation correction algorithm.

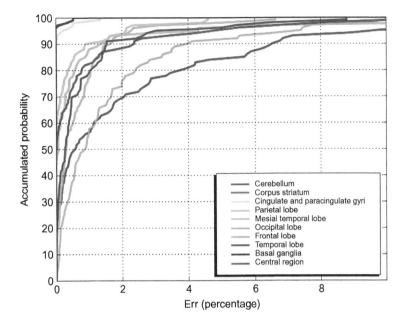

**FIGURE 3.16**

Cumulative distribution function of region-wise z-score errors.

are of general interest. We aggregate the errors between z-scores from VAC and those from AC with a real CT for different brain regions. This is shown as a CDF over 127 patients in Figure 3.16. For all cases, the brain regions that are most relevant to dementia diagnosis, that is, parietal lobe, temporal lobe, and cingulate cortex, have limited errors ≤2%. Hence, the effects of diagnosis are very minimal. (Please refer to Dewan et al. (2013) for more details of our method and validation.)

## 3.4.6 BONE SEGMENTATION IN MR FOR PET-MR ATTENUATION CORRECTION

Recently, a combination of PET and MRI (Judenhofer et al., 2008) has been proposed as a new multimodal diagnostic tool. However, MR cannot be directly used for AC since it is not capable of measuring transmission and attenuation of electrons directly. In order to recover the attenuation coefficients from MR, it is important to segment different tissues, for example, lung, fat, soft-tissue, bone. Among them, bone segmentation is particularly challenging yet not ignorable as bony structures often have the highest attenuation coefficients.

To tackle this difficult problem, we propose to build an articulated bone model offline. At runtime, an anatomy-aware articulated registration algorithm is designed to bring the bone model to the subject MR image (see Figure 3.17). Here, multi-landmark detection is employed to provide anatomical context information. Specifically, the landmarks detected in the subject MR are used to (1) crop the local ROIs for different bony structures, (2) initialize the registration of each bony structure, and (3) provide

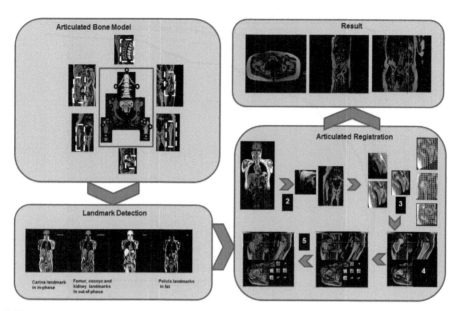

**FIGURE 3.17**

Workflow of MR bone segmentation.

the anatomical information to determine specific registration schemes for different bony structures. Validated on 241 cases from different clinical sites, our prototype can achieve success in 98% of cases.

## 3.5 CONCLUSION

In this chapter, we explored an information theoretic method to address the scheduling problem of multiple anatomical landmark detection. The key idea is to schedule vision tasks (detections of individual landmarks) in such an order that each operation achieves maximum expected information gain over all the tasks. More specifically, task dependency is modeled by conditional probability; the outcome of each task is assumed to be probabilistic as well, and the scheduling criterion is based on the reduction of the summed conditional entropy over all tasks. A Monte-Carlo simulation method is employed to efficiently evaluate information gain without estimating the conditional probability density functions. In this way, the proposed method is able to schedule multiple vision tasks very fast. Compared to existing scheduling methods, our method has two major advantages in scheduling multi-landmark detection. First, the probabilistic factors that influence the speed and performance of the scheduled systems are incorporated in the formulation of the scheduling criterion. Second, the proposed method schedules systems in an active way, that is, the schedule is adaptive to the image data in terms of achieving maximum information gain.

Based on our scheduling method, we built prototypes on various applications. Some representative ones are presented in this chapter. These applications cover different imaging modalities (CT, MR,

PET, radiograph, etc.) and clinical fields (oncology, orthopedics, neurology, etc.). Our method helps to achieve robust and accurate results in all applications.

The potential extension of this work exists in two aspects. First, from the perspective of optimization, the sequential decision-making process might not achieve the global optimal solution. A forward-backward strategy can be applied to improve it. The basic idea is to allow tasks being executed multiple times; that is, a task can be fired multiple times, as long as its execution can further reduce the system uncertainty. A good example is a second time detection of femoral heads using the localization results of iliac bifurcation. Second, considering the different accuracy requirements of different systems, a stop criterion based on information theory can be designed to increase the efficiency. In other words, instead of exhaustively executing all tasks, the scheduling method should actively stop running any task, as long as the system uncertainty is below the required level. For example, in the use case where landmarks are used to initialize a deformable model, if the detected landmarks are able to initialize a model accurately enough (depends on the robustness of the method of deformable segmentation), it is not necessary to detect the remaining landmarks.

## NOTE

a.   This should not be confused with the topic in operations research called online scheduling (Pruhs et al., 2003). In online scheduling problems, the basis assumption is that the tasks themselves are not known beforehand but rather come in an online fashion. This is not the case here.

## REFERENCES

Brucker, P., 2004. Scheduling Algorithms. Springer, Heidelberg.

Chhabra, A., Peng, Z., Zhou, X., Florin, C., Salganicoff, M., 2014. Knee joint space measurements on computer automatically aligned images vs conventional reconstructions. *Insights into Imaging,* Scientific session B-0969.

Chou, M.C., Liu, H., Queyranne, M., Simchi-Levi, D., 2006. On the asymptotic optimality of a simple on-line algorithm for the stochastic single-machine weighted completion time problem and its extensions Brownian models of open processing networks: canonical representation of workload. Oper. Res. 54, 464-474.

Cover, T., Thomas, J., 1991. Elements of Information Theory. John Wiley & Sons, New York.

Criminisi, A., Shotton, J., Robertson, D., Konukoglu, E., 2011. Regression forests for efficient anatomy detection and localization in CT studies. In: Medical Computer Vision. Recognition Techniques and Applications in Medical Imaging. Springer, Berlin, pp. 106-117.

Crow, F., 1984. Summed-area tables for texture mapping. Comp. Graphics, 18 (3), 207-212.

Denzler, J., Brown, C.M., 2002. Information theoretic sensor data selection for active object recognition and state estimation. IEEE Trans. PAMI 24, 145-157.

Dewan, M., Zhan, Y., Hermosillo, G., Jian, B., Zhou, X.S., 2013. Brain PET attenuation correction without CT: an investigation. International Workshop on Pattern Recognition in Neuroimaging (PRNI), June 2013, Philadelphia, PA, USA.

Farshidi, F., Sirouspour, S., Kirubarajan, T., 2005. Active multi-camera object recognition in presence of occlusion. Intelligent Robots and Systems Conference, August 2005, pp. 2718-2723.

Freund, Y., Schapire, R.E., 1997. A decision-theoretic generalization of on-line learning and an application to boosting. J. Comput. Syst. Sci. 55, 119-139.

Judenhofer, M., Wehrl, H., Newport, D., Catana, C., Siegel, S., Becker, M., Thielscher, A., Kneilling, M., Lichy, M., Eichner, M., et al., 2008. Simultaneous PET-MRI: a new approach for functional and morphological imaging. Nat. Med. 14 (4), 459-465.

Kreuchera, C., Kastellab, K., Hero, A.O., 2005. Sensor management using an active sensing approach. Signal Process. 85, 607-624.

Liu, D., Zhou, S.K., 2012. Anatomical landmark detection using nearest neighbor matching and submodular optimization. Medical Image Computing and Computer-Assisted Intervention Conference papers. Springer, Heidelberg, pp. 393-401.

Mehta, L., Thomas, S., 2012. The role of PET in dementia diagnosis and treatment. App. Rad. 41, 8-15.

Nam, I., 2001. Dynamic scheduling for a flexible processing network. Oper. Res. 49, 305-315.

Ostlere, S., 2007. Imaging the knee. Imaging 15, 217-241.

Peng, H., Long, F., Ding, C., 2005. Feature selection based on mutual information: criteria of max-dependency, max-relevance, and min-redundancy. IEEE Trans. PAMI 27, 1226-1238.

Pruhs, K., Sgall, J., Torng, E., 2003. Handbook of Scheduling: Algorithms, Models, and Performance Analysis. CRC Press, Boca Raton, FL.

Tao, Y., Peng, Z., Krishnan, A., Zhou, X.S., 2011. Robust learning-based parsing and annotation of medical radiographs. IEEE Trans. Med. Imaging 30 (2), 338-350.

Viola, P., Jones, M.J., 2004. Robust real-time face detection. Int. J. Comput. Vis. 57, 137-154.

Wikipedia, 2009. Landmark Point. http://en.wikipedia.org/wiki/Landmark-point.

Zhan, Y., Dewan, M., Zhou, X.S., 2009. Cross modality deformable segmentation using hierarchical clustering and learning. Medical Image Computing and Computer-Assisted Intervention Conference papers, pp. 1033-1041.

Zhan, Y., Dewan, M., Harder, M., Krishnan, A., Zhou, X.S., 2011. Robust automatic knee MR slice positioning through redundant and hierarchical anatomy detection. IEEE Trans. Med. Imaging 30, 2087-2100.

Zhan, Y., Dewan, M., Harder, M., Zhou, X.S., 2012. Robust MR spine detection using hierarchical learning and local articulated model. Medical Image Computing and Computer-Assisted Intervention Conference papers, pp. 141-148.

Zhang, S., Zhan, Y., Dewan, M., Huang, J., Metaxas, D.N., Zhou, X.S., 2012. Towards robust and effective shape modeling: sparse shape composition. Med. Image Anal. 16, 265-277.

Zhou, X.S., Comaniciu, D., Krishnan, A., 2003. Conditional feature sensitivity: a unifying view on active recognition and feature selection. 9th International Conference on Computer Vision, October 2003, Nice, France.

Zhou, X.S., Peng, Z., Zhan, Y., Dewan, M., Jian, B., Krishnan, A., Tao, Y., Harder, M., Grosskopf, S., Feuerlein, U., 2010. Redundancy, redundancy, redundancy: the three keys to highly robust anatomical parsing in medical images. Proceedings of the International Conference on Multimedia Information Retrieval, pp. 175-184.

# LANDMARK DETECTION USING SUBMODULAR FUNCTIONS

# 4

**D. Liu**

*Siemens Corporate Technology, Princeton, NJ, USA*

## CHAPTER OUTLINE

## 4.1 INTRODUCTION

An important area in medical image analysis is the development of methods for quickly finding the positions of certain anatomical structures, such as liver top, lung top, aortic arch, iliac artery bifurcation, femur head left and right, to name but a few. In multimodality image registration (such as positron emission tomography-computed tomography [PET-CT]) or in registration of follow-up scans, the fusion of multiple images can be initialized or guided by the positions of such anatomical structures

S. Kevin Zhou (Ed): Medical Image Recognition, Segmentation and Parsing. http://dx.doi.org/10.1016/B978-0-12-802581-9.00004-4

(Johnson and Christensen, 2002; Crum et al., 2004). In vessel centerline tracing, vessel bifurcations can provide the start and end points of certain vessels to enable fully automated tracing (Beck et al., 2010). In organ segmentation, the center position of an organ can provide the initial seed points to initiate segmentation algorithms (Rangayyan et al., 2009). In seminar reporting, automatically found anatomical structures can be helpful in configuring the optimal intensity window for display (Pauly and et al., 2011) or offer the text tooltips for structures in the scan (Seifert et al., 2010).

We define an anatomical landmark (or landmark in brief) as a distinct and unique point position in an image that coincides with an anatomical structure. Some anatomical landmarks have little ambiguity, such as the apex of the left or right lung in a CT image. Other landmarks such as the liver center lack distinctiveness, because the center of mass of the liver often does not coincide with a unique anatomical structure and becomes ill-defined. In such a case, one can define a hypothetical bounding box that tightly bounds the liver and define the liver center as the center of the bounding box.

We are interested in the problem of efficiently detecting a large number of landmarks from such scans, without reading DICOM tags or any textual information. This is challenging due to the presence of imaging noise, artifacts, and body deformation. The field of view is also unknown. A practical landmark detection method must meet the following requirements. First, it must be robust to deal with pathological or anomalous anatomies such as fluid-filled lungs, air-filled colons, inhomogeneous livers caused by different metastasis, and resected livers after surgical interventions, different contrast agent phases, scans of full or partial body regions, extremely narrow field of views, etc. Figure 4.1 shows some examples of CT scans that illustrate the challenges. Second, since landmark detection is mostly a preprocessing step for computationally heavier tasks such as CAD and registration, it must run fast so that more time can be allocated for heavier tasks.

State-of-the-art landmark detection methods are based on statistical learning (Viola and Jones, 2004). In this paradigm, each landmark has a dedicated detector (Zhan et al., 2008; Liu et al., 2010). In Okada et al. (2007), volumes have a consistent field of view, for example, the database consists of only liver scans. In such a case, it is possible to predefine a region of interest for each landmark

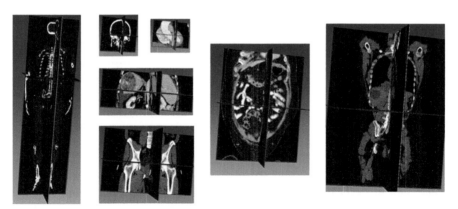

**FIGURE 4.1**

The database used in this chapter has thousands of 3D CT scans with different body regions and severe pathologies.

detector. In general, however, the position of each landmark can vary significantly across different scans; in most cases, some landmarks such as the head or toe are not even present in a body scan. Under such cases, running multiple detectors independently of each other can result in false detections (Peng et al., 2009; Liu et al., 2010). To handle the problem of false detections, one can exploit the spatial relationship information between landmarks to reduce false detections. A model for describing the spatial relationship between landmarks is the Markov Random Field (Besag, 1986; Bishop, 2006).

An important factor to consider when designing multiple landmark detectors is speed. Naively running each detector on the whole volume yields a time complexity proportional to the number of detectors and volume size. This poses significant computational resources when the number of landmarks of interest is large or when the volumes are large. More efficient detection can be achieved with a sequential method (Liu et al., 2010). Since the relative positions of landmarks in the human body are constrained (e.g., the kidney is below the heart in a typical CT scan), one can define a search range (subvolume) for each unknown landmark relative to the known landmark positions. Detecting a landmark within a local search range instead of within the whole volume achieves faster speed.

## 4.2 MULTIPLE LANDMARK DETECTION

Our goal in this chapter is to minimize the computational cost of sequential, multiple landmark detection. The computational cost is related to (i) the size of the image subspace (or *search space*) in which a detector is performing the search and (ii) the unit cost of the landmark detector. We will first focus on item (i) and later extend the framework to item (ii). The methods described in this chapter were first introduced in Liu et al. (2010) to minimize the total search range and later extended to minimize overall computation time in Liu and Zhou (2012) by modifying the cost function in the submodular formulation.

Having $n$ landmarks detected, with $N - n$ landmarks remaining to detect, which detector should one use next, and where should it be applied, so that the overall computational cost is minimized? These two questions are tightly related, and the answer is simple: *determine the search space for each detector based on the already detected landmarks and pick the detector that has the smallest search space.* We will show theoretical guarantees of the algorithm in Section 4.2.2, and then in Section 4.2.3 extend the algorithm to take multiple factors into account, including the size of the search space and the unit cost of the detector (classifier). In Section 4.3, we will discuss how to find the very first landmark, also called the anchor landmark, when none of the landmark positions are known *a priori*.

### 4.2.1 SEARCH SPACE

In sequential detection, landmarks already detected provide spatial constraints on the landmarks remaining to be detected. Consider an object consisting of $N$ distinct landmarks. Denote by

$$\Lambda_{(1):(n)} = \{l_{(1)} \prec l_{(2)} \prec \cdots \prec l_{(n)}\}, \quad n \leq N \tag{4.1}$$

the ordered set of detected landmarks. Denote by U the unordered set of landmarks that remains to be detected. For each landmark $l_i \in$ U, its search space $\Omega_{l_i}$ is determined jointly by landmarks in $\Lambda_{(1):(n)}$, for example, by the intersection of the individual search spaces,

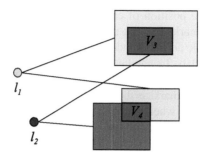

**FIGURE 4.2**

Illustration of the search space definition in Eq. (4.2). Detected landmarks $l_1$ and $l_2$ provide search spaces for undetected landmarks $l_3$ and $l_4$ (not shown). Final search spaces $V_3$ and $V_4$ for $l_3$ and $l_4$ are obtained by intersection. A greedy algorithm would prefer landmark $l_4$ over $l_3$ as the next landmark to detect since $V_4$ is smaller than $V_3$.

$$\Omega_{l_i}(\Lambda_{(1):(n)}) = \bigcap_{j, l_j \in \Lambda_{(1):(n)}} \Omega_{l_i}(\{l_j\}) \tag{4.2}$$

where $\Omega_{l_i}(\{l_j\})$ denotes the search space for landmark $l_i$ conditioned on the position of a detected landmark $l_j$. This is shown in Figure 4.2. This definition could be restrictive, so we will discuss alternatives in Section 4.2.3.

Denote the search volume (or search area) of search space $\Omega_{l_i}(\Lambda)$ as $V(\Omega_{l_i}(\Lambda))$, which calculates the volume of $\Omega_{l_i}(\Lambda)$. Without loss of generality, assume the search volume is the cardinality of the set of voxels (pixels) that fall within the search space. Define the constant $\Omega_\phi \equiv \Omega_k(\phi)$, $\forall k$, as the space of the whole image, which is a tight upper bound of the search space. The search volume has the following property:

**Theorem 4.1.** $\forall S \subseteq T$,

$$V(\Omega(S)) - V(\Omega(S \cup \{l\})) \geq V(\Omega(T)) - V(\Omega(T \cup \{l\})) \tag{4.3}$$

Set functions satisfying the above property are called *supermodular* (Schrijver, 2003).

Let us simplify the notation by omitting the subscript $l_i$ from $\Omega_{l_i}$. Define the complement $\overline{\Omega(S)} = \Omega_\phi \setminus \Omega(S)$, $\forall S$, where $\Omega_\phi$ has earlier been defined as the space of the whole volume.

**Lemma 4.1.** $\Omega(S \cup \{l\}) = \Omega(S) \cap \Omega(\{l\})$.
This follows from the definition.

**Lemma 4.2.** If $S \subseteq T$, then $\Omega(S) \supseteq \Omega(T)$.
Proof. $T = S \cup (T \setminus S) \Rightarrow$ From Lemma 4.1, $\Omega(T) = \Omega(S \cup (T \setminus S)) = \Omega(S) \cap \Omega(T \setminus S) \subseteq \Omega(S)$. $\quad\square$

**Lemma 4.3.** $\Omega(S) \setminus \Omega(S \cup \{l\}) = \Omega(S) \cap \overline{\Omega(\{l\})}$.
Proof. LHS $= \Omega(S) \setminus (\Omega(S) \cap \Omega(\{l\})) = \Omega(S) \cap \overline{(\Omega(S) \cap \Omega(\{l\}))} = \Omega(S) \cap (\overline{\Omega(S)} \cup \overline{\Omega(\{l\})}) = (\Omega(S) \cap \overline{\Omega(S)}) \cup (\Omega(S) \cap \overline{\Omega(\{l\})}) = $ RHS. $\quad\square$

**Lemma 4.4.** *If $\Omega(T) \subseteq \Omega(S)$, then $V(\Omega(S) \setminus \Omega(T)) = V(\Omega(S)) - V(\Omega(T))$.*

**Lemma 4.5.** *If $\Omega(T) \subseteq \Omega(S)$, then $V(\Omega(T) \leq V(\Omega(S))$.*
Finally we prove the supermodularity of $V(\Omega(.))$ in Theorem 4.1.

**Proof of Theorem 4.1.** From Lemma 4.2, $\Omega(S) \supseteq \Omega(T)$. Then $\Omega(S) \cap \overline{\Omega(\{l\})} \supseteq \Omega(T) \cap \overline{\Omega(\{l\})}$. From Lemma 4.3, we have $\Omega(S) \setminus \Omega(S \cup \{l\}) \supseteq \Omega(T) \setminus \Omega(T \cup \{l\})$. From Lemma 4.5, we have $V(\Omega(S) \setminus \Omega(S \cup \{l\})) \geq V(\Omega(T) \setminus \Omega(T \cup \{l\}))$. From Lemma 4.4, □

**Lemma 4.6.** *$F(.)$ in Eq. (4.5) is nondecreasing.*
*Proof.* From Lemmas 4.2 and 4.5, we have $\forall S \subseteq T$, we have $V(\Omega(T)) \leq V(\Omega(S))$, which shows $V(.)$ is nonincreasing. Consequently, $F(.)$ is nondecreasing. □

## 4.2.2 GREEDY ALGORITHM
The goal is to find the ordered set $\Lambda_{(2):(N)}$ that minimizes the cumulated search volume, that is,

$$\Lambda'_{(2):(N)} = \arg\min_{\Lambda_{(2):(N)}} \sum_{i=2}^{N} V\left(\Omega_{l_{(i)}}(\Lambda_{(1):(i-1)})\right) \tag{4.4}$$

Note that in Eq. (4.9) we do not include the first landmark $l_1$ as its search space is typically the whole image when no landmarks have been detected *a priori*. The first landmark can be detected using the method in Section 4.3.

Define the cost function $C_k(\Lambda) = V(\Omega_k(\Lambda)), \forall k$. A greedy algorithm for finding the ordering $\{l_{(1)}, \ldots, l_{(N)}\}$ that attempts to minimize the overall cost is to iteratively select the detector that yields the smallest cost. This is shown in Figure 4.3 and proceeds as follows.

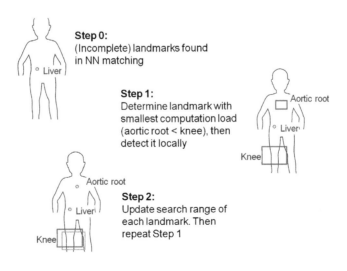

**Step 0:**
(Incomplete) landmarks found in NN matching

**Step 1:**
Determine landmark with smallest computation load (aortic root < knee), then detect it locally

**Step 2:**
Update search range of each landmark. Then repeat Step 1

**FIGURE 4.3**

Illustration of the greedy algorithm. Different box colors (red and blue) indicate search ranges provided by other landmarks (liver and aortic root).

Initialize $\Lambda = \{l_{(1)}\}$ **for** $j = 2, \ldots, N$ **do**
| $\quad l_{(j)} = \arg\min_k C_k(\Lambda_{(1):(j-1)})$ Append $l_{(j)}$ to the ordered set $\Lambda_{(1):(j-1)}$.
**end**

This simple algorithm has nice theoretical properties. Define

$$F_k(\Lambda) = C_k(\phi) - C_k(\Lambda) \tag{4.5}$$

Hence, $F_k(\phi) = 0$. From Lemma 4.6, $F_k(.)$ is a nondecreasing set function. From Eqs. (4.3) and (4.5), $\forall S \subseteq T$,

$$F_k(S) - F_k(S \cup \{l\}) \le F_k(T) - F_k(T \cup \{l\}) \tag{4.6}$$

which means $F_k(.)$ is *submodular* (Schrijver, 2003). Furthermore, since $C_k(\phi)$ is constant over $k$, Eq. (4.9) becomes

$$\Lambda'_{(2):(N)} = \underset{\Lambda_{(2):(N)}}{\operatorname{argmax}} \sum_{k=2}^{N} F_k(\Lambda_{(1):(k-1)}) \tag{4.7}$$

**Lemma 4.7.** $F(.) = \sum F_k(.)$ *is submodular if* $\forall k$, $F_k(.)$ *is submodular (Schrijver, 2003).*

Together, these properties bring us to the theorem that states the theoretical guarantee of the greedy algorithm.

**Theorem 4.2.** *If* $F(.)$ *is a submodular, nondecreasing set function and* $F(\phi) = 0$, *then the greedy algorithm finds a set* $\Lambda'$, *such that* $F(\Lambda') \ge (1 - 1/e) \max F(\Lambda)$ *(Nemhauser et al., 1978).*

Optimizing submodular functions is in general NP-hard (Lovasz, 1983). One must in principle calculate the values of $N!$ detector ordering patterns. Yet, the greedy algorithm is guaranteed to find an ordered set $\Lambda$ such that $F(.)$ reaches at least 63% of the optimal value.

Note that the ordering found by the algorithm is image-dependent, since the search space of the next detector is dependent on the position of the landmarks already detected. Therefore, the algorithm is not performing an "offline" scheduling of detectors. For another example, when the search space of a landmark is outside the image or if its detection score is too low, then this landmark is claimed missing. This would influence the subsequent detectors through the definition of the search space and affect the final ordering.

### 4.2.3 ANOTHER SEARCH SPACE CRITERIA

Another useful definition of search space can be stated as follows:

$$\Omega_{l_i}(\Lambda) = \min_{l \in \Lambda}\{\Omega_{l_i}(l)\} \tag{4.8}$$

In each round of the greedy algorithm, each detected landmark provides a search space candidate for each undetected landmark. Each undetected landmark then selects the smallest one among the provided candidates. The greedy algorithm then selects the undetected landmark that has the smallest search space. This is shown in Figure 4.4. We call this search space criteria the *min-rule* and the one in Section 4.2.1 the *intersection-rule*.

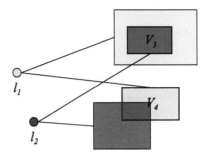

**FIGURE 4.4**

Illustration of the search space definition in Eq. (4.8). Detected landmarks $l_1$ and $l_2$ provide search spaces for undetected landmarks $l_3$ and $l_4$ (not shown). Final search spaces $V_3$ and $V_4$ for $l_3$ and $l_4$ are the minimum sets. This time, a greedy algorithm would prefer landmark $l_3$ over $l_4$ as the next landmark to detect since $V_3$ is smaller than $V_4$.

Since submodularity is closed under linear combination with nonnegative scalars (Schrijver, 2003), multiple submodular functions can be optimized simultaneously. For example, one could combine the min-rule and intersection-rule. Note that the set of individual search spaces $\{\Omega_{l_i}(\{l_j\})\}_{i,j=1,...,N}$ need not be the same for the min- and intersection-rules. Under this combination, some detectors could obtain a search range from the min-rule and some from the intersection-rule.

Denote $m_{l_i}(S) = \arg\min_{l \in S} \Omega_{l_i}(\{l\})$ as the landmark in the set of detected landmarks $S$ that provides the smallest search range for detector $l_i$. Here we show that this definition also satisfies Theorem 4.1.

***Lemma 4.8.*** $\forall S \subseteq T, V(\Omega(S)) \geq V(\Omega(T))$.
*Proof.* From definition, $\Omega(S) = \min_{l \in S} \Omega(\{l\})$, and $\Omega(T) = \min_{l \in T} \Omega(\{l\})$. Since $S \subseteq T$, we have $\Omega(S) \geq \Omega(T)$, and hence $V(\Omega(S)) \geq V(\Omega(T))$. □

***Proof of Theorem 4.1.***

**Case (i):** $m_{l_i}(T) = m_{l_i}(T \cup \{l\})$. This means including $l$ does not decrease the search space, and hence $V(\Omega(T)) = V(\Omega(T \cup \{l\}))$. But from Lemma 4.8, $V(\Omega(S)) \geq V(\Omega(S \cup \{l\}))$ always holds. Hence $V(\Omega(S)) - V(\Omega(S \cup \{l\})) \geq V(\Omega(T)) - V(\Omega(T \cup \{l\}))$.

**Case (ii):** $m_{l_i}(T) \neq m_{l_i}(T \cup \{l\})$. This means $l$ provides a smaller search space than any other landmark in $T$, and hence $m_{l_i}(\{l\}) = m_{l_i}(T \cup \{l\})$. Since $S \subseteq T$, we also have $m_{l_i}(\{l\}) = m_{l_i}(S \cup \{l\})$. Hence, $V(\Omega(S \cup \{l\})) = V(\Omega(T \cup \{l\}))$. But from Lemma 4.8, $V(\Omega(S)) \geq V(\Omega(T))$ always holds. Hence $V(\Omega(S)) - V(\Omega(S \cup \{l\})) \geq V(\Omega(T)) - V(\Omega(T \cup \{l\}))$. □

## 4.2.4 COST OF DETECTOR

The algorithm introduced so far only considered the search space. In practice, different detectors have different costs and this should be taken into account during optimization. For example, if we have two detectors, then the previous algorithm would select the next detector that has a smaller search space. However, this detector might have a much higher unit computational cost due to, for example, higher model complexity. One should multiply (and not linearly combine) search volume with the unit cost, since a detector is applied to *each* voxel within the search space and only the product reflects the cost correctly.

Fortunately, multiplication of a submodular function by a nonnegative scalar also maintains submodularity (Schrijver, 2003). Denote $q_i$ as the computational cost of detector $i$. The product $q_i C(\Omega_{l_i}(\Lambda))$ then considers the joint computational cost. Since $\forall i, q_i \geq 0, q_i C(\Omega_{l_i}(\Lambda))$ is submodular, the greedy algorithm can be applied and the same theoretical guarantees still hold.

The computational cost of a detector (classifier) can be estimated from, for example, the number of weak learners in boosting-based classifiers (Viola and Jones, 2004), the expected number of classifiers in a cascade of classifiers (Viola and Jones, 2004), or the empirical running time. Denote by $\alpha[l_j]$ the unit computation cost for evaluating the detector for landmark $l_j$. The goal is then to find the ordered set $\Lambda_{(1):(N)}$ that minimizes the *total computation*, that is,

$$\Lambda'_{(1):(N)} = \underset{\Lambda_{(1):(N)}}{\arg\min} \left\{ \alpha[l_{(1)}] \, V(\Omega[l_{(1)}]) + \sum_{i=2}^{N} \alpha[l_{(i)}] V(\Omega[l_{(i)}|\Lambda_{(1):(i-1)}]) \right\} \tag{4.9}$$

When $\alpha[l_j] = 1$ for all $j$, this reduces to searching the minimum overall search range. We find that unit computation cost is roughly proportional to the physical disk size needed to store the detector model; hence we set $\alpha[l_{(i)}]$ as the model disk size.

The *greedy algorithm* for finding the ordering $\{l_{(1)}, \ldots, l_{(N)}\}$ that attempts to minimize the overall cost proceeds as follows:

Initialize $\Lambda = \phi$.
**for** $j = 1, \ldots, N$ **do**
    $l_{(j)} = \arg\min_k \alpha[k] V(\Omega[k|\Lambda])$;
    Append $l_{(j)}$ to the ordered set $\Lambda$ so that the new $\Lambda = l_{(1)}, \ldots, l_{(j)}$.
**end**

In other words, in each round one triggers the detector that yields the smallest computation.

Again, *the greedy algorithm is guaranteed to find an ordered set $\Lambda$ such that the invoked cost is at least 63% of its optimal value (Liu et al., 2010)!* It is worth emphasizing that the ordering found by the algorithm is data-dependent and determined in run-time on the fly.

## 4.3 FINDING THE ANCHOR LANDMARK

One problem we have not addressed is how to initialize the greedy algorithm, since it requires at least one landmark to be already detected. This is the topic for this section. We provide two solutions: one is called sequential-anchoring, and the other one is called holistic-anchoring.

### 4.3.1 SEQUENTIAL-ANCHORING

The greedy algorithm finds an image-dependent ordering of detectors assuming at least one landmark $l_{(1)}$ has already been detected. We call $l_{(1)}$ the *anchor landmark*. Note that the anchor landmark can be a different landmark for different images.

Define $f(l)$ as the estimated frequency of appearance of landmark $l$ in an image. Then, define the ordering of trials

$$m_1 = \arg\max_l \{f(l_1), \ldots, f(l_N)\} \tag{4.10a}$$
$$m_2 = \arg\max_l \{f(l_1), \ldots, f(l_N)|m_1 \text{ not present}\} \tag{4.10b}$$
$$m_3 = \arg\max_l \{f(l_1), \ldots, f(l_N)|m_1, m_2 \text{ not present}\} \tag{4.10c}$$

and so on. We can use this ordering of trials to detect the anchor landmark. Intuitively, since landmark $m_1$ appears most frequently, searching for it in the first trial would reduce most significantly the need for a subsequent trial (whole-image search). Landmark $m_2$ is the most frequent landmark under the condition that $m_1$ does not exist in the volume. This conditioning is to avoid $m_2$ being a landmark that is in the vicinity of $m_1$, in which case if $m_1$ is occluded, most likely $m_2$ is also occluded.

Since all of the detectors have similar accuracy and computational cost, such an ordering based on conditional frequency performs well. However, if some detectors have very different accuracy or cost than the others, those characteristics should also be taken into account.

The system starts with detecting the anchor landmark and initiates the greedy algorithm. If the greedy algorithm determines a search space but the corresponding detector fails to find the landmark, the greedy algorithm simply proceeds to the next round. If all subsequent landmarks are not found, the system is restarted with a different anchor landmark. The chance that the system produces more false positives than running the detectors independently is low. This is because, while the false positive rate of each detector could be high, the chance that multiple detectors produce false positives within their assigned search spaces is exponentially low. In fact, there is a relationship between the overall false positive rate, detection rate, and the size of the individual search spaces. We have experiments and discussions on this topic in Section 4.5.1.

## 4.3.2 HOLISTIC-ANCHORING

The sequential-anchoring method follows the more traditional "sliding window" approach for detecting a landmark. In this section, we introduce the holistic-anchoring method, which is based on a fundamentally different philosophy.

Assume that a volume is represented by a $D$-dimensional feature vector. Given a query (unseen input) vector $x \in R^D$, the problem is to find the element $y^*$ in a finite set $Y$ of vectors to minimize the distance to the query vector:

$$y^* = \arg\min_{y \in Y} d(x, y) \tag{4.11}$$

where $d(.,.)$ is the Euclidean distance function. Other choices can be used too. Once $y^*$ is found, the coarse landmark position estimates are obtained through a "transfer" operation, as explained below.

In particular, we adopt a representation of the image using "global features" that provide a holistic description as in Torralba (2003), where a 2D image is divided into $4 \times 4$ regions, eight oriented Gabor filters are applied over four different scales, and the average filter energy in each region is used as a feature, yielding in total 512 features. For 3D volumes, we compute such features from nine 2D images, consisting of the sagittal, axial, and coronal planes that pass through 25%, 50%, and 75% of the respective volume dimension, resulting in a 4608-dimensional feature vector.

In practice, finding the closest (most similar) volume through evaluating the exact distances is too expensive when the database size is large and the data dimensionality is high. Two efficient approximations are used for speedup. Vector quantization (Lloyd, 1982) is used to address the database size issue and product quantization (Jegou et al., 2011) for the data dimensionality issue.

A quantizer is a function $q(.)$ mapping a $D$-dimensional vector $x$ to a vector $q(x) \in Q = \{q_i, i = 1, 2, \ldots, K\}$. The finite set $Q$ is called the codebook, which consists of $K$ centroids. The set of vectors mapped to the same centroid forms a Voronoi cell, defined as $V_i = \{x \in R^D | q(x) = q_i\}$. The $K$ Voronoi cells partition the space of $R^D$. The quality of a quantizer is often measured by the mean squared error between an input vector and its representative centroid $q(x)$. We use the $K$-means algorithm (Lloyd, 1982) to find a near-optimal codebook. During the search stage, which has a high speed requirement, distance evaluation between the query and a database vector consists of computing the distance between the query vector and the nearest centroid of the database vector.

These volume feature vectors are high dimensional (we use $D = 4608$ dimensions), which poses difficulty for a straightforward implementation of the $K$-means quantization described previously. A quantizer that uses only 1/3 bits per dimension already has $2^{1536}$ centroids. Such a large number of centroids makes it impossible to run the $K$-means algorithm in practice. Product quantization (Jegou et al., 2011) addresses this issue by splitting the high-dimensional feature vector into $m$ distinct subvectors as follows:

$$\underbrace{x_1, \ldots, x_{D^*}}_{u_1(x)}, \ldots, \underbrace{x_{D-D^*+1}, \ldots, x_D}_{u_m(x)} \tag{4.12}$$

The quantization is subsequently performed on the $m$ subvectors $q^1(u_1(x)), \ldots, q^m(u_m(x))$, where $q^i, i = 1, \ldots, m$ denote $m$ different quantizers. In the special case where $m = D$, product quantization is equivalent to scalar quantization, which has the lowest memory requirement but does not capture any correlation across feature dimensions. In the extreme case where $m = 1$, product quantization is equivalent to traditional quantization, which fully captures the correlation among different features but has the highest (and practically impossible, as explained earlier) memory requirement. We use $m = 1536$ and $K = 4$ (2 bits per quantizer).

Given a query, we use the aforementioned method to find the most similar database volume. Assume this database volume consists of $N$ landmarks with positions $\{s_1, \ldots, s_N\}$. We simply "transfer" these landmark positions to the query, as shown in Figure 4.5. In other words, the coarsely detected landmark positions are set as $\{s_1, \ldots, s_N\}$. As a result, we have obtained at least one anchor landmark. In practice, any one of the $s_i$ can be used as the anchor landmark.

## 4.3.3 COMPARING SEQUENTIAL-ANCHORING AND HOLISTIC-ANCHORING

The holistic-anchoring method requires a database sufficiently large so that, given a query, the best match in the training database indeed covers the same body region(s) as the query. We collect 2500 volumes annotated with 60 anatomical landmarks, including the left/right lung tops, aortic arch, femur heads, liver top, liver center, coccyx tip, etc. We use 500 volumes for constructing the training database and the remaining 2000 volumes for testing. To ensure that each query finds a good match, we construct the database of 100,000 volumes in a near-exhaustive manner: In each iteration, we randomly pick 1 of the 500 volumes and then randomly crop and slightly rotate it into a new volume before adding it to the database. The annotated anatomical landmark positions in the original volume are transformed accordingly. The system runs on an Intel Xeon 2.33 GHz CPU with 3 GB RAM (Figure 4.6).

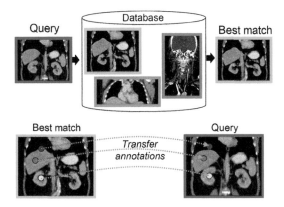

**FIGURE 4.5**

Coarse landmark detection, a 2D illustration. Real system operates on 3D volumes. Top: nearest neighbor search. Bottom: annotated positions of database volume are transferred to query.

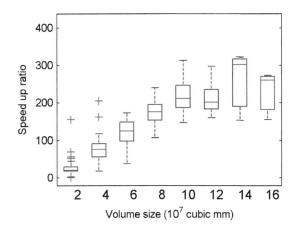

**FIGURE 4.6**

Speed-up ratio versus volume size when comparing holistic-anchoring and sequential-anchoring.

Registration-based methods are not applicable since the test volumes cover a large variety of body regions. If each region is detected separately, say, using Tu (2005), the total detection time is proportional to the number of regions, as detecting each region requires a scan over the whole volume. The work in Criminisi et al. (2009) reports a detection time around 2000 ms for nine landmarks, and median distance error around 22 mm on a GPU (parallelized) implementation. The work in Liu et al. (2010) has the highest accuracy and fastest speed, so we compare against this work in better detail. As in Figure 4.7, the implementation of Liu et al. (2010), which is tuned to a similar detection accuracy as shown in Table 4.1, has a detection time of 450 ms for six landmarks that define the presence of

|  | Median Time (ms) | Average of Median Errors (mm) |
|---|---|---|
| Sequential-anchoring | 450 | 28.6 |
| Holistic-anchoring | 5 | 29.9 |

**FIGURE 4.7**

The performance of detecting body regions using holistic-anchoring versus sequential-anchoring.

**Table 4.1 Median Detection Errors (mm) for Six Different Landmarks That Define Five Body Regions**

|  | Sequential-Anchoring | Holistic-Anchoring |
|---|---|---|
| Lung apex right | 24.1 | 27.1 |
| Skull base | 31.9 | 19.1 |
| Aortic root | 23.2 | 35.8 |
| Lung center | 20.6 | 24.5 |
| Sternum bottom | 37.3 | 35.1 |
| Liver center | 35.2 | 37.9 |

right lung, skull, aorta, sternum, and liver; but the maximum time is 4.9 s, significantly larger than the median. This poses a problem for time-critical subsequent tasks. The holistic-anchoring method has a nearly constant detection time of 5 ms, achieving a speed-up of 90 times while maintaining similar detection accuracy. The speed-up is even more significant if more regions are of interest as the detection does not depend on the number of regions. The holistic-matching code can be optimized and parallelized for faster speed. In general, a large detection error from holistic-matching, which is acceptable for initializing the greedy algorithm or for body region detection purposes, is due to the large variability in the landmark appearance and its relative location to other landmarks.

## 4.4 COARSE-TO-FINE DETECTION

In earlier discussions, we assumed each landmark is associated with a single detector. In implementation, a landmark has $R = 3$ detectors, each trained at different resolutions. Since training of landmark detectors is not the focus of this chapter, we refer the reader to prior work in Viola and Jones (2004) and Tu (2005). In detection, we employ a coarse-to-fine strategy. Such multiresolution techniques are frequently encountered when the solution to the original (high) resolution is either too complex to consider directly or is subject to large numbers of local minima. The general idea is to construct approximate, coarser versions of the problem and to use the solution of the coarser problems to guide solutions at finer scales.

We run the algorithm in Section 4.3 using the coarsest-resolution detectors only. We then define a local (small) search space around each detected landmark and run higher resolution detectors within the local search space. The overall approach is efficient, because the coarse-resolution detectors have already rejected most of the voxels in the image.

At the end, the posterior probability of position $x$ is taken from all resolutions using a log-linear model

$$p(x|I_{r_1},\ldots,I_{r_R}) \propto \exp\left(\sum_{i=1}^{R}\alpha_{r_i}\phi_{r_i}(x)\right) \tag{4.13}$$

where $I_{r_i}$ is the volume at resolution $r_i$, $p(x|I_{r_i})$ is the posterior probability from the detector with resolution $r_i$, and the potential functions are given by $\phi_{r_i}(x) = \log p(x|I_{r_i})$. This can be shown equivalent to a products-of-experts model (Hinton, 1999). We also experimented with the mixture-of-experts model (Jacobs et al., 1991) of the form

$$p(x|I_{r_1},\ldots,I_{r_R}) \propto \sum_{i=1}^{R}\alpha_{r_i}p(x|I_{r_i}). \tag{4.14}$$

While the products-of-experts tends to produce sharper classification boundaries, the mixture-of-experts tends to have a higher tolerance to poor probability estimates (Kittler et al., 1998). Our experiments suggest the use of the mixture-of-experts.

Notice that each position is associated with multiple subwindows at different resolutions, so a larger amount of local context is utilized. Using context in object detection is discussed in prior work (Viola and Jones, 2004; Tu, 2005). Our approach combines results from multiple resolutions and different subwindow sizes and hence is different from approaches where a single, optimal window size is determined (Viola et al., 2005).

In the following experiment, the database consists of 2046 volumes. We split the data into 70% training, 10% validation, and 20% testing, while avoiding splitting a patient with multiple scans into both training and testing. The pairwise search spaces, $\Omega_{l_i}(\{l_j\})$, for each pair of landmarks $l_i, l_j$, are cuboids estimated from training and validation data. Using only training data to define a tight cuboid for one landmark given another could result in too confined search spaces if the detectors have large errors in testing. We obtain this error information from the validation set and enlarge the cuboids accordingly.

We have 63 landmarks including positions such as the center, top, and bottom of organs, bones, and bifurcations of vessels. In Table 4.2, we show the speed of landmark detection when all landmarks are detected independently versus the proposed method with the min-rule. Q95 is the 95th percentile. $D_{8\text{ mm}}$

**Table 4.2 Detection Time (s) per Volume**

|  | Mean | Std | Q95 | Max. |
|---|---|---|---|---|
| Independent $D_{8\text{ mm}}$ $N = 63$ | 17.30 | 6.16 | 46.24 | 84.51 |
| Greedy $D_{8\text{ mm}}$ $N = 63$ | 1.14 | 0.47 | 1.92 | 2.44 |
| Independent $D_{8\text{ mm}}$ $N = 25$ | 6.72 | 6.40 | 17.73 | 35.00 |
| Greedy $D_{8\text{ mm}}$ $N = 25$ | 0.65 | 0.43 | 1.26 | 5.08 |
| Greedy $D_{4\text{ mm}}$ $N = 25$ | 1.30 | 0.87 | 3.30 | 6.11 |
| Greedy $D_{2\text{ mm}}$ $N = 25$ | 2.70 | 1.74 | 7.15 | 9.05 |

Notes: *N is the number of landmarks in the system.*

denotes the system using detectors trained at 8 mm resolution running the greedy method (without coarse-to-fine), $D_{4\,mm}$ uses the coarse-to-fine strategy with 8 and 4 mm resolution detectors, and $D_{2\,mm}$ uses detectors at all three (8, 4, and 2 mm) resolutions.

Table 4.2 also includes experiments where only a subset of 25 landmarks are used in the system. We observe that the detection time of the greedy approach is not linearly proportional to the number of landmarks. In fact, when using "fewer" landmarks, the maximum time "increased" from 2.44 to 5.08 s. This can be understood because the search space of each detector is provided by the landmarks already detected, some of which are not present in the 25-detector system.

The detection speed versus volume size is shown in Figure 4.8. The reason that smaller volumes do not consume much less time can be understood from Figure 4.9, which shows that smaller volumes often require more trials to find the anchor landmark. Since each trial requires a whole image search, detection time increases.

The detection errors of the coarse-to-fine strategy are shown in Table 4.3.

Two comparisons to recent literature can be made. First, the work in Criminisi et al. (2009) reported a detection time around 2 s for nine landmarks and mean distance error around 28 mm. The system achieves lower distance errors in less time even on a standard Intel Core2 Duo CPU 2.66 GHz (whereas they used a GPU implementation for speed-up). Second, the work in Zhan et al. (2008) reported larger distance errors (kidney error 9 mm, vs 6 mm when using coarse-to-fine 8 and 4 mm-resolution detectors) with detection time around 4 s for 6 landmarks, significantly slower than our system (1.3 s for 25 landmarks using coarse-to-fine 8 and 4 mm-resolution detectors).

In Table 4.4, we compare the different coarse-to-fine approaches discussed in Section 4.4. The baseline approach finds the top candidates at one resolution and initiates a finer-resolution detection around those top candidates. This has a shifting problem (much like in visual tracking) when only

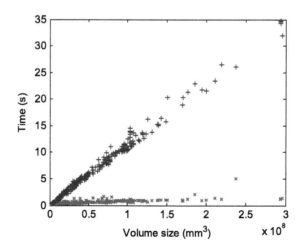

**FIGURE 4.8**

Detection time as a function of volume size. Blue (+): independent landmark detectors. Red (x): Greedy search.

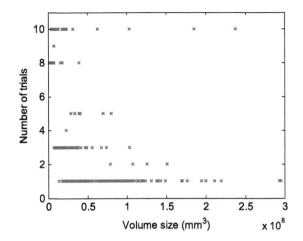

**FIGURE 4.9**

Number of trials to find the anchor landmark as a function of volume size.

**Table 4.3 Mean Distance Error in Millimeters**

|  | $D_{8\ mm}$ | $D_{4\ mm}$ | $D_{2\ mm}$ |
|---|---|---|---|
| TracheaBif. | 11.9 | 3.6 | 2.8 |
| L.LungTop | 22.2 | 3.5 | 3.2 |
| R.LungTop | 13.8 | 3.7 | 3.7 |
| LiverDome | 14.8 | 3.4 | 2.9 |
| L.Kidney | 13.6 | 6.7 | 6.3 |
| R.Kidney | 15.1 | 5.6 | 7.0 |

**Table 4.4 Distance Errors in Millimeters Comparing Coarse-to-Fine Detection Using the Product- and Mixture-of-Experts**

|  |  | Q25 | Q50 | Q95 |
|---|---|---|---|---|
| Iliac bifurcation | Baseline | 6.76 | 13.96 | 22.72 |
|  | Product | 4.67 | 8.43 | **11.56** |
|  | Mixture | **3.95** | **7.06** | 13.99 |
| Brachioc. artery | Baseline | 4.20 | 5.46 | 9.89 |
|  | Product | 4.30 | 6.83 | 11.46 |
|  | Mixture | **3.63** | **5.19** | **8.77** |
| *Bold indicates best outcome* |  |  |  |  |

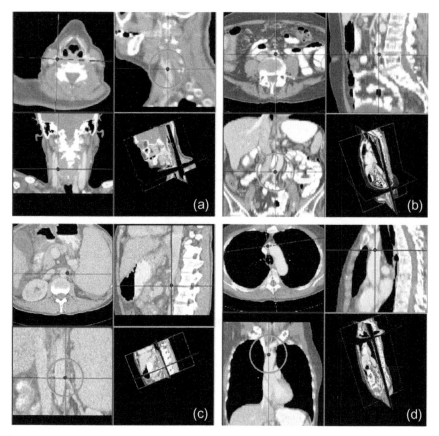

**FIGURE 4.10**

Detected results of (a) carotid, (b) iliac, (c) renal, and (d) brachiocephalic artery bifurcations.

neighboring resolutions are considered and information from the earliest resolutions are lost. The mixture-of-experts often has the most accurate results and has reasonable tolerance to outliers.

Some detection results of vessels are shown in Figure 4.10. Diseased vessels have high appearance variations, and yet we detect the carotid, iliac, renal, and brachiocephalic bifurcations with mean error 3.9, 7.2, 5.2, and 5.3 mm, respectively. When higher accuracy is desired for vessel detection, one may refer to the vascular landmark detection methods introduced in Liu et al. (2011).

Table 4.5 shows confusion matrices of 8 mm detectors. This will be discussed further in Section 4.5.1.

## 4.5 DISCUSSION

In this section, we discuss miscellaneous items that have been omitted in the previous sections.

**Table 4.5  Confusion Matrices**

|                | FP$_A$    | FN$_A$   | FP$_B$   | FN$_B$   |
|----------------|-----------|----------|----------|----------|
| SkullBase      | **0 (193)** | 0 [50]   | 1 (192)  | 0 [50]   |
| R.LungTop      | **0 (84)**  | 1 [114]  | 1 (83)   | 1 [114]  |
| LiverDome      | 0 (86)    | 2 [65]   | 0 (86)   | 2 [65]   |
| R.HipTip       | **0 (131)** | 0 [94]   | 1 (130)  | 0 [94]   |
| R.Knee         | 0 (265)   | 0 [12]   | 0 (265)  | 0 [12]   |
| LiverBott.     | 2 (33)    | 1 [33]   | 2 (33)   | 1 [33]   |
| TracheaBif.    | 0 (44)    | 0 [41]   | 0 (44)   | 0 [41]   |
| LiverCent.     | **0 (90)**  | 1 [136]  | 2 (88)   | 1 [136]  |
| L.HumerusHead  | 0 (96)    | 1 [12]   | 0 (96)   | 1 [12]   |
| R.HumerusHead  | 1 (80)    | 2 [7]    | 1 (80)   | 2 [7]    |
| L.LungTop      | **0 (61)**  | 1 [21]   | 1 (61)   | 1 [20]   |
| L.HipTip       | **0 (94)**  | **1 [46]** | 2 (92)   | 2 [45]   |
| L.FemurHead    | 0 (124)   | 0 [16]   | 0 (124)  | 0 [16]   |
| R.FemurHead    | 0 (120)   | 0 [16]   | 0 (120)  | 0 [16]   |
| CoccyxTip      | 0 (118)   | 0 [16]   | 0 (118)  | 0 [16]   |
| PubicSymph.Top | 0 (133)   | 0 [23]   | 0 (133)  | 0 [23]   |
| SternumTip     | 3 (51)    | 1 [22]   | 3 (51)   | 1 [22]   |
| AortaBend      | **0 (31)**  | 1 [53]   | 1 (30)   | 1 [53]   |
| Brachioceph.   | 1 (35)    | 3 [132]  | 1 (35)   | 3 [132]  |
| R.Kidney       | 2 (59)    | 5 [61]   | 2 (59)   | 5 [61]   |
| L.Kidney       | 0 (71)    | 0 [76]   | 0 (71)   | 0 [76]   |

Notes: *The first two columns (with subscript A) show the number of false positives and false negatives. Numbers in parentheses are the number of true negatives. Numbers in brackets are the number of true positives. The last two columns use detectors run independently. Detections with distance error larger than 5 voxels are false positives Entries in bold indicate best outcome.*

## 4.5.1  A SPATIAL CASCADE OF CLASSIFIERS

One might worry that a sequential detection approach could break down if the anchor landmark is incorrect or the first few detectors fail. Furthermore, the proposed search strategy was driven by computational cost considerations, and accuracy in terms of false positive rate and detection rate was not mentioned. Here we argue that the sequential "accept or reject" behavior of our method behaves similarly to a Viola-Jones cascade of classifiers (Viola and Jones, 2004). Intuitively, while the false positive rate of the first detector could be high, the rate that the first $n$ detectors all fail is significantly lower.

More formally, if each detector has false positive rate $f_i$ and detection rate $d_i$, the overall false positive rate and detection rate are $f = \prod f_i$ and $d = \prod d_i$ assuming independence. But $f$ and $d$ depend on the size of the search space, $\Omega_{l_i}(.)$. With a slight abuse of annotation, assume search space $\Omega_{l_i}$ is a cuboid, and $\lambda \Omega_{l_i}(.), \lambda > 0$ is an enlarged or shrunk cuboid with the same center. The operating point of the ROC curve can then be adjusted by tuning $\lambda$. As $\lambda$ increases, the individual detectors behave more independently and there is less cascade-effect. As $\lambda$ decreases, $d_i$ and $f_i$ decrease, and so do $d$ and $f$. Tuning individual classifiers to adjust the overall $f$ and $d$ is also presented in the Viola-Jones cascade of classifiers.

On the other hand, in the Viola-Jones cascade, classifiers of the "same" landmark are chained together. Here, classifiers of "different" landmarks are chained and provide robustness through their joint spatial relationship. As shown in Table 4.5, this geometric cascade indeed reduces false positives without sacrificing the detection rate. Such a robustness property is desirable and is typically implemented by random fields (Besag, 1986; Bishop, 2006) or voting procedures (Duda and Hart, 1972). If desired, one can still enforce a random field or perform voting on top of the methods introduced in this chapter.

## 4.5.2 SUBMODULARITY

The problem of maximizing a submodular function is of central importance, with special cases including Max Cut (Goemans and Williamson, 1995), maximum facility location (Cornuejols et al., 1977). While the graph Min Cut problem is a classical polynomial-time solvable problem, and more generally it has been shown that any submodular function can be "minimized" in polynomial time, maximization turns out to be an NP-hard problem (Schrijver, 2000). The work of Liu et al. (2010) is the first to apply the theory of submodularity to object detection. More specifically, we prove the submodularity of the cost functions based on two search space criteria.

## 4.5.3 INFORMATION GAIN AND ENTROPY

Several works use maximization of information gain or entropy as the objective function (Krause and Guestrin, 2005; Roy and Earnest, 2006; Zhan et al., 2008). Assume we have three landmarks, A, B, and C, with position $x_A, x_B, x_C$ distributed along a 1D line with position parameters ($\mu_A = 0, \Sigma_{AA} = 1$), ($\mu_B = 10, \Sigma_{BB} = 30$), ($\mu_C = 10, \Sigma_{CC} = 110$), and ($\Sigma_{AB} = 5, \Sigma_{AC} = 110, \Sigma_{BC} = 50$). This distribution could model the height of different people, with landmark A aligned with the CT scanner. Assume landmark A has already been detected. Which landmark should one detect next? The approach in Zhan et al. (2008) selects C since it yields a higher information gain than B. However, if the size of the search spaces of B and C are positively correlated with conditional covariance $\Sigma_{B|A}$ and $\Sigma_{C|A}$, the search space of B is actually smaller than the search space of C. Without considering other factors, this means the decision based on search space will be contrary to the one based on information gain. With different covariance matrices, the difference could be arbitrarily large. This can be understood when we realize that the objective of maximizing information gain does not have a direct relationship with saving computation time. The advantages of information gain mentioned in those works, however, should not be neglected. Therefore, a framework that gracefully trades off between information gain and computation time would be useful.

## 4.5.4 SPEED UPS

Other methods for reducing computational cost (from an algorithmic perspective, instead of hardware acceleration such as using GPU computing) in object detection include tree-structured search (Grimson,

1990), coarse-to-fine detection (Fleuret and Geman, 2001), cascade of classifiers (Viola and Jones, 2004), branch-and-bound (Lampert et al., 2008), reduction of classifier measurements (Sochman and Matas, 2005), and searching in marginal space (Zheng et al., 2009).

### 4.5.5 MULTIPLE OBJECTS OF THE SAME TYPE IN ONE IMAGE

In medical imaging, most anatomical structures have distinct appearances. Real-world image datasets (such as those obtained from hand-held cameras and camcorders) including the PASCAL dataset often contain multiple objects of the same class (type). In that scenario, the methods introduced in this chapter can be embedded in a parts-based framework such as Felzenszwalb and Huttenlocher (2005) and Felzenszwalb et al. (preprint) to speed up the search for object-parts.

### 4.5.6 SCALING UP TO MANY LANDMARKS

Our goal is to detect in the order of thousands of anatomical structures. With such a large number of detectors, the computational savings of the approach introduced in this chapter would be significant.

## 4.6 SUMMARY

In this chapter, we introduced a fast and accurate method to detect multiple landmarks. The method uses unary and pairwise context via a submodular formulation that aims to minimize the total computation for detecting landmark(s) and renders itself to a computationally efficiently greedy algorithm. The holistic-anchoring method leverages holistic contextual information in the medical data via the use of an approximate nearest neighbor matching to quickly identify the most similar database volume and transfer its landmark positions. The method has been successively validated on a database of 2500 CT volumes. The method can be applied to a variety of modalities such as CT and magnetic resonance imaging.

## REFERENCES

Beck, T., Bernhardt, D., Biermann, C., Dillmann, R., 2010. Validation and detection of vessel landmarks by using anatomical knowledge. In: Proc. SPIE Medical Imaging.

Besag, J., 1986. On the statistical analysis of dirty pictures. J. R. Stat. Soc. B-48, 259-302.

Bishop, C.M., 2006. Pattern Recognition and Machine Learning. Springer, Berlin, p. 383.

Cornuejols, G., Fischer, M., Nemhauser, G., 1977. On the uncapacitated location problem. Ann. Discrete Math. 1, 163-178.

Criminisi, A., Shotton, J., Bucciarelli, S., 2009. Decision forests with long-range spatial context for organ localization in CT volumes. In: MICCAI Workshop on Prob. Models for MIA.

Crum, W.R., Phil, D., Hartkens, T., Hill, D., 2004. Non-rigid image registration: theory and practice. Br. J. Radiol. 77, 140-153.

Duda, R.O., Hart, P.E., 1972. Use of the Hough transformation to detect lines and curves in pictures. Comm. ACM 15, 11-15.

Felzenszwalb, P., Huttenlocher, D., 2005. Pictorial structures for object recognition. Int. J. Comput. Vis. 61, 55-79.

Felzenszwalb, P., Girshick, R., McAllester, D., Ramanan, D., preprint. Object detection with discriminatively trained part based models. IEEE Trans. Pattern Anal. Mach. Intell.

Fleuret, F., Geman, D., 2001. Coarse-to-fine face detection. Int. J. Comput. Vis. 41, 85-107.

Goemans, M.X., Williamson, D.P., 1995. Improved approximation algorithms for maximum cut and satisfiability problems using semidefinite programming. J. ACM 42, 1115-1145.

Grimson, W., 1990. Object Recognition by Computer: The Role of Geometric Constraints. MIT Press, Cambridge, MA.

Hinton, G., 1999. Products of experts. In: Intl. Conf. Artificial Neural Networks (ICANN).

Jacobs, R., Jordan, M.I., Nowlan, S.J., Hinton, G.E., 1991. Mixtures of expert networks. Neural Comput. 3, 79-87.

Jegou, H., Douze, M., Schmid, C., 2011. Product quantization for nearest neighbor search. IEEE Trans. Pattern Anal. Mach. Intell. 33, 117-128.

Johnson, H., Christensen, G., 2002. Consistent landmark and intensity-based image registration. IEEE Trans. Med. Imaging 21, 450-461.

Kittler, J., Hatef, M., Duin, R., Matas, J., 1998. On combining classifiers. IEEE Trans. Pattern Anal. Mach. Intell. 20, 226-239.

Krause, A., Guestrin, C., 2005. Near-optimal nonmyopic value of information in graphical models. In: Conference on Uncertainty in Artificial Intelligence (UAI).

Lampert, C.H., Blaschko, M.B., Hofmann, T., 2008. Beyond sliding windows: object localization by efficient subwindow search. In: IEEE Conf. Computer Vision and Pattern Recognition.

Liu, D., Zhou, S.K., 2012. Anatomical landmark detection using nearest neighbor matching and submodular optimization. In: MICCAI.

Liu, D., Zhou, S.K., Bernhardt, D., Comaniciu, D., 2010. Search strategies for multiple landmark detection by submodular maximization. In: Proc. CVPR.

Liu, D., Zhou, S.K., Bernhardt, D., Comaniciu, D., 2011. Vascular landmark detection in 3D CT data. In: Proc. SPIE Medical Imaging.

Lloyd, S., 1982. Least square quantization in PCM. IEEE Trans. Inf. Theory 28, 129-137.

Lovasz, L., 1983. Submodular Functions and Convexity. Springer, Berlin, pp. 235-257 .

Nemhauser, G., Wolsey, L., Fisher, M., 1978. An analysis of the approximations for maximizing submodular set functions. Math. Program. 14, 265-294.

Okada, T., Shimada, R., Sato, Y., Hori, M., Yokota, K., Nakamoto, M., Chen, Y., Nakamura, H., Tamura, S., 2007. Automated segmentation of the liver from 3D CT images using probabilistic atlas and multilevel statistical shape model. In: Proc. MICCAI, pp. 86-93.

Pauly, O., et al., 2011. Fast multiple organs detection and localization in whole-body Mr Dixon sequences. In: MICCAI.

Peng, Z., Zhan, Y., Zhou, X.S., Krishnan, A., 2009. Robust anatomy detection from CT topograms. In: Proceedings of SPIE Medical Imaging.

Rangayyan, R., Banik, S., Rangayyan, R., Boag, G., 2009. Landmarking and Segmentation of 3D CT Images. Morgan & Claypool Publishers.

Roy, N., Earnest, C., 2006. Dynamic action spaces for information gain maximization in search and exploration. In: American Control Conference, pp. 6-11.

Schrijver, A., 2000. A combinatorial algorithm minimizing submodular functions in strongly polynomial time. J. Combin. Theory B80, 346-355.

Schrijver, A., 2003. Combinatorial Optimization, Polyhedra and Efficiency. Springer, Berlin.

Seifert, S., Kelm, M., Moeller, M., Mukherjee, S., Cavallaro, A., Huber, M., Comaniciu, D., 2010. Semantic annotation of medical images. In: SPIE Medical Imaging.

Sochman, J., Matas, J., 2005. Waldboost—learning for time constrained sequential detection. In: IEEE Conf. Computer Vision and Pattern Recognition.

Torralba, A., 2003. Contextual priming for object detection. Int. J. Comp. Vis. 53, 169-191.

Tu, Z., 2005. Probabilistic boosting-tree: learning discriminative models for classification, recognition, and clustering. IEEE Int. Conf. Comput. Vis. 2, 1589-1596.

Viola, P., Jones, M., 2004. Robust real-time face detection. Int. J. Comput. Vis. 57, 137-154.

Viola, P., Platt, J., Zhang, C., 2005. Multiple instance boosting for object detection. In: Proc. Advances in Neural Information Processing Systems (NIPS).

Zhan, Y., Zhou, X., Peng, Z., Krishnan, A., 2008. Active scheduling of organ detection and segmentation in whole-body medical images. In: MICCAI.

Zheng, Y., Georgescu, B., Ling, H., Zhou, S., Scheuering, M., Comaniciu, D., 2009. Constrained marginal space learning for efficient 3D anatomical structure detection in medical images. In: IEEE Conf. Computer Vision and Pattern Recognition.

~

# RANDOM FORESTS FOR LOCALIZATION OF SPINAL ANATOMY

5

**B. Glocker[1], E. Konukoglu[2] and D.R. Haynor[3]**

*Biomedical Image Analysis Group, Imperial College London, London, United Kingdom[1]*
*Martinos Center for Biomedical Imaging, MGH, Harvard Medical School, Boston, MA, USA[2]*
*Department of Radiology, University of Washington, Seattle, WA, USA[3]*

## CHAPTER OUTLINE

S. Kevin Zhou (Ed): Medical Image Recognition, Segmentation and Parsing. http://dx.doi.org/10.1016/B978-0-12-802581-9.00005-6

## 5.1 INTRODUCTION

Automatic localization of anatomical structures in medical scans is an important component in a wide range of clinical and research applications. Being able to parse a large database of images and extract semantic information about the presence and location of structures of interest is essential for automated quality control, data management, and decision support systems. Such *semantic imaging* enables, for example, smart image viewers which can support image-based diagnostic tasks by making the visual inspection of images more efficient. It is easy to imagine how a radiological image viewer that is equipped with semantic information could speed up the process of browsing through three-dimensional datasets. A simple click on an organ in a navigation bar would automatically adjust the multiplanar visualization to the region of interest and provide task-specific window/level settings. Additionally, semantic information can be used for querying large databases, for example, to identify similar cases, or for statistical modeling and population analysis in large imaging studies.

In this context, the spinal anatomy is of particular interest as the spine provides a natural, patient-specific coordinate system that is often used to describe the location of findings in surrounding tissue. The location of a lesion that is detected in an abdominal scan, for example, is often referred to by naming the closest vertebrae in the radiological report. Detection, localization, and identification of individual vertebrae is an extensively studied area of image analysis research (cf. Schmidt et al., 2007; Klinder et al., 2009; Alomari et al., 2011; Kelm et al., 2011; Zhan et al., 2012; Major et al., 2013). Applications which immediately benefit from spine localization include vertebra body segmentation (cf. Ayed et al., 2012), fracture detection (cf. Yao et al., 2012), longitudinal and multimodal registration (cf. Steger and Wesarg, 2012; Glocker et al., 2014), and statistical shape analysis (cf. Lecron et al., 2012). Furthermore, reliable vertebrae identification could greatly reduce the risk of wrong-level surgery (cf. Hsiang, 2011).

In this chapter, we will review two approaches for spine anatomy localization (cf. Glocker et al., 2012a, 2013) which are based on the same machine learning framework of random forests. Random forests, introduced by Breiman (2001), is a popular supervised learning technique which has been shown to often perform favorably compared to other methods (cf. Caruana et al., 2008). An excellent overview of random forests and their application in computer vision and medical image analysis is given by Criminisi et al. (2012). In particular for localization tasks, the random forest framework seems a very well-suited approach, as can be seen from many research papers, for example, on organ localization (Pauly et al., 2011; Cuingnet et al., 2012; Criminisi et al., 2013a,b; Gauriau et al., 2014), fitting of shape models (cf. Cootes et al., 2012), landmark detection (cf. Ebner et al., 2014), and vertebrae localization (cf. Roberts et al., 2012).

## 5.2 ANATOMY LOCALIZATION USING RANDOM FORESTS

In the following, we will discuss the framework of random forests as a general supervised, discriminative learning approach. Based on this framework, we will then see that *classification forests* and *regression forests* are particular instances of the same framework. Only a few components need to be changed to switch between classification and regression, while the main implementation is the same for both. Random forests belong to the class of ensemble methods that gain their predictive power by combining outputs of a set of independent (potentially weak) predictor functions. In random forests, each predictor function corresponds to a single decision tree.

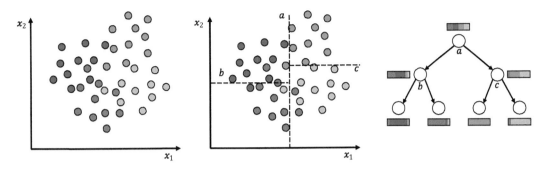

**FIGURE 5.1**

Illustration of data partitioning through a decision tree. Left: A toy classification dataset with two features $x_1$, $x_2$ and four categorical labels indicated by different colors. Middle: Data partitions corresponding to the split nodes of the decision tree. Right: A decision tree with three split nodes $a$, $b$, $c$ and four leaf nodes. The colored bars represent the distribution of training examples in each node.

Random forests, introduced by Breiman (2001), can be viewed as a randomized partitioning algorithm, which aims to group annotated input data into consistent clusters. The partitioning of the input data happens successively with respect to extracted feature values and some objective function that is defined in the space of annotations. The random forest method is an efficient way for finding discriminative features from a (potentially very large) set of candidate features, the *feature pool*. Feature learning is driven by the employed objective function and the annotations, hence the name supervised learning. As with most machine learning methods, random forests operates in two stages, *training* and *testing*. During training, the decision trees are constructed by finding the most discriminative features from which so-called *split functions* are determined which separate input data into (commonly) two subsets. The successive splitting of the input data within each decision tree yields clusters of data points from which statistical predictors are computed based on empirical distributions. During testing, those predictors are then used to make predictions for new data. The testing procedure of random forests is computationally extremely efficient as it only requires the evaluation of a few split functions when traversing the decision trees. The overall predictions are aggregations over individual tree predictions and are of probabilistic nature, that is, come with a confidence estimate. An illustration of a data partitioning through a decision tree is shown in Figure 5.1.

We now formalize those concepts and derive general algorithms for random forest training and testing before we discuss how to use this framework for anatomy localization.

## 5.2.1 RANDOM FORESTS

The goal of supervised, discriminative learning is to obtain the *posterior distribution p(y|x)*, where $x \in \mathbb{R}^M$ is an observation represented by its $M$-dimensional *feature vector*, and $y \in O^K$ is the $K$-dimensional output or *prediction* variable. The nature of the output $O$ depends on the type of problem at hand. If the output is *quantitative*, typically $O \subseteq \mathbb{R}$, the problems are called regression problems. If the output is *qualitative* (or categorical),[a] the problems are called classification problems. In the latter case, the output space often corresponds to a finite set of descriptive labels (or classes). Sometimes the elements of this finite set are represented by natural numbers; however, no metric or ordering is assumed on the elements. The differentiation of the output space is the main difference between classification and regression problems (cf. Hastie et al., 2009).

The posterior distribution provides probabilistic estimates over the different, possible predictions, and learning this distribution from a set of examples allows us to make predictions for new data. A common approach for making a prediction given the posterior is using the *maximum-a-posteriori* (MAP) estimate, $\hat{y} = \arg\max_y p(y|x)$.

We assume that a set of $N$ training examples $\mathcal{S} = \{(x^{(i)}, y^{(i)})\}_{i=1}^{N}$ is available from which we can learn the posterior distribution $p(x|y)$. In this context, the variables $y^{(i)}$ are also called the annotations. Random forests provide an effective way of learning and modeling the posterior, in particular, when the dimensionality $M$ of the feature space is high. In fact, in cases where the dimensionality is, say, $M < 100$, standard machine learning methods, such as variants of logistic or linear regression, might be more effective than random forests. However, in many image analysis applications, it is difficult to predefine a limited number of good (discriminative) features. One of the advantages of random forests is that it is sufficient to define potentially useful, parameterized feature types, which may be redundant or dependent. From the feature types, a large set, for example, $M \gg 1000$, of random features is generated and added to the feature pool $\mathcal{F}$ with $|\mathcal{F}| = M$. During random forest training the (few) most discriminative features are then sought within this pool. As mentioned previously, a random forest is an ensemble of $T$ decision trees, where each tree $t$ represents its own tree posterior $p^{(t)}(y|x)$. We will now describe the construction process of those trees, that is, the tree training.

### 5.2.1.1 Decision tree training

A binary[b] decision tree is an acyclic graph of hierarchically organized nodes, where each internal node (or *split node*) has exactly two child nodes, and nodes without children are called terminal nodes (or *leaf nodes*). The split nodes store split functions, and the leaf nodes store decisions. Decision tree training is the process of constructing a tree, starting with a single root node. For each tree $t$ a (sub)set of training examples $\mathcal{S}^{(t)} = \{(x^{(i)}, y^{(i)})\}_{i=1}^{n}$ is considered. For notational simplicity we will discard the tree dependent superscript in the following. Depending on the data, the employed objective function, and stopping criteria, a node either becomes a split node or a leaf node. Let us denote by $\mathcal{S}^{(j)}$ the training set reaching node $j$, where $\mathcal{S}^{(0)} = \mathcal{S}$ corresponds to the data at the root node. For split nodes, the data are partitioned into two disjoint sets $\mathcal{S}_L^{(j)}$ and $\mathcal{S}_R^{(j)}$ which are sent to the left and the right child nodes. The exact split depends on the parameters of a split function, and determining those parameters is the aim of a greedy optimization process. Most commonly used split functions are so-called axis-aligned functions $f_{m;\tau}$, defined as

$$f_{m;\tau}(x) = \begin{cases} 1 & \text{if } b_m \cdot x \geq \tau \\ 0 & \text{otherwise} \end{cases} \tag{5.1}$$

Here, $b_m$ is an $M$-dimensional binary vector with one nonzero entry at index $m$, and $\tau \in \mathbb{R}$ is a threshold. The vector $b_m$ selects one particular entry in the feature vector $x$ via the dot product $b_m \cdot x$, and the threshold defines whether the data point is added to the left or right subset, that is,

$\mathcal{S}_{\text{L}}^{(j)} = \{(x^{(i)}, y^{(i)}) : f_{m;\tau}^{(j)}(x^{(i)}) = 1\}$ and $\mathcal{S}_{\text{R}}^{(j)} = \{(x^{(i)}, y^{(i)}) : f_{m;\tau}^{(j)}(x^{(i)}) = 0\}$, respectively. The optimal split function parameters at each node $j$ are determined by maximizing the information gain, defined as

$$\text{IG}(b_m, \tau; j) = H(\mathcal{S}^{(j)}) - \sum_{k \in \{\text{L},\text{R}\}} \frac{|\mathcal{S}_k^{(j)}|}{|\mathcal{S}^{(j)}|} H(\mathcal{S}_k^{(j)}) \qquad (5.2)$$

where $H$ is a measure of entropy. The exact definition of this measure depends on the type of problem and the statistical representation of predictor functions, which will be discussed later. Intuitively, the information gain measures the increase of compactness or consistency of the data partitioning with respect to the annotations. Konukoglu et al. (2013) provide an alternative, generalized formulation of the tree training objective function in terms of cluster size.

Decision tree training stops at node $j$ when either no split yields an increased information gain, or if a stopping criteria holds. Commonly used stopping criteria include a maximum tree depth and a minimum number of training examples in each child node. If no further split is created, the node $j$ becomes a leaf node. Based on the arriving training examples $\mathcal{S}^{(j)}$, a statistical predictor $p^{(j)}(y|x)$ is computed using empirical distributions over the output variables $y^{(i)} \in O^K$. The specific form of those predictors, again, depends on the type of problem and the nature of the output space.

### Randomness
Injecting randomness into the training process is an important aspect of random forests, hence the naming. Randomness can be injected at two levels of the training process, at tree level and node level. At tree level the randomness concerns the subsampling of training examples (cf. *bagging* in Breiman, 2001). Each tree is trained on only a subset of training examples, which decorrelates trees, decreases the variance, and avoids overfitting. At node level, the randomness arises from the feature dimensions that are tested when optimizing the split function parameters. Only a small number of randomly chosen dimensions $M_j \ll M$ (e.g., a few hundred) are usually considered at each node. Again, this yields decorrelated trees but is also an important factor for the efficiency of the training process. As a rule of thumb, the number of random features per node is defined as $M_j = \sqrt{M}$.

### Optimization
The search for the best split function parameters, that is, selecting a feature dimension $m$ and a threshold $\tau$, commonly follows a randomized, greedy optimization strategy executed at each tree node. For each candidate feature dimension $m$ that is randomly chosen, a set of different thresholds, uniformly distributed along the range of feature responses, is evaluated. The parameter pair $(m, \tau)$ yielding the largest information gain is taken for defining the optimal split function $f_{m;\tau}$.

### 5.2.1.2 Decision tree testing
Once the decision trees are constructed, the ensemble can be used for making predictions on new data, which is a fairly straightforward and very efficient procedure. At so-called test time, only the feature vector $x$ is given for a test point. The test point is "pushed" through each tree where at each internal node the stored split functions are evaluated on the test point's feature vector. The result of the split function decides whether the test point is sent to the left or the right child. When the test point arrives at a leaf node, the stored statistics over training examples give the prediction for the test point. Thus, each tree $t$ yields a prediction in the form of a posterior $p^{(t)}(y|x)$ which captures empirical distributions

over the set of training examples that are most similar to the test point in the feature subspace. This observation has led to the interpretation of random forests as an approximate nearest neighbor method, as for example discussed by Konukoglu et al. (2013). The overall prediction is obtained by simple averaging

$$p(y|x) = \frac{1}{T}\sum_{t=1}^{T} p^{(t)}(y|x) \tag{5.3}$$

It should be noted that other aggregation rules are possible; averaging is only one possibility but probably the most widely used one. Another strategy is to weight each tree prediction according to some importance or confidence measure. A possible measure could take the consistency or compactness of leaf nodes into account. The weighting of tree predictions from less compact leaf nodes could be decreased accordingly.

We have now formalized the general framework of random forests and have seen the procedures that are necessary for training and testing. In the following, we will discuss two particular instances, regression forests and classification forests, that have been used for localization of spinal anatomy. We will start by specifying the notation and formal description of the spine localization problem.

## 5.2.2 SPINE ANATOMY LOCALIZATION

The spine is a bony structure, also referred to as the vertebral column, which consists of a set of individual vertebrae. Most human spines consist of 24 vertebrae, from which 7 belong to the cervical part of the spine (head and neck area; C1-C7), 12 form the thoracic part (rib cage; T1-T12), and 5 are part of the lumbar region (lower back; L1-L5). Each vertebra has a vertebral body, and in the following we will refer to the geometric center of this body as the location of the vertebra. Thus, vertebral locations (or centroids) resemble unique anatomical landmarks in human anatomy. In addition to the 24 vertebra centroids, we consider two more landmarks on the sacrum (S1, S2). This leads us to a spatial representation of the spine which is defined by a set of three-dimensional centroids $C = \{c_v\}_{v \in V}$ with $V = \{C1, \ldots, C7, T1, \ldots, T12, L1, \ldots, L5, S1, S2\}$ and $|V| = 26$. For notational simplicity, we refer to the centroids using indices from 1 to 26, $C = \{c_i\}_{i=1}^{26}$.

## 5.2.3 IMAGE FEATURES

As the aim is to build a system that allows us to localize the visible part of the vertebral column in images, we need to discuss the details of the imaging aspects. Let us start by defining an image as a function $I : \mathbb{R}^d \to \mathbb{R}^c$ that takes $d$-dimensional coordinates $p$ as input and returns $c$-dimensional vectors of intensity (or brightness) values. We write $I(p)$ to refer to the image values at a certain location. In our application of vertebrae localization in computed tomography (CT) images, the image dimension is $d = 3$, and the images are scalar-valued, that is, $c = 1$. We should note that absolute image coordinates are only meaningful within a particular image, that is, no registration between images is assumed anywhere in the system. In fact, in the particular CT databases that we will consider later for our experiments, no assumptions are made about which part of the spine is visible or to which extent. Images can contain only a few vertebrae from anywhere along the vertebral column, or they might contain the whole spine and even other anatomical parts, for example, the legs. The localization system should be able to detect which vertebrae are visible.

Image points are the data points in the random forest framework. To this end, each image point $p$ will be represented by a feature vector $x_p \in \mathbb{R}^M$, where each entry of the feature vector corresponds to the response of a particular feature evaluated on the image data. Those features should be efficient to compute and able to capture local and contextual information about the image point. A popular approach that allows the generation of many different features that fulfill those requirements is to employ so-called *box features*.

### 5.2.3.1 Randomized box features

Box features are relatively simple features based on computing mean intensity values within subareas of the images. A box, that is, a three-dimensional cuboid in our case, is parameterized by its three side lengths and a three-dimensional offset from an image point $p$. A randomized box feature can thus be generated by sampling the six box parameters taking a user-defined (and application dependent) range of values into account. Using integral images as suggested by Viola and Jones (2004), the sum of intensities within an arbitrarily sized box can be determined in constant time. Only eight values need to be read out from the integral images and with a specific order of additions and subtractions of those values one can reconstruct the sum of values. Dividing by the number of image points within the box gives the mean intensity value of the subarea of an image. Based on this, we make use of two types of features. The first one is a simple *one-box feature*, which takes a single box with an offset and returns the mean intensity within the box. The second one is a *two-box feature*, which takes two random boxes with offsets and returns the difference between their mean intensity values. The second one can be seen as a generalized, randomized version of the Haar-like two-rectangle feature as used by Viola and Jones (2004). While the one-box feature captures local and contextual appearance of structures in the surrounding of an image point, the second feature acts like a gradient feature by capturing intensity differences between local and contextual areas. While each individual feature is rather simple, and on its own probably not very informative, we will see that using the random forest framework to determine a chain of features along a path in a tree, those simple features can become very discriminative. In addition, the computational efficiency is beneficial for training *and* testing. During training a large number of features will be considered, and feature responses need to be computed on-the-fly at every tree node. Precomputing all feature responses for all training examples is not possible for large $M$ (size of the feature pool) as it would require too much memory. At test time, the efficient feature evaluation is obviously advantageous when predictions are computed for a large set of images. An illustration of the box features is shown in Figure 5.2.

### 5.2.4 REGRESSION FORESTS FOR LOCALIZATION

Considering the problem at hand of localizing anatomical landmarks of the spine, that is, the 26 centroids $\mathcal{C}$, in a given image, it seems tempting to formulate this problem as a regression problem. The task then becomes to predict the 78 quantitative parameters of the spine representation (26 times three-dimensional locations). However, since we cannot assume that images live in the same coordinate space, absolute centroid locations are only meaningful within one particular image but not in another one. Thus, we cannot directly use those coordinates from the training examples to learn a regression function. Instead, the output variable $y \in \mathbb{R}^{78}$ corresponds to a vector

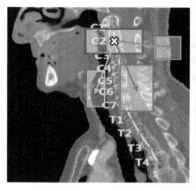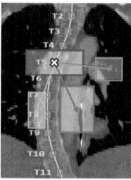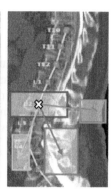

**FIGURE 5.2**

Illustration of random instances of box features for different image points in the cervical, thoracic, and lumbar region of the spine. Note that different box features capture different parts of the local and contextual appearance information.

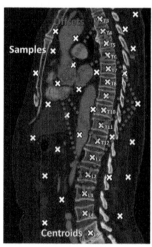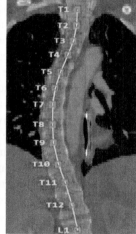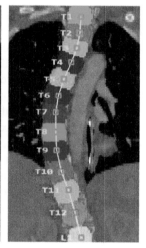

**FIGURE 5.3**

Illustration of the generation of training examples from vertebra centroid annotations for regression forests (left) and classification forests (middle, right). In regression forests, the output variable corresponds to relative offsets to the centroids. In classification forests, the output corresponds to categorical, point-wise vertebra labels.

of offsets between image coordinates $p$ and vertebrae centroids $C$. An illustration is shown in Figure 5.3. Given a training image with vertebrae centroid annotations, we can generate training examples $(x_p, y_p)$ from image points $p$, which are represented by their feature vectors $x_p$ and output $y_p = \left( (c_1 - p)^\top, (c_2 - p)^\top, \dots, (c_{26} - p)^\top \right)^\top$. The model for the empirical distribution stored at each leaf node of the decision trees can be chosen as a 78-dimensional multivariate normal distribution

$p(y|x) \triangleq \mathcal{N}_{78}(\bar{y}, \Sigma)$, where $\bar{y}$ corresponds to the mean over the output values of all training examples arriving in a leaf node, and $\Sigma$ is the covariance matrix. A useful property of the normal distribution as leaf node model is that it has a closed-form definition for the entropy which in the continuous case of regression is also called differential entropy. It is proportional to the logarithm of the determinant of the covariance matrix, $H_{\mathcal{N}} = \log|\Sigma|$.

Plugging this into Eq. (5.2) fully defines the objective function for regression tree training. An alternative to the differential entropy, which is often used in practice, is the trace of the covariance matrix, $H_{\mathcal{N}} = \text{tr}(\Sigma)$. Minimizing the trace often yields very similar partitions of training examples, although the covariances between different dimensions of the output space are ignored. However, this has the additional advantage that only the diagonal has to be stored in the leaf nodes, instead of the full matrix.

Both regression objective functions, the differential entropy and the trace, will lead to spatially consistent clusters of training examples, that is, clusters at leaf nodes that are spatially tight. Since the variance of the offset vectors is minimized, training examples tend to come from similar anatomical regions. At test time, image points extracted from the test image each make a prediction about the actual locations of the vertebrae. The predicted offsets $y_p$ are simply added to the location of the image point $p$, yielding a single *vote* for the vertebrae centroids $c_p = \left(p^\top + (y_{p;1}, y_{p;2}, y_{p;3}), \ldots, p^\top + (y_{p;24}, y_{p;25}, y_{p;26})\right)^\top$, where $y_{p;i}$ denotes the $i$th entry of the vector $y_p$. A posterior distribution of centroid locations $p(c_I|\mathcal{X}_I)$ in image $I$ can thus be obtained by collecting all votes (i.e., the predictions) from all test image points $\mathcal{X}_I = \{x_p\}_{p \in I}$ over all decision trees. In this context, regression forests are also denoted as Hough forests (cf. Gall et al., 2011) due to their similarity to the Hough transform.

### 5.2.4.1 Refinement stage

The posterior of centroids that is obtained from the regression forests could be directly used to obtain the MAP estimate. However, this does not yield very accurate results as can be seen in the experimental evaluation. The regression provides very good and robust estimates about the visible part of the spine and the rough locations of individual vertebrae. However, to obtain a much more accurate localization, a refinement stage based on a hidden Markov model (HMM) with statistical shape and appearance is employed in our earlier work (cf. Glocker et al., 2012a). We omit the exact details here, as we only focus on random forests, but it should be noted that the refinement step is quite essential. It makes use of local appearance of the test image and using dynamic programming fits the statistical model of the spine, making use of the posterior distribution obtained from the forest as a driving force. This process adds a generative model to the discriminative one provided by the regression forests.

## 5.2.5 CLASSIFICATION FORESTS FOR LOCALIZATION

Anatomy localization can also be formulated as a classification problem where each image point of a test image is classified as being part of a particular anatomical structure (or background). From such a dense classification, locations of structures such as centroids can then be derived, for example by computing the center of mass. However, training a classification forest would actually require a set of training examples where the output variable $y$ corresponds to categorical labels. Since in our case we are given a set of images with centroid annotations, we need a way of transforming those sparse annotations into dense, point-wise classification maps. Note, obtaining those maps manually is time-consuming and not feasible for a large set of images. In contrast, the sparse centroid annotations can be obtained quite efficiently. We use a simple transform based on Euclidean distances which assigns each image point in a training image a categorical label $l \in \mathcal{L} = \mathcal{V} \cup \{B\}$, where $B$ is the background label. The label corresponds to the vertebra centroid that is closest to the image point, $l_p = \arg\min_{v \in \mathcal{V}} \|p - c_v\|$, and image points whose smallest distance to a centroid is larger than a threshold are assigned the background label. The threshold can be set depending on the expected size of each vertebral body, or one can use one global threshold according to the average size. We use a threshold of 20 mm for all vertebrae. An illustration is shown in Figure 5.3. This process allows the generation of training examples $(x_p, y_y)$ with $y_p = l_p$. The model for the empirical distribution that is stored at each leaf node of the decision trees is based on a simple histogram over categorical labels. The measure of entropy is defined as the Shannon entropy $H = -\sum_{y \in \mathcal{L}} p(y|x) \log p(y|x)$. Plugging this into Eq. (5.2) fully defines the objective function for classification tree training.

One problem that often arises in classification concerns unbalanced classes with respect to the distribution of training examples. The nature of the problem often yields more training examples for some classes (or labels) than for others. This can have an adverse effect on the classifier which will have a bias in prediction toward classes with more training examples. To overcome this problem in classification forests a common approach is to reweight the histogram counts before computing the empirical distributions during tree training. To this end, the counts for each class at the root node are stored and used for reweighting every time a class distribution is computed at a node. At the root node, this yields a uniform distribution over classes. The reweighting factor for each class is determined as $|\mathcal{S}^{(0)}|/|\mathcal{S}^{(0)}_{y=l}|$, where $\mathcal{S}^{(0)}_{y=l}$ corresponds to the set of training examples at the root node with a categorical label $y = l$. The reweighting compensates for unbalanced classes and commonly yields more balanced decision trees.

### 5.2.5.1 Refinement stage

Similar to the regression approach, a refinement stage is employed to estimate accurate locations of vertebrae after testing. Here, we need to transform the dense classification maps back to sparse centroids. In our earlier work (cf. Glocker et al., 2013), we employ a centroid estimation strategy using mean shift (Fukunaga and Hostetler, 1975) and an additional outlier removal step. Note that the classification maps that we obtain from the random forest are probabilistic, that is, we obtain probabilities $p(y_p|x_p)$ for the labels at every image point $p$. Using the probabilities, the mean shift algorithm estimates the modes of the underlying spatial label distributions. Exact details are omitted here but can be found in our original paper. It should be noted that the same refinement stage based on a HMM that was introduced for the regression forests could be used in the case of classification. However, we found that the HMM model is too restrictive when it comes to pathological cases, as later discussed in the experiments.

## 5.2.6 REGRESSION vs CLASSIFICATION

One conceptual difference between regression forests and classification forests in the context of anatomy localization is the way the predictions are used. In the case of regression, theoretically, every image point can contribute to the final prediction. Their individual votes are aggregated which adds a certain level of robustness. Intuitively, each image point in a test image is asked "what it believes where the structures of interest are." This is different in the case of classification, where every image point is asked "whether it believes it is part of a structure of interest or not." In our experimental evaluation, we found that both questions can lead to accurate results, but it highly depends on the nature of the input data. Regression seems suitable when there is no significant change in global shape and spatial arrangement of the structures, for instance in a population of healthy subjects. In highly pathological cases, the classification approach seems more suitable to capture local shape and appearance while being invariant to global changes. In an earlier work on organ segmentation (cf. Glocker et al., 2012b), we formulated a joint regression-classification framework which aims at combining the advantages of both classification and regression forests. Whether such an approach is suitable for the task of anatomy localization would be worth exploring. In the following section, we present an experimental evaluation of the two different localization approaches on two spine CT databases.

## 5.3 EXPERIMENTAL COMPARISON

We performed an experimental comparison of the two different random forest approaches, regression forests and classification forests, for the task of spine anatomy localization. To this end, we made use of two different data collections of CT images, one with only few and one with quite severe spinal pathologies. We quantified the performance of the methods on those data collections in terms of localization accuracy. We should note that although this comparison does not compare regression versus classification in an isolated manner, since the localization results of both approaches depend on the refinement stage, it still provides some insights into the advantages and disadvantages of the two approaches, in particular, with respect to normal versus pathological anatomy.

### 5.3.1 LOCALIZATION DATASETS

Before we discuss the quantitative evaluation, we provide some details about the two data that is used for the experiments. We make use of two CT data collections namely the *Normal CT* and *Spine CT* datasets (see Figure 5.4).

#### 5.3.1.1 Normal CT

The *Normal CT* dataset consists of 200 CT scans, mostly from trauma patients. It is a heterogeneous collection from different clinical centers with varying imaging hardware. The dataset is called "normal" as both shape and appearance of the spine in those images appear healthy, that is, patients did not necessarily suffer from a problem with the spine. In fact, the majority of the cases have nonspine-related pathologies. The visible body parts, that is, the field-of-views, for the scans vary significantly. In some cases, only four vertebrae are visible, while others correspond to whole-body scans. The number of slices along the main body axis varies between 51 and 2058, with an average of 240 slices. The interslice distances vary between 0.5 and 6.5 mm. All visible vertebrae in all 200 CT scans were manually annotated by identifying the centroids of vertebral bodies.

#### 5.3.1.2 Spine CT

The *Spine CT* dataset consists of 224 CT scans of spine patients and has been made publicly available.[c] The data have been acquired at the Department of Radiology, University of Washington, Seattle, USA. Images were acquired with a General Electric multidetector CT scanner with varying slice thickness and

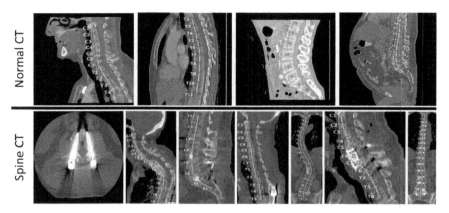

**FIGURE 5.4**

Example images with annotations from the two CT data collections.

a standard bone algorithm. The cohort was chosen at random from those patients who had two or more cross-sectional studies. The field-of-view along the main body axis varies and usually between 5 and 15 vertebrae are visible. The CT slices are focused on the spine with a very narrow field-of-view in the in-plane dimensions. Thus, not much contextual information from surrounding anatomical structures is available. Spinal pathologies include basically everything that can affect shape and appearance, from high-grade scoliosis, kyphosis, fractures, and implants. The collection contains pre- and postoperative scans with partly severe imaging artifacts. All visible vertebrae in all 224 CT scans have been manually annotated by identifying the centroids of vertebral bodies.

## 5.3.2 EXPERIMENTAL SETUP

We performed two separate evaluations, one on each of the data collections. This allowed us to compare the performance of the two localization approaches on different data. In both cases, we randomly split the data into two equally sized sets, each once used for training and once for testing in a twofold cross-validation. For the *Spine CT* dataset, we made sure that scans from the same patient are in the same subset. We first describe the metrics for error quantification, before we report the parameter settings for the two methods.

### 5.3.2.1 Error quantification

The evaluation of vertebrae localization and identification is carried out by considering different criteria. We also evaluated individually the performance within the cervical, thoracic, and lumbar regions of the spine. The performance metrics are described in the following.

### Localization error

For each correctly detected vertebra we determine the distances (in millimeters) between estimated vertebrae centroids and reference positions. The mean and standard deviations are reported.

Identification rates

A vertebra is considered to be correctly identified if the predicted centroid is within 2 cm of the reference one and if the closest centroid among all annotated ones is the correct one.

### 5.3.2.2 Parameter settings

For the comparative analysis, the general forest parameters for the two approaches are identical. Both the regression forest and the classification forest consist of 20 trees each with a maximum tree depth of 24. A minimum of eight training examples per node are guaranteed and used as a tree growing stopping criterion. The total number of box features in the feature pool is set to 10,000. At each node we randomly choose 100 features and evaluate potential splits for 10 uniformly distributed thresholds during split node optimization. The ranges for the box sizes and offsets vary between the approaches. The regression forest makes use of longer range features which capture more contextual information. The maximum box size is set to 50 mm, while the maximum offset is set to 75 mm. The classification forest on the other hand relies on more local information. Hence, the maximum box size is set to 30 mm, while the maximum offset is set to 40 mm. In all our experiments, the CT images are downsampled to an isotropic voxel resolution of 2 mm. For the regression forest, 5% of image points are randomly sampled uniformly from each image for training and testing. For the classification forest, we use all image points with HU values above 100, which are points more likely to correspond to bony structures. The parameters for the subsequent refinement stages are provided in our original works (cf. Glocker et al., 2012a, 2013).

### 5.3.3 RESULTS

The main results are summarized in Table 5.1. Given are the median, mean, and standard deviations of the localization errors and the identification rates overall and per spinal region. The regression forests perform slightly better on the *Normal CT* dataset compared to the classification forests. On the *Spine CT* collection, however, the classification forests are clearly superior. In Figure 5.5, we also provide the localization error statistics per vertebra. In particular in the lower thoracic and lumbar regions, the regression forests struggle to obtain good localization results. Those are the areas that are mostly affected by spinal pathologies in the *Spine CT* dataset.

---

## 5.4 CONCLUSION

From the experimental evaluation and comparison of regression forests and classification forests for the task of spine anatomy localization, we draw the following conclusions. Both approaches can be employed in time-critical applications. Using the sampling strategies as described in Section 5.3.2.2 enables per image testing times of only a few minutes (including the refinement stages) (see Figure 5.6). Forest testing itself takes in both cases less than a minute. In terms of accuracy, it should be noted that there is a significant difference between the raw forest output and the refined estimates (also cf. Glocker et al., 2012a). Both approaches rely on postprocessing steps for refinement. Regression forests provide a very robust and efficient initial estimate about the visible anatomy and rough locations (within centimeters), but do not yield very accurate estimates in terms of localization error. The regression

**Table 5.1 Summary of the Quantitative Comparison of Regression Forests and Classification Forests for the Task of Vertebrae Localization**

| Method | | Regression Forests | | | | Classification Forests | | | |
|---|---|---|---|---|---|---|---|---|---|
| Data | Region | Median | Mean | Std | Id. Rates (%) | Median | Mean | Std | Id. Rates (%) |
| Normal CT | All | **5.4** | **9.7** | **11.2** | **80** | 7.6 | 11.5 | 14.1 | 76 |
| | Cervical | 6.5 | 8.2 | 6.1 | 73 | **6.3** | **7.7** | **4.4** | **78** |
| | Thoracic | **5.5** | **9.9** | **10.8** | **77** | 8.7 | 12.4 | 11.6 | 67 |
| | Lumbar | **5.3** | **9.4** | **12.0** | **86** | 6.6 | 10.6 | 16.9 | 86 |
| Spine CT | All | 14.8 | 20.9 | 20.0 | 51 | **8.8** | **12.4** | **11.2** | **70** |
| | Cervical | 11.5 | 17.0 | 17.7 | 54 | **5.9** | **7.0** | **4.7** | **80** |
| | Thoracic | 12.7 | 19.0 | 20.5 | 56 | **9.8** | **13.8** | **11.8** | 62 |
| | Lumbar | 23.2 | 26.6 | 19.7 | 42 | **10.2** | **14.3** | **12.3** | **75** |

Note: Localization errors are given in millimeters. Bold numbers indicate which of the two methods has better performance.

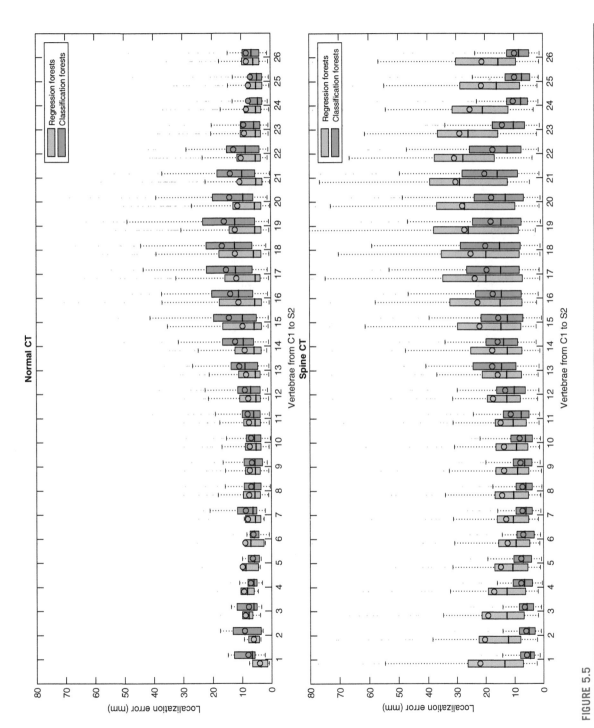

**FIGURE 5.5**

Statistics of localization errors per vertebra for regression forests and classification forests on the two different CT data collections. Largest errors occur for both methods in the lower thoracic and upper lumbar area.

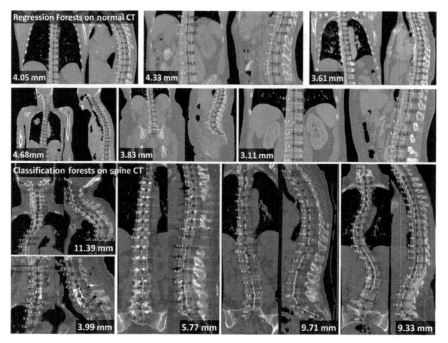

**FIGURE 5.6**

Visual results for vertebrae localization using regression forests (top) and classification forests (bottom) on the *Normal CT* and *Spine CT* data collection, respectively.

approach seems particularly well suited for rather normal cases, that is, cases where there are no large anatomical variations in shape and appearance. In those cases, the aggregation of votes from image points from the whole image domain results in the robustness of the method. Classification forests, on the other hand, are able to handle abnormal cases as they make only local decisions about whether a point belongs to a certain anatomy. Those predictions can be highly accurate but often contain many false positives and need a clean-up stage as part of the postprocessing. While we have explored a joint regression/classification approach in an earlier work (cf. Glocker et al., 2012b), recently the most accurate applications of random forests involve some sort of cascading. One strategy is to consider using forests within an auto-context framework (cf. Tu and Bai, 2010) where predictions of an earlier stage are used as features in subsequent stages. Another successful strategy is to implement a global-to-local hierarchy of forests (cf. Ebner et al., 2014; Gauriau et al., 2014) where predictions are made subsequently and refined in each stage. Using a sophisticated cascade of classifiers or regressors can even make the postprocessing step unnecessary. In some applications, the accuracy of the localization is not critical. In a recent work (cf. Glocker et al., 2014), we employed the classification forests successfully within a longitudinal registration pipeline. The estimates about vertebra centroids eliminate the registration initialization issues, and we could show that using location priors determined with a forest drastically reduces the number of failed registrations.

## NOTES

a. Sometimes the term *discrete* is used to refer to classification, which is, however, not a very appropriate differentiation from regression, as discrete spaces can be quantitative.
b. Binary trees are the most commonly used type of decision trees, although $n$-ary trees with $n > 2$ have been proposed in the literature.
c. See http://spineweb.digitalimaginggroup.ca. Note that in the meantime the number of annotated datasets that are available has been increased to 242.

## REFERENCES

Alomari, R.S., Corso, J.J., Chaudhary, V., 2011. Labeling of lumbar discs using both pixel- and object-level features with a two-level probabilistic model. IEEE Trans. Med. Imaging 30 (1), 1-10.

Ayed, I.B., Punithakumar, K., Minhas, R., Joshi, R., Garvin, G.J., 2012. Vertebral body segmentation in MRI via convex relaxation and distribution matching. In: Medical Image Computing and Computer-Assisted Intervention—MICCAI 2012. Springer, Heidelberg, pp. 520-527.

Breiman, L., 2001. Random forests. Mach. Learn. 45 (1), 5-32.

Caruana, R., Karampatziakis, N., Yessenalina, A., 2008. An empirical evaluation of supervised learning in high dimensions. In: Proceedings of the 25th International Conference on Machine Learning, pp. 96-103.

Cootes, T.F., Ionita, M.C., Lindner, C., Sauer, P., 2012. Robust and accurate shape model fitting using random forest regression voting. In: Computer Vision—ECCV 2012. Springer, Heidelberg, pp. 278-291.

Criminisi, A., Shotton, J., Konukoglu, E., 2012. Decision forests: a unified framework for classification, regression, density estimation, manifold learning and semi-supervised learning. Found. Trends Comput. Graphics Vision 7 (2/3), 81-227.

Criminisi, A., Robertson, D., Konukoglu, E., Shotton, J., Pathak, S., White, S., Siddiqui, K., 2013a. Regression forests for efficient anatomy detection and localization in computed tomography scans. Med. Image Anal. 17 (8), 1293-1303.

Criminisi, A., Robertson, D., Pauly, O., Glocker, B., Konukoglu, E., Shotton, J., Mateus, D., Möller, A.M., Nekolla, S., Navab, N., 2013b, Anatomy detection and localization in 3D medical images. In: Decision Forests for Computer Vision and Medical Image Analysis. Springer, London, pp. 193-209.

Cuingnet, R., Prevost, R., Lesage, D., Cohen, L.D., Mory, B., Ardon, R., 2012. Automatic detection and segmentation of kidneys in 3D CT images using random forests. In: Medical Image Computing and Computer-Assisted Intervention. Springer, pp. 66-74.

Ebner, T., Stern, D., Donner, R., Bischof, H., Urschler, M., 2014. Towards automatic bone age estimation from MRI: localization of 3D anatomical landmarks. In: Medical Image Computing and Computer-Assisted Intervention. Springer, Heidelberg, pp. 421-428.

Fukunaga, K., Hostetler, L., 1975. The estimation of the gradient of a density function, with applications in pattern recognition. IEEE Trans. Inf. Theory 21 (1), 32-40.

Gall, J., Yao, A., Razavi, N., Van Gool, L., Lempitsky, V., 2011. Hough forests for object detection, tracking, and action recognition. IEEE Trans. Pattern Anal. Mach. Intell. 33 (11), 2188-2202.

Gauriau, R., Cuingnet, R., Lesage, D., Bloch, I., 2014. Multi-organ localization combining global-to-local regression and confidence maps. In: Medical Image Computing and Computer-Assisted Intervention. Springer, Heidelberg, pp. 337-344.

Glocker, B., Feulner, J., Criminisi, A., Haynor, D.R., Konukoglu, E., 2012a, Automatic localization and identification of vertebrae in arbitrary field-of-view CT scans. In: Medical Image Computing and Computer-Assisted Intervention. Springer, Heidelberg, pp. 590-598.

Glocker, B., Pauly, O., Konukoglu, E., Criminisi, A., 2012b, Joint classification-regression forests for spatially structured multi-object segmentation. In: Computer Vision—ECCV 2012. Springer, Heidelberg, pp. 870-881.

Glocker, B., Zikic, D., Konukoglu, E., Haynor, D.R., Criminisi, A., 2013. Vertebrae localization in pathological spine CT via dense classification from sparse annotations. In: Medical Image Computing and Computer-Assisted Intervention. Springer, Heidelberg, pp. 262-270.

Glocker, B., Zikic, D., Haynor, D.R., 2014. Robust registration of longitudinal spine CT. In: Medical Image Computing and Computer-Assisted Intervention. Springer, Heidelberg, pp. 251-258.

Hastie, T., Tibshirani, R., Friedman, J., Hastie, T., Friedman, J., Tibshirani, R., 2009. The Elements of Statistical Learning, vol. 2, 1. Springer, Berlin.

Hsiang, J., 2011. Wrong-level surgery: a unique problem in spine surgery. Surg. Neurol. Int. 2, 47.

Kelm, B.M., Zhou, S.K., Suehling, M., Zheng, Y., Wels, M., Comaniciu, D., 2011. Detection of 3D spinal geometry using iterated marginal space learning. In: Medical Computer Vision. Recognition Techniques and Applications in Medical Imaging. Springer, Heidelberg, pp. 96-105.

Klinder, T., Ostermann, J., Ehm, M., Franz, A., Kneser, R., Lorenz, C., 2009. Automated model-based vertebra detection, identification, and segmentation in CT images. Med. Image Anal. 13 (3), 471-482.

Konukoglu, E., Glocker, B., Zikic, D., Criminisi, A., 2013. Neighbourhood approximation using randomized forests. Med. Image Anal. 17 (7), 790-804.

Lecron, F., Boisvert, J., Mahmoudi, S., Labelle, H., Benjelloun, M., 2012. Fast 3D spine reconstruction of postoperative patients using a multilevel statistical model. In: Medical Image Computing and Computer-Assisted Intervention—MICCAI 2012. Springer, Heidelberg, pp. 446-453.

Major, D., Hladuvka, J., Schulze, F., Buehler, K., 2013. Automated landmarking and labeling of fully and partially scanned spinal columns in CT images. Med. Image Anal. 17 (8), 1151-1163.

Pauly, O., Glocker, B., Criminisi, A., Mateus, D., Möller, A.M., Nekolla, S., Navab, N., 2011. Fast multiple organ detection and localization in whole-body Mr Dixon sequences. In: Medical Image Computing and Computer-Assisted Intervention. Springer, Heidelberg, pp. 239-247.

Roberts, M.G., Cootes, T.F., Adams, J.E., 2012. Automatic location of vertebrae on DXA images using random forest regression. In: Medical Image Computing and Computer-Assisted Intervention. Springer, Heidelberg, pp. 361-368.

Schmidt, S., Kappes, J., Bergtholdt, M., Pekar, V., Dries, S., Bystrov, D., Schnörr, C., 2007. Spine detection and labeling using a parts-based graphical model. In: Information Processing in Medical Imaging, pp. 122-133.

Steger, S., Wesarg, S., 2012. Automated skeleton based multi-modal deformable registration of head&neck datasets. In: Medical Image Computing and Computer-Assisted Intervention. Springer, Heidelberg, pp. 66-73.

Tu, Z., Bai, X., 2010. Auto-context and its application to high-level vision tasks and 3D brain image segmentation. IEEE Trans. Pattern Anal. Mach. Intell. 32 (10), 1744-1757.

Viola, P., Jones, M.J., 2004. Robust real-time face detection. Int. J. Comput. Vis. 57 (2), 137-154.

Yao, J., Burns, J.E., Munoz, H., Summers, R.M., 2012. Detection of vertebral body fractures based on cortical shell unwrapping. In: Medical Image Computing and Computer-Assisted Intervention. Springer, Heidelberg, pp. 509-516.

Zhan, Y., Maneesh, D., Harder, M., Zhou, X.S., 2012. Robust MR spine detection using hierarchical learning and local articulated model. In: Medical Image Computing and Computer-Assisted Intervention. Springer, Heidelberg, pp. 141-148.

# INTEGRATED DETECTION NETWORK FOR MULTIPLE OBJECT RECOGNITION

**M. Sofka**[1,2]

*Security Business Group, Cisco Systems, Prague, Czech Republic*[1]
*Department of Computer Science, Czech Technical University, Prague, Czech Republic*[2]

## CHAPTER OUTLINE

## 6.1 INTRODUCTION

Recognizing multiple objects or anatomical structures has many applications in medical imaging systems, for example, in multiobject visual tracking, to initialize segmentation of the structures or to provide accurate measurements. The goal of the recognition is to find the pose parameters of all structures of interest relative to the origin of the image coordinate system, camera, or other structures and to assign the correct object class label to the structures. In the first step, a model is constructed from a set of training examples to capture the statistics of the object class. The parameters are then found during inference by applying the model on a new image. In generative models, the probability model consists of the object appearance variations conditioned on the pose and a probability model of appearance variations of the background along with the prior probabilities of each class. The inference is computed by evaluating the posterior probabilities using the Bayes' theorem. In practice, it is very hard to model all variations of the structures since the structure shape, shadows and occlusions, image characteristics, and acquisition parameters can vary significantly. Discriminative models are more tractable. The probability model consists of an object presence or class label conditioned on the appearance. The inference typically computes the posterior probability given a set of discrete parameter values. Multiscale and sampling techniques are used to make the process efficient.

The robustness of the variations in the photometric appearance of the structures is achieved by features that are invariant to intensity transformations. One example of such features are Haar features that compare intensity statistics computed in adjacent rectangular windows of various configurations (Viola and Jones, 2004). Other popular feature types are local binary patterns that relate the intensity values of a pixel to those of its neighbors. When combined with histograms of oriented gradients (Dalal and Triggs, 2005), invariance to small geometric transformations is achieved by computing local histograms of the features. Larger geometric transformations can be directly modeled by decomposing a structure into parts (Felzenszwalb et al., 2010) and considering the statistical relationships between the parts and the structure of interest. Local detectors can then be improved by modeling the interdependence of objects using contextual (Kumar and Hebert, 2006; Hoiem et al., 2008; Desai et al., 2011) and semantic information. Spatial information can also be disregarded altogether resulting in a bag-of-features model (Lampert et al., 2009). As an alternative to manually engineered features, hierarchical feature representations can be learned from large databases (Sermanet et al., 2014).

State-of-the-art approaches to multiobject detection (Viola and Jones, 2004; Felzenszwalb et al., 2010) rely on an individual detector for each object class followed by postprocessing to prune spurious detections within and between classes. Detecting multiple objects jointly rather than individually has the advantage that the spatial relationships between objects can be exploited. This is done implicitly in deep neural networks, where the relationships are encoded by hidden layers (Sermanet et al., 2014). Obtaining a joint model of multiple objects involves the estimation of a large number of parameters which increases the requirements on the training time and the size of the annotation database. In situations where this is not practical, the multiobject detection task has been solved by multiple individual object detectors connected by a spatial model. Relative locations of the objects provide constraints that help to make the system more robust by focusing the search in regions where the object is expected based on locations of the other objects. Modeling long-range dependencies is straightforward in these models. The most challenging aspect of these algorithms is designing detectors that are fast and robust, modeling the spatial relationships between objects, and determining the order of object dependencies. In this chapter, we propose a multiobject recognition system that addresses these challenges.

The exposition starts in Section 6.2 by presenting a general framework for multiobject recognition without considering contextual dependencies between objects. The recognition is accomplished by a discriminative appearance model of each individual object. Section 6.3 then describes a sequential sampling framework, where the interdependence between objects is modeled by a transition distribution. The distribution specifies the "transition" of a pose of one object to a pose of another object as detailed in Section 6.3.1. This process relies on the strong prior information present in medical images of a human body. Together, all detectors and any associated processing form the integrated detection network (IDN) presented in Section 6.3.2. Section 6.3.3 explains how to determine the size of the context region (detection scale) and which objects to detect first in an optimal way. The chapter concludes by highlighting examples of IDN applications in Section 6.4 and by final remarks in Section 6.5.

## 6.2 INDEPENDENT MULTIOBJECT RECOGNITION

This section starts by discussing the independent recognition, where the spatial relationships between objects are not explicitly modeled. The next section then describes a technique that takes advantage of previously recognized objects to improve the recognition of a new object.

The state of the modeled object $s$ is denoted as $\theta_s$, where $\theta_s = \{\pi_s, y_s\}$. The first term, $\pi_s$, denotes the pose $\pi_s = \{\mathbf{p}, \mathbf{r}, \mathbf{s}\}$ with the position $\mathbf{p}$, orientation $\mathbf{r}$, and size $\mathbf{s}$ of the object $s$. The second term, $y_s$, denotes the object label. The set of observations for an object $s$ is obtained from the image neighborhood $V_s$. The neighborhood $V_s$ is specified by the coordinates of a bounding box within an $N$-dimensional image $V$, $V : R^N \rightarrow I$, where $I$ is the image intensity. The images are typically two or three dimensional. The observations computed from $V_s$ are features with a likelihood $f(V_s|\theta_s)$. They represent the appearance of each object and are assumed conditionally independent given the state $\theta_s$.

The task of object recognition consists of detecting the object instance inside the image $V$ and identifying the object class, both of which are accomplished by using observations computed from the image. The object $s$ is detected by estimating the pose parameters $\pi_s$ and classified by assigning the label $y_s$. The likelihood $f(V_s|\theta_s)$ can be formulated as:

$$f(V_s|\theta_s) = f(V_s|\pi_s, y_s) = f(y_s, \pi_s|V_s)\frac{f(V_s)}{f(y_s, \pi_s)} = f(y_s|\pi_s, V_s)f(\pi_s|V_s)\frac{f(V_s)}{f(y_s, \pi_s)} \qquad (6.1)$$

The term $f(y_s|\pi_s, V_s)$ denotes the posterior of the object class label with object pose $\pi_s$ given the observations from $V_s$. The term $f(\pi_s|V_s)$ is the posterior of the pose given observations. The term $f(y_s, \pi_s)$ denotes the prior on the labels and pose parameters and is estimated from the training data. The term $f(V_s)$ is set to a uniform distribution.

The object recognition can be accomplished by sliding a window, where the window defines the neighborhood $V_s$ at each step. The observations from $V_s$ are used to classify the window by assigning the class label. The object classifier is therefore represented by the model $f(y_s|V_s)$, which is the posterior of the object class within the image neighborhood $V_s$:

$$f(y_s|V_s) = \int_{\pi_s} f(y_s|\pi_s, V_s)f(\pi_s|V_s)\, d\pi_s \qquad (6.2)$$

In practice, the probability of the anatomical structure $s$ being detected is evaluated using a discrete set of pose parameter values $\{\pi_s\}$ and a binary (object vs background) or multiobject classifier.

The set of best instance parameters $\hat{\theta}_s = \{\hat{\pi}_s, \hat{y}_s\}$ for each object $s$ is then estimated using the observations from $V_s$:

$$\{\hat{\pi}_s, \hat{y}_s\} = \arg\max_{y_s, \pi_s} P(y_s|\pi_s, V_s)P(\pi_s|V_s) \qquad (6.3)$$

To leverage the power of a large annotated dataset, discriminative classifier (probabilistic boosting tree [PBT], Tu, 2005) is used to best decide between positive and negative examples of the object. PBT combines a binary decision tree with boosting, letting each tree node be an AdaBoost classifier. This way, the misclassified positive or negative examples early on can still be correctly classified by children nodes. Other classification approaches can be used as well.

## 6.3 SEQUENTIAL SAMPLING FOR MULTIOBJECT RECOGNITION

Similarly to the individual detection of single objects, the goal of the multiobject detection is to estimate the likelihood of the observations given object parameters. The sequence of parameters of multiple objects is denoted as $\theta_{0:s} = \{\theta_0, \theta_1, \ldots, \theta_s\}$ and the sequence of volumes to compute the observations

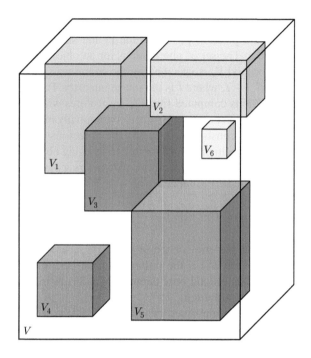

**FIGURE 6.1**

In multiobject detection, the set of observations is a sequence of image patches $\{V_s\}$. The sequence specifies a spatial order of structures. The structures are detected in this order, which is automatically determined.

as $V_{0:s} = \{V_0, V_1, \ldots, V_s\}$. It is possible to construct such a sequence since there exists prior knowledge for determining the image neighborhoods $V_0, V_1, \ldots, V_s$. The image neighborhoods in the sequence $V_{0:s}$ might overlap and can have different sizes (Figure 6.1). An image neighborhood $V_i$ might even be the entire volume $V$. The order in this sequence is determined manually based on the expert knowledge or automatically based on the posterior probability of object poses in the ground truth region (see more details following).

It is clear that the conditional likelihood model $P(V_{0:s}|\theta_{0:s})$ is now much more complicated. The posterior of the object classes $f(y_{0:s}|\pi_{0:s}, V_{0:s})$ involves the dependence of all instance labels jointly on all pose parameters and all observations. Such a large search space is computationally prohibitive both in training and in inference. Since the likelihood models in practical situations lead to intractable exact inference, approximation by Monte Carlo methods, also known as particle filtering or sequential estimation, has been widely adopted.

Sequential estimation techniques (Doucet et al., 2001) estimate the object state $\theta_s$ using observations from $V_{0:s}$ in a sequential spatial order. This way, the posterior distribution of the parameters (state) of each anatomical structure is estimated based on all observations so far. This concept is used to solve the multiobject detection problem by recursively applying *prediction* and *update* steps to obtain the posterior distribution $f(\theta_{0:s}|V_{0:s})$. The prediction step computes the probability density of the state of the object $s$ using the state of the previous object, $s - 1$, and previous observations of all objects up to $s - 1$:

$$f(\boldsymbol{\theta}_{0:s}|V_{0:s-1}) = f(\boldsymbol{\theta}_s|\boldsymbol{\theta}_{0:s-1})f(\boldsymbol{\theta}_{0:s-1}|V_{0:s-1}) \qquad (6.4)$$

The state dynamics, that is, relationships between object poses, are modeled with an initial distribution $f(\boldsymbol{\theta}_0)$ and a transition distribution $f(\boldsymbol{\theta}_s|\boldsymbol{\theta}_{0:s-1})$. Note that here the first-order Markov transition $f(\boldsymbol{\theta}_s|\boldsymbol{\theta}_{s-1})$ is not used since any detected object can depend on any other previously detected object. When detecting the object $s$, the observation $V_s$ is used to compute the estimate during the update step as:

$$f(\boldsymbol{\theta}_{0:s}|V_{0:s}) = \frac{f(V_s|\boldsymbol{\theta}_s)f(\boldsymbol{\theta}_{0:s}|V_{0:s-1})}{f(V_s|V_{0:s-1})} \qquad (6.5)$$

where $f(V_s|V_{0:s-1})$ is the normalizing constant.

As simple as they seem, these expressions do not have analytical solution in general. This problem is addressed by drawing $m$ weighted samples $\{\boldsymbol{\theta}_{0:s}^j, w_s^j\}_{j=1}^m$ from the distribution $f(\boldsymbol{\theta}_{0:s}|V_{0:s})$, where $\{\boldsymbol{\theta}_{0:s}^j\}_{j=1}^m$ is a realization of state $\boldsymbol{\theta}_{0:s}$ with weight $w_s^j$.

In most practical situations, sampling directly from $f(\boldsymbol{\theta}_{0:s}|V_{0:s})$ is not feasible. The idea of importance sampling is to introduce a *proposal distribution* $p(\boldsymbol{\theta}_{0:s}|V_{0:s})$, which includes the support of $f(\boldsymbol{\theta}_{0:s}|V_{0:s})$. This is better than sampling the parameter space uniformly (Viola and Jones, 2004; Tu, 2005), since sampling from the proposal distribution (Liu et al., 2001) focuses on regions of high probability. This saves computational time, as fewer samples are required, and increases robustness compared to the case where the same number of samples would be drawn uniformly.

It is now useful to discuss the concept of weighted samples. A set of weighted random samples $\{\boldsymbol{\theta}_{0:s}^j, w_s^j\}_{j=1}^m$ is called *proper* with respect to $f$, if for any square integrable function $h(\cdot)$ (Doucet et al., 2001)

$$E[h(\boldsymbol{\theta}_{0:s}^j)w_s^j] = cE_f h(\boldsymbol{\theta}_{0:s}) \qquad (6.6)$$

where $c$ is a normalizing constant common to all $m$ samples. Note that $\boldsymbol{\theta}$ estimated as $\sum_{j=1}^m w_s^j h(\boldsymbol{\theta}_{0:s}^j)$ does not depend on the normalizing constant of $f$, that is, $c$ does not need to be known. In order for the samples from the proposal $p(\boldsymbol{\theta}_{0:s}|V_{0:s})$ to be proper, the weights are defined as

$$\tilde{w}_s^j = \frac{f(V_{0:s}|\boldsymbol{\theta}_{0:s}^j)f(\boldsymbol{\theta}_{0:s}^j)}{p(\boldsymbol{\theta}_{0:s}^j|V_{0:s})}$$

$$w_s^j = \frac{\tilde{w}_s^j}{\sum_{i=1}^m \tilde{w}_s^i} \qquad (6.7)$$

Since the current states do not depend on observations from other objects then

$$p(\boldsymbol{\theta}_{0:s}|V_{0:s}) = p(\boldsymbol{\theta}_{0:s-1}|V_{0:s-1})p(\boldsymbol{\theta}_s|\boldsymbol{\theta}_{0:s-1}, V_{0:s}) \qquad (6.8)$$

Note that $V_s$ was left out of the first term since the states in the sequence $\boldsymbol{\theta}_{0:s-1}$ do not depend on it. The states are computed as

$$f(\boldsymbol{\theta}_{0:s}) = f(\boldsymbol{\theta}_o) \prod_{j=1}^s f(\boldsymbol{\theta}_j|\boldsymbol{\theta}_{0:j-1}) \qquad (6.9)$$

Substituting Eqs. (6.8) and (6.9) into Eq. (6.7), we have

$$\tilde{w}_s^j = \frac{f(V_{0:s}|\theta_{0:s}^j)f(\theta_{0:s}^j)}{p(\theta_{0:s-1}^j|V_{0:s-1})p(\theta_s^j|\theta_{0:s-1}^j, V_{0:s})} \tag{6.10}$$

$$= \tilde{w}_{s-1}^j \frac{f(V_{0:s}|\theta_{0:s}^j)f(\theta_{0:s}^j)}{f(V_{0:s-1}|\theta_{0:s-1}^j)f(\theta_{0:s-1}^j)p(\theta_s^j|\theta_{0:s-1}^j, V_{0:s})} \tag{6.11}$$

$$= \tilde{w}_{s-1}^j \frac{f(V_s|\theta_s^j)f(\theta_s^j|\theta_{0:s-1}^j)}{p(\theta_s^j|\theta_{0:s-1}^j, V_{0:s})} \tag{6.12}$$

In this chapter, the transition prior $f(\theta_s^j|\theta_{0:s-1}^j)$ is adopted as the proposal distribution. Compared to the more general proposal, $p(\theta_s^j|\theta_{0:s-1}^j, V_{0:s})$, the most recent observation is missing. In practice, this does not pose a problem in detection since the predicted samples are near the likelihood peaks. The importance weights are then calculated as:

$$\tilde{w}_s^j = \tilde{w}_{s-1}^j f(V_s|\theta_s^j) \tag{6.13}$$

Other proposal distributions to leverage relations between multiple objects can also be designed.

When detecting each object, the sequential sampling produces the approximation of the posterior distribution $f(\theta_{0:s}|V_{0:s})$ using the samples from the detection of the previous object as follows:

1. Obtain $m$ samples from the proposal distribution, $\theta_s^j \sim p(\theta_s^j|\theta_{0:s-1}^j)$.
2. Reweight each sample according to the importance ratio

$$\tilde{w}_s^j = \tilde{w}_{s-1}^j f(V_s|\theta_s^j) \tag{6.14}$$

Normalize the importance weights.
3. Resample the particles using their importance weights to obtain more particles in the peaks of the distribution. Finally, compute the approximation of $f(\theta_{0:s}|V_{0:s})$:

$$f(\theta_{0:s}|V_{0:s}) \approx \sum_{j=1}^{m} w_s^j \delta(\theta_{0:s} - \theta_{0:s}^j) \tag{6.15}$$

where $\delta$ is the Dirac delta function.

## 6.3.1 THE OBSERVATION AND TRANSITION MODELS

The key components of the sequential sampling framework are the *observation* and *transition* models. The observation model $f(V_s|\theta_s)$ in the update step describes the appearance of each object and is obtained from Eq. (6.1). This corresponds to the likelihood of a hypothesized state that gives rise to observations. As mentioned earlier, the model is based on a deterministic model learned using a large annotated database of images. The transition model in the prediction step describes the way states are propagated between the image neighborhoods. Relying on the anatomical context the transition kernel is based on a pairwise dependency

$$f(\boldsymbol{\theta}_s|\boldsymbol{\theta}_{0:s-1}) = f(\boldsymbol{\theta}_s|\boldsymbol{\theta}_j), \quad j \in \{0, 1, \ldots, s-1\} \tag{6.16}$$

Please note that a state of *any* previously detected object is used to compute the transition. This is less restrictive than a Markovian process, $f(\boldsymbol{\theta}_s|\boldsymbol{\theta}_{s-1})$, which would always use the immediate precursor. The distribution $f(\boldsymbol{\theta}_s|\boldsymbol{\theta}_j)$ is modeled as a Gaussian estimated from the training data. The statistical model captures spatial relationships between the structures while ignoring abnormal configurations that may be caused by a disease progression. During detection, the predictions are used as the best available estimates even for abnormal cases.

### 6.3.2 INTEGRATED DETECTION NETWORK

The computational speed and robustness of the recognition system is increased by hierarchical processing. Further performance improvements are obtained by starting from structures that are easier to detect and constraining the detection of the other structures by exploiting spatial configurations. This design results in a large number of observation and transition models such that multiple structures can be efficiently recognized. The models and any intermediate processing are managed by the IDN. As shown in Figure 6.2 (left), IDN is a pairwise, feed-forward network. IDN consists of *nodes* that perform operations on the input *data* and produce zero or more output data. The operations, such as candidate sample detection, propagation, and aggregation, are only related to each other through data connections. This makes it possible to easily add new nodes and data types to an existing network.

In detection, one major problem is how to effectively propagate detection candidate samples across the levels of the hierarchy. This typically involves defining a search range at a fine level where the candidates from the coarse level are refined. Incorrect selection of the search range leads to higher computational cost, lower accuracy, or drift of the coarse candidates toward incorrect refinements. The search range in IDN is part of the model that is learned from the training data. One difficulty of sequential processing of multiple structures is in selecting the order of detections such that the overall performance is maximized. The IDN detection schedule is designed to minimize the uncertainty of the detections, as described in the next section.

### 6.3.3 DETECTION ORDER SELECTION

The spatial order of detections in IDN is automatically determined during training. The goal is to select the order such that the posterior probability $P(\boldsymbol{\theta}_{0:s}|V_{0:s})$ is maximized in the neighborhood region around the ground truth. Since determining this order has exponential complexity in the number of objects, a greedy approach is adopted. The training data are first split into two sets.

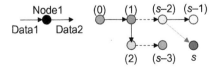

**FIGURE 6.2**

IDN consists of *nodes* that operate on *data* (left). Illustration of the IDN and order selection (right). See text for details.

Using the first set, all object detectors are trained individually to obtain posterior distributions $f(\boldsymbol{\theta}_0|V_0), f(\boldsymbol{\theta}_1|V_1), \ldots, f(\boldsymbol{\theta}_s|V_s)$. The second set is used for order selection as shown in Figure 6.2 (right) as follows.

Suppose that the detection order is determined up to $s-1$, $\boldsymbol{\theta}_{(0)}, \boldsymbol{\theta}_{(1)}, \ldots, \boldsymbol{\theta}_{(s-1)}$. The order selection aims to add to the network the best pair $[s, (j)]$ (or feed-forward path) that maximizes the expected value of the following score $S[s, (j)]$ over both $s$ and $(j)$ computed from the second training set:

$$
S[s, (j)] = \int_{\substack{\boldsymbol{\theta}_s \in \Omega(\tilde{\boldsymbol{\theta}}_s) \\ \boldsymbol{\theta}_{(0:s-1)} \in \Omega(\tilde{\boldsymbol{\theta}}_{(0:s-1)})}} f(\boldsymbol{\theta}_{(0:s-1)}|V_{(0:s-1)}) f(\boldsymbol{\theta}_s|\boldsymbol{\theta}_{(j)}) f(V_s|\boldsymbol{\theta}_s)\, d\boldsymbol{\theta}_s d\boldsymbol{\theta}_{(0:s-1)} \qquad (6.17)
$$

where $\Omega(\tilde{\boldsymbol{\theta}})$ is the neighborhood region around the ground truth $\tilde{\boldsymbol{\theta}}$. The expected value is approximated as the sample mean of the cost computed for all examples of the second training data set.

During hierarchical detection, larger object context is considered at coarser image resolutions resulting in robustness against noise, occlusions, and missing data. High detection accuracy is achieved by focusing the search in a smaller neighborhood at the finer resolutions. The resolution level and the size of the image neighborhoods $\{V_i\}$ can be selected using the same mechanism as the order selection by introducing additional parameters (Sofka et al., 2014). Choosing the scale automatically is advantageous since objects have different sizes and the size of the context neighborhood is also different.

## 6.4 APPLICATIONS

This section highlights applications where IDN is effective in recognizing multiple anatomical structures. The first application is to recognize landmarks in brain magnetic resonance imaging scans (Sofka et al., 2012). A total of 384 volumes were used for training and 127 for testing with the average volume size of $130 \times 130 \times 101$ voxels after resampling to 2 mm isotropic resolution. In each volume, the system detects crista galli (CG), occipital bone (OB), the anterior of the corpus callosum (ACC), the posterior of the corpus callosum (PCC), and the brain stem (STEM). The average detection error is 2.37 mm. Example detections are shown in Figure 6.3.

The second application shows how to automatically detect and measure anatomical structures in fetal head ultrasound volumes (Sofka et al., 2014). A total of 1982 volumes were used for training and 107 for testing. The average volume size was $186 \times 123 \times 155$ voxels after resampling to 1 mm isotropic resolution. The IDN produced a standardized visualization plane with correct orientation and centering as well as the biometric measurement of the anatomy. The plane parameters and the measurement were derived from the pose of the anatomical structure. The following measurements were obtained (Figure 6.4): cerebellum, cisterna magna, lateral ventricles, occipitofrontal diameter, biparietal diameter, and head circumference. The average measurement error was below 2 mm and within the inter-user variability.

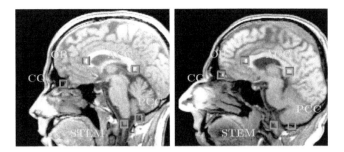

**FIGURE 6.3**

Automatic recognition results (blue) and ground truth reference (red) of five landmarks in two brain magnetic resonance imaging scans: crista galli (CG), occipital bone (OB), the anterior of the corpus callosum (ACC), the posterior of the corpus callosum (PCC), and the brain stem (STEM).

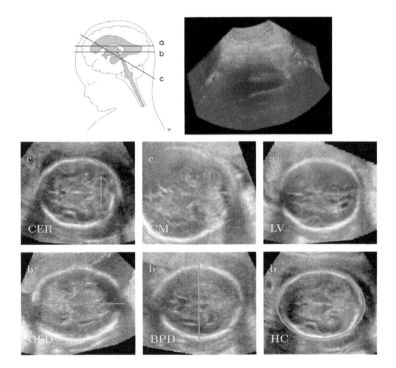

**FIGURE 6.4**

Automatic fetal head and brain (AFHB) system provides automatic measurements at three standardized planes: ventricular (a), thalamic (b), and cerebellar (c) from a 3D ultrasound volume. Shown are example results for cerebellum (CER), cisterna magna (CM), lateral ventricles (LV), occipitofrontal diameter (OFD), biparietal diameter (BPD), and head circumference (HC).

## 6.5 CONCLUSIONS

This chapter presented the IDN for recognizing multiple objects by exploiting their relative spatial configurations. Modeling interdependence of objects introduces additional constraints that make it possible to achieve high localization accuracy. The approach is motivated by sequential estimation techniques that estimate a spatial order of probability distributions for a sequence of objects. The computation requires a likelihood of a hypothesized state (object pose and label) that gives rise to observations and a transition model that describes the way the states are propagated between objects. Sampling techniques have been used to approximate the posterior distribution and make the modeling tractable. At each step, the prediction step involves sampling from the proposal distribution of the current state conditioned on the history of states and the history of observations. The posterior distribution of the pose (state) of each anatomical structure is then estimated during the update step based on the prediction and all observations so far. The observations are features computed from image neighborhoods surrounding the anatomies. The likelihood of a hypothesized state that gives rise to observations is based on a deterministic model learned using a large annotated database of images. The transition model that describes the way the poses of anatomical structures are related is Gaussian.

The modular nature of the IDN makes it straightforward to adopt different observation and transition models. These models can capture more intricate object relationships (e.g., context from multiple previously detected objects) or introduce application-specific constraints. All these properties contribute to the improved detection and classification accuracy which makes the IDN an attractive choice for multiobject recognition tasks.

## REFERENCES

Dalal, N., Triggs, B., 2005. Histograms of oriented gradients for human detection. In: Proc. CVPR, vol. 1, pp. 886-893.

Desai, C., Ramanan, D., Fowlkes, C., 2011. Discriminative models for multi-class object layout. Int. J. Comput. Vis. 95 (1), 1-12.

Doucet, A., De Freitas, N., Gordon, N., 2001. Sequential Monte Carlo Methods in Practice. Springer-Verlag, New York.

Felzenszwalb, P., Girshick, R., McAllester, D., Ramanan, D., 2010. Object detection with discriminatively trained part based models. IEEE Trans. Pattern Anal. Machine Intell. 32 (9), 1627-1645. ISSN 0162-8828.

Hoiem, D., Efros, A., Hebert, M., 2008. Putting objects in perspective. Int. J. Comput. Vis. 80 (1), 3-15.

Kumar, S., Hebert, M., 2006. Discriminative random fields. Int. J. Comput. Vis. 68 (2), 179-201.

Lampert, C.H., Blaschko, M., Hofmann, T., 2009, Dec. Efficient subwindow search: a branch and bound framework for object localization. IEEE Trans. Pattern Anal. Mach. Intell. 31 (12), 2129-2142.

Liu, J.S., Chen, R., Logvinenko, T., 2001. A theoretical framework for sequential importance sampling with resampling. In: Doucet, A., De Freitas, N., Gordon, N. (Eds.), Sequential Monte Carlo Methods in Practice. Springer-Verlag, New York, pp. 225-242.

Sermanet, P., Eigen, D., Zhang, X., Mathieu, M., Fergus, R., LeCun, Y., 2014. Overfeat: integrated recognition, localization and detection using convolutional networks. In: International Conference on Learning Representations.

Sofka, M., Ralovich, K., Zhang, J., Zhou, S.K., Comaniciu, D., 2012. Progressive data transmission for anatomical landmark detection in a cloud. Methods Inform. Med. 51 (3), 268-278.

Sofka, M., Zhang, J., Good, S., Zhou, S.K., Comaniciu, D., 2014. Automatic detection and measurement of structures in fetal head ultrasound volumes using sequential estimation and integrated detection network (IDN). IEEE Trans. Med. Imaging 33 (5), 1054-1070.

Tu, Z., 2005. Probabilistic boosting-tree: learning discriminative models for classification, recognition, and clustering. In: Proc. ICCV, vol. 2, pp. 1589-1596.

Viola, P., Jones, M.J., 2004. Robust real-time face detection. Int. J. Comput. Vis. 57 (2), 137-154.

# ORGAN DETECTION USING DEEP LEARNING

7

**H.-C. Shin[1], M. Orton[2], D.J. Collins[2], S. Doran[2] and M.O. Leach[2]**

*National Institutes of Health, Bethesda, MD, USA[1]*
*Cancer Research UK Cancer Imaging Centre,*
*Institute of Cancer Research and Royal Marsden Hospital, London, United Kingdom[2]*

## CHAPTER OUTLINE

S. Kevin Zhou (Ed): Medical Image Recognition, Segmentation and Parsing. http://dx.doi.org/10.1016/B978-0-12-802581-9.00007-X

## 7.1 INTRODUCTION

Imaging findings are now regarded as valid output measures in treatment trials. One of the fundamental requirements for a successful cancer clinical trial is to be able to identify lesions, so that their progression over the course of treatment can be followed. Traditionally, this would involve a radiologist using his or her skill and experience to outline slice-by-slice each or some of the tumors present. The outlining is rarely achieved for all slices in a three-dimensional (3D) dataset in clinical practice, and it is highly operator-dependent. This time-consuming and tedious task is a clear rate-limiting step in scaling-up the clinical trials involving patient images.

*Artificial intelligence* (AI) tries to build intelligent agents, which can perform some time-consuming and tedious tasks for us. Artificial intelligence is relevant to any intellectual task, and it is being applied in many aspects of our daily life, for example, from washing machines to web search engines and car navigation systems. At present, artificial intelligence comprises a large variety of subfields, and this chapter addresses the subfield of *machine learning*, modeling the *learning* behavior of humans and building systems to do that.

However, medical image analysis still remains a challenging application area for artificial intelligence. A wide variety of image modalities are now available in the clinic (such as magnetic resonance imaging [MRI] and positron emission tomography-computed tomography [PET-CT]), where new multi modal medical images provide more information about the imaged tissues for diagnosis. Additionally, patient data typically contain many abnormalities, where tissue types and the shapes of the organs in these datasets differ widely. Also, we rarely understand the underlying mechanisms of the human body in detail. For these reasons, obtaining ground-truth examples for an artificial intelligence to learn patterns or decision rules from medical images can be difficult, complicating the implementation of such an intelligent system for automatic image analysis.

An algorithmic framework to learn decision rules or useful data representation by itself can be beneficial for the automated interpretation of medical images. Important information in the data can be "mined" by a data-driven artificial *learning* approach, in the environment where it is difficult to collect the examples to support learning the patterns or decision rules, and where underlying mechanisms of the human body are not fully understood.

Deep learning demonstrates the framework for the application of artificial intelligence for automatic medical image analysis, more specifically: *artificial learning* or *machine learning*. The important aspect of deep learning is the study and application of the *unsupervised feature learning*, modeling the "self-learning" or "self-teaching" behavior of humans, and demonstrating such algorithms for medical image analysis.

The examples introduced in this chapter use patient images obtained by MRI. MR images provide the most comprehensive information about the characteristics of soft tissues and therefore are well suited for cancer diagnosis. Different MRI techniques are typically used to diagnose a patient, as images obtained from different imaging techniques provide different information about the tissues being imaged and highlight different tissue characteristics in the image.

It is challenging to relate a different information modality (such as a timeseries) to the base image modality or to relate images obtained by different imaging techniques as the difference images look slightly different from each other. Different organs ("liver," "kidney," and "spleen") and tissue types ("white matter," "cerebrospinal fluid," and "tumor") with diverse characteristics should be recognized by analyzing the images from different modalities.

With deep learning, *unsupervised feature learning* is applied to the patient MR images to *learn* the semantics in medical images in the form of a set of numbers (*features*), where they are learned from unlabeled or minimally labeled datasets in a "self-taught" manner. The central idea used in this chapter is to achieve learning by applying the structure of artificial neurons (logistic regression) and their extended forms—artificial neural networks. The approaches introduced in this chapter can help in scaling-up imaging trials by clearing the rate-limiting step of finding clinically relevant images for patient treatment and medical research.

## 7.2 RELATED LITERATURE

The overall aim of the approach introduced in this chapter is to learn the object classes in a minimally labeled dataset: in other words, only a weakly supervised training is required to train a classifier. So-called "part-models" for the self-learning of object classes were studied for 2D images by Weber et al. (2000), Fergus et al. (2003), Bernstein and Amit (2005), Torralba et al. (2007), and Felzenszwalb et al. (2010), in order to achieve object detection in such weakly supervised settings. In the work presented in this chapter, a deep network model is used to learn features and part-based object class models in an unsupervised setting.

Ji et al. (2013) used 3D convolutional neural networks (CNNs) to perform human-action recognition in video sequences. In this case, the CNNs were trained with labeled datasets and a large number of labeled examples were required. Furthermore, the action recognition was performed on a sub-window within a video sequence, which had to be preselected by a tracking algorithm, and the performance of the action-recognition was dependent on the tracking algorithm. By contrast, a generative model for learning latent information was applied for action recognition by Niebles et al. (2008) and it did not require a tracking algorithm to recognize a human action, where the spatio temporal features were learned from video sequences in an unsupervised manner. Based on the learned spatio temporal features, "interest points" were detected within a video sequence, and multiple actions could be recognized in a single video, based on those interest points. In a similar manner, we use a deep learning model to learn the latent information in a 4D medical image dataset.

Deep learning has attracted much interest recently and has been used in a number of application areas. Many studies have shown how hierarchical structures in images can be learned using deep architectures with application to object recognition (Ranzato et al., 2007; Yu et al., 2009; Glorot et al., 2011; Lee et al., 2011; Sohn et al., 2011; Zeiler et al., 2011). Object recognition and tracking in videos with deep networks was shown by Bazzani et al. (2011), where a graphical model was used in addition to unsupervised feature learning via restricted Boltzmann machines (RBMs) by Rumelhart et al. (1986). Deep neural networks for classification of fMRI brain images were studied by Schmah et al. (2008), where RBMs were used to classify the stage and action of a volume while the images were taken.

Deep learning of multi modal features was recently studied by Ngiam et al. (2011). The approach demonstrated in this chapter is similar, and a stacked autoencoder (SAE) model is used for separately learning both visual and temporal features. Independent subspace analysis, a deep neural network model for unsupervised multi modal feature learning, was suggested by Le et al. (2011), whereas in the study done by Li and Prakash (2011) and the many previous action-recognition studies appearing in Le et al. (2011) the objective was to recognize the action a video sequence represents. This also applies to the work of Ngiam et al. (2011), where the objective was to use multi modal feature learning to classify the whole video sequence as a single category. In the approach presented in this chapter, we aim to use unsupervised feature learning to recognize several objects within a given multi modal dataset.

Previous studies of automated object detection in medical images have tended to concentrate on brain images, especially detecting brain tumors. This is largely because both the shape and properties of the brain are more homogeneous across individuals than is the case for other parts of the body; for example, segmentation of multiple sclerosis (MS) lesions is reported by Geremia et al. (2010), Corso et al. (2008), Clark et al. (1998), and Farhangfar et al. (2009). In all of these cases, the disease tends to change the overall shape of the brain relatively little, whereas substantial shape changes can be observed with diseased abdominal organs. Moreover, tumor is not an organ type but is a collection of abnormal tissues, which makes the approach to tumor segmentation different from object detection with a pattern recognition approach.

The abdominal region contains many important organs and therefore segmentation techniques have considerable potential to aid automated diagnosis and radiotherapy planning. Multi-organ detection was demonstrated in computed tomography (CT) images by Okada et al. (2006), in contrast-enhanced abdominal CT images by Linguraru and Summers (2011), and in whole-body Dixon MRI sequences by Pauly et al. (2011). In all of these cases, a clearly labeled training dataset was required. Multi-organ segmentation on CT images using active learning with a minimal supervisory training set was demonstrated by Iglesias et al. (2011), although in this study, a clinical expert's presence was required for the consecutive labeling during the active learning process. Also, the organs in the dataset in the studies are not largely abnormal as is the case in our data with tumors.

---

## 7.3 METHODS

### 7.3.1 LOGISTIC REGRESSION

Logistic regression (Bishop et al., 2006, pp. 205-206) is one of the most popular algorithms for binary classification problems—to classify a given data sample $x$ to a binary class $y$ of being true (1) or false (0)—for example, "liver" or "nonliver." The logistic sigmoid function is often denoted as $g(z)$:

$$g(z) = \frac{1}{1 + e^{-z}} \tag{7.1}$$

The term "sigmoid" means S-shaped, and it is also known as a *squashing function*, as it maps the whole real range of $z$ into [0, 1] in the $g(z)$. This simple function has two useful properties that: (1) it can be used to model a conditional probability distribution and (2) its derivative has a simple form.

As can be seen from the plot of the sigmoid function in Figure 7.1, for the sigmoid function $g(z) \to 0$ as $z \to -\infty$, and $g(z) \to 1$ as $z \to +\infty$. This property can be used for modeling a conditional probability distribution $p(y = 0|x)$ or $p(y = 1|x)$, as cumulative distribution functions for many common probability distributions will be sigmoidal as shown in Figure 7.1. In fact, a supervised learning approach to binary classification is to obtain the parameters $w_0$, $w_1$ to model the conditional probability of $p(y = 1|x; w_0, w_1)$ or $p(y = 0|x; w_0, w_1)$:

$$p(y = 1|x; w_0, w_1) = g(w_0 + w_1 x) \tag{7.2}$$

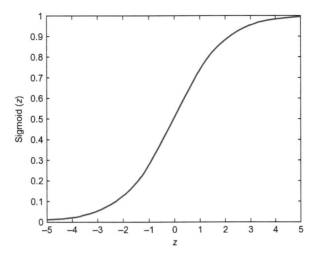

**FIGURE 7.1**

Logistic sigmoid function $g(z) = \frac{1}{1+e^{-z}}$.

$$p(y = 0|x; w_0, w_1) = 1 - g(w_0 + w_1 x) \tag{7.3}$$

where this form of discrete probability distribution is called the *Bernoulli distribution*, $w_0$ is the offset or *bias* term, and $w_1$ is the *weight* which is responsible for the slope of the modeling function.

Letting $\mathbf{x} \in \mathbb{R}^{(k+1)\times 1} = \{x_0, x_1, x_2, \dots, x_k\}$ with $x_0 = 1$ and similarly for the corresponding weights $\mathbf{w} \in \mathbb{R}^{(k+1)\times 1} = \{w_0, w_1, w_2, \dots, w_k\}$, the preceding equations can be written more compactly as:

$$p(y|\mathbf{x}, \mathbf{w}) = g(\mathbf{w}^T \mathbf{x})^y (1 - g(\mathbf{w}^T \mathbf{x}))^{(1-y)} \tag{7.4}$$

An illustration of the sigmoid conditional probability distribution model for input data of dimension $k$ is shown in Figure 7.2, with $z = w_0 + \sum_{j=1}^{k} w_j x_j$.

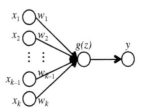

**FIGURE 7.2**

An illustration of the sigmoid conditional probability distribution model, where $z = w_0 + \sum_{j=1}^{k} w_j x_j$.

## 7.3.2 NEURAL NETWORKS

While only a binary decision (*true/false*) can be made using logistic regression, multiple choice decisions can be made using neural networks (Bishop et al., 2006, pp. 225-284). In the same way that biological neural networks are formed as a connected collection of single neurons, artificial neural networks are an extended form of logistic regression. In effect, neural networks are equivalent to running several logistic regressions at the same time.

Figure 7.3(a) shows a neural network with four input units and two output units. Each circle in the input and output of the network is called a *unit*, where the collection of the input units is called the *input layer*, and the collection of the output units is called the *output layer*. The links connecting the layers are called *weights*. As can be seen in Figure 7.3(b), each part of the network corresponding to each output unit $y_i$ is effectively a logistic regression model. Compared to the logistic regression model in Figure 7.2 though, the weights are now indexed differently, as there are more output units and therefore more weights correspondingly. Each weight is now indexed as $w_{ji}$, where the subscript $i$ corresponds to its input unit and $j$ corresponds to its output unit. The "hypothesis" of the neural network model $h_{\mathbf{w}}(x)$ is a collection of logistic sigmoid functions $g(z)$ (Eq. 7.1).

A multilayer neural network can be constructed by feeding the output neuron of a given layer into the input of the next layer of neurons. Activation of each output neuron with or without the bias term $w_0$ can be fed into the next set of neural networks as an input. The layers between the input and output layers are called *hidden layers*, and a multilayer neural network with an arbitrary number of hidden layers can be constructed. Successive connection of neural networks results in some useful characteristics of its modeling function. A major advantage of multilayer neural networks is that they can model a nonlinear function, which is not possible with a single-layer neural network. More details can be found in the literature, for example, in Duda et al. (2000, pp. 282-287) and Bishop (1995, pp. 116-121).

An example of a multilayer neural network is shown in Figure 7.4. Three neural network layers are fed forward, such that the output of a network becomes the input of the next network. Neural networks with structures similar to this are called *feed forward* neural networks.

With more networks and layers, there is additional superscript notation to each parameter—a superscript ($l$), which denotes a parameter's corresponding layer. For example, the $i$th activation in the $l$th layer is denoted with the additional superscript ($l$): $a_i^{(l)}$. In addition, a bias term $+1$ is introduced,

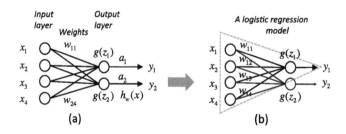

**FIGURE 7.3**

(a) A neural network with four input units and two output units. A subnetwork for each output unit is effectively a logistic regression model (b).

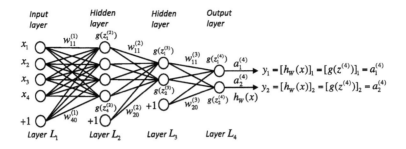

**FIGURE 7.4**

An example of a multilayer neural network. It is a feed forward network with three neural networks between four layers. The first and last layers are called the input layer and the output layer, and the layers between them are called the hidden layers. The +1's are the biases where the weights to the biases are $w_{j0}^{(l)}$ for the $j$th input in the $l$th layer, and $[\cdot]_k$ denotes the $k$th element of the hypothesis function.

where the weights to the biases are $w_{j0}^{(l)}$ for the $j$th input in the $l$th layer. Note that the bias was notated as $w_0$ in logistic regression. As there can be multiple layers of logistic units in neural networks, the bias $w_0$ in logistic regression is distinguished from the input +1 and its weight $w_{j0}$, to make a clearer distinction between the *inputs* and the *weights*.

### 7.3.2.1 Cost function

For the cost function of a neural network with $L$ layers, we start by extending the cost function of the logistic regression model for $K$ classes:

$$J_{\mathbf{w}}(\mathbf{X}) = \frac{1}{m} \sum_{i=1}^{m} \sum_{k=1}^{K} \left[ -y_k^{(i)} \log\left( \left[ h_{\mathbf{w}}(\mathbf{x}^{(i)}) \right]_k \right) - (1 - y_k^{(i)}) \log\left( 1 - \left[ h_{\mathbf{w}}(\mathbf{x}^{(i)}) \right]_k \right) \right] \tag{7.5}$$

where $[h_{\mathbf{w}}(\mathbf{x})]_k$ is the $k$th element of the hypothesis function, computed as:

$$[h_{\mathbf{w}}(\mathbf{x})]_k = \left[ g(\mathbf{z}^{(L)}) \right]_k \tag{7.6}$$

The logistic sigmoid function $g(\cdot)$ is as before, and $\mathbf{z}^{(L)}$ is the input to the final layer, which is obtained by propagating the following equation for $l = 2$ to $L$:

$$\mathbf{z}^{(l)} = \mathbf{w}^{(l-1)^T} \mathbf{a}^{(l-1)} \tag{7.7}$$

The activation for the input layer is the input data, such that $\mathbf{a}^{(1)} = \mathbf{x}$, because there is no previous layer of networks for the input layer. The bias term +1 can be added in each layer propagation. To include the bias term in Eq. (7.7), it can be noted as $a_0^{(l)}$, where the corresponding weight is then notated as $w_{j0}^{(l)}$.

### 7.3.2.2 Backpropagation

As multilayer neural networks are composed of multiple layers of logistic units fed-forward, it is not straightforward to compute the gradient of the cost function to train the networks. Backpropagation is an algorithm proposed by Rumelhart (1995) to efficiently compute the gradient of the cost function for feed forward neural networks. The basic idea of the backpropagation algorithm is that information is sent alternately forwards and backwards through the network, whereby the errors $\delta_j$ are computed and *backpropagated*, to obtain the derivatives of the layers.

The algorithm states:

**1.** Perform a feedforward pass, computing the activations $a_j^{(l)}$ for the layers $L_2, L_3, \ldots, L_n$.

**2.** For each output unit $k$ in the output layer $n_l$, compute the error term as

$$\delta_k^{(n_l)} = (a_k^{(n_l)} - y_k) \tag{7.8}$$

**3.** For each node $i$ in the previous hidden layers, compute the error term as

$$\delta_i^{(l)} = \left( \sum_{j=1}^{n_{l+1}} w_{ji}^{(l)} \delta_j^{(l+1)} \right) g'(z_i^{(l)}) \tag{7.9}$$

where $n_{l+1}$ is the number of units in layer $l$'s succeeding layer $(l+1)$, and $g'(z_i^{(l)})$ is the gradient of the $i$th unit's logistic sigmoid function in the $l$th layer.

**4.** Having computed all of the error terms $\delta_i^{(l)}$ after a forward-pass and a backward-pass, compute the desired partial derivatives, which are given as:

$$\frac{\partial}{\partial w_{ji}^{(l)}} J_{\mathbf{W}}(\mathbf{X}) = a_j^{(l)} \delta_i^{(l+1)} \tag{7.10}$$

## 7.3.3 SPARSE AUTOENCODERS

An *autoencoder* (Hinton and Zemel, 1994) neural network is a symmetrical neural network for unsupervised feature learning, consisting of three layers (input/output layers and hidden layer). The autoencoder learns an approximation to the identity function, so that the output $\hat{\mathbf{x}}^{(i)}$ is similar to the input $\mathbf{x}^{(i)}$ after the feed forward propagation in the networks:

$$\hat{\mathbf{x}}^{(i)} \approx h_{\mathbf{W}}(\mathbf{x}^{(i)}) \tag{7.11}$$

where the $h_{\mathbf{W}}(\cdot)$ is the hypothesis of the autoencoder neural network model. With the separate notations for the weights of input $\mathbf{W}$ and the bias $\mathbf{b}$, the cost function of an autoencoder can be written as:

$$J(\mathbf{W}, \mathbf{b}; \mathbf{X}, \hat{\mathbf{X}}) = \frac{1}{m} \sum_{i=1}^{m} \left( \frac{1}{2} \| h_{\mathbf{W}, \mathbf{b}}(\mathbf{x}^{(i)}) - \hat{\mathbf{x}}^{(i)} \|^2 \right) \tag{7.12}$$

A sparse autoencoder is an autoencoder model with an additional sparse constraint in its cost function, to learn a nonreplicative and overcomplete feature set (Bengio et al., 2007; Marc' Aurelio Ranzato et al., 2007; Lee et al., 2008; Vincent et al., 2008; Larochelle et al., 2009). The cost function of the sparse autoencoder can be written using the notations already introduced for describing feed-forward neural networks as:

$$J(\mathbf{W}, \mathbf{b}; \mathbf{X}, \hat{\mathbf{X}}) = \left[ \frac{1}{m} \sum_{i=1}^{m} \left( \frac{1}{2} \| h_{\mathbf{W}, \mathbf{b}}(\mathbf{x}^{(i)}) - \hat{\mathbf{x}}^{(i)} \|^2 \right) \right]$$

$$+ \frac{\lambda}{2} \sum (w_{ji})^2 + \beta \sum \mathrm{KL}(\rho \| \hat{\rho}_j) \tag{7.13}$$

where $\beta$ is a hyperparameter (sparsity penalty weight) to control the importance of the sparsity penalty term relative to the rest of the terms in the cost function, and $\lambda$ controls the regularization of the weight parameters. The term $\mathrm{KL}(\rho \| \hat{\rho}_j)$ stands for the Kullback-Leibler (KL) divergence (Kullback and Leibler, 1951), which is a standard function for measuring the difference of two distributions (Guo et al., 2007; Pitié et al., 2007). Used as the sparsity penalty term for the sparse autoencoders, the KL divergence measures the difference between a Bernoulli random variable with mean $\rho$ and a Bernoulli random variable with mean $\hat{\rho}_j$:

$$\mathrm{KL}(\rho \| \hat{\rho}_j) = \rho \log \frac{\rho}{\hat{\rho}_j} + (1 - \rho) \log \frac{1 - \rho}{1 - \hat{\rho}_j} \tag{7.14}$$

The KL-divergence reaches its minimum of 0 at $\hat{\rho}_j = \rho$ and approaches $\infty$ as $\hat{\rho}_j$ diverges from $\rho$ nearing 0 or 1. Therefore, minimizing this penalty term will cause $\hat{\rho}_j$ to be close to $\rho$. Some other measures than the KL-divergence can also be used for the sparsity penalty term, such as L2-distance between $\rho$ and $\hat{\rho}_j$ or using the Chi-square kernel (Zhou et al., 2012).

An example of a sparse autoencoder network for input data with dimension of $\mathbf{x} \in \mathbb{R}^{4 \times 1}$ (e.g., each sample consists of four observations) is shown in Figure 7.5. Each unit in the input layer $x_i$ is the single data point in the input data $\mathbf{x}$, where it is fed-foward to the hidden layer via the weights $\mathbf{W}^{(1)}$ and an optional bias $+1$ with the weights to the bias $\mathbf{b}^{(1)}$:

$$\mathbf{z}^{(2)} = \mathbf{W}^{(1)}\mathbf{x} + \mathbf{b}^{(1)} \tag{7.15}$$

The *symmetry* of the autoencoder arises from trying to approximate the identity function, thereby setting the dimension of the input and output layers the same, while the dimension of the hidden layer is configurable.

### 7.3.3.1 Training sparse autoencoders

Sparse autoencoders are trained using the backpropagation algorithm, in the same way as feed forward neural networks are trained for classification as in Section 7.3.2. The only differences from Section 7.3.2 in training sparse autoencoders are

- The objective is to minimize the squared-error cost function (Eq. 7.12) rather than to maximize the likelihood function (or minimize the negative log-likelihood function (Eq. 7.5)).
- For the second-layer derivatives, there is the sparsity penalty term (Eq. 7.14) to consider in the cost function.

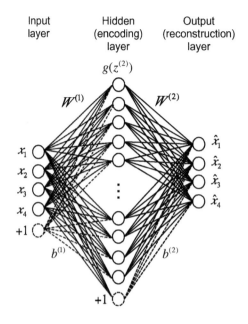

**FIGURE 7.5**

A single-layer sparse autoencoder with encoding bias and decoding bias for an input data of dimension $\mathbf{x} \in \mathbb{R}^{4\times1}$. The weights for the input data ($\mathbf{W}^{(1)}, \mathbf{W}^{(2)}$) are shown as straight lines, where the weights for the biases ($\mathbf{b}^{(1)}, \mathbf{b}^{(2)}$) are shown as dotted lines. The weights for the input ($\mathbf{W}^{(1)}$) and output layers ($\mathbf{W}^{(2)}$) are called the encoding matrix and decoding matrix, respectively.

## 7.3.4 STACKED SPARSE AUTOENCODERS

Stacked sparse autoencoders—a deep learning architecture of sparse autoencoders—are built by stacking additional unsupervised feature learning layers and can be trained greedily for each additional layer (Bengio et al., 2007). By applying a pooling operation after each layer, features of progressively larger input regions are encoded.

### 7.3.4.1 Max-pooling and translational invariance

Pooling (Hubel and Wiesel, 1965) is an operation often used in deep learning networks to reduce the amount of computation required to train the networks especially with large input dimensions, while not losing any important information for feature learning and classification. There are some different forms of pooling operations such as *max-pooling* (based on *max* operation), *mean-pooling* (based on *mean* operation), as well as some advanced forms of pooling such as probabilistic max-pooling (Lee et al., 2009) and differentiable pooling (Zeiler and Fergus, 2012).

Also, *translational invariance* can be achieved by applying a pooling operation, meaning that a region or object can become invariant to (small) translations after the application of pooling. Translational invariance is a highly desirable property in many tasks such as object recognition and audio recognition. For example, we would wish an image-based face detection system to detect a face even when a person faces slightly up or down (rotational translation), or the person has slightly

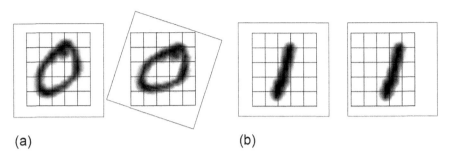

**FIGURE 7.6**

Translational invariance is a highly desirable property in many tasks such as object recognition. For example, a handwritten digit recognition system should recognize a digit as "0" even when there is rotational translation (a). This applies similarly to locational translation that both inputs to the 5 × 5 receptive field should be recognized as the digit "1" (b). The handwritten digits are from LeCun and Cortes (1998).

moved in the image (locational translation). An example of translational invariance being necessary for handwritten digit recognition is shown in Figure 7.6 for (a) rotational translation and (b) locational invariance.

For 2D max-pooling in the $M \times M$ image space where each location (pixel) of the image corresponds to an input $x_i$, max-pooling after the feature encoding $\mathbf{W}x_i$ can be applied to capture a larger spatial proximity of the features (e.g., a part of an organ represented by the features):

$$\mathbf{y} = \max\{|\mathbf{W}x_1, \mathbf{W}x_2, \ldots, \mathbf{W}x_R|\} \tag{7.16}$$

where $\mathbf{W}$ is the encoding matrix (or a feature set, distinct for each layer), $x_1, \ldots, x_R$ are the input vectors to the max-pooling operation with $R = M^2$, and the max and modulus functions are applied element-wise.

## 7.4 EXPERIMENTS
### 7.4.1 DATASET

Dynamic contrast enhanced MRI (DCE-MRI) is a dynamic MRI technique, where a series of images are acquired over time with a contrast agent injection to observe the behavior of the contrast change in the MR images. Different contrast enhancement behavior due to the different vascular structure of each voxel in a body can be measured as a sequential series of 3D images. Figure 7.7 shows a DCE-MRI scan of a patient with a liver tumor, a series of 3D images taken over time, which therefore forms a 4D image.

The datasets used in this section are DCE-MRI scans from two studies of liver metastases and one study of kidney metastases:

- Dataset A: scans of 46 patients with liver metastases, each containing 7-12 contiguous coronal slices with image size $256 \times 256$, repeated at $T = 40$ time points.

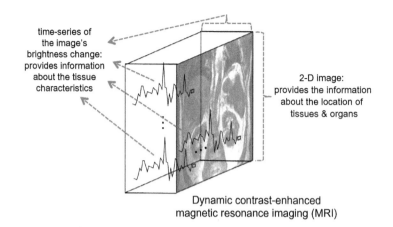

**FIGURE 7.7**

A 4D DCE-MRI scan of a liver patient for 40 time points with volume size of 256 × 256 × 7. Each pixel of an image slice in a volume gives a time series of its brightness over 40 images.

- Dataset B: scans of 3 patients with kidney metastases, each containing 14 contiguous coronal slices with size 256 × 267, repeated at $T = 40$ time points.
- Dataset C: scans of 29 patients with liver metastases from a clinical trial, each containing 14 contiguous coronal slices with image size 209 × 256, repeated at $T = 40$ time points.

In this section, subsets of Dataset A were used for the training, subsets of Dataset B for the cross-validation (CV), and Dataset C was used for the final visualization and test. By dividing the dataset as such, a general applicability of the learned models can be tested for any new previously unseen dataset.

Labeled samples are collected by drawing "rough" outlines encompassing tissues of multiple organ types as shown in Figure 7.8. The outlines were drawn by a nonmedical-expert and subsequently adjusted and confirmed by a radiologist, such that the outlines encompass all the tissues of a given organ type and the labeling is correct, even though the outlines are not very accurate. These labeled samples are used to train the final classifiers (as a "rough guidance") and for evaluating the results using unsupervised feature learning.

## 7.4.2 LEARNING AN OVERCOMPLETE TEMPORAL AND VISUAL FEATURE SET

The single-layer sparse autoencoder (Eq. 7.13) is used to learn the temporal features from the dataset, where each time series is a 40-element input vector ($\mathbf{x}^{(i)} \in \mathbb{R}^{40 \times 1}$). Approximately $1.3 \times 10^4$ time series signals were randomly sampled from the complete set of contrast uptake curves in the training dataset, excluding the background and regions affected by breathing motion.

There are many existing reports on the application of deep learning to classification using the purely spatial features found in 2D images. In this section, we will describe the features learned from 2D image-space as the "visual features," in order to have a clear distinction from temporal features with spatial pooling.

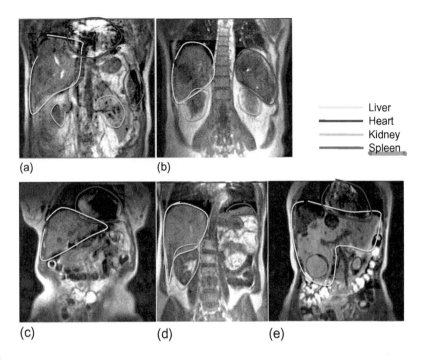

**FIGURE 7.8**

Labelling organs. The shapes of the organs vary substantially, and the shape of liver with metastases can be very abnormal (e). Regions were labeled as described in the main text. Note how the exact outline of the organs is not always clear. Uncertainty in identifying the spleen was high, as it is difficult to distinguish from the other nearby organs, for example in (d).

Two-dimensional visual features are learned from approximately $1.3 \times 10^4$ image patches (of certain size—see Section 7.4.5) randomly sampled from the first image slice in each time-series (before the contrast agent is injected). Each patch of size $mps_1 \times mps_1$ is unrolled into a 1D vector to train the sparse autoencoder in the same way as for the timeseries signals. The first image slice in each time-series is used as a "natural" (MR) image of the organs without any artifacts (e.g., contrast enhancement, where the behavior of the enhancement progression in time is different between tissue/organ types), to achieve similar visual feature learning from natural images in other studies. Background regions or regions affected by breathing motion are excluded when acquiring the samples.

The overcomplete visual feature set with 256 features learned using a single-layer sparse autoencoder is shown in Figure 7.9, together with the overcomplete 256 temporal feature set also learned using a single-layer sparse antoencoder. They represent an overcomplete set of 256 temporal features, and there is no obvious redundancy or repetition of trivial signals (Figure 7.9(a)). The visual bases in Figure 7.9(b) are learned from $8 \times 8$ image patches and show Gabor-like edge detectors of different orientations and locations, which are coherent with the results of the previous studies of Marc' Aurelio Ranzato et al. (2007) and Goodfellow et al. (2009).

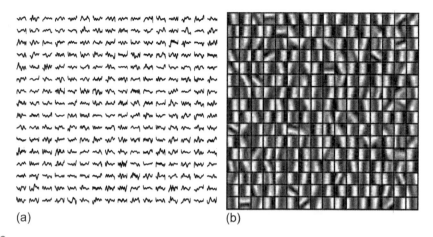

(a)                                                    (b)

**FIGURE 7.9**

The 256 overcomplete (a) temporal and (b) 8 × 8 size visual feature sets learned by unsupervised sparse feature learning using single-layer sparse autoencoders.

## 7.4.3 PART-BASED MODEL WITH SPATIAL FEATURE MATCHING

In the first feature learning layer of SAEs, visual features are learned for a certain spatial dimension $(M \times M)$ and temporal features are matched for the spatial dimension with max-pooling. Features of the next level spatial hierarchy—object parts with a larger region of translationally invariant feature sets— are captured by successive unsupervised feature learning on the max-pooled output of the features to learn the features of larger input regions, based on what it has learned for a smaller input region. Max-pooling in the visual feature learning network is applied such that each layer captures the same sized 2D spatial area as the temporal feature learning layer.

With the features learned for a certain spatial dimension, we would wish that these correspond to object parts (parts of the organs), so that part-based object detection can be performed as has been done for 2D images by Weber et al. (2000), Fergus et al. (2003), Bernstein and Amit (2005), Torralba et al. (2007), and Felzenszwalb et al. (2010), and for action recognition in video sequences by Niebles et al. (2008), where Niebles et al. (2008) called the parts the "interest-points." The spatial regions (parts) of the visual feature dimension and max-pooling size will be referred to as the "patches."

This can be compared with the "bag-of-words" model for image classification by Sivic et al. (2005) and Nowak et al. (2006), where the application of sequential unsupervised feature learning combined with max-pooling for learning features of progressively larger regions is conceptually similar to the spatial pyramid matching model by Felzenszwalb et al. (2010) and Lazebnik et al. (2006). In the case of the approach presented in this chapter, however, features are learned in the image-space as well as in the temporal-space; therefore, it can be called the "bag of spatial and temporal words."

Since we wish that this "bag of spatial and temporal words," in other words "spatial- and/or temporal-patches," be classified as parts of certain organs or not-of-interest as a part-based model, a classifier network is connected at the output of the feature learning networks. Examples of the model of two-layer stacked sparse autoencoder networks for learning hierarchical visual features and temporal features, each with a classifier network as the final layer, are shown in Figure 7.10.

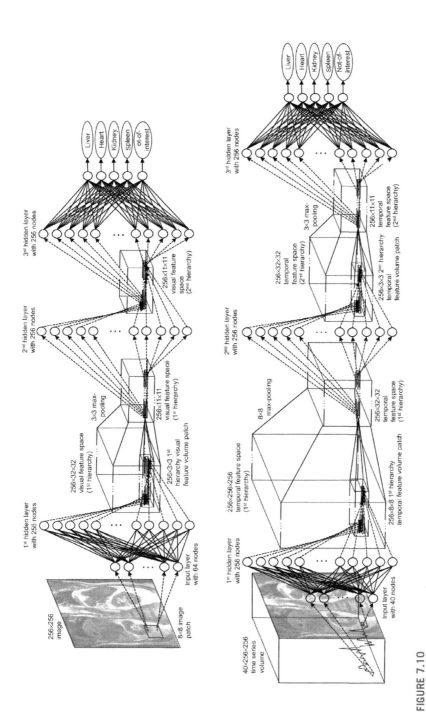

**FIGURE 7.10**

An overall architecture of two-layer visual feature learning networks (top) and temporal feature extraction networks (bottom), where the structure of the architectures (including the number of nodes, pooling size, etc.) is optimized. The first and second hidden layers are unsupervised feature learning networks, and the third hidden layer is a classification network, which is trained with supervision to classify patches of different organs.

## 7.4.4 ANALYSIS AND COMPARISON WITH OTHER METHODS

The extent to which the learned features can represent the object classes in the dataset (organs) is evaluated by the patch-wise classification accuracy of organs, based on the labels obtained from the roughly drawn regions of interest (ROIs) as shown in Figure 7.8. Since the labeled regions include voxels from outside of the intended organ, the accuracy cannot be 100%, even with a perfect classification. However, as the labeled regions contain more correct voxels than incorrect voxels, we assume that higher accuracy corresponds to a better classification performance in general.

The unsupervised feature learning methods using SAEs are compared to principal components analysis (PCA), as PCA is a popular unsupervised feature learning method. PCA is therefore also evaluated as to whether it can learn hierarchical features when applied successively with max-pooling, using 16 principal components for projection of the input data. The SAE are tested also with both 16 (SAE-16) and 256 (SAE-256) learned features to make a fair comparison with PCA using 16 features, and to see the effect of the number of SAE learned features and overcompleteness on classification performance.

In addition, a single-layer convolutional network (1-CNN) is tested to evaluate the effect of pretraining on the features, as well as a single convolutional network using HOG visual features and discrete Fourier transformed (DFT) temporal features. Classification is done with a single-layer classifier network, where the parameters for the training are chosen by a CV test on small subsets of the data. With the best parameters so derived, the final accuracy is reported after additional training and CV using larger subsets of the dataset. Unsupervised feature learning and classifier training use only Dataset A, and classification is performed only with Dataset B, to show the applicability of the features learned unsupervised to an unseen dataset.

## 7.4.5 COORDINATE-ASCENT-LIKE OPTIMIZATION OF HYPERPARAMETERS

Deep networks are known to be difficult to train, and this certainly applies to the stacked sparse autoencoder training as well, where there are many hyperparameters affecting the behavior of the model. The hyperparameters required for training the sparse autoencoders are the target mean activation $\rho$, number of hidden units $s_2$, the weight of the sparsity penalty $\beta$, and the weight decay parameter $\lambda$. The window size for visual feature learning and max-pooling is introduced for the first layer of SAEs (mps$_1$), as well as the max-pooling size for the second layer of SAEs (mps$_2$).

Five parameters should be tested for both temporal and visual feature learning ($\rho$, $s_2$, $\beta$, $\lambda$, and mps$_1$) with the first feature learning layer. If we wish to test five values for each of the parameters, a total of $5^{5 \times 2} = 9,765,625$ combinations of hyperparameters should be tested, and if we wish to test the full combinations for the second feature learning layer, the number of combinations will increase by approximately a power of 2.

These are too many combinations to perform a full search to find the best set of hyperparameters. Therefore, it was proposed (Shin et al., 2013) to use a coordinate-ascent-like method to optimize these for each layer together with the patch and pooling sizes, optimizing each parameter while the others are fixed, and repeating this process for a certain number of iterations until the performance converges. For each iteration in the optimization of first feature learning layers, five values for $\beta = \{1, 3, 9, 27, 81\}$ and mps$_1 \in \{6, 8, 9, 12, 16\}$ are tested, and six values for $\lambda \in \{10^{-4}, 3 \times 10^{-4}, 10^{-3}, 3 \times 10^{-3}, 10^{-2}, 3 \times 10^{-2}\}$, $\rho \in \{10^{-3}, 3 \times 10^{-3}, 10^{-2}, 3 \times 10^{-2}, 0.1, 0.3\}$, and $s_2 \in \{9, 16, 32, 64, 128, 256\}$ are tested.

Tests and searches also evaluated were whether whitening the images prior to visual feature training is helpful, and if so, what parameter combinations are optimal. Six combinations for image-whitening parameters were assessed for training visual features. For more details about the image whitening and its effect on visual feature learning, see Bell and Sejnowski (1997) and Coates et al. (2011). The ranges and intervals for each parameter value are chosen based on the previous research (Goodfellow et al., 2009; Shin et al., 2011) and some initial experiments on a small set of hyperparameter combinations.

For the second feature learning layers, the first-layer hyperparameters were fixed as they were optimized for the first layer, and the combinations of only the second-layer feature learning were tested. However, the window sizes for the max-pooling and visual feature learning were tested for the first and second layers individually ($mps_1$, $mps_2$), to assess (i) whether learning features for a large spatial area in the first layer are sufficient if $mps_1$ is set large for the first-layer optimization, or (ii) whether learning features for progressively larger regions with feature propagation work better in this case.

The progress of patch-wise classification accuracy along the coordinate-ascent-like optimization is shown in Figure 7.11, for first- and second-layer SAEs and PCAs, where only the window sizes and the hyperparameters for image whitening are tested for PCAs. We can see that the accuracies increase gradually along the progress of the optimization, while they converge to an optimum after some iterations. The optimal parameters found for image whitening were [Spectrum − Decay = 1, Cutoff − Frequency = 0.3] for the SAEs, and [Spectrum − Decay = 0.3, Cutoff − Frequency = 0.3] for PCA. Details about the parameters for the image-whitening procedure used here can be found in Vedaldi and Fulkerson (2008). The optimal values of the other parameters of all the methods compared are shown in Table 7.1, together with the classification accuracies achieved with the parameters and methods. The average F1-score ($F1_{avg}$) of each individual object class (liver, heart, kidney, spleen, not-of-interest) is shown for comparison later in Section 7.4.7 in Table 7.2.

## 7.4.6 UNSUPERVISED LEARNING OF OBJECT CLASSES

In this section, we will assess whether the object classes in the dataset are learned in an unsupervised manner ("self-taught learned") by the unsupervised feature learning with the SAEs training. For this purpose, 1500 randomly sampled patches for each organ class are visualized in the feature spaces, using the features examined previously in Table 7.1. Please note that the "roughly" labeled samples are used to sample the patches for the assessment, but the feature learning is performed on randomly sampled patches in the training dataset without using any labeled information.

The patches of organ classes in feature spaces are shown in Figure 7.12 in 2D scatter plots, where PCA is used to reduce the dimension of the feature space by a factor of 2 in order to aid visualization. It is noticeable that the object classes are very well captured by the 16 temporal features learned by single-layer unsupervised sparse feature learning (TE-L1-SAE-16). The object classes are reasonably well separated with 1-convolutional DFT temporal features (TE-DFT), but less so with 1-convolutional PCA (TE-L1-PCA) or 1-convolutional temporal features alone (TE-1-CNN). It is not obvious from the plots whether the overcomplete methods (with 256 features) have learned features that better discriminate the organ classes and may therefore be expected to give better classification performance. This can be due to the dramatic dimensionality reduction needed for visualization (from 256 to 2), as the classification performance with those features shows good results in Table 7.1. Overall, temporal features have better classification performance than visual-only features.

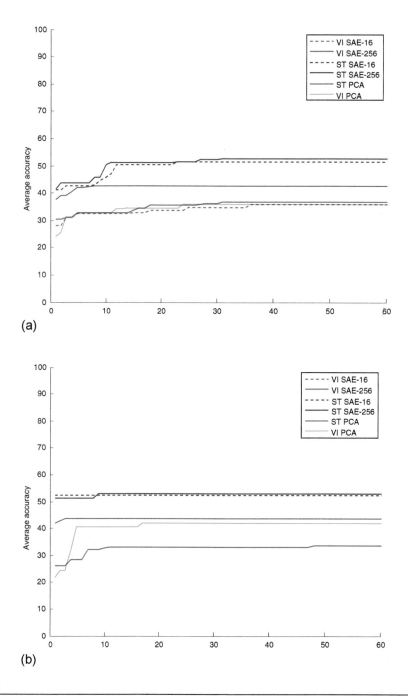

**FIGURE 7.11**

Average accuracies during the hyperparameter optimization processes for spatio temporal (ST) features and visual (VI) features, each with PCA, SAEs with 16 features (SAE-16) and 256 features (SAE-256). A single hyperparameter is optimized at a time sequentially in the grid of hyperparameter space, where the objective is to achieve higher average accuracy on all of the organ types in the CV dataset. (a) Parameter optimization process on first layer. (b) Parameter optimization process on second layer.

**Table 7.1 Part-Based Classification Accuracies and the Stacked Sparse Autoencoder (SAE) Hyperparameters (Including Patch and Pooling Sizes) Used with: First and Second Level Hierarchy (L1 and L2); Visual and Temporal Features (VI and TE); 16 and 256 Learned Features**

| Method | $mps_1$ | $mps_2$ | acc | $F1_{avg}$ |
|---|---|---|---|---|
| VI L1 PCA | 16 | n/a | 36.09 | 0.33 |
| VI L2 PCA | 16 | 6 | 29.70 | 0.33 |
| TE L1 PCA | 16 | n/a | 42.33 | 0.48 |
| TE L2 PCA | 9 | 6 | 35.74 | 0.42 |
| VI HOG | 6 | 2 | 28.28 | 0.30 |
| TE DFT | 12 | n/a | 41.90 | 0.50 |
| VI 1-CNN | 12 | n/a | 35.46 | 0.34 |
| TE 1-CNN | 16 | n/a | 45.57 | 0.53 |

| Method | $\rho$ | $\lambda$ | $\beta$ | $mps_1$ | $mps_2$ | acc | $F1_{avg}$ |
|---|---|---|---|---|---|---|---|
| VI L1 SAE-16 | 0.3 | 0.003 | 1 | 16 | n/a | 36.00 | 0.30 |
| VI L2 SAE-16 | 0.1 | 0.0001 | 3 | 12 | 3 | 33.24 | 0.30 |
| TE L1 SAE-16 | 0.01 | 0.003 | 1 | 16 | n/a | 51.71 | 0.53 |
| TE L2 SAE-16 | 0.01 | 0.0001 | 1 | 6 | 3 | 30.68 | 0.23 |
| VI L1 SAE-256 | 0.3 | 0.0001 | 27 | 16 | n/a | 36.37 | 0.33 |
| VI L2 SAE-256 | 0.03 | 0.0001 | 1 | 16 | 3 | 36.12 | 0.38 |
| TE L1 SAE-256 | 0.003 | 0.0001 | 1 | 16 | n/a | 51.68 | 0.56 |
| TE L2 SAE-256 | 0.1 | 0.0001 | 1 | 6 | 3 | 53.10 | 0.54 |

Notes: *Baseline models are compared with their average classification accuracies for organs (acc), and the average F1-score ($F1_{avg}$) of each individual object class's score is shown for comparison later in Section 7.4.7 with Table 7.2.*

Figure 7.12 appears to show nearly perfect categorization of self-learned features for the TE-L1-SAE-16 approach, but the reason the classification accuracy is not higher than that in Table 7.1 can be seen in Figure 7.13. Figure 7.13 shows 1500 randomly sampled patches of a new subset of the training dataset (liver patient dataset) and CV dataset (kidney patient dataset), each encoded with the same temporal features used in Figure 7.12. Although the TE-L1-SAE-16 features separate the organ classes very well in the new subset of the training dataset, the separation is not nearly as clear in the CV dataset. This performance reduction could be mitigated by unsupervised feature learning on a larger subset of (more heterogeneous) training data, but it is technically challenging to train on a very large-scale dataset. In Figure 7.13, the patches of the CV dataset encoded with the TE-L1-DFT and TE-L2-PCA features—which showed good separation of the organ classes with the training data—are also shown, and they too show less clear separation in the CV dataset.

**Table 7.2 Model and Hyperparameters of Visual and Temporal Features for Each Organ Class for the Context-Specific Feature Learning**

**Visual Features**

| Organ | Model | $\rho$ | $\lambda$ | $\beta$ | $mps_1$ | $mps_2$ | $F1_{tmp}$ | $acc_{opt}$ | $acc_{1+/-}$ |
|---|---|---|---|---|---|---|---|---|---|
| Liver | L2-256 | 0.03 | 0.0001 | 1 | 16 | 3 | 0.53 | 58.10 | 52.57 |
| Heart | L2-256 | 0.03 | 0.0001 | 1 | 16 | 3 | 0.43 | 63.25 | 55.23 |
| Kidney | L1-256 | 0.3 | 0.0001 | 27 | 16 | n/a | 0.32 | 52.97 | 49.82 |
| Spleen | L2-256 | 0.03 | 0.0001 | 1 | 16 | 3 | 0.51 | 73.21 | 61.45 |
| NOI | L2-256 | 0.03 | 0.0001 | 1 | 16 | 3 | 0.35 | 60.38 | 59.88 |

**Temporal Features**

| Organ | Model | $\rho$ | $\lambda$ | $\beta$ | $mps_1$ | $mps_2$ | $F1_{tmp}$ | $acc_{opt}$ | $acc_{1+/-}$ |
|---|---|---|---|---|---|---|---|---|---|
| Liver | L1-256 | 0.3 | 0.0001 | 27 | 16 | n/a | 0.50 | 64.78 | 57.46 |
| Heart | L1-256 | 0.3 | 0.0001 | 1 | 16 | n/a | 0.81 | 84.88 | 84.54 |
| Kidney | L2-256 | 0.3 | 0.0001 | 1 | 9 | 3 | 0.72 | 81.82 | 79.16 |
| Spleen | L2-256 | 0.01 | 0.0001 | 1 | 6 | 3 | 0.54 | 78.44 | 73.13 |
| NOI | L1-16 | 0.3 | 0.0001 | 1 | 8 | 3 | 0.58 | 58.09 | 52.01 |

**Combined**

| Organ | $acc_{1}$ | $acc_{12}$ |
|---|---|---|
| Liver | 66.80 | 62.62 |
| Heart | 68.35 | 65.59 |
| Kidney | 68.28 | 79.41 |
| Spleen | 66.97 | 63.44 |
| NOI | 70.61 | 62.01 |

Notes: The classification accuracy with the chosen model for each organ class $acc_{opt}$ is shown for the CV dataset for all organs except for heart (which does not appear in the CV data and so is tested on a subset of the training dataset). Accuracy with a higher $\rho$ autoencoder layer ($acc_{1+/-}$) is compared with that of the first/second layer giving the optimal accuracy ($acc_{opt}$). Some organ classes benefit from combined features, while it is better to use temporal features only for some organ classes. The average F1-score in picking the parameters in the optimization process in Table 7.1 is also shown: $F1_{tmp}$. NOI = not-of-interest.

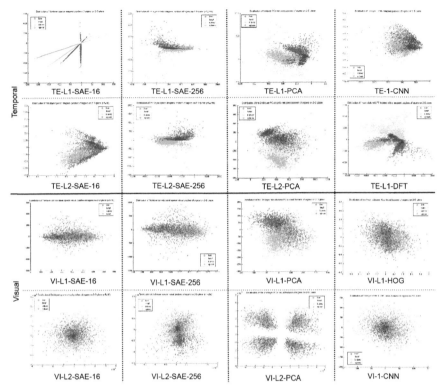

**FIGURE 7.12**

Scatter plots showing 1500 randomly sampled patches of the organ object classes (red: liver, yellow: heart, green: kidney, blue: spleen) in the training dataset with each of the feature learning methods and projected onto 2D space using PCA.

## 7.4.7 CONTEXT-SPECIFIC FEATURE LEARNING

Different organ classes have different properties, and therefore it seems reasonable to suppose that the task of separating a given organ class from all other classes might be best achieved by learning the optimal feature for that particular organ, rather than by training on the average separation performance for all classes. Applying this in the context of action recognition as in Niebles et al. (2008), the question would be: Can one obtain better performance with a feature learning model optimized specifically for "hand waving," for example, rather than using the same feature learning model that simultaneously tries to classify, say, "running" and all the other different actions studied?

It is usually time-consuming and difficult to design a new feature-learning model for every object class, but deep learning architecture requires very little modification to achieve that. In this study, a model with the same basic design for both visual and temporal feature learning was applied. Moreover, features of different characteristics can be learned by tuning the hyperparameters in the learning model, as studied by Goodfellow et al. (2009).

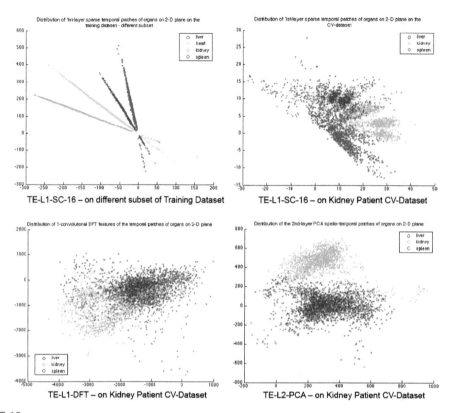

**FIGURE 7.13**

Scatter plots showing 1500 randomly sampled patches of a different subset of the training dataset and the CV liver patient dataset. The patches are processed and displayed in the same way as for Figure 7.12. Since the scans of the CV dataset are focused on the kidneys, heart does not appear in those images due to its anatomical location; therefore, heart is absent in the CV dataset. We can see sparse autoencoder encoding (top two plots) gives better separation of organ types than the other feature learning methods compared (DFT and PCA—bottom two plots).

In principle one would optimize the hyperparameters in Table 7.1 separately for each object class, but the computational resource required to do this exceeded that which was available for this study (Section 7.4.5). Instead, during the hyperparameter optimization process in Section 7.4.5 and Table 7.1, the parameter sets with the best F1-scores of each object class were picked along the trajectory of the optimization process.

The reason F1-scores are used instead of accuracies for assessing the classification performance for each organ class is because, in this case, the true/false label is biased for each class to the other classes. For example, with 1500 samples obtained for each of the 5 organ classes, the accuracy for a mostly failed liver classification except for 1 sample, for instance, will still be as high as $0.7999 = (1500 \times 4 - 1)/(1500 \times 5)$, while the F1-score is $\approx 0$, providing a more unbiased measure for such a

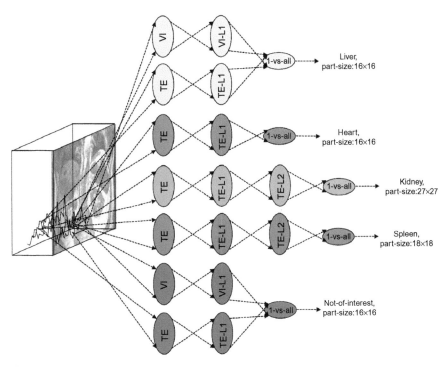

**FIGURE 7.14**

A conceptual visualization of the usage of context-specific features with SAEs in classification. Patches of different modalities are sampled from the dataset and go through different feature networks to be classified as an object part of an organ category.

case. The best F1-scores for each object class along the optimization process of overall classification accuracies in Table 7.1 are shown in Table 7.2 as $F1_{tmp}$, with their corresponding hyperparameter sets.

One-vs-all classifiers are trained by logistic regression using the parameter sets with the same inputs as the multi-class classifier networks. The final classification performance for the individual features optimized for each organ class is evaluated as accuracies ($acc_{opt}$) on an equal number of true/false labels for each organ class, where they are shown in Table 7.2. For the results using visual and temporal features only, the accuracy with the *first* autoencoder layer is denoted by $acc_{l+/-}$ if $acc_{opt}$ was achieved by the *second* autoencoder layer, whereas $acc_{l+/-}$ represents the accuracy with the *second* autoencoder layer if the $acc_{opt}$ was achieved by the *first* autoencoder layer. A shallow combined representation of multi modal features (Ngiam et al., 2011) is examined as well for both hierarchy autoencoders, and their classification accuracies both with first ($acc_{l_1}$) and second ($acc_{l_2}$) autoencoder layers are shown in the right-hand section of the table. The final classifier network with the context-specific feature learning model for each object class is shown in Figure 7.14.

Here, we observe that (1) Organ-specific parameter selections generally give improved performance, although not always by a large amount. (2) Temporal features alone give good classification performance for heart, kidney, and spleen. (Note: The heart was classified on a different dataset, because of its absence on the validation set—see caption to Figure 7.13.) (3) Generally, the second-layer visual features showed better performance than the first-layer features, while this was not evident for the temporal features, which had a worse performance for liver and heart. (4) Shallow combination of the first-layer visual and temporal features showed better performance than features of either modality alone for liver and "not-of-interest" (NOI) tissues, although the increase in accuracy for liver was small.

It is also possible to draw some conclusions from these results about the parameter settings for deep network models with SAEs: (1) The optimized sparsity $\rho$ in the second layer tends to be lower than that in the first layer to capture fewer and larger size higher hierarchy features. (2) The weight decay parameter $\lambda$ and the regularization parameter $\beta$ affect the behavior of the autoencoder less than the sparsity parameter $\rho$ does. (3) In the temporal domain, a larger feature set (256) was selected for organs than for NOI tissues (16 features)—this is probably because NOI does not represent a specific object class, and so the fewer features that are used, the less prone is the model to overfitting specific background entities in the training data.

## 7.4.8 PART-BASED MULTI-ORGAN DETECTION

The best feature set for each organ class can be chosen from the results in Table 7.2: TE-L1-256 features for heart, TE-L2-256 for kidney and spleen, the combined L1-16 features for NOI, and the combined L1-256 features for liver. Some of the part-based organ detection results in training, CV, and the test dataset are shown in Figure 7.15. As might be expected, the results reflect the organs at which the image datasets themselves were targeted. Thus, liver is better recognized on the scans whose purpose was to image liver tumors, and kidney in renal cell carcinoma patients.

### 7.4.8.1 Probabilistic part-based organ detection

As more patches are classified correctly than incorrectly to their corresponding category of organs, it is reasonable to perform organ detection based on a probabilistic part-based model, first by generating a probability map for each organ, and then by selecting a threshold to generate a binary mask, using the features selected in Table 7.2. The probability map is generated using 1000 randomly sampled patches, where they are sampled on the nonbackground regions and the regions not affected by breathing motion.

The patches iterate through randomly sampled locations $(i, j)$ in an image, and its score for being an organ $A$ is increased by 1 unit if the location $(i, j)$ is in a patch classified as the organ $A$. On the other hand, if $(i, j)$ is in the patch but the classifier returns a different class, we subtract 0.2 from the score, because the average false classification rate for the organ classes is $\approx 0.2$ (from Table 7.2). The final scores after all patches have been considered are normalized by dividing by the maximum score in the image, to get a probability map for an organ $A$ in an image. An example of a probability map—total likelihood scores of each organ class normalized to formulate a probability—is shown as heat maps in Figure 7.16.

For the final organ detection, a number of simple postprocessing steps are performed. From the probability map, the largest, contiguous regions are obtained for which the probability is larger than a preset threshold, except for kidney, where two such regions are obtained using our prior anatomical knowledge that there are more likely to be two kidneys than one. There are cases where only one kidney appears in the image, and these cases are accounted for by ignoring any regions that are smaller than 200 pixels. The thresholds are organ-specific (see Table 7.3) and were selected by examining the pixel-wise

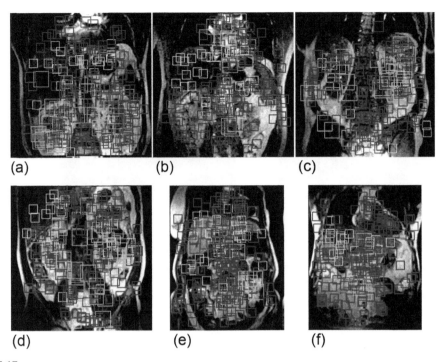

**FIGURE 7.15**

Classification results of part-based organ detection (yellow: liver, magenta: heart, cyan: kidney, red: spleen, blue: not-of-interest (NOI)). (a and b) Liver patient training dataset, (c and d) kidney patient CV dataset, and (e and f) liver patient from a clinical trial. The patch size for liver and heart is $16 \times 16$, for kidney $27 \times 27$, for spleen $18 \times 18$, and for NOI $24 \times 24$. The various parameters including the patch sizes for each organ class are chosen based on the results shown in Table 7.2.

precision (true positives/(true positives + false positives)) and recall (true positives/(true positives + false negatives)) on the CV dataset. Convex hull processing (Andrew, 1979) is then applied to the final regions for each object category to outline the regions smoothly, using the bwconvhull function of the MATLAB® Image Processing Toolbox library.

Some examples of the final visualization of multi-organ detection are shown in Figure 7.17. Organs are generally well detected, but the performance of the algorithm varies from patient to patient. Encouragingly, even unusually large livers and those with metastases are correctly assigned to the liver organ class. Notice that this method of performing organ recognition does not lead to mutually exclusive regions, something which is a consequence of independently generating and processing the probability maps for each organ.

Pixel-wise precision and recall scores on the CV kidney patient dataset and object-wise precision and recall scores on the test liver patient dataset from a clinical trial are shown in Table 7.3. All of the organ types are well detected with an average 0.60 in precision and 0.80 in recall.

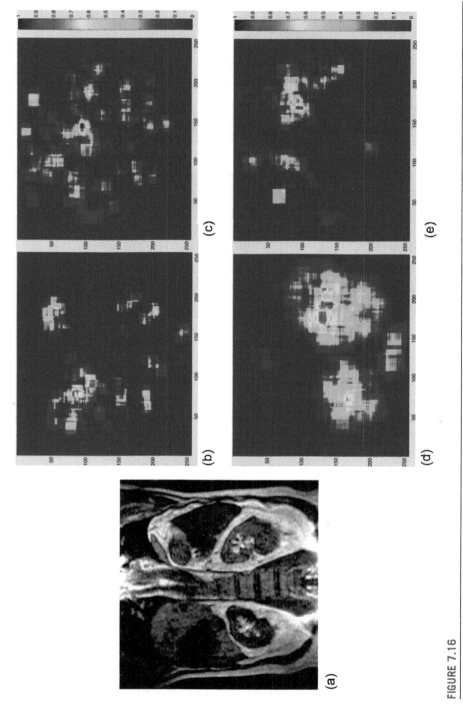

**FIGURE 7.16**

Source image of a liver tumor patient (a), with probability maps for: (b) liver, (c) heart, (d) kidney, and (e) spleen.

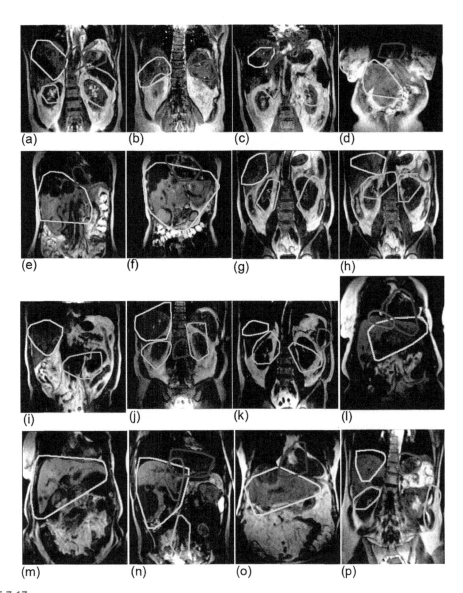

**FIGURE 7.17**

Some examples of the final multi-organ detection (yellow: liver, magenta: heart, cyan: kidney, red: spleen) on training dataset (a–f), CV dataset (g–k), and test dataset (l–p). Liver and kidney are well detected, whereas spleen is less well detected. In some images, the detected heart region also contains aorta (a and j), which is probably because the signal uptake pattern in the aorta and the heart is similar. The liver class detected includes both normal appearing tissues and tumor tissues. Liver tumor is seen in most of the liver patient images (a–f and l–p), with some largely abnormal liver shapes (e and n).

**Table 7.3 Selected Threshold and Pixel-Wise Precision/Recall with the Threshold for the Organ Classes on the CV Dataset, Except Heart Which Was Validated on the Training Dataset**

|  | Threshold | Pixel-Prec./Recall | Object-Prec./Recall |
|---|---|---|---|
| Liver | 0.1 | 0.86/0.32 | 0.96/0.91 |
| Heart | 0.2 | 0.83/0.25 | 0.57/0.67 |
| Kidney | 0.4 | 0.45/0.31 | 0.46/0.91 |
| Spleen | 0.3 | 0.45/0.37 | 0.40/0.72 |

Note: *Object-wise precision/recall was validated on the test dataset of a clinical trial.*

## 7.5 CONCLUSIONS

The challenges for object detection in patient datasets are (1) the organs with diseases are sometimes grossly abnormal; (2) the shape of the organs shown by slices in a 3D medical image differ between slices in ways that are sometimes challenging even for a trained radiologist; and (3) it is hard to obtain many training datasets and the ground truth is hard to define.

Deep learning methods enable us to learn hierarchical features in a data-driven, unsupervised manner. In the experiment demonstrated in this chapter, organ classes are learned without detailed human input, and only a "roughly" labeled dataset was required to train the classifier for multiple organ detection. A robust detection of multiple organs can be further conveyed for finer segmentation using more a precisely labeled training dataset or to enable disease identification by distinguishing anomalies in the detected organ regions.

Tremendous achievements have been made more recently in natural image classification with the introduction of very large dataset (ImageNet dataset (Deng et al., 2009) with about 1.2 million natural images) and with parallel processing via modern graphics processing units, for example, by Krizhevsky et al. (2012), Erhan et al. (2014), and Simonyan and Zisserman (2015). Further work should also investigate the potential of natural image analysis for application to medical images.

## ACKNOWLEDGMENTS

We acknowledge the support received from the CRUK and EPSRC Cancer Imaging Centre in association with the MRC and Department of Health (England) grant C1060/A10334, also NHS funding to the NIHR Biomedical Research Centre.

## REFERENCES

Andrew, A., 1979. Another efficient algorithm for convex hulls in two dimensions. Inf. Process. Lett. 9 (5), 216-219.

Bazzani, L., Larochelle, H., Murino, V., Ting, J.A., Freitas, N.D., 2011. Learning attentional policies for tracking and recognition in video with deep networks. In: Proceedings of the 28th International Conference on Machine Learning (ICML-11), pp. 937-944.

Bell, A.J., Sejnowski, T.J., 1997. The "independent components" of natural scenes are edge filters. Vis. Res. 37 (23), 3327-3338.

Bengio, Y., Lamblin, P., Popovici, D., Larochelle, H., 2007. Greedy layer-wise training of deep networks. Adv. Neural Inf. Process. Syst. 19, 153.

Bernstein, E.J., Amit, Y., 2005. Part-based statistical models for object classification and detection. In: IEEE Computer Society Conference on Computer Vision and Pattern Recognition, 2005. vol. 2, pp. 734-740.

Bishop, C.M., 1995. Neural Networks for Pattern Recognition. Oxford University Press, New York.

Bishop, C.M., et al., 2006. Pattern Recognition and Machine Learning, vol. 4. Springer, New York.

Clark, M.C., Hall, L.O., Goldgof, D.B., Velthuizen, R., Murtagh, F.R., Silbiger, M.S., 1998. Automatic tumor segmentation using knowledge-based techniques. IEEE Trans. Med. Imaging 17 (2), 187-201.

Coates, A., Ng, A.Y., Lee, H., 2011. An analysis of single-layer networks in unsupervised feature learning. In: International Conference on Artificial Intelligence and Statistics, pp. 215-223.

Corso, J.J., Sharon, E., Dube, S., El-Saden, S., Sinha, U., Yuille, A., 2008. Efficient multilevel brain tumor segmentation with integrated Bayesian model classification. IEEE Trans. Med. Imaging 27 (5), 629-640.

Deng, J., Dong, W., Socher, R., Li, L.J., Li, K., Fei-Fei, L., 2009. Imagenet a large-scale hierarchical image database. IEEE Conference on Computer Vision and Pattern Recognition, 2009, pp. 248-255.

Duda, R.O., Hart, P.E., Stork, D.G., 2000. Pattern Classification and Scene Analysis, second ed. Wiley-Interscience, Oxford.

Erhan, D., Szegedy, C., Toshev, A., Anguelov, D., 2014. Scalable object detection using deep neural networks. In: IEEE Conference on Computer Vision and Pattern Recognition, Ohio, USA.

Farhangfar, A., Greiner, R., Szepesvári, C., 2009. Learning to segment from a few well-selected training images. Proceedings of the 26th Annual International Conference on Machine Learning. ACM, pp. 305-312.

Felzenszwalb, P.F., Girshick, R.B., McAllester, D., Ramanan, D., 2010. Object detection with discriminatively trained part-based models. IEEE Trans. Pattern Anal. Mach. Intell. 32 (9), 1627-1645.

Fergus, R., Perona, P., Zisserman, A., 2003. Object class recognition by unsupervised scale-invariant learning. In: IEEE Computer Society Conference on Computer Vision and Pattern Recognition, 2003. Proceedings, vol. 2. IEEE, p. II-264.

Geremia, E., Menze, B.H., Clatz, O., Konukoglu, E., Criminisi, A., Ayache, N., 2010. Spatial decision forests for MS lesion segmentation in multi-channel MR images. In: Medical Image Computing and Computer-Assisted Intervention. Springer, Heidelberg, pp. 111-118.

Glorot, X., Bordes, A., Bengio, Y., 2011. Domain adaptation for large-scale sentiment classification: a deep learning approach. In: Proceedings of the 28th International Conference on Machine Learning (ICML-11), pp. 513-520.

Goodfellow, I., Le, Q., Saxe, A., Lee, H., Ng, A.Y., 2009. Measuring invariances in deep networks. Adv. Neural Inf. Process. Syst. 22, 646-654.

Guo, J., Liu, F., Zhu, Z., 2007. Estimate the call duration distribution parameters in GSM system based on Kl divergence method. In: IEEE International Conference on Wireless Communications Networking and Mobile Computing, 2007. WiCom, 2007, pp. 2988-2991.

Hinton, G.E., Zemel, R.S., 1994. Autoencoders, minimum description length, and helmholtz free energy. Adv. Neural Inf. Process. Syst. 6, 3.

Hubel, D.H., Wiesel, T.N., 1965. Receptive fields and functional architecture in two nonstriate visual areas (18 and 19) of the cat. J. Neurophysiol. 28, 229-289.

Iglesias, J.E., Konukoglu, E., Montillo, A., Tu, Z., Criminisi, A., 2011. Combining generative and discriminative models for semantic segmentation of CT scans via active learning. In: Information Processing in Medical Imaging. Springer, Heidelberg, pp. 25-36.

Ji, S., Xu, W., Yang, M., Yu, K., 2013. 3D convolutional neural networks for human action recognition. IEEE Trans. Pattern Anal. Mach. Intell. 35 (1), 221-231.

Krizhevsky, A., Sutskever, I., Hinton, G., 2012. Imagenet classification with deep convolutional neural networks. Adv. Neural Inf. Process. Syst. 25, 1106-1114.

Kullback, S., Leibler, R.A., 1951. On information and sufficiency. Ann. Math. Stat. 22 (1), 79-86.

Larochelle, H., Bengio, Y., Louradour, J., Lamblin, P., 2009. Exploring strategies for training deep neural networks. J. Mach. Learn. Res. 10, 1-40.

Lazebnik, S., Schmid, C., Ponce, J., 2006. Beyond bags of features: spatial pyramid matching for recognizing natural scene categories. In: IEEE Computer Society Conference on Computer Vision and Pattern Recognition, 2006, vol. 2. IEEE, pp. 2169-2178.

Le, Q.V., Zou, W.Y., Yeung, S.Y., Ng, A.Y., 2011. Learning hierarchical invariant spatio-temporal features for action recognition with independent subspace analysis. In: 2011 IEEE Conference on Computer Vision and Pattern Recognition, pp. 3361-3368.

LeCun, Y., Cortes, C., 1998. MNIST handwritten digit database. AT&T Labs (online). Available at: http://yann.lecun.com/exdb/mnist.

Lee, H., Ekanadham, C., Ng, A., 2008. Sparse deep belief net model for visual area V2. Adv. Neural Inf. Process. Syst. 20, 873-880.

Lee, H., Grosse, R., Ranganath, R., Ng, A.Y., 2009. Convolutional deep belief networks for scalable unsupervised learning of hierarchical representations. In: Proceedings of the 26th Annual International Conference on Machine Learning. pp. 609-616.

Lee, H., Grosse, R., Ranganath, R., Ng, A.Y., 2011. Unsupervised learning of hierarchical representations with convolutional deep belief networks. Commun. ACM 54 (10), 95-103.

Li, L., Prakash, B.A., 2011. Time series clustering: complex is simpler! In: Proceedings of the 28th International Conference on Machine Learning, pp. 185-192.

Linguraru, M.G., Summers, R.M., 2011. Multi-organ automatic segmentation in 4D contrast-enhanced abdominal CT. In: 5th IEEE International Symposium on Biomedical Imaging: From Nano to Macro, 2008. pp. 45-48.

Marc' Aurelio Ranzato, Y., Boureau, L., LeCun, Y., 2007. Sparse feature learning for deep belief networks. Adv. Neural Inf. Process. Syst. 20, 1185-1192.

Ngiam, J., Khosla, A., Kim, M., Nam, J., Lee, H., Ng, A., 2011. Multimodal deep learning. In: Proceedings of the 28th International Conference on Machine Learning, pp. 689-696.

Niebles, J.C., Wang, H., Fei-Fei, L., 2008. Unsupervised learning of human action categories using spatial-temporal words. Int. J. Comput. Vis. 79 (3), 299-318.

Nowak, E., Jurie, F., Triggs, B., 2006. Sampling strategies for bag-of-features image classification. In: Computer Vision—ECCV 2006. Springer, Heidelberg, pp. 490-503.

Okada, T., Yokota, K., Hori, M., Nakamoto, M., Nakamura, H., Sato, Y., 2006. Construction of hierarchical multi-organ statistical atlases and their application to multi-organ segmentation from CT images. In: Medical Image Computing and Computer-Assisted Intervention. Springer, Heidelberg, pp. 502-509.

Pauly, O., Glocker, B., Criminisi, A., Mateus, D., Möller, A.M., Nekolla, S., Navab, N., 2011. Fast multiple organ detection and localization in whole-body Mr Dixon sequences. In: Medical Image Computing and Computer-Assisted Intervention. Springer, Heidelberg, pp. 239-247.

Pitié, F., Kokaram, A.C., Dahyot, R., 2007. Automated colour grading using colour distribution transfer. Comput. Vis. Image Underst. 107 (1), 123-137.

Ranzato, M., Huang, F.J., Boureau, Y.L., LeCun, Y., 2007. Unsupervised learning of invariant feature hierarchies with applications to object recognition. In: IEEE Conference on Computer Vision and Pattern Recognition, 2007. pp. 1-8.

Rumelhart, D.E., 1995. Back Propagation: Theory, Architectures, and Applications. Psychology Press, Hove.

Rumelhart, D., McClelland, J.L., Group, P.R., et al., 1986. Parallel Distributed Processing: Explorations in the Microstructure of Cognition: Psychological and Biological Models, vol. 2. MIT Press, Cambridge, MA.

Schmah, T., Hinton, G.E., Small, S.L., Strother, S., Zemel, R.S., 2008. Generative versus discriminative training of RBMS for classification of fMRI images. Adv. Neural Inf. Process. Syst. 21, 1409-1416.

Shin, H.C., Orton, M., Collins, D.J., Doran, S., Leach, M.O., 2011. Autoencoder in time-series analysis for unsupervised tissues characterisation in a large unlabelled medical image dataset. In: 10th International Conference on Machine Learning and Applications and Workshops, 2011, vol. 1. IEEE, pp. 259-264.

Shin, H.C., Orton, M.R., Collins, D.J., Doran, S.J., Leach, M.O., 2013. Stacked autoencoders for unsupervised feature learning and multiple organ detection in a pilot study using 4D patient data. IEEE Trans. Pattern Anal. Mach. Intell. 35 (8), 1930-1943.

Simonyan, K., Zisserman, A., 2015. Very deep convolutional networks for large-scale image recognition. In: International Conference on Learning Representations.

Sivic, J., Russell, B.C., Efros, A.A., Zisserman, A., Freeman, W.T., 2005. Discovering objects and their location in images. In: Tenth IEEE International Conference on Computer Vision, 2005. vol. 1. IEEE, pp. 370-377.

Sohn, K., Jung, D.Y., Lee, H., Hero, A.O., 2011. Efficient learning of sparse, distributed, convolutional feature representations for object recognition. In: 2011 IEEE International Conference on Computer Vision. IEEE, pp. 2643-2650.

Torralba, A., Murphy, K.P., Freeman, W.T., 2007. Sharing visual features for multiclass and multiview object detection. IEEE Trans. Pattern Anal. Mach. Intell. 29 (5), 854-869.

Vedaldi, A., Fulkerson, B., 2008. VLFeat: an open and portable library of computer vision algorithms. Available at: http://www.vlfeat.org/.

Vincent, P., Larochelle, H., Bengio, Y., Manzagol, P.A., 2008. Extracting and composing robust features with denoising autoencoders. In: Proceedings of the 25th International Conference on Machine Learning. pp. 1096-1103.

Weber, M., Welling, M., Perona, P., 2000. Towards automatic discovery of object categories. In: IEEE Conference on Computer Vision and Pattern Recognition, 2000, vol. 2. IEEE, pp. 101-108.

Yu, K., Xu, W., Gong, Y., 2009. Deep learning with kernel regularization for visual recognition. Adv. Neural Inf. Process. Syst. 22. 1889-1896.

Zeiler, M.D., Fergus, R., 2012. Differentiable pooling for hierarchical feature learning. Available at: http://arxiv.org/abs/1207.0151.

Zeiler, M.D., Taylor, G.W., Fergus, R., 2011. Adaptive deconvolutional networks for mid and high level feature learning. In: 2011 IEEE International Conference on Computer Vision. IEEE, pp. 2018-2025.

Zhou, G., Sohn, K., Lee, H., 2012. Online incremental feature learning with denoising autoencoders. In: International Conference on Artificial Intelligence and Statistics, pp. 1453-1461.

# AUTOMATIC SEGMENTATION AND PARSING ALGORITHMS

# A PROBABILISTIC FRAMEWORK FOR MULTIPLE ORGAN SEGMENTATION USING LEARNING METHODS AND LEVEL SETS

8

## S. Kevin Zhou and D. Xu

*Medical Imaging Technologies, Siemens Healthcare Technology Center, Princeton, NJ, USA*

## CHAPTER OUTLINE

S. Kevin Zhou (Ed): Medical Image Recognition, Segmentation and Parsing. http://dx.doi.org/10.1016/B978-0-12-802581-9.00008-1

## 8.1 INTRODUCTION

Multiple organ segmentation is essential to a multitude of clinical applications. For computer-aid diagnosis systems that aim to detect lesions in the abdominal organs such as liver, kidneys, and spleen (Kobatake, 2007), it is a prerequisite to segment these organs. For radiation therapy planning (Qatarneh et al., 2003; Kaus et al., 2007), multiple organ segmentation is a must-have feature for commercial software. For planning liver surgeries such as resection and transplant (Fan et al., 2000), it is helpful to clearly visualize right lung, liver, and right kidneys. In addition, quantitative measures like 3D shape variability and organ volume size variability can be computed as an indication of disorders (Tsushima and Endo, 2000). From the scanner perspective, precise segmentation of organs from a planning scan enables the so-called semantic scanning for diagnosis, which improves the scanning workflow as less manual intervention is needed, consistently images only desired body regions, and emits less radiation to patients when compared with a conventional scanning procedure.

Although remarkable progress has been made in segmenting organs, the field still confronts a lot of challenges to obtain results that can be used in clinical applications. The first challenge is the *significant shape and appearance variations* caused by a multitude of factors: sensor noise/artifact, patient difference and motion, pathology and contrast agents, partial scan and field of view, soft tissue, etc. The second challenge lies in *stringent accuracy and speed requirements*. Image reading and diagnosis allow almost no room for mistake. In spite of the high accuracy requirement, the demand for speedy processing does not diminish. A speedy work flow is crucial to any radiology lab that strives for high throughput. Few radiologists or physicians can wait for hours or even minutes to obtain the analysis results.

In this chapter, we present a fully automatic approach for multiple organ segmentation that addresses these challenges. It robustly handles body scans with partial presence of the organs and guarantees no overlapping between two neighboring organs. It runs fast. For example, in our computed tomography (CT) experiment, it takes about 80 s to segment 10 organs (left and right lungs, liver, heart, left and right kidneys, spleen, bladder, prostate, and rectum) with an accuracy close to inter-user variability.

We leverage the fact that, unlike images of natural scenes, medical images of humans manifest strong context, which will be formally defined in Section 8.2. Figure 8.1 shows the contextual positions of multiple organs. In addition, we collect a large dataset of medical images with annotations. Therefore, we design a *context learning* method to characterize the statistical relationships among images, landmarks, and organs in a *discriminative* fashion for effective and efficient landmark and organ parsing.

The chapter is structured as follows. In Section 8.2, we review the literature about how to segment multiple organs. We then present an overview of the proposed solution in a probabilistic formulation in Section 8.3.1 and elaborate the details about individual organ detection and segmentation and joint organ segmentation in Sections 8.3.2 and 8.3.3, respectively. We present the experimental results in Section 8.4 and discuss various issues related to our solution. Section 8.5 concludes the chapter.

## 8.2 LITERATURE REVIEW

There is a large literature on segmenting a single organ such as lung, liver, prostate, etc. Since our intent is to segment multi-organs, we will skip reviewing single organ segmentation and focus on previous

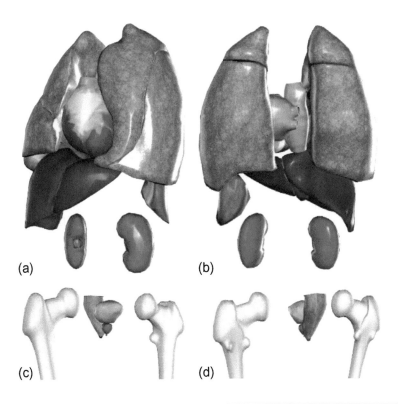

**FIGURE 8.1**

Graphical illustration of contextual positions of multiple organs. (a, b) The anterior and posterior views of seven organs in chest and upper abdomen: left and right lungs, liver, heart, left and right kidneys, and spleen. (c, d) The anterior and posterior views of three organs in lower abdomen in CT: bladder, prostate, and rectum. The left and right femoral heads are included for better illustration.

*Image courtesy to BioDigital Human https://www.biodigital.com/.*

segmentation work that involves at least two neighboring organs. If two organs are not direct neighbors, single organ segmentation can be applied to segment each organ. Because we focus on body organs, we also skip reviewing the literature for segmenting neighboring brain structures. The multi-organ segmentation approaches reviewed here can be roughly divided into several categories: atlas-based, deformable models, energy minimization, learning-based, and others.

## Atlas-based

Park et al. (2003) build a probabilistic atlas of abdomen consisting of 4 organs (i.e., liver, kidneys, and spinal cord) using 32 noncontrast abdominal CT scans and use it for automatic segmentation of the organs. In Zhou and Bai (2007), segmentation of multiple abdominal organs is achieved by combining an atlas with fuzzy connectedness. Okada et al. (2008) construct hierarchical multi-organ statistical atlases for automatic segmentation of liver, vena cava, and gallbladder from CT images. Organ regions are initialized using probabilistic atlases and subsequently refined by multilevel, multi-organ statistical shape models. Fenchel et al. (2008) use a statistical atlas to label anatomical structures in MR fast view scans. Suzuki et al. (2012) address the missing organ issue in multi-organ segmentation by including an explicitly missing organ detection module that tests the abnormality of postsurgical organ motion and organ-specific intensity homogeneity into an atlas-guided segmentation solution. Wolz et al. (2012) further extend the atlas approach to create hierarchically weighted subject-specific atlases for multi-organ segmentation from abdominal CT images.

## Deformable models

Yang et al. (2004) present level set based 3D deformable models that incorporate neighborhood constraints for segmentation of multiple objects from 3D medical images. The joint density functions of the neighboring objects are learned to capture the variations of the neighboring shape and position relationships from a set of training images. Costa et al. (2007) present a fully automatic method for localization and segmentation of prostate and bladder from CT scans. First, a heuristic bladder model is used to locate and segment the bladder and a statistical shape prior is included in a 3D deformation model to fit the prostate. Then an adaptive nonoverlapping constraint is introduced to arbitrate the evolution of both structures.

## Energy minimization

Yan et al. (2005) introduce an energy functional that features the competition between neighboring shape models for avoiding overlapping while incorporating both prior shape information and interactions between deformable models. Shimizu et al. (2007) propose an energy minimization method for extracting 12 organs, including liver, spleen, left and right kidneys, heart, gallbladder, pancreas, portal vein between the spleen and liver, stomach wall, esophagus, abdominal aorta, and inferior vena cava, from noncontrast 3D abdominal CT images. The energy function takes into account the hierarchy and exclusiveness between organs as well as uniformity of gray values.

## Learning-based

Kohlberger et al. (2011) use learning-based marginal space learning (MSL) models to automatically detect the organs (liver, heart, and kidneys) from CT scans, then leverage learned boundary detectors to segment multiple organs and finally invoke the level set optimization to refine the organ segmentation. Lu et al. (2012) follow a similar learning-based approach but followed with an information-theory-based boundary deformation for final segmentation of prostate, bladder, and rectum from CT scans.

## Other approaches

Linguraru et al. (2010) construct a 4D graph and use the graph cut algorithm to simultaneously segment four abdominal organs (liver, spleen, and kidneys) from contrast-enhanced CT scans with two phases, the phase information being the fourth dimension. Uzunbaş et al. (2013) integrate deformable and graphical models for multi-organ segmentation in a collaborative fashion. Recently, segmentation and registration are combined for more accurate organ segmentation (Lu et al., 2010).

## 8.3 PROPOSED METHOD

We first present a probabilistic framework in Section 8.3.1, which decomposes a highly complex problem into three simpler subproblems. The first is multiple landmark detection described in other chapters in this book, the second is to estimate the organ, and the third is to segment multiple organs. We use the method described in Chapter 4 to detecting multiple landmarks. In Section 8.3.2, we elaborate a learning approach for individual organ pose estimation and segmentation. In Section 8.3.3, we discuss a multilevel set approach for joint organ segmentation refinement.

### 8.3.1 PROBABILISTIC FRAMEWORK FOR AUTOMATIC PARSING OF LANDMARKS AND ORGANS

We denote a 3D volume by $\mathbf{V}$, and a landmark position by $\mathbf{p} = [x, y, z] \in \mathbb{R}^3$. An organ is specified by a mesh $\mathcal{M} = (\mathcal{P}, \mathcal{T})$ consisting of a set of points, $\mathcal{P} = \{\mathbf{v}_i \in \mathbb{R}^3\}_{i=1}^N$, and a single set of triangle indices, $\mathcal{T} = \{\triangle_j \in \mathbb{Z}^3\}_{j=1}^M$. In addition to the mesh representation, an organ can also be described by other representations such as binary mask, level set function, etc. In this work, we use the level set function $\phi$. Furthermore, for each organ we define its pose by $\theta = \{\mathbf{t}, \mathbf{r}, \mathbf{s}\}$, including the position $\mathbf{t} \in \mathbb{R}^3$, the orientation $\mathbf{r} \in \mathbb{R}^3$ as three Euler angles, and the scale $\mathbf{s} \in \mathbb{R}^3$ using three anisotropic scale parameters.

Considering the relationships between landmarks and organs, the most general formulation of detecting $N$ landmarks $\mathbf{p}_{1:N} = \{\mathbf{p}_1, \mathbf{p}_2, \ldots, \mathbf{p}_N\}$, estimating $M$ organ poses $\theta_{1:M} = \{\theta_1, \theta_2, \ldots, \theta_M\}$, and segmenting $M$ organs $\mathcal{M}_{1:m} = \{\mathcal{M}_1, \mathcal{M}_2, \ldots, \mathcal{M}_M\}$ from a 3D body scan $\mathbf{V}$ in a probabilistic sense[a] is to model the joint posterior probability $P(\mathbf{p}_{1:N}, \theta_{1:M}, \mathcal{M}_{1:M}|\mathbf{V})$ and find, say, its mode as the solution. This is, however, difficult to achieve due to high complexity. Using the chain rule,

$$P(\mathbf{p}_{1:N}, \theta_{1:M}, \mathcal{M}_{1:M}|\mathbf{V}) = P(\mathbf{p}_{1:N}|\mathbf{V})P(\theta_{1:M}|\mathbf{p}_{1:N}, \mathbf{V})P(\mathcal{M}_{1:M}|\theta_{1:M}, \mathbf{p}_{1:N}, \mathbf{V}),$$

we break down a highly complex problem into three simpler tasks:

1. ($T_1$) Multiple landmark detection using $P(\mathbf{p}_{1:N}|\mathbf{V})$ or equivalent.
2. ($T_2$) Estimating organ poses using $P(\theta_{1:M}|\mathbf{p}_{1:N}, \mathbf{V})$ or equivalent.
3. ($T_3$) Segmenting multiple organs using $P(\mathcal{M}_{1:M}|\mathbf{p}_{1:N}, \theta_{1:M}, \mathbf{V})$ or equivalent.

For ($T_1$) multiple landmark detection, we refer the readers to other chapters in this book.
For ($T_2$) organ pose estimation, we assume that each organ pose is conditionally independent:

$$P(\theta_{1:M}|\mathbf{p}_{1:N}, \mathbf{V}) = \prod_{m=1}^M P(\theta_m|\mathbf{p}_{1:N}, \mathbf{V})$$

That is, we estimate each organ pose independently, which allows us to use the same pose estimation pipeline for all organs. We use the MSL approach (Zheng et al., 2007, 2008, 2009a) to model $P(\theta_i|\mathbf{p}_{1:N}, \mathbf{V})$ based on unitary context, which refers to the local regularity surrounding a single object. This is detailed in Section 8.3.2.

For ($T_3$) multiple organ segmentation, we assume that the organ meshes do not depend on the landmarks if the organ poses are known:

$$P(\mathcal{M}_{1:M}|\theta_{1:M}, \mathbf{p}_{1:N}, \mathbf{V}) = P(\mathcal{M}_{1:M}|\theta_{1:M}, \mathbf{V})$$

Further, we take a two-step approach.

1. ($T_{3.1}$) The first step is to segment each organ individually, which again allows the use of the same processing pipeline based on machine learning and unitary context.
2. ($T_{3.2}$) The second step is to refine the segmentation and avoid organ overlap using a joint level set framework and pairwise context, which refers to the joint regularities between two objects.

Mathematically, the two-step approach is described by introducing intermediate mesh variables $\mathcal{N}_{1:M}$ in the formulation.

$$
\begin{aligned}
P(\mathcal{M}_{1:M}|\theta_{1:M}, \mathbf{V}) &= \int_{\mathcal{N}_{1:M}} P_{\text{indiv}}(\mathcal{N}_{1:M}|\theta_{1:M}, \mathbf{V}) P_{\text{joint}}(\mathcal{M}_{1:M}|\mathcal{N}_{1:M}, \theta_{1:M}, \mathbf{V}) \, d\mathcal{N}_{1:M} \\
&= \int_{\mathcal{N}_{1:M}} \prod_{m=1}^{M} P_{\text{indiv}}(\mathcal{N}_m|\theta_m, \mathbf{V}) P_{\text{joint}}(\mathcal{M}_{1:M}|\mathcal{N}_{1:M}, \mathbf{V}) \, d\mathcal{N}_{1:M} \\
&\approx P_{\text{joint}}(\mathcal{M}_{1:M}|\hat{\mathcal{N}}_{1:M}, \mathbf{V})
\end{aligned}
\tag{8.1}
$$

Here, we assume that

$$
P_{\text{indiv}}(\mathcal{N}_{1:M}|\theta_{1:M}, \mathbf{V}) = \prod_{m=1}^{M} P_{\text{indiv}}(\mathcal{N}_m|\theta_m, \mathbf{V})
$$

and

$$
P_{\text{joint}}(\mathcal{M}_{1:M}|\mathcal{N}_{1:M}, \theta_{1:M}, \mathbf{V}) = P_{\text{joint}}(\mathcal{M}_{1:M}|\mathcal{N}_{1:M}, \mathbf{V})
$$

and also use the "winner-take-all" approximation

$$
P_{\text{indiv}}(\mathcal{N}_{1:M}|\theta_{1:M}, \mathbf{V}) \approx \delta(\mathcal{N}_{1:M} - \hat{\mathcal{N}}_{1:M})
$$

with

$$
\hat{\mathcal{N}}_m = \arg\max_{\mathcal{N}_m} P_{\text{indiv}}(\mathcal{N}_m|\theta_m, \mathbf{V})
$$

Therefore, maximizing $P(\mathcal{M}_{1:M}|\theta_{1:M}, \mathbf{V})$ requires first maximizing $P_{\text{indiv}}(\mathcal{N}_m|\theta_m, \mathbf{V})$, which solves ($T_{3.1}$), and then maximizing $P_{\text{joint}}(\mathcal{M}_{1:M}|\hat{\mathcal{N}}_{1:M}, \mathbf{V})$, which solves ($T_{3.2}$). We use a discriminating learning method to solve the individual organ segmentation problem as covered in Section 8.3.2. As shown in Section 8.3.3, joint segmentation is solved using a level set formulation that uses the implicit $\phi$ representation. So, instead of using $P_{\text{joint}}(\mathcal{M}_{1:M}|\hat{\mathcal{N}}_{1:M}, \mathbf{V})$, we use

$$
P_{\text{joint}}(\phi_{1:M}|\phi_{1:M}^0, \mathbf{V}) = \exp\{-E(\phi_{1:M}|\phi_{1:M}^0, \mathbf{V})/\sigma\}
$$

where $E$ is an energy function to be minimized, $\phi$ is equivalent to $\mathcal{M}$, and $\phi^0$ to $\hat{\mathcal{N}}$.

Figure 8.2 schematically shows the proposed hierarchical, feedforward parsing solution. We first detect a cohort of anatomical landmarks, which offers the constraints for organ pose estimation. We further individually detect the organ poses and then segment the organs using learning methods. Finally, we refine the organ segmentation and avoid organ overlapping using a level set method. In Sofka et al.

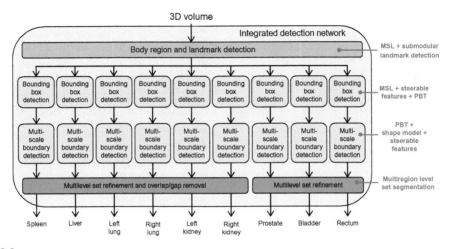

**FIGURE 8.2**

The schematic illustration of the proposed method.

(2011, 2014), the integrated detection network (IDN) method is presented. In this work, we also utilize this framework to implement the previous scheme.

The IDN is proposed to simplify design, modification, tuning, and implementation of sophisticated detection systems. It is a feedforward network consisting of nodes that perform operations on the input data and produce zero or more output data. The operations, such as candidate detection, propagation, and aggregation, are only related to each other through data connections. This makes it possible to easily add new nodes and data types to an existing network. The same network is used in both detection and training which enables rapid prototyping and algorithm evaluation. Furthermore, the basic network building blocks (such as a rigid detector encapsulating position, orientation, and size detection) can be designed and interconnected into complex hierarchies. Such a flexible design makes it easy to manage large-scale detection systems.

## 8.3.2 DISCRIMINATIVE LEARNING FOR SINGLE ORGAN POSE ESTIMATION AND SEGMENTATION

### 8.3.2.1 Organ pose and statistical shape model

In an offline training step, a set of CT images complete with manual annotation of the organs of interest is used to learn the statistical shape models of the shape variation. The input annotation meshes are first brought into correspondence using coherent point drift (Myronenko and Song, 2010) so that each annotation mesh has the same number of points and a consistent triangulation. Other surface-based methods for shape registration (Shen and Davatzikos, 2000; Zhang et al., 2013) can be used too. Each annotation mesh, $\mathcal{M}_k = (\mathcal{P}_k, \mathcal{T})$, then consists of a set of points, $\mathcal{P}_k = \{\mathbf{v}_{ki} \in \mathbb{R}^3\}_{i=1}^I$, and a single set of triangle indices, $\mathcal{T} = \{\triangle_j \in \mathbb{Z}^3\}_{j=1}^J$.

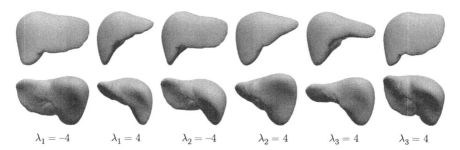

$\lambda_1 = -4 \qquad \lambda_1 = 4 \qquad \lambda_2 = -4 \qquad \lambda_2 = 4 \qquad \lambda_3 = 4 \qquad \lambda_3 = 4$

**FIGURE 8.3**

The variability of statistical liver shape model by using one of the first three basis vectors to represent the shape. The top and bottom lines display the front and back views, respectively.

The variability in the point coordinates is modeled through a low-dimensional linear basis giving a prior shape model,

$$\mathcal{S} = (\{\hat{v}\}_{i=1}^I, \{U_j\}_{j=1}^J) \tag{8.2}$$

that consists of a mean shape $\{\hat{v}\}_{i=1}^I$ and a set of linear basis shapes, $U_j = \{u_{ij}\}_{i=1}^I$. The linear basis is empirically estimated by performing principal component analysis (PCA) on the input annotation meshes, where the corresponding meshes are first aligned using Procrustes analysis. Figure 8.3 shows the top three PCA shape components of the statistical liver shape model.

A mesh in the *span* of the basis can be approximated by modulating the linear shape vectors and applying a similarity transform

$$g(v_i; \{\lambda_j\}, \mathbf{t}, \mathbf{r}, \mathbf{s}) = \mathbf{t} + \mathbf{T}(\mathbf{s}, \mathbf{r}) \sum_j (\hat{v}_i + \mathbf{u}_{ij}\lambda_j) \tag{8.3}$$

where $\mathbf{T}$ is the similarity transformation specified by a rotation, $\mathbf{r}$, and scale, $\mathbf{s}$, and $\mathbf{t}$ is a translation vector, and $\{\lambda_j\}$ are the shape coefficients. In our experiment, we empirically find that this linear modeling is good at handling a wide range of shapes. To better handle abnormal shapes or outliers, robust modeling of shapes (Zhang et al., 2012) could be helpful.

Each training shape can be approximated in the same manner, meaning each training shape has an associated pose and shape coefficient vector. In the following description of the image-based detection procedure, the relationship between these parameters and the image features is modeled with machine learning so that the parameters of the shape model can be inferred on unseen data.

### 8.3.2.2 MSL for organ pose detection

For the estimation of the pose configuration of each organ, the state of each object is compactly represented with nine parameters including the position $\mathbf{t} \in \mathbb{R}^3$, orientation as Euler angles $\mathbf{r}$, and scale, $\mathbf{s}$, of the object: $\theta = \{\mathbf{t}, \mathbf{r}, \mathbf{s}\}$. For computational efficiency these three sets of parameters are treated as a chain of dependent estimates (Ling et al., 2008):

$$P(\theta|\mathbf{p}_{1:N}, \mathbf{V}) = P(\mathbf{t}|\mathbf{p}_{1:N}, \mathbf{V})P(\mathbf{r}|\mathbf{t}, \mathbf{V})P(\mathbf{s}|\mathbf{t}, \mathbf{r}, \mathbf{V}) \tag{8.4}$$

where $P(\mathbf{t}|\mathbf{p}_{1:N}, \mathbf{V})$ is the position detector, $P(\mathbf{r}|\mathbf{t}, \mathbf{V})$ the position-orientation detector, and $P(\mathbf{s}|\mathbf{t}, \mathbf{r}, \mathbf{V})$ the position-orientation-scale detector. All three detectors are learned using probabilistic boosting tree (PBT) (Tu, 2005), with the position detector using the 3D Haar-like features and the other two using the steerable features. Splitting up the pose estimation in this way reduces the dimensionality of each subproblem allowing fewer particles to be used during estimation. Zheng et al. (2007) report an example of MSL computational efficiency on heart chamber detection from cardiac CT, which achieves a computation reduction of almost six orders of magnitude when compared with exhaustive scanning.

MSL significantly reduces the learning complexity too as the bootstrapping happens between different stages. This bootstrapping procedure significantly reduces the amount of negatives and hence makes the learning of binary classifiers amenable; otherwise, it is simply too hard to learn the classifiers due to the dominance of negatives. In Zheng et al. (2009b), experiments show that MSL significantly outperforms full space learning in terms of both accuracy and speed.

After the organ pose is detected, the mean shape of the organ is used as an initial segmentation. This initial shape is further refined for better segmentation. Rather than searching for all of the shape coefficients directly, estimation of the first three PCA coefficients $\lambda = \{\lambda_1, \lambda_2, \lambda_3\}$ in Eq. (8.3) is also done in the MSL framework by augmenting the pose parameter $\theta$ with $\lambda$: $\theta = [\mathbf{t}, \mathbf{r}, \mathbf{s}, \lambda]$. In practice, the candidates from the pose estimation process are augmented with three PCA coefficients sampled uniformly over the range of coefficients observed in the training data,

$$P(\theta|\mathbf{p}_{1:N}, \mathbf{V}) = P(\mathbf{t}|\mathbf{p}_{1:N}, \mathbf{V})P(\mathbf{r}|\mathbf{t}, \mathbf{V})P(\mathbf{s}|\mathbf{t}, \mathbf{r}, \mathbf{V})P(\lambda|\mathbf{t}, \mathbf{r}, \mathbf{s}, \mathbf{p}_{1:N}, \mathbf{V}) \tag{8.5}$$

The observation model, $P(\lambda|\theta, \mathbf{p}_{1:N}, \mathbf{V})$, is empirically modeled with a discriminative PBT classifier that uses steerable features evaluated on surface points of the synthesized mesh (Zheng et al., 2007).

### 8.3.2.3 Organ segmentation using boundary detector and freeform deformation

The first three PCA coefficients give a coarse approximation to the boundary of the organ in the image. In order for the shape model to be expressive enough for all real instances, a large number of basis functions may be needed (e.g., the order of hundreds). Instead of estimating all of the $\lambda$ coefficients directly as previously, the freeform refinement takes an iterative surface deformation approach, which is similar to the one proposed by the active shape model (Cootes et al., 1995).

Starting with the initialized shape from above, the freeform refinement seeks to find the most probable mesh, $\mathcal{N}$, in the space of the linear shape model:

$$\max_{\mathcal{N}} P_{\text{indiv}}(\mathcal{N}|\theta, V) \quad \text{s.t.} \quad \mathcal{N} \in \text{span}(\mathcal{S}) \tag{8.6}$$

where $P_{\text{indiv}}(\mathcal{N}|\theta, V)$ is approximated by integrating over the surface:

$$P_{\text{indiv}}(\mathcal{N}|\theta, V) = \frac{1}{I} \sum_{\mathbf{v}_i} f(\mathbf{v}_i|V) \tag{8.7}$$

Here the per-point posterior is directly approximated by a discriminative classifier. Letting $y_i = \{-1, +1\}$ be a random variable denoting the presence of a surface at point $\mathbf{v}_i$ along normal $\mathbf{n}_i$:

$$f(\mathbf{v}_i|V) = P(y_i = +1|\mathbf{v}_i, \mathbf{n}_i, V) \tag{8.8}$$

The statistical classifier for the boundary can take into account different cues such as raw image intensity, spatial texture, or distance to anatomical structures in order to discriminate between surface points either on or off the organ boundary. We use the PBT classifier (Tu, 2005) that automatically selects the best set of steerable features. If only healthy cases exist, the classifier will pick features like image gradient or raw intensity. However, robustness to pathological cases can be obtained by ensuring pathological cases exist in training.

Instead of performing a coupled high-dimensional optimization for all points simultaneously, local search within a predefined range $\{-\tau, \tau\}$ is performed for each vertex to find the best displacement along the normal, $\mathbf{v}_i \leftarrow \mathbf{v}_i + d_i \mathbf{n}_i$:

$$d_i = \arg \max_{-\tau \leq d \leq \tau} f(\mathbf{v}_i + d\mathbf{n}_i | V) \tag{8.9}$$

The resulting shape is projected onto the shape-space and surface normals are updated. This interleaved displacement and regularization process is iterated several times. In latter iterations, $\tau$ is reduced, and the shape is allowed to vary from the span $(S)$. In these iterations, instead of regularizing by projecting into the shape space, a simple mesh smoothing is used to regularize the displaced mesh (Ling et al., 2008).

## 8.3.3 MULTILEVEL SET FOR JOINT ORGAN SEGMENTATION REFINEMENT

Although the learning-based segmentation subsystem already provides good individual organ segmentation results, they usually exhibit small overlaps between adjacent organ boundaries or gaps where the true organ boundaries coincide. However, the mesh representation is not well suited to detect and remove local overlaps and gaps. The level set implicit representation, on the other hand, is amenable to such a task. With the ultimate target of finding the correct separating boundary between two or multiple neighboring organs in mind, we further propose a multilevel set-based joint segmentation approach, which not only refines the segmentation boundary accuracy, removes local overlaps and gaps, but also finds the true separating boundary given that enough image information is available. In particular, we propose an energy function consisting of a series of energy terms that encourages data fidelity, smooth boundary, overlap removal, gap filling, and proximity to the initial segmentation.

### 8.3.3.1 From mesh to level set function

We initialize signed distance functions $\phi_i^0 : \mathbb{R}^3 \Rightarrow \mathbb{R}$ from each of the result meshes $\hat{\mathcal{N}}_i$, by employing a fast mesh voxelization algorithm. The boundary information then is encoded implicitly in the zero crossings of the $\phi_i$, that is, $\hat{\mathcal{N}}_i := \{\mathbf{x}|\phi_i^0(\mathbf{x}) = 0, |\nabla\phi^0| = 1\}$, with $|\nabla\phi^0| = 1$ denoting the so-called distance-property, and $\phi > 0$ inside the object and $< 0$ outside, see Chan and Vese (2001) and the references therein. Furthermore, we employ a narrow-banded level set scheme, which maintains the distance-property in a small narrow-band of $\pm 2$ voxels from the zero crossing. In addition to the distance functions, we still keep the mesh vertex points and track them along with the evolving zero crossing as described in Kohlberger et al. (2009), since they provide point-wise correspondences to the mean shape of the PCA model employed in the preceding learned-based boundary detection step.

### 8.3.3.2 Data fidelity

For each organ, this refining level set segmentation is realized by employing gradient descent iteration to converge to a minimum of an associated energy functional $E(\phi_i)$, given the initial distance maps as starting points, see Chan and Vese (2001) and the references therein. As a data-fidelity energy term, we here employ

$$E_p(\phi) = -\alpha \int_\Omega H(\phi) \log p_{in}(\mathbf{V}(\mathbf{x})|\phi) + (1 - H(\phi)) \log p_{out}(\mathbf{V}(\mathbf{x})|\phi) \, d\mathbf{x}$$

with $H$ denoting the Heaviside step function, $\mathbf{V}(\mathbf{x})$ being the voxel intensity at $\mathbf{x}$, and $p_{in/out}$ referring to nonparametric probability estimates of the intensities inside and outside, respectively, of the current segment $\phi$ using a Parzen density estimator with a Gaussian kernel (see Cremers et al. (2007) for further details), and $\alpha$ being a constant weight.

### 8.3.3.3 Boundary smoothness

In order to add robustness against noisy data, we incorporate the boundary smoothness regularization term

$$E_c(\phi) = \int_\Omega \gamma_{l(\mathbf{x})} |\nabla H(\phi)| \, d\mathbf{x}, \quad \text{with} \quad l(\mathbf{x}) = \arg \min_{i=1,\ldots,N} \|\mathbf{x} - v_i\|_{\mathcal{L}_2} \tag{8.10}$$

which employs a weight $\gamma_{l(\mathbf{x})}$ that varies with the location on the boundary. The latter is realized by assigning fixed weights $\{\gamma_i\}$ to each of the correspondence points $\{v_i\}$ on the mean shape of the PCA shape model, which then are tracked along during the zero-crossing evolution; see Kohlberger et al. (2009) for more details.

### 8.3.3.4 Disjoint constraint to remove overlaps

Assume that two adjacent organs A and B imperfectly overlap each other to a certain degree; see, for example, Figure 8.4(a). By representing these two surfaces using level set functions $\phi_A$ and $\phi_B$, locations $\tilde{\mathbf{x}}$ inside the overlapping region are exclusively characterized by $\phi_A(\tilde{\mathbf{x}}) > 0$ and $\phi_B(\tilde{\mathbf{x}}) > 0$, and thus provide a much simpler overlap indicator compared to any other based on an explicit shape representation. Subsequently, additional energy terms which explicitly penalize overlaps usually are of the form

$$E_o(\phi_A, \phi_B) := \int_\Omega H(\phi_A(\mathbf{x})) \, H(\phi_B(\tilde{\mathbf{x}})) \, \phi_B(\tilde{\mathbf{x}}) \, d\mathbf{x} \tag{8.11}$$

where the first product in the integrand is unequal zero only inside the overlap regions; see Figure 8.4(b). In addition to similar terms such as proposed in Mansouri et al. (2006), we propose to also multiply with the second distance function $\phi_B$ which makes $E_o$ smoother at the presence of small overlaps and thereby decreases oscillations during gradient descent. The corresponding energy gradient reads (Paragios, 2002):

$$\frac{\partial \phi_A}{\partial t} = -\frac{\partial E_o}{\partial \phi_A} = -\delta_\epsilon(\phi_A) \, H_\epsilon(\phi_B(\tilde{\mathbf{x}})) \, \phi_B(\tilde{\mathbf{x}}) \tag{8.12}$$

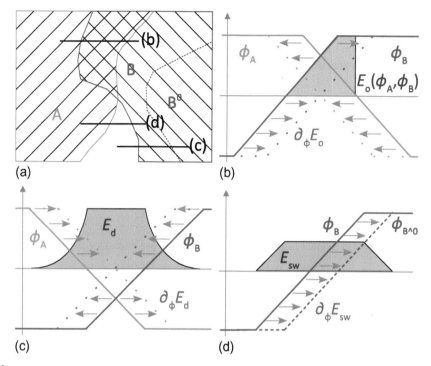

**FIGURE 8.4**

Imposing geometric constraints to remove overlaps (b) and gaps (c) from an existing segmentation, while controlling the deviation from a given shape locally (d). Note that (b)–(d) are 1D-cuts along the black lines in (a).

### 8.3.3.5 Local proximity constraint to fill gaps

With regard to removing erroneous gaps between adjacent segmentation boundaries, we add the following energy to the total energy functional:

$$E_d(\phi_A, \phi_B) := \frac{1}{2} \int_\Omega \beta_{l(\mathbf{x})} (\phi_A(\mathbf{x}) + \phi_B(\tilde{\mathbf{x}}) + D)^2 \, d\mathbf{x} \qquad (8.13)$$

with $D = 0$ for the time being, and $\{\beta_i\}$ being correspondence points-bound weights with $\beta_i = 0$ at points where no boundary coincidence ought to be enforced, and $\beta_i > 0$ at locations where boundaries of A and B ought to coincide. As shown in Figure 8.4(c), $\phi_A$ and $\phi_B$ cancel each other out if their zero crossings coincide and thus the integrand becomes zero. As an extension, one can enforce the two boundaries to not touch but stay in a predefined distance $D > 0$ from each other. The gradient descend partial differential equation (PDE) of $E_d$ w.r.t. $\phi_A$ reads:

$$\frac{\partial \phi_A}{\partial t} = -\frac{\partial E_d}{\partial \phi_A} = -\beta_{l(\mathbf{x})} (\phi_A(\mathbf{x}) + \phi_B(\tilde{\mathbf{x}}) + D) \qquad (8.14)$$

which shows that $\phi_A$ increases at locations where $\phi_B < D$, and thus expands its representing boundary, and decreases at locations where $\phi_B > D$, that is, shrinks the boundary.

### 8.3.3.6 *Template constraint*

Finally, we add a third geometric term, which ensures that the level set result is sufficiently similar to a learning-based contour, that is, the refined boundary is sought only in the vicinity of its initialization. To that end, we use the term

$$E_{sw}(\phi, \phi^0) := \frac{1}{2} \int_\Omega \omega_{l(\mathbf{x})}^{in} \, H(\phi_P(\mathbf{x}) - \phi(\mathbf{x})) + \omega_{l(\mathbf{x})}^{out} \, H\left(\phi(\mathbf{x}) - \phi^0(\mathbf{x})\right) \, d\mathbf{x} \tag{8.15}$$

which is an extension of the approach shown in Rousson and Paragios (2002) in the sense that it applies region-specific weights $\{\omega_i^{in}\}$ to the shape dissimilarity measure between the current $\phi$ and the template shape $\phi^0$ (which is the initial one here), as well as applying different weights for deviations outside or inside of the template shape. See Figure 8.5 for a local weight map. Technically, note that the first term of the integrand is nonzero only if the zero-crossing of $\phi$ resides inside the zero-crossing of $\phi^0$, that is the current boundary is smaller than the template shape boundary; see Figure 8.4(d). Vice versa, the second term measures local expansions relative to the template shape boundary, by becoming nonzero only where $\phi(\mathbf{x}) > \phi^0(\mathbf{x})$.

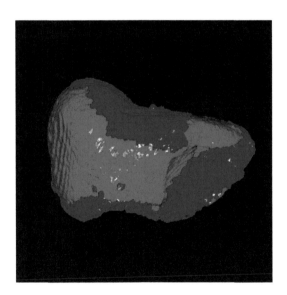

**FIGURE 8.5**

Visualization of the manually set local weights $\{\omega_i^{out}\}$ of the outward template constraint (red: 50, blue: 0.2) for the liver. These weights are bound to point-based shape correspondences in relation to a fixed model shape and thereby allow for a region-specific control over the different geometrical constraints during the level set segmentation.

The corresponding energy gradient clearly shows that the proposed energy term has the desired effect:

$$\frac{\partial \phi}{\partial t} = -\frac{\partial E_{sw}}{\partial \phi} = \omega_{l(\mathbf{x})}^{in} \delta_\epsilon \left( \phi^0(\mathbf{x}) - \phi(\mathbf{x}) \right) - \omega_{l(\mathbf{x})}^{out} \delta_\epsilon \left( \phi(\mathbf{x}) - \phi^0(\mathbf{x}) \right) \tag{8.16}$$

that is, increasing $\phi$ at locations where $\phi < \phi^0$, and decreasing it in the opposite case.

### 8.3.3.7 Interleaved multi-energy minimization

Finally, all of the proposed energy terms are combined into energy minimizations for each organ $\{\phi_i\}$:

$$\min_{\phi_i} E_p(\phi_i) + E_c(\phi_i) + \sum_{j \in \mathcal{A}_i(j)} E_o(\phi, \phi_j) + \sum_{j \in \mathcal{P}_i(j)} E_d(\phi, \phi_j) + E_{sw}(\phi_i, \phi_i^0) \tag{8.17}$$

which are mutually coupled by the disjoint and proximity terms ($\mathcal{A}_i$: indices of organs adjacent to organ $i$, $\mathcal{P}_i$: indices of organs with which organ $i$ shares a mutual proximity constraint). Consequently, minimizers $\{\tilde{\phi}_i\}$ of these individual energies depend on each other. We leverage interleaved gradient descent iterations to yield the desired segmentation improvements in practice. Specifically, we carry out a descent along the negative gradients of the $N$ per-organ energies in lockstep, while using the segmentation results $\{\phi_i^{t-1}\}$ of the previous joint iteration to compute the coupled energy gradients $\partial E_i(\phi_i; \{\phi_i^{t-1}\})/\partial \phi_i$. The descent for a particular energy is terminated if a given maximum number of iterations has been reached, or if the maximum norm of its gradient falls below a given threshold, that is, the segmentation boundary $\phi_i$ changes less than a chosen tolerance (see Figure 8.6).

### 8.3.3.8 Fast implementation

We also implemented an interleaved binary Split Bregman method (Goldstein et al., 2010) to tackle the multilevel set problem for fast computation. It casts Eq. (8.17) as a totally convex optimization problem and uses the Split Bregman method to find the optimal solution. It has been demonstrated in Goldstein et al. (2010) that this method allows one to use much larger time steps than the conventional multilevel set methods that are based on gradient descent, which implies that less iteration number and computation time is needed for obtaining comparable segmentation results. Our evaluation results show that the Split Bregman method is about 30% times faster than the gradient descent method, while they yield comparable high-quality segmentation.

---

## 8.4 EXPERIMENTAL RESULTS

We collected a challenging database of hundreds of CT scans, featuring different variations. They are from different clinical sites and acquired by CT machines manufactured by Siemens and other vendors. With a median image resolution about 1/1/2 mm ($x/y/z$), they contain different body regions: pure head and neck, thorax, runoff, lower abdomen, and combinations of these body regions, and might carry contract agents at different contrast phases. Finally, different pathologies, mostly oncological such as liver tumors, lung nodules, prostate cancer, etc., are present in the database.

The annotations are done separately for different organs as not all scans contain all organs. Table 8.2 lists the number of annotations we amassed for organs, respectively. Over 10 randomly selected cases are annotated by at least 2 experts in order to measure the inter-user variability.

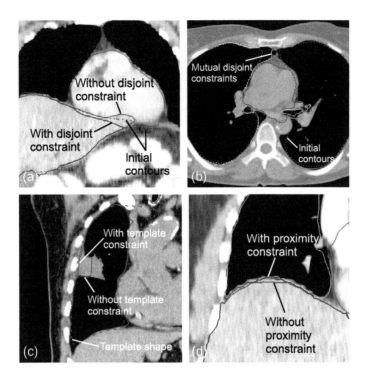

**FIGURE 8.6**

Effect of the different proposed geometric constraints. Whereas the disjoint constraint (a) + (b) can be used to remove overlaps between initial segmentations, the template constraint (c) can bind the level set zero-crossing to the initial one in a location-specific manner. With the proximity constraint (d), coincidence of shared boundaries can be imposed locally.

We measure the segmentation accuracy by the following two commonly used metrics: average symmetric absolute surface distance (ASD) and dice similarity coefficient (DSC).

- *Average symmetric ASD.* Given two surface meshes $\mathcal{X}$ and $\mathcal{Y}$ and the distance $d(\mathbf{x} \longrightarrow \mathcal{Y})$ as the smallest distance of node $\mathbf{x}$ in mesh $\mathcal{X}$ to mesh $\mathcal{Y}$ in a Euclidean space, imposing the comparison direction $\mathcal{X} \longrightarrow \mathcal{Y}$, the ASD is defined as

$$\text{ASD} = \frac{1}{2}(d_{\text{mean}}(\mathcal{X} \longrightarrow \mathcal{Y}) + d_{\text{mean}}(\mathcal{Y} \longrightarrow \mathcal{X})), \tag{8.18}$$

$$d_{\text{mean}}(\mathcal{X} \longrightarrow \mathcal{Y}) = \frac{1}{\| \mathcal{X} \|} \sum d(\mathbf{x} \longrightarrow \mathcal{Y}) \tag{8.19}$$

where $\| \mathcal{X} \|$ is the cardinality of $\mathcal{X}$. The smaller the distance ASD is, the more accurate the segmentation is.
- *DSC.* On a voxel-by-voxel basis, one can define four classes: true positives (TP) are voxels inside the object of interest in automatic and reference segmentation; true negatives (TN) are voxels

labeled as background in both segmentations; false positives (FP) are voxels detected as foreground but in reality belonging to the background (over-segmentation); and false negatives (FN) are voxels belonging to the object of interest that are spuriously classified as background (under-segmentation). The DSC is well established for segmentation validation purposes:

$$DSC = \frac{2 \times TP}{2 \times TP + FP + FN} \tag{8.20}$$

The value of DSC lies in the range of [0, 1]. The higher the DSC is, the more accurate the segmentation is.

Our system was implemented in C++ and compiled using Visual Studio 2012. In the experiments following, timing results are reported for an Intel Xeon 64-bit machine running Windows Server 2008 (Intel Xeon CPU X5650 @2.67 GHZ) with 24 threads unless otherwise specified. Most of our source code runs in multi-threads for speedup. No graphics processor unit (GPU) computation was involved.

The overall detection pipeline is shown in Figure 8.2. We first present experimental details of the learning-based approach for pose detection and segmentation of a single organ and then move onto the level-set approach for joint organ segmentation refinement. In CT organ segmentation, we detected five landmarks of skull base, liver top, trachea, pubic symphysis, and aortic root and use them to narrow the search range of the position detection for organs.

## 8.4.1 RESULTS OF LEARNING-BASED APPROACH FOR A SINGLE ORGAN

Figure 8.7 shows the detailed scheme for individual organ pose estimation and segmentation using the liver as a working example. MSL is first applied at 3 mm resolution to detect position candidates, then position-orientation candidates, and finally position-orientation-scale candidates (e.g., the candidates for rigid bounding box). After that, the PCA detector is invoked to detect the candidates for the top three PCA coefficients for the liver shape. Boundary detectors coupled with regularization are then

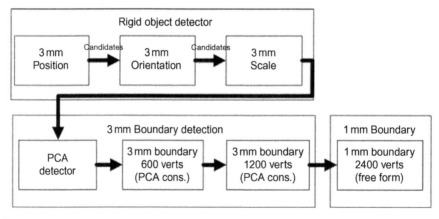

**FIGURE 8.7**

The subnetwork for learning-based liver segmentation from CT scans.

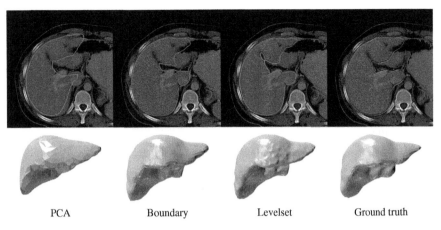

          PCA                   Boundary                  Levelset               Ground truth

**FIGURE 8.8**

One sample result of liver segmentation after PCA detector, learning-based boundary deformation, and level set refinement, respectively.

applied to refine the liver shape three times in a hierarchical manner from 3 to 1 mm and from a coarse mesh of 600 vertexes, a refined mesh of 1200 vertexes to a final mesh of 2400 vertexes. The first two times the PCA shape projection is used as regularization and the third time a simple mesh smoothing as regularization. All detectors are learned using PBT.

Using 433 datasets with liver annotations, we performed a fourfold cross-validation. Table 8.1 lists the segmentation accuracy of different stages. It is evident that the accuracy increases as the stage proceeds. Figure 8.8 shows the segmentation results obtained at different stages. Our experimental results on other organs exhibit similar improving trends as the stage proceeds.

**Table 8.1 The CT Multi-Organ Segmentation Results (Fourfold Cross Validation) in terms of Symmetric Mesh-Mesh Distance and DSC**

|  | Mean | Q50 | Q80 | No. of Cases |
|---|---|---|---|---|
| *ASD* | | | | |
| Liver (3 mm, 600 vert.) | $2.60 \pm 1.46$ | 2.23 | 2.83 | 433 |
| Liver (3 mm, 1200 vert.) | $2.35 \pm 1.35$ | 2.04 | 2.59 | |
| Liver (1 mm, 2400 vert.) | $1.70 \pm 1.34$ | 1.34 | 1.96 | |
| *DSC* | | | | |
| Liver (3 mm, 600 vert.) | $0.93 \pm 0.03$ | 0.94 | 0.96 | 433 |
| Liver (3 mm, 1200 vert.) | $0.94 \pm 0.03$ | 0.95 | 0.97 | |
| Liver (1 mm, 2400 vert.) | $0.95 \pm 0.03$ | 0.96 | 0.97 | |

## 8.4.2 RESULTS OF MULTILEVEL SET APPROACH FOR MULTIPLE ORGANS

We benchmarked the overall system on manually annotated datasets in order to study the overall accuracy improvement yielded by multilevel set refinement. The parameters are tuned empirically for best performance. After the joint gradient descent had converged w.r.t. each energy of the level set segmentation, the final meshes were extracted from the level set maps via the marching cube algorithm.

Test sets for the different organs (excluding heart) are listed in Table 8.2. For heart results, refer to Zheng et al. 2010. Fourfold cross-validation is performed. From the results in Tables 8.2 and 8.3, we observe the following:

- The proposed segmentation system yields the segmentation accuracies ranging from 1.06 mm (0.97) for left lung, 2.89 mm (0.94) for liver, to 2.84 mm (0.76) for prostate in terms of ASD (DSC). They are fairly close to inter-user variability.
- The proposed multilevel set segmentation brings improvements for almost all organs except liver. For right lung, the improvement is very noticeable, reducing the ASD from 2.09 to 1.17 mm. When we inspect the liver results, we note that the multilevel set part in fact does a fairly good job to resolve the overlapping between liver and its neighboring organs, but it has a tendency to oversegment into the nearby soft tissues such as fat under skin, while the learning-based part does not. For rectum, we skip the level-set refinement part as it does not further improve the segmentation performance.

**Table 8.2 The CT Multi-Organ Segmentation Results (Fourfold Cross Validation) in terms of Symmetric Mesh-To-Mesh Distance**

| ASD (mm) | Mean | Q50 | Q80 | Inter-User | No. of Cases |
|---|---|---|---|---|---|
| Liver, learning | 1.70 ± 1.34 | 1.34 | 1.96 | | 433 |
| Liver, level set | 2.19 ± 1.20 | 1.89 | 2.45 | 2.23 ± 0.84 | |
| Spleen, learning | 2.38 ± 5.94 | 1.76 | 2.19 | | 311 |
| Spleen, level set | 2.37 ± 6.94 | 1.59 | 1.91 | 1.99 ± 0.57 | |
| L. lung, learning | 1.97 ± 0.45 | 1.91 | 2.19 | | 203 |
| L. lung, level set | 1.06 ± 0.18 | 1.03 | 1.16 | 1.78 ± 0.66 | |
| R. lung, learning | 2.09 ± 0.63 | 1.91 | 2.30 | | 214 |
| R. lung, level set | 1.17 ± 0.41 | 1.03 | 1.27 | 1.61 ± 0.43 | |
| L. kidney, learning | 1.51 ± 0.42 | 1.45 | 1.79 | | 402 |
| L. kidney, level set | 1.36 ± 0.49 | 1.28 | 0.62 | 1.50 ± 0.33 | |
| R. kidney, learning | 1.56 ± 0.41 | 1.52 | 1.83 | | 356 |
| R. kidney, level set | 1.43 ± 0.52 | 1.37 | 1.78 | 1.67 ± 0.31 | |
| Prostate, learning | 2.87 ± 1.60 | 2.47 | 3.61 | | 217 |
| Prostate, level set | 2.84 ± 1.31 | 2.49 | 3.32 | 3.10 ± 0.49 | |
| Bladder, learning | 2.39 ± 2.07 | 1.88 | 2.79 | | 304 |
| Bladder, level set | 2.39 ± 2.02 | 1.92 | 2.78 | 1.85 ± 0.30 | |
| Rectum, learning | 4.25 ± 1.94 | 3.74 | 5.12 | 3.27 ± 1.87 | 160 |

Note: The median image resolution about 1/1/2 mm (x/y/z).

**Table 8.3 The CT Multi-Organ Segmentation Results (Fourfold Cross Validation) in terms of DSC**

| DSC | Mean | Q50 | Q80 | Inter-User | No. of Cases |
|---|---|---|---|---|---|
| Liver, learning | 0.95 ± 0.03 | 0.96 | 0.97 | | 433 |
| Liver, level set | 0.94 ± 0.03 | 0.95 | 0.97 | 0.94 ± 0.02 | |
| Spleen, learning | 0.89 ± 0.06 | 0.91 | 0.93 | | 311 |
| Spleen, level set | 0.90 ± 0.06 | 0.91 | 0.93 | 0.90 ± 0.03 | |
| L. lung, learning | 0.94 ± 0.01 | 0.95 | 0.97 | | 203 |
| L. lung, level set | 0.97 ± 0.01 | 0.97 | 0.97 | 0.95 ± 0.01 | |
| R. lung, learning | 0.92 ± 0.03 | 0.92 | 0.94 | | 214 |
| R. lung, level set | 0.97 ± 0.01 | 0.97 | 0.97 | 0.97 ± 0.02 | |
| L. kidney, learning | 0.92 ± 0.03 | 0.93 | 0.96 | | 402 |
| L. kidney, level set | 0.93 ± 0.03 | 0.94 | 0.97 | 0.92 ± 0.02 | |
| R. kidney, learning | 0.92 ± 0.03 | 0.92 | 0.94 | | 356 |
| R. kidney, level set | 0.93 ± 0.03 | 0.93 | 0.95 | 0.92 ± 0.02 | |
| Prostate, learning | 0.76 ± 0.12 | 0.79 | 0.86 | | 217 |
| Prostate, level set | 0.76 ± 0.12 | 0.79 | 0.86 | 0.73 ± 0.06 | |
| Bladder, learning | 0.89 ± 0.06 | 0.91 | 0.94 | | 304 |
| Bladder, level set | 0.87 ± 0.10 | 0.89 | 0.94 | 0.89 ± 0.02 | |
| Rectum, learning | 0.72 ± 0.11 | 0.75 | 0.86 | 0.78 ± 0.11 | 160 |

- There are still segmentation outliers as indicated by the large standard deviation values for, say, spleen and the fact that median ASD is always smaller than the mean for all organs. In general, the standard deviation for automatic segmentation is larger than that of the inter-user variability. However, overall the number of outliers is low, as the 80% is quite close to the median.

The average run time for the full detection pipeline is about 80 s, which includes about 60 s for detecting and segmenting 10 organs individually (roughly 10 s per organ) and about 20 s for the fast implementation of multilevel set based on the Split Bregman method. The whole pipeline with the gradient descent-based level set implementation takes an extra 20 s, totaling about 100 s.

## 8.5 CONCLUSIONS

We have presented a fully automatic framework for multiple organ segmentation along with multiple landmark detection from a 3D body scan. We have mitigated the complexity of this problem by breaking it into multiple simple tasks, thereby leading to a hierarchical solution, and utilized a probabilistic formulation to mathematically describe the statistical relationships among landmark, organs, and 3D images. In particular, we have depicted a series of machine learning-based methods to take advantage of anatomical context manifested in the human body and exemplified by annotated datasets when addressing simple tasks: MSL and boundary deformation for individual organ pose detection and segmentation, multilevel set method for joint organ segmentation refinement and overlap removal. We have experimented with the whole solution on a database of over hundreds of CT scans and achieved a segmentation accuracy close to the inter-user variability while running fast, taking about 80 s for parsing a CT scan.

The current solution can be further improved for more efficiency and effectiveness and better addressing clinical challenges, following the research directions along better handling of severe pathologies and extreme conditions, more efficient computation, more effective discriminative learning approaches, and using a larger database and fewer annotations.

## NOTE

a. This can also be argued from a joint optimization perspective. In later sections, we do adopt the viewpoint of optimization as needed.

## REFERENCES

Chan, T.F., Vese, L.A., 2001. Active contours without edges. IEEE Trans. Image Process. 10 (2), 266-277.

Cootes, T.F., Taylor, C.J., Cooper, D.H., Graham, J., et al., 1995. Active shape models—their training and application. Comput. Vis. Image Underst. 61 (1), 38-59.

Costa, M., Delingette, H., Novellas, S., Ayache, N., 2007. Automatic segmentation of bladder and prostate using coupled 3D deformable models. In: Medical Image Computing and Computer-Assisted Intervention—MICCAI 2007. Springer, Heidelberg, pp. 252-260.

Cremers, D., Rousson, M., Deriche, R., 2007. A review of statistical approaches to level set segmentation: integrating color, texture, motion and shape. Int. J. Comput. Vis. 72 (2), 195-215.

Fan, S.T., Lo, C.M., Liu, C.L., Yong, B.H., Chan, J.K.F., Ng, I.L., 2000. Safety of donors in live donor liver transplantation using right lobe grafts. Arch. Surg. 135, 336-340.

Fenchel, M., Thesen, S., Schilling, A., 2008. Automatic labeling of anatomical structures in MR fastview images using a statistical atlas. In: Medical Image Computing and Computer-Assisted Intervention—MICCAI 2008. Springer, Heidelberg, pp. 576-584.

Goldstein, T., Bresson, X., Osher, S., 2010. Geometric applications of the split Bregman method: segmentation and surface reconstruction. J. Sci. Comput. 45 (1-3), 272-293.

Kaus, M.R., Brock, K.K., Pekar, V., Dawson, L.A., Nichol, A.M., Jaffray, D.A., 2007. Assessment of a model-based deformable image registration approach for radiation therapy planning. Int. J. Radiat. Oncol. Biol. Phys. 68 (2), 572-580.

Kobatake, H., 2007. Future CAD in multi-dimensional medical images: project on multi-organ, multi-disease CAD system. Comput. Med. Imaging Graph. 31 (4/5), 258-266.

Kohlberger, T., Uzunbaş, M.G., Alvino, C., Kadir, T., Slosman, D.O., Funka-Lea, G., 2009. Organ segmentation with level sets using local shape and appearance priors. In: Medical Image Computing and Computer-Assisted Intervention—MICCAI 2009. Springer, Heidelberg, pp. 34-42.

Kohlberger, T., Sofka, M., Zhang, J., Birkbeck, N., Wetzl, J., Kaftan, J., Declerck, J., Zhou, S., 2011. Automatic multi-organ segmentation using learning-based segmentation and level set optimization. In: Medical Image Computing and Computer-Assisted Intervention—MICCAI 2011. Springer, Heidelberg, pp. 338-345.

Ling, H., Zhou, S.K., Zheng, Y., Georgescu, B., Suehling, M., Comaniciu, D., 2008. Hierarchical, learning-based automatic liver segmentation. In: Proc. IEEE Conference on Computer Vision and Pattern Recognition, pp. 1-8.

Linguraru, M., Pura, J., Chowdhury, A., Summers, R., 2010. Multi-organ segmentation from multi-phase abdominal CT via 4D graphs using enhancement, shape and location optimization. In: Medical Image Computing and Computer-Assisted Intervention—MICCAI 2010. Springer, Heidelberg, pp. 89-96.

Lu, C., Chelikani, S., Chen, Z., Papademetris, X., Staib, L.H., Duncan, J.S., 2010. Integrated segmentation and nonrigid registration for application in prostate image-guided radiotherapy. In: Medical Image Computing and Computer-Assisted Intervention—MICCAI 2010. Springer, Heidelberg, pp. 53-60.

Lu, C., Zheng, Y., Birkbeck, N., Zhang, J., Kohlberger, T., Tietjen, C., Boettger, T., Duncan, J., Zhou, S., 2012. Precise segmentation of multiple organs in CT volumes using learning-based approach and information theory. In: Medical Image Computing and Computer-Assisted Intervention—MICCAI 2012. Springer, Heidelberg, pp. 462-469.

Mansouri, A.R., Mitiche, A., Vázquez, C., 2006. Multiregion competition: a level set extension of region competition to multiple region image partitioning. Comput. Vis. Image Underst. 101 (3), 137-150.

Myronenko, A., Song, X., 2010. Point set registration: coherent point drift. IEEE Trans. Pattern Anal. Mach. Intell. 32 (12), 2262-2275.

Okada, T., Yokota, K., Hori, M., Nakamoto, M., Nakamura, H., Sato, Y., 2008. Construction of hierarchical multi-organ statistical atlases and their application to multi-organ segmentation from CT images. In: Medical Image Computing and Computer-Assisted Intervention—MICCAI 2008. Springer, Heidelberg, pp. 502-509.

Paragios, N., 2002. A variational approach for the segmentation of the left ventricle in cardiac image analysis. Int. J. Comput. Vis. 50 (3), 345-362.

Park, H., Bland, P.H., Meyer, C.R., 2003. Construction of an abdominal probabilistic atlas and its application in segmentation. IEEE Trans. Med. Imaging 22 (4), 483-492.

Qatarneh, S.M., Noz, M.E., Hyoeynmaa, S., Maguire Jr., G.Q., Kramer, E.L., Crafoord, J., 2003. Evaluation of a segmentation procedure to delineate organs for use in construction of a radiation therapy planning atlas. Int. J. Med. Inform. 69 (1), 39-55.

Rousson, M., Paragios, N., 2002. Shape priors for level set representations. In: ECCV 2002. Springer, Heidelberg, pp. 78-92.

Shen, D., Davatzikos, C., 2000. An adaptive-focus deformable model using statistical and geometric information. IEEE Trans. Pattern Anal. Mach. Intell. 22 (8), 906-913.

Shimizu, A., Ohno, R., Ikegami, T., Kobatake, H., Nawano, S., Smutek, D., 2007. Segmentation of multiple organs in non-contrast 3D abdominal CT images. Int. J. Comput. Assist. Radiol. Surg. 2 (3), 135-142.

Sofka, M., Ralovich, K., Birkbeck, N., Zhang, J., Zhou, S.K., 2011. Integrated detection network (IDN) for pose and boundary estimation in medical images. In: 2011 IEEE International Symposium on Biomedical Imaging: From Nano to Macro, pp. 294-299.

Sofka, M., Zhang, J., Good, S., Zhou, S.K., Comaniciu, D., 2014. Automatic detection and measurement of structures in fetal head ultrasound volumes using sequential estimation and integrated detection network (IDN). IEEE Trans. Med. Imaging 33 (5), 1054-1070.

Suzuki, M., Linguraru, M., Okada, K., 2012. Multi-organ segmentation with missing organs in abdominal CT images. In: Medical Image Computing and Computer-Assisted Intervention—MICCAI 2012. Springer, Heidelberg, pp. 418-425.

Tsushima, Y., Endo, K., 2000. Spleen enlargement in patients with nonalcoholic fatty liver. Dig. Dis. Sci. 45 (1), 196-200.

Tu, Z., 2005. Probabilistic boosting-tree: learning discriminative models for classification, recognition, and clustering. In: IEEE Int. Conf. Comput. Vis., pp. 1589-1596.

Uzunbaş, M.G., Chen, C., Zhang, S., Pohl, K.M., Li, K., Metaxas, D., 2013. Collaborative multi organ segmentation by integrating deformable and graphical models. In: Medical Image Computing and Computer-Assisted Intervention—MICCAI 2013. Springer, Heidelberg, pp. 157-164.

Wolz, R., Chu, C., Misawa, K., Mori, K., Rueckert, D., 2012. Multi-organ abdominal CT segmentation using hierarchically weighted subject-specific atlases. In: Medical Image Computing and Computer-Assisted Intervention—MICCAI 2012. Springer, Heidelberg, pp. 10-17.

Yan, P., Shen, W., Kassim, A., Shah, M., 2005. Segmentation of neighboring organs in medical image with model competition. In: Medical Image Computing and Computer-Assisted Intervention—MICCAI 2005. Springer, Heidelberg, pp. 270-277.

Yang, J., Staib, L.H., Duncan, J.S., 2004. Neighbor-constrained segmentation with level set based 3-D deformable models. IEEE Trans. Med. Imaging 23 (8), 940-948.

Zhang, S., Zhan, Y., Dewan, M., Huang, J., Metaxas, D.N., Zhou, X.S., 2012. Towards robust and effective shape modeling: sparse shape composition. Med. Image Anal. 16 (1), 265-277.

Zhang, S., Zhan, Y., Cui, X., Gao, M., Huang, J., Metaxas, D., 2013. 3D anatomical shape atlas construction using mesh quality preserved deformable models. Comput. Vis. Image Underst. 117 (9), 1061-1071.

Zheng, Y., Barbu, A., Georgescu, B., Scheuering, M., Comaniciu, D., 2007. Fast automatic heart chamber segmentation from 3D CT data using marginal space learning and steerable features. In: IEEE Int. Conf. Comput. Vis., pp. 1-8.

Zheng, Y., Barbu, A., Georgescu, B., Scheuering, M., Comaniciu, D., 2008. Four-chamber heart modeling and automatic segmentation for 3-D cardiac CT volumes using marginal space learning and steerable features. IEEE Trans. Med. Imaging 27 (11), 1668-1681.

Zheng, Y., Georgescu, B., Ling, H., Zhou, S., Scheuering, M., Comaniciu, D., 2009a. Constrained marginal space learning for efficient 3D anatomical structure detection in medical images. In: IEEE Conference on Computer Vision and Pattern Recognition, pp. 194-201.

Zheng, Y., Lu, X., Georgescu, B., Littmann, A., Mueller, E., Comaniciu, D., 2009b, Robust object detection using marginal space learning and ranking-based multi-detector aggregation: application to left ventricle detection in 2D MRI images. In: IEEE Conference on Computer Vision and Pattern Recognition, pp. 1343-1350.

Zheng, Y., Vega-Higuera, F., Zhou, S.K., Comaniciu, D., 2010, "Fast and Automatic Heart Isolation in 3D CT Volumes: Optimal Shape Initialization," Proc. Int'l Workshop on Machine Learning in Medical Imaging.

Zhou, Y., Bai, J., 2007. Multiple abdominal organ segmentation: an atlas-based fuzzy connectedness approach. IEEE Trans. Inf. Technol. Biomed. 11 (3), 348-352.

# LOGISMOS: A FAMILY OF GRAPH-BASED OPTIMAL IMAGE SEGMENTATION METHODS

# 9

**I. Oguz, H. Bogunović, S. Kashyap, M.D. Abràmoff, X. Wu and M. Sonka**

*Iowa Institute for Biomedical Imaging, University of Iowa, Iowa City, IA, USA*

## CHAPTER OUTLINE

S. Kevin Zhou (Ed): Medical Image Recognition, Segmentation and Parsing. http://dx.doi.org/10.1016/B978-0-12-802581-9.00009-3

## 9.1 INTRODUCTION

The task of optimally identifying three-dimensional surfaces representing object boundaries, surfaces over time (4D), or surfaces in higher-dimensional applications is important in segmentation and quantitative analysis of volumetric images. In addition to single standalone surfaces, many surfaces that need to be identified appear in mutual interactions. These surfaces are *coupled* in a way that their topology and relative positions are usually known and appear in some specific relationship. Clearly, incorporating such surface-interrelation information into the segmentation task with some precision will further improve its accuracy and robustness. Simultaneous segmentation of coupled surfaces in volumetric images is an underexplored topic, especially when more than two are involved.

A polynomial-time method exists for $nD$ ($n \geq 3$) optimal hypersurface detection with hard smoothness constraints, making globally optimal surface segmentation in volumetric images practical (Wu and Chen, 2002; Li et al., 2004a). By modeling the problem with a weighted *geometric graph*, the method transforms the task into computing a minimum $s\text{-}t$ cut in a directed graph, which simplifies the problem and consequently solves it in polynomial time. Note that the general method of graph cut optimization is used as the underlying optimization method in the layered optimal graph image segmentation of multiple objects and surfaces (LOGISMOS) framework, which accounts for a possibly confusing terminological similarity between direct graph cut segmentation (Boykov and Jolly, 2000, 2001; Boykov and Kolmogorov, 2004) and the LOGISMOS optimal surface segmentation methods reported here. Nevertheless, the two approaches are principally different (Sonka et al., 2015).

## 9.2 LAYERED OPTIMAL GRAPH IMAGE SEGMENTATION OF MULTIPLE OBJECTS AND SURFACES

The *LOGISMOS* optimal surface segmentation facilitates simultaneous detection of $k$ ($k \geq 2$) interrelated surfaces by modeling the $nD$ problem in an $(n + 1)$-D geometric graph (or simply *graph*), where the $(n + 1)$th dimension holds special arcs that control interrelations between pairs of sought surfaces (Li et al., 2004b, 2006; Yin et al., 2010). The apparently daunting combinatorial explosion in computation is avoided by employing $s\text{-}t$ cut optimizer applied to a properly transformed geometric graph constructed as described previously. As such, the difference between the direct graph-cut approaches (Boykov and Jolly, 2000, 2001; Boykov and Kolmogorov, 2004) and the LOGISMOS methods is in the graph construction and use of mutual contextual constraints while utilizing the generally identical graph optimizer.

Like other graph-search-based segmentation methods, the LOGISMOS approach first builds a graph that contains information about the boundaries of the target objects in the input images and then searches the graph for a segmentation solution. However, to make this approach work effectively for segmentation problems, several key issues must be handled: (i) how to obtain relevant information about the target object boundaries; (ii) how to capture such information in a graph; and (iii) how to search the graph for the *optimal* surfaces of the target objects. The general approach consists of five main steps, which constitute a high-level solution to these three key issues. Of course, in solving different segmentation problems, variations of these steps may be applied and specific cases outlined in this chapter demonstrate the flexibility.

While a very brief outline of the LOGISMOS approach is given in the remainder of this section, graph construction details, overview of numerous variations of the LOGISMOS approach, and strategies yielding efficient solutions can be found in Wu et al. (2007) and Sonka et al. (2015).

## 9.2.1 OPTIMAL SURFACE SEGMENTATION

1. *Presegmentation.* Given an input image, a presegmentation is performed to obtain an approximation to the (unknown) surfaces for target object boundaries. This gives useful information on the topological structures of the target object(s). The topological correctness of the presegmentation is important because LOGISMOS is topology-preserving, that is, the final segmentation will be equivalent topologically to the presegmentation. However, the exact boundary position of the presegmentation is not crucial since it will be optimized in the subsequent steps of the LOGISMOS framework. Several approximate surface detection methods are available, such as active appearance models, level sets, and atlas-based registration. For surfaces with a geometry that is known to be relatively simple (e.g., terrain-like, cylindrical, or spherical surfaces), this first step is trivial since it is known *a priori*.

2. *Mesh generation.* From the resulting approximate segmentation(s), a mesh is computed. The mesh is used to specify the structure of a graph $G_B$, called the *base graph*. $G_B$ defines the neighboring relations among voxels on the sought (optimal) surfaces. Voronoi diagram and Delaunay triangulation algorithms or isosurfacing methods (e.g., marching cubes) can be used for mesh generation. Figure 9.1(a) shows an example presegmentation mesh for the lung surface. For simple surfaces, this step may be trivial, since in many cases a mesh can be obtained easily.

3. *Resampling along graph columns.* For each vertex $v$ on the sought surfaces, a vector of candidate points is created that is expected to contain $v$. This is done by resampling the input image along a ray or path intersecting every vertex $u$ of the mesh (one ray per mesh vertex). We note that the elements in $v$ do not have to be equidistant in image space (Abràmoff et al., 2014). The direction of the ray is either an approximate normal of the meshed surface at $u$, defined by a center point/line of the target object, or otherwise derived from the presegmentation object shape. These vectors of

**FIGURE 9.1**

LOGISMOS graph construction for the lung surface. (a) Presegmentation mesh. (b) The graph columns constructed using the ELF method (Section 9.3.3). Colors represent individual columns. (c) Column structure inside the presegmentation surface. The surface and columns are clipped along the white rectangle shown in (a) to reveal the inside of the surface. Outside the surface is shown in white, inside is shown in pink.

candidate points form a new, resampled image. Figure 9.1(b and c) shows a possible configuration for the paths taken by these voxel vectors for the lung segmentation task.

4. *Graph construction.* A weighted directed graph $G$ is built on the vectors of candidate points in the image that resulted from the resampling. Each candidate-point vector corresponds to a list of nodes in $G$ (called a *column*). $G$ is a *geometric* graph since it is naturally embedded in an $nD$ space ($n \geq 3$). Neighboring relations among points on the surfaces are represented by adjacency relations among the columns of $G$, as specified by the arcs in the base graph $G_B$. Each column contains exactly one vertex located on the sought surfaces. The arcs of $G$ are used to enforce constraints on the surfaces, such as smoothness and intersurface separation constraints. The intensity of each point location in the vectors is related to the cost of the corresponding node in $G$. The node costs of $G$ can also encode edge-based and region-based cost functions. Information on the constraints and cost functions of a target segmentation problem needs to be obtained. If multiple surfaces of a single object, or surfaces of multiple objects, are to be segmented, multiple graphs as described previously are joined by graph arcs, which specify pairwise topological relationships between surfaces and/or objects and can also encode multisurface/multiobject constraints. By linking these specific-surface subgraphs together, a single graph results (Figure 9.2 and following).

5. *Graph search.* The graph construction scheme ensures that the sought optimal surfaces correspond to an *optimal closed set* in the weighted directed graph $G$ (Wu and Chen, 2002; Li et al., 2006). Thus, the sought optimal surfaces are obtained by searching for an optimal closed set in $G$ using efficient closed set algorithms in graph theory and can be achieved by using standard *s-t* cut algorithms.

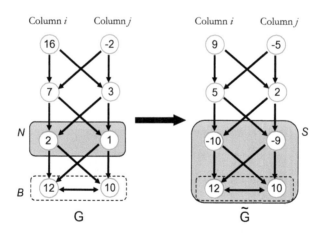

**FIGURE 9.2**

LOGISMOS graph structure. Graph nodes are organized along columns representing the search space and each node is associated with an unlikeliness cost. Pairs of subsequent nodes in a given column are connected via intracolumn arcs. Neighboring columns are connected via intercolumn arcs, which control the smoothness of the final surface. These two types of arcs are essential for converting the min-cost/max-flow problem in $G$ to the problem of finding the minimum closed set on the equivalent graph $\tilde{G}$. Note that the costs are transformed between $G$ and $\tilde{G}$ in this process; see Sonka et al. (2015), Li et al. (2006), and Wu and Chen (2002) for details.

A key innovation of this method is its nontrivial graph construction, aiming to transform the surface segmentation problem into computing a minimum *closed set* in a node-weighted directed graph. A closed set Z in a digraph is a subset of nodes such that all successors of any nodes in Z are also contained in Z. The *cost* of a closed set is the total cost of the nodes in the set. The minimum closed set problem is to search for a closed set with the minimum cost, which can be solved in polynomial time by computing a minimum *s-t* cut in a derived arc-weighted digraph (Hochbaum, 2001).

Figure 9.2 shows the LOGISMOS graph structure for the simplest scenario of a single-surface segmentation. This graph contains intracolumn arcs between successive nodes in each column, and intercolumn arcs between neighboring columns, which encode surface smoothness constraints. These two types of arcs are common to all LOGISMOS applications. More complicated use cases, such as simultaneous segmentation of multiple surfaces or objects, use additional arc types to encode the mutual relationships of these entities, as will be illustrated in Sections 9.3–9.5.

Designing appropriate cost functions is of paramount importance for any graph-based segmentation method. In real-world problems, the cost function usually reflects either a region-based or edge-based property of the surface to be identified and can be defined using a multiscale approach.

A typical edge-based cost function aims to position the boundary surface accurately in the volumetric image. An advanced version of an edge-based cost function may utilize a combination of the first and second derivatives of the image intensity function (Sonka et al., 1997) and may consider preferred directions of the identified surface. The combination of the first and second derivatives permits fine-tuning of the cost function to maximize border positioning accuracy.

The object boundaries do not have to be defined by gradients. For example, the 3D Chan-Vese functional can be used:

$$C(S, a_1, a_2) = \int_{\text{inside}(S)} (I(x, y, z) - a_1)^2 \, dx \, dy \, dz + \int_{\text{outside}(S)} (I(x, y, z) - a_2)^2 \, dx \, dy \, dz$$

in which $a_1$ and $a_2$ are the mean intensities in the interior and exterior of the surface $S$ and the energy $C(S, a_1, a_2)$ is minimized when $S$ coincides with the object boundary and best separates the object and background with respect to their mean intensities (Wu et al., 2011).

Another approach to cost function design is to use machine learning-based approaches. Here, we train classifiers to learn the expected boundary information from a set of annotated images. The unseen test image is run through the trained classifier which predicts the unlikeliness costs for all the nodes.

## 9.3 MULTIOBJECT MULTISURFACE LOGISMOS FOR KNEE JOINT SEGMENTATION

In this section, we demonstrate the application of the LOGISMOS algorithm to segment 3D magnetic resonance imaging (MRI) scans of the knee joint. The knee joint is one of the most complex joints in the human body, consisting of the femur (thigh bone), the tibia (shin bone), the patella (knee cap), and the fibula (a smaller bone running alongside the tibia). Articular cartilage is found covering the ends of each of these bones in the regions where they come in contact with each other. The algorithm presented here focuses on simultaneously segmenting bones and articular cartilages of the two primary bones, that is, the femur and tibia.

Osteoarthritis (OA) is currently the leading cause of functional disability; it leads to loss of articular cartilages over time. Several large-scale clinical trials for developing a disease modifying osteoarthritis drug (DMOAD) are underway. Imaging is crucial in these studies to determine the effect of such drugs on disease progression. In particular, MRI has been shown to provide more objective quantitative results than scoring methods used for radiographs and is more sensitive to cartilage losses (Sharma et al., 2008). Automated segmentation of knee MRI scans allows more objective and more efficient quantification of cartilage loss than manual segmentation by trained radiologists, which can take several hours of effort and is prone to inter/intra observer variability and operator-induced biases.

However, the complex anatomy of the knee joint, the challenges from the MR appearance of the cartilage, osteophyte, and surface fibrillation make fully automated segmentation a challenging task. In particular, the closely positioned cartilage and bone surfaces at the interface of the tibia and femur are highly difficult to distinguish from each other. As a result, methods utilizing independent segmentation of the surfaces frequently fail. The LOGISMOS approach consistently delivers simultaneous segmentation of these mutually interacting surfaces and objects, which allows increased accuracy for each surface and improves the overall robustness of the method.

Several segmentation algorithms have been previously proposed for this task. Dodin et al. (2011) propose using a ray casting technique to segment the bones of the femur and tibia. They formulate the problem by decomposing the MR images into multisurface layers localizing the boundaries of bones and several partial segmentation objects which are merged to obtain the final complete bone segmentation. In Fripp et al. (2010), a fully automated segmentation method is proposed for nonpathological knees. A 3D active shape model is used as initialization to extract the bone-cartilage interface; the cartilage is then segmented using a deformable model with patient-specific tissue estimation. More recently, Lee et al. (2014) proposed building a multilabel atlas which is merged using a locally weighted voting scheme followed by region adjustment. These and other existing methods combine locally optimal schemes to obtain a final segmentation, which can be inadequate especially in the presence of substantial cartilage atrophy. In contrast, LOGISMOS segmentation is guaranteed to achieve the globally optimal solution with respect to the cost function.

## 9.3.1 PRESEGMENTATION AND MESH GENERATION

The presegmentation approach consists of three main steps: the volume of interest (VOI) detection, initialization by fitting a shape model, and single-surface graph segmentation.

In order to reduce the computational time, we detect the VOI which includes the femur and the tibia bone and the corresponding articular cartilages and crop the input MRI accordingly. The detection of the VOI is done by an AdaBoost classifier (Freund and Schapire, 1995) previously trained on manually delineated VOIs. The features used for this task are the response to nine different 3D Haar-like filters, using a multiscale approach.

Mean shape meshes $\bar{S}_0$ for the femur and tibia bones were created from a training set. Using VOI bounds, the bone-specific mesh is fitted by affine registration. This approach ensures a well-defined mesh topology defining the bone structure, which is very important for the LOGISMOS approach because the topology of the final segmentations of both the bone and the cartilage surfaces is defined by this initial mesh.

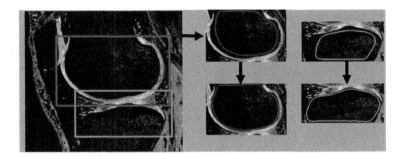

**FIGURE 9.3**

Presegmentation of the knee. Left: The VOI bound extraction for the femur (red) and tibia (green). Top row: Affine fitting of the mean shapes $\bar{\mathcal{S}}_0$. Bottom row: Accurate patient-specific bone structure $\mathcal{S}$ obtained via single-surface LOGISMOS segmentation.

After fitting $\bar{\mathcal{S}}_0$, a single-surface LOGISMOS segmentation is performed independently for the femur and the tibia bones. This results in highly accurate patient-specific bone mesh structures $\mathcal{S}$ (Figure 9.3). The cost function and graph column construction used for this step are the same as those employed in the multisurface multiobject version presented in the following.

## 9.3.2 RESAMPLING ALONG GRAPH COLUMNS

The graph column construction is a crucial step in mesh-based graph optimization techniques. Graph columns based on the normal to the mesh surface fail as two or more graph columns may intersect, which can lead to self-intersecting segmentation results. Instead, we adopt a graph column construction approach based on the concept of electric lines of force (ELF). It is well-known in electric field theory that, given an electric field formed by multiple charged particles, the lines of force exhibit a nonintersection property. We mimic this behavior by simulating charged particles placed at each vertex of the mesh surface and computing the electric field these particles form, using Coulomb's law; the graph columns follow the ELF and are therefore guaranteed not to intersect each other.

However, we modify the ELF computation to adapt to a surface representation by nonuniformly distributed vertices on a mesh. Two main issues are addressed with the modification:

1. The vertices ($v_i$) of the mesh surface are assigned a positive charge based on the sum of the surface areas associated with the triangles $t_j$ adjacent to $v_i$. This modification allows for coping with the nonuniform distribution of vertices along the surface.
2. In the ELF computation, the radius of influence ($r_i$) of each vertex $v_i$ is given by the distance from $v_i$ to the point where the ELF is being evaluated. Changing the contribution of this radius from $r^2$ to $r^m$ ($m > 2$) decreases the influence of more distant vertices, making it more robust.

This results in the following formulation of the ELF field:

$$\hat{E} = \sum_i \frac{\sum_j \text{AREA}(t_j)}{r_i^m} \hat{\mathbf{r}}_i \tag{9.1}$$

where $v_i \in t_j$ and $m > 2$.

### 9.3.3 GRAPH CONSTRUCTION AND GRAPH SEARCH

As discussed in Section 9.2, multiple surfaces and objects are modeled as subgraphs that are connected via special arcs to form a single graph in the LOGISMOS framework. Using the presegmentation mesh ($S$), a subgraph is thus constructed for the bone and cartilage surfaces of the femur and tibia, with graph columns built using the ELF approach. For each of these four subgraphs, we use the intracolumn and intercolumn arcs as described in Section 9.2.

Next, we introduce pairwise intersurface arcs between the bone and cartilage subgraphs of each of the objects to enforce minimum and maximum surface separation constraints between these surfaces. However, only parts of the bone are covered by articular cartilage while the remaining portions have no cartilage. Using region-detection classifiers, columns that do not have cartilage are identified and their minimum surface separation constraint is set to zero, while the regions identified with articular cartilage have a nonzero minimum separation constraint.

The knee anatomy is such that the portions of the femoral and tibial cartilage are in close apposition and a key constraint is that these surfaces do not cross each other. This desired behavior is accomplished by introducing interobject arcs between the corresponding columns of the two objects. However, this is challenging because the topology of the two meshes is different and no straightforward one-to-one correspondence exists between the two sets of vertices. To establish suitable correspondences, we estimate an approximate medial sheet for mapping vertices between the two objects (Figure 9.4).

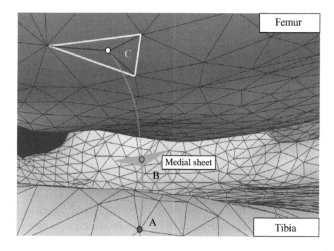

**FIGURE 9.4**

Constraint point mapping example: Each tibia vertex A in the region of interaction is pushed forward toward the medial sheet, using the ELF field implied by the tibia (solid blue line). The intersection point B of the ELF curve and the medial sheet is determined. This point is then back-propagated along the ELF field implied by the femur (dotted line). The point of intersection between the ELF curve and the femur surface is marked as the constraint point C. This constraint point is connected to nearby femur vertices using intercolumn arcs. The ELF path computed in this process is used to create graph columns shared by the two objects, linked together by interobject arcs enforcing the minimum and maximum interobject separation constraints. The same procedure is repeated to create constraint points from the femur to the tibia.

For each vertex A determined to be in the region of interaction between the two objects, the vertex is pushed forward toward the opposite object, along the ELF field implied by the first object. The point B where this pushed-forward arc from the first object intersects the medial sheet is determined. This point is back-propagated to the second object along the ELF field implied by the second object. The point C where this pulled-back arc intersects the second object is defined as a constraint point. Each constraint point thus computed is connected to the nearby vertices of the second surface via intercolumn arcs. The path constructed in this process is used to construct a shared column between the two objects; interobject arcs are introduced between these columns to enforce minimum and maximum separation constraints between the two objects. This ensures that the two cartilage surfaces do not overlap. Note that in this application, both the graph construction and the interobject mapping employ the ELF field strategy.

### 9.3.4 COST FUNCTION DESIGN

The knee segmentation employs a classifier-based cost function. The femur and tibia have specific random forest classifiers, (Breiman, 2001) trained for the bone and the cartilage surfaces, respectively. A breakdown of the classifiers used per object is shown in Figure 9.5.

For each node, the costs assigned are based on the unlikeliness of the associated bone or cartilage surface to occur at that image location. These costs at each of the nonvoxel locations are defined as the probability output of the corresponding classifier. The classifiers make use of steerable packets to collect neighborhood information for each node (Kashyap et al., 2013). These are input to the previously trained bone and cartilage classifiers, which output the unlikeliness of the node being on the target surface.

The images from which the classification features are collected have a resolution of 0.36 mm × 0.36 mm × 0.7 mm for both training and testing datasets used in the experiments presented here. For the bone classifiers, the features collected are a combination of Gaussian gradient images with kernel sizes of 0.36, 0.7, and 1.4 mm, and eigenvalues of Hessian images with kernel sizes of 0.5, 1.0, and

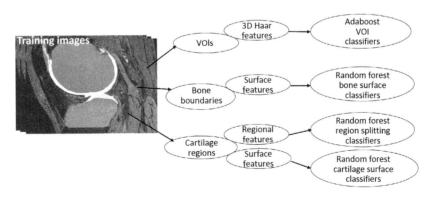

**FIGURE 9.5**

Use of classifiers for the knee segmentation task. Note that the femur and tibia each have a separate set of classifiers.

2.0 mm. The cartilage detection employs two sets of classifiers: a classifier for detecting the region where the cartilage is likely to occur on the surface and a classifier to determine the cartilage surface cost. In addition to the features used for the bone classifier, Laplacian gradient images with kernel sizes of 0.7 and 1.4 mm are collected along with Gabor texture features and higher order statistics of mean, variance, skewness, kurtosis of underlying image intensity per steerable packet for the cartilage classifiers.

Once the graph construction is complete, we translate the problem into the equivalent minimum-cost closed set problem, which is solved using standard min-cut/max-flow optimization algorithms.

### 9.3.5 SUBPLATE DETECTION

The OA research community has developed guidelines for a standardized approach to partition the femur and tibia cartilage into subplates (Eckstein et al., 2006). We have developed a fully automated nomenclature-compliant subplate detection algorithm (Kashyap et al., 2013). The overall list of subplates detected by this algorithm and their terminology is described in Figure 9.6(a). The

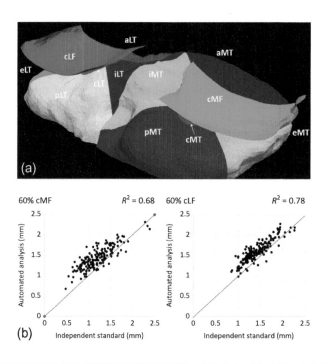

**FIGURE 9.6**

(a) Automated subplate division of the cartilage. The 60% central lateral (cLF) and central medial femur (cMF) are shown. Each medial (MT) and lateral tibia (LT) regions are subdivided as: central (cLT/cMT), interior (iLT/iMT), exterior (eLT/eMT), anterior (aLT/aMT), and posterior (pLT/pMT) regions, respectively. (b) Correlation of thickness values between the manual and LOGISMOS segmentation for individual patients for the 60% cMF and 60% cLF. Both plates show that the thickness measures are in high agreement with $R^2$ values of 0.68 and 0.78, respectively. The dotted line is the identity line displayed for reference purposes.

LOGISMOS segmentation results are analyzed using these automatically determined subplates to quantify regional cartilage thickness loss. The study of focal losses in load-bearing regions of the cartilage in this manner has been shown to be more effective than analyzing the full cartilage (Sharma et al., 2008).

## 9.3.6 CASE STUDY

### Datasets and study design

The data used to evaluate our method was provided by the Osteoarthritis Initiative (OAI) which is available for public access (OAI, 2015). All MR acquisitions were done using a Dual Echo Steady State (DESS) pulse sequence with an in-plane resolution of 0.36 mm × 0.36 mm and a slice thickness of 0.7 mm, resulting in 384 × 384 × 160 voxels. Two different studies were undertaken to validate the LOGISMOS algorithm for knee segmentation.

For the first study, 88 datasets with baseline (BL) and 12-month follow-up (12M) scans were used (176 3D MRI in total). Manual segmentations were provided by the OAI for these scans. The aim of this experiment was to quantify the border positioning errors and the cartilage thickness errors between LOGISMOS results and the corresponding manual segmentations in each subplate.

For the second study, 131 datasets with BL and 48-month follow-up (48M) scans were used, resulting in a total of 262 3D MR datasets. The aim of this experiment was to explore the applicability of our algorithm to longitudinal studies, by assessing the agreement of the thickness loss quantified by our algorithm with the clinical prognosis. No manual segmentations were available for this dataset.

### Accuracy of LOGISMOS in comparison with manual segmentation

The LOGISMOS algorithm was used to segment the 176 MRI scans in the first dataset. Four subjects were excluded from further study because of presegmentation failure. The subplate division algorithm was used on both the manual segmentations and the automated LOGISMOS results. In this experiment, we focused on the four main subplate regions: 60% cLF, 60% cMF, LT, and MT.

Table 9.1 presents the signed and unsigned border positioning errors as well as the thickness errors in each plate. The average signed border positioning error for both the cartilage and the bone surfaces is smaller than the in-plane voxel resolution of 0.36 mm, indicating good agreement between the LOGISMOS results and manual segmentations. Furthermore, the cartilage thickness errors are also at subvoxel level, suggesting high accuracy.

Figure 9.6(b) shows the correlation of the thickness measurements between the manual segmentations and the LOGISMOS results for the 60% cLF and cMF plates. The LOGISMOS thickness quantification showed a strong correlation with the manual segmentation in both plates. We note that this is a very challenging dataset including patients with known pathology; the satisfactory performance of LOGISMOS in this challenging dataset is therefore highly encouraging.

### Applicability of LOGISMOS to longitudinal studies

For the second experiment, LOGISMOS was used to segment 262 MRI datasets. The resulting surfaces were divided into subplates for analysis. While no manual segmentations were available for this dataset, each patient in this study had a BL Kellgren-Lawrence (KL) score of 2 or 3 (Kellgren et al., 1957). The KL score classifies the severity of OA by measuring the joint space narrowing on radiographs of the

**Table 9.1 Signed and Unsigned Surface Positioning Errors and the Cartilage Thickness Errors for the 60% cLF , 60% cMF, LT, and MT Plates**

| Plate Name | Signed | | | Unsigned | | |
| --- | --- | --- | --- | --- | --- | --- |
| | Cartilage Surface Error (mm) | Bone Surface Error (mm) | Thickness Error (mm) | Cartilage Surface Error (mm) | Bone Surface Error (mm) | Thickness Error (mm) |
| 60 % cLF | $-0.04 \pm 0.21$ | $0.10 \pm 0.11$ | $-0.17 \pm 0.14$ | $0.36 \pm 0.15$ | $0.22 \pm 0.07$ | $0.19 \pm 0.11$ |
| 60 % cMF | $-0.03 \pm 0.25$ | $0.18 \pm 0.32$ | $-0.23 \pm 0.18$ | $0.45 \pm 0.18$ | $0.32 \pm 0.27$ | $0.25 \pm 0.16$ |
| cLT | $0.02 \pm 0.21$ | $0.09 \pm 0.27$ | $-0.12 \pm 0.17$ | $0.44 \pm 0.13$ | $0.29 \pm 0.23$ | $0.17 \pm 0.13$ |
| MT | $0.05 \pm 0.28$ | $0.12 \pm 0.27$ | $-0.13 \pm 0.18$ | $0.55 \pm 0.18$ | $0.30 \pm 0.22$ | $0.18 \pm 0.14$ |

patient. KL grades of 2 or more are considered a clear indicator that the patient has an onset of OA and cartilage loss will accelerate over the subsequent years. Therefore, we hypothesized that for larger load-bearing plates such as cLF/cMF and cLT/cMT, the losses in cartilage would be significant over the 48M duration of the study.

To test this hypothesis, we analyzed the thickness losses over time for all the subplates described in Section 9.3.5. Figure 9.7 presents the thickness quantification at each time point. The differences in thickness between BL and 48M were statistically significant for almost all the larger load-bearing plates, confirming our hypothesis.

These two studies indicate that the LOGISMOS approach achieves high segmentation accuracy in a fully automated framework. Segmenting a 3D dataset (for every time-point) required $\approx$7 min after the classifiers were loaded into the memory. The overall analysis process had a memory requirement

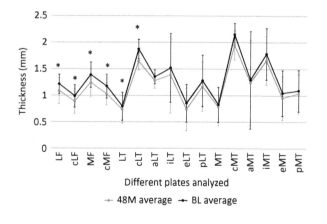

**FIGURE 9.7**

Longitudinal study analyzing 131 patients with KL grades of 2 or 3. We observe a general trend toward thickness loss between the two time points across all plates. The larger load-bearing plates showed statistically significant thickness loss (denoted by asterisk).

of $\approx$20 GB. On average, the signed surface positioning errors were lower than the in-plane voxel resolution of 0.36 mm.

Our method holds promise as a tool for quantitative evaluation of cartilage thinning in longitudinal studies. The obtained assessment of longitudinal thinning of the cartilage (Figure 9.7) demonstrates the ability to quantitatively assess temporal cartilage changes in the main subplates, indicating the clinical relevance of our method. With increasing efforts toward creating DMOADs, our highly accurate automated technique addresses a crucial need for consistent quantitative analysis of large patient populations in clinical trials.

## 9.4 MULTISURFACE MULTIIMAGE CO-SEGMENTATION: RETINAL OCT

In this section, we demonstrate the use of LOGISMOS in segmenting retinal layers across multiple spatially overlapping volumes imaged with optical coherence tomography (OCT). OCT has become an indispensable tool for noninvasive high-resolution 3D volumetric imaging of the retina and its layered structure (Figure 9.8). In particular, the thickness of retinal layers is relevant to the diagnosis and management of a variety of ocular diseases such as age-related macular degeneration, diabetic-retinopathy, and glaucoma, the three most common causes of blindness in the developed world. Thus, their accurate and reproducible segmentation is of great clinical importance (Abràmoff et al., 2010).

When consistency between multiple segmentations is required, it is attractive to exploit the additional information available from the overlapping areas rather than discarding it as redundant, especially in low contrast and noisy images such as OCT. Such a requirement typically occurs in two applications: extending the imaged field of view by creating a 3D mosaic of images (small spatial overlap) or segmenting images forming a 4D longitudinal dataset (large spatial overlap). However, it is not immediately clear how to effectively combine the multiple information sources available in the areas of overlap.

Here, we utilize LOGISMOS to perform simultaneous co-segmentation of multiple surfaces assuring consistent segmentation across the overlapping images (Figure 9.9). After spatial alignment, all the images are segmented simultaneously, imposing *a priori* interimage-intrasurface constraints for each pair of overlapping images, which penalizes deviations from the expected surface-height differences. The methodology was originally reported in Bogunovic et al. (2014).

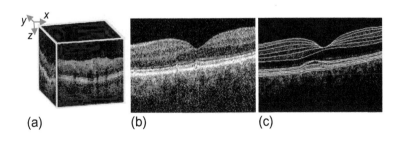

(a)          (b)          (c)

**FIGURE 9.8**

(a) Retinal OCT volume and (b) its cross section (B-scan). (c) Corresponding retinal layer segmentation.

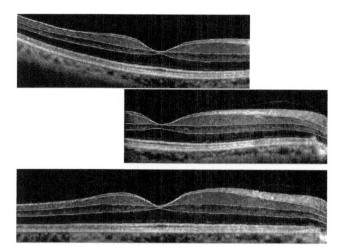

**FIGURE 9.9**

Multisurface multiimage co-segmentation. Top: B-scan slices of two overlapping volumes. Aligned OCT volumes are segmented simultaneously (co-segmentation). Bottom: co-segmentation result shown on single composite (wide-field) B-scan, after stitching and flattening of the composite OCT.

The layered and flat structure of the retina makes it naturally suitable for LOGISMOS as the layer interfaces represent an ordered series of smooth terrain-like surfaces. Thus, the presegmentation is simply a plane and the base graph $G_B$ is just a 4-connected grid. In addition, there is no need for image resampling as the voxels forming the 3D image can be used directly as voxel vectors that form the columns along the $z$-direction (depth-axis) of the geometric graph.

## 9.4.1 METHODOLOGY OVERVIEW

The multisurface multiimage co-segmentation task is modeled as an energy minimization problem where, in addition to basic LOGISMOS elements enforcing shape and context (Song et al., 2013), inconsistencies in the overlapped areas are penalized. This can be formulated as follows. We start with an ordered set of $N$ surfaces $S = \{S_1, \ldots, S_N\}$ across $M$ overlapping images $\mathcal{I} = \{I_1, \ldots, I_M\}$. Surface $S_i$ is assumed to be positioned *above* the surface $S_{i+1}$, along the $z$-axis (depth-axis). We then pose the co-segmentation as the minimization of:

$$E(\mathcal{S}) = \sum_{i=1}^{N} \sum_{j=1}^{M} E_{\text{image}}(S_i^j) + \alpha \sum_{i=1}^{N} \sum_{j=1}^{M} E_{\text{shape}}(S_i^j) + \beta \sum_{i=1}^{N-1} \sum_{j=1}^{M} E_{\text{context}}(S_i^j, S_{i+1}^j)$$

$$+ \gamma \sum_{i=1}^{N} \sum_{l,m \in O} E_{\text{overlap}}(S_i^l, S_i^m) \qquad (9.2)$$

where $S_i^j$ denotes $i$th surface of $j$th image. The parameters $\alpha$, $\beta$, and $\gamma$ weigh the contributions of the energy terms and their values depend on the application, which have to be determined by observing the performance on a training set of images.

The term $E_{\text{image}}$ is the energy associated with how well a surface fits the underlying image information, that is, a surface is expected to lie along an intensity gradient. The term $E_{\text{shape}}$ incorporates prior shape information on smoothness of a surface. The term $E_{\text{context}}$ incorporates prior pair-wise context information, that is, the expected separation (distance) between neighboring pairs of surfaces.

Here, we specifically introduce an additional term $E_{\text{overlap}}$ to enforce a consistent surface co-segmentation in the areas covered by the set $O$ of pairwise overlapping images. More specifically, for any surface:

$$E_{\text{overlap}}(S^l, S^m) = \sum_{p \in S^l \stackrel{\triangle}{=} q \in S^m} f_o(d_{pq}^{l,m} - \bar{d}_{pq}^{l,m}) \tag{9.3}$$

where $p$ and $q$ are the anatomically corresponding "column" vectors of the same surfaces in two images while $d_{pq}^{l,m} = S^l(p) - S^m(q)$ is their difference. The $\bar{d}$ denotes *a priori* expected difference remaining after alignment. In order for the above functional to be optimally solvable in polynomial time, $f_o$ has to be a convex function (Ishikawa, 2003) and typically implements prior *hard* (Garvin et al., 2009) or *soft* (spring-like) (Song et al., 2013) constraints.

It should be noted that, although surface consistency across the images is enforced by the previous functional, this does not guarantee consistency of layer thicknesses (distances between pairs of surfaces). That is a more difficult problem as it involves satisfying constraints of not just two, but four variables: $S_i^l(p) - S_{i+1}^l(p) = S_i^m(q) - S_{i+1}^m(q)$. Such higher order, nonsubmodular functions do not have known transformations to the max-flow min-cut problem on a graph, hence currently finding their optimum is intractable (Kolmogorov and Zabih, 2004).

### 9.4.2 COST FUNCTIONS FOR RETINAL OCT

The cost function that forms $E_{\text{image}}$ is specific to each image forming the multiimage OCT setting. As the surfaces lie on a transition between layers, the cost is taken to be proportional to the inverted vertical gradient magnitude. Depending on the surface of interest, a gradient computation is used that favors either dark-to-bright or bright-to-dark transitions.

A method able to segment up to 11 surfaces (10 layers) in a single OCT image was presented in Quellec et al. (2010). In practice, due to large computational requirements imposed by segmenting such a large number of surfaces and the dense resolution of OCT, a hierarchical and multiscale approach is utilized. The basic idea is to detect the intraretinal surface in the higher resolution image constrained by the intraretinal surface segmented in the lower resolution images. Furthermore, the surfaces are hierarchically detected starting from the most easily detectable, that is, starting with the surfaces exhibiting the strongest features and ending with the most subtle interfaces.

### 9.4.3 OVERLAP CONSTRAINT ARCS

A subgraph is created for each of the $M$ images. For each subgraph, intraimage arcs are the same as in basic LOGISMOS, where intraimage-intercolumn arcs impose smoothness within the image and intraimage-intersurface impose context, that is, allowed distance (min and max) between a pair of surfaces within the same image. The newly introduced interimage-intrasurface arcs are implementing

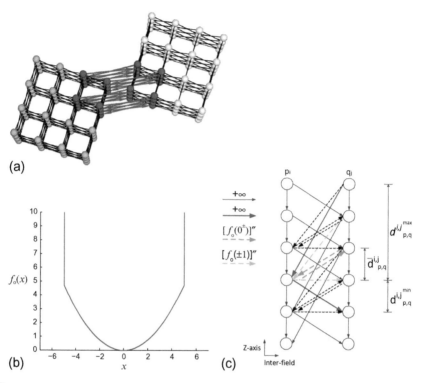

**FIGURE 9.10**

Graph construction. (a) Example of two subgraphs $G_n^l$ and $G_n^m$ of the same surface $S_n$, with their intra- and intercolumn arcs (in black), and interimage-intrasurface arcs (in red). The nodes belonging to the area of overlap are highlighted (in red). (b) Function $f_o$ implementing the overlap constraints. (c) Interimage-intrasurface arc construction where dashed arrows denote the arcs implementing soft constraints while solid ones denote arcs implementing the hard constraints.

*Source: Bogunovic et al. (2014)*

function $f_o$ in Eq. (9.3). Because we expect segmentations to be consistent in the overlap areas, soft constraints are imposed to encourage expected shape change or surface distance value within the limits of hard constraints. The graph construction with the emphasis on the newly introduced interimage-intrasurface arcs is shown in Figure 9.10. Alternatively, if we do expect small anatomical differences then soft constraints should be removed and only hard ones kept.

### Interimage-intrasurface arcs

To implement $f_o(\cdot)$, a set of arcs is constructed in-between subgraphs $G_n^l$ and $G_n^m$, corresponding to a pair of overlapping images $(I_l, I_m)$ of the same surface. To assure consistent segmentation of the surface in the overlapped area we use soft constraints, bounded by hard ones to limit the number of arcs and lower the computational burden. After alignment there is an expected column-specific shift $\bar{d}_{pq}^{l,m}$ between a pair of surfaces belonging to the overlapping pair of images $(I_l, I_m)$. First, we add the arcs with $+\infty$

weights, imposing the hard constraint $|d_{pq}^{l,m} - \bar{d}_{pq}^{l,m}| \leq H_{pq}^{l,m}$. The arcs connect $v_n^l(x, y, z) \in p_l(x, y)$ to node $v_n^m(x, y, \max(z - \bar{d}_{pq}^{l,m} - H_{pq}^{l,m}, 0)) \in q_m(x, y)$ and $v_n^m(x, y, z) \in q_m(x, y)$ to node $v_n^l(x, y, \max(z + \bar{d}_{pq}^{l,m} - H_{pq}^{l,m}, 0)) \in p_l(x, y)$. Second, we add the soft constraint, weighted arcs in-between the hard constraint ones. For each $h = d_{pq}^{l,m} - \bar{d}_{pq}^{l,m}$, where $-H_{pq}^{l,m} < h < H_{pq}^{l,m}$, if $[f_o(h)]' \geq 0$, an arc is added from $v_n^l(x, y, z) \in p_l(x, y)$ to node $v_n^m(x, y, \max(z - \bar{d}_{pq}^{l,m} - h, 0)) \in q_m(x, y)$ with weight $[f_o(h)]''$. If $[f_o(h)]' \leq 0$, an arc is added from $v_n^m(x, y, z) \in q_m(x, y)$ to node $v_n^l(x, y, \max(z + \bar{d}_{pq}^{l,m} + h, 0)) \in p_l(x, y)$ with the same weight $[f_o(h)]''$. The $[f_o(h)]'$ and $[f_o(h)]''$ are the discrete equivalents of first and second derivative of $f_o$, respectively. Using this construction, the total weight of the arcs cut by the surface set $S$ between two subgraphs $G^l$ and $G^m$ on column $p$ equals the value of the overlap prior penalty $f_o(d_{pq}^{l,m} - \bar{d}_{pq}^{l,m})$. Additional details can be found in Song et al. (2013) and Bogunovic et al. (2014).

The large number of the previously introduced arcs does increase the required computational resources. A potential resource optimization step would be to rely only on a decimated subset of spatial correspondences (red arcs in Figure 9.10(a)). As the intraretinal surfaces are spatially smooth, the segmentation accuracy should not be affected, while the graph complexity would be substantially decreased.

## 9.4.4 CASE STUDY

The value of our approach is demonstrated on the task of segmenting intraretinal layers from a set of overlapping OCT images. Two scenarios are considered: forming segmentation of a wide field of view of the retina and segmenting layers from a set of repeated OCT scans. Our underlying assumption is that the imaged anatomy has undergone little or no change between image acquisitions. After the co-segmentation, the images and the segmented surfaces are stitched together using the Voronoi-diagram-based parcellation to obtain a single composite OCT result. The performance is compared to the alternative scenario where each volume is segmented independently. The gold standard was taken to be the average of manual surface tracings performed by two ophthalmologists who traced the nerve fiber layer (NFL), and ganglion cell and inner plexiform layers (GCL + IPL), which are of high clinical importance.

### Mosaic co-segmentation
To create an extended field of view, a nine-field acquisition was performed where the scanned subject sequentially fixates on spots forming a $3 \times 3$ grid. For 2D en-face group alignment we employed a standard wide-field mosaicing workflow (Brown and Lowe, 2006). The method's accuracy and reproducibility were evaluated on such nine-field acquisitions from 10 patients with glaucoma. The average unsigned co-segmented surface position error ($4.58 \pm 1.46$ µm) was comparable to the average difference between manual surface tracings performed by ophthalmologists ($5.86 \pm 1.72$ µm). Independently segmenting the fields can produce pronounced artifacts in the overlapped areas (Figures 9.11 and 9.12). Such inconsistencies are avoided when employing our new co-segmentation approach, obtaining artifact-free thickness maps irrespective of the utilized stitching technique, and more accurate layer segmentations as was confirmed by quantitative analysis (Bogunovic et al., 2014).

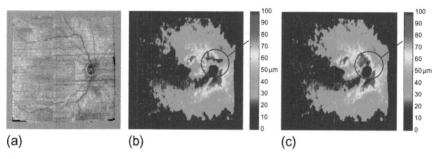

**FIGURE 9.11**

(a) Two-dimensional projection image of the nine-field stitched composite OCT. Surface segmentation shown as a composite NFL thickness map for (b) independent segmentation, and (c) co-segmentation. The overlayed circles denote the area where co-segmentation avoids stitching artifacts.

*Source: Bogunovic et al. (2014)*

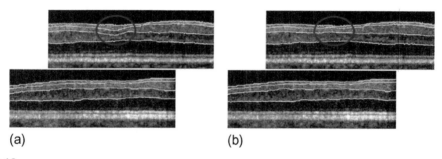

**FIGURE 9.12**

Surface segmentation across overlapping B-scans for (a) independent segmentation, and (b) co-segmentation. The overlayed circles highlight areas where independent segmentation produces erroneous and inconsistent results as opposed to the co-segmentation.

## Longitudinal co-segmentation

For the longitudinal co-segmentation scenario, the method was evaluated on repeated macula-centered OCT images from 16 patients with glaucoma (Figure 9.13). The second scan was registered to the first one, and the surfaces were co-segmented. The unsigned surface positioning error averaged over all the surfaces was significantly smaller in both time-points. As expected, the segmentation consistency between the two time-points of all three layer thicknesses was significantly better ($p < 0.01$) for the co-segmentation approach.

## Computational resources

The resources required by the multifield co-segmentation reflect that the number of nodes in the constructed graph is multiplied by $M$ and the soft constraints additionally introduce a large number of arcs. Compared to the sequential nine-field independent segmentations that required $\approx 3.5$ GB of

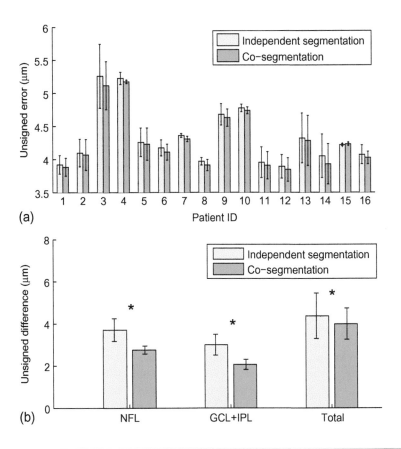

**FIGURE 9.13**

(a) Mean unsigned error over the surfaces across both time points for independent and co-segmentation. (b) Layer thickness variability of longitudinal scans expressed as the mean unsigned difference between the two scans for NFL, GCL + IPL, and the total retinal thickness (asterisk denotes statistical significance).

memory and took ≈10 min to complete, the co-segmentation approach required ≈70 GB of memory and took ≈35 min (Linux, 2.5 GHz AMD Opteron, 256 GB RAM).

Overall, the results demonstrated that, as opposed to the current state of the art which segments layers in each of the images independently, the proposed LOGISMOS co-segmentation method obtains consistent segmentation results across the overlapped and registered areas, producing more accurate, reproducible, and artifact-free results. The improvement was particularly pronounced in the segmentation of surfaces, which are difficult to segment as they are not always accompanied by strong gradients or other image features. In those cases, the extra information available by having the same area multiply imaged can be utilized by the co-segmentation to achieve more robust results. The obtained multifield co-segmentation has been successfully used on 122 glaucoma patients to predict local visual acuity from OCT, demonstrating the clinical relevance of this approach (Bogunovic et al., 2015).

## 9.5 COMPLEX MULTISURFACE GEOMETRY: LOGISMOS-B FOR BRAIN CORTEX

In this section, we use the human brain cortex as an example of LOGISMOS-based segmentation for multiple surfaces with complex geometry, originally proposed in Oguz and Sonka (2014b). The white matter (WM) and gray matter (GM) surfaces of the cortex are simultaneously segmented. In this scenario, while the same graph-based segmentation principles apply, the construction of the graph itself is more involved. In particular, the choice of the method for building the columns of the geometric graph is crucial to the successful segmentation of complex objects.

It is important that the graph columns never intersect each other, and that each ray intersects the desired surface exactly once. Without these properties, it is impossible to maintain the desired topology of the segmentation results, as intersections between the two surfaces and self-intersections become viable, damaging the integrity of the cortical sheet. We use a new approach for building the columns of this geometric graph to segment the highly convoluted human cortical surface, using generalized gradient vector flows (GGVF) (Xu and Prince, 1998), which allow for spatially varying amounts of smoothing based on the magnitude of the input gradient field. This technique is fundamental to the successful segmentation of the human cortex and other similarly complex-shaped surfaces.

As previously discussed, multiple surfaces of an object are represented by introducing duplicates of the entire graph (base graph and the associated columns) and introducing intersurface arcs which encode hard constraints on minimum and maximum surface separation in the LOGISMOS framework. In this application, we use the WM surface of the cortex (i.e., the WM–GM boundary) as the base graph, and both the WM surface and the pial surface (i.e., the GM-CSF boundary) are considered to be mutually interacting, nonintersecting surfaces of the same object. The surface separation constraints are set by considering the expected range of cortical thickness from the literature. This variant of the general LOGISMOS framework is called LOGISMOS-B (B for brain).

### 9.5.1 COLUMN CONSTRUCTION BASED ON GGVF

In this section, we discuss the efficient construction of nonintersecting graph columns using the GGVF approach. To this end, the gradient of the T1-weighted (T1w) image is computed after bias-field correction. This gradient map is masked with a skull-strip mask and rescaled such that the maximum vector magnitude is equal to 1. Using this initial edge map $f$, the GGVF field $\tilde{\mathbf{v}}$ is given by the equilibrium solution of

$$\mathbf{v_t} = g(|\nabla f|)\nabla^2\mathbf{v} - h(|\nabla f|)(\mathbf{v} - \nabla f) \tag{9.4}$$

where $g()$ and $h()$ are weighting functions between the smoothing term and the data term (Xu and Prince, 1998). The smoothing term seeks to produce a smoothly varying vector field, whereas the data term penalizes against large deviations from the input. The weighting functions are dependent on the gradient of the edge map, which can be leveraged to reduce smoothing near strong gradients. We follow the recommendation for weighting functions for GGVF from (Xu and Prince, 1998):

$$g(|\nabla f|) = e^{-(|\nabla f|/\kappa)} \tag{9.5}$$
$$h(|\nabla f|) = 1 - g(|\nabla f|) \tag{9.6}$$

In this setup, $\kappa$ is the only remaining free parameter for controlling the amount of global smoothing.

The partial differential equation specifying GGVF can be implemented using an explicit finite difference scheme, as in Xu and Prince (1998). Such an implementation has been shown to be numerically stable if the time step $\Delta t$ is sufficiently small, specifically, if $\Delta t \leq \frac{\Delta x \Delta y \Delta z}{8 g_{max}}$, where $\Delta x$, $\Delta y$, and $\Delta z$ are the spatial sample intervals and $g_{max}$ is the maximum value of the weighting function $g()$ over the input edge map.

After computing the GGVF field, the graph columns are built by integrating through the GGVF vector field, starting at the base graph. The step size $\Delta$ for the integration is equivalent to the node spacing along each column. Any nodes along a column that require more than 180° rotation of the step direction are discarded, to avoid "zigzags" in the graph columns in flat-intensity regions with vanishing gradients.

Figure 9.14 shows the different column building strategies. Using the normal directions (Figure 9.14a, d, g) results in straight paths for the graph columns, which is adequate for grid-based OCT applications (Section 9.4) but inappropriate for highly folded cortical surfaces. The curved paths of ELF (Figure 9.14b, e, h; Section 9.3.3) offer a substantial improvement over the normal directions

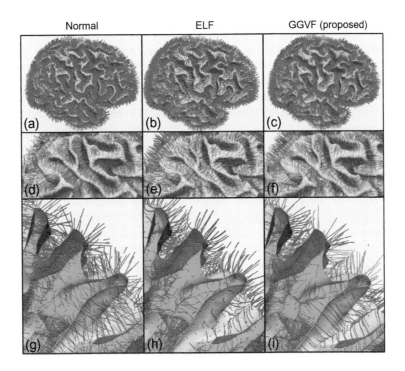

**FIGURE 9.14**

Construction of graph columns. (a–c) Whole brain; (d–f) zoomed in view; (g–i) zoomed in view with cross-sectional clipping for illustrating the interior of the surface. The outside of the WM surface is shown in white, the inside in green, and the graph columns in red.

*Source: Oguz and Sonka (2014b)*

and are useful in the context of nonplanar shapes such as the knee segmentation task. While in theory these do not intersect each other, their computation becomes extremely expensive given the very large graph sizes needed for representing the cortex. Various heuristics can be used to speed up the computation, but this jeopardizes the nonintersection property. Additionally, ELF columns are heavily dependent on the preliminary segmentation, which makes it more difficult to recover from poor initialization. The GGVF columns (Figure 9.14c, f, i) yield nonoverlapping paths that converge to an approximation of the medial surface while providing a regular coverage of the space, in a computationally efficient way. Intersecting graph columns, whether computed via normal vectors or heuristic ELF implementations, lead to very poor segmentation results as neither the topology of the surfaces nor their interactions with each other can be maintained. The GGVF-based column construction avoids these problems.

## 9.5.2 COST FUNCTION

The cost function used for the WM surface is the inverse gradient magnitude of the T1w image. For the GM surface, a weighted sum of the first- and second-order derivatives of the T1w image is used (Sonka et al., 1997). If available, the gradient of the T2-weighted (T2w) image can be used for improving the GM surface placement, as well as in the tissue classification step for generating the base graph. A surface segmentation approach simultaneously considering image data from two or more registered image sources was first reported in Han et al. (2011). In the cortical surface segmentation application, both the T1w and T2w images are smoothed using gradient anisotropic diffusion filtering for five iterations prior to gradient computation. Note that when both T1w and T2w images are available, each associated gradient map is scaled to the intensity range $[0 \ldots 1]$ to simplify the weighting of these cost components against each other.

## 9.5.3 REGIONALLY AWARE SEGMENTATION

One of the strengths of the LOGISMOS framework is that it naturally allows using different segmentation parameters in different regions of the surface. For the cortical surface reconstruction, we exploit this feature by using different graph construction parameters as well as different constraints in different regions of the brain to leverage *a priori* anatomical knowledge (von Economo, 1929) and expected image appearance. For this purpose, a rough parcellation of the base graph is obtained via atlas-based segmentation, which allows identifying the region that each graph column belongs to.

The heuristic described previously to avoid zigzags is relaxed regionally in the thickest parts of the cortex, where the relatively large GM patch often means a flat intensity region with vanishing gradients; the heuristic may thus cause the desired GM boundary location to be excluded from the search space. The cingulate and the temporal gyrus, which are among the thickest parts of the cortex, are thus using a relaxed heuristic as well as less strict smoothness constraints to allow for desired graph behavior between these regions and the neighboring areas.

Anatomy-driven minimum surface separation constraints are used to allow more robust segmentation. The visual cortex and the postcentral sulcus, which are known to be among the thinnest parts of the cortex, are allowed a reduced surface separation, that is, 2 mm as opposed to 2.5 mm elsewhere on the brain. Finally, the WM and GM surfaces are allowed to collapse onto each other near the amygdala, where there is no separate cortical layer. The cost function is also modified locally to discourage the cortical surface from entering the amygdala.

Similar localized adjustments can be made to the cost function and the graph construction parameters based on any additional *a priori* information, such as in the presence of known tumors.

### 9.5.4 PIPELINE OVERVIEW

The GGVF-based column construction of the LOGISMOS-B graph is somewhat sensitive to initialization: while the accuracy of the presegmentation with respect to surface placement is irrelevant, it is crucial that the branching structure of the WM is accurately captured by the initial surface. LOGISMOS-B cannot grow new branches or remove existing ones, since the path and reach of the streamlines of the GGVF vectors are determined by the starting points of the path integration. Therefore, it is important to design a preprocessing pipeline for the algorithm to generate a topologically accurate WM surface approximation that represents all of the main branches of the true WM surface.

The main steps toward achieving this goal are atlas-based tissue classification and bias-field correction, hemispheric splitting of the brain, filling of the subcortical structures and ventricles, and mesh-based postprocessing to achieve spherical topology.

We start by processing the T1w MRI volume of the subject through the BRAINSABC software (Kim and Johnson, 2013; Johnson, 2015). BRAINSABC deformably registers the input image to an atlas and performs joint tissue classification and bias-field correction using an expectation-maximization algorithm (Van Leemput et al., 1999). This procedure generates classification of each image voxel into one of the predefined tissue classes such as WM, GM, cerebellar WM, and cerebellar GM, as well as nonbrain tissue types such as the skull. Afterwards, all voxels that were classified as brain tissue are combined, and the resulting binary image is morphologically dilated using a spherical structuring element ($r = 1$ mm) to create a skull-strip mask.

Next, the cerebral cortex is split into two hemispheres by detecting the plane of maximal symmetry. Note that the two hemispheres are considered separately from this point onward. For each hemisphere, the largest connected component of the voxels belonging to the WM tissue class (excluding the brainstem and cerebellar WM) is extracted. Then, the "holes" in the WM surface, such as the subcortical structures and the ventricles, are filled in, in order to remove any WM boundaries that do not follow the inner surface of the cortical ribbon. Then, any remaining topological handles and holes are detected and removed following the methodology in Jaume et al. (2005). This technique detects the topological defects and removes them by either filling them in or cutting them apart, based on the route that would modify the least number of voxels. The resulting surface is of spherical topology and it forms an approximation of the WM surface, which is used for constructing the LOGISMOS-B graph for final segmentation.

Given an accurate segmentation of the cortical ribbon, we use the popular thickness computation method based on the Laplace equation (Jones et al., 2000). In this volumetric approach, the Laplace equation given by $\nabla^2 u(x) = 0$ is set up using the input WM and GM segmentations as boundary conditions ($u(x) = 1$ and $u(x) = -1$, respectively). The smooth gradient of $u$, $v = \frac{\nabla u}{\|\nabla u\|}$ is used to compute streamlines, which are guaranteed to not intersect each other and provide a one-to-one correspondence between the inner and outer boundaries of the cortical ribbon. The length of each streamline is reported as the local thickness measurement.

### 9.5.5 CASE STUDY

Datasets

We use two datasets to evaluate our method. The first dataset from Johns Hopkins University (JHU) (Shiee et al., 2014) consists of five multiple sclerosis (MS) patients and five healthy controls. These images have isotropic resolution of (1 mm$^3$) for the controls and (0.83 mm$^3$) for the MS patients. Manual landmarks are identified by two independent raters in seven clusters on both WM and GM surfaces. Each cluster (calcarine, central sulcus, cingulate, parieto-occipital, superior frontal, superior temporal, and Sylvian fissure) has 30 landmarks per hemisphere. A total of 7 clusters $\times$ 2 hemispheres $\times$ 2 surfaces $\times$ 30 landmarks $\times$ 2 raters $=$ 1680 landmarks are available per subject or 16,800 landmarks total. The second dataset consists of 73 healthy subjects from the publicly available IXI database (IXI, 2015), collected at the IoP in London. These images have a resolution of $0.937 \times 0.937 \times 1.2$ mm$^3$.

FreeSurfer

We evaluate our segmentations by comparing to FreeSurfer (Dale et al., 1999), which is a popular software suite (version 5.1 was used). Its approach is based on skull-stripping followed by segmentation via surface deformation with topological constraints to prevent self-intersections. Gradient descent is used to optimize the deformation energy; however, self-intersections are detected and avoided by reducing the step size accordingly. Note that this method, like all gradient-based optimization methods, is prone to converging to local minima, unlike our LOGISMOS method which guarantees a globally optimal solution with respect to the employed cost function.

Evaluation of surface placement accuracy

The surface placement accuracy is quantitatively evaluated by computing signed and unsigned distances between the automatically computed surfaces and the manually placed landmarks. Figure 9.15(a) shows that LOGISMOS-B has significantly less bulk error (measured by unsigned distances) as well as significantly less surface placement bias (consistent over- or under-segmentation, measured by signed distances) than FreeSurfer. Figure 9.16 shows representative FreeSurfer and LOGISMOS-B surfaces in the same dataset for qualitative evaluation. We observe that the FreeSurfer surface reconstruction is less than ideal especially for the MS patients; note the missing chunk of tissue for the rightmost subject near the inferior temporal gyrus, as well as the fused appearance of the gyri throughout the brain for all MS subjects, especially in comparison to the LOGISMOS-B surfaces. More detailed slice-by-slice study of the FreeSurfer results indicates that most of these problems are likely caused by local minima of the cost function created by the edges of the MS lesions. LOGISMOS-B is robust to such problems due to its global optimization.

One of the strengths of the LOGISMOS framework is its computational efficiency, due to the existence of low-order polynomial-time solutions. In the JHU dataset, the average run time for LOGISMOS-B was 2 h 55 min, compared to 9 h 55 min for FreeSurfer. We note that over 2.5 h of this time was spent in preprocessing, and the LOGISMOS step itself only took 8 min on average. The complete graph (including both surfaces) consisted of $\approx$5 million nodes per subject. Since most of the preprocessing steps such as hemisphere splitting and tissue classification are already computed as part of routine processing pipelines, the additional computational burden for LOGISMOS-B is minimal.

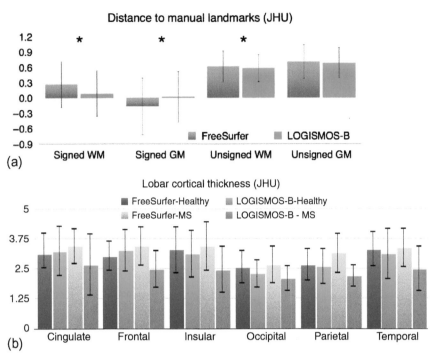

**FIGURE 9.15**

(a) The signed and unsigned distance error between the automatically computed surfaces and the manual landmarks in the JHU dataset. Asterisks indicate statistically significant differences. (b) Lobar cortical thickness comparison between the healthy controls and MS patients (JHU). Mean ± std. deviation are reported in millimeters.

## Evaluation of derived cortical thickness measurements

A very popular end goal for cortical surface reconstruction is the analysis of cortical thickness measurements derived from the surfaces. A direct evaluation of the cortical thickness accuracy is difficult given the inherent difficulty of creating manual thickness measurements in the 3D convoluted cortex. Therefore, we present an indirect evaluation based on known patterns in thickness differences, as originally reported in Oguz and Sonka (2014a).

Figure 9.15(b) compares the cortical thickness in the healthy and MS groups from the JHU dataset. The FreeSurfer measurements disagree with the known fact that MS patients exhibit cortical thinning (e.g., Sailer et al., 2003 and references therein). LOGISMOS-B, in contrast, reproduces this expected pattern. In fact, in addition to the diffuse overall thinning in the whole brain, LOGISMOS-B reports a marked focal thinning in the frontal and temporal lobes, in close agreement with Sailer et al. (2003). The inaccurate FreeSurfer reconstruction for MS subjects, especially the artificially enlarged GM segmentation (Figure 9.16), likely leads to the higher reported cortical thickness in the MS patients compared to healthy subjects. The robust LOGISMOS-B accurately captures the thinning in MS patients, both diffusely and focally.

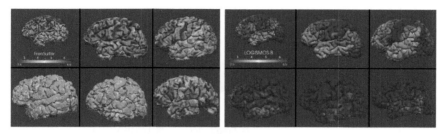

**FIGURE 9.16**

Illustrative GM surfaces from the JHU dataset, created by FreeSurfer and LOGISMOS-B. Top row, healthy, bottom, MS patients. The color map indicates local cortical thickness.

*Source: Oguz and Sonka (2014a)*

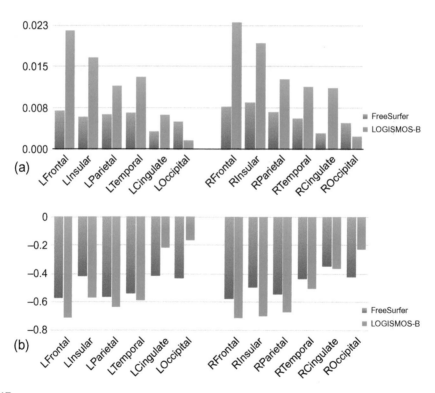

**FIGURE 9.17**

(a) Annual thinning rate of the cortex (IXI dataset). (b) Correlation of cortical thickness and subject age.

Figure 9.17 shows a regression analysis of cortical thickness against subject age in the healthy controls from the IXI dataset. Overall, LOGISMOS-B reports a more rapid thinning per year (as indicated by the slope) and a stronger correlation with age than FreeSurfer. In particular, LOGISMOS-B reports average thinning of 0.022 mm/year in the frontal lobe, but a low correlation and only 0.002 mm/year thinning in the occipital lobe, closely matching the literature. FreeSurfer reports only 0.008 mm/year thinning in the frontal lobe and 0.005 mm/year thinning and a rather strong correlation in the occipital lobe. The similarity of these two rates and their mismatch with published literature indicate that FreeSurfer is either overestimating occipital thinning or underestimating frontal thinning, or, likely, both. LOGISMOS-B also shows a greater range of these age effects on thickness, which should translate into higher statistical power in studies compared to FreeSurfer, which report relatively homogeneous thinning rates. These findings illustrate the high accuracy of the LOGISMOS-B approach and its relevance for neuroimaging studies.

## 9.6 FUTURE DIRECTIONS

The LOGISMOS approach is under continuing development and a number of extensions to the original have been reported.

One of the frequently occurring segmentation problems is simultaneous segmentation of mutually interacting regions and surfaces: a solution to this task that combines LOGISMOS with the Boykov's graph cut approach is given in Song et al. (2011).

Use of LOGISMOS approaches for multimodality image segmentation (e.g., simultaneous segmentation of cancerous tumors in PET/CT image data) (Han et al., 2011) and in the time-sequence domain (Chen et al., 2013) are other useful extensions of the original framework.

The *just-enough-interaction* (JEI) paradigm achieves image segmentation in a sequence of two main steps—automated image segmentation followed by expert-guided modifications (Sun et al., 2013a,b). The goal of this two-step process is to achieve sufficient segmentation correctness in all analyzed cases, even if the initial automated segmentation is locally imperfect. Importantly, graph *s-t* cut optimization can be applied iteratively without restarting the optimization process from scratch. This property of the *s-t* cut graph optimization is utilized when LOGISMOS is employed in both the first and second steps of the JEI approach. Once LOGISMOS produces the initial automated segmentation, user interactions can identify desirable surface locations in areas of local inaccuracy. These interactions are used to locally modify the respective local/regional graph costs, and a new graph optimization solution can be obtained iteratively and very efficiently in close to real time after each such interaction. As a result, the two-step method uses LOGISMOS in both steps and contributes to the resulting surface detection by employing a highly efficient user-guided approach (Sun et al., 2013a,b).

The LOGISMOS image segmentation strategy has evolved from a theoretical proof of single-surface solution optimality to a powerful and multifaceted family of approaches offering great flexibility and high accuracy of surface positioning in volumetric image data, using approximate image presegmentation for initialization. The reliance of the solution on highly flexible cost functions, the ability to incorporate *a priori* information directly in the segmentation process, the ability to locally modify the solution-affecting constraints, and the guarantee of global optimality are all intriguing properties of this approach, suggesting that many novel extensions will likely be developed in the future. While all examples given here demonstrated LOGISMOS' applications to medical image analysis tasks, the utility of the LOGISMOS strategy goes well beyond medical imaging. The LOGISMOS techniques can be applied to any multisurface, multiobject, multimodality, and/or surface-region segmentation problems for which $n$-dimensional volumetric data are available and topologically correct approximate presegmentation obtainable. The availability of efficient expert-guided JEI methods is further strengthening the utility of the presented approaches, facilitating LOGISMOS' applicability to complicated, difficult, and/or atypical data and offering solutions in cases where other approaches may fail.

## ACKNOWLEDGMENTS

This research was funded, in part, by NIH-NIBIB grant R01-EB004640 and NSF CAREER Award CCF-0844765. We are grateful to Jerry Prince for providing the JHU brain MRI dataset; Young H. Kwon and Pavlina Kemp for performing manual tracings of retinal layers in OCT; Douglas B. Critser for acquiring retinal OCT scans; and Teresa Kopel for database management. The OAI is a public-private partnership comprised of five contracts (N01-AR-2-2258; N01-AR-2-2259; N01-AR-2-2260; N01-AR-2-2261; N01-AR-2-2262) funded by the National Institutes of Health, a branch of the Department of Health and Human Services, and conducted by the OAI Study Investigators. Private funding partners include Merck Research Laboratories; Novartis Pharmaceuticals Corporation, GlaxoSmithKline; and Pfizer, Inc. Private sector funding for the OAI is managed by the Foundation for the National Institutes of Health. This manuscript was prepared using an OAI public use data set and does not necessarily reflect the opinions or views of the OAI investigators, the NIH, or the private funding partners.

## REFERENCES

Abràmoff, M.D., Garvin, M.K., Sonka, M., 2010. Retinal imaging and image analysis. IEEE Rev. Biomed. Eng. 3, 169-208.

Abràmoff, M.D., Wu, X., Lee, K., Tang, L., 2014. Subvoxel accurate graph search using non-Euclidean graph space. PLoS ONE 9 (10), e107763.

Bogunovic, H., Sonka, M., Kwon, Y.H., Kemp, P., Abramoff, M.D., Wu, X., 2014. Multi-surface and multi-field co-segmentation of 3-D retinal optical coherence tomography. IEEE Trans. Med. Imaging 33 (12), 2242-2253.

Bogunovic, H., Kwon, Y.H., Rashid, A., Lee, K., Critser, D.B., Garvin, M.K., Sonka, M., Abramoff, M.D., 2015. Relationships of retinal structure and Humphrey 24-2 visual field thresholds in patients with glaucoma. Invest. Ophthalmol. Vis. Sci. 56 (1), 259-271.

Boykov, Y., Jolly, M.P., 2000. Interactive organ segmentation using graph cuts. In: Proc. Medical Image Computing and Computer-Assisted Intervention, Pittsburgh, PA, USA, pp. 276-286.

Boykov, Y., Jolly, M.P., 2001. Interactive graph cuts for optimal boundary & region segmentation of objects in $N$-D images. In: Proc. International Conference on Computer Vision, vols. 1935-I, pp. 105-112.

Boykov, Y., Kolmogorov, V., 2004. An experimental comparison of min-cut/max-flow algorithms for energy minimization in vision. IEEE Trans. Pattern Anal. Mach. Intell. 26 (9), 1124-1137.

Breiman, L., 2001. Random forests. Mach. Learn. 45 (1), 5-32.

Brown, M., Lowe, D.G., 2006. Automatic panoramic image stitching using invariant features. Int. J. Comput. Vis. 74 (1), 59-73.

Chen, M., Zheng, Y., Wang, Y., Müller, K., Lauritsch, G., 2013. Automatic 3D motion estimation of left ventricle from C-arm rotational angiocardiography using a prior motion model and learning based boundary detector. International Conference on Medical Image Computing and Computer-Assisted Intervention, vol. 16, Pt 3, pp. 90-97.

Dale, A.M., Fischl, B., Sereno, M.I., 1999. Cortical surface-based analysis. I. Segmentation and surface reconstruction. NeuroImage 9 (2), 179-194.

Dodin, P., Martel-Pelletier, J., Pelletier, J.P., Abram, F., 2011. A fully automated human knee 3D MRI bone segmentation using the ray casting technique. Med. Biol. Eng. Comput. 49 (12), 1413-1424.

Eckstein, F., Ateshian, G., Burgkart, R., Burstein, D., Cicuttini, F., Dardzinski, B., Gray, M., Link, T.M., Majumdar, S., Mosher, T., Peterfy, C., Totterman, S., Waterton, J., Winalski, C.S., Felson, D., 2006. Proposal for a nomenclature for magnetic resonance imaging based measures of articular cartilage in osteoarthritis. Osteoarthr. Cartilage 14 (10), 974-983.

Freund, Y., Schapire, R.E., 1995. A decision-theoretic generalization of on-line learning and an application to boosting. In: Computational Learning Theory, pp. 23-37.

Fripp, J., Crozier, S., Warfield, S.K., Ourselin, S., 2010. Automatic segmentation and quantitative analysis of the articular cartilages from magnetic resonance images of the knee. IEEE Trans. Med. Imaging 29 (1), 55-64.

Garvin, M.K., Abramoff, M.D., Wu, X., Russell, S.R., Burns, T.L., Sonka, M., 2009. Automated 3-D intraretinal layer segmentation of macular spectral-domain optical coherence tomography images. IEEE Trans. Med. Imaging 28 (9), 1436-1447.

Han, D., Bayouth, J., Song, Q., Taurani, A., Sonka, M., Buatti, J., Wu, X., 2011. Globally optimal tumor segmentation in PET-CT images: a graph-based co-segmentation method. In: Proc. of 22nd International Conference on Information Processing in Medical Imaging (IPMI), Lecture Notes in Computer Science, vol. 6801. Springer, Kloster Irsee, Germany, pp. 245-256.

Hochbaum, D., 2001. A new-old algorithm for minimum-cut and maximum-flow in closure graphs. Networks 37 (4), 171-193.

Ishikawa, H., 2003. Exact optimization for Markov random fields with convex priors. IEEE Trans. Pattern Anal. Mach. Intell. 25 (10), 1333-1336.

IXI, 2015. IXI. http://biomedic.doc.ic.ac.uk/brain-development/index.php?n=Main.Datasets.

Jaume, S., Rondao, P., Macq, B., 2005. Open topology: a toolkit for brain isosurface correction. Insight J. http://hdl.handle.net/1926/50

Johnson, H., 2015. BRAINSABC. https://github.com/BRAINSia/BRAINSTools.

Jones, S.E., Buchbinder, B.R., Aharon, I., 2000. Three-dimensional mapping of cortical thickness using Laplace's equation. Hum. Brain Mapp. 11 (1), 12-32.

Kashyap, S., Yin, Y., Sonka, M., 2013. Automated analysis of cartilage morphology. In: Proc. of the IEEE International Symposium on Biomedical Imaging, pp. 1300-1303.

Kellgren, J., Lawrence, J., et al., 1957. Radiological assessment of osteo-arthrosis. Ann. Rheum. Dis. 16 (4), 494-502.

Kim, E.Y., Johnson, H.J., 2013. Robust multi-site MR data processing: iterative optimization of bias correction, tissue classification, and registration. Front. Neuroinform. 7, 29.

Kolmogorov, V., Zabih, R., 2004. What energy functions can be minimized via graph cuts? IEEE Trans. Pattern Anal. Machine Intell. 26 (2), 147-159.

Lee, J.G., Gumus, S., Moon, C.H., Kwoh, C.K., Bae, K.T., 2014. Fully automated segmentation of cartilage from the MR images of knee using a multi-atlas and local structural analysis method. Med. Phys. 41 (9), 092303.

Li, K., Wu, X., Chen, D.Z., Sonka, M., 2004a, Efficient optimal surface detection: theory, implementation and experimental validation. In: Proc. SPIE International Symposium on Medical Imaging: Image Processing, vol. 5370, pp. 620-627.

Li, K., Wu, X., Chen, D.Z., Sonka, M., 2004b, Globally optimal segmentation of interacting surfaces with geometric constraints. In: Proc. IEEE Conf. on Computer Vision and Pattern Recognition, vol. I, pp. 394-399.

Li, K., Wu, X., Chen, D.Z., Sonka, M., 2006. Optimal surface segmentation in volumetric images—a graph-theoretic approach. IEEE Trans. Pattern Anal. Mach. Intell. 28 (1), 119-134.

OAI, 2015. The Osteoarthritis Initiative. https://oai.epi-ucsf.org/datarelease/.

Oguz, I., Sonka, M., 2014a. Robust cortical thickness measurement with LOGISMOS-B. In: International Conference on Medical Image Computing and Computer-Assisted Intervention, vol. 8673, pp. 722-730.

Oguz, I., Sonka, M., 2014b. LOGISMOS-B: layered optimal graph image segmentation of multiple objects and surfaces for the brain. IEEE Trans. Med. Imaging 33 (6), 1220-1235.

Quellec, G., Lee, K., Dolejsi, M., Garvin, M.K., Abramoff, M.D., Sonka, M., 2010. Three-dimensional analysis of retinal layer texture: identification of fluid-filled regions in SD-OCT of the macula. IEEE Trans. Med. Imaging 29 (6), 1321-1330.

Sailer, M., Fischl, B., Salat, D., Tempelmann, C., Schönfeld, M.A., Busa, E., Bodammer, N., Heinze, H.J., Dale, A., 2003. Focal thinning of the cerebral cortex in multiple sclerosis. Brain 126 (Pt 8), 1734-1744.

Sharma, L., Eckstein, F., Song, J., Guermazi, A., Prasad, P., Kapoor, D., Cahue, S., Marshall, M., Hudelmaier, M., Dunlop, D., 2008. Relationship of meniscal damage, meniscal extrusion, malalignment, and joint laxity to subsequent cartilage loss in osteoarthritic knees. Arthritis Rheum. 58 (6), 1716-1726.

Shiee, N., Bazin, P.L., Cuzzocreo, J.L., Ye, C., Kishore, B., Carass, A., Calabresi, P.A., Reich, D.S., Prince, J.L., Pham, D.L., 2014. Reconstruction of the human cerebral cortex robust to white matter lesions: method and validation. Hum. Brain Mapp. 35 (7), 3385-3401.

Song, Q., Chen, M., Bai, J., Sonka, M., Wu, X., 2011. Surface-region context in optimal multi-object graph based segmentation: Robust delineation of pulmonary tumors. In: Proc. of 22nd International Conference on Information Processing in Medical Imaging, Lecture Notes in Computer Science, vol. 6801. Springer, Kloster Irsee, Germany, pp. 61-72.

Song, Q., Bai, J., Garvin, M.K., Sonka, M., Buatti, J.M., Wu, X., 2013. Optimal multiple surface segmentation with shape and context priors. IEEE Trans. Med. Imaging 32 (2), 376-386.

Sonka, M., Reddy, G.K., Winniford, M.D., Collins, S.M., 1997. Adaptive approach to accurate analysis of small-diameter vessels in cineangiograms. IEEE Trans. Med. Imaging 16 (1), 87-95.

Sonka, M., Hlavac, V., Boyle, R., 2015. Image Processing, Analysis, and Machine Vision, fourth ed. Cengage Learning, New York, NY.

Sun, S., Sonka, M., Beichel, R., 2013a. Graph-based IVUS segmentation with efficient computer-aided refinement. IEEE Trans. Med. Imaging 32 (8), 1536-1549.

Sun, S., Sonka, M., Beichel, R., 2013b. Lung segmentation refinement based on optimal surface finding utilizing a hybrid desktop/virtual reality user interface. Comput. Med. Imaging Graph. 37 (1), 15-27.

Van Leemput, K., Maes, F., Vandermeulen, D., Suetens, P., 1999. Automated model-based tissue classification of MR images of the brain. IEEE Trans. Med. Imaging 18 (10), 897-908.

von Economo, C., 1929. The Cytoarchitectonics of the Human Cerebral Cortex. Oxford University Press, London.

Wu, X., Chen, D.Z., 2002. Optimal net surface problems with applications. In: Proc. of the 29th International Colloquium on Automata, Languages and Programming, pp. 1029-1042.

Wu, X., Chen, D.Z., Li, K., Sonka, M., 2007. The layered net surface problems in discrete geometry and medical image segmentation. Int. J. Comput. Geometry Appl. 17 (3), 261-296.

Wu, X., Dou, X., Wahle, A., Sonka, M., 2011. Region detection by minimizing intraclass variance with geometric constraints, global optimality, and efficient approximation. IEEE Trans. Med. Imaging 30 (3), 814-827. ISSN 0278-0062. http://dx.doi.org/10.1109/TMI.2010.2095870.

Xu, C., Prince, J.L., 1998. Generalized gradient vector flow external forces for active contours. Signal Process. 71 (2), 131-139.

Yin, Y., Zhang, X., Williams, R., Wu, X., Anderson, D.D., Sonka, M., 2010. LOGISMOS—layered optimal graph image segmentation of multiple objects and surfaces: Cartilage segmentation in the knee joint. IEEE Trans. Med. Imaging 29 (12), 2023-2037.

# A CONTEXT INTEGRATION FRAMEWORK FOR RAPID MULTIPLE ORGAN PARSING

# 10

**N. Lay[1], S. Kevin Zhou[1], D. Yang[2] and N. Birkbeck\*,[3]**

*Siemens Corporate Technology, Princeton, NJ, USA[1]*
*Rutgers, New Brunswick, NJ, USA[2]*
*Google, Mountain View, CA, USA[3]*

## CHAPTER OUTLINE

---

*This author contributed to this work while at Siemens Corporate Technology.

S. Kevin Zhou (Ed): Medical Image Recognition, Segmentation and Parsing. http://dx.doi.org/10.1016/B978-0-12-802581-9.00010-X

## 10.1 INTRODUCTION

Algorithms for segmenting anatomical structures in medical imaging are often targeted to individual structures (Yang and Duncan, 2004; Ling et al., 2008; Zheng et al., 2009; Zhou, 2010). Instead, when the problem is posed as the joint segmentation of multiple organs, constraints can be formulated between the organs, for example, nonoverlapping, and the combined formulation allows for a richer prior model on the joint shape of the multiple structures of interest. Such multiorgan segmentation is often posed with atlas-based or level-set-based formulation due to the ease with which geometric constraints can be modeled (Shimizu et al., 2007; Kohlberger et al., 2011).

However, level set methods are computationally demanding and still require a decent initialization so as not to fall into a local minimum. Discriminative learning-based methods are often an alternative approach to initializing such segmentations (e.g., Kohlberger et al., 2011), but, again, these methods often treat the initialization of each organ as an independent problem. While solving the single organ segmentation problem with learning-based methods can be fast (e.g., Zheng et al., 2009), in order to achieve efficient multiobject segmentation, often a tree-like search structure has to be imposed on the detection order of the structures (Liu et al., 2010; Sofka et al., 2010).

The sequential ordering is used to avoid evaluating local classifiers everywhere in the image and to ensure a sane organ configuration. However, as shapes of adjacent structures are often correlated, the appearance of neighboring image patches is often consistent, meaning image patterns commonly associated with one organ, say the liver, are likely to appear next to the right kidney. Instead of modeling dependency among structures at the algorithm level, for example, with generative models (Sofka et al., 2010), the correlation between such *global image context* and the shapes can be learned directly (e.g., Zhou et al., 2007; Criminisi et al., 2009, 2010; Zhou, 2010).

One method to utilize global contextual cues is to regress the position of the organ bounding boxes from each voxel location in the image (Zhou et al., 2007; Criminisi et al., 2009, 2010; Zhou, 2010). Others suggested that this global information alone may not be accurate enough and further improved the accuracy using a cascade of locally trained regressors (Cuingnet et al., 2012).

In this work, we propose a novel integration of both local and global discriminative information for efficient multiple organ segmentation. Unlike other learning-based approaches, we do not rely on a tree-like dependency structure of organ detections to obtain an efficient detection algorithm. Instead, our global image context is only sparsely sampled, allowing us to derive an efficient detection algorithm: global context is used to hypothesize locations that need to be evaluated with the local discriminative classifier. Our nonparametric representation of global image context models correlations in the target shape, allowing us to jointly localize landmarks on multiple target organs. We impose a constraint on the distribution of allowable shapes, enabling us to initialize a likely shape from only a few landmarks per organ. The initialized shape is then deformed using a learned discriminative boundary detector to better fit the image appearance. We demonstrate that the combination of local and global image context outperforms either local or global context alone, and illustrate the use of the proposed joint landmark detection, robust shape initialization, and discriminative boundary deformation to segment up to six organs in either computed tomography (CT) or magnetic resonance (MR) data in *roughly 1-3 s* with segmentation in MR data taking *less than 1 s*. The segmentation accuracy is *fairly close to inter-user variability*.

## 10.2 RELATED LITERATURE

Marginal space learning (MSL) is an effective learning-based approach to segmenting single organs in 3D volumes (Zheng et al., 2008). In MSL, the pose estimation problem is decomposed into subproblems of first estimating position, then orientation, then scale, and finally the coarse shape coefficients. The decomposition into subproblems keeps the learning-based parameter estimation at each phase tractable. Our proposed approach decomposes the shape estimation problem into more tractable components. However, instead of decomposing the problem into inhomogeneous components (e.g., position, orientation, scale), we subdivide the shape estimation problem into that of estimating a set of landmarks.

Detecting a set of landmarks to initialize the segmentation of organs has been proposed before in the medical imaging literature (e.g., Sofka et al., 2011; Zhang et al., 2011). Like these methods, our approach can utilize a sparse shape representation or a statistical point distribution model. However, the main difference is that we use local and global image context to simultaneously localize landmarks on multiple organs instead of using sliding window approaches to independently identify landmarks on a single organ. While detection-only approaches for landmark localization can be efficient (e.g., Liu et al., 2010), such efficient search strategies often give priority to certain landmarks. Thus, a different ordering of the landmarks in the search can give different detection results. Our combination of local and global information can also achieve efficient detection and does not suffer from this limitation.

We indirectly infer the shape of multiple organs from the image. Other approaches, such as the shape regression machine (Zhou et al., 2007; Zhou, 2010), propose to localize the shape using detection but to regress directly the low dimensional coefficients of a point distribution model from the image intensities. Instead, as learning-based detection is known to work well for keypoints, we pose the shape estimation problem as estimating multiple landmarks rather than shape coefficients directly. The shape regression machine approach also combines a classifier to aggregate the contribution of a regressor from multiple positions, but our detection strategy is founded as a sampling method to approximate the expectation of the landmark positions.

With regard to the use of regression to estimate multiple structures in medical image volumes, Criminisi et al. (2009) have used regression forests to identify the axis-aligned bounding box of multiple organs in CT volumes. In contrast to their approach, where each voxel votes for the offset to the coordinates that define an axis aligned bounding box, our approach obtains landmarks on the shape of the object, meaning our method obtains not only a bounding box but also a segmentation. Further, our product of experts formulation leads to an effective way of sampling to estimate landmark positions. This means our approach only needs to be applied to a small subset of voxels during testing rather than every voxel in the volume.

Classifiers have also been combined with the forest-based regression framework in Hough forests (Gall and Lempitsky, 2009). In Hough forests, the classification of a pixel into foreground/background is interleaved into regression trees. If a given patch is considered foreground, it will predict the object center. Our application of local discriminative classifiers differs in two ways. First, our regressor and classifiers are using two pieces of information to predict a landmark: a global patch to predict landmark positions and local patches around the predictions to *verify* the predictions. Second, we do not distinguish between foreground and background, so each position in the image may contribute to the final position of a landmark. In our application, this classification problem is a simpler problem because the appearance at a landmark location versus a nonlandmark location is likely more coherent than the appearance of all foreground versus background pixels.

Nearest neighbor (NN) forests have been developed in Konukoglu et al. (2013). Our work employs binary space partitioning (BSP) regression trees, which are loosely similar to *k-d* trees; *k-d* trees are used for efficient nearest neighbor searches. Hence our BSP trees behave like a kind of nearest neighbor regressor. We also describe a *Region Clustering* tree that can be described by the nearest neighbor forest framework.

## 10.3 METHODS

We aim to segment $C$ organ shapes, $\mathbf{S} = [\mathbf{S}_1, \ldots, \mathbf{S}_C]$, given a volumetric image $\mathbf{I}$. We denote the set of all voxels in the image $\mathbf{I}$ by $\Omega$ and its size by $|\Omega|$. We assume that there exists a set of $D$ corresponding landmarks, $\mathbf{X} = [\mathbf{x}_1, \ldots, \mathbf{x}_D]$, on the multiple shapes $\mathbf{S}$ and decompose the problem into estimating (i) the landmarks given the image using the posterior $P(\mathbf{X}|\mathbf{I})$ defined in Section 10.3.1 and (ii) the shapes given the landmarks and the image using energy minimization in Section 10.3.2. We use the notation $[\mathbf{x}, \ldots, \mathbf{x}]_D$ to represent repeating $\mathbf{x}$ in $D$ times.

### 10.3.1 JOINT LANDMARK DETECTION USING CONTEXT INTEGRATION

To jointly detect the landmarks, we integrate both local and global image context using a product rule into one posterior probability $P(\mathbf{X}|\mathbf{I})$:

$$P(\mathbf{X}|\mathbf{I}) = P^{\mathrm{L}}(\mathbf{X}|\mathbf{I})P^{\mathrm{G}}(\mathbf{X}|\mathbf{I}) \tag{10.1}$$

where $P^{\mathrm{L}}(\mathbf{X}|\mathbf{I})$ and $P^{\mathrm{G}}(\mathbf{X}|\mathbf{I})$ are local and global context posteriors, respectively.

#### 10.3.1.1 Local context posterior

Though not necessarily true, we assume that the landmarks are *locally independent*:

$$P^{\mathrm{L}}(\mathbf{X}|\mathbf{I}) = \prod_{i=1}^{D} P^{\mathrm{L}}(\mathbf{x}_i|\mathbf{I}) \tag{10.2}$$

For modeling $P^{\mathrm{L}}(\mathbf{x}_i|\mathbf{I})$, we exploit the local image context to learn a discriminative detector for landmark $\mathbf{x}_i$ (using, e.g., probabilistic boosting tree [PBT] (Tu, 2005)), that is,

$$P^{\mathrm{L}}(\mathbf{x}_i|\mathbf{I}) = \omega_i^{\mathrm{L}}(+1|\mathbf{I}[\mathbf{x}_i]) \tag{10.3}$$

with $\mathbf{I}[\mathbf{x}_i]$ being the local image patch centered at $\mathbf{x}_i$ and $\omega_i^{\mathrm{L}}(+1|\cdot)$ the local context detector for landmark $\mathbf{x}_i$.

### 10.3.1.2 Global context posterior

We integrate global evidence from all voxels in $\Omega$.

$$P^{G}(\mathbf{X}|\mathbf{I}) = \sum_{\mathbf{y}\in\Omega} P^{G}(\mathbf{X}|\mathbf{I}, \mathbf{y})P(\mathbf{y}|\mathbf{I}) = |\Omega|^{-1} \sum_{\mathbf{y}\in\Omega} P^{G}(\mathbf{X}|\mathbf{I}[\mathbf{y}]) \tag{10.4}$$

In Eq. (10.4), we assume a uniform prior probability $P(\mathbf{y}|\mathbf{I}) = |\Omega|^{-1}$ and $P^{G}(\mathbf{X}|\mathbf{I}[\mathbf{y}])$ is the probability of the landmarks at $\mathbf{X}$ when observing the image patch $\mathbf{I}[\mathbf{y}]$ at a location $\mathbf{y}$.

To learn $P^{G}(\mathbf{X}|\mathbf{I}[\mathbf{y}])$, we leverage annotated data sets and a "randomized" $K$-NN approach (Friedman et al., 2001). We later consider another kind of NN approach that optimizes spatial neighborhood locality. For a complete set of training images with annotated landmarks, we randomly form $K$ subsets. From each subset of images with corresponding landmarks, we construct a training database $\{(\mathbf{J}_n, d\mathbf{X}_n)\}_{n=1}^{N}$ consisting of $N$ pairs of image patch $\mathbf{J}$ and relative shift $d\mathbf{X}$ in an iterative fashion.

---

**for** $n=1, \ldots, N$ **do**
    Randomly sample in the subset an image, say $\tilde{\mathbf{J}}$, with landmarks $\tilde{\mathbf{X}}$
    Randomly sample a voxel location, say $\mathbf{z}$, from $\Omega$
    Set the image patch $\mathbf{J}_n = \tilde{\mathbf{J}}[\mathbf{z}]$
    Set the relative shift $d\mathbf{X}_n = \tilde{\mathbf{X}} - [\mathbf{z}, \ldots, \mathbf{z}]_D$.
**end for**

---

For a test image patch $\mathbf{I}[\mathbf{y}]$, we first find its NN $\hat{\mathbf{J}}_k$ from each subset; this way we find its $K$ neighbors $\{\hat{\mathbf{J}}_1, \ldots, \hat{\mathbf{J}}_K\}$ along with their corresponding shift vectors $\{d\hat{\mathbf{X}}_1[\mathbf{y}], \ldots, d\hat{\mathbf{X}}_K[\mathbf{y}]\}$. How to efficiently find the NN for each subset is elaborated later. We then simply approximate $P^{G}(\mathbf{X}|\mathbf{I}[\mathbf{y}])$ as

$$P^{G}(\mathbf{X}|\mathbf{I}[\mathbf{y}]) = K^{-1} \sum_{k=1}^{K} \delta(\mathbf{X} - [\mathbf{y}, \ldots, \mathbf{y}]_D - d\hat{\mathbf{X}}_k[\mathbf{y}]) \tag{10.5}$$

Figure 10.1 graphically illustrates how the approach works. It also gives an example of the local, global, and joint posteriors. Even though the local detector may be inaccurate, it is only being applied at locations predicted from the global context, meaning it is possible to get a highly peaked posterior when integrating evidence from local and global context.

### 10.3.1.3 MMSE and MAP estimate for landmark location

The expected landmark location $\bar{\mathbf{X}}$, also the minimum mean square error (MMSE) estimate, is computed as

$$\bar{\mathbf{X}} = \sum_{\mathbf{X}} \mathbf{X}\, P(\mathbf{X}|\mathbf{I}) = \sum_{\mathbf{X}} \mathbf{X}\, P^{L}(\mathbf{X}|\mathbf{I})P^{G}(\mathbf{X}|\mathbf{I}) \tag{10.6}$$

$$= \frac{1}{K|\Omega|} \sum_{\mathbf{X}} \sum_{\mathbf{y}\in\Omega} \sum_{k=1}^{K} \mathbf{X} \prod_{i=1}^{D} \omega_i^{L}(+1|\mathbf{I}[\mathbf{x}_i])\delta(\mathbf{X} - [\mathbf{y}, \ldots, \mathbf{y}]_D - d\hat{\mathbf{X}}_k[\mathbf{y}])$$

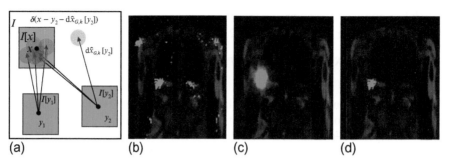

**FIGURE 10.1**

(a) An illustration of how image patches (green) predict the landmark location using global context and Eq. (10.5) and then these predictions are combined with local context at (blue) **x**. (b) Detection scores for a landmark on the top left of the liver in a low-resolution MR FastView 3D volume, where local context gives spurious responses. (c) Global context gives a coarse localization. (d) The integration of local and global detection gives a fine scale density.

Using the local independence and vector decomposition, it can be shown that the expected location $\bar{\mathbf{x}}_i$ for a single landmark is computed as

$$\bar{\mathbf{x}}_i = K^{-1}|\Omega|^{-1} \sum_{\mathbf{y} \in \Omega} \sum_{k=1}^{K} (\mathbf{y} + d\hat{\mathbf{x}}_{k,i}[\mathbf{y}]) \omega_i^{\mathrm{l}}(+1 | \mathbf{I}[\mathbf{y} + d\hat{\mathbf{x}}_{k,i}[\mathbf{y}]]) \tag{10.7}$$

Equation (10.7) implies an efficient scheme—evaluating the local detector only for the locations predicted from the global context posterior instead of the whole image. Since the predicted locations are highly clustered around the true location, this brings the first significant reduction in computation. Similarly, the maximum a posterior (MAP) estimate $\hat{\mathbf{x}}_i$ can be derived as

$$\hat{\mathbf{x}}_i = \arg\max_{\mathbf{x}} \omega_i^{\mathrm{l}}(+1 | \mathbf{I}[\mathbf{x}]) \sum_{\mathbf{y} \in \Omega} \sum_{k=1}^{K} \delta(\mathbf{x} - \mathbf{y} - d\hat{\mathbf{x}}_{k,i}[\mathbf{y}]) \tag{10.8}$$

### 10.3.1.4 Sparsity in global context
The global context from all voxels is highly redundant as neighboring patches tend to predict nearby landmark locations. Therefore, we can "sparsify" the global context by constructing the subset $\Omega_\ell$ from the full voxel set $\Omega$; for example, we can skip every other $l$ voxels. This brings the second significant reduction in computation complexity by $O(l^3)$.

### 10.3.1.5 Efficient approximate NN search with BSP trees
Computing the expected landmark location in Eq. (10.7) relies on the ability to compute the NN from the training database of $\{\mathbf{J}_n, d\mathbf{X}_n\}_{n=1}^N$ for one subset of training images. The time and space efficiency of this operation is influenced by two factors: the size of the database, $N$, and the dimension of the points,

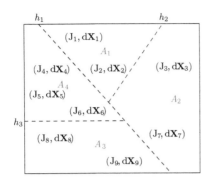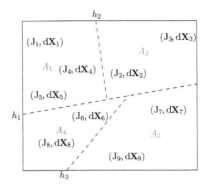

**FIGURE 10.2**

Two BSP trees for different subsets of the training data are used to partition the space into convex regions (e.g., the leafs), $A_j$, using a set of hyperplanes $h_l$. Instead of searching over all entries within a leaf of the tree to find an exact NN, we simply store the average relative offset vector for the training samples that fell into the leaf.

$D$, in the database. With, for example, 100 training volumes of dimension $128^3$, we have a potential database size of $N = 128^3 \times 100 > 209$ million. Furthermore, in order to have enough contextual information, an image patch $J_n$, with size up to $32^3$ voxels, is used, meaning that the NN query must be performed in a high dimensional space of up to $D = 32{,}768$.

For efficiency, we relax the requirement of finding the exact nearest Euclidean neighbor to that of finding an approximate NN. We then take a similar approach to local sensitive hashing (Datar and Indyk, 2004) and build multiple hash indexes on the data (Figure 10.2). However, instead of using a hash function, we construct a random BSP tree that is similar to a random projection tree (Dasgupta and Freund, 2008). At each node of our BSP tree, we choose a random hyperplane to split the data. Unlike random projection trees, which choose the split hyperplane uniformly random on a $D$-dimensional hypersphere, we restrict the hyperplanes to be Haar wavelets. We have two reasons for doing this: (1) Haar wavelets provide a class of features often used to discriminate appearance in classification problems and (2) any Haar feature can be instantaneously evaluated using an integral image. Further, instead of storing all training sample patches in their respective leaf nodes within the tree, we choose a single representative relative shift vector—this way the space requirements are dependent on the size of the tree instead of $O(ND)$.

In our experiments, we typically form $K = 10$ subsets and hence train 10 BSP-trees with each tree built up to depth 10. This means that an approximate NN match for a single tree is computed using at most 10 Haar wavelet evaluations, and all $K = 10$ approximate neighbors can be found in as little as 100 Haar wavelet evaluations.

### 10.3.1.6 Region Clustering forest

Another perspective to landmark prediction with a decision tree-like structure is to consider the region in the image from where a landmark is predicted. A decision tree partitions an image into disjoint regions based on some feature space. Each disjoint region in the image is described by a single leaf.

See, for example, Figure 10.3. When learning a piecewise constant landmark offset regressor, some ideal properties include

1. **Contiguity**
   Leaves of a decision tree ought to describe one contiguous region of the image.
2. **Locality**
   Leaves of a decision tree ought to describe a spatially compact region of the image.

A piecewise constant landmark offset regressor can only be reliable if the prediction originates from a single contiguous region in the image. This is shown in Figure 10.3 and leads to property 1. But this is not sufficient for a reliable prediction. A leaf that describes a relatively large and contiguous region of the image cannot be expected to predict accurately either. An example can be seen from Figure 10.3(a) where one leaf describes a region as large as the volume itself. This ultimately leads to property 2 where a leaf ought to describe a more localized region.

To attempt to meet these properties, we consider a loss function that measures the spatial locality of the training example positions

$$\ell(T) = \sum_{L \in T} \sum_{V \in L} \frac{1}{|V|} \sum_{x \in V} (x - \mu_V)^2 \tag{10.9}$$

Here $T$ is a trained decision tree (which we will refer to as a Region Clustering tree), $L$ is a leaf vertex in $T$, $V$ is an observed set of points in a volume falling in leaf $L$, $x$ is a point falling in volume $V$, and $\mu_V$ is the mean of all points in $V$. Each Random Tree $T$ is a different approximate minimum of $\ell(T)$. It is noteworthy to point out that this formulation involves no ground truth. Hence, it is a purely unsupervised method, which is closely related to the Neighborhood Approximation Forest (Konukoglu et al., 2013).

To approximately optimize Eq. (10.9) in a decision tree framework, consider optimizing the loss (Eq. 10.11) for each decision tree node. Denote

$$H(S) = \sum_{V \in S} \frac{1}{|V|} \sum_{x \in V} (x - \mu_V)^2 \tag{10.10}$$

where $H(S)$ is a measure of spatial locality, $|\cdot|$ is the cardinality, $S$ is a training sample, $V$ is a set of points that fall in a distinct volume, $x$ are points in $V$, and $\mu_V$ is the mean of the points in $V$, then

$$\ell(A, B) = \frac{|A|}{|A \cup B|} H(A) + \frac{|B|}{|A \cup B|} H(B) \tag{10.11}$$

Here, $|\cdot|$ is the cardinality, $A$ and $B$ are partitions in the feature space, $V$ is a set of points that fall in a distinct volume, $x$ are points in $V$, and $\mu_V$ is the mean of the points in $V$. A direct optimization of Eq. (10.11) is problematic due to the following corner cases:

1. $H(S)$ is already optimal
   Any partitioning of the training sample $S$ into $A, B$ will be optimal. There are infinitely many solutions.
2. $\ell(A, B) = H(S)$
   No partitioning of $S$ will improve the spatial locality.

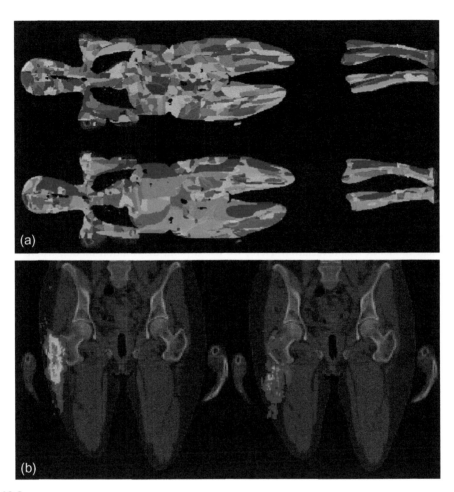

**FIGURE 10.3**

Leaf map and voting map examples of a Region Clustering and BSP tree. The Region Clustering tree leaves often describe relatively localized regions in the volumetric image. Contrast this with BSP which, for example, exhibits a single leaf (most purple regions) describing a region as large as the image itself. Consequently, Region Clustering produces higher quality predictions. (a) Leaf map of one depth 10 tree from both Region Clustering (top) and BSP (bottom). Each color generally corresponds to one leaf (but there are leaves that share colors). (b) Region Clustering (left) and BSP (right) voting maps for a landmark on the femoral head surface using a single tree. Only voxels with 10 or more votes are colored. More patches vote in the vicinity of the femoral head with Region Clustering than they do with BSP.

To avoid these corner cases, we instead consider the reduction of loss. This instead becomes a *gain* function.

$$IG(A, B) = 1 - \frac{\ell(A, B)}{H(S)} \tag{10.12}$$

where the denominator $H(S)$ is the measure of the spatial locality of the original training examples $S$. The effect of partitioning $S$ into $A, B$ produces an average locality of $\ell(A, B)$ and $IG(A, B)$ measures the reduction of spatial locality, where $IG(A, B) = 0$ means no reduction and $IG(A, B) = 1$ is full reduction. The corner cases are then easily avoided since $H(S) = 0$ is easily checked and $\ell(A, B) = H(S)$ always results in $IG(A, B) = 0$.

## 10.3.2 SHAPE INITIALIZATION USING ROBUST MODEL ALIGNMENT

An initial segmentation for each organ is then aligned to the sparse detected landmarks through the use of a statistical model of shape variation. Here, we use a point distribution model, where each organ shape is represented as a mean shape or mesh with $M$ mesh nodes, $\bar{\mathbf{V}} = [\bar{\mathbf{v}}_1, \bar{\mathbf{v}}_2, \ldots, \bar{\mathbf{v}}_M]$, plus a linear combination of a set of $N$ eigenmodes, $\mathbf{U}_n = [\mathbf{u}_{1,n}, \mathbf{u}_{2,n}, \ldots, \mathbf{u}_{M,n}]$, with $1 \leq n \leq N$.

As a complete organ shape is characterized by only a few coefficients that modulate the eigenmodes, the point distribution model can be used to infer a shape from a sparse set of landmark points. Given a set of detected landmarks, $\{\mathbf{x}_i\}$, the best fitting instance of the complete shape is found by minimizing the following robust energy function:

$$(\beta, \{a_n\}) = \operatorname{argmin}_{\beta, \{a_n\}} \sum_i \psi \left( \left\| \mathbf{x}_i - T_\beta \left\{ \bar{\mathbf{v}}_{\pi(i)} + \sum_{n=1}^N a_n \mathbf{u}_{\pi(i),n} \right\} \right\|^2 \right) + \sum_{n=1}^N a_n^2 \Big/ \lambda_n \tag{10.13}$$

where the function $\pi(i)$ maps the landmark $\mathbf{x}_i$ to the corresponding mesh index in $\bar{\mathbf{V}}$, the function $T_\beta\{\cdot\}$ is a 9D similarity transform parameterized by the vector $\beta = [t_x, t_y, t_z, \theta_x, \theta_y, \theta_z, s_x, s_y, s_z]$, and $\lambda_n$ are the corresponding eigenvalues. The first term measures the difference between a predicted shape point under a hypothesis transformation from the detected landmark, and the second term is a prior keeping the eigenmodes responsible for smaller variation closer to zero. As we typically only have a few landmarks, and have a principal component analysis (PCA) model for a larger number of vertices, using no prior term gives rise to an ill-posed problem. Finally, $\psi$ is a robust norm, reducing the effect of outliers. We use $\psi(s^2) = s$.

## 10.3.3 DISCRIMINATIVE BOUNDARY REFINEMENT

Using the initialization from Section 10.3.2, a fine refinement of the points on the surface mesh is obtained by iteratively displacing each vertex along its surface normal, $\mathbf{v}_i \leftarrow \mathbf{v}_i + \mathbf{n}_i \hat{\tau}_i$. The best displacement for each point is obtained by maximizing the output of a discriminative classifier (Ling et al., 2008):

$$\hat{\tau}_i = \operatorname{argmax}_{\tau_i} \omega^B(+1 | \mathbf{v}_i + \mathbf{n}_i \tau_i) \tag{10.14}$$

Here, $\omega^B(+1|\cdot)$ is the boundary detector that scores whether the point, $\mathbf{v}_i + \mathbf{n}_i\tau_i$, is on the boundary of the organ being segmented. Regularity is incorporated in the previously independent estimated displacements by projecting the resulting mesh onto the linear subspace spanned by the linear shape model, as in the active shape model (ASM) (Cootes et al., 1995).

## 10.4 OBJECT CONTEXT

As an extension to global and local context, it is possible to introduce the notion of *object context*. Object context factors in object-specific cues such as the edge of an object. Object context can help further localize landmark predictions. Where the objective was originally purely landmark detection, we aim to segment the unknown shape directly. The objective of segmentation is to estimate an unknown shape, $S$, given a volumetric image $I$. The shape $S$ is comprised of vertexes $\{\mathbf{v}_i \in \mathbb{R}^3\}_{i=1}^N$, normals $\{\mathbf{n}_i \in \mathbb{R}^3\}_{i=1}^N$, and triangles $\{\mathbf{t}_j \in \{1, 2, \ldots, N\}^3\}_{j=1}^T$. We would furthermore like to segment $M$ such shapes $S_m$ from image $I$. For the sake of simplicity, we will ignore the triangle information as these remain constant for each mesh. That is, the shape $S_m = \{(\mathbf{v}_{im}, \mathbf{n}_{im})\}_{i=1}^{N_m}$.

For simplicity of notation, we will denote $S = \cup_{m=1}^M S_m = \{\mathbf{v}_i, \mathbf{n}_i\}_{i=1}^D$ as the set of all mesh vertexes and normals combined. As with local and global context, the mesh vertexes are jointly detected by sampling a posterior defined by the product of global and *object* context

$$P(S|I) = P^O(S|I)P^G(S|I) \tag{10.15}$$

where $P^O(S|I)$ and $P^G(S|I)$ are object and global context posteriors, respectively. For simplicity, the object context posterior assumes independence among the mesh vertexes and is thus defined as

$$P^O(S|I) = P^O((\mathbf{v}_1, \mathbf{n}_1), (\mathbf{v}_2, \mathbf{n}_2), \ldots, (\mathbf{v}_D, \mathbf{n}_D)|I) \approx \prod_{i=1}^D P^O(\mathbf{v}_i, \mathbf{n}_i|I) \tag{10.16}$$

We model each independent posterior $P(\mathbf{v}_i, \mathbf{n}_i|I)$ with a discriminative classifier (using, e.g., PBT, Tu 2005), that is

$$P^O(\mathbf{v}_i, \mathbf{n}_i|I) = h_i^L(+1|I[\mathbf{v}_i], \mathbf{n}_i) \tag{10.17}$$

with $I[\mathbf{v}_i]$ being the local image patch centered at $\mathbf{v}_i$ and $h_i^L(+1|\cdot)$ being the object context detector for mesh vertex $(\mathbf{v}_i, \mathbf{n}_i)$.

To model the global context posterior, we integrate over all voxels in $\Omega$

$$P^G(S|I) = \sum_{\mathbf{x} \in \Omega} P^G(S|I, \mathbf{x})P(\mathbf{x}|I) = |\Omega|^{-1} \sum_{\mathbf{x} \in \Omega} P^G(S|I[\mathbf{x}]) \tag{10.18}$$

where we assume $P(\mathbf{x}|I) = |\Omega|^{-1}$ and that $P^G(S|I[\mathbf{x}])$ is the probability of the shape $S$ given the image patch $I[\mathbf{x}]$.

The mesh vertexes can be predicted through expectation

$$E[\mathbf{V}] = \sum_{\mathbf{X}} \mathbf{X}P(S|I) = \sum_{\mathbf{X} \in \Omega} \sum_{\|\mathbf{N}\|=1} \mathbf{X}P^O((\mathbf{X}, \mathbf{N})|I)P^G((\mathbf{X}, \mathbf{N})|I) \tag{10.19}$$

## 10.5 AUTOMATIC MESH VERTEX SELECTION

The object context posterior $P^O(S|I)$ adds overhead during detection. This is especially apparent under the assumption of independence of mesh vertexes. This system does not scale well for high-resolution meshes. As a consequence, we consider predicting coarse resolution meshes and then upsampling these in a postprocessing step. The postprocessing can also serve as a regularization where some predictions can be inaccurate. As described in Section 10.3.2, we use robust PCA to serve both purposes. Since our formulation treats meshes as points and normals, the objective is to identify a sparse set of vertexes to predict. In the Local + Global context work presented here and in Lay et al. (2013), landmarks were manually picked on the surface of the mesh for each structure. We propose an automated way to sample mesh vertexes based on a discriminative boundary classifier $h(+1|I[\mathbf{v}], \mathbf{n})$. This boundary classifier is later used to define the object context posterior $P^O(S|I)$. The mesh vertexes are picked as follows.

Figure 10.4 motivates the use of this strategy. Some locations on the mesh are confusing and not well described by a boundary classifier. This especially helps produce more accurate mesh initializations during detection since the object context posterior will generally produce a high response near the boundary.

---

**Input**: Volumetric images with corresponding registered annotation meshes $(I_n, M_n)$, $n = 1, 2, \ldots, N$, and a minimum distance $D$ between two selected mesh vertexes.
**Output**: A subset of mesh vertex indexes $Q \subseteq \{1, 2, \ldots, |V|\}$

Initialize visit labels for each mesh vertex $L_i = $ Unvisited, $i = 1, 2, \ldots, |V|$
Initialize mesh vertex probability sum $p_i = 0$, $i = 1, 2, \ldots, |V|$
Initialize $\tilde{V} = \emptyset$
**for** $n=1,2,\ldots,|V|$ **do**
    For every mesh vertex $(\mathbf{v}_i, \mathbf{n}_i) \in M_n$, set $p_i \leftarrow p_i + h(+1|I_n[\mathbf{v}_i], \mathbf{n}_i)$
**end for**
Rank $p_i$ from greatest to least
**for** $n=1,2,\ldots,|V|$ **do**
  **if** $L_n == $ Unvisited **then**
  Set $L_n \leftarrow$ Visited
  Append $Q \leftarrow Q \cup \{n\}$
  Dilate the "Visited" label to all vertexes within $D$ units of distance from $V_n$
    **end if**
**end for**

---

## 10.6 INCOMPLETE ANNOTATIONS

One practical limitation in all formulations of the landmark regressor is the required presence of all landmarks in training cases. However, medical images are often targeted to specific body regions, thus limiting the field of view. In such cases, each training volume may only have a subset of the landmarks

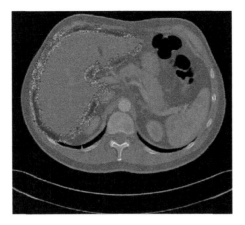

**FIGURE 10.4**

A boundary probability map on a liver annotation mesh. The boundary responses shown only range from $0.75 \leq h(+1|I[\mathbf{v}],\mathbf{n}) \leq 1$. Mesh vertexes that correspond to prominent geometric features (such as the liver tip) do not necessarily correspond with a *reliable* boundary probability.

of interest. It is possible to deal with partial landmark annotations by introducing a binary vector that indicates the presence or absence of landmarks for a given training example.

## 10.7 EXPERIMENTS

Our system was implemented in C++ using OpenMP and compiled using Visual Studio 2008. In the experiments following, timing results are reported for an Intel Xeon 64-bit machine running Windows Server 2008 and using 16 threads. We illustrate results of the Local + Global approach on segmenting six organs in MR scans (Section 10.7.1) and five organs in CT (Section 10.7.2). We additionally show preliminary results of *Object* context on 11 organs in CT scans (Section 10.7.3).

### 10.7.1 LUNGS, HEART, LIVER, AND KIDNEYS IN MR LOCALIZER SCANS

We tested our approach on a challenging set of MR localizer scans acquired using a fast continuously moving table technique (syngo TimCT FastView, Siemens). Such scans are often used for MR examination planning to increase scan reproducibility and operator efficiency. A total of 185 volumes having 5 mm isotropic spacing were split into a training set of 135 and test set of 50. These data are challenging due to the low resolution, weak boundaries, inhomogeneous intensity within scan, and varying image contrast across scans. For this example, we used $K = 10$ NN. The local detectors were also trained on 5 mm resolution using a PBT (Tu, 2005) and a combination of Haar and image gradient features. A total of 33 landmarks were selected on the 6 organs, with 6 landmarks each on the liver and the lungs, and 5 landmarks each on the kidneys and heart.

First, we demonstrate the effectiveness of integrating local and global context with respect to accuracy and evaluation time. Table 10.1 illustrates median errors for all landmark positions averaged

**Table 10.1 Accuracy (Measured in Millimeters) and Timing Results for the Landmark Detection Using Local, Global, and Local + Global Context Posterior**

|  | Global | | Local | | Local + Global | |
|---|---|---|---|---|---|---|
| Spacing | Time (s) | Median | Time | Median | Time (s) | Median |
| 1 (5 mm) | 2.76 | **25.0 ± 17.4** | 1.91 | 16.4 ± 10.6 | – | – |
| 5 (25 mm) | 0.92 | 39.9 ± 33.4 | – | – | 2.11 | **12.9 ± 7.52** |
| 7 (35 mm) | 0.91 | 54.1 ± 54.1 | – | – | 0.91 | 13.0 ± 7.56 |
| 15 (75 mm) | **0.89** | 79.0 ± 85.6 | – | – | **0.23** | 14.1 ± 8.25 |

*Bold values indicate smallest values in their respective column.*

over the testing set. For the local context detector and Local + Global posterior, we used the MMSE estimate. While it is possible to get better speedup with a sparse sampling of the global context when computing the expected value, we noticed that the MAP estimate gave better results, as we reported in the table. Obtaining the MAP estimate requires populating a probability image and scanning through the image to get the MAP estimate (this is proportional to the number of landmarks, which is why no speedup is reported in the table). Besides, the accuracy of the global context posterior suffers from sparse sampling, and even with dense sampling it still performs worse than the Local + Global method. On the other hand, it is evident that a sparser sampling of the volume has little impact on the accuracy of the Local + Global method. The local classifier is computed using a constrained search over the volume (e.g., using bounds for the landmark positions relative to the image, Zheng et al., 2009), but achieves worse accuracy and is still slower than our combined Local + Global posterior modeling.

The shape landmarks are used to infer the shape of all the organs (see Figure 10.5). We compare the resulting segmentation results at several phases to a state-of-the-art hierarchical detection using

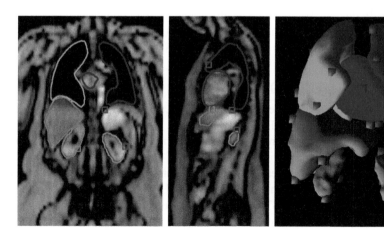

**FIGURE 10.5**

An illustration of the landmarks in 3D and automatic segmentation results. Our method is robust to a few failed landmarks.

MSL (Zheng et al., 2009) that is known as both fast and accurate. For the MSL setup, the kidneys were predicted from the liver bounding box, meaning the kidney search range was more localized, allowing the detection to be faster (the lungs were predicted relative to the heart in a similar manner). Table 10.2 illustrates the timing and accuracy results for the 50 unseen test cases using both MSL and our method. The accuracy is gauged by symmetric surface-to-surface distance. Figure 10.6 illustrates two qualitative results.

The fast landmark detection and robust shape initialization can provide an approximate shape in as little as 0.33 s (for spacing of 75 mm, e.g., 15 voxels). The improvement of our initialization on the liver and lungs over the MSL approach is likely due to our use of more landmarks to capture more variations associated with complex anatomies than MSL, which fits shapes of varying complexities into a rigid bounding box. On the other hand, for both kidneys with fewer variations in the shape but more in the appearance, MSL performs better as it considers kidney as a whole. The discriminative boundary deformation significantly improves the segmentation accuracy for both approaches, which yield comparable overall accuracy for all organs. Our approach is more efficient, for example, over five times faster if we skip every 12th voxel (65 mm) in the global context. With a skipping factor of 75 mm, we achieved segmentation of six organs *within 1 s* and with accuracy almost as good as the best quality! Both methods perform fairly close to inter-user variability.[a]

One potential concern with relying on far-away global context information is that the reliability of the detection and segmentation may degrade or vary when given a subvolume. To investigate this, we evaluated the lung, liver, and heart segmentation accuracy on the same subset of unseen volumes, but this time we cropped the volumes 10 cm below the lung and heart, meaning that the kidneys and liver are not present. In these cropped volumes, using a spacing factor of 50 mm, we find the accuracy of our Local + Global method to be consistent with that in Table 10.2, where right lung accuracy was $3.57 \pm 1.32$, heart accuracy was slightly worse at $4.53 \pm 2.39$, and the left lung was $3.22 \pm 1.02$. Although the global model may predict instances of missing organs (e.g., the kidney and liver), these detections can be pruned by thresholding the local classifier scores or by identifying missing organs as those with a low average boundary detector score.

## 10.7.2 PROSTATE, BLADDER, RECTUM, AND FEMORAL HEADS IN CT SCANS

In this second data set, we detect the prostate, bladder, rectum, and femoral heads in CT scans. The detection and segmentation of these structures is useful for radiation therapy planning. These data exhibit challenges in weak boundaries between soft tissues, complex shapes in rectum and femoral head, large-scale variation in bladder, etc. A total of 145 cases were used, with 100 randomly selected for training and the remaining 45 used in testing. The volumes were isotropically resampled to have a resolution of 3 mm. Six manually selected landmarks were identified on each of the objects, with the exception of the bladder, which used seven as it had large variability. And a similar configuration as described in the previous section was used to train the local and global context models.

Table 10.3 shows the timing and accuracy results for the final segmentation compared to an MSL pipeline. Even with a spacing factor of 36 mm, our Local + Global model behaves similarly to or better than MSL on all organs except for the bladder while giving an overall speedup of six times over MSL. MSL seems to better handle the large-scale variability observed in the bladder. Our approach significantly outperforms MSL for rectum, possibly because of the aforementioned reason—the rectum shape varies a lot and landmark-based shape initialization is better. Both approaches achieved accuracy

**Table 10.2** Accuracy (Measured in Millimeters) and Timing for Segmentation Results Using Our Approach Compared to the State-of-the-Art MSL Model on the MR FastView Data

| | Skip (mm) | Time (s) | Liver | R. Kidney | L. Kidney | R. Lung | Heart | L. Lung |
|---|---|---|---|---|---|---|---|---|
| **Detection and Shape Initialization** | | | | | | | | |
| MSL | – | 5.50 | 9.21 ± 1.82 | **3.44 ± 1.16** | **3.08 ± 1.21** | 7.29 ± 1.64 | 5.98 ± 1.59 | 7.42 ± 1.71 |
| | 25 | 2.21 | **7.41 ± 1.91** | 4.10 ± 1.34 | 4.31 ± 1.81 | **6.60 ± 1.74** | **5.64 ± 1.41** | **6.72 ± 1.55** |
| | 35 | 1.01 | 7.43 ± 1.95 | 4.18 ± 1.39 | 4.39 ± 1.89 | 6.67 ± 1.79 | 5.69 ± 1.40 | 6.78 ± 1.53 |
| Local + Global | 50 | 0.55 | 7.55 ± 2.03 | 4.36 ± 1.43 | 4.57 ± 1.93 | 6.77 ± 1.86 | 5.78 ± 1.48 | 6.83 ± 1.64 |
| | 60 | 0.39 | 7.63 ± 1.95 | 4.59 ± 1.52 | 4.70 ± 1.98 | 6.86 ± 1.91 | 5.92 ± 1.53 | 6.91 ± 1.68 |
| | 75 | **0.33** | 7.94 ± 2.21 | 5.13 ± 1.77 | 5.38 ± 2.90 | 6.97 ± 1.95 | 5.98 ± 1.57 | 6.88 ± 1.75 |
| **With Boundary Refinement** | | | | | | | | |
| MSL | – | 6.36 | 4.87 ± 1.46 | **2.26 ± 0.61** | **2.12 ± 0.68** | 3.67 ± 0.95 | **3.99 ± 1.36** | 3.55 ± 0.97 |
| | 25 | 2.89 | **4.07 ± 0.99** | 2.33 ± 0.68 | 2.41 ± 1.61 | **3.56 ± 0.96** | 4.02 ± 1.50 | **3.35 ± 0.83** |
| | 35 | 1.60 | 4.08 ± 0.99 | 2.37 ± 0.69 | 2.47 ± 1.72 | 3.57 ± 0.98 | 4.02 ± 1.52 | **3.35 ± 0.83** |
| BSP | 50 | 1.13 | 4.09 ± 1.01 | 2.37 ± 0.73 | 2.48 ± 1.66 | 3.57 ± 0.95 | 4.06 ± 1.62 | 3.36 ± 0.83 |
| | 60 | 0.97 | 4.08 ± 1.00 | 2.42 ± 0.79 | 2.42 ± 1.57 | 3.57 ± 0.97 | 4.07 ± 1.63 | 3.35 ± 0.84 |
| | 75 | **0.89** | 4.17 ± 1.14 | 2.51 ± 1.00 | 2.84 ± 2.51 | 3.57 ± 0.95 | 4.11 ± 1.64 | 3.37 ± 0.83 |
| Inter-user variability | | | 4.07 ± 0.93 | 1.96 ± 0.43 | 2.10 ± 0.51 | 3.79 ± 0.36 | 4.54 ± 0.88 | 3.52 ± 0.63 |

*Bold values indicate smallest value in their respective column excluding Inter-user variability.*

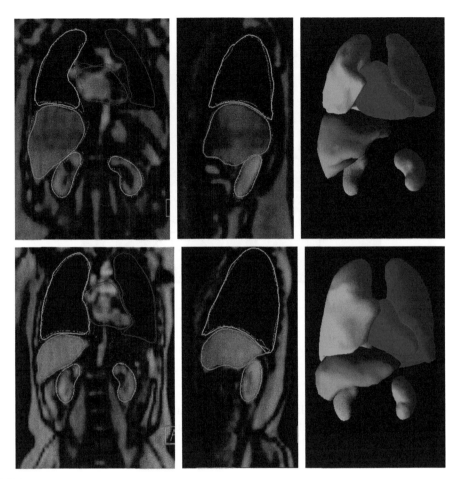

**FIGURE 10.6**

Qualitative results of the MR FastView segmentation (solid) on unseen cases with ground truth (dotted).

**Table 10.3 Accuracy and Timing for Segmentation Results Using Our Model Compared to the State-of-the-Art MSL Model on CT Prostate, Bladder, Rectum, and Femoral Heads**

| | | | Detection, Shape Initialization, and Boundary Refinement | | | | |
|---|---|---|---|---|---|---|---|
| | Skip (mm) | Time (s) | Prostate | Bladder | Rectum | R. Fem | L. Fem |
| MSL | – | 9.67 | $3.57 \pm 2.01$ | **$2.59 \pm 1.70$** | $4.36 \pm 1.70$ | $1.89 \pm 0.99$ | $2.05 \pm 1.27$ |
| BSP | 10 (30 mm) | 1.76 | **$3.35 \pm 1.40$** | $3.08 \pm 2.25$ | **$3.97 \pm 1.43$** | **$1.88 \pm 0.78$** | **$1.90 \pm 1.18$** |
| | 12 (36 mm) | 1.36 | $3.48 \pm 1.53$ | $3.17 \pm 2.28$ | $3.98 \pm 1.49$ | $1.93 \pm 1.00$ | $2.23 \pm 1.76$ |
| | 15 (45 mm) | 1.09 | $3.70 \pm 1.64$ | $3.28 \pm 2.42$ | $4.03 \pm 1.48$ | $2.04 \pm 1.18$ | $2.25 \pm 2.04$ |
| | Inter-user variability | | $3.03 \pm 1.15$ | $2.03 \pm 0.11$ | $2.93 \pm 1.10$ | $1.29 \pm 0.12$ | $1.16 \pm 0.21$ |

*Bold values indicate smallest value in their respective column and excluding Inter-user variability.*

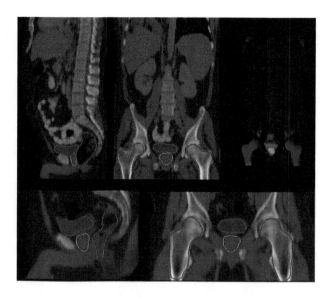

**FIGURE 10.7**

An illustration of the segmentation results on two of the CT prostate data sets. These data have wildly varying dimensions, some being full body scans and others localized near the prostate. Our method works well across this variation and handles large variability in shape and appearance of the organs, such as drastic changes in appearance in the rectum.

fairly close to the inter-user variability except for the rectum.[b]  We achieved a speed of just over 1 s by skipping every 16th voxel, with decent accuracy. Figure 10.7 shows two of the automatic CT segmentations on unseen images. The femoral accuracy of the femoral head is limited by the low resolution of our mesh and is due to using a 3 mm isotropic resolution. However, this serves as a good initialization for voxel-based refinement using graph cut or random walker.

## 10.7.3 OBJECT CONTEXT IN CT SCANS

Object context with region clustering was tested on a CT segmentation problem. The objective was to segment: lungs, liver, spleen, kidneys, bladder, prostate, rectum, and femoral heads in CT images. Some challenges include varying fields of view, missing annotations, and an imbalanced number of annotations for each structure. Table 10.4 provides details of the quantity of images and annotations considered. Collectively, 1191 distinct CT volumes were used to train this system.

To prepare the system for training, all annotations for each structure were registered. Using the resulting correspondence meshes, a PCA shape model was created for each structure. Then a boundary classifier $h(+1|I[\mathbf{x}], \mathbf{n})$ was trained for each structure using the annotations as the ground truth. Due to scalability issues, we consider only coarse meshes during training and detection with the forest as described in Section 10.3.1.6. However, high-resolution meshes are fit to the coarse detections in the robust PCA phase of detection. The coarse meshes were automatically selected as described in Section 10.5.

**Table 10.4 Number of Annotations per Structure**

| Structure | Annotations | Mesh Vertexes | Test Data |
|---|---|---|---|
| Liver | 433 | 7 | 50 |
| L. kidney | 404 | 5 | 50 |
| R. kidney | 361 | 6 | 50 |
| Spleen | 314 | 7 | 50 |
| L. lung | 205 | 8 | 50 |
| R. lung | 217 | 8 | 50 |
| Prostate | 100 | 6 | 45 |
| Bladder | 100 | 7 | 45 |
| L. femur | 94 | 5 | 45 |
| R. femur | 91 | 6 | 45 |
| Rectum | 100 | 6 | 45 |
| Total | 1191 | 71 | – |

A total of 71 mesh vertexes were collectively sampled on all the structures considered (see Table 10.4). After sampling coarse meshes for each structure, the system was trained as described in Section 10.3. The forest uses trees that learn decision criteria based on Haar features. The Haar features are as large as 10 cm × 10 cm × 10 cm in dimension.

We additionally combine our boundary classifier with a position classifier $h(+1|I[\mathbf{x}])$. And this is due to the observation that the boundary classifier describes the entire structure boundary and not a specific location on the structure boundary. Coupling the two classifiers allows for a more localized response around the ground truth that is also closer to the structure boundary. Thus, our object context per-vertex posterior is defined as

$$P^O(\mathbf{v}_i, \mathbf{n}_i|I) = h_i^b(+1|I[\mathbf{v}_i], \mathbf{n}_i)h_i^p(+1|I[\mathbf{v}_i])$$

where $h_i^b(+1|I[\mathbf{v}], \mathbf{n})$ is the boundary classifier and $h_i^p(+1|I[\mathbf{v}])$ is the position classifier. The boundary and position classifiers use steerable and Haar features, respectively.

For mesh initialization and refinement, we use robust PCA as in Lay et al. (2013) as well as ASM (Cootes et al., 1995) with the discriminative boundary classifier.

The system was tested on 50 unseen cases for liver, spleen, left and right kidneys, and left and right lungs while the remaining structures were tested on 45 cases. Prostate, bladder, rectum, and left and right femoral heads were compared directly with Lay et al. (2013) for both the Local + Global and MSL pipelines using identical test setup. However, where Local + Global evaluates on a fixed grid, we evaluate on a random subset of voxels totaling 0.1% of the voxels in the entire volume. This should be approximately the same as considering a grid with 10 voxel skips. Table 10.5 provides an overview of the performance between the three systems. We also consider the inter-user variability for comparison.

The addition of the boundary classifier in the object context as well as the strategic mesh vertex sampling is largely responsible for the performance boost. These collectively produce more

**Table 10.5 Error in Millimeters on Unseen Cases**

| Structure | Object | Local + Global | MSL | IUV |
|---|---|---|---|---|
| Liver | 4.54 ± 2.86 | – | – | – |
| L. kidney | 3.07 ± 1.98 | – | – | – |
| R. kidney | 2.77 ± 1.22 | – | – | – |
| Spleen | 2.51 ± 1.18 | – | – | – |
| L. lung | 5.25 ± 2.19 | – | – | – |
| R. lung | 5.28 ± 3.42 | – | – | – |
| Prostate | **2.83 ± 1.16** | 3.35 ± 1.40 | 3.57 ± 2.01 | 3.03 ± 1.15 |
| Bladder | 2.87 ± 2.96 | 3.08 ± 2.25 | **2.59 ± 1.70** | 2.03 ± 0.11 |
| Rectum | **3.89 ± 1.83** | 3.97 ± 1.43 | 4.36 ± 1.70 | 2.93 ± 1.10 |
| L. femur | 2.22 ± 0.65 | **1.90 ± 1.19** | 2.05 ± 1.27 | 1.29 ± 0.12 |
| R. femur | 2.03 ± 0.96 | **1.88 ± 0.78** | 1.89 ± 0.99 | 1.16 ± 0.21 |

Notes: *Object outperforms Local + Global on three of five structures and offers similar accuracy on the femoral heads. Local + Global is described in Section 10.3.1, MSL is marginal space learning, and IUV is inter-user variability. Bold values indicate smallest values between Object, Local + Global and MSL columns.*

accurate mesh initializations than Local + Global. However, the performance regression in the left and right femur is counterintuitive. The boundary classifier produces more accurate predictions on these structures. The likely cause of this is a combination of imbalanced training examples and randomness in training. Since each tree was trained on 100 random volumes out of the 1191 cases, it is possible that the trees were exposed to relatively few examples of femur annotations. This contrasts with Local + Global, which was trained on volumes that included all annotations of every structure.

## 10.8 CONCLUSIONS

In this work, we proposed a fusion of local and global context, coupled with discriminative models, for rapid multi-organ segmentation. Exploiting sparsity of the nonparametric global context led to a fast algorithm: the global context is only evaluated at sparse regions and is used to predict hypotheses for all landmarks simultaneously. By robustly fitting statistical shape model to these landmarks and deforming the fitted shape using a learned boundary detector, we achieved segmentation accuracy comparable to inter-user variability.

Although our approach is already efficient, we feel that there is still room for improvement. Specifically, the local detectors often get evaluated on the same voxel multiple times; a simple caching of classifier results could be used to improve efficiency. Along a similar line, if results are cached, there may also be benefit in having a multi-class classifier be used to model the local posterior. We will also investigate how to further improve the segmentation accuracy for organs with simple shape but large variability in appearance like kidney or in scale like bladder.

## NOTES

a.  The inter-user variability was measured over 10 randomly selected unseen test cases.
b.  The inter-user variability was measured over five randomly selected unseen test cases.

## REFERENCES

Cootes, T.F., Taylor, C.J., Cooper, D.H., Graham, J., 1995. Active shape models their training and application. Comput. Vis. Image Underst. 61, 38-59.

Criminisi, A., Shotton, J., Bucciarelli, S., 2009. Decision forests with long-range spatial context for organ localization in CT volumes. In: MICCAI-PMMIA Workshop.

Criminisi, A., Shotton, J., Robertson, D.P., Konukoglu, E., 2010. Regression forests for efficient anatomy detection and localization in CT studies. In: MICCAI-MVC Workshop, Lecture Notes in Computer Science, vol. 6533, pp. 106-117.

Cuingnet, R., Prevost, R., Lesage, D., Cohen, L.D., Mory, B., Ardon, R., 2012. Automatic detection and segmentation of kidneys in 3D CT images using random forests. In: MICCAI, pp. 66-74.

Dasgupta, S., Freund, Y., 2008. Random projection trees and low dimensional manifolds. In: Proceedings of the 40th Annual ACM Symposium on Theory of Computing, STOC '08. ACM, New York, NY, USA, pp. 537-546.

Datar, M., Indyk, P., 2004. Locality-sensitive hashing scheme based on p-stable distributions. In: SCG '04: Proceedings of the Twentieth Annual Symposium on Computational Geometry. ACM Press, New York, pp. 253-262.

Friedman, J., Hastie, T., Tibshirani, R., 2001. The Elements of Statistical Learning, vol. 1. Springer, Berlin.

Gall, J., Lempitsky, V., 2009. Class-specific Hough forests for object detection. In: Proceedings IEEE Conference Computer Vision and Pattern Recognition.

Kohlberger, T., Sofka, M., Zhang, J., Birkbeck, N., Wetzl, J., Kaftan, J.N., Declerck, J., Zhou, S.K., 2011. Automatic multi-organ segmentation using learning-based segmentation and level set optimization. In: MICCAI, pp. 338-345.

Konukoglu, E., Glocker, B., Zikic, D., Criminisi, A., 2013. Neighbourhood approximation using randomized forests. Med. Image Anal. 17 (7), 790-804.

Lay, N., Birkbeck, N., Zhang, J., Zhou, S.K., 2013. Rapid multi-organ segmentation using context integration and discriminative models. In: Information Processing in Medical Imaging, pp. 450-462.

Ling, H., Zhou, S.K., Zheng, Y., Georgescu, B., Suehling, M., Comaniciu, D., 2008. Hierarchical, learning-based automatic liver segmentation. In: CVPR, Los Alamitos, CA, USA.

Liu, D., Zhou, K., Bernhardt, D., Comaniciu, D., 2010. Search strategies for multiple landmark detection by submodular maximization. In: CVPR.

Shimizu, A., Ohno, R., Ikegami, T., Kobatake, H., Nawano, S., Smutek, D., 2007. Segmentation of multiple organs in non-contrast 3D abdominal CT images. Int. J. Comput. Assist. Radiol. Surg. 2, 135-142.

Sofka, M., Zhang, J., Zhou, S.K., Comaniciu, D., 2010. Multiple object detection by sequential Monte Carlo and hierarchical detection network. In: CVPR, http://www.sofka.com/HDN/.

Sofka, M., Wetzl, J., Birkbeck, N., Zhang, J., Kohlberger, T., Kaftan, J., Declerck, J., Zhou, S.K., 2011. Multi-stage learning for robust lung segmentation in challenging CT volumes. In: Proceedings of the 14th International Conference on Medical Image Computing and Computer-Assisted Intervention (MICCAI 2011), Toronto, Canada.

Tu, Z., 2005. Probabilistic boosting-tree: learning discriminative models for classification, recognition, and clustering. In: ICCV, pp. 1589-1596.

Yang, J., Duncan, J.S., 2004. 3D image segmentation of deformable objects with joint shape-intensity prior models using level sets. Med. Image Anal. 8 (3), 285-294.

Zhang, S., Zhan, Y., Dewan, M., Huang, J., Metaxas, D.N., Zhou, X.S., 2011. Sparse shape composition: a new framework for shape prior modeling. In: CVPR, pp. 1025-1032.

Zheng, Y., Barbu, A., Georgescu, B., Scheuering, M., Comaniciu, D., 2008. Four-chamber heart modeling and automatic segmentation for 3-D cardiac CT volumes using marginal space learning and steerable features. IEEE Trans. Med. Imaging 27 (11), 1668-1681.

Zheng, Y., Georgescu, B., Ling, H., Zhou, S.K., Scheuering, M., Comaniciu, D., 2009. Constrained marginal space learning for efficient 3D anatomical structure detection in medical images. In: CVPR, pp. 194-201.

Zhou, S.K., 2010. Shape regression machine and efficient segmentation of left ventricle endocardium from 2D B-mode echocardiogram. Med. Image Anal. 14 (4), 563-581.

Zhou, S.K., Zhou, J., Comaniciu, D., 2007. A boosting regression approach to medical anatomy detection. In: IEEE Conference on Computer Vision and Pattern Recognition, 2007. CVPR'07, pp. 1-8.

# MULTIPLE-ATLAS SEGMENTATION IN MEDICAL IMAGING

# 11

**G. Sanroma[1,2], G. Wu[1], M. Kim[1], M.A. González Ballester[2,3] and D. Shen[1]**

*Department of Radiology and BRIC, University of North Carolina at Chapel Hill, Chapel Hill, NC, USA[1]*
*Department of Information and Communication Technologies, Pompeu Fabra University, Barcelona, Spain[2]*
*Catalan Institution for Research and Advanced Studies, Barcelona, Spain[3]*

## CHAPTER OUTLINE

## 11.1 INTRODUCTION

Modern imaging technologies have led to a rapid increase in the availability of medical imaging data. In order to allow for quantitative analysis of these data it is necessary to extract some high-level information from the images. One example of this type of information is the delineation of the anatomical structures. Morphological analysis of anatomical data has many applications. For example, accurate delineation of a tumor from computed tomography images is required for cancer treatment in radiotherapy (Keall et al., 2006; Khan et al., 2009c). In neurosciences, the shape of the hippocampus is the key to characterize neurological diseases such as Alzheimer's disease (AD) and schizophrenia

S. Kevin Zhou (Ed): Medical Image Recognition, Segmentation and Parsing. http://dx.doi.org/10.1016/B978-0-12-802581-9.00011-1

**231**

(Elias et al., 2000; Amieva et al., 2008), where the hippocampus needs to be segmented from magnetic resonance (MR) images before its shape can be analyzed. The problem is that manual delineation of anatomical structures is expensive and prone to subjective bias and, thus, automatic segmentation methods are highly useful. In fact, automatic segmentation is an active research topic in the medical image analysis field.

Multiple-atlas segmentation (MAS) aims to automatically segment the anatomical structures on a target image by transferring the ground-truth annotations from a set of atlases through image registration. By using multiple atlases, MAS encompasses a larger anatomical variability than single-atlas-based counterpart methods and, therefore, it can achieve more accurate labeling results.

There are two types of MAS methods: the ones that build a probabilistic representation (i.e., a probabilistic atlas) from the set of annotated atlases, and the ones that directly use the individual atlases in the set. There is evidence pointing to the superior performance of the second type of method (Babalola et al., 2009), which we will denote as nonparametric methods since they do not build any parametric representation from the atlas-set. One possible reason for their success is that they allow for using the subset of atlases better suited for segmenting each particular target subject (rather than using a probabilistic atlas built from *all* the atlases). Another hypothesis is that the multiple pairwise registrations required to warp each individual atlas onto the target image might be more robust than relying on a single pairwise registration between the probabilistic atlas and the target image. In this chapter, we will focus on the nonparametric methods using each individual atlas in the set, referred to hereinafter simply as MAS.

The goal of MAS is to segment a target image, denoted as $T$, using a set of atlas images, denoted as $A_1, \ldots, A_m$, and their corresponding label maps, denoted as $L_1, \ldots, L_m$, with $L_i(x) \in \{0, 1\}$ indicating whether voxel $x \in \Omega$ belongs to the structure of interest (1) or not (0).

There are three steps involved in MAS, namely, atlas selection, image registration, and label fusion.

- In the *atlas selection* step, we select the atlases that are most anatomically similar to the target subject, denoted by the index-set $S_T \subset \{1, \ldots, m\}$. Although early MAS methods use all the available atlases or simply select them randomly, later methods show the benefit of using a subset of accurately selected atlases. In Section 11.2, we will review different measures regarding anatomical similarity for atlas selection and we will show how both the type of similarity measurement and the number of atlases used affect the eventual segmentation performance.

- In the *image registration* step, we bring the atlases into correspondence with the target image by computing the spatial transformations that maximize the similarity with the target image. The goal of this step is to align each atlas to the target image so that their transformed label maps, denoted as $\tilde{L}_i$, can be propagated onto the target image. The two types of transformations used are linear and deformable. In Section 11.3, we will discuss the impact of this step on the segmentation performance.

- In the *label fusion* step, we compute the estimated segmentation on the target image, denoted as $\hat{F}$, by combining the decisions from the propagated atlas label maps. In Section 11.4, we will categorize the existing label fusion methods into the following three types: (i) *weighted voting* methods decide the target labels as a weighted average of the atlas labels. (ii) *Probabilistic* methods formulate label fusion in a Bayesian framework (some of these methods include the weighted voting rule as a particular case). (iii) *Machine learning-based* methods use supervised learning to model the relationships between complex image features and anatomical labels. Machine learning-based methods are often used in combination with the weighted voting or probabilistic approaches.

Once the estimated target label map is obtained, denoted as $\hat{F}$, we compute the segmentation accuracy by measuring the overlap with the *true* target label map, denoted as $F$. The dice similarity coefficient (DSC) is usually employed as a measure of overlap. It is expressed as:

$$\text{DSC}\left(\hat{F}, F\right) = \frac{2 \times \#\left(\hat{F} \cap F\right)}{\#\left(\hat{F} \cup F\right)} \tag{11.1}$$

where $\hat{F} = \{x | \hat{F}(x) = 1\}$ and $F = \{x | F(x) = 1\}$ denote the sets of locations containing foreground labels on the estimated $\hat{F}$ and true $F$ target label maps, respectively, $\cap$ and $\cup$ denote the set intersection and set union, respectively, and $\#(\cdot)$ denotes the cardinality of the set.

In Sections 11.2–11.4, we will review in detail the atlas selection, image registration, and label fusion steps, respectively, and in Section 11.5, we will give some concluding remarks.

## 11.2 ATLAS SELECTION

The use of multiple atlases raises the question of which atlases to use. Early works on MAS just pick the atlases randomly (Heckemann et al., 2006a). Under random selection, segmentation accuracy improves as the number of atlases increases. This is because combining the decision of multiple atlases tends to correct random errors made by the individual atlases, which is one of the core ideas underpinning MAS (Section 11.4 describes in more detail the ways of combining atlas decisions).

Segmentation performance can be considerably improved by using the subset of atlases best representing the anatomy of the to-be-segmented target image, compared to selecting them randomly. The reason is that, by discarding dissimilar atlases, we filter out the unrelated anatomical characteristics to the target image. A critical issue consists of defining a similarity function that reflects the anatomical similarity between an atlas $A_i$ and the target image $T$. One widely used similarity measure for atlas selection is normalized mutual information (MI) (Studholme et al., 1999), although we can use other measures such as cross correlation (CC) or the inverse of the sum of squared differences (SSD). The intuition of selecting the atlases based on image similarity is that the more similar the images are after registration, the most accurate the alignment is of their anatomical structures.

MI measures the statistical dependency of two variables. In the case of two medical images, the higher their MI, the more correlated they are and, hence, the more similar they are. It is defined as

$$\rho_i^T \equiv \text{MI}\left(\tilde{T}, \tilde{A}_i\right) = \frac{H\left(\tilde{T}\right) + H\left(\tilde{A}_i\right)}{H\left(\tilde{T}, \tilde{A}_i\right)} \tag{11.2}$$

where $H(\cdot)$ and $H(\cdot, \cdot)$ denote the marginal and joint entropies, respectively, and the tilde indicates that the images have been registered before evaluating their similarity.

MI-based selection outperforms random selection in terms of segmentation accuracy (Heckemann et al., 2006a; Aljabar et al., 2009; Lotjonen et al., 2010). Before computing the similarity between two images, spatial correspondence must be obtained through image registration. Selection after deformable registration is more accurate than after linear registration (Rohlfing et al., 2004; Lotjonen et al., 2010). Furthermore, tailoring the similarity measurement to a region of interest (ROI) of the to-be-segmented structure is even better than comparing the whole image (Wu et al., 2007).

Let us denote as $S_T \subseteq \{1,\dots,m\}$ the set of indices of the $k$ selected atlases with the highest similarity scores $\rho_i^T$. That is, $\#(S_T) = k$ and

$$\rho_i^T > \rho_j^T, \quad \forall i \in S_T, \ \forall j \notin S_T \tag{11.3}$$

Unlike the case of random selection, optimal segmentation performance in the case of image similarity-based selection is achieved when using a subset of the best $k < m$ atlases rather than when using them all (Klein et al., 2008; Aljabar et al., 2009; Lotjonen et al., 2010; Sanroma et al., 2014). This justifies the importance of accurate atlas selection. Another advantage is that using a subset of atlases usually increases the segmentation speed compared to using them all, especially if atlas selection is done prior to the registration step.

Figure 11.1 compares the segmentation performance of random selection (RND) versus selection based on MI with respect to the number of atlases used, where the majority vote rule (see Section 11.4) has been used to fuse the labels.

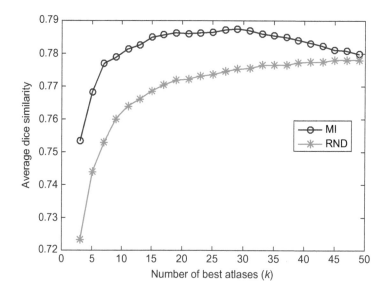

**FIGURE 11.1**

Each location in the plot shows the average DSC obtained in 66 leave-one-out hippocampus segmentation experiments. Green and blue plots correspond to random selection (averaged over 10 randomizations) and the selection by MI, respectively. Vertical axis shows segmentation performance. Horizontal axis shows the number of atlases used.

As we can see, image similarity-based selection outperforms random selection. Image similarity-based selection experiences a dramatic increase during the best few atlases. Then, optimal performance is maintained for a range of best atlases, and finally it starts to decrease above a certain number of best atlases. One explanation for this phenomenon is that including less similar atlases into the set tends to push the segmentation estimates toward the population mean which is less likely to be close to the true target segmentation than the segmentation estimates obtained using a subset of the most similar atlases (Aljabar et al., 2009). On the other hand, performance by random selection increases asymptotically as the number of atlases increases. This is consistent with the fact that errors introduced by random selection are more likely to be random, which falls into the type of errors that can be corrected by consecutively adding more atlases (Heckemann et al., 2006a).

Aljabar et al. (2009) found that, using MI-based selection, segmentation accuracy starts to decrease when using further than the best 20 atlases (out of 274 available atlases). On the other hand, Lotjonen et al. (2010) and Sanroma et al. (2014) found that segmentation accuracy starts to drop when using approximately more than half of the available atlases (in databases containing ≤50 atlases).

van Rikxoort et al. (2010) proposed an iterative method for automatically determining the number of atlases where, at each iteration, the target image was segmented by adding the next best atlas to the set of atlases from the previous iteration. They considered that the optimal results were reached when the estimated segmentations between two consecutive iterations only varied slightly.

Some methods select the atlases based on the distance between the images in a manifold. The motivation is that the manifold better captures the anatomical similarity compared to using the original image space. Different techniques have been used to compute the manifold such as spectral graph theory (Wolz et al., 2010), locality preserving projections (Cao et al., 2011), and Laplacian eigenmaps (Lombaert et al., 2014). All these methods use the distance in the manifold to select the atlases. However, the manifold is still built based on image similarity measurements.

So far, most of the methods use image similarity as a surrogate measurement of the anatomical similarity. To get further insight into the accuracy of image similarity for selecting good atlases, it is interesting to see how many of the best atlases selected by image similarity are actually the best ones, in terms of segmentation performance. We measure the number of common atlases between the top $k$ atlases according to MI and the top $k$ atlases according to ground-truth DSC (Eq. 11.1) with the target labels. If the number of common atlases is equal to $k$, then it means that MI perfectly selects the $k$ best performing atlases. Figure 11.2 shows the average number of optimal (blue) and nonoptimal (gray) atlases selected by MI for labeling the hippocampus in 66 images. The different bars in the plot show the selection results for different numbers of selected atlases ($k$). As we can see from the figure, atlases selected by MI always contain less than 50% of the best performing atlases, especially when using small sets of atlases.

In light of the limitation of image similarity in selecting optimal atlases, a different kind of method uses supervised learning to devise new similarity measurements that correlate better with the true segmentation performance. The main idea is to use the training set of atlases to learn the relationships between the features extracted from each pair of images and their eventual segmentation performance (determined by the DSC between their label maps). In this way, given a target image, we can estimate the segmentation performance of each of the atlases by applying the learned relationships to the extracted image features. For example, Sanroma et al. (2014) proposed to learn a new similarity function between a target and an atlas image with the following form:

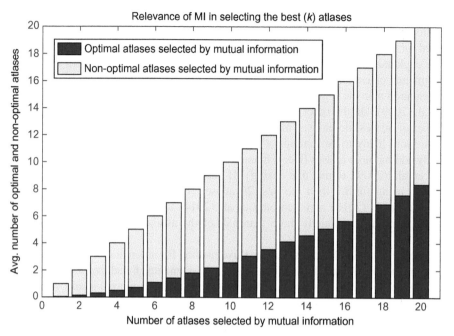

**FIGURE 11.2**

Number of optimal (blue) and nonoptimal (gray) atlases selected by MI. Each bar shows the average results of 132 leave-one-out hippocampus labeling experiments (left and right). Specifically, at each leave-one-out experiment, 1 subject was used as the target subject and the remaining 65 as the atlases.

$$\rho_i^T = \vec{v}^\top \cdot \Phi\left(\tilde{T}, \tilde{A}_i\right) \tag{11.4}$$

where $\Phi(\cdot)$ is a function that computes pairwise differences between HOG features (Dalal and Triggs, 2005) of the linearly aligned target and atlas images and $\vec{v}$ is a (column) vector that captures the relationships between the pairwise HOG differences and the eventual segmentation performance (in terms of DSC). Such relationships in $\vec{v}$ are learned so that the similarity function of Eq. (11.4) ranks the atlases as similarly as possible to how they would be ranked using the ground-truth DSC with the unknown target label map. Using the set of atlases as a training set, the goal is to find the weighting vector $\vec{v}$ satisfying the following constraints:

$$\vec{v}^\top \cdot \Phi\left(\tilde{A}_t, \tilde{A}_i\right) > \vec{v}^\top \cdot \Phi\left(\tilde{A}_t, \tilde{A}_j\right), \quad \forall i \in S_t^\star, \ \forall j \notin \{S_t^\star \cup \{t\}\}, \ \forall t \tag{11.5}$$

where $A_t$ is the atlas acting as the target image and $S_t^\star$ is the set of indices of the best remaining atlases in the training set for segmenting the target image according to the ground-truth DSC. This problem falls within the learning to rank framework and can be solved using support vector machine (SVM)-rank (Joachims, 2002).

Along similar lines, Konukoglu et al. (2012) presented a supervised method using random forests for predicting neighborhoods under arbitrary distance metrics. They presented experiments of predicting the closest brain MR images to a given image in terms of the amount of deformation required to warp one image onto the other. Although they did not specifically address the problem of atlas selection, their method can be easily adapted to predict the optimal atlases by substituting the similarity metric.

To get further insight into the performance of each of these previously described methods, we present hippocampus labeling experiments on 66 subjects in the ADNI dataset (http://adni.loni.ucla.edu/). Atlas selection is performed on the linearly aligned images by FLIRT in the FSL toolbox (Smith et al., 2004) with 12 degrees of freedom and the default parameters. Label fusion is performed by majority voting on the nonrigidly aligned images by the diffeomorphic demons (Vercauteren et al., 2009).

Figure 11.3 shows the segmentation performance with respect to the number of best atlases by the following atlas selection strategies: (i) MI (Aljabar et al., 2009), (ii) neighborhood approximation forests (NAF) (Konukoglu et al., 2012), (iii) HOG + SVM-rank (HSR) (Sanroma et al., 2014), and (iv) optimal selection by the groung-truth (GTR) Dice similarity of Eq. (11.1). Although selection by ground-truth DSC is infeasible in practice because the target label map is unknown, it is interesting to show the theoretical upper bound that can be reached under ideal selection. Vertical axes show the average segmentation accuracy over all target images and horizontal axes show the number of atlases.

Learning-based methods targeted at the expected segmentation accuracy (red and magenta) outperform selection by image similarity (blue). Importantly, the best segmentation performance of all the methods is obtained by using a subset of the best atlases rather than all (Klein et al., 2008; Aljabar et al., 2009; Lotjonen et al., 2010; Sanroma et al., 2014), thus confirming the importance of atlas selection. We can also see the huge gap between the performance of selection by image similarity (blue) and optimal selection (black) (Lotjonen et al., 2010; Sanroma et al., 2014). This gap is partially overcome by the learning-based methods (red and magenta). Optimal selection (GTR) achieves its best performance when using only the best 10-15 atlases, whereas addition of subsequent atlases deteriorates the segmentation performance. The more accurate the selection method, the fewer atlases it requires to reach the optimal segmentation performance. All the methods converge to the same performance when all the atlases are used and, hence, there is no selection at all (52 atlases in Figure 11.3).

These results show that atlas selection has an important effect in segmentation results, and that image similarity is not highly correlated to segmentation performance. Learning-based methods, on the other hand, obtain significant improvements, but there is still room for improvement compared to the upper bound by optimal selection.

Selection by ground-truth DSC cannot be used in practice because the label map of the target image is unknown. An alternative strategy consists of iteratively estimating the target label map and selecting the best atlases according to their DSC with this tentative label map (Isgum et al., 2009; Langerak et al., 2010). This iterative process of tentative label map update and atlas selection has shown better performance than image similarity for selecting good atlases (Langerak et al., 2010).

Another interesting idea is to use registration loops to estimate the segmentation performance between an atlas and a target image (Datteri et al., 2011; Goksel et al., 2013). A registration loop consists of several concatenated pairwise registrations involving both atlas and target images. Using the assumption that segmentation errors accumulate along the loop and given that segmentation errors between any pair of atlases is known, segmentation errors between any pair of target and atlas images can be estimated by solving a set of linear equations.

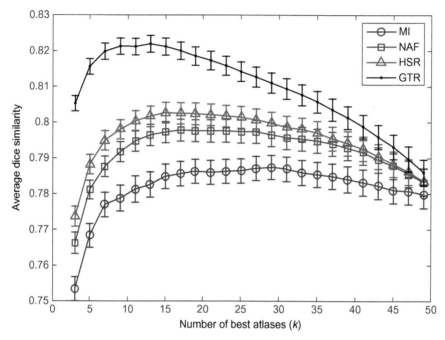

**FIGURE 11.3**

Blue, magenta, red, and black curves show the segmentation performance achieved by four different atlas selection methods (MI, NAF, HSR, and GTR) on segmenting the hippocampus of 66 target images. Labels have been fused with the majority vote rule. Vertical axis shows the segmentation performance, and horizontal axis shows the number of atlases used.

## 11.3 IMAGE REGISTRATION

Image registration brings the set of atlases into spatial correspondence with the target image so that the labels can be directly propagated. After this step, the possible label values on each target point are entirely determined by the position of this point.

Correspondence is derived by the spatial transformation that maximizes the image similarity between each atlas and the target image. That is, we seek the spatial transformation $\varphi$ such that the transformed atlas image $\tilde{A}_i \equiv \varphi(A_i)$ is as similar to the target image $T$ as possible. More formally,

$$\max_{\varphi} \{\text{sim}(T, \varphi(A_i)) + \lambda \cdot \text{reg}(\varphi)\} \tag{11.6}$$

where $\text{sim}(\cdot, \cdot)$ is some similarity measurement between two images and $\text{reg}(\cdot)$ is a regularization term controlling the flexibility of the transformation with the scalar $\lambda$ regulating its strength. The transformed label map according to the computed transformation, denoted as $\tilde{L}_i \equiv \varphi(L_i)$, will then be used for label fusion.

We distinguish two types of registration according to its transformation model: linear and deformable registration (Goshtasby, 2005). Linear registration includes rotation, scaling, translation, and other affine transformations, whereas deformable registration allows for locally warping the atlases to the target image.

Registration is usually carried out as a standalone process regardless of the segmentation. There is a wide range of literature studying this process and comparing different alternatives (Goshtasby, 2005; Klein et al., 2009; Ou et al., 2014). Following the scope of this chapter, we will focus on the works that study the relationship between image registration and the performance of MAS.

As mentioned in the introduction, it is hypothesized that the advantage of nonparametric versus parametric MAS is partly due to the multiple pairwise registrations between the atlases and the target image. Following this line of thought, we can extend nonparametric MAS by generating, not one, but multiple registrations for *each* atlas. It has been shown that the increase in the number of registrations leads to improved segmentation performance (Wang et al., 2013a), thus providing some evidence confirming the hypothesis of the multiple pairwise registrations.

Another important issue concerns the impact of the accuracy of these registrations on the segmentation performance. In one study by Depa et al. (2011), the authors proposed to register the atlases to a common space rather than directly to the target image. The multiple pairwise registrations between the atlases and the target image were then obtained via the common space, which is faster but less accurate than registering each atlas directly to the target image. Results showed that segmentation performance using this approach was statistically indistinguishable from the one obtained by directly registering the atlases to the target image. These results suggest that the registration accuracy is (to a certain extent) not crucial for MAS performance as long as we use multiple pairwise registrations.

## 11.4 LABEL FUSION

Label fusion is used to combine the decisions from the multiple atlases to produce the final segmentation on the target image. Each atlas image $A_i$ and label map $L_i$ are registered onto the target image $T$ (for notational simplicity we drop here the tilde denoting the registered image $\tilde{A}_i$ and label map $\tilde{L}_i$). The segmentation label on each target voxel $x$, denoted as $\hat{F}(x)$, is obtained by combining the labels on the corresponding atlas locations $L_i(x)$. The simplest way, known as the majority vote rule, assigns the label with the highest number of votes. More specifically:

$$\hat{F}(x) = \arg \max_{l \in \{0,1\}} \left\{ \sum_{i \in S_T} \delta\left(L_i(x) = l\right) \right\} \tag{11.7}$$

where $\delta(\cdot)$ is the delta function returning 1 if the argument is true, and 0 otherwise, and $S_T \subseteq \{1, \ldots, m\}$ is the subset of indices of the selected atlases, as defined in Eq. (11.3) in Section 11.2.

Combining the decisions from multiple atlases by the majority vote rule outperforms any single atlas-based segmentation scenario as demonstrated by Rohlfing et al. (2004). The reason is that combining multiple decisions tends to correct random errors made by the individual atlases (such random errors may arise from either the variability in individual registrations or the random variability in the labels of individual voxels (Heckemann et al., 2006a,b)). However, in real applications some correlation may exist in the error patterns, and thus more sophisticated fusion strategies are needed to compensate for these errors (see Section 11.4.1.2).

We categorize the existing label fusion approaches into the following types:

- *Weighted voting* approaches determine the target labels as a weighted combination of atlas labels, where weights denote the importance of each atlas.
- *Probabilistic* approaches formulate label fusion using the Bayes' probability rules. Some of these methods include weighted voting approaches as particular cases.
- *Machine learning-based* approaches use supervised learning to model the relationship between the appearance features and the anatomical labels.

## 11.4.1 WEIGHTED VOTING

The most common way of fusing the atlas labels to obtain the target segmentation is the weighted voting rule. It consists of computing the label at each target point $x$ as a weighted average of the atlas labels, as follows:

$$\hat{F}(x) = \arg\max_l \left\{ \sum_{i \in S_T} \omega_i(x) \cdot \delta(L_i(x) = l) \right\} \tag{11.8}$$

where $\omega_i(x)$ is a spatially varying weight denoting the importance of the $i$th atlas in determining the target label at location $x$. Note that the majority vote rule of Eq. (11.7) is a particular case of weighted voting by assigning the same weight to all the atlases.

We distinguish between two types of methods: the first type computes the weights based on the estimation of the local segmentation performance of each atlas independently. The second type computes the weights so as to minimize the correlations between the error patterns of pairs of atlases. These second types of methods are especially suited in the case that the errors made by the atlases are not random but correlated, which is the most common case in a real scenario.

### 11.4.1.1 Independent weighting

Image similarity is the most widely used heuristic for estimating the local segmentation performance of each individual atlas. It is based on the intuition that the more similar an atlas is to the target image, the more accurate the registration of the anatomical structures and, hence, the higher the segmentation performance. The weights denoting the local importance of each atlas are then computed based on the similarity between the local image patches. One widely used similarity measure between two image patches in the target and atlas image, respectively, is the exponential of the negative SSD:

$$\omega_i(x) = \exp\left( -\gamma \cdot \sum_{y \in \mathcal{N}_x} (T(y) - A_i(y))^2 \right) \tag{11.9}$$

where $\gamma$ is a normalization parameter and $\mathcal{N}_x$ is the spatial neighborhood defining the image patches centered at $x$. Other similarity measurements can be used such as MI and CC (Artaechevarria et al., 2009). Despite image similarity being the most commonly used metric, other methods use empirical measurements of the segmentation confidence on the set of atlases (Khan et al., 2009a,b; Sdika, 2010; Zhang et al., 2011).

The local weighted voting strategy of Eq. (11.8) assumes that there is a one-to-one correspondence between the atlas and target images after registration and, hence, the target label at location $x$, denoted

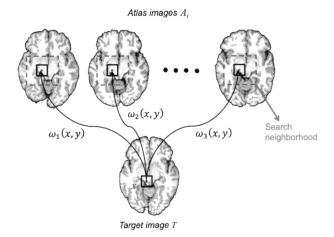

Atlas images $A_i$

$\omega_2(x,y)$

$\omega_1(x,y)$

$\omega_3(x,y)$

Search neighborhood

Target image $T$

**FIGURE 11.4**

One-to-many correspondences in label fusion. Corresponding atlas points are sought in a local neighborhood (blue-dashed boxes). Black boxes denote the image patches used to estimate the segmentation performance based on similarity measurements.

as $\hat{F}(x)$, is computed using the atlas contributions at the same corresponding location, denoted as $L_i(x)$ in Eq. (11.8). However, registration errors might violate such a one-to-one correspondence assumption and, hence, better robustness can be obtained by also considering the atlas labels in a spatial neighborhood. According to this new strategy, target labels are determined as follows:

$$\hat{F}(x) = \arg\max_l \left\{ \sum_{i \in S_T} \sum_{y \in \mathcal{N}'_x} \omega_i(x,y) \cdot \delta(L_i(y) = l) \right\} \qquad (11.10)$$

where $\mathcal{N}'_x$ is the spatial neighborhood for searching for potential atlas correspondences and $\omega_i(x,y)$ denotes the estimated segmentation performance derived from assigning the atlas label at point $y \in \mathcal{N}'_x$ to the target label at point $x$, where the segmentation performance is usually estimated using local patch similarity measurements, such as the one denoted in Eq. (11.9).

Figure 11.4 shows a one-to-many correspondences scenario that allows for searching for candidate atlas correspondences in a certain neighborhood (blue-dashed boxes in Figure 11.4).

This one-to-many correspondences assumption notably improves label fusion performance compared to assuming one-to-one correspondences (Rousseau et al., 2011). Moreover, it obtains good segmentation results even using linear registration (Coupé et al., 2011). In fact, the one-to-many correspondences strategy is adopted by many later label fusion methods.

This strategy of computing local fusion weights based on patch-wise comparisons is referred to as patch-based labeling (PBL). The accuracy of PBL largely relies on the ability of identifying the *true* corresponding atlas patches (i.e., those with the same central label as the underlying target point) by means of image similarity measurements. Sparse representations have been also used for improving PBL by reducing the contributing atlas labels to only a few relevant ones, thus reducing the chances of introducing misleading atlas labels. Sparse PBL (SPBL) computes the weights as a regression problem with sparsity constraints, as follows:

$$\min_{\vec{w}} \left\{ \|\vec{t} - A\vec{w}\|_2^2 + \lambda \|\vec{w}_1\| \right\} \tag{11.11}$$

where $\vec{w} \in \mathbb{R}^n$ is a (column) vector containing the estimated weights associated with each atlas patch, $\vec{t} \in \mathbb{R}^p$ is a column vector representing the intensities within the target patch (centered at $x$) and $A = [\vec{a}_1, \ldots, \vec{a}_j, \ldots, \vec{a}_n] \in \mathbb{R}^{p \times n}$ is a matrix of stacked atlas patches in the neighborhood $\mathcal{N}'_x$ of the target patch, where each $\vec{a}_j$ is a column vector of intensities. The first term of Eq. (11.11) is the data fitting term ensuring that similar atlas patches to the target patch (in terms of SSD) receive high weights. The second term is the $\ell_1$-norm regularization enforcing that only a few atlas patches bear nonzero weight. The combination of both terms, controlled by parameter $\lambda$, makes SPBL more robust than traditional PBL by its ability to use only a few relevant patches in label fusion (Tong et al., 2012, 2013; Zhang et al., 2012).

Recently, there have been many extensions to further improve the labeling accuracy of SPBL. First, instead of labeling each target point individually, it is more reasonable to impose those similar neighboring target points to be labeled using similar patterns of contributing atlases. This can be achieved by labeling a group of target points simultaneously (rather than one-by-one) and enforcing (i) the weighting vector for each point to be as sparse as possible; and (ii) the weighting vectors to have similar sparsity patterns. To that end, $\ell_{2,1}$-norm regularization is used in Wu et al. (2012) to replace the $\ell_1$-norm in the conventional SPBL. Consider the matrix $W \in \mathbb{R}^{n \times m}$, where each column $\vec{w}_i, i = 1, \ldots, m$ contains the sought weights vector for each of the $m$ target points to be jointly labeled. Minimizing the $\ell_{2,1}$-norm, defined as $\|W\|_{2,1} = \sum_{i=1}^{n} \sqrt{\sum_{j=1}^{m} W_{ij}^2}$, encourages the weights vectors for all the target points to share similar sparsity patterns.

To achieve a higher level of accuracy during the label fusion procedure, it is important that the chosen patch similarity measurement accurately captures the tissue/shape appearance of the anatomical structure. One limitation of existing state-of-the-art label fusion methods is that they often apply a fixed size image patch throughout the entire label fusion procedure. Doing so may affect the fidelity of the patch similarity measurement, which in turn may not adequately capture complex tissue appearance patterns expressed by the anatomical structure. To address this limitation, Wu and Shen (2014) and Wu et al. (2015) proposed a hierarchical structure-sensitive label fusion method by adding three new label fusion contributions.

First, each image patch is characterized by a multi-scale feature representation that encodes both local and semi-local image information. This is done by replacing the simple image intensities used in the conventional PBL by a multi-layered patch representation where the innermost layers encode image intensities at lower scales and the outermost layers encode the image intensities at larger scales. Doing so will increase the accuracy of the patch-based similarity measurement. Figure 11.5 shows the multi-layered patch representation.

Other similar methods have replaced the image intensities by other kinds of more informative features. For example, Guo et al. (2014) applied a stacked auto-encoder (Hinton et al., 2006; Hinton and Salakhutdinov, 2006) to learn the intrinsic feature representations for image patches and use the learned low-dimensional feature representations to replace the intensities in label fusion. This method has been demonstrated to be successful in segmenting the hippocampus from challenging infant brain MR images.

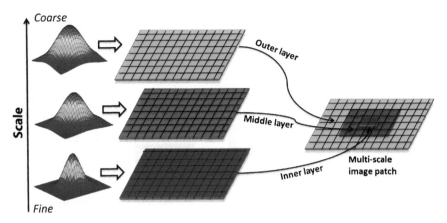

**FIGURE 11.5**

The construction of the multi-scale image patch by adaptively replacing the intensity values with convolved intensity values via different Gaussian filters.

Second, to limit the possibility of the patch-based similarity measurement being wrongly guided by the presence of multiple anatomical structures in the same image patch, each atlas image patch is further partitioned into a set of label-specific partial image patches according to the existing labels. Since image information has now been semantically divided into different patterns, these new label-specific atlas patches make the label fusion process more specific and flexible. This is integrated into the sparse regression-based label fusion of Eq. (11.11) by partitioning each atlas patch in the matrix of neighboring atlas patches (denoted as $A$ in Eq. (11.11)) into multiple columns according to the different anatomical structures contained in the patch. Figure 11.6 shows the integration of the structure-specific patches into the sparse-regression-based label fusion.

Finally, in order to correct target points that are mislabeled during label fusion, a hierarchical approach is used to improve the label fusion results. In particular, a coarse-to-fine iterative label fusion approach is used that gradually reduces the patch size.

In the following, we demonstrate the accuracy of some of the representative label fusion methods covered so far in hippocampus labeling experiments. Accurate delineation of the hippocampus is important in many neuroscience studies because of the relationships of the morphology of hippocampus with dementias such as AD. In this experiment, we randomly select 23 normal control (NC) subjects, 22 mild cognitive impairment (MCI) subjects, and 21 AD subjects from the ADNI dataset (http://adni.loni.ucla.edu/). The following three preprocessing steps have been performed on all subject images: (1) Skull removal by a learning-based meta-algorithm (Shi et al., 2012); (2) N4-based bias field correction (Tustison et al., 2010); and (3) intensity standardization to normalize the intensity range (Madabhushi and Udupa, 2006). Semi-automated hippocampal volumetry was carried out using a commercial high-dimensional brain mapping tool (Medtronic Surgical Navigation Technologies, Louisville, CO), which has been validated and compared to manual tracing of the hippocampus (Hsu et al., 2002). In this experiment, we regard the hippocampal segmentations from ADNI as the ground truth.

A leave-one-out strategy is used to compare the label performance of *PBL* (Coupé et al., 2011; Rousseau et al., 2011), *SPBL* (Zhang et al., 2012), and hierarchical structure-sensitive PBL (*HSSPBL*)

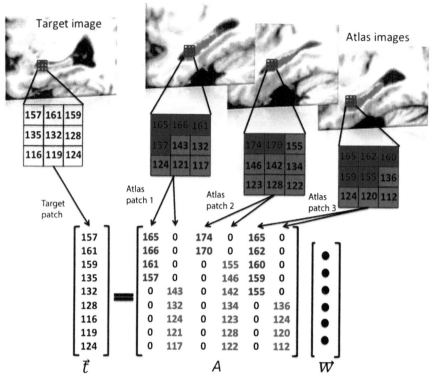

**FIGURE 11.6**

The integration of the structure-specific patches into the sparse regression-based label fusion of Eq. (11.11). Atlas intensity patches are split according to their underlying anatomical information.

(Wu et al., 2015). In each leave-one-out experiment, affine registration is first performed by FLIRT in the FSL toolbox (Smith et al., 2004) with 12 degrees of freedom and the default parameters (i.e., normalized MI similarity metric, and a search range of $\pm 20$ mm in all directions). Then after the affine registration, a deformable registration is performed using the diffeomorphic demons (Vercauteren et al., 2009) method with the default registration parameters (i.e., smoothing sigma 1.8, and iterations in low, middle, and high resolutions as $20 \times 10 \times 5$).

Using all 66 leave-one-out cases, the mean and standard deviation of the DSC from the hippocampus labelling results are calculated and reported in Table 11.1. A few important observations can be made. Compared to the other two methods, the HSSPBL achieves the highest DSCs, obtaining approximately a 1.9% and 1.2% improvement over the PBL and SPBL methods, respectively. The computation times by the three label fusion methods are also reported in the last row of Table 11.1. The computation environment of our experiments is 8 CPUs @ 3.0 GHz and 16 GB RAM.

Since the improvement in label fusion is usually obtained around the boundary of hippocampus, it is interesting to examine the labelling results at the hippocampus surface. To perform this experiment, we first construct the ground-truth hippocampus surface mask and also the estimated hippocampus surface mask. Then the distance at each vertex between the two surfaces is computed. Table 11.2 shows

**Table 11.1 Dice Ratio Mean, Standard Deviation, and Mean Computation Time Results for PBL, SPBL, and HSSPBL When Used to Label the Hippocampus**

|  | PBL | SPBL | HSSPBL |
|---|---|---|---|
| Dice ratio | $85.2 \pm 3.5$ | $87.3 \pm 3.4$ | $88.5 \pm 2.2$ |
| Time (s) | 75 | 128 | 618 |

**Table 11.2 Maximum Surface Distance Results When Used to Label the Hippocampus (Unit: mm)**

|  | PBL | SPBL | HSPBL$^{+,*}$ |
|---|---|---|---|
| Mean | $0.410 \pm 0.150$ | $0.380 \pm 0.100$ | $0.334 \pm 0.090$ |
| Max | 4.359 | 3.742 | 2.450 |

Note: *Symbols "$^+$" and "$^*$" indicate significant improvement ($p < 0.05$) over the PBL and SPBL methods, respectively.*

the values of the averaged surface-to-surface distance and the maximum surface-to-surface distance by PBL, SPBL, and HSSPBL. We further perform the paired $t$-tests upon the surface distances. We observe that HSSPBL has significant improvement ($P < 0.05$) over PBL, and SPBL.

### 11.4.1.2 Joint weighting

Estimating the weight of each atlas independently only produces unbiased segmentation estimates in the case that the anatomical characteristics are equally distributed among the atlases. However, it is usually the case that some anatomical characteristics are overrepresented and, therefore, segmentation results are biased toward reproducing the particular errors of these characteristics. One solution to this problem is to jointly minimize the correlation of the participating atlases when choosing the weights instead of computing them independently. In this way, we enforce the contributing atlas patches to be anatomically varied and thus enforce the most represented anatomical characteristics not to accumulate the majority of the weights.

As described in Eq. (11.8), the target label $\hat{F}(x)$ is computed as a weighted average of the atlas labels $L_i(x)$, where the weight $\omega_i(x)$ denotes the importance of a particular atlas at a particular location. In order to avoid the bias toward the overrepresented characteristics, we seek to minimize the correlation among the contributing atlas patches and thus maximize the anatomical variability. This can be expressed by the following quadratic optimization problem (Wang et al., 2011, 2013b):

$$\min_{\vec{w}} \left\{ \vec{w}^\top M \vec{w} \right\} \quad \text{subject to} \quad \sum_{i=1}^{n} \vec{w}(i) = 1 \tag{11.12}$$

where $\vec{w} = [\omega_1(x), \ldots, \omega_i(x), \ldots, \omega_n(x)]$ is a vector containing the weight for each atlas patch and $M \in \mathbb{R}^{n \times n}$ is a pairwise dependency matrix where each element $M(i,j)$ denotes the probability of the $i$th and $j$th atlas patches both having the same error patterns at location $x$.

In order to be comparable to the previous label fusion methods, the joint probability of error $M(i,j)$ can be estimated based on image intensity differences, as follows:

$$M(i,j) = \left[ \sum_{y \in \mathcal{N}_x} |T(y) - A_i(y)| \cdot |T(y) - A_j(y)| \right]^p \tag{11.13}$$

where $p$ is a gain exponent. Note that, in the case of an individual atlas, the probability of error, denoted as $M(i,i)$, is exactly the SSD. Intuitively, the joint probability of error in Eq. (11.13) is large when the intensity differences between the atlases and the target image are large and also their error patterns are strongly correlated. Other measurements can also be used to estimate the joint probability of error in labeling the target image, such as measurements based on empirical evidence gathered from the set of atlases (Wang and Yushkevich, 2012).

Figure 11.7 shows the ideas of PBL using independent and joint weights, respectively, where the dependencies used by each method to compute the weights are represented in the form of a graph. As we can see, independent weighting only accounts for the relationship between each individual atlas patch and the to-be-labeled target patch, whereas the joint weighting strategy also takes into account the pairwise dependencies between the atlas patches by means of the pairwise dependency matrix $M$.

It is obvious that the patch dependency of Eq. (11.13) is only measured by the intensity error pattern, which is, however, not directly related to the goal of label fusion. Wu et al. (2012, 2014) model the pairwise patch dependency by analyzing the correlation of their morphological error patterns and also the labeling consensus among atlases. The patch dependencies are further recursively updated based on the latest labeling results to correct the possible labeling errors, which falls into the type of problems that can be solved by the expectation-maximization (EM) framework. The objective function in their joint label fusion method is

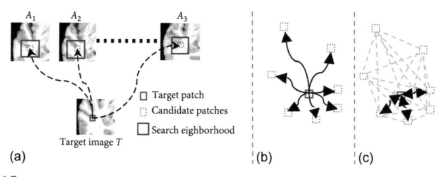

**FIGURE 11.7**

Overview of the PBL and Joint PBL. As shown in (a), the target patch (red box) seeks contributions from all possible candidate atlas patches (pink boxes) in a small search neighborhood (blue box). The schematic graphs in (b) and (c) show the dependencies used by PBL and Joint PBL, respectively.

$$\min_{\vec{w}} \left\{ \|\vec{t} - A\vec{w}\|_2^2 + \alpha \vec{w}^{\mathsf{T}} M \vec{w} + \lambda \|\vec{w}\|_1 \right\} \tag{11.14}$$

where the first term is the data-fitting term penalizing the reconstruction errors of the target patch in the same way as done by SPBL (Eq. 11.11), the second term accounts for the pairwise dependencies between the atlas patches as done by Joint PBL (Eq. 11.12), and the last term enforces sparsity in the resulting weighs vector $\vec{w}$. The importance of each term is regulated by the scalars $\alpha$ and $\lambda$. As said, Wu et al. (2012, 2014) have taken into account both the correlation of the error patterns and also the labeling consensus among atlases when modeling the pairwise dependency matrix $M \in \mathbb{R}^{n \times n}$. More specifically, each element $M(i,j)$ is defined as

$$M(i,j) = (1-r) \cdot \phi_{ij}^{\mathrm{E}} + r \cdot \phi_{ij}^{\Lambda} \tag{11.15}$$

where $r$ is a scalar balancing the correlation of the error pattern, denoted as $\phi_{ij}^{\mathrm{E}}$, and the labeling consensus, denoted as $\phi_{ij}^{\Lambda}$. These two terms are defined as follows:

$$\phi_{ij}^{\mathrm{E}} = \delta \left( L_i(x) = L_j(x) \right) \cdot \left[ \|e_i\|_2^2 \cdot \left[ \mathrm{NCC}\left(e_i, e_j\right) + 1 \right] \cdot \|e_j\|_2^2 \right] \tag{11.16}$$

$$\phi_{ij}^{\Lambda} = 1 - \frac{\delta \left( L_i(x) = \hat{F}(x) \right) + \delta \left( L_j(x) = \hat{F}(x) \right)}{2}$$

where $e_i = (a_i - \vec{t})$ and $e_j = (a_j - \vec{t})$ denote the error intensity patterns between the atlas and target patches, "NCC" denotes the normalized cross correlation, and $\hat{F}(x)$ denotes the tentative target label at voxel $x$.

The method alternates between two steps: (1) estimation of the tentative target label map $\hat{F}$ using the weighted voting rule, where the weights for each atlas point are computed as denoted in Eq. (11.14), and (2) estimation of the pairwise dependency matrix $M \in \mathbb{R}^{n \times n}$ as defined in Eqs. (11.15) and (11.16).

We compare the proposed Joint Sparse PBL method (JSPBL) with the independent weighting alternative PBL (Coupé et al., 2011; Rousseau et al., 2011) and its sparse extension SPBL (Zhang et al., 2012). We use the same experimental setting as in the previous section. Briefly, we randomly select 23 NC subjects, 22 MCI subjects, and 21 AD subjects from the ADNI dataset (http://adni.loni. ucla.edu/). We regard the hippocampal segmentations from ADNI as the ground truth. In each leave-one-out experiment, affine registration is first performed by FLIRT in the FSL toolbox (Smith et al., 2004) with 12 degrees of freedom and the default parameters, and deformable registration is performed using the diffeomorphic demons (Vercauteren et al., 2009) method.

Using all 66 leave-one-out cases, the mean and standard deviation of the DSC from the hippocampus label results are calculated and reported in Table 11.3. As we can see, JSPBL outperforms the rest of the methods.

In order to show the importance of the parameters $\alpha$ and $\lambda$ in Eq. (11.14) controlling the importance of pairwise dependency term and the sparsity of the weights, Figure 11.8 shows the results obtained by varying these parameters in labeling a subset of 15 randomly selected subjects. It is worth noting that the results reported in Table 11.3 use the optimal values for these parameters, namely, $\alpha = 0.5$ and $\lambda = 0.1$.

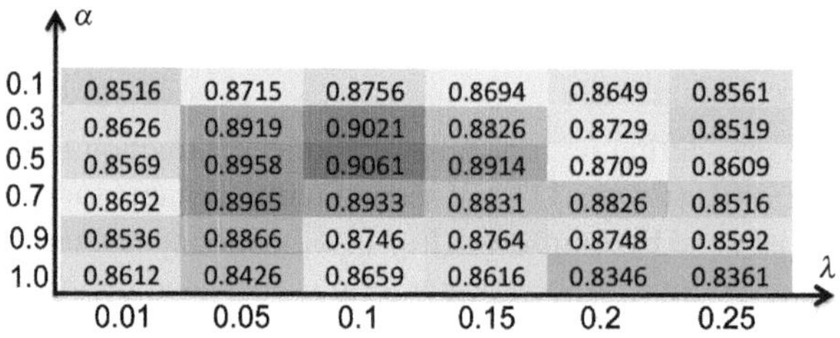

**FIGURE 11.8**

Segmentation performance for different values of parameters $\alpha$ and $\lambda$.

**Table 11.3 Dice Ratio Mean and Standard Deviation for PBL, SPBL, and JSPBL When Used to Label the Hippocampus**

|  | PBL | SPBL | JSPBL |
|---|---|---|---|
| Dice ratio | $85.2 \pm 3.5$ | $87.3 \pm 3.4$ | $88.7 \pm 2.2$ |

## 11.4.2 PROBABILISTIC

Probabilistic approaches formulate label fusion in a Bayesian manner. We distinguish between two types of these methods. The first ones iteratively estimate both the target labels and the performance level estimates using the EM algorithm (Dempster et al., 1977), that is, the so-called STAPLE (Warfield et al., 2004), and the second ones are motivated by the weighted voting strategy.

### 11.4.2.1 Staple

Estimating the performance of each atlas for segmenting the target image is a central problem in multi-atlas label fusion. It consists of assigning a score to each atlas based on their agreement with the true target labels $F$, so that atlases with higher agreement have higher contribution. The problem is that the true target segmentation is not available, so most methods use surrogate measurements, such as image similarity, to approximate the true label similarity. STAPLE follows a different approach by directly estimating the performance parameters that best agree with a probabilistic estimate of the target labels. More formally, performance parameters for each atlas, denoted as $\boldsymbol{\theta} = \{\theta_1, \ldots, \theta_m\}$, are sought to maximize the joint likelihood of the atlas and target labels, denoted as $P(\boldsymbol{L}, F|\boldsymbol{\theta})$. Since target labels are missing, the joint likelihood function is substituted by its conditional expectation given some tentative parameter estimates. Thus, performance parameters are estimated in STAPLE as follows:

$$\hat{\boldsymbol{\theta}} = \arg\max_{\boldsymbol{\theta}} P(\boldsymbol{L}, F|\boldsymbol{\theta}) \simeq \arg\max_{\boldsymbol{\theta}} E\left[\log P(\boldsymbol{L}, F|\boldsymbol{\theta}) | \boldsymbol{L}, \boldsymbol{\theta}^{(0)}\right] \quad (11.17)$$

$$= \arg\max_{\boldsymbol{\theta}} \left\{ \sum_F \log P(\boldsymbol{L}, F|\boldsymbol{\theta}) \cdot P\left(F|\boldsymbol{L}, \boldsymbol{\theta}^{(0)}\right) \right\}$$

where $\boldsymbol{\theta}^{(0)}$ denotes the tentative parameter estimates and $\boldsymbol{L} = \{L_1, \ldots, L_m\}$ denotes the atlas label maps.

This is a two-step process known as the EM algorithm. In the E-step, we compute the conditional expectation given the parameter estimates from previous iteration $\boldsymbol{\theta}^{(n-1)}$. In the M-step, we find the new parameters $\boldsymbol{\theta}^{(n)}$ that maximize the conditional expectation. This procedure is carried out iteratively until convergence. The properties of the EM algorithm guarantee that agreement with the *true* target labels is improved after each update of the performance parameters.

Multiple extensions have been presented to the original STAPLE algorithm. For example, Asman and Landman (2011) note that performance estimation is biased by the voxels with low variability, such as those in big uniform regions. They improve STAPLE's performance by giving more importance to the voxels with higher variability, such as those in smaller structures or near the boundaries. Recall that STAPLE characterizes the performance of each atlas globally. Asman and Landman (2012) propose instead to use local performance parameters $\theta_{ix}$ of each atlas at each location $x$. Further improvements can be achieved by allowing STAPLE to fuse probabilistic (i.e., $L_i(x) = [0 \ldots 1]$) rather than binary atlas labels (i.e., $L_i(x) = \{0, 1\}$) (Akhondi-Asl and Warfield, 2013). This implies the need for more sophisticated decision functions at each target point than simply the registered atlas labels (see Section 11.4.3.1 for more details about using classifiers in label fusion). Finally, Asman and Landman (2014) adapt STAPLE to handle hierarchical anatomical annotations, where the higher levels of the hierarchy contain coarser structures that are subsequently decomposed into finer structures at the lower levels.

Image similarity has also been introduced in STAPLE. The basic idea is to weigh the contribution of each atlas location using local image similarity measurements with the corresponding target location. For example, Cardoso et al. (2013) used a ranking-based strategy to discard the most dissimilar atlas patches in STAPLE. This shows the benefit of atlas selection at a local rather than a global level. Nonlocal STAPLE Asman and Landman (2013) introduced the one-to-many correspondence assumption of PBL by considering also the neighboring atlas locations in STAPLE.

### 11.4.2.2 Probabilistic weighted voting

The weighted voting rule can also be motivated from a Bayesian perspective. Consider a model where the label at each target voxel $F(x)$, with $x \in \Omega$, is generated by a particular atlas $L_i(x)$, $i \in \{1, \ldots, n\}$. Let us introduce the membership variable $Q : \Omega \rightarrow \{1, \ldots, n\}$ assigning each target voxel an atlas index responsible for its label. Obviously, both the target labels and the membership variable are unknown. Similarly, as in STAPLE, we can express the probability of the target labels by marginalizing over the missing data, in this case the membership variable. This is formulated as follows (Sabuncu et al., 2010):

$$\hat{F} = \arg\max_F P(F|T, A, L) = \arg\max_F \left\{ \sum_Q \{p(Q) \cdot P(F|Q, T, A, L)\} \right\} \quad (11.18)$$

$$= \arg\max_F \sum_Q \left\{ p(Q) \cdot \prod_{x \in \Omega} \{ p(F(x)|L_{Q(x)}) \cdot p(T(x)|A_{Q(x)}) \} \right\}$$

where $A$ and $L$ denote the set of atlas images and labels, respectively, and $Q(x)$ denotes the atlas contributing to target label at location $x$.

The EM algorithm is used to iteratively update the membership variable $Q$ and to compute maximum-a-posterior estimates of the target labels $\hat{F}$. The prior on the membership variable $p(Q)$ controls the spatial smoothness of the atlas contributions. In one extreme, each atlas contributes independently to each target voxel (local weighted voting), and in the other extreme, each atlas contributes to the whole image (global weighted voting). The term $p\left(F(x)|L_{Q(x)}\right)$ enforces spatial smoothness by accounting for the registered atlas labels at each location, and the term $p\left(T(x)|A_{Q(x)}\right)$ controls the strength of each atlas based on the local image similarity. Extensions of this model have been presented to deal with multimodality images (Iglesias et al., 2013) and to handle one-to-many correspondences as in PBL (Bai et al., 2013).

## 11.4.3 MACHINE LEARNING-BASED

Machine learning has been extensively applied to detect anatomical structures in medical images (Zhou, 2014). In the context of MAS, machine learning has been used to model the relationships between the observable image features and the underlying anatomical labels. The set of atlas images is used along with their corresponding label maps to learn the classification rules leading to optimal labeling performance. Usually, more complex image features are used than simple image intensities. The target labels are obtained by applying the learned classification rule to the extracted target image features. Compared to the conventional label fusion approaches that derive the target labels by image registration, machine learning-based approaches are able to capture more complex relationships between image appearance and anatomical labels.

Among the multiple methods applying machine learning to MAS, we will focus on the ones following the nonparametric approach described in this chapter. These are (i) the ones that learn a classifier from each atlas, and then use the conventional label fusion techniques to combine their decisions, and (ii) the ones that learn a specific classifier to label each target point individually. These latter ones substitute conventional label fusion approaches but are similar in spirit to PBL (Coupé et al., 2011; Rousseau et al., 2011) in that they use neighboring atlas patches and labels to learn the classifier.

We will discard the methods that build a single classifier using all the atlases since they are more related to the parametric approaches and, hence, do not involve any atlas selection or label fusion steps (Morra et al., 2008, 2010; Tu et al., 2008).

### 11.4.3.1 One classifier per atlas

These methods learn a different classifier from each atlas, and then apply them independently to the target image. The multiple decisions from the set of classifiers are combined using conventional label fusion methods. The advantage of these methods is that the decision from each atlas is obtained using a classifier instead of simply using the registered atlas labels. Although classifiers can capture more complex relationships, deciding the labels based exclusively on the visual features can lead to some spatial inconsistency. This inconsistency is usually compensated by adding a term representing the prior probability of each label at each location.

One technique falling into this category obtains the label decisions from the multiple atlases using a nearest neighbor classifier based on the observed visual features (Weisenfeld and Warfield, 2011). The multiple decisions are then probabilistically combined using STAPLE (Section 11.4.2.1). To ensure spatial smoothness, a prior probability term is included based on the registered atlas label at each location.

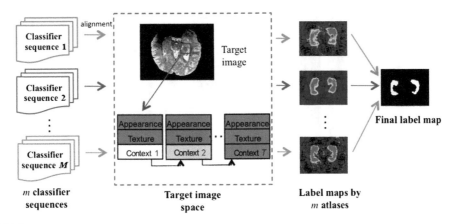

**FIGURE 11.9**

Application of the ACM-based classifier for labeling the hippocampi.

Random forests (Breiman, 2001; Criminisi and Shotton, 2013) have also been used to learn a classifier from each atlas, the so-called atlas forest (AF) (Zikic et al., 2013). The multiple decisions from each AF are then combined by simple averaging. To overcome the spatial inconsistency arising from labeling each target point based exclusively on its visual features, label priors from a probabilistic atlas are combined with the AF decisions to decide the final labels. A number of features are used mostly based on differences between mean intensities of local cuboids around each point.

Auto-context models (ACM) (Tu and Bai, 2010) have also been used for MAS (Kim et al., 2013). In this approach, a cascade of classifiers is learned from each atlas. Each classifier in the cascade learns to assign labels based on the observed image features and the context features. Image features include intensity, location, and neighborhood features (such as intensity mean, variance, gradient, and curvature in a small neighborhood), Haar features (Viola et al., 2001), and texture features based on the gray level co-occurrence matrix (Haralick et al., 1973). Contextual features consist of the classification results from the previous classifier in the cascade in a spatial neighborhood. In the application stage, as shown in Figure 11.9, the multiple cascades of classifiers are applied to the target image and classification results from each atlas are obtained. The multiple tentative segmentations from each classifier are finally fused by local weighted averaging.

One of the advantages of using ACM for MAS is that the spatial smoothness of the results is implicitly enforced by the context features, and there is no need to enforce any spatial prior using a probabilistic atlas. Figure 11.10 shows how labeling results are gradually improved at each iteration of the ACM.

### 11.4.3.2 One classifier per point

These methods learn a classifier for each target point using the training set of neighboring atlas patches and labels. The classifier encodes the relationships between visual features and anatomical labels at each particular location. Therefore, spatial consistency is implicitly enforced, and there is no need to use spatial priors. They follow the spirit of PBL methods in that neighboring atlas patches and labels are used to decide the label on each target point. The difference is that, instead of using the weighted

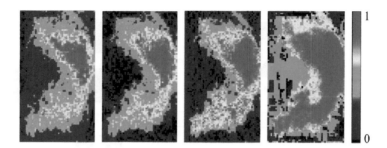

**FIGURE 11.10**

The hippocampus classification map at each iteration of the ACM.

average based on patch similarity, they decide the label by applying the learned relationships to the target features.

One of the simplest strategies applies the $k$-nearest-neighbor classifier to assign the label on each target point (Arzhaeva et al., 2007). This consists of finding the $k$ most similar atlas patches in the feature space and then assigning the probability of the target label, accordingly. This strategy turns out to be very similar to the weighted vote rule used in PBL. The difference is that the most similar patches are equally taken into account instead of using a weighted sum based on patch similarity. They extract the image features using multi-scale Gaussian derivative filters.

A more sophisticated method uses polynomial regression to model the relationships between image appearance and anatomical labels (Wang et al., 2011). For each target location, a polynomial regression model is learned using the training set of neighboring atlas image patches and labels. The regression model is then applied to the target patch to decide its center label.

SVM (Cortes and Vapnik, 1995) have also been used to learn the optimal classification rule based on the image appearances and anatomical labels in the set of neighboring atlas locations (Hao et al., 2014; Bai et al., 2015). Original intensities, image gradients, and context features were used in Bai et al. (2015). The outputs of various filters such as first- and second-order gradients, and Sobel and Laplacian operators were used as image features in Hao et al. (2014).

## 11.5 CONCLUSIONS

In this chapter, we have covered the topic of MAS. We have focused on the nonparametric approaches that directly use the individual atlases in the set, rather than building a probabilistic atlas. The distinguishing steps of these methods are the atlas selection, image registration, and label fusion steps.

The atlas selection step selects the atlases most anatomically similar to the target image. It has been shown that using a subset of anatomically similar atlases leads to better segmentation results than using all the available atlases. This is because results using all the available atlases tend to be closer to the population mean, which is not necessarily representative of the target image. We have seen different criteria to select the atlases. Although selecting the atlases based on their similarity with the target image is better than random selection, it is still far from optimal. More advanced approaches use machine learning to approximate a similarity score better correlated with optimal selection. This leads to better performance than selecting the atlases based on image similarity, but there is still a gap compared to optimal selection.

The registration step computes approximate correspondences between each atlas and the target image by means of a spatial transformation. We have seen that the increase of the number of pairwise registrations between the atlases and the target image leads to better segmentation performance.

The label fusion step decides the labels on the target image by combining the individual decisions from the multiple atlases. The most widely used strategy is the weighted voting rule, where target labels are decided as a weighted average of the atlas labels. Different label fusion methods differ in the way they compute the weights. The most common way is to use image similarity measurements. More advanced methods use image regression techniques with sparsity constraints to set the weights. The main idea of these latter methods is to decrease the number of contributing atlas patches to only a few relevant ones in order to reduce the chances of introducing misleading information. Conventional weighted voting approaches perform well when all the anatomical characteristics are equally represented among the set of atlases. However, this is not usually the case, since some anatomical characteristics are overrepresented in the set of atlases. In such case, labeling results of the conventional weighted voting are biased toward committing the typical errors of the most represented characteristics. This can be overcome by using strategies to set the weights that enforce the variability in the anatomical characteristics of the atlas patches used for label fusion. Machine learning has also been used in label fusion. The main idea is to learn the optimal classification rules by taking into account the relationships between the image features and the underlying anatomical labels.

MAS has developed rapidly in the last 10 years. Many developments have been made both in the atlas selection and the label fusion steps since the introduction of the majority vote rule using all the available atlases. Recent developments show an increasing trend in the use of machine learning techniques in the different steps of MAS.

# REFERENCES

Akhondi-Asl, A., Warfield, S.K., 2013. Simultaneous truth and performance level estimation through fusion of probabilistic segmentations. IEEE Trans. Med. Imaging 32 (10), 1840–1852.

Aljabar, P., Heckemann, R.A., Hammers, A., Hajnal, J.V., Rueckert, D., 2009. Multi-atlas based segmentation of brain images: atlas selection and its effect on accuracy. Neuroimage 46 (3), 726–738.

Amieva, H., Goff, M.L., Millet, X., Orgogozo, J., Pérès, K., Barberger-Gateau, P., Jacqmin-Gadda, H., Dartigues, J., 2008. Prodromal Alzheimer's disease: successive emergence of the clinical symptoms. Ann. Neurol. 64, 492–498.

Artaechevarria, X., Munoz-Barrutia, A., de Solorzano, C.O., 2009. Combination strategies in multi-atlas image segmentation: application to brain MR data. IEEE Trans. Med. Imaging 28 (8), 1266–1277.

Arzhaeva, Y., Rikxoort, E.M.V., Ginneken, B.V., 2007. Automated segmentation of caudate nucleus in MR brain images with voxel classification. In: Heimann, T., Styner, M., van Ginneken, B. (Eds.), 3D Segmentation in the Clinic: A Grand Challenge, Medical Image Computing and Computer Assisted Intervention (MICCAI 2007), Brisbane (Australia), pp. 65–72.

Asman, A.J., Landman, B.A., 2011. Robust statistical label fusion through consensus level, labeler accuracy, and truth estimation (collate). IEEE Trans. Med. Imaging 30 (10), 1779–1794.

Asman, A.J., Landman, B.A., 2012. Formulating spatially varying performance in the statistical fusion framework. IEEE Trans. Med. Imaging 31 (6), 1326–1336.

Asman, A.J., Landman, B.A., 2013. Non-local statistical label fusion for multi-atlas segmentation. Med. Image Anal. 17 (2), 194–208.

Asman, A.J., Landman, B.A., 2014. Hierarchical performance estimation in the statistical label fusion framework. Med. Image Anal. 18 (7), 1070–1081.

Babalola, K.O., Patenaude, B., Aljabar, P., Schnabel, J., Kennedy, D., Crum, W., Smith, S., Cootes, T., Jenkinson, M., Rueckert, D., 2009. An evaluation of four automatic methods of segmenting the subcortical structures in the brain. Neuroimage 47 (4), 1435–1447.

Bai, W., Shi, W., O'Regan, D.P., Tong, T., Wang, H., Jamil-Copley, S., Peters, N.S., Rueckert, D., 2013. A probabilistic patch-based label fusion model for multi-atlas segmentation with registration refinement: application to cardiac MR images. IEEE Trans. Med. Imaging 32 (7), 1302–1315.

Bai, W., Shi, W., Ledig, C., Rueckert, D., 2015. Multi-atlas segmentation with augmented features for cardiac MR images. Med. Image Anal. 19 (1), 98–109.

Breiman, L., 2001. Random forests. Mach. Learn. 45 (1), 5–32.

Cao, Y., Yuan, Y., Li, X., Turkbey, B., Choyke, P.L., Yan, P., 2011. Segmenting images by combining selected atlases on manifold. In: MICCAI. LNCS.

Cardoso, M.J., Leung, K., Modat, M., Keihaninejad, S., Cash, D., Barnes, J., Fox, N.C., Ourselin, S., 2013. Steps: similarity and truth estimation for propagated segmentations and its application to hippocampal segmentation and brain parcelation. Med. Image Anal. 17 (6), 671–684.

Cortes, C., Vapnik, V., 1995. Support-vector networks. Mach. Learn. 20 (3), 273–297.

Coupé, P., Manjón, J., Fonov, V., Pruessner, J., Robles, M., Collins, D.L., 2011. Patch-based segmentation using expert priors: application to hippocampus and ventricle segmentation. Neuroimage 54 (2), 940–954.

Criminisi, A., Shotton, J., 2013. Decision Forests for Computer Vision and Medical Image Analysis. Springer Publishing Company, Berlin.

Dalal, N., Triggs, B., 2005. Histograms of oriented gradients for human detection. In: International Conference on Computer Vision and Pattern Recognition.

Datteri, R., Asman, A., Landman, B., Dawant, B., 2011. Estimation of registration accuracy applied to multi-atlas segmentation. In: MICCAI.

Dempster, A.P., Laird, N.M., Rubin, D.B., 1977. Maximum likelihood from incomplete data via the EM algorithm. J. R. Stat. Soc. Ser. B 39 (1), 1–38.

Depa, M., Holmvang, G., Schmidt, E.J., Golland, P., Sabuncu, M.R., 2011. Towards efficient label fusion by pre-alignment of training data. In: MICCAI, pp. 38–46.

Elias, M., Beiser, A., Wolf, P., Au, R., White, R., D'Agostino, R., 2000. The preclinical phase of Alzheimer disease: a 22-year prospective study of the Framingham cohort. Arch. Neurol. 57, 803–813.

Goksel, O., Gass, T., Vishnevsky, V., Szekely, G., 2013. Estimation of atlas-based segmentation outcome: leveraging information from unsegmented images. In: ISBI.

Goshtasby, A.A., 2005. 2-D and 3-D Image Registration: For Medical, Remote Sensing, and Industrial Applications. Wiley-Interscience, Oxford.

Guo, Y., Wu, G., Commander, L.A., Szary, S., Jewells, V., Lin, W., Shen, D., 2014. Segmenting hippocampus from infant brains by sparse patch matching with deep-learned features. In: Medical Image Computing and Computer-Assisted Intervention—MICCAI, Boston, MA, USA, pp. 308–315.

Hao, Y., Wang, T., Zhang, X., Duan, Y., Yu, C., Jiang, T., Fan, Y., 2014. Local label learning (LLL) for subcortical structure segmentation: application to hippocampus segmentation. Hum. Brain Mapp. 35 (6), 2675–2697.

Haralick, R.M., Shanmugam, K., Dinstein, I.H., 1973. Textural features for image classification. IEEE Trans. Syst. Man Cybern. 6 (3), 610–621.

Heckemann, R.A., Hajnal, J.V., Aljabar, P., Rueckert, D., Hammers, A., 2006a. Automatic anatomical brain MRI segmentation combining label propagation and decision fusion. Neuroimage 33 (1), 115–126.

Heckemann, R.A., Hajnal, J.V., Aljabar, P., Rueckert, D., Hammers, A., 2006b, Multiclassifier fusion in human brain MR segmentation: modelling convergence. In: MICCAI.

Hinton, G.E., Salakhutdinov, R.R., 2006. Reducing the dimensionality of data with neural networks. Science 313 (5786), 504–507.

Hinton, G.E., Osindero, S., Teh, Y.W., 2006. A fast learning algorithm for deep belief nets. Neural Comput. 18 (7), 1527–1554.

Hsu, Y.Y., Schuff, N., Du, A.T., Mark, K., Zhu, X., Hardin, D., Weiner, M.W., 2002. Comparison of automated and manual MRI volumetry of hippocampus in normal aging and dementia. J. Magn. Reson. Imaging 16, 305–310.

Iglesias, J.E., Sabuncu, M.R., Leemput, K.V., 2013. A unified framework for cross-modality multi-atlas segmentation of brain MRI. Med. Image Anal. 17 (8), 1181–1191.

Isgum, I., Staring, M., Rutten, A., Prokop, M., Viergever, M.A., van Ginneken, B., 2009. Multi-atlas-based segmentation with local decision fusion: application to cardiac and aortic segmentation in CT scans. IEEE Trans. Med. Imaging 28 (7), 1000–1010.

Joachims, T., 2002. Optimizing search engines using click through data. In: Proceedings of the Eighth ACM SIGKDD International Conference on Knowledge Discovery and Data Mining.

Keall, P., Mageras, G., Balter, J., Emery, R., Forster, K., Jiang, S., Kapatoes, J., Low, D., Murphy, M., Murray, B., Ramsey, C., Herk, M.V., Vedam, S., Wong, J., Yorke, E., 2006. The management of respiratory motion in radiation oncology report of AAPM task group 76. Med. Phys. 33 (10), 3874–3900.

Khan, A.R., Cherbuin, N., Wen, W., Anstey, K., Sachdev, P.S., Faisal, B.M., 2009a. Optimal weights for local multi-atlas fusion using supervised learning and dynamic information (superdyn): validation on hippocampus segmentation. Neuroimage 56 (1), 126–139.

Khan, A.R., Chung, M.K., Faisal, B.M., 2009b, Robust atlas-based brain segmentation using multi-structure confidence-weighted registration. In: G.-Z. Yang, Hawkes, D.J., Rueckert, D., Noble, J.A., Taylor, C.J. (Eds.), MICCAI. Springer, pp. 549–557.

Khan, F., Bell, G., Antony, J., Palmer, M., Balter, P., Bucci, K., Chapman, M.J., 2009c. The use of 4D CT to reduce lung dose: a dosimetric analysis. Med. Dosim. 34 (4), 273–278.

Kim, M., Wu, G., Li, W., Wang, L., Son, Y.D., Cho, Z.H., Shen, D., 2013. Automatic hippocampus segmentation of 7.0 tesla MR images by combining multiple atlases and auto-context models. Neuroimage 83, 335–345.

Klein, S., van der Heide, U.A., Lips, I.M., van Vulpen, M., Staring, M., Pluim, J.P.W., 2008. Automatic segmentation of the prostate in 3D MR images by atlas matching using localized mutual information. Med. Phys. 35 (4), 1407–1417.

Klein, A., Andersson, J., Ardekani, B.A., Ashburner, J., Avants, B.B., Chiang, M.C., Christensen, G.E., Collins, D.L., 2009. Evaluation of 14 nonlinear deformation algorithms applied to human brain MRI registration. Neuroimage 46 (3), 786–802.

Konukoglu, E., Glocker, B., Zikic, D., Criminisi, A., 2012. Neighbourhood approximation forests. In: MICCAI.

Langerak, T.R., van der Heide, U.A., Kotte, A.N.T.J., Viergever, M.A., van Vulpen, M., Pluim, J.P.W., 2010. Label fusion in atlas-based segmentation using a selective and iterative method for performance level estimation (simple). IEEE Trans. Med. Imaging 29 (12), 2000–2008.

Lombaert, H., Zikic, D., Criminisi, A., Ayache, N., 2014. Laplacian forests: semantic image segmentation by guided bagging. In: MICCAI.

Lotjonen, J.M., Wolz, R., Koikkalainen, J.R., Thurfjell, L., Waldemar, G., Soininen, H., Rueckert, D., 2010. Fast and robust multi-atlas segmentation of brain magnetic resonance images. Neuroimage 49 (3), 2352–2365.

Madabhushi, A., Udupa, J., 2006. New methods of MR image intensity standardization via generalized scale. Med. Phys. 33 (9), 3426–3434.

Morra, J.H., Tu, Z., Apostolova, L.G., Green, A.E., Avedissian, C., Madsen, S.K., Parikshak, N., Hua, X., Toga, A.W., Clifford, R.J., Weiner, M.W., Thompson, P.M., 2008. Validation of a fully automated 3D hippocampal segmentation method using subjects with Alzheimer's disease mild cognitive impairment, and elderly controls. Neuroimage 43 (1), 59–68.

Morra, J.H., Tu, Z., Apostolova, L.G., Green, A.E., Toga, A.W., Thompson, P.M., 2010. Comparison of Adaboost and support vector machines for detecting Alzheimer's disease through automated hippocampal segmentation. IEEE Trans. Med. Imaging 29 (1), 30–43.

Ou, Y., Akbari, H., Bilello, M., Da, X., Davatzikos, C., 2014. Comparative evaluation of registration algorithms in different brain databases with varying difficulty: results and insights. IEEE Trans. Med. Imaging 33 (10), 2039–2065.

Rohlfing, T., Brandt, R., Menzel, R., Maurer Jr., C.R., 2004. Evaluation of atlas selection strategies for atlas-based image segmentation with application to confocal microscopy images of bee brains. Neuroimage 21 (4), 1428–1442.

Rousseau, F., Habas, P.A., Studholme, C., 2011. A supervised patch-based approach for human brain labeling. IEEE Trans. Med. Imaging 30 (10), 1852–1862.

Sabuncu, M.R., Yeo, B.T.T., Leemput, K.V., Fischl, B., Golland, P., 2010. A generative model for image segmentation based on label fusion. IEEE Trans. Med. Imaging 29 (10), 1714–1729.

Sanroma, G., Wu, G., Gao, Y., Shen, D., 2014. Learning to rank atlases for multiple-atlas segmentation. To appear in IEEE Transactions on Medical Imaging.

Sdika, M., 2010. Combining atlas based segmentation and intensity classification with nearest neighbor transform and accuracy weighted vote. Med. Image Anal. 14 (2), 219–226.

Shi, F., Wang, L., Dai, Y., Gilmore, J., Lin, W., Shen, D., 2012. Label: pediatric brain extraction using learning-based meta-algorithm. Neuroimage 62, 1975–1986.

Smith, S.M., Jenkinson, M., Woolrich, M.W., Beckmann, C.F., Behrens, T.E.J., Johansen-Berg, H., Bannister, P.R., Luca, M.D., Drobnjak, I., Flitney, D.E., Niazy, R.K., Saunders, J., Vickers, J., Zhang, Y., Stefano, N.D., Brady, J.M., Matthews, P.M., 2004. Advances in functional and structural MR image analysis and implementation as FSL. Neuroimage 23, S208–S219.

Studholme, C., Hill, D., Hawkes, D., 1999. An overlap invariant entropy measure of 3D medical image alignment. Pattern Recogn. 32 (1), 71–86.

Tong, T., Wolz, R., Hajnal, J.V., Rueckert, D., 2012. Segmentation of brain MR images via sparse patch representation. In: STMI.

Tong, T., Wolz, R., Coupé, P., Hajnal, J.V., Rueckert, D., 2013. Segmentation of MR images via discriminative dictionary learning and sparse coding: application to hippocampus labeling. Neuroimage 76 (1), 11–23.

Tu, Z., Bai, X., 2010. Auto-context and its application to high-level vision tasks and 3D brain image segmentation. IEEE Trans. Pattern Anal. Mach. Intell. 32 (10), 1744–1757.

Tu, Z., Narr, K., Dollár, P., Dinov, I.D., Thompson, P.M., Toga, A.W., 2008. Brain anatomical structure segmentation by hybrid discriminative/generative models. IEEE Trans. Med. Imaging 27 (4), 495–508.

Tustison, N., Avants, B., Cook, P., Zheng, Y., Egan, A., Yushkevich, P., Gee, J., 2010. N4ITK: improved N3 bias correction. IEEE Trans. Med. Imaging 29 (6), 1310–1320.

van Rikxoort, E.M., Isgum, I., Arzhaeva, Y., Staring, M., Klein, S., Viergever, M.A., Pluim, J.P.W., van Ginneken, B., 2010. Adaptive local multi-atlas segmentation: application to the heart and the caudate nucleus. Med. Image Anal. 14, 39–49.

Vercauteren, T., Pennec, X., Perchant, A., Ayache, N., 2009. Diffeomorphic demons: efficient non-parametric image registration. Neuroimage 45 (1, Suppl. 1), S61–S72.

Viola, P., Jones, M., 2001. Rapid object detection using a boosted cascade of simple features. In: CVPR.

Wang, H., Yushkevich, P.A., 2012. Dependency prior for multi-atlas label fusion. In: ISBI, pp. 892–895.

Wang, H., Suh, J.W., Das, S.R., Pluta, J., Altinay, M., Yushkevich, P.A., 2011. Regression-based label fusion for multi-atlas segmentation. In: CVPR, pp. 1113–1120.

Wang, H., Pouch, A.M., Takabe, M., Jackson, B., Gorman, J.H., Gorman, R.C., Yushkevich, P.A., 2013a, Multi-atlas segmentation with robust label transfer and label fusion. In: IPMI

Wang, H., Suh, J.W., Das, S.R., Pluta, J., Craige, C., Yushkevich, P.A., 2013b. Multi-atlas segmentation with joint label fusion. IEEE Trans. Pattern Anal. Mach. Intell. 35 (3), 611–623.

Warfield, S.K., Zou, K.H., Wells, W.M., 2004. Simultaneous truth and performance level estimation (staple): an algorithm for the validation of image segmentation. IEEE Trans. Med. Imaging 23 (7), 903–921.

Weisenfeld, N.I., Warfield, S.K., 2011. Learning likelihoods for labeling (L3): a general multi-classifier segmentation algorithm. In: MICCAI, pp. 322–329.

Wolz, R., Aljabar, P., Hajnal, J.V., Hammers, A., Rueckert, D., 2010. Leap: learning embeddings for altas propagation. Neuroimage 49 (2), 1316–1325.

Wu, G., Shen, D., 2014. Hierarchical label fusion with multiscale feature representation and label-specific patch partition. In: MICCAI, Boston, USA.

Wu, M., Rosano, C., Lopez-Garcia, P., Carter, C.S., Aizenstein, H.J., 2007. Optimum template selection for atlas-based segmentation. Neuroimage 34, 1612–1618.

Wu, G., Wang, Q., Zhang, D., Shen, D., 2012. Robust patch-based multi-atlas labeling by joint sparsity regularization. In: STMI.

Wu, G., Wang, Q., Zhang, D., Nie, F., Huang, H., Shen, D., 2014. A generative probability model of joint label fusion for multi-atlas based brain segmentation. Med. Image Anal. 18 (6), 881–890.

Wu, G., Kim, M., Sanroma, G., Wang, Q., Munsell, B., Shen, D., 2015. Hierarchical multi-atlas label fusion with multi-scale feature representation and label-specific patch partition. Neuroimage 106 (1), 34–46.

Zhang, D., Wu, G., Jia, H., Shen, D., 2011. Confidence-guided sequential label fusion for multi-atlas based segmentation. In: MICCAI, vol. 6893, pp. 643–650.

Zhang, D., Guo, Q., Wu, G., Shen, D., 2012. Sparse patch-based label fusion for multi-atlas segmentation. In: Yap, P.-T., Liu, T., Shen, D., Westin, C.-F., Shen, L. (Eds.), MBIA, Elsevier.

Zhou, S.K., 2014. Discriminative anatomy detection: classification vs regression. Pattern Recogn. Lett. 43, 25–38.

Zikic, D., Glocker, B., Criminisi, A., 2013. Atlas encoding by randomized forests for efficient label propagation. In: Mori, K., Sakuma, I., Sato, Y., Barillot, C., Navab, N. (Eds.), MICCAI. Springer, pp. 66–73.

# AN OVERVIEW OF THE MULTI-OBJECT GEOMETRIC DEFORMABLE MODEL APPROACH IN BIOMEDICAL IMAGING

# 12

**A. Carass and J.L. Prince**

*Department of Electrical and Computer Engineering, The Johns Hopkins University, Baltimore, MD, USA*

## CHAPTER OUTLINE

S. Kevin Zhou (Ed): Medical Image Recognition, Segmentation and Parsing. http://dx.doi.org/10.1016/B978-0-12-802581-9.00012-3

## 12.1 INTRODUCTION

Deformable models have been fundamental for image segmentation since the seminal paper of Kass, Witkin, and Terzopoulos (Kass et al., 1988). A deformable model, also known as a *snake* or *active contour*, is an energy minimizing, deformable curve that is influenced by internal and external forces that pull the model toward object contours. External forces move the curve to desirable image features (such as image gradient), while internal forces ensure desirable properties of the curve (such as smoothness). As we think of the evolution of the curve occurring over time, some literature will use the term speeds for forces. Strictly speaking, speeds are forces that are applied along the direction normal to the evolving curve, while forces can have a non-normal component. If we restrict ourselves to thinking about closed curves, we can then naturally think of an implicit representation arising from level sets (Osher and Sethian, 1988; Sethian, 1996; Chan and Vese, 2001; Osher and Fedkiw, 2003). This approach is referred to as geometric deformable models (GDMs) (Caselles et al., 1993, 1997; Malladi et al., 1995) with the evolution of the curve being defined implicitly based on the evolution of the level set function. Signed distance functions (SDFs) are commonly used for the level set function (Osher and Fedkiw, 2003), with the SDF simply being the distance to the object boundary with the sign distinguishing the interior (negative) and exterior (positive) of the object. Evolution of GDMs is handled by updating the values of the level set function based on decreasing the cost of an associated energy. If the level set function at a voxel goes from being positive to negative, then the voxel has moved from the outside to the inside of the object.

There have been numerous explorations of segmentation through multi-object level set-based methods (Paragios and Deriche, 2000; Samson et al., 2000; Vese and Chan, 2002; Angelini et al., 2004; Tsai et al., 2004; Zimmer and Olivo-Marin, 2005; Brox and Weickert, 2006; Mansouri et al., 2006; Pohl et al., 2007; Fan et al., 2008; Kohlberger et al., 2011; Li and Kim, 2011; Al-Shaikhli et al., 2014; Günther et al., 2014) with several relevant review articles on the topic (Tai and Chan, 2004; Cremers et al., 2007). The most basic approach is to use $M$ level sets to handle $M$ objects, in which case the label $i$ for the $i$th object is assigned when the $i$th level set $\phi_i$ is negative. There are two important factors to consider in relation to multiple object level set methods: intersections/overlaps and gaps. Situations that involve overlaps may not be entirely unwelcome when considering crossing fibers in diffusion imaging. In general, however, overlaps can cause confusion: *How can two objects occupy the same space?* Those instances involving multiple objects in the same space may be better handled by multiple objects; in the example of crossing fibers objects can be defined for the fibers before and after the crossing region and another object specifically for the crossing fibers (Bazin et al., 2011). Gaps, at least in biomedical imaging, are usually an undesirable occurrence that make little or no biological sense—a clinician would be very concerned to find a gap between a patient's brain and their spine. Both gaps and overlaps can occur with the direct use of $M$ level sets, unless all the level sets are moved in synchrony. One approach to deal with this has been the introduction of coupled forces (Paragios and Deriche, 2000; Samson et al., 2000; Zimmer and Olivo-Marin, 2005) to avoid these situations; however, they do not come with any guarantees and can in practice still allow gaps and overlaps.

An alternative solution that ensures no overlaps or gaps is the multiphase (MP) approach (Vese and Chan, 2002) which can represent $M$ objects with $\log_2 M$ level sets. It was clearly a significant step forward, substantially reducing the computational burden as $M$ increases. However, MP has three shortcomings: (1) its image-based external force term is not easily generalized; (2) internal forces are applied to the level set functions rather than the objects, so as the lengths of level set functions are minimized it may not be the case for the boundaries themselves; and (3) the evolution can encounter pixels that can only be changed if two level sets are updated simultaneously, a problem that is more prone to occur with more objects.

Topological flexibility was originally claimed to be one of the main selling points of GDMs (McInerney and Terzopoulos, 1995; Delingette and Montagnat, 2000). However, in the last decade, there have been numerous works (Han et al., 2003; Bazin et al., 2007; Cardoso et al., 2011a,b; Gao et al., 2013) espousing the benefits of using topology to improve the accuracy of results, though there are works dating back over several decades (Rosenfeld, 1970; Malandain et al., 1993; Bertrand, 1994; Rosenfeld et al., 1998). In particular, when a specific anatomy has a known topology, it should be preserved. For example, if asked to segment a hand into its fingers, palm, and wrist, you would not allow any finger to be connected to the palm twice or for there to be multiple palm objects. In this way, knowledge of the components and the homology of each component leads to a natural desire to seek out the target that has this correct topology.

Han et al. (2003) introduced the concept of a topology-preserving geometric deformable model (TGDM). TGDM constrains a traditional GDM preventing the evolving implicit surface from ever changing topology. The introduced constraint, based on the simple point criteria (SPC) (Bertrand, 1994), checks the topology of an object implied by its evolving level set and restricts the level set from changing sign if the sign change will lead to the object changing topology. Thus, a simple point is a point which would not change the topology of an object, at the current evolution, whether it is added to or removed from the object. TGDM operated in the domain of a foreground object and a background object; however, the concept can be extended to a multi-object environment, which is reviewed in Section 12.2.2.

In this chapter, we explore the applications of the multi-object geometric deformable model (MGDM) (Fan et al., 2008; Bogovic et al., 2013b). It is a level set segmentation framework that guarantees no overlaps or gaps, and evolves a very small number of level set derived functions independently of the number of regions. MGDM can apply to all existing types of speed functions that have been previously reported in the literature, and it can enforce object relationships and topological constraints on individual objects as well as on groups of objects. A unique feature of MGDM is that it can apply differing speeds to the same object at different boundaries depending on the defined relationships with its neighbors. By neighbor relationships, we mean consistent connectivity between objects. MGDM takes the objects and converts these relationships into a small number of distance functions and label functions, where the label functions at a voxel retain information about the voxel's current label and the label of some of its nearest neighbors. In $N$ dimensions, MGDM requires $N$ distance functions and $N$ label functions, a condition that is independent of the number of objects under consideration. As MGDM is a multi-object extension to the conventional geometric level set formulation, it follows that all previously reported forces can be used to move object boundaries. Overlaps and gaps are avoided as the evolving functions provide a partition of the image, under the assumption that the initialization had no overlaps or gaps. The $N$ label functions allow us to know the current speeds to consider for each object boundary interaction. The topology of objects is enforced using a multi-object variant of the SPC (Bertrand, 1994), with similar implications for groups of objects. As MGDM is based on SDFs to represent the objects, it can resolve boundary locations to subvoxel resolution.

In Section 12.2, we provide an overview of the mathematical framework that underpins MGDM and a description of the multi-object SPC for maintaining the topology of objects and groups of objects. In Section 12.3, we revisit the classical example of a topologically consistent hand segmentation first demonstrated in Han et al. (2003) for the case of multiple objects. In Section 12.4, we provide several applications of MGDM in real world biomedical imaging segmentation. We conclude with a discussion of the advantages and disadvantages of the framework.

## 12.2 METHODS
### 12.2.1 FRAMEWORK

MGDM (Fan et al., 2008; Bogovic et al., 2013b) is a multi-object extension to the conventional geometric level set formulation of active contours (Caselles et al., 1993; Malladi et al., 1995; Caselles et al., 1997). It uses a decomposition of the SDFs of all objects that enables efficient contour evolution while preventing object overlaps and gaps from forming. We consider $M$ objects $O_1, O_2, \ldots, O_M$ that cover a domain $\Omega$ with $O_i \cap O_j = \emptyset$ for all $i \neq j$ and $\cup_i O_i = \Omega$. Let $\phi_i$ be the SDF for $O_i$ defined as

$$\phi_i(x) = \begin{cases} -d_x(O_i), & x \in O_i \\ d_x(O_i), & x \notin O_i \end{cases} \tag{12.1}$$

where

$$d_x(O_i) = \min_{y \in \partial O_i} \|x - y\| \tag{12.2}$$

is the shortest distance by the Euclidean norm from the point $x \in \Omega$ to the boundary of $O_i$, denoted $\partial O_i$. In a conventional multi-object segmentation formulation, each object is moved according to a speed function $f_i(x)$ defined for each object using the standard partial differential equation (PDE) for level set evolution,

$$\frac{\partial \phi_i(x)}{\partial t} = f_i(x)|\nabla \phi_i(x)| \quad \text{for } i = 1, \ldots, M. \tag{12.3}$$

The level set evolution is typically implemented using a narrow band method (Chopp, 1993; Adalsteinsson and Sethian, 1995), which allows the updates of the level set to occur in a small neighborhood around the zero level set of all objects.

MGDM does not use this conventional formulation. It instead uses a unique representation of the objects and their level set functions, thus removing the requirement to store the level set functions for each object separately. This alternative representation additionally enables a convenient capability to encode boundary-specific speed functions in the deformable model. By boundary specific, we mean the boundary between objects $O_i$ and $O_j$, which can have a different set of forces acting on it than the entire boundary of object $O_i$ that is specified in Eq. (12.3). We define a set of label functions that specify the object at $x$ and all successively nearest neighboring objects

$$L_0(x) = i \iff x \in O_i$$

$$L_1(x) = \arg\min_{j \neq L_0(x)} d_x(O_j)$$

$$L_2(x) = \arg\min_{j \neq \{L_0(x), L_1(x)\}} d_x(O_j) \tag{12.4}$$

$$\vdots$$

$$L_{N-1}(x) = \underset{j \neq \{L_k(x)\}_{k=0,\dots,N-2.}}{\arg\min} d_x(O_j)$$

We note that the function $L_0(x)$ is the current label at the voxel $x$, whereas $L_1(x)$ is the label of the first nearest neighbor to $x$, and $L_j(x)$ is the label of the $j$th nearest neighbor to $x$. We then define functions that give the distance to each successively distant object

$$\varphi_0(x) = d_x(L_1(x))$$
$$\varphi_1(x) = d_x(L_2(x)) - d_x(L_1(x))$$
$$\varphi_2(x) = d_x(L_3(x)) - d_x(L_2(x)) \qquad (12.5)$$

$$\vdots$$

$$\varphi_{N-2}(x) = d_x(L_{N-1}(x)) - d_x(L_{N-2}(x)).$$

Thus, $\varphi_0(x)$ is the shortest distance required to travel from $x$ to reach its nearest neighbor $L_1(x)$, and $\varphi_1(x)$ is the additional distance required to travel to reach the second nearest neighbor of $x$ having already traveled $\varphi_0(x)$, and $\varphi_j(x)$ is the distance required to travel from the $(j-1)$th neighbor of $x$ to reach its $j$th neighbor. Together, these functions describe a local "object environment" at each point $x$. It can be shown that the SDFs at $x$ for all objects can be reconstructed from these functions (see Bogovic et al. (2013b) for details). Examples of $L_0(x)$, $L_1(x)$, $\varphi_0(x)$, and $\varphi_1(x)$ for the initialization of one of our experiments can be seen in Figure 12.1.

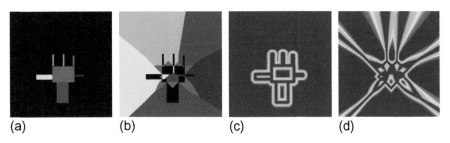

|  (a) | (b) | (c) | (d) |

**FIGURE 12.1**

Shown are the label functions (a) $L_0(x)$ and (b) $L_1(x)$ for the initialization of our hand segmentation experiment (see Section 12.3 for details). $L_0(x)$ corresponds to the initial segmentation, and $L_1(x)$ is the label of the first nearest neighbor. The color used for each object's label is identical for $L_0(x)$ and $L_1(x)$, while (c) and (d) show $\varphi_0(x)$ and $\varphi_1(x)$, respectively. Recall that $\varphi_0(x)$ is the distance from $x$ to its nearest neighbor, and $\varphi_1(x)$ is the additional distance needed to reach the second nearest neighbor. The color scale goes from 0 (blue) to a maximum of 25 pixels (red).

We observe that the SDFs of the closest objects can be approximated using just three label functions and three distance functions in 3D:

$$\hat{\phi}_i(x) = \begin{cases} -\varphi_0(x), & i = L_0(x) \\ \varphi_0(x), & i = L_1(x) \\ \varphi_0(x) + \varphi_1(x), & i = L_2(x) \\ \varphi_0(x) + \varphi_1(x) + \varphi_2(x), & i \neq L_{0,1,2}(x) \end{cases} \tag{12.6}$$

where the notation $i \neq L_{0,1,2}(x)$ means $i \neq L_0(x)$ and $i \neq L_1(x)$ and $i \neq L_2(x)$. This is readily extended to $N$ label functions and $N$ distance functions in $N$-dimensional settings. The $\hat{\phi}_i(x)$'s are level set functions sharing the same zero level sets as the true SDFs; they give a valid representation of the boundary structure of all the objects—details and conditions of the stability of this approximation are in Bogovic et al. (2013b). Therefore, storing just these six functions (three label functions and three distance functions) is sufficient to describe the local object environment of every point in the domain for any number of objects. This represents an important computational improvement over traditional multi-object level set frameworks; for example, note that Brox and Weickert (2006) required $M$ functions and Vese and Chan (2002) used $\log_2 M$ functions.

The second computational savings of MGDM comes about by realizing that the evolution equations, given in Eq. (12.3), can be carried over by updating the distance functions instead of the SDFs, as follows

$$\frac{\partial \psi_k(x)}{\partial t} = \frac{1}{2}(f_{L_k}(x) - f_{L_{k+1}}(x)), \quad k = 2, 1, 0 \tag{12.7}$$

for all $x$ in the narrow band. Evolving these distance functions must be carried out by starting with $\psi_2$, then $\psi_1$, and finally $\psi_0$; any changes to the ordering of object neighbors during this process are reflected by changes in the associated label functions. Reconstruction of the continuous level set boundaries of the actual objects themselves need not be carried out until after the very last iteration of the evolution. To accomplish this, an isosurface algorithm is run on each level set function $\hat{\phi}_i(x)$, and the object boundaries will have subvoxel resolution by virtue of the level set representation and subvoxel resolution of isosurface algorithms.

Since MGDM keeps track of both the object label and its nearest neighbor at each $x$, the updated Eq. (12.7) is very fast to carry out. Furthermore, it can use both object-specific and boundary-specific speed functions. Given the index of the object and its neighbor stored at each $x$, a simple index into a lookup table gives the appropriate speed functions to use for that object and particular boundary.

## 12.2.2 TOPOLOGY PRESERVATION

Like TGDM (Han et al., 2003), which maintains single-object topology using the SPC, MGDM is capable of preserving multiple object relationships using the digital homeomorphism constraint (DHC), which is an extension of the SPC to multiple objects (Bazin et al., 2007; Bazin and Pham, 2008). We therefore use the DHC in MGDM to maintain proper object topology (when desired). This is readily achieved by checking the SPC in a structured manner for the various objects. In particular, we consider the foreground object $O_i$ with a corresponding background object of $\cup_{j \neq i} O_j$ for each voxel that is being considered for addition to or removal from $O_i$ during the current evolution. This, however, only guarantees the topology of $O_i$; it could introduce situations where the topology of $O_i$ is preserved but $O_i$ is allowed to touch $O_k$ from which it had previously been kept separate or the changing voxel means that structures around $O_i$ become disconnected. To prevent this, we have to consider the foreground object $O_i \cup O_k$ with a background object of $\cup_{j \neq i,k} O_j$ and again test the SPC for each voxel in the current evolution of the level set that wishes to change into or out of the foreground object $(O_i \cup O_k)$. We require one more check to guarantee topology preservation: given a voxel $x$ that wishes to change from object $O_i$ to $O_k$, we need to know if the relationship between $O_i$, $O_k$, and a third object $O_l$ would be changed if we allow $x$ to change between $O_i$ and $O_k$. Thus, we need to consider the foreground object $O_i \cup O_k \cup O_l$ with a corresponding background object of $\cup_{j \neq i,k,l} O_j$, for each $l \neq i,k$.

This can be summarized with the following statement (Bazin and Pham, 2008):

> A digital homeomorphism is a transformation, for a given segmentation of space into $N$ objects $O_1, \dots, O_N$, that allows any point $x$ to change from $O_i$ to $O_j$ if and only if $x$ is a simple point for each of the foreground objects $O_i$, $O_j$, $\{O_i \cup O_k\}_{k \neq j}$, $\{O_j \cup O_k\}_{k \neq i}$, $\{O_i \cup O_k \cup O_l\}_{k,l \neq j}$, and $\{O_j \cup O_k \cup O_l\}_{k,l \neq i}$, with appropriately constructed background objects.

The DHC extends the SPC by noting that simple points are object dependent. We note that the DHC holds regardless of the connectivity choice (6-connected vs 26-connected) for the digital objects.

## 12.3 SEGMENTATION OF A MULTI-OBJECT HAND

In the work of Han et al. (2003), the authors (among other things) demonstrated a topologically consistent segmentation of a hand illustration. The purpose of the example is to establish the correctness of their algorithm and also to highlight the flaws with traditional GDMs. We provide a similar, illustrative example, for a multi-object segmentation of a hand. Figure 12.2 shows a 2D example that illustrates the multi-object capabilities of MGDM. The image to segment is shown in Figure 12.2(a), with MGDM being driven by two region forces derived from the original image and an outline of the palm (Figure 12.2(b)). These two region forces act upon the seven foreground objects, allowing the palm object to dominate within the region provided by Figure 12.2(b), outside of which the fingers or wrist dominate the force balance. The initialization for MGDM is shown in Figure 12.2(e), consisting of a wrist (purple), palm (red), thumb (yellow), and four fingers (shades of green and blue). Figure 12.2(f) and (g) shows intermediate results during the evolution of the objects, while Figure 12.2(h) shows the final result of MGDM after the segmentation has remained unchanged for a predetermined number of iterations. Figure 12.2(c) and (d) displays a zoomed portion of Figure 12.2(a) and (d), respectively, showing the middle and ring fingers. Enforcing topology preservation during the evolution guarantees that the initialization, all intermediate segmentations, and the final result have the same topology, which in this case means the middle and ring fingers can never touch.

For this experiment, the speed terms on object boundary $(i,j)$ take the form

$$F_{(i,j)}(\mathbf{x}) = \sum_{k=0}^{1} -\beta_{(i,j,k)} \left[ (I_k(\mathbf{x}) - \mu_{(k,j)})^2 - (I_k(\mathbf{x}) - \mu_{(k,i)})^2 \right] \qquad (12.8)$$

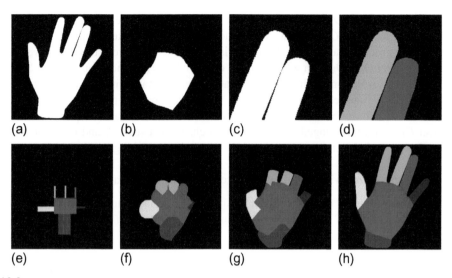

**FIGURE 12.2**

Shown are (a) the original illustration of a hand to be segmented, (b) an outline of the palm, with (c) and (d) showing a zoomed portion of the original image and final segmentation, demonstrating the effects topology preservation has on MGDM. While (e) is the initialization of MGDM with seven foreground objects, (f) and (g) are two intermediate segmentations from the evolution, and (h) is the final result after MGDM has converged.

where $I_k(\mathbf{x})$ is the intensity of the pixel location $\mathbf{x}$ in the $k$th region image; the two region images are shown in Figure 12.2(a) and (b). Here $\mu_{(k,i)}$ is a threshold for the desired intensity of object $i$ in region image $k$, and $\beta_{(i,j,k)}$ is a weight determining the strength of these forces relative to each other. In region image 0—the whole hand—the fingers and wrist have the same $\beta_{(i,j,0)} = \beta$ with the background, and have no corresponding $\beta_{(i,j,0)}$ with each other as they do not touch in the initialization. The palm object has $\beta_{(i,j,0)} = 0$ for all other objects (background and the foreground objects of wrist and fingers) meaning that unless there are other forces the palm object will not contract or expand. However, in region image 1—which is the outlined palm—the palm object has a $\beta_{(i,j,1)} = 2\beta$ with the other background and foreground objects; thus the palm object will dominate within the outlined palm region image, expanding to fill the region completely. As both of our region images are simple binary images, we can set $\mu_{(k,i)}$ equal to 1 for all foreground objects (see Figure 12.3).

## 12.4 APPLICATIONS

In this section, we provide three applications of MGDM in biomedical image analysis; these include cell segmentation in fluorescence images (Section 12.4.1), retinal tissue cell segmentation in optical coherence tomography (OCT) (Section 12.4.2), and cerebellum lobule parcellation from magnetic resonance images (Section 12.4.3) of the whole brain.

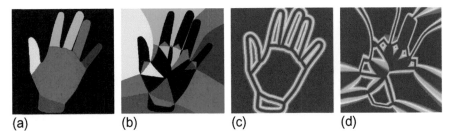

(a)          (b)          (c)          (d)

**FIGURE 12.3**

Shown are the label functions (a) $L_0(x)$ and (b) $L_1(x)$ for the converged result of our hand experiment. $L_0(x)$ corresponds to the final segmentation, $L_1(x)$ is the label of the first nearest neighbor of the final segmentation. Shown in (c) and (d) are the final versions of $\varphi_0(x)$ and $\varphi_1(x)$, respectively. See Figure 12.1 for the initial versions of each of these functions.

## 12.4.1 CELL SEGMENTATION

We study human umbilical vein endothelial cells (HUVECs) which have been stained with DAPI and VE-cadherin, so that the cell nuclei appear blue and cell junctions appear green in fluorescence images. The goal is to segment each individual cell within the available fluorescence images; example images are shown in Figure 12.4, with the individual color channels for the image more clearly showing the cell nuclei in blue and the cellular junctions in green. To achieve this, we will use MGDM to represent each cell as a different object. We identify the cell nuclei and use them as the initialization of our multiple objects. This is followed by an enhancement of the cell junction walls, from which we construct forces which we use to evolve our initialization at the cell nuclei outward to the enhanced cell junction walls. Thus, we determine the extent of each cell within the domain of the image. This result is based in part on work presented in Yang et al. (2013).

### 12.4.1.1 Nucleus detection

To initialize the segmentation, we identify the cell nuclei from the blue channel of the HUVEC (Figure 12.4(b)) RGB images. An initial estimation of the cell nuclei can be achieved by selecting all connected components within the blue channel image above a certain size threshold. To avoid situations where two cell nuclei are touching, due to clustering, and cannot be correctly distinguished, we use a contour analysis on the cell boundary. To test if the cell boundary under evaluation should be divided, a contour distance map is computed and a candidate cut is generated by detecting local minima of the contour distance map. The candidate cuts are evaluated by checking the similarity of the segmented contours to an ellipse. Cell nuclei are sequentially detected in this manner until all connected components within the image have been evaluated for separation.

### 12.4.1.2 Cell junction enhancement

Given that we now have an initialization of cell nucleus, we use the cell junction network (Figure 12.4(c)) to drive this initialization to the extents of the cells. The cell junction image suffers from several defects: bright intensities throughout the image not associated with cell boundaries; the cell junctions have an inconsistent appearance; and are indistinguishable in some areas. To overcome these

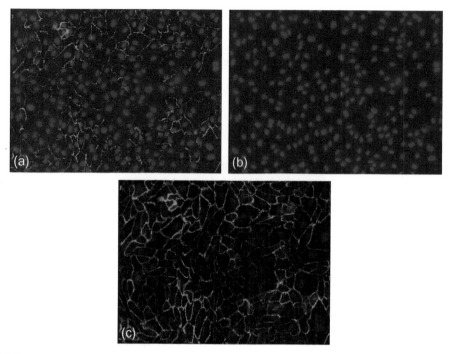

**FIGURE 12.4**

An example fluorescence image of human umbilical vein endothelial cells (HUVECs); shown are (a) the original image immunostained for DAPI (blue) and VE-cadherin (green), with (b) showing the blue channel containing cell nuclei, and (c) showing the green channel which contains the cell junction network.

issues, we enhance the curvilinear structure by applying an order-statistic filter and then computing the principle curvature of the image intensity surface.

Our order-statistic filter replaces the pixel value with in the $k$th largest value over a small neighborhood around the pixel. This eliminates the bright spots within the images without affecting the curvilinear structure. To enhance the cell junction network, the Hessian matrix is computed, which is a matrix of second-order derivatives of a smooth version of the image. The principle curvatures indicate the directions along which the local surface has the greatest and least curvature. We use the first principle curvature to identify the curvilinear structure in the image and suppress frequency intensity variations. The smooth intensity peaks at the cell nuclei are actively suppressed, and the cell junction becomes a nice curvilinear structure and weak cell junctions are enhanced. A more detailed explanation of the cell junction enhancement is available in Yang et al. (2013).

### 12.4.1.3 MGDM cell segmentation

Gradient vector flow (GVF) (Xu and Prince, 1998) is a widely used advection force to drive an active contour to an object boundary. It is computed as a diffusion of the gradient vectors of the edge map derived from the image. GVF has the advantages of large capture range and can force object contours into boundary concavities. A weighted sum of GVF and the gradient field, both computed on our cell junction enhanced image, provides the external force used to drive MGDM. We also include an internal force made up of a pressure-based speed—to ensure none of our initializations vanish—and a curvature smoothing-based speed. The internal pressure force is only applied to the cell objects and not the background object. If $c$ is the enhanced cell junction image, then the level set speed for the boundary $(i, j)$ comes from the GVF field obtained by finding the vector field $\mathbf{v}_{i,j}$ that minimizes

$$E = \int_{\mathbf{x}} \mu \|\mathbf{v}_{i,j}\|^2 + \|\nabla c\|^2 \|\mathbf{v}_{i,j} - \nabla c\|^2 \tag{12.9}$$

where $\mu$ is a weighting term. With a resulting vector field speed given by

$$f^b_{(i,j)}(\mathbf{x}) = -\mathbf{v}_{i,j}(\mathbf{x}) \cdot \nabla \hat{\phi}_i(\mathbf{x}). \tag{12.10}$$

The force description for boundary $(i, j)$ can then be summarized by

$$F_{(i,j)}(\mathbf{x}) = \alpha \kappa - \epsilon \left[ \mathbf{v}_{i,j}(\mathbf{x}) \cdot \nabla \phi_i(\mathbf{x}) \right] + \zeta |\nabla \phi_i(\mathbf{x})| \tag{12.11}$$

where $\kappa$ denotes the mean curvature of the boundary, with $\alpha$, $\epsilon$, and $\zeta$ being the weights of the competing forces. Results for the cell segmentations of a zoomed portion of Figure 12.4 are shown in Figure 12.5, along with the corresponding original image, and the blue and green image channels.

## 12.4.2 RETINAL LAYER SEGMENTATION

OCT has become a standard clinical tool for observing ophthalmological diseases. It allows microscopic imaging of the human retina, enabling the unprecedented study of ocular diseases. The OCT interferometric technique detects reflected or back-scattered light from tissue by passing a beam of light through the lens of the eye and observes the reflection interference with a reference beam originating from the same light source. This signal describes a reflectivity profile along the beam axis, representing a depth profile along the beam, known as an A-scan. Multiple adjacent A-scans are used to create two-dimensional (B-scans) and three-dimensional image volumes; an example image is shown in Figure 12.6 along with several labels. As depth images, the OCT data naturally provide thickness measurements of the cellular layers within the retina. To make this information readily available to clinicians we must segment the retinal layers. We present an automated algorithm for identifying (in order from the vitreous to the choroid) the RNFL, GCIP, INL, OPL, ONL, IS, OS, and RPE (refer to the figure for definitions). The GCIP is actually a merging of the GCL and IPL, as the boundary between the two is hard to discern. This application of MGDM originally appeared in Carass et al. (2014).

### 12.4.2.1 Retinal layer processing overview

First, as is common in the literature, we estimate the boundaries of the vitreous and choroid within the retina. We use these boundaries and a regression-based mapping to transform the retinal space between the vitreous and choroid to a computational domain in which layers are approximately flat, which we refer to as *flat space*. In the original space, we use a random forest (RF) layer boundary estimation (Lang et al., 2013) to compute probabilities for the boundaries of each layer and then also map these to flat space. We use the boundary probabilities to drive MGDM, providing a segmentation in flat space which is then mapped back to the original space.

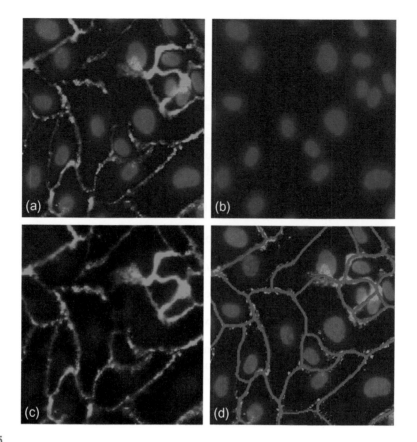

**FIGURE 12.5**

(a) Shows a zoomed region of the image in Figure 12.4(a), with the corresponding (b) cell nuclei (blue channel), (c) the cell junction network (green channel), and (d) the boundaries output by MGDM overlaid on the original image as orange contours.

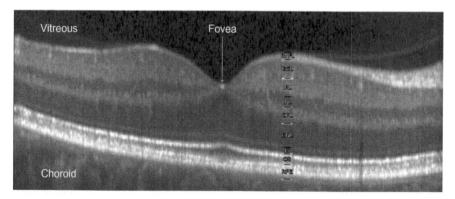

**FIGURE 12.6**

A typical B-scan with annotations indicating the locations of the vitreous, choroid, and fovea, the image has been rescaled by a factor of three along each A-scan for display purposes. The markings denote various layers: retinal nerve fiber (RNFL); ganglion cell (GCL); inner plexiform (IPL); inner nuclear (INL); outer plexiform (OPL); outer nuclear (ONL); inner segment (IS); outer segment (OS); and retinal pigment epithelium (RPE).

### 12.4.2.2 Retinal layer preprocessing

The data are preprocessed in a similar fashion to Lang et al. (2013), which we briefly describe here. The data undergo intensity normalization, which is necessary because of automatic intensity rescaling and automatic real-time averaging which occurs on the OCT scanner, both of which can cause differences in the dynamic ranges of B-scans intra-subject. The normalization uses a robust maximum $I_m$ and linearly rescales intensities from the range $[0, I_m]$ to the range $[0, 1]$, with values greater than $I_m$ being clamped at 1. The robust maximum, $I_m$, is found by first median filtering each individual A-scan within the same B-scan using a kernel size of 15 pixels. The robust maximum is set to a value that is 5% larger than the maximum intensity of the entire median-filtered image.

We next identify the macular retina by estimating the inner limiting membrane (ILM) and the Bruch's membrane (BrM) (providing initial estimates that are updated later). The ILM is the boundary that separates the RNFL from the vitreous and the BrM separates the RPE from the choroid. Vertical derivatives (i.e., along the A-scan) of a Gaussian smoothed image ($\sigma = 3$ pixels) are computed and the largest positive derivative is associated with the ILM while the largest negative derivative below the ILM is associated with the BrM. Using these two sets of gradient extrema, positive and negative, we associate each with a boundary, the ILM and BrM, respectively. These are of course inaccurate estimates prone to error; we provide a minor correction in the preprocessing phase by independently median filtering the two collections. Any point that is more than 15 voxels from the median filtered curve is removed as an outlier and an interpolated point replaces it in the collection. The ILM and BrM are further refined within the MGDM portion of the segmentation.

### 12.4.2.3 Retinal flat space

We use a computational domain, which we refer to as flat space, to help improve the speed and parameter choices for MGDM. We geometrically transform each subject image to a space in which all retina layers of the subject are approximately flat. This transform was learned based on manual segmentations of 37 subjects. We converted the positions of the boundaries between the manually delineated retinal layers into proportional distances between the BrM (which is given a distance of 0) and the ILM (which is given a distance of 1). An estimate of the foveal centers of all 37 subjects is derived based on the thinnest distance between the ILM and BrM within a small search window about the center of the macula, with the fovea then being used as the origin for each scan. For each aligned A-scan, we compute the interquartile mean of the proportional positions of each of the seven retinal layer boundaries between the ILM and BrM.

To transform a *new subjects* OCT scan to flat space, we use the estimated ILM and BrM boundaries and the foveal center, as outlined above. From the learned regression on the 37 subjects, we estimate the positions of seven internal boundaries for each A-scan. A-scans are then resampled interpolating new values at the estimated boundary positions and at ten equally spaced vertices between these boundary positions. An example of an OCT scan transformed from its native space into flat space can be seen in Figure 12.7; more details are available in Carass et al. (2014).

### 12.4.2.4 Retinal boundary probability map

Probabilities for the position of the nine boundaries within the retinal space are computed based on a trained RF (Breiman, 2001). The RF is trained on a set of image features and corresponding manual delineations derived from a training set of OCT images. The trained RF can be applied to the image

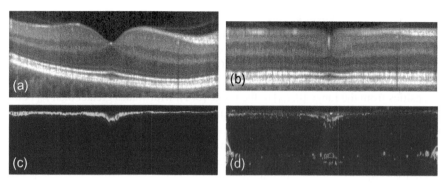

**FIGURE 12.7**

Shown is (a) the original image in native space. In flat space are (b) the original image, (c) a heat map of the probabilities for one of the boundaries (ILM), and (d) the *y*-component of the GVF field for that same boundary. The color scale in (c) represents 0 as blue and 1 as white. The images have been rescaled by a factor of three along each A-scan for display purposes.

features derived from a new OCT image and used to estimate the probabilities of the locations of nine retinal boundaries within the new OCT image. There are 27 features used in RF training and classifying; the details of the features used can be found in Lang et al. (2013).

Given a new image, the RF classifier is applied to all of the voxels, producing for each voxel the probability that the voxel belongs to each boundary. Since the RF classification is carried out on the original OCT image, the boundary probabilities are assigned to the voxels of the original OCT image. The RF training data and validation have all been previously completed in each subject's native space; for this reason we have kept the probability estimation from the RF in the subject's own native space. Examples showing these nine probability maps are shown in Lang et al. (2013). Here, we add an additional step to this process: transforming the estimated boundary probability maps to flat space. This allows us to carry out segmentation in flat space while utilizing features (and probabilities) developed on the original images. A probability map for the ILM boundary is shown in flat space in Figure 12.7(c).

### 12.4.2.5 MGDM segmentation in flat space

The MGDM framework allows control over the movement of the boundaries of our 10 retinal objects (8 retinal layers plus the choroid and scale complex, and the vitreous) in order to achieve the final segmentation in flat space. For this retinal layer segmentation example, we use two speed functions to drive MGDM (see Figure 12.8). The first speed function is the inner product of a GVF (Xu and Prince, 1998) field computed for each of the boundary probability maps with the gradient of the associated SDF. We compute nine GVF fields for each of the retinal boundaries. GVF ensures a large capture range, the entire computational domain, greatly simplifying the initialization. Our second speed function within MGDM is a curvature speed term (Caselles et al., 1993, 1997; Malladi et al., 1995). As we expect retinal layers to be predominately flat and the curvature naturally encourages flat surfaces, this is a perfect regularizer to use in flat space. We segment all the retinal layers simultaneously as well as those

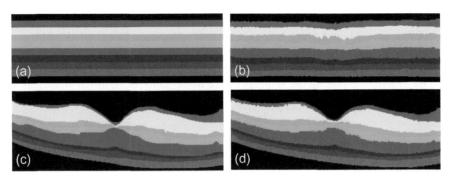

**FIGURE 12.8**

Shown in flat space are (a) the MGDM initialization, and (b) the MGDM result. A manual segmentation of the same subject is shown in (c) and the MGDM result mapped back to the native space of the subject is shown in (d). The original OCT data are shown in Figure 12.7(a). The images have been rescaled by a factor of three along each A-scan for display purposes.

portions of vitreous and choroid that are included in our computational domain. The equations for the boundaries $(i, j)$ are similar to Eq. (12.11) with the pressure force weight $\zeta$ set to zero.

## 12.4.3 CEREBELLUM PARCELLATION

The cerebellum of vertebrates is a very complex structure, which plays a critical role in eye movement, speech, balance, fine motor control, motor learning, and cognition (Ito, 1984; Schmahmann, 1991). These functionalities are compartmentalized within the cerebellum to particular regions. In particular, we note, disease-related cerebellum degeneration is region specific and can be related to patterns of symptoms (Ying et al., 2006). The cerebellum consists of a thin sheet of highly convoluted gray matter (GM) wrapped around a central mass of white matter (WM) known as the corpus medullare (CM). The branching WM jutting out from the CM create subdivisions, which are the 10 lobules and are referred to by the roman numerals I-X. With prominent fissures leading to natural groupings of the lobules into lobes: the anterior lobe (lobules I-V); the middle lobe (lobules VI-VII); and the caudal lobe (lobules VIII-X). Using MGDM we generate a 28-label parcellation of the cerebellum. This approach to using MGDM to segment the cerebellum originally appeared in Bogovic et al. (2013a). Images are preprocessed with topology-preserving anatomy driven segmentation (TOADS) Bazin and Pham (2008) to provide a cerebellum mask.

### 12.4.3.1 Cerebellum atlas creation

A cohort of 15 subjects (9 females) is used for atlas construction, with a subject MPRAGE acquired on a 3.0 T MR scanner (Intera, Phillips Medical Systems, The Netherlands). The parameters of the MPRAGE are: 132 slices, axial orientation, 1.1 mm slice thickness, 8° flip angle, TE = 3.9 ms, TR = 8.43 ms, field of view of $21.2 \times 21.2$ cm, matrix $256 \times 256$ (resolution: $0.828125 \times 0.828125 \times 1.1$ mm). A human expert rater manually labeled the cerebellar lobules from these images. A group-wise registration was performed using all subjects in the cohort using the symmetric image normalization (SyN) algorithm (Avants et al., 2008). The ground truth labels were transformed to the group mean, and a probability map for each object was computed. The atlas was corrected to ensure that all lobules were connected to the CM, and that lobules are connected to the adjacent lobules in the rostral and caudal directions. An additional output of the registration is a mean cerebellum image, which serves as a target for the segmentation of a new subject's cerebellum. The new unseen image is registered, using SyN, to the mean template placing the subjects image in the same space as our statistical atlas of the cerebellum objects.

### 12.4.3.2 Boundary classification within the cerebellum

As image intensity is not a sufficient discriminator for cerebellar lobules; we classify voxels into boundary or nonboundary for the edge between object $i$, $O_i$, and object $j$, $O_j$. We denote this boundary as $(i, j)$ with the understanding that $(i, j)$ is equivalent to $(j, i)$, and our classifier for the boundary is $c_{i,j}$. We thus estimate

$$p = p_\mathbf{x}(c_{i,j}|I) \tag{12.12}$$

which is the conditional probability that $\mathbf{x}$ is on the boundary $(i, j)$ given the image intensity $I$. Our level set speed for the $(i, j)$ boundary is given by the GVF field of the conditional probability map, obtained by finding the vector field $\mathbf{v}_{i,j}$ that minimizes

$$E = \int_\mathbf{x} \mu \|\mathbf{v}_{i,j}\|^2 + \|\nabla p\|^2 \|\mathbf{v}_{i,j} - \nabla p\|^2. \tag{12.13}$$

With a resulting vector field speed given by

$$f^b_{(i,j)}(\mathbf{x}) = -\mathbf{v}_{i,j}(\mathbf{x}) \cdot \nabla \hat{\phi}_i(\mathbf{x}) \tag{12.14}$$

which we note only affects the evolution of the distance function $\varphi_0$ where $x$'s nearest boundary is $(i, j)$. Rather than using image intensity in $p_\mathbf{x}(c_{i,j}|I)$, we use a set of features computed at $\mathbf{x}$ which are the eigenvalues of the image Hessian computed at various scales (see Bogovic et al. (2013a) for complete details). An RF (Breiman, 2001) is used to train the classifier from the feature vector. The conditional probabilities are computed in the natural way for each of the boundary pairs $(i, j)$ for voxels within a small distance of the boundary $(i, j)$. The conditional probabilities are corrected using a fast marching topology approach (Bazin et al., 2007), which removes extraneous regions from the result. Finally, a GVF field is computed from the topology corrected probability map.

### 12.4.3.3 MGDM boundary evolution on the cerebellum

The forces driving each boundary $(i, j)$ with the MGDM cerebellum segmentation are the probabilistic atlas, image intensity, tissue classification, and the GVF boundary classification field. Each boundary

$(i, j)$ combines these speeds in a unique way, the weights $(\alpha, \beta, \gamma, \delta, \epsilon)$ for which are learned from the training cohort of 15 subjects. The general form of these is

$$F_{(i,j)}(\mathbf{x}) = \alpha\kappa - \beta\left[(I(\mathbf{x}) - \mu_j)^2 - (I(\mathbf{x}) - \mu_i)^2\right] - \gamma\left[l_j(\mathbf{x}) - l_i(\mathbf{x})\right]$$
$$- \delta\left[r_{\text{CSF}}(\mathbf{x}) - r_{\text{GM}}(\mathbf{x})\right] - \epsilon\left[\mathbf{v}_{i,j}(\mathbf{x}) \cdot \nabla\phi_i(\mathbf{x})\right] \tag{12.15}$$

where $\kappa$ denotes the mean curvature of the boundary, $I(\mathbf{x})$ the intensity at $\mathbf{x}$, $\mu_i$ the mean intensity in object $i$, $l_i(\mathbf{x})$ the probability of finding object $i$ at $\mathbf{x}$ from the probabilistic atlas, and $r_{\text{tissue}}(\mathbf{x})$ the membership function of a tissue class derived from TOADS (Bazin and Pham, 2008). Example results are shown in Figure 12.9.

## 12.5 DISCUSSION AND CONCLUSION

The MGDM approach presents a compact representation while implicitly coupling objects as proposed by Brox and Weickert (2006). An advantage of MGDM over Brox and Weickert (2006), is the avoidance of a "gap-filling" term, as object boundaries are evolved implicitly coupling objects. The number of functions required by MGDM is $2N$ in an $N$-dimensional setting regardless of the number of objects, $M$, being tracked. This represents a significant saving in the case of Brox and Weickert which required $M$ functions, and potentially in comparison to the MP approach of Vese and Chan (2002) which uses $\log_2 M$ functions, assuming of course that $M \gg 2N$.

The approximation that occurs within MGDM's representation of the level sets up to the $N$th nearest neighbor in a $N$-dimensional space can give rise to some issues. The level sets $\hat{\phi}_i(x)$ correctly represent the true level set and SDFs at the boundary of objects with the proviso that the objects are more than a voxel thick and no more than $(N + 1)$ objects are meeting at a voxel in the $N$-dimensional case. The problem of $(N+1)$ objects meeting can be overcome by increasing the number of stored label functions and distance maps.

A key advantage of MGDM is its ability to conveniently reflect different speeds on different boundaries between objects. Because the first and second label functions identify the object and its nearest neighbor, these boundary-specific speeds are readily indexed and used when appropriate. The OCT segmentation method, for example, illustrated this procedure by using a separate GVF speed for each retinal boundary. The cerebellum parcellation approach used a separate membership function for each pair of lobule boundaries while using a single speed for the boundaries representing cerebellum and background. While not fully illustrated in the examples shown here, it should be clear that all of the creative techniques that have been used in deformable models in the past can also be incorporated in MGDM as needed—and these can be applied on an object-by-object or boundary-by-boundary basis.

We note that a fully functional and general MGDM software module, written in Java, is available at http:/www.nitrc.org/projects/mgdm. The computation of the speeds that are used in the examples described here can be carried out, in some cases, using standard image processing techniques found in MATLAB, MIPAV, and ITK, for example. The computation of GVF is carried out using a module from the JIST (Lucas et al., 2010) image processing toolkit found at http://www.nitrc.org/projects/jist.

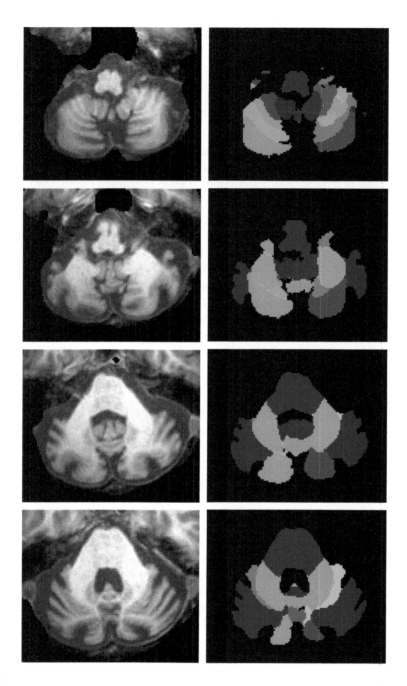

**FIGURE 12.9**

Axial slices showing an MR image of a cerebellum and the corresponding cerebellar segmentation achieved through MGDM.

## ACKNOWLEDGMENTS

We would like to thank Peter C. Searson, Director of the Johns Hopkins Institute for Nanobiotechnology, for providing the human umbilical vein endothelial cells in Section 12.4.1. This work was supported in part by the NIH/NINDS grant R01-NS056307 and the NIH/NEI grants R21-EY022150 and R01-EY024655.

## REFERENCES

Adalsteinsson, D., Sethian, J.A., 1995. A fast level set method for propagating interfaces. J. Comput. Phys. 118, 269–277.

Al-Shaikhli, S.D.S., Yang, M.Y., Rosenhahn, B., 2014. Multi-region labeling and segmentation using a graph topology prior and atlas information in brain images. Comput. Med. Imaging Graph. 38 (8), 725–734.

Angelini, E.D., Song, T., Mensh, B.D., Laine, A., 2004. Multi-phase three-dimensional level set segmentation of brain MRI. In: 7th International Conference on Medical Image Computing and Computer Assisted Intervention (MICCAI 2004), Lecture Notes in Computer Science, vol. 3216. Springer, Berlin, Heidelberg, pp. 318–326.

Avants, B.B., Epstein, C.L., Grossman, M., Gee, J.C., 2008. Symmetric diffeomorphic image registration with cross-correlation: evaluating automated labeling of elderly and neurodegenerative brain. Med. Image Anal. 12 (1), 26–41.

Bazin, P.L., Pham, D.L., 2008. Homeomorphic brain image segmentation with topological and statistical atlases. Med. Image Anal. 12 (5), 616–625.

Bazin, P.L., Ellingsen, L., Pham, D., 2007. Digital homeomorphisms in deformable registration. In: Proceedings of the 20th International Conference on Information Processing in Medical Imaging (IPMI 2007), Lecture Notes in Computer Science, vol. 4584. Springer, Berlin, Heidelberg, pp. 211–222.

Bazin, P.L., Ye, C., Bogovic, J.A., Shiee, N., Reich, D.S., Prince, J.L., Pham, D.L., 2011. Direct segmentation of the major white matter tracts in diffusion tensor images. NeuroImage 58 (2), 458–468.

Bertrand, G., 1994. Simple points, topological numbers and geodesic neighborhood in cubic grids. Pattern Recogn. Lett. 15 (10), 1003–1011.

Bogovic, J.A., Bazin, P.L., Ying, S.H., Prince, J.L., 2013a, Automated segmentation of the cerebellar lobules using boundary specific classification and evolution. In: Proceedings of the 23rd International Conference on Information Processing in Medical Imaging (IPMI 2013), pp. 62–73.

Bogovic, J.A., Prince, J.L., Bazin, P.L., 2013b. A multiple object geometric deformable model for image segmentation. Comp. Vis. Image Underst. 117 (2), 145–157.

Breiman, L., 2001. Random forests. Mach. Learn. 45 (1), 5–32.

Brox, T., Weickert, J., 2006. Level set segmentation with multiple regions. IEEE Trans. Imag. Proc. 15 (10), 3213–3218.

Carass, A., Lang, A., Hauser, M., Calabresi, P.A., Ying, H.S., Prince, J.L., 2014. Multiple-object geometric deformable model for segmentation of macular OCT. Biomed. Opt. Express 5 (4), 1062–1074.

Cardoso, M.J., Clarkson, M.J., Modat, M., Ourselin, S., 2011a, Longitudinal cortical thickness estimation using Khalimsky's cubic complex. In: Fichtinger, G., Martel, A., Peters, T. (Eds.), 14th International Conference on Medical Image Computing and Computer Assisted Intervention (MICCAI 2011), Lecture Notes in Computer Science, vol. 6892. Springer, Berlin, Heidelberg, pp. 467–475.

Cardoso, M.J., Clarkson, M.J., Modat, M., Ourselin, S., 2011b, On the extraction of topologically correct thickness measurements using Khalimsky's cubic complex. In: Székely, G., Hahn, H.K. (Eds.), Information Processing in Medical Imaging, Lecture Notes in Computer Science, vol. 6801. Springer, Berlin, Heidelberg, pp. 159–170.

Caselles, V., Catté, F., Coll, T., Dibos, F., 1993. A geometric model for active contours in image processing. Numer. Math. 66 (1), 1–31.

Caselles, V., Kimmel, R., Sapiro, G., Sbert, C., 1997. Minimal surfaces based object segmentation. IEEE Trans. Pattern Anal. Mach. Intell. 19, 394–398.

Chan, T.F., Vese, L.A., 2001. Active contours without edges. IEEE Trans. Imag. Proc. 10 (2), 266–277.

Chopp, D.L., 1993. Computing minimal surfaces via level set curvature flow. J. Comput. Phys. 106 (1), 77–91.

Cremers, D., Rousson, M., Deriche, R., 2007. A review of statistical approaches to level set segmentation: integrating color, texture, motion and shape. Int. J. Comp. Vis. 72 (2), 195–215.

Delingette, H., Montagnat, J., 2000. New algorithms for controlling active contour shape and topology. In: Proceedings of the European Conference on Computer Vision (ECCV) 2000, Lecture Notes in Computer Science, vol. 1843. Springer, Berlin, Heidelberg, pp. 381–395.

Fan, X., Bazin, P.L., Prince, J.L., 2008. A multi-compartment segmentation framework with homeomorphic level sets. In: 2008 IEEE Conference on Computer Vision and Pattern Recognition (CVPR), pp. 1–6.

Gao, M., Chen, C., Zhang, S., Qian, Z., Metaxes, D.N., Axel, L., 2013. Segmenting the papillary muscles and the trabeculae from high resolution cardiac CT through restoration of topological handles. In: Proceedings of the 23rd International Conference on Information Processing in Medical Imaging (IPMI 2013), Lecture Notes in Computer Science, vol. 7917. Springer, Berlin, Heidelberg, pp. 184–195.

Günther, C., Meinke, M., Schröder, W., 2014. A flexible level-set approach for tracking multiple interacting interfaces in embedded boundary methods. Comput. Fluids 102, 182–202.

Han, X., Xu, C., Prince, J.L., 2003. A topology preserving level set method for geometric deformable models. IEEE Trans. Pattern Anal. Mach. Intell. 25 (6), 755–768.

Ito, M., 1984. The Cerebellum and Neural Control. Raven, New York.

Kass, M., Witkin, A., Terzopoulos, D., 1988. Snakes: active contour models. Int. J. Comp. Vis. 1, 321–331.

Kohlberger, T., Sofka, M., Zhang, J., Birkbeck, N., Wetzl, J., Kaftan, J., Declerck, J., Zhou, S.K., 2011. Automatic multi-organ segmentation using learning-based segmentation and level set optimization. In: 14th International Conference on Medical Image Computing and Computer Assisted Intervention (MICCAI 2011), Lecture Notes in Computer Science, vol. 6893. Springer, Berlin, Heidelberg, pp. 338–345.

Lang, A., Carass, A., Hauser, M., Sotirchos, E.S., Calabresi, P.A., Ying, H.S., Prince, J.L., 2013. Retinal layer segmentation of macular OCT images using boundary classification. Biomed. Opt. Express 4 (7), 1133–1152.

Li, Y., Kim, J., 2011. Multiphase image segmentation using a phase-field model. Comput. Math. Appl. 62 (2), 737–745.

Lucas, B.C., Bogovic, J.A., Carass, A., Bazin, P.L., Prince, J.L., Pham, D.L., Landman, B.A., 2010. The Java Image Science Toolkit (JIST) for rapid prototyping and publishing of neuroimaging software. Neuroinformatics 8 (1), 5–17.

Malandain, G., Bertrand, G., Ayache, N., 1993. Topological segmentation of discrete surfaces. Int. J. Comp. Vis. 10 (2), 183–197.

Malladi, R., Sethian, J.A., Vemuri, B.C., 1995. Shape modeling with front propagation: a level set approach. IEEE Trans. Pattern Anal. Mach. Intell. 17, 158–175.

Mansouri, A.R., Mitiche, A., Vázquez, C., 2006. Multiregion competition: a level set extension of region competition to multiple region image partitioning. Comput. Vis. Image Underst. 101 (3), 137–150.

McInerney, T., Terzopoulos, D., 1995. Topologically adaptable snakes. In: Proceedings of the International Conference on Computer Vision (ICCV) 1995, pp. 840–845.

Osher, S.J., Fedkiw, R., 2003. Level Set Methods and Dynamic Implicit Surfaces. Springer, New York.

Osher, S., Sethian, J.A., 1988. Fronts propagating with curvature-dependent speed: algorithms based on Hamilton-Jacobi formulations. J. Comput. Phys. 79, 12–49.

Paragios, N., Deriche, R., 2000. Coupled geodesic active regions for image segmentation: a level set approach. In: Proceedings of the European Conference on Computer Vision (ECCV) 2000, Lecture Notes in Computer Science, vol. 1843. Springer, Berlin, Heidelberg, pp. 224–240.

Pohl, K.M., Kikinis, R., Wells, W.M., 2007. Active mean fields: solving the mean field approximation in the level set framework. In: Proceedings of the 20th International Conference on Information Processing in Medical Imaging (IPMI 2007), Lecture Notes in Computer Science, vol. 4584. Springer, Berlin, Heidelberg, pp. 26–37.

Rosenfeld, A., 1970. Connectivity in digital pictures. J. ACM 17 (1), 146–160.

Rosenfeld, A., Kong, T.Y., Nakamura, A., 1998. Topology-preserving deformations of two-valued digital pictures. Graph. Models Image Process. 60 (1), 24–34.

Samson, C., Blanc-Feraud, L., Aubert, G., Zerubia, J., 2000. A level set model for image classification. Int. J. Comp. Vis. 40 (3), 187–197.

Schmahmann, J.D., 1991. An emerging concept. The cerebellar contribution to higher function. Arch. Neurol. 48, 1178–1187.

Sethian, J.A., 1996. A fast marching level set method for monotonically advancing fronts. Proc. Natl. Acad. Sci. USA 93, 1591–1595.

Tai, X.C., Chan, T.F., 2004. A survey on multiple level set methods with applications for identifying piecewise constant functions. Int. J. Numer. Anal. Model 1 (1), 25–47.

Tsai, A., Wells, W., Tempany, C., Grimson, E., Willsky, A., 2004. Mutual information in coupled multi-shape model for medical image segmentation. Med. Image Anal. 8 (4), 429–445.

Vese, L.A., Chan, T.F., 2002. A multiphase level set framework for image segmentation using the Mumford and Shah model. Int. J. Comp. Vis. 50 (3), 271–293.

Xu, C., Prince, J.L., 1998. Snakes, shapes, and gradient vector flow. IEEE Trans. Imag. Proc. 7 (3), 359–369.

Yang, Z., Bogovic, J.A., Carass, A., Ye, M., Searson, P.C., Prince, J.L., 2013. Automatic cell segmentation in fluorescence images of confluent cell monolayers using multi-object geometric deformable model. Proc. SPIE Med. Imaging 8669, 866904–866908.

Ying, S.H., Choi, S.I., Perlman, S.L., Baloh, R.W., Zee, D.S., Toga, A.W., 2006. Pontine and cerebellar atrophy correlate with clinical disability in SCA2. Neurology 66 (3), 424–426.

Zimmer, C., Olivo-Marin, J.C., 2005. Coupled parametric active contours. IEEE Trans. Pattern Anal. Mach. Intell. 27 (11), 1838–1842.

# ROBUST AND SCALABLE SHAPE PRIOR MODELING VIA SPARSE REPRESENTATION AND DICTIONARY LEARNING

# 13

**S. Zhang[1], Y. Zhan[2] and D.N. Metaxas[3]**

*Department of Computer Science, University of North Carolina at Charlotte, Charlotte, NC, USA[1]*
*Computer-Aided Diagnosis and Therapy Research and Development, Siemens Healthcare, Malvern, PA, USA[2]*
*Department of Computer Science, Rutgers University, Piscataway, NJ, USA[3]*

## CHAPTER OUTLINE

## 13.1 INTRODUCTION

In various applications of medical image segmentation, the deformable model has achieved tremendous success, which should be attributed to its joint employment of shape and appearance characteristics. While appearance features provide low-level clues of organ boundaries, shape imposes high-level knowledge to infer and refine a deformable model. However, in some medical image analysis, appearance cues are relatively weaker or even misleading. In those cases, the best "guess" of the organ boundaries can only come from shape priors, which should be effectively modeled from training shapes. Effective shape modeling is confronting these challenges: (1) shape variation is complex and cannot always be modeled by a parametric probability distribution; (2) a shape instance derived from image appearance cues (input shape) may have gross errors; and (3) local details of the input shape are difficult to preserve if they are not statistically significant in the training data. The traditional deformable model, for example, active shape model (ASM) (Cootes et al., 1995), as well as its extensions (Nahed et al., 2006; Heimann and Meinzer, 2009), cannot tackle them in a uniform way. Section 13.2.1 reviews some related work regarding shape prior models.

Recently, a new nonparametric method has been proposed to tackle these three challenges in a unified framework (Zhang et al., 2012a,b). Instead of assuming any parametric model of shape statistics, this method incorporates shape priors on-the-fly through *Sparse Shape Composition*. More specifically, there are two sparsity observations: (1) Given a large shape repository of an organ, a shape instance of the same organ can be approximated by the composition of a sparse set of instances in the shape repository; and (2) gross errors from local appearance cues might exist but these errors are sparse in spatial space. This setting shows three major advantages: (1) general—there is no assumption of a parametric distribution model (e.g., a unimodal distribution assumption in ASM), which facilitates the modeling of complex shape statistics; (2) robust—since it explicitly models gross errors, erroneous information from appearance cues can be effectively detected and removed; and (3) comprehensive—it exploits information from all training shapes. Thus, it is able to recover detail information even if the detail is not statistically significant in training data. By incorporating these two sparsity priors into traditional deformable models, the model becomes robust to gross errors and can preserve shape details.

Although Sparse Shape Composition effectively models shape prior and tackles three challenges in a unified framework, it still has limitations in terms of run-time efficiency, particularly under two situations. First, there are a large number of training data available and all of them are straightforwardly included in the training repository. Second, in practice, many 3D deformable models have many thousands of points in order to give an accurate description of organ shapes. In both scenarios, Sparse Shape Composition needs to solve a large-scale sparse optimization problem, which has high computational complexity. Compared to traditional shape modeling methods, Sparse Shape Composition might exhibit relatively low speed.

In this chapter, we present a shape prior-based segmentation framework aiming to achieve robust segmentation in the presence of weak/misleading appearance cues. Particularly, we employ Sparse Shape Composition to model shape priors in our model. We also improve this shape prior in two aspects. First, a sparse dictionary learning technique is employed to compute a compact codebook (i.e., dictionary), which can well represent the original database. Instead of using all data for model selection, we perform Sparse Shape Composition on this learned dictionary, improving the computational efficiency. Second, instead of modeling global shape priors, we decompose the deformable surface to multiple parts and build shape models on them independently. The partition is accomplished by the affinity propagation method (Frey and Dueck, 2007) using both geometry and appearance features. Besides the run-time efficiency, this strategy also facilitates a better shape modeling, since the shape statistics of the local subsurface often has more compact distribution than the global surface. In the following sections, we introduce the related work, details of Sparse Shape Composition, and its evaluations.

## 13.2 RELATED WORK
### 13.2.1 SHAPE PRIOR MODELS

Following the seminal work, ASM, many other methods have been proposed to alleviate problems in three categories: (1) complex shape variations, (2) gross errors of input, and (3) loss of shape details.

To model complex shape variations, a classical solution is to use a mixture of Gaussians to represent 2D shape variation (Cootes and Taylor, 1997). Manifold learning techniques can also be used to learn a nonlinear shape prior to alleviate this problem (Etyngier et al., 2007; Zhang et al., 2011). However, it is still possible that shape variation is too complex to model with any parametric probability distribution. Thus, shape prior models are desirable to be able to model any specific shape. Pohl et al. (2004) have proposed to couple the PCA-based shape modeling with a maximum *a posteriori* estimation problem which will be solved through an expectation maximization framework. This allows the system to accommodate shapes that differ somewhat from those modeled by the principal component analysis (PCA). Thus, it is not restricted to the modes of variations presented in the shape model but models patient-specific abnormalities. Some methods were also proposed to decompose the shape space into multiple subspaces. Representative studies include patient-specific shape statistics (Yan and Kruecker, 2010) or a subject-specific dynamical model (Zhu et al., 2009, 2010) to constrain the deformable contours.

To handle outliers of input data, Duta and Sonka (1998) propose detecting and correcting outliers by using the variance information from the point distribution model (PDM). If a point is considered an outlier, it is corrected based on the position of its neighbors. Lekadir et al. (2007) employ a shape metric based on the ratio of landmark distances to detect outliers. Other methods try to decrease outliers' influence using the weighting of residuals. Rogers and Graham (2002) evaluate the use of M-estimators, image match and random sample consensus (RANSAC) (Fischler and Bolles, 1981) for this purpose. In a concluding evaluation, RANSAC was the most effective of these three methods. Nahed et al. (2006) proposed to use a robust point matching algorithm (Chui and Rangarajan, 2003) which rejects outliers and finds the best-fitting model. Missing landmarks/boundaries is also a special case of outliers. Yan et al. (2010) tried to use partial ASM to address this problem of the missing boundary in image segmentation.

To preserve local shape details, sparse PCA (Sjostrand and et.al., 2007) has been proposed to obtain sparser modes and produces near-orthogonal components. Thus each mode only affects locally clustered landmarks and captures more detail information, and is able to represent anatomically meaningful variables from a data set. Some other methods divide the shape model into several independently modeled parts, such as the hierarchical approach (Davatzikos et al., 2003). A hierarchical representation of a shape is introduced by using its wavelet transform, followed by a PCA on the wavelet coefficients. Thus, parts information can be represented by wavelet. Since the smaller parts exhibit less variation, they can be captured with fewer training samples than the variations for the full shape.

### 13.2.2 SPARSITY METHODS AND DICTIONARY LEARNING

Sparsity methods have been widely investigated recently. It shows that a sparse signal can be recovered from a small number of its linear measurements with high probability (Candes et al., 2006; Donoho, 2006). To solve these problems of sparsity priors, one can either use greedy methods such as basis pursuit (Chen et al., 2001), matching pursuit (MP) (Mallat and Zhang, 1993), orthogonal matching pursuit (OMP) (Chen et al., 1989; Pati et al., 1993), and stagewise OMP (stOMP) (Donoho et al., 2006), or use $\ell_1$-norm relaxation and convex optimization (Candes et al., 2006; Figueiredo et al., 2007; Kim et al., 2007).

The sparsity prior has been widely used in computer vision and multimedia communities, such as, but not limited to, robust face recognition (Wright et al., 2009; Wagner et al., 2012), image alignment (Peng et al., 2012), image restoration (Mairal et al., 2009), deconvolution of low-dose perfusion computed tomography (CT) (Fang et al., 2013, 2014, 2015), and atlas-based segmentation (Wu et al., 2014). Specifically, Wright et al. (2009) have contended both theoretically and experimentally to show that sparse representation is critical for high-performance classification of high-dimensional data such as face images. It also demonstrates that the choice of features is less important than the number of features used, and occlusion and corruption can be handled uniformly and robustly with this framework. We have investigated sparse representation for shapes instead of images or videos.

Furthermore, when training dataset has thousands or millions of samples, it may not be feasible to use all of them due to the computational consideration. It is necessary to learn a compact dictionary to represent the original dataset by minimizing the reconstruction errors. Finding the compact dictionary has been extensively studied in signal processing community. We briefly introduce some relevant techniques. Dictionary learning typically consists of the sparse coding and codebook update. Greedy algorithms such as MP (Mallat and Zhang, 1993) and OMP (Chen et al., 1989; Pati et al., 1993) can be employed for finding sparse coefficients (coding). Extensive study of these algorithms shows that if the sought solution is sparse enough, these greedy techniques can obtain the optimal solution (Tropp, 2004). To update the codebook, the method of optimal direction (Engan et al., 1999) and K-SVD (Aharon et al., 2006) are two effective approaches. Although both of them result in similar results, we use K-SVD to learn our dictionary because of its better convergence rate in empirical observations.

## 13.3 SEGMENTATION FRAMEWORK

To achieve generality, our segmentation framework is designed in the spirit of "data-driven." Figure 13.1 shows the workflow of our segmentation system, which consists of offline learning and runtime segmentation stages. In offline learning, images along with the manually labeled ground truths are employed to learn the appearance and shape characteristics of the organ under study.

Appearance characteristics are obtained through learning landmark detectors and a set of spatially adaptive boundary detectors. More specifically, landmark/boundary detection is formulated as a classification problem. A large number of features are extracted using overcomplete Haar wavelets. These features are selected and optimally aggregated using the AdaBoost classification algorithm. Shape characteristics are extracted from a set of manually delineated organ contours/surfaces. A shape repository is constructed using these organ contours/surfaces. It will be exploited to derive shape priors during runtime.

Runtime segmentation starts from the initialization of the model (represented by a 2D contour or a 3D triangular surface) based on automatically detected landmarks and shape priors. The contour/surface then deforms under the guidance of both image appearance cues and shape priors. Deformation is usually formulated as the optimization of an energy function consisting of external/image and internal/shape terms, and in practical implementations it is usually performed in two steps iteratively. First, the surface model deforms to local places where the learning-based boundary detectors generate

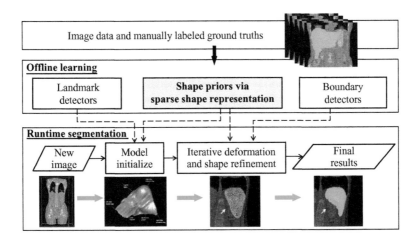

**FIGURE 13.1**

The workflow of our segmentation framework consisting of the offline learning and online testing modules. Gray blocks indicate the proposed methods and modules.

higher responses. Next, the locally deformed surface is refined by the shape priors derived from the shape repository. These two steps will be repeated until convergence.

Although learning-based landmark/boundary detectors can tackle reasonable appearance variations (Zhan et al., 2008, 2009), they might generate wrong responses in the presence of severe imaging artifacts/diseases, and hence mislead the deformable model. In this scenario, shape prior is the only information source to initialize/correct the deformable surface. (Note that shape priors are employed in both landmark-based model initialization and shape refinement in Figure 13.1.) Therefore, the effective modeling of shape priors becomes extremely critical to achieve a robust segmentation. This will be the major topic in the remainder of this chapter. (For more details of appearance modeling, please refer to Zhan et al. (2008, 2009).)

## 13.4 SPARSE SHAPE COMPOSITION
### 13.4.1 METHODOLOGY

Instead of assuming any parametric probabilistic distributions of the shape statistics, our shape prior model is based on two observations: (1) After being aligned to a common canonical space, any shape can be approximated by a sparse linear combination of other shape instances in the same shape category. Approximation residuals might come from inter-subject variations. (2) If the shape to be approximated is derived by appearance cues, residual errors might include gross errors from landmark/boundary detections. But such errors are sparse as well. Accordingly, we aim to incorporate shape priors *on-the-fly* through shape composition, that is, a shape derived by appearance cues is refined by the approximation of a set of annotated shape instances following the two sparsity observations. It is worth mentioning that sparsity has been adopted in segmentation algorithms in different manners, such as the sparse information models (Florin et al., 2007), which reconstruct a 3D surface from 2D sparse subcomponents, and multi-atlas based or patch-driven methods (Liao et al., 2013; Wu et al., 2014).

## Notations and basic framework

Explicit parametric shape representation is employed to model a shape instance, that is, a curve (2D) or a triangular mesh (3D) consisting of a set of vertices. To describe the $i$th shape in the training data, the coordinates of all its vertices are concatenated into a vector $d_i \in \mathbb{R}^n$, where $n$ is the product of the number of vertices in each shape by the dimension. Thus the training repository can be represented as a matrix $D = [d_1, d_2, \ldots, d_k] \in \mathbb{R}^{n \times k}$, where $k$ is the number of shapes. In our framework, all $d_i, i = 1, 2, 3, \ldots, k$ are prealigned using generalized Procrustes analysis (Goodall, 1991). $y \in \mathbb{R}^n$ is the vector of a newly input shape which needs to be constrained or refined. Our basic framework assumes that after proper alignment, any input shape $y$ can be approximately represented as a weighted linear combination of existing data $d_i, i = 1, 2, 3, \ldots, k$, and the parts which cannot be approximated are noises. We denote $x = [x_1, x_2, \ldots, x_k]^T \in \mathbb{R}^k$ as the coefficients or weights. Thus, the value of $x$ for the linear combination is found by minimizing the following loss function:

$$\underset{x,\beta}{\arg\min} \|T(y, \beta) - Dx\|_2^2 \tag{13.1}$$

where $T(y, \beta)$ is a global transformation operator with parameter $\beta$. It aligns the input shape $y$ to the mean shape of existing data $D$. $x$ and $\beta$ are computed by solving Eq. (13.1). Thus, the input shape $y$ is constrained or refined as $Dx$ and transformed back by the inverse of the transformation matrix using parameter $\beta$.

## Sparse linear combination

The limitations of Eq. (13.1) are twofold. First, the data matrix $D$ may be overcomplete ($k > n$) when the number of shapes is larger than the length of $d_i$. Thus, the system may not have a unique solution. More constraints of the coefficient $x$ are needed. Second, the input shape, including the noises, may be perfectly represented if any linear combination can be used. A more appropriate assumption is that the input shape can be approximately represented by a *sparse* linear combination of existing data. This way, the problem is reformulated as:

$$\underset{x,\beta}{\arg\min} \|T(y, \beta) - Dx\|_2^2 \tag{13.2}$$

$$\text{s.t. } \|x\|_0 \leq k_1$$

where $\| \cdot \|_0$ is the $\ell_0$-norm counting the nonzero entries of a vector, and $k_1$ is the predefined sparsity number. Such formulation ensures that the number of nonzero elements in $x$ is smaller than $k_1$. The value of $k_1$ depends on specific applications, and is discussed in the experiment section.

## Non-Gaussian errors

The formulation Eq. (13.2) works well for many scenarios. However, there is still one limitation in Eq. (13.2). Since the loss function is based on $\ell_2$-norm, it assumes that the error model follows a Gaussian distribution. Thus, it is sensitive to large noises or gross errors of the input shape, caused by image occlusion or points missing. Such a problem happens frequently in many applications. In these cases, some errors can be very large, but they are relatively sparse compared to the whole data.

To alleviate this problem, we explicitly model the error as a sparse vector $e \in \mathbb{R}^n$ by reformulating the problem as:

$$\underset{x,e,\beta}{\arg\min} \|T(y,\beta) - Dx - e\|_2^2 \tag{13.3}$$

$$\text{s.t. } \|x\|_0 \leq k_1, \quad \|e\|_0 \leq k_2$$

where $k_2$ is the sparsity number of $e$. When solving Eq. (13.3), $e$ captures sparse but large errors which are caused by occlusion or point missing. When there is no such error, the $\ell_2$-norm loss function can deal with it well and $e$ will be all zeros. Thus, $e$ is a good supplement which specifically handles non-Gaussian and sparse errors. Note that, unlike the formulation in the robust face recognition (Wright et al., 2009), we do not assume that the misalignment is small and thus explicitly model the transformation with parameter $\beta$ in Eq. (13.3).

## Convex relaxation

Equation (13.3) is an NP hard problem owing to the nonconvex $\ell_0$-norm. Thanks to the recent proof of the sparse representation theorem (Donoho, 2004), $\ell_1$-norm relaxation can be employed to make the problem convex while still preserving the sparsity property. The optimization problem is then transformed to Eq. (13.3)

$$\underset{\mathbf{x},\mathbf{e},\beta}{\arg\min} \|T(\mathbf{v},\beta) - D\mathbf{x} - \mathbf{e}\|_2^2 + \lambda_1 \|\mathbf{x}\|_1 + \lambda_2 \|\mathbf{e}\|_1 \tag{13.4}$$

However, to solve Eq. (13.4), we still need to simultaneously optimize multiple variables and deal with the nonlinearity if $T(\mathbf{v},\beta)$ is modeled as a rigid or similarity transformation. Our solution is to use an EM style algorithm (or alternating minimization) to solve Eq. (13.4). In the "E" steps, the transformation parameter $\beta$ is estimated using Procrustes analysis. In the "M" steps, with a fixed $\beta$, Eq. (13.4) becomes a typical linear inverse problem, which can be solved by a typical convex solver. (In this study, we use interior-point convex optimization solver (Nesterov and Nemirovsky, 1994; Grant and Boyd, 2008).) The "E" and "M" steps are iteratively performed until $\mathbf{x}$, $\mathbf{e}$, and $\beta$ converge.

## Computational complexity analysis

By optimizing Eq. (13.4), shape priors are in fact incorporated *on-the-fly* through shape composition. Compared to traditional statistical shape models, for example, the ASM, our method is able to remove gross errors from local appearance cues and preserve shape details even if they are not statistically significant. However, on the other hand, the optimization of Eq. (13.4) increases the computational cost, hence, limits the run-time efficiency of the Sparse Shape Composition. Recall the definition of the objective function; the computational cost is determined by the size of the shape repository matrix $D \in \mathbf{R}^{2N \times K}$. More specifically, the computational complexity of the interior-point convex optimization solver is $\mathcal{O}(N^2 K)$ per iteration (Nesterov and Nemirovsky, 1994), which means the computational cost will increase quickly with the increase of (1) $K$, number of the shape instances in the shape repository; and (2) $N$, number of vertices of a shape. Note that $\mathcal{O}(N^2 K)$ is the computational complexity for *one* iteration. Empirically, with larger $K$ and $N$, it usually takes more iterations to convergency, which further decreases the algorithm speed.

Accordingly, the run-time efficiency of our method will be particularly low in two scenarios. First, in some applications, for example, 2D lung localization in X-ray images, a large number of training shapes (a large $K$) are available due to the relatively lower cost of manual/semi-automatic annotations. Second, a large number of vertices (a large $N$), are necessary to describe shape details. This is usually the case in 3D segmentation problems. Therefore, we design two novel strategies to increase the run-time efficiency of our method, which will be detailed next.

## 13.4.2 EXPERIMENTS

We evaluate this Sparse Shape Composition by automatically locating the lung in X-ray images. Radiography (X-ray) is the most frequently used medical imaging modality due to its fast imaging speed and low cost. About one-third of radiograph examinations are chest radiographs. It is used to reveal various pathologies including abnormal cardiac sizes, pneumonia shadow, and mass lesions. The automation of pathology detection often requires robust and accurate lung segmentation. The major challenges of lung segmentation in radiography come from large variations of lung shapes, lung disease, and a pseudo-boundary close to the diaphragm. In a chest X-ray, the position, size, and shape of lungs often provide important clinical information. Therefore, in this experiment, we try to locate the left or right lung using landmark detection and shape inference. Out of 367 X-ray images (all images are from different patients), 200 are used as training data, and the other 167 are used for testing purposes. In this study, we select training samples to ensure a good coverage of different ages and genders (according to information from the DICOM header). The number of training samples is determined empirically. The ground truths are binary masks of manual segmentation results. A 2D contour is extracted from each mask. To obtain the landmarks for training purposes, we manually select six specific points (e.g., corner points) on the contour, and then evenly and automatically interpolate a fixed number of points between two neighboring landmarks along the contour (around 106 points in total after interpolation). Thus, a rough one-to-one correspondence is obtained for both landmarks and shapes. Since the detected landmarks may not be accurate or complete, shape prior is necessary to infer a shape from them. When applying this model, we constantly use the same parameter values for all X-ray images, that is, $\lambda_1 = 50$ and $\lambda_2 = 0.15$.

In this study, we compare the sparsity-based shape prior modeling with other state-of-the-art methods. For a fair comparison, we intentionally embed different shape models into the same organ localization framework. (It is not fair to compare completely different end-to-end systems, for example, our system versus ASM system, since the performance difference, if any, cannot be solely attributed to shape prior modeling.) More specifically, the same learning-based algorithm (Zhan et al., 2008) is used to detect landmarks for shape inference (organ localization). Furthermore, the shape is inferred from the detected landmarks directly without iteratively deforming and fitting to the image boundary. The reasons for this setting are twofold. First, enough instances of iterative deformations may eventually bring the shape to the image boundary accurately because of the deformation strategy. It is then difficult to evaluate the performance of shape prior models. Thus, we apply the inference method only once without the deformation. Second, such a one-step inference process is very fast and already good enough as the input for some clinical applications, such as a computer-aided diagnosis program. The compared methods are listed as the following: (1) PA: Procrustes analysis is used to find a similarity transformation to fit a mean shape to detected landmarks. (2) SMS: It is the Shape Model Search module in ASM, which employs the PCA method to refine the input shape. Note that we are not using the entire ASM framework including boundary detection and iterative fitting. We focus on the key module of ASM inducing shape prior information. (3) R-SMS: The shape model search step in the robust ASM (Rogers and Graham, 2002) method uses the RANSAC framework to remove the influence of erroneous detections. (4) SI-NN: It stands for shape inference using $k$ nearest neighbors. It uses nearest neighbors to find the closest prototypes in the expert's structure annotations. The distance metric we used is based on the $\ell_2$ distance between corresponding points. (5) TPS: Thin-plate-spline (Bookstein, 1989) is used to deform the mean shape to fit detected landmarks. TPS is a nonrigid and local deformation technology and has been used in robust point matching applications (TPS-RPM) (Chui and Rangarajan, 2003). (6) SSC2: It is the sparse learning shape method without modeling $e$.

Some representative and challenging cases are shown in Figures 13.2–13.4. In Figure 13.2, there are some misdetections which are considered as gross errors. The Procrustes analysis, SMS method, SI-NN algorithm, and TPS cannot handle such cases. R-SMS is not sensitive to outliers and performs

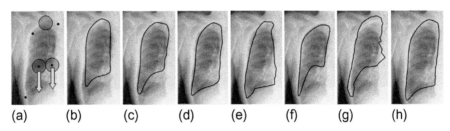

(a)       (b)       (c)       (d)       (e)       (f)       (g)       (h)

**FIGURE 13.2**

Comparisons of the right lung localization. (a) Detected landmarks are marked as black dots. There are two detection errors and one point missing (marked as circles, and the arrows point to the proper positions). (b) Similarity transformation from Procrustes analysis. (c) Shape Model Search module in ASM, using PCA-based method. (d) Shape Model Search in Robust ASM, using RANSAC to improve the robustness. (e) Shape inference method using nearest neighbors. (f) Thin-plate-spline. (g) Sparse representation without modeling $e$. (h) The proposed method.

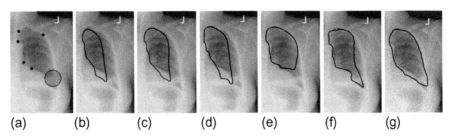

(a)       (b)       (c)       (d)       (e)       (f)       (g)

**FIGURE 13.3**

Comparisons of the left lung localization. There is one point missing (marked by a circle), and this lung has a very special shape, which is not captured by the mean shape or its variations. Compared methods are the same as Figure 13.2.

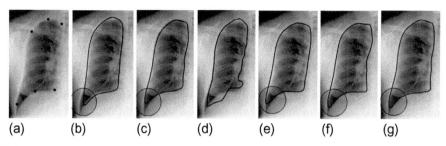

**FIGURE 13.4**

Comparisons of the right lung localization. All six detections are roughly accurate. Thus there is no gross error. The regions marked by circles show the difference of preserved details. Compared methods are the same as Figure 13.2.

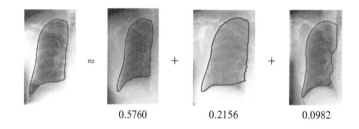

**FIGURE 13.5**

Three shape components with largest weights from our model. The left image means the result in Figure 13.4. The three components have weights 0.5760, 0.2156, and 0.09822, respectively.

better. SSC2 also fails to handle such non-Gaussian errors since $e$ is not modeled. SSC can successfully capture such misdetected points in $e$ and generate a reasonable shape.

In Figure 13.3, the underlying shape of the lung is special and different from most other lung shapes (see the mean shape in Figure 13.3(b)). Furthermore, there is a missing point. Neither a transformed mean shape or its variations can represent such a shape. TPS is very flexible and able to generate special shapes. However, it fails to handle the missing point. SSC roughly captures the correct shape and generates a better result than the others.

In Figure 13.4, all six detections are correct. However, the shape's details are not preserved using the mean shape or its variations, since the variations of the bottom left tip are not the major variation modes. Both SSC2 and SSC discover more detail information than other methods. Thus, a sparse linear combination is sufficient to recover such details, even if the gross error $e$ is not modeled. Figure 13.5 shows three SSC-selected shape components with largest weights which generate the result in Figure 13.4. Two of them do have certain levels of detail information in the bottom left region, although they are still different from the input shape. It demonstrates that our model can discover meaningful shape components, and the final shape composition result can well approximate the testing data. Please note that our model cannot "create" local shape details without the support of local appearance cues.

Instead, our method aims to "preserve" shape details derived by appearance cues given these details exist in our shape repository. In particular, our method is able to preserve local shape details even when they are not statistically significant in the shape space.

Cases in Figures 13.3 and 13.4 are actually similar to "abnormal testing cases" since they are different from most other shapes in the database. To handle such abnormal shapes, our database needs to contain shape instances with similar local abnormalities. However, our method is still more efficient in abnormal shape modeling than other statistical shape models, owing to two reasons. First, our method only requires that abnormal shape instances exist in the database. In contrast, other methods, for example, ASM, cannot model abnormal shapes unless these shape instances form principal components in the shape space, which often requires a large number of abnormal shape instances in the training set. Second, our method is able to approximate an abnormal shape instance that never appears in the dataset. For example, we can approximate a lung shape with abnormalities in both apex and lateral tip regions with the linear combination of a lung shape with apex abnormality and another lung shape with lateral tip abnormality.

To quantitatively compare different methods, we report the mean values and standard deviations of sensitivity and specificity between binary masks in Figure 13.6. Note that the specificity is always good in all methods. The reason is that the size of either left or right lung is relatively small compared to the whole chest X-ray image. Hence, most "true negatives" can be correctly found. Thus, we also report dice similarity coefficient (DSC), which is a good complement to the other two measurements. DSC is defined as: $2 \times \text{TP}/(2 \times \text{TP} + \text{FP} + \text{FN})$, where TP, FP, and FN stand for true positive, false positive, and false negative, respectively. Generally Procrustes analysis, TPS, and SMS achieve good performances, especially when landmarks are correctly detected. However, they are sensitive to non-Gaussian errors. R-SMS can handle this problem because of the RANSAC method, but sometimes it fails to deal with the multimodal distribution of shapes. SI-NN is a good nonparametric method. However, it may not be able to represent shapes which do not appear in the training data. The sparse linear combination by SSC2 can approximate such shapes and it generally performs better than the others. Without modeling error $e$, this method still fails to recover a correct shape. In our method, although the parameter for $e$ is set to a relatively small value, it still contributes to the performance of the model. It performs the best in terms of sensitivity and DSC, without sacrificing the specificity. The standard deviations in Figure 13.6 show that SSC also achieves the best stability among all compared methods.

The experiments are performed on a PC with 2.4 GHz Intel Quad CPU, 8 GB memory, with Python 2.5 and C++ implementations. The whole framework is fully automatic. As it benefits from the FISTA algorithm, our algorithm is very efficient. Given this scale of data, it takes around 0.5 s to infer a shape from the landmarks.

## 13.5 DICTIONARY LEARNING FOR COMPACT REPRESENTATIONS
### 13.5.1 METHODOLOGY

Assume $K$ is the number of training samples, the computational complexity of the sparse optimization for each iteration is comparable to the cost of solving a least-squares problem (i.e., $\mathcal{O}(N^2 K)$), when using interior-point methods (Nesterov and Nemirovsky, 1994). One factor that affects the run-time efficiency is $K$, the number of shape instances in matrix $D$. In many applications of medical image

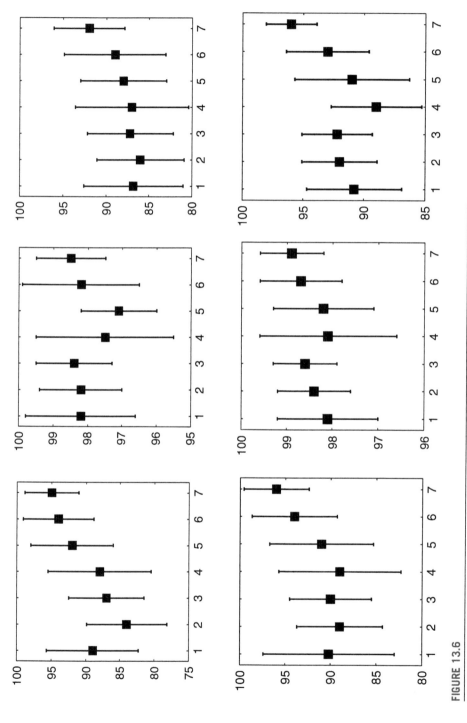

**FIGURE 13.6**

Mean values ($\mu$) and standard deviations ($\sigma$) of $P$, $Q$, and DSC from the left lung (first row) and right lung (second row) of all testing data. In each figure, the $y$-axis is the performance of $P$, $Q$, or DSC. The $x$-axis means seven methods (from left to right) in the same order as Figure 13.2. Squares denote $\mu$, segments denote $\sigma$.

analysis, the amount of training data is usually limited ($\sim$100) due to the high cost of manual annotations. In such cases, we can simply include all samples in the matrix $D$, since Eq. (13.4) can still be efficiently solved. However, in some other applications, for example, lung localization in chest X-ray images, one can potentially get thousands of training data samples using some semi-automatic tools. In this scenario, including all shape instances in $D$ will dramatically decrease the algorithm speed.

In fact, owing to the similar shape characteristics across the population, these thousands of shape instances usually contain lots of redundant information. Instead of including all of them, a standard approach is to construct a dictionary $D$ with a much more compact size. Note that compact size is not the only requirement of the shape dictionary. Since Sparse Shape Composition is our ultimate goal (see Eq. (13.4)), this shape dictionary should also have the sparse representation capability, that is, any shape in the population can be approximated by a sparse set of elements in the dictionary. To learn such a shape dictionary, we employ the K-SVD algorithm (Aharon et al., 2006).

Mathematically, K-SVD aims to optimize the following objective function with respect to the dictionary $D$ and coefficient $X$:

$$\underset{D,X}{\arg\min}\{\|Y - DX\|_2^2\} \tag{13.5}$$

$$\text{s.t. } \forall i, \quad \|x_i\|_0 \leq L \tag{13.6}$$

where matrix $Y \in \mathbf{R}^{n \times K}$ represents the entire dataset (all training shapes in our case), $D \in \mathbf{R}^{n \times k}(k \ll K)$ is the unknown dictionary that may be overcomplete, and matrix $X$ is the sparse coefficients. Denote $y_i$ as the $i$th column of $Y$, $x_i$ as the $i$th column of $X$, then $y_i$ and $x_i$ are the $i$th shape vector and coefficient vector, respectively, with dimensionality, $y_i \in \mathbf{R}^n$ and $x_i \in \mathbf{R}^k$. This equation contains two important properties of the learned dictionary $D$. First, $k \ll K$ indicates the dictionary has a much more compact size. Second, $\forall i, \|x_i\|_0 \leq L$ guarantees the sparse representation capability of the dictionary.

In the K-SVD algorithm, Eq. (13.6) is optimized by two alternative steps, sparse coding and codebook update. Sparse coding is a greedy method which can approximate an input data by finding a sparse set of elements from the codebook. Codebook update is to generate a better dictionary, given sparse coding results. These two steps are alternately performed until convergence.

## Sparse coding stage

The K-SVD algorithm starts from a random $D$ and $X$ and the sparse coding stage uses pursuit algorithms to find the sparse coefficient $x_i$ for each signal $y_i$. OMP (Chen et al., 1989; Pati et al., 1993) is employed in this stage. OMP is an iterative greedy algorithm that selects at each step the dictionary element that best correlates with the residual part of the signal. Then it produces a new approximation by projecting the signal onto those elements already selected (Tropp, 2004).

## Codebook update stage

In the codebook update stage K-SVD aims to update $D$ and $X$ iteratively. In each iteration, $D$ and $X$ are fixed except only one column $d_i$ and the coefficients corresponding to $d_i$ ($i$th row in $X$), denoted as $x_T^i$. Equation (13.5) can be rewritten as:

$$\left\| Y - \sum_{j=1}^{k} d_j x_T^j \right\|_F^2 = \left\| \left( Y - \sum_{j \neq i} d_j x_T^j \right) - d_i x_T^i \right\|_F^2 \tag{13.7}$$

$$= \left\| E_i - d_i x_T^i \right\|_F^2 \tag{13.8}$$

We need to minimize the difference between $E_i$ and $d_i x_T^i$ with fixed $E_i$, by finding alternative $d_i$ and $x_T^i$. Since SVD finds the closest rank-1 matrix that approximates $E_i$, it can be used to minimize Eq. (13.7). Assume $E_i = U \Sigma V^T$; $d_i$ is updated as the first column of $U$, which is the eigenvector corresponding to the largest eigenvalue. $x_T^i$ is updated as the first column of $V$ multiplied by $\Sigma(1, 1)$. The updated $x_T^i$ may not always guarantee sparsity. A simple but effective solution is to discard the zero entries corresponding to the old $x_T^i$.

The learned dictionary $D$ will be used in Eq. (13.4) at run-time. It is worth noting that an element in $D$ might not be the same as any shape instances in the training set. In other words, the learned shape dictionary consists of virtual shape instances which might not exist in the real world. However, these virtual shapes do have sparse composition capability with a much more compact size, which can highly improve the run-time efficiency of our Sparse Shape Composition.

## 13.5.2 EXPERIMENTS

We use the same application (i.e., lung localization) to evaluate this algorithm. We use a large dataset to test the performance of dictionary learning. Out of 1037 scans, 800 are used as training, and the other 237 are used as testing. Five dictionaries are learned from 800 training data samples, whose sizes are 256, 128, 64, 32, and 16, respectively. Then we compare the performance of Sparse Shape Composition using either these dictionaries or using all data. Figure 13.7 shows two visual comparisons of shape inference results. An interesting observation is that using a compact dictionary sometimes can achieve relatively better results than using all the data. The reason is that K-SVD not only well generalizes the training data, but also removes noise when computing the compact dictionary. When the dictionary size

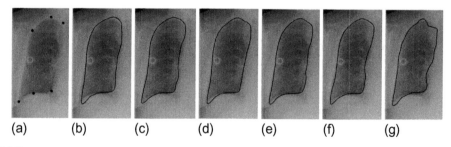

(a)   (b)   (c)   (d)   (e)   (f)   (g)

**FIGURE 13.7**

Comparison of Sparse Shape Composition using different dictionaries. Figure (a) is the detected landmarks. Figure (b) is the shape inference result of using all training data. Figures (c)–(g) are results of using different sizes (800, 256, 128, 64, 32, and 16) of dictionaries learned from K-SVD.

**Table 13.1 Comparison of Computational Efficiency of Using Sparse Shape Composition With All Data or With Compact Dictionaries**

| All Data | Dict (256) | Dict (128) | Dict (64) | Dict (32) | Dict (16) |
|---|---|---|---|---|---|
| 31.7 s | 6.8 s | 4.3 s | 2.1 s | 0.5 s | 0.1 s |

is smaller than a threshold (e.g., 16); however, its performance drops quickly. Thus, a certain number of elements is still necessary for a meaningful dictionary.

Figure 13.8 shows quantitative comparisons of our method. We choose Procrustes analysis as the baseline method, which fits the mean shape to detected landmarks using the similarity transformation found by minimizing least square errors. We also compare the performance of Sparse Shape Composition using all training data, or using compact dictionaries with sizes 256, 128, 64, 32, and 16. The results are consistent with the visual comparison in Figure 13.7, that is, compact dictionaries can achieve comparable or even better performance as using all data, when the dictionary size is larger than a threshold. When only few instances are used as the dictionary, it actually degenerates to the simplest case, that is, only using mean shape as the Procrustes analysis. Thus a dictionary with size 16 achieves similar performance to the Procrustes method.

Another significant benefit of using a compact dictionary is the computational efficiency. Table 13.1 shows the computational time of compared methods. The experiments of computational time are performed on a PC with 2.4 GHz Intel Quad CPU, 8 GB memory, with Python 2.5 and C++ implementations. Grant and Boyd (2008) is employed to solve convex functions. Using a compact dictionary significantly decreases the computational time of shape inference using Sparse Shape Composition.

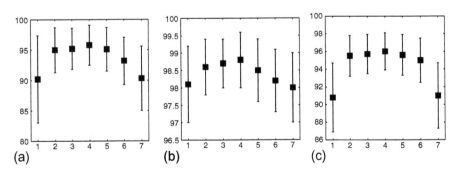

**FIGURE 13.8**

Quantitative comparison. From left to right: baseline method using Procrustes analysis (mean shape only), Sparse Shape Composition using all data, or using dictionaries with size 256, 128, 64, 32, and 16, respectively. (a) Sensitivity; (b) specificity; and (c) DSC.

## 13.6 MESH PARTITION FOR LOCAL SPARSE SHAPE COMPOSITION
### 13.6.1 METHODOLOGY

Recall the computational complexity of the solver $\mathcal{O}(N^2K)$. In practice, many 3D deformable models include many thousands of vertices (i.e., large $N$) to give an accurate description of organ shapes. The optimization of Eq. (13.4) thus has high computational complexity. If the whole surface can be divided into $p$ partitions with about $\frac{N}{p}$ vertices in each partition, the computational complexity is decreased to only $\mathcal{O}((\frac{N}{p})^2K)$ for each partition, which is $\frac{1}{p^2}$ of the original one.

Fortunately, our Sparse Shape Composition method inherently supports the partition of the surface by estimating a sparse linear combination from an incomplete input. Assume $\mathbf{v}_{\text{sub}} = \mathbf{S}\mathbf{v}$ is a subset of all vertices in shape $\mathbf{v}$, where $\mathbf{S}$ is a binary diagonal matrix, which indicates if the $i$th vertex is in the subset ($\mathbf{S}_{ii} = 1$). Equation (13.3) can then be naturally extended as:

$$\underset{\mathbf{x},\mathbf{e},\beta}{\arg\min} \|T(\mathbf{v}_{\text{sub}}, \beta) - \mathbf{S}\mathbf{D}\mathbf{x} - \mathbf{S}\mathbf{e}\|_2^2, \quad \text{s.t. } \|\mathbf{x}\|_0 < k_1, \quad \|\mathbf{e}\|_0 < k_2 \qquad (13.9)$$

Equation (13.9) can be solved using the same $\ell_1$-norm relaxation and EM optimization. The only difference is that the optimized $\mathbf{x}$ will be finally applied on the full space of $D$, such that the entire input shape is refined.

The remaining problem is how to divide the surface efficiently. In this study, affinity propagation clustering (Frey and Dueck, 2007) is employed to divide the model shape into multiple partitions. Since one-to-one correspondences are already constructed among all shapes, affinity propagation only needs to perform once for the model shape. The similarity used in the affinity propagation is defined as the combination of the image similarity and geodesic distances between vertices (Zhan et al., 2009):

$$s(v_i, v_j) = 1 - \frac{1}{K} \sum_{k=1}^{K} \left[ \alpha G\left(v_i^k, v_j^k\right) + (1 - \alpha)C\left(F\left(v_i^k\right), F\left(v_j^k\right)\right) \right] \qquad (13.10)$$

where $K$ is the number of training subjects, and $v_i^k$ denotes the $i$th vertex of the $k$th subject. $G\left(v_i^k, v_j^k\right)$ denotes the geodesic distance between $v_i^k$ and $v_j^k$. $C\left(F\left(v_i^k\right), F\left(v_j^k\right)\right)$ denotes the Euclidean distance between the image feature vector calculated at $v_i^k$ and $v_j^k$. It is worth noting that there are two additional benefits of partitioning the entire surface in our deformable segmentation framework. First, since organ boundaries may have a heterogeneous appearance, as shown in Figure 13.9, the partitioning of the surface also facilitates the training of local boundary detectors, which only deal with training samples with much fewer feature variations. Second, since local shape statistics often lie in a more compact space than global ones, shape priors built on subsurface are expected to improve the performance of shape modeling as well.

In our implementation, each divided partition is further "dilated" for several levels to produce overlaps with neighboring partitions. Finally, partitions are converted to a set of indication matrices $\mathbf{S}_1, \mathbf{S}_2, \ldots, \mathbf{S}_p$ used in Eq. (13.9). The optimization problem defined on the entire surface is thus decomposed to a set of subproblems. Each partition is refined independently but the refined partitions are averaged in these overlapping regions to guarantee the smoothness of the entire surface. The merit of Eq. (13.9) is actually beyond the support of surface partition. One extreme situation of Eq. (13.9) is that $\mathbf{S}$ becomes very sparse and only includes a few vertices (usually with the most distinctive

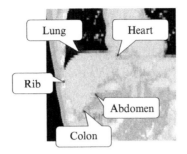

**FIGURE 13.9**

An example of liver boundaries from CT images. It includes boundaries between liver and rib, lung, heart, abdomen, and colon that show heterogeneous appearance in local shapes.

appearance/geometry characteristics). In this situation, Eq. (13.9) indeed becomes the shape inference method, which is the first step of our runtime segmentation system. Again, by incorporating shape priors with the assumption of "sparse gross errors," our initialization method becomes robust to erroneous landmark detections due to severe diseases/imaging artifacts. In addition, Eq. (13.9) also supports a multi-resolution/hierarchical scheme, which has been widely employed to improve the efficiency and robustness of deformable segmentation (Langs et al., 2010). In our implementation, only a small set of sparsely distributed vertices are used as driving vertices to estimate a rough segmentation of the initial stages. As the iterations increase, more and more vertices join the driving set to gradually reach accurate segmentation.

## 13.6.2 EXPERIMENTS

We evaluate this mesh partition strategy using 3D low-dose CT data from PET-CT. To decrease radiations to patients, CT images in PET-CT scans usually have low dose and large slice thickness, which result in low contrast and fuzzy boundaries between organs. Hence, organ segmentation in whole body PET-CT becomes more challenging than traditional CT (Ling et al., 2008). In our experiment, the 3D ground truth of low-dose CT is manually segmented by multiple clinical experts. Out of 67 CT scans, 40 are used to train the landmark detector and also used to construct the shape repository $D$. The other 27 are left for testing. To obtain the one-to-one correspondence for vertices among all shapes, we choose one shape as a reference and register it to all the others using an improved adaptive-focus deformable model (Shen and Davatzikos, 2000; Zhang et al., 2013). Each shape has 1096 vertices and 2088 triangles. Twenty vertices are selected as landmarks for model initialization. They are critical anatomical landmarks or have discriminative appearance features. Thus, they are relatively easy to detect using our landmark detectors.

Since Sparse Shape Composition is not efficient in dealing with a large number of vertices, we can evenly select a subset of vertices for Sparse Shape Composition for acceleration purpose, that is, the multi-resolution scheme. However, this approach ignores much information since only part of the shape is considered. Instead of using a subset, we use mesh partitioning to generate local shape partitions,

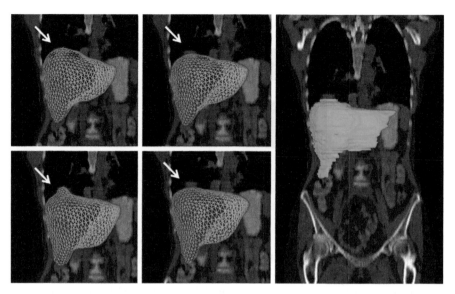

**FIGURE 13.10**

Initialization results (first row) and deformation results (second row) from the corresponding initialization. Compared methods are Procrustes analysis (first column) and our method (second column). The rightmost figure is the ground truth. Procrustes analysis incorrectly includes part of the lung because of the artifacts inducing by breath (see the marked arrow).

and then apply Sparse Shape Composition on these local shapes. This approach not only improves the computational efficiency, but also well models local shape statistics.

We compared our method with: (1) Procrustes analysis (Goodall, 1991), which finds a similarity transformation to fit a mean shape to detected landmarks; (2) shape prior used in ASM (Cootes et al., 1995), which employs the PCA method to learn shape statistics and refine the input shape. For a fair comparison, same landmark/boundary detectors and deformation strategy are used in all methods. They only differ in model initialization and model refinement, which involve shape priors.

Figures 13.10 and 13.11 show some visual results of two different cases in 3D. Figure 13.10 compares the landmark detection-based initialization. Since the image contrast of low-dose CT is very low and there are breathing artifacts in the lung region, the landmark detector may easily fail to locate correct positions. Our method is less sensitive to such errors. Its initialization result is already very close to the object boundary. We also compare the deformation results starting from different initializations. A better initialized model also benefits the deformation performance. Figure 13.11 compares the refinement results after deformation, starting from the same initialized model. Note that the refined shape may not be exactly on the image boundary since this part is just a regularization step without considering any image information. The refined shape of PCA shape prior follows the mean shape and the its variations, but it incorrectly includes a large part of the kidney. The shape from our method is more specific to this image and is more accurate.

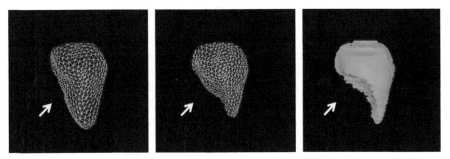

**FIGURE 13.11**

The refinement results. From left to right: PCA results, our method, the ground truth. PCA method incorrectly includes a large part of the kidney.

**Table 13.2 Quantitative Comparisons of the Mean Values and Standard Deviations of the Distances (Voxel) Between Surfaces**

| Method | Figure 13.10(Init) | Figure 13.11 | All Data |
|---|---|---|---|
| Procrustes analysis | 2.26 ± 1.72 | 3.67 ± 3.34 | 3.96 ± 3.21 |
| PCA prior | 2.26 ± 1.72 | 1.81 ± 2.10 | 2.16 ± 1.68 |
| Sparse, whole shape | **1.31 ± 0.95** | 1.37 ± 0.96 | 1.25 ± 0.92 |
| Sparse, mesh partition | **1.31 ± 0.95** | **1.10 ± 0.87** | **1.13 ± 0.83** |

Note: *The first column compares initialization results. Values in bold indicate the best performance in that column.*

To quantitatively evaluate the 3D segmentation accuracy, we report the mean value and standard deviation of the distances between shape surfaces in Table 13.2. The surface mesh is divided into 30 regions. Our framework achieves the best performance. The standard deviations in Table 13.2 show that our method also achieves the best stability among all methods. Sparse prior with mesh partitioning is slightly better than the same prior with whole shape. Note that the initialization step is the same for both settings, that is, using multi-resolution scheme. To further evaluate the benefit of mesh partitioning, we also compare the running time. The shape refinement step takes several minutes when applied to the whole surface directly. Using mesh partitioning, it significantly improves the efficiency and only takes 2-3 s. The whole system takes around 20 s (a Python implementation on a PC with 2.4 GHz Intel Quad CPU) to segment liver in a $512 \times 512 \times 300$ CT volume, including data loading, initialization, deformation, and shape refinement. Note that the shape refinement module not only improves the robustness of the deformable model, but also decreases the iteration times of deformation since it helps avoid local minima of image information.

## 13.7 DISCUSSION

In this chapter, we introduce a deformable model with novel shape prior modeling.[a] Different from traditional shape models, which usually model shape statistics in a parametric way, we incorporate shape priors on-the-fly through Sparse Shape Composition. It is able to handle gross errors, model complex shape variations, and preserve shape details in a unified framework. Hence, our deformable model becomes robust to weak or misleading appearance cues. We further designed two strategies to improve the computational efficiency of the Sparse Shape Composition. First, given a large number of training shape instances, K-SVD is used to learn a much more compact but still informative shape dictionary. Second, if shape instances have a large number of vertices, affinity propagation method is used to partition the surface into small subregions, on which the Sparse Shape Composition is performed locally. Both strategies dramatically decrease the scale of the sparse optimization problem and thus speed up the algorithm. The experiments show the following facts: (1) This implicitly incorporated shape constraint benefits the interpretation of images. Such shape-based information improves the robustness and accuracy of low-level algorithms. Therefore, Sparse Shape Composition is able to effectively model shape priors and achieves better performance than the smoothness shape prior, Procrustes analysis, and PCA-based shape prior. (2) The sparse linear combination of shape repository is able to well approximate an input shape if the input does not have gross errors. The $\ell_1$-norm constraint of $e$ handles the non-Gaussian residuals caused by occlusion, miss detection, or point missing. (3) Our method is able to use a subset of vertices on the contour and surface as the input. Sparse learning is applied on this subset and computes a group of coefficients. Such coefficients are then used to combine the whole contour or surfaces, which generate reasonable results. This property can seamlessly incorporate with a multi-resolution scheme. Our method can naturally extend to multi-resolution without significant overhead of implementation or computational complexity. (4) When the number of training data are huge (e.g., thousands), it is infeasible to simply stack all shapes into the data matrix since Sparse Shape Composition could not handle them efficiently. In this case, a dictionary learning technique is employed to learn a compact dictionary, whose size is much smaller than the whole dataset. This compact dictionary highly improves the computational efficiency without sacrificing segmentation accuracy. (5) When the shape data contain thousands of vertices, solving the convex problem becomes time consuming. A multi-resolution scheme can decrease the computational time. However, it also ignores some information since it only uses a subset of the whole shape. We use a mesh partitioning method to model local shape priors instead of the whole shape. In this way, we can decrease the running time and effectively model the local priors as well. (6) This shape prior method is applied to handle problems related to diverse medical imaging modalities, for example, X-ray or CT. It shows good generality to different imaging modalities and shape dimensions. We expect to apply this method to more applications in the future.

## NOTE

a. Source code is available at http://research.rutgers.edu/~shaoting/robust_segmentation.html.

# REFERENCES

Aharon, M., Elad, M., Bruckstein, A., 2006. K-SVD: an algorithm for designing overcomplete dictionaries for sparse representation. In: IEEE Transaction Signal Processing, pp. 4311–4322.

Bookstein, F., 1989. Principal warps: thin-plate splines and the decomposition of deformations. IEEE Trans. Pattern Anal. Mach. Intell. 11 (6), 567–585.

Candes, E., Romberg, J., Tao, T., 2006. Robust uncertainty principles: exact signal reconstruction from highly incomplete frequency information. IEEE Trans. Inf. Theory 52 (2), 489–509.

Chen, S., Billings, S.A., Luo, W., 1989. Orthogonal least squares methods and their application to non-linear system identification. Int. J. Control. 50, 1873–1896.

Chen, S.S., Donoho, D.L., Saunders, M.A., 2001. Atomic decomposition by basis pursuit. SIAM J. Sci. Comput. 43 (1), 129–159.

Chui, H., Rangarajan, A., 2003. A new point matching algorithm for non-rigid registration. Comput. Vis. Image Underst. 89 (2–3), 114–141.

Cootes, T.F., Taylor, C.J., 1997. A mixture model for representing shape variation. In: Image and Vision Computing, pp. 110–119.

Cootes, T., Taylor, C., Cooper, D., Graham, J., 1995. Active shape model—their training and application. Comput. Vis. Image Underst. 61, 38–59.

Davatzikos, C., Tao, X., Shen, D., 2003. Hierarchical active shape models, using the wavelet transform. IEEE Trans. Med. Imaging 22 (3), 414–423.

Donoho, D.L., 2004. For most large underdetermined systems of equations, the minimal L1-norm near-solution approximates the sparsest near-solution. Commun. Pure Appl. Math. 59 (7), 907–934.

Donoho, D.L., 2006. Compressed sensing. IEEE Trans. Inf. Theory 52 (4), 1289–1306.

Donoho, D.L., Tsaig, Y., Drori, I., Luc Starck, J., 2006. Sparse solution of underdetermined linear equations by stagewise orthogonal matching pursuit. IEEE Trans. Inf. Theory 58 (2), 1094–1121.

Duta, N., Sonka, M., 1998. Segmentation and interpretation of MR brain images. an improved active shape model. IEEE Trans. Med. Imaging 17 (6), 1049–1062.

Engan, K., Aase, S., Hakon Husoy, J., 1999. Method of optimal directions for frame design. In: IEEE International Conference on Acoustics, Speech, and Signal Processing, vol. 5, pp. 2443–2446.

Etyngier, P., Segonne, F., Keriven, R., 2007. Shape priors using manifold learning techniques. In: International Conference on Computer Vision, pp. 1–8.

Fang, R., Chen, T., Sanelli, P.C., 2013. Towards robust deconvolution of low-dose perfusion CT: sparse perfusion deconvolution using online dictionary learning. Med. Image Anal. 17 (4), 417–428.

Fang, R., Karlsson, K., Chen, T., Sanelli, P.C., 2014. Improving low-dose blood-brain barrier permeability quantification using sparse high-dose induced prior for Patlak model. Med. Image Anal. 18 (6), 866–880.

Fang, R., Zhang, S., Chen, T., Sanelli, P., 2015. Robust low-dose CT perfusion deconvolution via tensor total-variation regularization. IEEE Trans. Med. Imaging. 34 (7), 1533–1548.

Figueiredo, M., Nowak, R., Wright, S., 2007. Gradient projection for sparse reconstruction: application to compressed sensing and other inverse problems. IEEE J. Sel. Top. Sign. Process. 1 (4), 586–597. ISSN 1932-4553.

Fischler, M.A., Bolles, R.C., 1981. Random sample consensus: a paradigm for model fitting with applications to image analysis and automated cartography. Commun. ACM 24 (6), 381–395.

Florin, C., Paragios, N., Funka-Lea, G., Williams, J., 2007. Liver segmentation using sparse 3D prior models with optimal data support. In: Information Processing in Medical Imaging, pp. 38–49.

Frey, B., Dueck, D., 2007. Clustering by passing messages between data points. Science 315 (5814), 972.

Goodall, C., 1991. Procrustes methods in the statistical analysis of shape. J. R. Stat. Soc. 53, 285–339.

Grant, M., Boyd, S., 2008. CVX: MATLAB software for disciplined convex programming.

Heimann, T., Meinzer, H.P., 2009. Statistical shape models for 3D medical image segmentation: a review. Med. Image Anal. 13 (4), 543–563.

Kim, S., Koh, K., Lustig, M., Boyd, S., Gorinevsky, D., 2007. An interior-point method for large-scale L1-regularized least squares. IEEE J. Sel. Top. Sign. Proces. 1 (4), 606–617. ISSN 1932-4553.

Langs, G., Paragios, N., Essafi, S., 2010. Hierarchical 3D diffusion wavelet shape priors. In: International Conference on Computer Vision, pp. 1717–1724.

Lekadir, K., Merrifield, R., Yang, G.Z., 2007. Outlier detection and handling for robust 3D active shape models search. IEEE Trans. Med. Imaging 26, 212–222.

Liao, S., Gao, Y., Lian, J., Shen, D., 2013. Sparse patch-based label propagation for accurate prostate localization in CT images. IEEE Trans. Med. Imaging 32 (2), 419–434.

Ling, H., Zhou, S., Zheng, Y., Georgescu, B., Suehling, M., Comaniciu, D., 2008. Hierarchical, learning-based automatic liver segmentation. In: IEEE Conference on Computer Vision and Pattern Recognition, pp. 1–8.

Mairal, J., Bach, F., Ponce, J., Sapiro, G., Zisserman, A., 2009. Non-local sparse models for image restoration. In: International Conference on Computer Vision, pp. 2272–2279.

Mallat, S., Zhang, Z., 1993. Matching pursuits with time-frequency dictionaries. In: IEEE Transaction Signal Processing, pp. 3397–3415.

Nahed, J.A., Jolly, M.P., Yang, G.Z., 2006. Robust active shape models: a robust, generic and simple automatic segmentation tool. In: International Conference on Medical Image Computing and Computer Assisted Intervention.

Nesterov, Y., Nemirovsky, A., 1994. Interior point polynomial methods in convex programming. Stud. Appl. Math. 13, 1993.

Pati, Y.C., Rezaiifar, R., Krishnaprasad, P., 1993. Orthogonal matching pursuit: recursive function approximation with applications to wavelet decomposition. In: Twenty-Seventh Asilomar Conference on Signals, Systems and Computers, pp. 40–44.

Peng, Y., Ganesh, A., Wright, J., Xu, W., Ma, Y., 2012. RASL: robust alignment by sparse and low-rank decomposition for linearly correlated images. IEEE Trans. Pattern Anal. Mach. Intell. 34 (11), 2233–2246.

Pohl, K., Warfield, S., Kikinis, R., Grimson, W., Wells, W., 2004. Coupling statistical segmentation and PCA shape modeling. In: Medical Image Computing and Computer-Assisted Intervention. Springer, pp. 151–159.

Rogers, M., Graham, J., 2002. Robust active shape model search. In: European Conference on Computer Vision, pp. 517–530.

Shen, D., Davatzikos, C., 2000. An adaptive-focus deformable model using statistical and geometric information. IEEE Trans. Pattern Anal. Mach. Intell. 22 (8), 906–913.

Sjostrand, K., et.al., 2007. Sparse decomposition and modeling of anatomical shape variation. IEEE Trans. Med. Imaging 26 (12), 1625–1635.

Tropp, J.A., 2004. Greed is good: algorithmic results for sparse approximation. In: IEEE Transaction Information Theory, pp. 2231–2242.

Wagner, A., Wright, J., Ganesh, A., Zhou, Z., Mobahi, H., Ma, Y., 2012. Toward a practical face recognition system: robust alignment and illumination by sparse representation. IEEE Trans. Pattern Anal. Mach. Intell. 34 (2), 372–386.

Wright, J., Yang, A., Ganesh, A., Sastry, S., Ma, Y., 2009. Robust face recognition via sparse representation. IEEE Trans. Pattern Anal. Mach. Intell. 31 (2), 210–227.

Wu, G., Wang, Q., Zhang, D., Nie, F., Huang, H., Shen, D., 2014. A generative probability model of joint label fusion for multi-atlas based brain segmentation. Med. Image Anal. 18 (6), 881–890.

Yan, P., Kruecker, J., 2010. Incremental shape statistics learning for prostate tracking in TRUS. In: International Conference on Medical Image Computing and Computer Assisted Intervention, pp. 42–49.

Yan, P., Xu, S., Turkbey, B., Kruecker, J., 2010. Discrete deformable model guided by partial active shape model for TRUS image segmentation. IEEE Trans. Biomed. Eng. 57 (5), 1158–1166.

Zhan, Y., Zhou, X.S.Z., Peng, Z., Krishnan, A., 2008. Active scheduling of organ detection and segmentation in whole-body medical images. In: International Conference on Medical Image Computing and Computer Assisted Intervention, pp. 313–321.

Zhan, Y., Dewan, M., Zhou, X.S., 2009. Cross modality deformable segmentation using hierarchical clustering and learning. In: International Conference on Medical Image Computing and Computer Assisted Intervention, pp. 1033–1041.

Zhang, W., Yan, P., Li, X., 2011. Estimating patient-specific shape prior for medical image segmentation. In: International Symposium on Biomedical Imaging, pp. 1451–1454.

Zhang, S., Zhan, Y., Dewan, M., Huang, J., Metaxas, D.N., Zhou, X.S., 2012a. Towards robust and effective shape modeling: sparse shape composition. Med. Image Anal. 16 (1), 265–277.

Zhang, S., Zhan, Y., Metaxas, D.N., 2012b. Deformable segmentation via sparse representation and dictionary learning. Med. Image Anal. 16 (7), 1385–1396.

Zhang, S., Zhan, Y., Cui, X., Gao, M., Huang, J., Metaxas, D., 2013. 3D anatomical shape atlas construction using mesh quality preserved deformable models. Comput. Vis. Image Underst. 117 (9), 1061–1071.

Zhu, Y., Papademetris, X., Sinusas, A., Duncan, J., 2009. A dynamical shape prior for LV segmentation from RT3D echocardiography. In: International Conference on Medical Image Computing and Computer Assisted Intervention, pp. 206–213.

Zhu, Y., Papademetris, X., Sinusas, A., Duncan, J., 2010. Segmentation of the left ventricle from cardiac MR images using a subject-specific dynamical model. IEEE Trans. Med. Imaging 29 (3), 669–687.

# RECOGNITION, SEGMENTATION AND PARSING OF SPECIFIC OBJECTS

# SEMANTIC PARSING OF BRAIN MR IMAGES

# 14

**C. Ledig and D. Rueckert**

*Department of Computing, Biomedical Image Analysis Group, Imperial College London, London, United Kingdom*

## CHAPTER OUTLINE

S. Kevin Zhou (Ed): Medical Image Recognition, Segmentation and Parsing. http://dx.doi.org/10.1016/B978-0-12-802581-9.00014-7

## 14.1 INTRODUCTION

The extraction of a single or multiple anatomical meaningful region of interest (ROI) from a subject's brain magnetic resonance (MR) image is essential for computer-aided diagnosis and therapy planning, as well as for the extraction of biomarkers which are clinically useful (e.g., in clinical trials). The process of subdividing an image into distinct regions is referred to as *segmentation*. Once a brain MR image is segmented into its individual anatomical components, volumes or shape-related measures can be readily quantified. In addition, the microstructure tissue properties of anatomical regions can be assessed via multi-modal imaging, for example, diffusion weighted MR imaging.

The process of semantic segmentation refers to the labeling of pixels or voxels into anatomically meaningful regions. In the context of the segmentation of brain MR images, this often includes tissue segmentation as well as the parcellation of tissues into distinct regions. For example, gray matter (GM) may be subdivided into cortical GM and subcortical GM. The cortical GM may be further subdivided into the temporal lobe, occipital lobe, parietal lobe, and frontal lobe. Each lobe can be further subdivided in line with knowledge from anatomical or cytoarchitectonic brain atlases such as the Brodmann atlas (Brodmann, 1909). Similarly, subcortical GM can be further differentiated into structures such as thalamus, putamen, and basal ganglia. Semantic segmentation is heavily dependent on *a priori* knowledge about the location and relationship of different anatomical structures in the brain. In most cases, this knowledge is represented in the form of atlases of the human brain.

In this chapter, we provide an overview of existing atlas-based segmentation methods (Section 14.2). Even though most techniques are applicable to the segmentation of other organs or structures as well as other imaging modalities, particular focus is placed on methods for the segmentation of T1-weighted (T1w) MR brain images into anatomical structures. In Section 14.3, we also describe several publicly available brain atlases that are essential for the incorporation of semantic knowledge into the segmentation process.

## 14.2 ATLAS-BASED SEGMENTATION METHODS

In atlas-based methods, the segmentation of a brain image is inferred by aligning $M$ brain atlases denoted by $\mathbf{A_m}$ with $m = 1,\ldots,M$. A brain atlas is usually created by an expert by manually or semi-automatically annotating a given volumetric brain image. The term *atlas* comprises the annotated atlas intensity image, $\mathbf{I_m^A}$, and the corresponding reference segmentation, $\mathbf{L_m^A}$, thus $\mathbf{A_m} = \{\mathbf{I_m^A}, \mathbf{L_m^A}\}$. A single brain atlas is shown in Figure 14.1. A detailed overview of commonly used brain atlases is provided in Section 14.3.

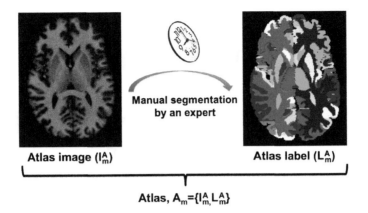

**Atlas image ($I_m^A$)**    **Atlas label ($L_m^A$)**

Manual segmentation
by an expert

**Atlas, $A_m = \{I_m^A, L_m^A\}$**

**FIGURE 14.1**

A brain atlas $\mathbf{A_m}$ consists of an intensity image $I_m^A$ with corresponding segmentation $L_m^A$. The reference segmentation is ideally created manually by an expert who follows a detailed segmentation protocol. This process is very time consuming and not scalable, as it can only be performed on a small number of images.

The aim of whole-brain segmentation is to segment a target image $\mathbf{I_{tgt}}$ into $K$ distinct structural ROIs. The unsegmented image $\mathbf{I_{tgt}} \in \Omega$ is indexed as $\mathbf{I_{tgt}} = \{y_1, y_2, \ldots, y_N\}$ where $y_i \in \mathbb{R}^+$. Here $y_i$ ($i = 1, \ldots, N$) denotes the intensity value of the $i$th voxel. The corresponding, inferred label map $\mathbf{L_{tgt}}$ is indexed accordingly as $\mathbf{L_{tgt}} = \{l_1, l_2, \ldots, l_N\}$. The probabilistic (or soft) segmentation is denoted by $\mathbf{P_{tgt}} = \{\mathbf{p_1}, \mathbf{p_2}, \ldots, \mathbf{p_N}\}$, where $\mathbf{p_i}$ is a $k$-valued vector with $\|\mathbf{p_i}\|_1 = 1$ and $\mathbf{p_i}(k) \geq 0$ describes the probability of voxel $i$ belonging to structure $k \in \{1, \ldots, K\}$. It can be observed that the label map $\mathbf{L_{tgt}}$ is defined as:

$$l_i = \arg\max_k \mathbf{p_i}(k) \tag{14.1}$$

If $\mathbf{p_i}$ is multi-modal $l_i$ can be chosen as any of the modes, for example, at random (Heckemann et al., 2006).

In the following an overview over widely used atlas-based segmentation approaches and their essential building blocks, *brain extraction*, *atlas alignment*, *label fusion*, and *segmentation refinement* is provided. A schematic illustration of this procedure is provided in Figure 14.2.

## 14.2.1 BRAIN EXTRACTION

A prerequisite of most anatomical segmentation approaches is the availability of a binary brain mask discriminating the actual brain from nonbrain tissue such as the skull, the neck or the eyes. The calculation of this mask is, however, not trivial. Many brain extraction methods tend to produce either too restrictive or too generous masks and there is no consensus of what constitutes an ideal brain mask (Eskildsen et al., 2012).

A rough categorization can be made by distinguishing manual approaches (Eritaia et al., 2000), semi-automatic approaches (Freeborough et al., 1997), and automatic approaches (Sandor and Leahy, 1997; Smith, 2002; Ségonne et al., 2004; Leung et al., 2011; Eskildsen et al., 2012; Manjón et al., 2014;

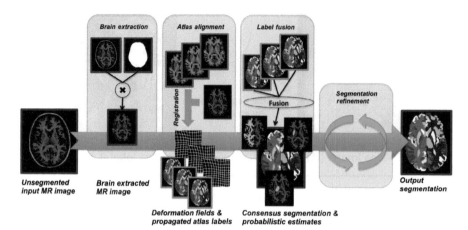

**FIGURE 14.2**

Schematic illustration of a typical segmentation pipeline with the common building blocks: brain extraction, atlas alignment, label fusion, and segmentation refinement. The unsegmented target image and the estimated segmentation are outlined in blue, the atlas images are outlined in red, and the propagated atlas labels in orange, respectively.

Heckemann et al., 2015). Approaches that require user interaction usually require substantial expertise, have poor inter- and intra-rater reliability and are very time consuming, which can be prohibitive when large databases are to be analyzed (Freeborough et al., 1997; Warfield et al., 2004; Eskildsen et al., 2012). Skull-stripping is not the focus of this chapter but a brief overview over existing approaches is provided in the following.

### 14.2.1.1 Deformable models
Sandor and Leahy (1997) (brain surface extractor, BSE) employ an edge-detector and morphological operations to calculate a brain mask. In Smith (2002) and Ségonne et al. (2004), a deformable model is automatically fit to the brain surface. Smith (2002) (brain extraction tool, BET) calculate the center of gravity and an approximate radius of the head by thresholding the image using robust minimum/maximum estimates of the image intensities. Based on this information a brain surface tessellation is initialized that iteratively evolves. The process is constrained by both intensity and smoothness terms. Ségonne et al. (2004) obtain an initial estimate of the brain mask using a watershed algorithm. The surface of this approximate but robust estimate is then employed as initialization of an active contour model (Kass et al., 1988) that integrates both geometric and atlas-based information (Ségonne et al., 2004). A quantitative comparison of these methods (Sandor and Leahy, 1997; Smith, 2002; Ségonne et al., 2004) can be found in Fennema-Notestine et al. (2006).

### 14.2.1.2 Database of extracted reference images
More recent and potentially more accurate methods for brain extraction rely on a database of brain extracted reference magnetic resonance (MR) images (Leung et al., 2011; Eskildsen et al., 2012; Manjón et al., 2014). In Leung et al. (2011), the authors nonrigidly align the reference images to the

subject that is to be extracted (cf. Section 14.2.2) and perform label fusion (cf. Section 14.2.3.1). In Heckemann et al. (2015) an atlas-based approach was developed with particular focus on robustness that relies on iterative refinement of the brain mask. Other approaches such as Eskildsen et al. (2012) and Manjón et al. (2014) follow a patch-based label fusion approach using linear registration only (cf. Section 14.2.3.4). Approaches for brain extraction tend to employ similar methodology to the techniques for the segmentation of anatomical structures. A comprehensive summary of relevant literature is provided in Leung et al. (2011) or Eskildsen et al. (2012).

In the remainder of this review it is assumed that $\mathbf{I}_{tgt}$ and the atlas images $\mathbf{I}_m^A$ are brain extracted. Skull-stripping the atlas images is often trivial as the corresponding expert label maps $\mathbf{L}_m^A$ can be binarized and employed as mask. The calculation of accurate brain masks for images which contain pathologies is, however, more complicated.

## 14.2.2 ATLAS-TO-IMAGE REGISTRATION

To exploit the labeling information encoded in the atlases most segmentation methods rely on aligning each individual atlas $\mathbf{A}_m$ with $\mathbf{I}_{tgt}$. This process is commonly referred to as *image registration* and usually driven by the image intensities of the corresponding images.

Image registration is highly complex and an active area of research that received continuous attention over the last decades. Therefore, it is only briefly discussed here. A comprehensive overview and evaluation of established registration approaches can be found in Zitová and Flusser (2003), Klein et al. (2009), and Sotiras et al. (2013).

### 14.2.2.1 Formulation of the registration problem

In general, image registration seeks to calculate a transformation $\phi : \Omega \to \Omega$ that transforms a source (moving) image $\mathbf{I}_{src}$ such that its similarity with a target (fixed) image $\mathbf{I}_{tgt}$ is maximized. The process of image registration is shown in Figure 14.3. For a given similarity measure $\mathcal{S}(\cdot,\cdot) : \mathbb{R}^N \times \mathbb{R}^N \to \mathbb{R}$ the optimization problem can be formulated as:

$$\hat{\phi} = \arg\min_{\phi}[-\mathcal{S}(\mathbf{I}_{tgt}, \phi(\mathbf{I}_{src})) + \mathcal{R}(\phi)] \tag{14.2}$$

Here, $\mathcal{R}$ is a regularization term. In nonrigid registration, regularization of the usually ill-posed optimization problem is an important factor to encourage smooth and ideally even diffeomorphic transformations (Rueckert et al., 1999; Vercauteren et al., 2009).

### 14.2.2.2 Similarity measures

To quantify image similarity several measures have been proposed. Common choices for $\mathcal{S}$ include sum of squared differences (SSD), mutual information (MI) (Collignon et al., 1995; Viola and Wells III, 1997), normalized mutual information (NMI) (Studholme et al., 1999), or cross-correlation (CC). A definition of these similarity measures is provided in Table 14.1. The basic assumption of SSD is that intensities of perfectly matched images are identical (Roche et al., 1999). This assumption can be relaxed when using CC (affine relationship) or MI/NMI (statistical relationship) (Roche et al., 1999; Artaechevarria et al., 2009). SSD and CC are often used to register images from the same modality/sequence, while the statistical measures have been successfully applied for multi-modal registration.

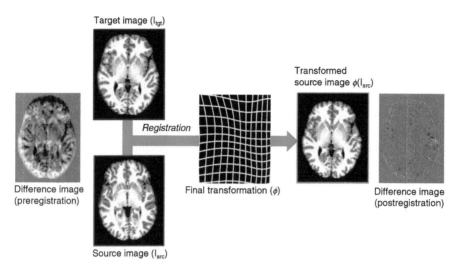

**FIGURE 14.3**

Schematic process of registering a source image $\mathbf{I}_{src}$ to a target image $\mathbf{I}_{tgt}$ with calculated transformation $\phi$. The difference image of $\mathbf{I}_{src}$, $\phi(\mathbf{I}_{src})$, and $\mathbf{I}_{tgt}$ is shown before and after registration, respectively. The target image is outlined in blue, the source image is outlined in red (before) and orange (after registration).

**Table 14.1 Overview Over Possible Measures to Quantify Similarity Between Two Images I and J: SSD, MI, NMI, and CC**

| Measure | Definition | Value Range | Similarity/Dissimilarity |
|---------|-----------|-------------|--------------------------|
| SSD $(\mathbf{I}, \mathbf{J})$ | $\sum_{i=1}^{N}(I(i) - J(i))^2$ | SSD $\geq 0$ | Dissimilarity |
| MI $(\mathbf{I}, \mathbf{J})$ | $H(\mathbf{I}) + H(\mathbf{J}) - H(\mathbf{I}, \mathbf{J})$ | MI $\geq 0$ | Similarity |
| NMI $(\mathbf{I}, \mathbf{J})$ | $\frac{H(\mathbf{I}) + H(\mathbf{J})}{H(\mathbf{I}, \mathbf{J})}$ | $1 \leq$ NMI $\leq 2$ | Similarity |
| CC $(\mathbf{I}, \mathbf{J})$ | $\frac{\mathrm{Cov}(\mathbf{I}, \mathbf{J})}{\sqrt{\mathrm{Var}(\mathbf{I})}\sqrt{\mathrm{Var}(\mathbf{J})}}$ | $-1 \leq$ CC $\leq 1$ | Similarity |

*Notes: Note that SSD is a measure of dissimilarity. MI and NMI require the calculation of individual histograms $(h_I, h_J)$ and the joint histogram $(h_{I,J})$ of the intensity images. The measures can then be calculated based on the joint, $H(\mathbf{I}, \mathbf{J})$, and the marginal entropies, $H(\mathbf{I})$ and $H(\mathbf{J})$.*

### 14.2.2.3 Transformation models

In image registration the degrees of freedom of $\phi$ are essential as they determine the level of detail of the computed transformations. Generally, it can be distinguished between *rigid*, *affine*, and *nonrigid* image alignment.

Rigid registration establishes the optimal alignment of two images by allowing translations and rotations only. Affine registration additionally compensates for transformations that include shear and scale. The recovery of both rigid and affine transformations requires the solution of a low-dimensional optimization problem that can be solved efficiently. An accurate affine transformation is usually a crucial prerequisite for a subsequent nonrigid registration (Rueckert et al., 1999).

The aim of nonrigid registration is the recovery of a deformation field that brings both images into optimal alignment. Here, the deformation field can be described by a transformation model, which is often built on cosine or B-spline basis functions (Ashburner et al., 1998; Rueckert et al., 1999; Andersson et al., 2007; Klein et al., 2009; Modat et al., 2010). Next to these approaches, nonparametric methods that do not model the transformation explicitly have been successfully applied. Popular examples include the so-called Demons algorithm (Thirion, 1998; Vercauteren et al., 2009) or the symmetric registration method proposed in Avants et al. (2008). The parameter space of the resulting optimization problem is large and can exceed millions of parameters, especially if no transformation model is used (Klein et al., 2009; Vercauteren et al., 2009).

In the context of atlas alignment for image segmentation, it should be noted that nonrigid transformations can be calculated at different levels of detail. For example, when an explicit transformation model based on B-spline basis functions is used, the control point spacing and thus the number of parameters can be varied. Usually a finer control point spacing yields a more accurate registration result; however, it comes at a substantially increased computational cost.

### 14.2.2.4 Large deformation registration problem

The accurate registration of an atlas and unsegmented MR image can be difficult if the target image differs from the available atlases due to general anatomical variability or pathological changes. Also intensity inhomogeneities or noise can facilitate an accurate registration difficult (Vovk et al., 2007).

There have been several methods proposed to address the large deformation registration problem in adult brains in the context of Alzheimer's disease (AD). In Heckemann et al. (2010), the authors proposed multi-atlas propagation with enhanced registration (Heckemann et al., 2010, 2011) (MAPER). MAPER employs automatically calculated brain tissue segmentations to guide the registration process. This allows a robust image alignment, even if the target image shows severe brain atrophy. In another approach, Wolz et al. (2010a) described an iterative approach to improve segmentation accuracy by propagating atlas labels over a learned manifold while refining intermediate segmentations based on image intensities using graph-cuts (GC) (cf. Section 14.2.4). It was shown by Gerber et al. (2010) that coordinates within a low-dimensional space, a nonlinear manifold, allow for a meaningful image comparison and statistical tests.

A manifold of the anatomical variation in a given data set is also learned in Hamm et al. (2010). In this work, it was shown that the problem of recovering a large deformation between two images can be simplified by solving a series of small deformation registration problems (Hamm et al., 2010). The small deformations are calculated along the shortest path between the images on the learned manifold (Hamm et al., 2010).

In the following, $\phi_m$ denotes the calculated transformation from the atlas space of $\mathbf{A_m}$ to the coordinate system of $\mathbf{I}_{tgt}$. Once the atlases $\mathbf{A_m}$ have been propagated based on $\phi_m$ and the label maps, $\mathbf{L_m^A}$, reside in the same coordinate system as the unsegmented target image, $\mathbf{I}_{tgt}$, a consensus segmentation can be inferred using a variety of label fusion techniques (cf. Section 14.2.3).

## 14.2.3 LABEL FUSION

### 14.2.3.1 Majority vote fusion

In majority vote fusion (MVF), also called "vote-rule" or "decision" fusion, each of the $M$ propagated atlas labels $\mathbf{L_m^A}$ contributes equally to the final segmentation. A certain voxel is thus labeled according to the opinion on which the majority of the propagated atlas segmentations agree. Formally the probability of voxel $i$ being labeled as structure $k$ can be calculated as:

$$\mathbf{p_i}(k) = \frac{1}{M} \sum_{m=1}^{M} \delta(L_m^A(i), k) \tag{14.3}$$

Here, $\delta(\cdot, \cdot)$ is the Kronecker delta defined as:

$$\delta(v, w) = \begin{cases} 1 & \text{if } v = w \\ 0 & \text{otherwise} \end{cases} \tag{14.4}$$

The actual segmentation estimate, $\mathbf{L_{tgt}}$, is then readily inferred through Eq. (14.1).

MVF was first described by Rohlfing et al. (2004) where it was applied to the segmentation of bee brains. Heckemann et al. (2006) successfully employed MVF to segment MR brain images and presented a model that describes the basic assumption of label fusion. In this model, it is assumed that there are two major sources of segmentation errors: (1) *Systematic errors* ($\epsilon_{sys}$) due to deviations of the (manual) reference segmentation from the true segmentation or due to consistent registration bias. (2) *Random errors* ($\epsilon_{rand}$) introduced due to inaccuracies in individual reference labels or image registrations (Heckemann et al., 2006). With this assumption random errors can be corrected by fusing several label estimates. However, the systematic errors asymptotically limit the segmentation accuracy as the number of fused atlases increases (Heckemann et al., 2006). In Heckemann et al. (2006), the following relation is suggested to model the segmentation accuracy $\text{SI}_{model}$, measured as Dice coefficient (Dice, 1945) or so-called similarity index (SI), dependent on the number of atlases $K$:

$$\text{SI}_{model} = 1 - \epsilon_{sys} - \frac{\epsilon_{rand}}{\sqrt{K}} \tag{14.5}$$

Figure 14.4 shows the schematic process and the qualitative behavior of label fusion approaches using the model from Eq. (14.5). According to Artaechevarria et al. (2009), MVF is the most simple and most popular label fusion strategy, and does not require any *a priori* knowledge except for the actual segmentations that are to be fused. MVF has its origins in the more general combination of classifiers as, for example, Xu et al. (1992), Kittler et al. (1998), or Kuncheva (2004).

### 14.2.3.2 Atlas selection

If only a single atlas from a given atlas database is to be used, a carefully selected atlas that is similar to $\mathbf{I_{tgt}}$ allows a higher segmentation accuracy than choosing an atlas at random. This was confirmed in a variety of applications, such as the segmentation of computed tomography (CT) images of the head (Han et al., 2008) or the segmentation of bee brains (Rohlfing et al., 2004) and human brains in MR images (Wu et al., 2007).

However, the fusion of multiple atlases (e.g., using MVF) substantially outperforms the segmentation based on a single atlas only (Rohlfing et al., 2004; Heckemann et al., 2006; Aljabar et al., 2009).

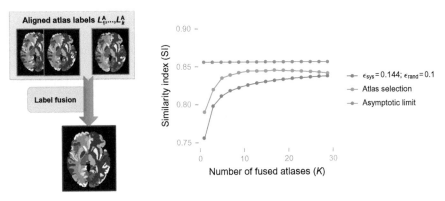

**FIGURE 14.4**

Left: Schematic process of fusing $K$ atlas labels that have been aligned to the target image into a consensus segmentation. Right: Illustrations of the increasing segmentation accuracy with increasing number of fused atlas labels. The model described in Eq. (14.5) is shown for $\epsilon_{sys} = 0.144$, $\epsilon_{rand} = 0.1$ (red) with corresponding asymptotic limit (blue). A qualitative plot indicating the increased accuracy when atlas selection is used is also shown (green). The diagram is based on and adapted from Heckemann et al. (2006) and Aljabar et al. (2009).

Klein et al. (2007) and Aljabar et al. (2009) thus suggested to combine these approaches and perform label fusion on a *selection* of atlases from a larger database.

As selection criterion, the image similarity between the aligned atlas images and $\mathbf{I}_{tgt}$ can be calculated using a variety of similarity measures such as SSD, MI (Collignon et al., 1995; Viola and Wells III, 1997; Klein et al., 2007), NMI (Studholme et al., 1999; Wu et al., 2007), or CC (Aljabar et al., 2009) (cf. Table 14.1). Further, image similarity can be assessed on different alignment levels, for example, after affine or nonlinear registration (Rohlfing et al., 2004; Klein et al., 2007; Wu et al., 2007), but also in a template space (Aljabar et al., 2009). When the selection is performed in a template space all atlas images can be preregistered to this template. This reduces the computational burden dramatically as during atlas selection a single registration, aligning $\mathbf{I}_{tgt}$ to the template, suffices. Only the selected atlases are then aligned with $\mathbf{I}_{tgt}$ in a nonrigid fashion (Aljabar et al., 2009). In addition to image similarity, other criteria such as characteristics of the required deformation to align the images (Rohlfing et al., 2004) or meta-information (age, sex, etc.) (Aljabar et al., 2009) can be used.

In summary, atlas selection addresses two limitations of standard multi-atlas label fusion: First, the accurate nonlinear alignment (cf. Section 14.2.2) of numerous atlases to the unsegmented image, $\mathbf{I}_{tgt}$, is computationally intensive. Second, it was shown that there is an asymptotic limit of the segmentation accuracy caused by systematic and anatomical variations (Heckemann et al., 2006; Aljabar et al., 2009). Segmentation results can substantially improve up to around 20 selected atlases (Heckemann et al., 2006; Aljabar et al., 2009) (cf. Figure 14.4). However, using more atlases with an anatomy that increasingly differs from $\mathbf{I}_{tgt}$ might even deteriorate segmentation accuracy (Aljabar et al., 2009). Nevertheless, it should be noted that the ideal number of selected atlases might be strongly dependent on the quality of the atlases, the anatomical variability of the subjects and the ROI that is to be segmented.

### 14.2.3.3 Weighted vote fusion

Instead of selecting atlases, and thus potentially neglecting relevant information, another approach is to weight the contribution of each individual atlas. A detailed description and comparison of this category of label fusion can be found in Artaechevarria et al. (2009).

In globally weighted fusion (GWF), the probabilistic label estimates are calculated based on *global*, atlas-dependent voting weights $w_m^g$ as:

$$\mathbf{p_i}(k) = \frac{\sum_{m=1}^{M} w_m^g \delta(L_m^A(i), k)}{\sum_{k'=1}^{K} \sum_{m=1}^{M} w_m^g \delta(L_m^A(i), k')} \tag{14.6}$$

Here, the voting weight, $w_m^g$, of each atlas is generally determined by the image similarity of the transformed atlas MR images, $\mathbf{I_m^A}$, and the subject image $\mathbf{I}_{tgt}$. Potential measures to quantify this similarity of intensity images include SSD, MI, NMI, or CC (Artaechevarria et al., 2009). The calculation of global voting weights based on these measures, $w_m^{gSSD}$, $w_m^{gCC}$, $w_m^{gMI}$, and $w_m^{gNMI}$, is described in Table 14.1. As the SSD increases with increasing image *dissimilarity* the voting weight is defined as the inverse of the actual SSD, $w_m^{gSSD} = \text{SSD}(\mathbf{I_m^A}, \mathbf{I}_{tgt})^{-1}$. Artaechevarria et al. (2009) further introduced a gain parameter, $p$, that potentiates the respective weights, for example, $(w_m^{gNMI})^p$. However, it was found that the segmentation result is usually not very sensitive toward this parameter and the optimal choice depends on the dataset (Artaechevarria et al., 2009).

Segmentation accuracy can be further increased by calculating *local* voting weights, $w_m^l(i)$, within a location-specific region (Artaechevarria et al., 2009). These regions can be, for example, a spherical or cubical neighborhood of the voxel under consideration. The size of the neighborhood is a tunable parameter; however, a neighborhood radius of $r = 5$ was shown to yield good results (Artaechevarria et al., 2009). In locally weighted fusion (LWF), the probabilistic segmentation estimates are calculated as:

$$\mathbf{p_i}(k) = \frac{\sum_{m=1}^{M} w_m^l(i) \delta(L_m^A(i), k)}{\sum_{k'=1}^{K} \sum_{m=1}^{M} w_m^l(i) \delta(L_m^A(i), k')} \tag{14.7}$$

It was shown that weighted fusion overall outperforms MVF (Artaechevarria et al., 2009; Sabuncu et al., 2010). LWF is usually superior to GWF and particularly useful in image regions with high contrast (Artaechevarria et al., 2009; Sabuncu et al., 2010). The ideal fusion strategy is thus dependent on the brain anatomy that is to be segmented. LWF with SSD often performs well (Artaechevarria et al., 2009; Wang et al., 2013). However, when compared to NMI, SSD is more sensitive to noise in low-contrast regions and relies on the assumption of similar intensity profiles of the images (Roche et al., 1999; Artaechevarria et al., 2009).

### 14.2.3.4 Patch-based label fusion

Inspired by the work on nonlocal means filtering for image denoising (Buades et al., 2005; Coupé et al., 2008), Coupé et al. (2010) proposed a *patch-based* approach to address the problem of label fusion. Patch-based label fusion was subsequently described thoroughly in Rousseau et al. (2011) and Coupé et al. (2011). In patch-based label fusion techniques, image patches of the unsegmented image are locally compared to image patches in the atlas images. Usually patches are defined as three-dimensional (3D) volumes of a given diameter. For a fixed patch in $\mathbf{I}_{tgt}$ with center voxel $i$, $P(\mathbf{I}_{tgt}, i)$, numerous

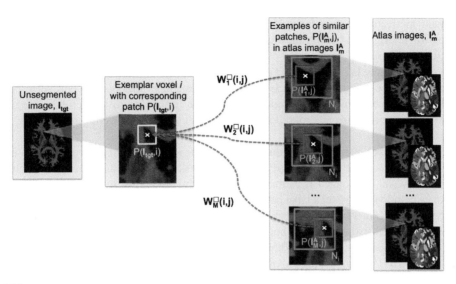

**FIGURE 14.5**

Illustration of the weight calculation when segmenting one example voxel $i$. The weights, $w_m^{\square}(i,j)$, are determined between the fixed reference patch, $P(\mathbf{I}_{\text{tgt}}, i)$ (yellow), and atlas patches, $P(\mathbf{I}_{\mathbf{m}}^{\mathbf{A}}, j)$ (red). For each atlas image several atlas patches that are shifted within a local search neighborhood (cyan) are considered. With a weighted voting approach a probabilistic segmentation (cf. Eq. 14.8) is obtained. Illustration adapted and modified from Coupé et al. (2011) and Rousseau et al. (2011).

patches in $\mathbf{I}_{\mathbf{m}}^{\mathbf{A}}$ are taken into account. Specifically, all patches with center $j$, $P(\mathbf{I}_{\mathbf{m}}^{\mathbf{A}}, j)$, with the spatial constraint that $j$ lies within a defined neighborhood, $\mathcal{N}_i$, of $i$ are considered. Both the size of the 3D patches (patch size) and the size of the neighborhood (search window size) are parameters that need to be chosen. An illustration of this process is provided in Figure 14.5. The exact label fusion procedure can be formalized as:

$$\mathbf{p_i}(k) = \frac{\sum_{m=1}^{M} \sum_{j \in \mathcal{N}_i} w_m^{\square}(i,j) \delta(L_m^A(j), k)}{\sum_{k'=1}^{K} \sum_{m=1}^{M} \sum_{j \in \mathcal{N}_i} w_m^{\square}(i,j) \delta(L_m^A(j), k')} \tag{14.8}$$

Here $w_m^{\square}(i,j)$ is a weight that is calculated based on the similarity of the patch $P(\mathbf{I}_{\text{tgt}}, i)$, centered at voxel $i$ in $\mathbf{I}_{\text{tgt}}$, and the patch $P(\mathbf{I}_{\mathbf{m}}^{\mathbf{A}}, j)$, centered at voxel $j$ in atlas $\mathbf{I}_{\mathbf{m}}^{\mathbf{A}}$. A common definition (Buades et al., 2005; Coupé et al., 2011; Rousseau et al., 2011) of this similarity measure is:

$$w_m^{\square}(i,j) = \exp \frac{-\|P(\mathbf{I}_{\text{tgt}}, i) - P(\mathbf{I}_{\mathbf{m}}^{\mathbf{A}}, j)\|^2}{Nh} \tag{14.9}$$

Here, $\| \cdot \|$ is the $L2$-norm and $N$ is the number of voxels in the patches. Further, $h$ is a decay parameter that requires tuning (Coupé et al., 2011). If $h \to \infty$ all patches are weighted equally; if $h \to 0$ only the best matching patch is selected. Potentially, $w_m^{\square}(i,j)$ might be set to zero below a given threshold (Coupé et al., 2011).

The main motivation for patch-based label fusion is to remove the computationally expensive requirement of nonrigidly aligning the reference atlases (cf. Section 14.2.2). The patch-based formulation further relaxes the assumption of a one-to-one mapping between the atlas images, $\mathbf{I}_m^A$, and the unsegmented image, $\mathbf{I}_{tgt}$ (Rousseau et al., 2011). An approximate alignment, using, for example, affine registration (Coupé et al., 2011), is sufficient to establish reasonable patch correspondences. Nevertheless, it must be noted that nonrigid alignment can further improve patch-based segmentation as it allows the more rigorous incorporation of topological constraints (Coupé et al., 2011; Rousseau et al., 2011).

In patch-based label fusion one can discriminate *point-wise* and *multipoint* estimators (Rousseau et al., 2011). In Eq. (14.8), a point-wise estimator is described, in which the label probability of each individual voxel (or point) $i$ is estimated individually. In contrast to this, multipoint estimators calculate at each individual voxel a label patch estimate (Rousseau et al., 2011). Specifically, instead of considering only the center label, $L_m^A(j)$ (cf. Eq. 14.8), label information from the whole patch centered at $j$ is fused into a patch estimate. While point-wise estimators are commonly used and computationally more efficient, it was shown that multipoint estimators can potentially increase segmentation accuracy (Rousseau et al., 2011). More details on multipoint estimators can be found in Katkovnik et al. (2010) and Rousseau et al. (2011).

Recent advances in patch-based segmentation include the application of sparsity techniques (Tong et al., 2013) or the efficient search of patch correspondences using the PatchMatch algorithm (Barnes et al., 2009; Shi et al., 2014; Ta et al., 2014). Next to image segmentation, it was proposed to employ patch-based methods to grade subjects according to clinical variables (Coupé et al., 2012a,b). In this patch-based grading approach, a meaningful clinical label, for example, AD or healthy control (HC), is associated with each patch of a reference database. Instead of fusing anatomical labels, $L_m^A(j)$, these clinical labels are fused in Eq. (14.8) within a region. It was shown that the resulting grading value allows the accurate discrimination of different AD disease states (Coupé et al., 2012a,b).

### 14.2.3.5 Joint label fusion

The label fusion techniques that were presented so far treat each atlas independently from the others for the calculation of voting weights. Thus, none of these approaches takes into account that similar or, in general, correlated atlases might produce similar segmentation errors (Wang et al., 2013). To address this limitation Wang et al. (2013) introduced an approach called joint label fusion (JLF) in which the joint probability distribution of two atlases producing the same labeling error is explicitly modeled.

In particular, the authors aim to minimize the expected error between the true, yet unknown, segmentation of $\mathbf{I}_{tgt}$ and the consensus segmentation estimate $\mathbf{L}_{tgt}$. This optimization problem can be solved once dependency matrices $\mathbf{M}_i$ of size $M \times M$ are established that model the likelihood that a pair of the $M$ available atlases make an identical error at voxel $i$. In Wang et al. (2013), the authors calculate the correlation of the intensity similarity of two atlases with respect to $\mathbf{I}_{tgt}$. A local estimation of $\mathbf{M}_i$ is obtained by performing the similarity computation in a local neighborhood of the corresponding voxel $i$. More details on JLF can be found in Wang et al. (2013).

Many approaches ranking among the top performing methods are based on JLF strategies that incorporate the nonlocal patch-based concept. This was confirmed for the segmentation of various anatomies in recent segmentation challenges (Landman and Warfield, 2012; Asman et al., 2013). For example, JLF performs very well for the segmentation of the brain into distinct ROIs (Landman and Warfield, 2012; Asman et al., 2013), but also for the segmentation of the myocardium (Asman et al., 2013; Bai et al., 2015).

### 14.2.3.6 Statistical label fusion

With origins in the popular simultaneous truth and performance level evaluation (STAPLE) (Warfield et al., 2004) algorithm, there is another category of statistical label fusion approaches. Given several manual label sets, STAPLE was proposed to simultaneously estimate the performance-level parameters of each expert rater and the most probable ground truth. The STAPLE algorithm computes a probabilistic estimate of the true segmentation (Warfield et al., 2004). For the sake of consistency with existing literature the commonly used notation is employed to outline the STAPLE algorithm. This notation is slightly different in comparison to the rest of this section. This also accommodates the fact that STAPLE was originally described for the estimation of a ground truth from several expert reference segmentations rather than for the fusion of automatic label estimates. The following description is adapted from Warfield et al. (2004), where more details about the exact implementation of STAPLE can be found.

Let $\mathbf{D}$ be a $N \times M$ matrix that describes the decisions of $M$ raters (or atlases) at $N$ voxels. Let $\mathbf{T}$ be a vector of size $N$ indicating the true but unknown segmentation. For $K$ possible labels $\mathbf{D}$ and $\mathbf{T}$ are indexed as $D_{im} \in \{1, \ldots, K\}$ and $T_i \in \{1, \ldots, K\}$. The goal of the STAPLE algorithm is to estimate a performance tensor $\hat{\theta}$ of size $M \times K \times K$ that maximizes the log-likelihood of observing the complete data $(\mathbf{D}, \mathbf{T})$. Here, element $\theta_{ms's}$ quantifies the probability that rater $m$ decides on label $s'$ given that the true label is $s$. For a probability mass function $f(\mathbf{D}, \mathbf{T}|\theta)$ that describes the probability of observing the complete data, $\hat{\theta}$ can be calculated by solving:

$$\hat{\theta} = \arg\max_{\theta} \ln f(\mathbf{D}, \mathbf{T}|\theta) \tag{14.10}$$

The solution of this problem would be trivial if the true segmentation $\mathbf{T}$ were known. As $\mathbf{T}$ is, however, unknown Warfield et al. (2004) suggested to employ the expectation-maximization (EM) algorithm to solve Eq. (14.10). In this approach, a ground truth $\mathbf{T}$ is estimated in the expectation-step and the ideal performance parameters $\hat{\theta}$ found in the aximization-step. This is repeated iteratively until the model converges. Convergence to a local maximum of Eq. (14.10) is guaranteed (Warfield et al., 2004). There are different strategies to initialize $\theta$ in the first iteration (Warfield et al., 2004). Furthermore, spatial prior information can be incorporated through probabilistic priors or smoothness constraints based on Markov random fields (MRFs) (Warfield et al., 2004).

Next to the basic STAPLE algorithm outlined previously, there have been several successful attempts to incorporate both image intensity information (Asman and Landman, 2013; Cardoso et al., 2013) and the concept of nonlocal patch-based approaches into the STAPLE framework (Asman and Landman, 2013). Many other extensions include formulations that allow the application to data with missing labels (Landman et al., 2012), local estimation of rater performances (Asman and Landman, 2012; Commowick et al., 2012), or the fusion of probabilistic decisions (Akhondi-Asl and Warfield, 2013).

## 14.2.4 REFINEMENT OF IMAGE SEGMENTATIONS

The segmentation estimates obtained by multi-atlas label fusion, as described in the previous Section 14.2.3, can be further improved. In the following, two successful strategies to the refinement of image segmentations are presented: the refinement of segmentations based on image intensities and the refinement based on classifiers that were trained to correct systematic bias of a segmentation method.

### 14.2.4.1 Intensity-based refinement

The probabilistic segmentation estimates, $\mathbf{P}_{tgt}$, obtained by automatic label fusion techniques (cf. Section 14.2.3) can be refined based on the image intensities of $\mathbf{I}_{tgt}$. It was shown that modifying image segmentations based on the actual image intensities can substantially improve segmentation results (van der Lijn et al., 2008; Wolz et al., 2009; Lötjönen et al., 2010; Ledig et al., 2015).

Using Bayes' theorem the refinement task is often modeled as calculating the maximum-a-posteriori (MAP) estimate as:

$$\mathbf{L}_{tgt} = \arg\max_{\mathbf{L}} p(\mathbf{L}|\mathbf{I}_{tgt}) = \arg\max_{\mathbf{L}} \frac{p(\mathbf{I}_{tgt}|\mathbf{L})p(\mathbf{L})}{p(\mathbf{I}_{tgt})} = \arg\max_{\mathbf{L}} p(\mathbf{I}_{tgt}|\mathbf{L})p(\mathbf{L}) \tag{14.11}$$

Assuming voxel-wise independence the image likelihood, $p(\mathbf{I}_{tgt}|\mathbf{L})$, can be calculated as $\prod_{i=1}^{N} p(y_i|l_i)$ where $p(y_i|l_i)$ is given by a predefined intensity model. The probability of a segmentation, $p(\mathbf{L})$, is often modeled based on spatial prior knowledge and smoothness constraints between adjacent labels. Since the target image is fixed, the optimization problem is independent of $p(\mathbf{I}_{tgt})$.

Two popular approaches to solve the optimization problem stated in Eq. (14.11) are based on GC (Greig et al., 1989; Boykov et al., 2001; van der Lijn et al., 2008; Wolz et al., 2009) or the EM algorithm (Van Leemput et al., 1999; Lötjönen et al., 2010; Ledig et al., 2015).

### 14.2.4.2 Expectation-maximization optimization

The widely used EM-optimization was presented for image segmentation by Van Leemput et al. (1999). For the sake of consistency with existing literature, in the following paragraph the notation is employed that was also used in Van Leemput et al. (1999), Cardoso et al. (2011), and Ledig et al. (2015).

Based on a Gaussian mixture model (GMM) it is assumed that given the intensity characteristics $\Phi = \{(\mu_1, \sigma_1), (\mu_2, \sigma_2), \ldots, (\mu_K, \sigma_K)\}$ of $K$ structural classes, the likelihood of observing intensity $y_i$ at voxel $i$ is given as:

$$f(y_i|\Phi) = \sum_k f(y_i|\mathbf{z_i} = \mathbf{e_k}, \Phi)f(\mathbf{z_i} = \mathbf{e_k}) \tag{14.12}$$

Here, it is assumed that the probability of a voxel $i$ to have intensity $y_i$, $f(y_i|\mathbf{z_i} = \mathbf{e_k}, \Phi)$, given that it belongs to class $k$, $(\mathbf{z_i} = \mathbf{e_k})$ is described by a normal distribution (Wells III et al., 1996; Van Leemput et al., 1999; Zhang et al., 2001; Cardoso et al., 2011; Ledig et al., 2015). Thus, $f(y_i|\mathbf{z_i})$ is modeled as $f(y_i|\mathbf{z_i} = \mathbf{e_k}, \Phi) = \mathcal{G}_k(y_i)$ where $\mathcal{G}_k$ denotes the Gaussian distribution with corresponding parameters $(\mu_k, \sigma_k)$. The prior probability $f(\mathbf{z_i} = \mathbf{e_k})$ that a voxel $i$ belongs to structure $k$ is given by the probabilistic label estimates after multi-atlas label propagation, $\mathbf{P}_{tgt}^{prior}$ (cf. Section 14.2.3). By assuming that voxels are statistically independent, the probability of observing the complete image $\mathbf{I}_{tgt}$, given that the model parameters $\Phi$ are known in iteration $m$, is given by $f(\mathbf{I}_{tgt}|\Phi^{(m)}) = \prod_i f(y_i|\Phi^{(m)})$. In the EM approach, this model is solved by interleaving the expectation of the probabilities of each voxel $i$ to belong to structure $k$, $p_{ik}^{(m)}$, and the maximization of the model by updating the model parameters $\Phi^{(m)}$. It is assumed that the probabilities, $p_{ik}^{(m+1)}$, are known in iteration $(m+1)$, so that the model parameters, $\Phi$, can be updated as:

$$\mu_k^{(m+1)} = \frac{\sum_{i=1}^N p_{ik}^{(m+1)} y_i}{\sum_{i=1}^N p_{ik}^{(m+1)}} \quad , \quad \sigma_k^{(m+1)} = \sqrt{\frac{\sum_{i=1}^N p_{ik}^{(m+1)} \left( y_i - \mu_k^{(m+1)} \right)^2}{\sum_{i=1}^N p_{ik}^{(m+1)}}} \tag{14.13}$$

Given the updated model parameters the estimate of the class probabilities in the next iteration is given as:

$$p_{ik}^{(m+1)} = \frac{f(y_i | \mathbf{z_i} = \mathbf{e_k}, \Phi^{(m)}) f(\mathbf{z_i} = \mathbf{e_k})}{\sum_{k'=1}^K f(y_i | \mathbf{z_i} = \mathbf{e_{k'}}, \Phi^{(m)}) f(\mathbf{z_i} = \mathbf{e_{k'}})} \tag{14.14}$$

Usually the model converges after a few iterations.

Smoothness of the final segmentation can be enforced with a global and stationary MRF, which can be integrated using the mean field approximation (Zhang, 1992), following the example of Van Leemput et al. (1999), Cardoso et al. (2011), or Ledig et al. (2015). This also allows the incorporation of topological knowledge next to the spatial information provided by the prior estimates. The MRF energy function is usually calculated based on the probabilistic label estimates in iteration $m$, in the first-order neighborhood of each image voxel. A connectivity matrix, $G$ of size $K \times K$, can be defined that describes the connectivity between class $k$ and $j$. Usually $G$ is defined as:

$$G(k, j) = \begin{cases} 0, & \text{if } k = j \\ \beta, & \text{if structures } k \text{ and } j \text{ share a boundary} \\ \gamma, & \text{if structures } k \text{ and } j \text{ are distant} \end{cases} \tag{14.15}$$

Here $\beta$ and $\gamma$, with $0 \le \beta \le \gamma$, are parameters describing the penalty for certain neighborhood configurations.

Images of substantially deformed or abnormal brains pose great challenges to the label fusion techniques described in Section 14.2.3 as the atlas images are difficult to align due to, for example, existing pathology in the target. This results in inaccurate spatial *a priori* information limiting the potential of refinement techniques based on intensities. It was shown that explicitly relaxing the spatial priors $\mathbf{P}_{\text{tgt}}^{\text{prior}}$ based on image intensities can substantially improve segmentation results (Cardoso et al., 2011; Ledig et al., 2015). In Ledig et al. (2015), the authors proposed a method called multi-atlas label propagation with expectation-maximization based refinement (MALP-EM) with a prior relaxation technique to successfully segment abnormal MR images.

### 14.2.4.3 Graph-cut optimization

The optimization problem in Eq. (14.11) can be rewritten (Greig et al., 1989; van der Lijn et al., 2008) as a minimization problem by taking the negative logarithm as:

$$\mathbf{L}_{\text{tgt}} = \arg\min_{\mathbf{L}}(-\ln p(\mathbf{I}_{\text{tgt}}|\mathbf{L}) - \ln p(\mathbf{L})) = \arg\min_{\mathbf{L}}(E_{\text{intensity}}(\mathbf{L}) + E_{\text{prior}}(\mathbf{L})) \tag{14.16}$$

This amended formulation allows the definition of a network graph for which a minimum cut can be calculated based on the Ford-Fulkerson max-flow/min-cut algorithm (Greig et al., 1989). In Eq. (14.16), the intensity (or data) term, $E_{\text{intensity}}(\mathbf{L}) = -\sum_{i=1}^{N} \ln p(y_i|l_i)$, quantifies the agreement of the image data, $\mathbf{I}_{\text{tgt}}$, with the intensity model. A common choice for the intensity model of $p(y_i|l_i)$ is a Gaussian probability distribution with label-specific parameters $(\mu_{l_i}, \sigma_{l_i})$ (van der Lijn et al., 2008; Wolz et al., 2010b). The second term, $E_{\text{prior}}(\mathbf{L})$, incorporates both spatial prior information provided through the probabilistic segmentation estimates (e.g., obtained through label fusion) and smoothness constraints which are often modeled through MRFs (van der Lijn et al., 2008; Wolz et al., 2010b). The cost function that is minimized by GC can then be summarized as:

$$E(\mathbf{L}) = \underbrace{-\sum_{i=1}^{N} \ln p(y_i|l_i)}_{E_{\text{intensity}}} \underbrace{-\sum_{i=1}^{N} \ln p(l_i)}_{E_{\text{spatial prior}}} + \underbrace{\sum_{i=1}^{N} \sum_{j\in\mathcal{N}_i} G(l_i, l_j)}_{E_{\text{smoothness prior}}} \quad (14.17)$$

Here, $p(l_i)$ is the prior probability that voxel $i$ has label $l_i$. It can be calculated using label fusion (cf. Section 14.2.3) so that $p(l_i) = \mathbf{p_i}(l_i)$. Furthermore $\mathcal{N}_i$ is the set of voxels neighboring voxel $i$ and as in Eq. (14.15) $G(l_i, l_j)$ penalizes nonsmooth label configurations ($G(l_i, l_j) > 0$ for $l_i \neq l_j$). The individual energy terms can be multiplied with weighting factors to control their individual contribution (Song et al., 2006; van der Lijn et al., 2008; Wolz et al., 2010b).

GC optimization was first introduced for binary segmentation problems (Greig et al., 1989; Boykov et al., 2001; Boykov and Kolmogorov, 2004) for which a global optimum can be found. However, the optimization problem can also be formulated as a multiway cut problem and employed for the segmentation of multiple labels (Boykov et al., 2001; Boykov and Kolmogorov, 2004; Song et al., 2006). For multiway cut problems, Boykov et al. (2001) presented an algorithm that efficiently calculates approximate solutions of the global minima with optimality bounds. GC optimization typically assigns one strict label to each voxel.

Based on GC, Wolz et al. (2010b) proposed a framework to measure longitudinal changes by building a 4D graph based on edges between both spatially and temporally neighboring voxels.

### 14.2.4.4 Learning-based refinement

Learning-based refinement is based on the assumption that a substantial fraction of falsely labeled image voxels is due to systematic bias of the employed segmentation method (Wang et al., 2011). Systematic bias often originates in different definitions of manual segmentation protocols or inaccurate translation of the manual protocol to the automatic method (Wang et al., 2011). The assumption made by Wang et al. (2011) is similar to the one made by Heckemann et al. (2006): In the work by Heckemann et al. (2006), the authors described segmentation inaccuracies in the context of multi-atlas label propagation as a combination of random variability of propagated labels and systematic errors.

The main contribution of Wang et al. (2011) is the proposal to explicitly learn systematic segmentation errors with respect to reference segmentations using machine learning. Specifically, features based on image intensities and label context are extracted in a local neighborhood of each voxel and combined with spatial information. These features are subsequently employed to train error detection and error correction classifiers using AdaBoost (Freund and Schapire, 1995) with respect to reference segmentations (Wang et al., 2011). These classifiers have been shown to allow a significant

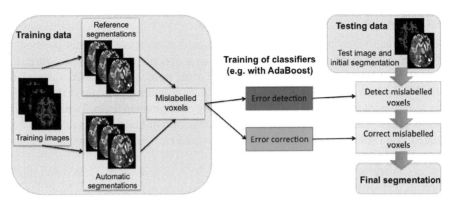

**FIGURE 14.6**

Schematic process of training classifiers for the detection and correction of systematic segmentation bias. This illustration corresponds to the variant named *explicit bias correction* in Wang et al. (2011). Note that for binary segmentation tasks the error detection and error correction classifiers are identical. Illustration adapted and modified from Wang et al. (2011).

reduction of systematic bias in the context of many applications. In the original work, Wang et al. (2011) presented substantial improvements when the method was employed to correct automatically calculated hippocampus segmentations, brain masks and brain tissue segmentations.

A schematic illustration of the method is provided in Figure 14.6. More details on learning-based refinement can be found in Wang et al. (2011).

## 14.2.5 REMARKS

Recently several segmentation challenges were held in conjunction with international conferences. The methods with particularly good performance for segmenting brain data were often based on JLF (cf. Section 14.2.3.5) and corrected for systematic segmentation bias (cf. Section 14.2.4.2) (Landman and Warfield, 2012; Asman et al., 2013).

The careful design and implementation of each individually outlined building block, *brain extraction*, *atlas alignment*, *label fusion*, and *label refinement*, is essential and critical to realize a segmentation approach that is both accurate and robust. Failure or inaccuracies within a single of these "modules" is likely to negatively impact the final segmentation result. It is tempting to consider each of these blocks separately to reduce the complexity of the task. This further allows the independent implementation, tuning and validation of each module. It should be mentioned, however, that there is some evidence that more complex approaches that model and solve several building blocks jointly (e.g., registration and segmentation) can increase accuracy (Ashburner and Friston, 2005). Nevertheless, in practice the theoretical advantages of these joint models might be outweighed by the previously mentioned merits of a modular approach.

## 14.3 BRAIN ATLASES FROM MR IMAGES

Atlases of the human brain can be considered as maps that associate a spatial position within the brain with structural or functional information such as a specific anatomical structure. Early brain atlases were created based on a single subject or a small number of selected subjects (Mazziotta et al., 1995). While these early atlases provided great insight into brain anatomy they were limited in their ability to represent the large intersubject variability of the human brain. To address this problem, probabilistic population atlases were created from a population of brain images that were aligned with and segmented in a common reference or so-called stereotaxic space, for example, in Shattuck et al. (2008).

Popular stereotaxic spaces are given by the MNI-305[a] (Evans et al., 1993) and the MNI-152[b] (Mazziotta et al., 1995) brain templates, which are available through the Montreal Neurological Institute (http://www.mni.mcgill.ca/) (MNI). Both templates were created by averaging the contributing MR intensity images (305 and 152, respectively) in a common space after linear image registration (Evans et al., 1993; Mazziotta et al., 1995). The MNI-152 template was built by the International Consortium for Brain Mapping (ICBM) from images acquired with better contrast and at a higher resolution than the images on which the MNI-305 template is based.[b] The stereotaxic spaces described by these template images can serve as targets to align individual atlases of an atlas database (Hammers et al., 2003; Shattuck et al., 2008), such as the ones described in this section. The propagated atlas labels can then be averaged using label fusion techniques (cf. Section 14.2.3) to create a probabilistic brain atlas. It must be noted that the characteristics of the resulting probabilistic atlas, such as spatial variability of individual structures, directly depends on the chosen template space (e.g., MNI-305, MNI-152) and the registration approach (e.g., affine or nonrigid transformation model). As a consequence, based on atlas databases such as the ones described in the following, a variety of probabilistic atlases can be created that can be tailored to a particular application.

A broader description and history of atlases of the human brain can be found in Mazziotta et al. (1995) and Shattuck et al. (2008).

In this chapter, the focus is, however, on nonprobabilistic brain atlases that can be aligned with a specific target image. As many individual brain atlases need to be aligned, this approach is computationally more expensive than the alignment with a single atlas only. However, accuracy of the estimated target segmentation can be substantially improved based on *subject-specific* atlases created using label fusion (cf. Section 14.2.3).

In the following, five publicly available nonprobabilistic brain atlases based on T1-weighted MR images are introduced. The reviewed brain atlases were selected because they are widely used, publicly available, and contain manually annotated anatomical labels for both cortical and noncortical structures. An overview of key characteristics of these atlases is given in Table 14.2.

However, next to this selection of brain atlases there are alternatives available. For example, Klein et al. (2009) employed next to the IBSR18 (cf. Section 14.3.2) and LBPA40 (cf. Section 14.3.4) atlases, the CUMC12 (Columbia University Medical Center) and MGH10 (Massachusetts General Hospital) brain atlas to evaluate 14 established registration algorithms. Furthermore, Klein and Tourville (2012) recently created a detailed protocol to label human cortices. Based on this protocol MR images from 101 healthy participants, with origins in nine different publicly available data sets, were segmented. The expert labels for all images[c] were obtained by manually editing label maps that were calculated using FreeSurfer (http://surfer.nmr.mgh.harvard.edu/, Fischl and Dale, 2000; Fischl et al., 2002, 2004) (FreeSurfer) to correspond with the protocol.

**Table 14.2 Overview of Key Characteristics of the Five Selected Atlas Databases**

| Atlas | N | Male/Female | Age (Mean [Min; Max]) | ROIs | C1 | C2 | Literature | URL |
|-------|---|-------------|----------------------|------|----|----|-----------|-----|
| AAL | 1 | 1/0 | Young adult | 116 | No | No | Tzourio-Mazoyer et al. (2002) | AAL-1/2 |
| IBSR18 | 18 | 4/14 | 38 [7; 71] | 34 | Yes | Yes | – | IBSR-1 |
| Hammers | 30 | 15/15 | 31[a] [20; 54] | 83 | No | No | Hammers et al. (2003), Hammers et al. (2007), and Gousias et al. (2008) | Hammers-1 |
| LPBA40 | 40 | 20/20 | 29.2 [19; 39] | 56 | No | No | Shattuck et al. (2008) | LPBA-1 |
| NMM | 30[b] | 10/20 | 34.3 [18; 90] | 134 | Yes | Yes | Marcus et al. (2007), and Worth and Tourville (2013) | NMM-1/2/3 |

[a] *Median.*
[b] *Atlas consists of 35 images as five subjects were scanned twice.*
*C1: cortical ROIs contain only grey matter tissue.*
*C2: all brain tissue including ventricles is annotated. For example, AAL, Hammers, and LPBA atlases contain unannotated white matter (WM).*
*AAL-1: http://www.gin.cnrs.fr/spip.php?article217.*
*AAL-2: http://www.bic.mni.mcgill.ca/ServicesAtlases/Colin27Highres.*
*IBSR-1: http://www.nitrc.org/projects/ibsr.*
*Hammers-1: http://biomedic.doc.ic.ac.uk/brain-development/index.php?n=Main.Adult.*
*LPBA-1: http://www.loni.usc.edu/atlases/Atlas_Detail.php?atlas_id=12.*
*NMM-1: http://Neuromorphometrics.com/.*
*NMM-2: http://www.cma.mgh.harvard.edu/manuals/segmentation/.*
*NMM-3: http://www.braincolor.org.*

## 14.3.1 AAL ATLAS

The *Automated Anatomical Labeling (AAL) brain atlas*[d] (Tzourio-Mazoyer et al., 2002) distinguishes 116 ROIs and is based on a single MR template image with a resolution of 1 mm × 1 mm × 1 mm. The template[e] was obtained by averaging 27 T1w MR scans of a male individual to increase the signal-to-noise ratio (SNR) (Holmes et al., 1998; Tzourio-Mazoyer et al., 2002). The MR template was then segmented manually into distinct ROIs based on 2D axial slices. The ROIs were outlined only on every second axial slice (Tzourio-Mazoyer et al., 2002). The atlas segmentations available for download[d] are, compared to the MR template, of a lower resolution of 2 mm × 2 mm × 2 mm. The AAL atlas was constructed with a focus on measuring activation patterns within the defined ROIs in functional imaging. To avoid missing some structure-related activity due to a too-conservative definition of ROIs and to account for inter-subject variability, structures were outlined quite generously, even beyond the GM boundary (Tzourio-Mazoyer et al., 2002).

In total, the template is divided into 116 anatomical structures including the cortical gyri but also the hippocampus, subcortical structures such as amygdala, caudate nucleus, putamen, pallidum, thalamus and 26 labels subdividing the cerebellum (Tzourio-Mazoyer et al., 2002). Structures in the left and right hemisphere are treated separately. Ventricles were not segmented. The visualization of the atlas in Figure 14.7 clearly shows the generous definition of ROIs, including more than one tissue type.

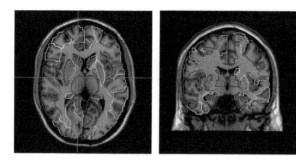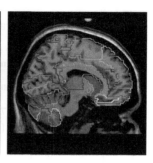

**FIGURE 14.7**

The AAL atlas in axial (left), coronal (middle), and sagittal (right) view plane. T1w MR template with overlaid segmentation contours in a color scheme that provides a good contrast between adjacent labels. The cross-hair in the axial view indicates the position of the illustrated coronal and sagittal slice.

## 14.3.2 IBSR18 ATLAS

The Internet Brain Segmentation Repository (IBSR) V2.0[f] atlas consists of T1w MR images acquired from 18 subjects (14 male/4 female, mean age [min; max] of 14 subjects 38 years [7; 71][g]). The slice thickness of all images is 1.5 mm. However, the in-plane resolution varies from 0.8371 mm × 0.8371 mm to 1 mm × 1 mm. All images were positionally normalized by rotating the images into the Talairach orientation. Expert segmentations of 34 anatomical structures[h] were created manually.

The annotated structures include, for example, hippocampus, amygdala, caudate, pallidum, putamen, thalamus, inferior lateral ventricle, and lateral ventricle. The cerebellum is split into cerebellum cortex and cerebellum white matter (WM). Structures in the left and right hemisphere are discriminated. Cortical annotations include cortical GM only. An example of a subject of the IBSR atlas is shown in Figure 14.8.

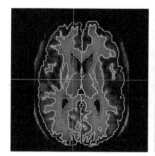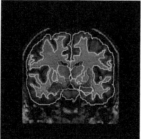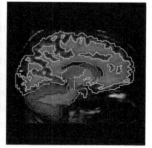

**FIGURE 14.8**

An example of a subject (IBSR01, male, 37 years) of the IBSR atlas in axial (left), coronal (middle), and sagittal (right) view plane. T1w MR template with overlaid segmentation contours.

### 14.3.3 HAMMERS ATLAS

The *Hammers brain atlas*[i] (Hammers et al., 2003, 2007; Gousias et al., 2008) consists of 30 T1w MR images with corresponding segmentations distinguishing 83 ROIs. The images were acquired from young healthy adults (15 male/female, median age [min; max] of all subjects 31 years [20; 54]) and resliced to an isotropic resolution of 0.9375 mm × 0.9375 mm × 0.9375 mm (Hammers et al., 2003; Gousias et al., 2008). All images were acquired at 1.5 Tesla (T) with the same scanner (Gousias et al., 2008). Originally, Hammers et al. (2003) annotated 49 distinct anatomical regions of 20 subjects. Delineations were done in native space. This work was subsequently extended to 30 subjects and by further subdividing the 49 regions into a total of 83 ROIs (Hammers et al., 2007; Gousias et al., 2008). Following a well-defined protocol (Hammers et al., 2003), the MR images were manually annotated on 2D slices in structure-specific orientations. Subsequent control of difficult cases was conducted by a trained specialist (Hammers et al., 2003). An intra-rater reliability study indicates good reliability (Hammers et al., 2007). Hammers et al. (2003) further created a probabilistic brain atlas by aligning the individual segmentations to the MNI-152[b] template space using statistical parametric mapping (http://www.fil.ion.ucl.ac.uk/spm/, Ashburner and Friston, 1997; Ashburner et al., 1998; Ashburner and Friston, 2005) (SPM).

Each of the 30 MR images is divided into 83 ROIs subdividing the cortex, ventricles, and noncortical structures such as the hippocampus, amygdala, caudate nucleus, pallidum, putamen, and thalamus. There is no finer separation within the cerebellum. Structures in the left and right hemisphere form separate ROIs. GM and WM are combined in one common label for most cortical ROIs (Hammers et al., 2003). An example of a subject of the Hammers atlas is shown in Figure 14.9.

### 14.3.4 LPBA40 ATLAS

The LONI Probabilistic Brain Atlas (LPBA)[j] consists of T1w MR images acquired from 40 healthy volunteers (20 male/female, mean age [min; max] of all subjects 29.2 years [19; 39]) (Shattuck et al., 2008). All images were acquired at the same scanner at 1.5 T and subsequently *rigidly* aligned to the MNI-305[a] (Evans et al., 1993) template space. Images were further resampled to an

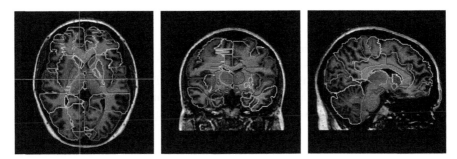

**FIGURE 14.9**

An example of a subject (a01) of the Hammers atlas in axial (left), coronal (middle), and sagittal (right) view plane. T1w MR template with overlaid segmentation contours.

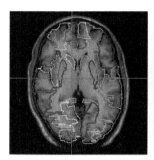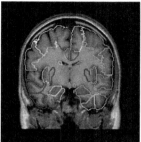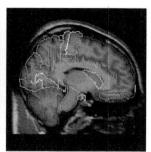

**FIGURE 14.10**

An example of a subject (S01) of the LPBA atlas in axial (left), coronal (middle), and sagittal (right) view plane. T1w MR template with overlaid segmentation contours.

isotropic resolution of 1 mm × 1 mm × 1 mm (Shattuck et al., 2008). Manual delineation of the images into 56 distinct ROIs was then performed in template space following a detailed protocol (Shattuck et al., 2008). Rater-reliability was assessed. Several versions of a probabilistic atlas were produced by employing different techniques (e.g., SPM) to *nonrigidly* align the individual segmentations to the MNI-305 template space (Shattuck et al., 2008). However, the individual 40 annotated nonprobabilistic atlases are available.

The atlas distinguishes hippocampus, caudate, putamen, cerebellum, and brainstem but mainly parcellates cortical ROIs (Shattuck et al., 2008). Amygdala, pallidum, and thalamus are absent. There is no finer separation within the cerebellum. Structures in the left and right hemisphere form individual ROIs. Cortical structures potentially contain WM that lies between sulci or in the vicinity of cortical GM (Shattuck et al., 2008). An example of a subject of the LPBA atlas is shown in Figure 14.10.

## 14.3.5 NMM ATLAS

The *Neuromorphometrics (NMM) brain atlas*[k] consists of a continuously growing number of manually annotated T1w MR brain images (Worth and Tourville, 2013). The currently available annotated images can be obtained with an academic license for an annual fee. Recently, a subset of 35 images was used as "gold standard" and was made freely available in the course of the "MICCAI 2012 Grand Challenge and Workshop on Multi-Atlas Labeling" (Landman and Warfield, 2012). In the following, a description of these 35 images is provided.

The 35 images were taken from the Open Access Series of Imaging Studies (OASIS) database and acquired from 30 individuals (Marcus et al., 2007). Repeat scans were acquired of five of the subjects in a second session within 90 days of the original scan (Marcus et al., 2007). All images were acquired at 1.5 T at the same scanner (Marcus et al., 2007). Images from the OASIS database were corrected for bias field inhomogeneities and positionally normalized.[l] The MR images with corresponding segmentations are resampled to a resolution of 1 mm × 1 mm × 1 mm. A description of relevant subsets including information on gender and age is provided in Table 14.3.

**Table 14.3 Overview of Relevant NMM Subsets With Respective Age and Gender Information**

| Subset | Number of Images/Subjects | Gender (Male/Female) | Age (Mean [Min; Max]) |
|---|---|---|---|
| Complete | 35/30 | 10/20 | 34.3 [18; 90] |
| Atlas | 30/30 | 10/20 | 34.3 [18; 90] |
| Repeat | 10/5 | 2/3 | 24.6 [20; 29] |
| Training | 15/15 | 5/10 | 23 [19; 34] |
| Test | 20/15 | 5/10 | 45.7 [18; 90] |

Note: *Definition of TRAINING and TEST set as used in the MICCAI 2012 Grand Challenge.*

The manual segmentation into 138 anatomical structures has been carried out by experts[m] according to publicly available protocols.[n] All manual segmentations were quality controlled by another expert.[1] As suggested by Landman and Warfield (2012), the small regions "vessel" and "cerebral exterior" were excluded in both the left and the right hemisphere. Thus, the atlas comprises effectively 134 ROIs of which 36 are noncortical and 98 cortical. The noncortical structures comprise several ROIs such as amygdala, caudate nucleus, hippocampus, pallidum, putamen, and thalamus. The cerebellum is subdivided into WM, cerebellum exterior, and the cerebellar vermal lobules. Cortical ROIs contain a single tissue type (cortical GM) only. Without any further subdivision, cerebral WM is pooled together in one ROI for the left and right brain hemisphere, respectively. The 134 ROIs contain 63 distinct anatomical structures which have symmetric counterparts in their opposite hemisphere, in total 126 paired ROIs. The remaining eight unpaired structures are: third ventricle, fourth ventricle, brain stem, CSF, optic chiasm, cerebellar vermal lobules I-V, cerebellar vermal lobules VI-VII, and cerebellar vermal lobules VIII-X. Examples of brain MR images of a young male subject (20 years) and a rather old female subject (90 years) are illustrated with overlaid manual segmentation outlines in Figure 14.11.

## 14.4 CONCLUSIONS

In this chapter, we have reviewed several approaches for the semantic segmentation of brain MR images. These approaches are nearly always atlas-based segmentation techniques that can fully make use of *a priori* knowledge that is encoded in the atlases. The large number of different techniques in this area demonstrates that this is still an active area of research. The performance of current state-of-the-art techniques is starting to approach that of human observers in terms of accuracy. However, the robustness of current approaches is not yet comparable to human observers. This is especially true in cases where pathologies are present in the MR images that are not present in the atlases.

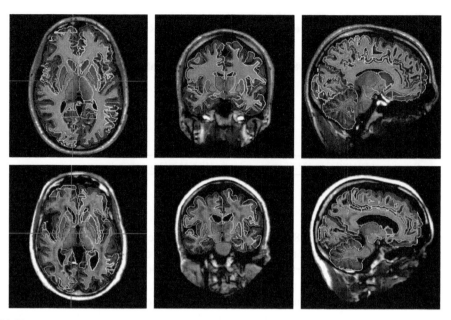

**FIGURE 14.11**

Two examples of subjects of the NMM atlas in axial (left), coronal (middle), and sagittal (right) view plane. T1w MR images of a male subject aged 20 years (OAS1_0285, top) and a female subject aged 90 years (OAS1_0083, bottom) with overlaid segmentation contours.

## NOTES

a. http://www.bic.mni.mcgill.ca/ServicesAtlases/MNI305.
b. http://www.bic.mni.mcgill.ca/ServicesAtlases/ICBM152Lin.
c. http://mindboggle.info/.
d. http://www.gin.cnrs.fr/spip.php?article217.
e. http://www.bic.mni.mcgill.ca/ServicesAtlases/Colin27Highres.
f. http://www.nitrc.org/projects/ibsr.
g. No exact age provided for four subjects.
h. The readme file describes 39 anatomical structures. In contrast to this description labels for cerebral exterior (left/right), exterior (left/right), and amygdala anterior (left/right) are missing while CSF is an additional label not mentioned in the description ($39 - 6 + 1 = 34$).
i. http://biomedic.doc.ic.ac.uk/brain-development/index.php?n=Main.Adult.
j. http://www.loni.usc.edu/atlases/Atlas_Detail.php?atlas_id=12.
k. http://www.neuromorphometrics.com/.
l. http://www.neuromorphometrics.com/wp-content/uploads/2013/07/DescriptionofLabeledScans.pdf.
m. Provided by Neuromorphometrics, Inc. (http://Neuromorphometrics.com/) under academic subscription.
n. http://www.cma.mgh.harvard.edu/manuals/segmentation/ and http://www.braincolor.org.

# REFERENCES

Akhondi-Asl, A., Warfield, S.K., 2013. Simultaneous truth and performance level estimation through fusion of probabilistic segmentations. IEEE Trans. Med. Imaging 32 (10), 1840–1852.

Aljabar, P., Heckemann, R.A., Hammers, A., Hajnal, J.V., Rueckert, D., 2009. Multi-atlas based segmentation of brain images: atlas selection and its effect on accuracy. NeuroImage 46 (3), 726–738.

Andersson, J., Jenkinson, M., Smith, S., 2007. Non-linear registration, AKA spatial normalisation. Technical Report TR07JA2, FMRIB Centre, Oxford, UK.

Artaechevarria, X., Munoz Barrutia, A., Ortiz, C.D.S., 2009. Combination strategies in multi-atlas image segmentation: application to brain MR data. IEEE Trans. Med. Imaging 28 (8), 1266–1277.

Ashburner, J., Friston, K., 1997. Multimodal image coregistration and partitioning: a unified framework. NeuroImage 6 (3), 209–217.

Ashburner, J., Friston, K.J., 2005. Unified segmentation. NeuroImage 26 (3), 839–851.

Ashburner, J., Hutton, C., Frackowiak, R., Johnsrude, I., Price, C., Friston, K., 1998. Identifying global anatomical differences: deformation-based morphometry. Hum. Brain Mapp. 6 (5-6), 348–357.

Asman, A.J., Landman, B.A., 2012. Formulating spatially varying performance in the statistical fusion framework. IEEE Trans. Med. Imaging 31 (6), 1326–1336.

Asman, A.J., Landman, B.A., 2013. Non-local statistical label fusion for multi-atlas segmentation. Med. Image Anal. 17 (2), 194–208.

Asman, A., Akhondi-Asl, A., Wang, H., Tustison, N.J., Avants, B.B., Warfield, S.K., Landman, B.A., 2013. MICCAI 2013 Segmentation Algorithms, Theory and Applications (SATA) Challenge Results Summary, URL https://masi.vuse.vanderbilt.edu/workshop2013/images/1/1b/SATA_2013_Proceedings.pdf.

Avants, B.B., Epstein, C.L., Grossman, M., Gee, J.C., 2008. Symmetric diffeomorphic image registration with cross-correlation: evaluating automated labeling of elderly and neurodegenerative brain. Med. Image Anal. 12 (1), 26–41.

Bai, W., Shi, W., Ledig, C., Rueckert, D., 2015. Multi-atlas segmentation with augmented features for cardiac MR images. Med. Image Anal. 19 (1), 98–109.

Barnes, C., Shechtman, E., Finkelstein, A., Goldman, D.B., 2009. PatchMatch: a randomized correspondence algorithm for structural image editing. ACM Trans. Graph. 28 (3), 24:1–24:11.

Boykov, Y., Kolmogorov, V., 2004. An experimental comparison of min-cut/max-flow algorithms for energy minimization in vision. IEEE Trans. Pattern Anal. Mach. Intell. 26 (9), 1124–1137.

Boykov, Y., Veksler, O., Zabih, R., 2001. Fast approximate energy minimization via graph cuts. IEEE Trans. Pattern Anal. Mach. Intell. 23 (11), 1222–1239.

Brodmann, K., 1909. Vergleichende Lokalisationslehre der Großhirnrinde: In ihren Prinzipien Dargestellt auf Grund des Zellenbaues. Verlag von Johann Ambrosius Barth.

Buades, A., Coll, B., Morel, J., 2005. A review of image denoising algorithms, with a new one. Multiscale Model. Simul. 4 (2), 490–530.

Cardoso, M.J., Clarkson, M.J., Ridgway, G.R., Modat, M., Fox, N.C., Ourselin, S., 2011. LoAd: a locally adaptive cortical segmentation algorithm. NeuroImage 56 (3), 1386–1397.

Cardoso, M.J., Leung, K., Modat, M., Keihaninejad, S., Cash, D., Barnes, J., Fox, N.C., Ourselin, S., 2013. STEPS: similarity and truth estimation for propagated segmentations and its application to hippocampal segmentation and brain parcelation. Med. Image Anal. 17 (6), 671–684.

Collignon, A., Maes, F., Delaere, D., Vandermeulen, D., Suetens, P., Marchal, G., 1995. Automated multi-modality image registration based on information theory. In: International Conference on Information Processing in Medical Imaging (IPMI), vol. 3, pp. 263–274.

Commowick, O., Akhondi-Asl, A., Warfield, S.K., 2012. Estimating a reference standard segmentation with spatially varying performance parameters: local MAP STAPLE. IEEE Trans. Med. Imaging 31 (8), 1593–1606.

Coupé, P., Yger, P., Prima, S., Hellier, P., Kervrann, C., Barillot, C., 2008. An optimized blockwise nonlocal means denoising filter for 3-D magnetic resonance images. IEEE Trans. Med. Imaging 27 (4), 425–441.

Coupé, P., Manjón, J.V., Fonov, V., Pruessner, J., Robles, M., Collins, D.L., 2010. Nonlocal patch-based label fusion for hippocampus segmentation. In: Lecture Notes in Computer Science, MICCAI 2010, pp. 129–136.

Coupé, P., Manjón, J.V., Fonov, V., Pruessner, J., Robles, M., Collins, D.L., 2011. Patch-based segmentation using expert priors: application to hippocampus and ventricle segmentation. NeuroImage 54 (2), 940–954.

Coupé, P., Eskildsen, S.F., Manjón, J.V., Fonov, V.S., Collins, D.L., 2012a. Simultaneous segmentation and grading of anatomical structures for patient's classification: application to Alzheimer's disease. NeuroImage 59 (4), 3736–3747.

Coupé, P., Eskildsen, S.F., Manjón, J.V., Fonov, V.S., Pruessner, J.C., Allard, M., Collins, D.L., 2012b. Scoring by nonlocal image patch estimator for early detection of Alzheimer's disease. NeuroImage Clin. 1 (1), 141–152.

Dice, L.R., 1945. Measures of the amount of ecologic association between species. Ecology 26 (3), 297–302.

Eritaia, J., Wood, S.J., Stuart, G.W., Bridle, N., Dudgeon, P., Maruff, P., Velakoulis, D., Pantelis, C., 2000. An optimized method for estimating intracranial volume from magnetic resonance images. Magn. Reson. Med. 44 (6), 973–977.

Eskildsen, S.F., Coupé, P., Fonov, V., Manjón, J.V., Leung, K.K., Guizard, N., Wassef, S.N., Østergaard, L.R., Collins, D.L., 2012. BEaST: brain extraction based on nonlocal segmentation technique. NeuroImage 59 (3), 2362–2373.

Evans, A.C., Collins, D.L., Mills, S.R., Brown, E.D., Kelly, R.L., Peters, T.M., 1993. 3D statistical neuroanatomical models from 305 MRI volumes. In: Nuclear Science Symposium and Medical Imaging Conference—NSS/MIC 1993, IEEE Conference Record, vol. 3, pp. 1813–1817.

Fennema-Notestine, C., Ozyurt, I.B., Clark, C.P., Morris, S., Bischoff-Grethe, A., Bondi, M.W., Jernigan, T.L., Fischl, B., Segonne, F., Shattuck, D.W., Leahy, R.M., Rex, D.E., Toga, A.W., Zou, K.H., Brown, G.G., 2006. Quantitative evaluation of automated skull-stripping methods applied to contemporary and legacy images: effects of diagnosis, bias correction, and slice location. Hum. Brain Mapp. 27 (2), 99–113.

Fischl, B., Dale, A.M., 2000. Measuring the thickness of the human cerebral cortex from magnetic resonance images. Proc. Natl Acad. Sci. 97 (20), 11050–11055.

Fischl, B., Salat, D.H., Busa, E., Albert, M., Dieterich, M., Haselgrove, C., van der Kouwe, A., Killiany, R., Kennedy, D., Klaveness, S., Montillo, A., Makris, N., Rosen, B., Dale, A.M., 2002. Whole brain segmentation: automated labeling of neuroanatomical structures in the human brain. Neuron 33 (3), 341–355.

Fischl, B., van der Kouwe, A., Destrieux, C., Halgren, E., Ségonne, F., Salat, D.H., Busa, E., Seidman, L.J., Goldstein, J., Kennedy, D., Caviness, V., Makris, N., Rosen, B., Dale, A.M., 2004. Automatically parcellating the human cerebral cortex. Cereb. Cortex 14 (1), 11–22.

Freeborough, P.A., Fox, N.C., Kitney, R.I., 1997. Interactive algorithms for the segmentation and quantitation of 3-D MRI brain scans. Comput. Meth. Prog. Biomed. 53 (1), 15–25.

Freund, Y., Schapire, R.E., 1995. A decision-theoretic generalization of on-line learning and an application to boosting. In: Computational Learning Theory, Lecture Notes in Computer Science, vol. 904. Springer, Berlin, Heidelberg, pp. 23–37.

Gerber, S., Tasdizen, T., Fletcher, P.T., Joshi, S., Whitaker, R., 2010. Manifold modeling for brain population analysis. Med. Image Anal. 14 (5), 643–653.

Gousias, I.S., Rueckert, D., Heckemann, R.A., Dyet, L.E., Boardman, J.P., Edwards, A.D., Hammers, A., 2008. Automatic segmentation of brain MRIs of 2-year-olds into 83 regions of interest. NeuroImage 40 (2), 672–684.

Greig, D.M., Porteous, B.T., Seheult, A.H., 1989. Exact maximum a posteriori estimation for binary images. J. R. Stat. Soc. Ser. B (Methodol.) 51 (2), 271–279.

Hamm, J., Ye, D.H., Verma, R., Davatzikos, C., 2010. GRAM: a framework for geodesic registration on anatomical manifolds. Med. Image Anal. 14 (5), 633–642.

Hammers, A., Allom, R., Koepp, M., Free, S.L., Myers, R., Lemieux, L., Mitchell, T.N., Brooks, D.J., Duncan, J.S., 2003. Three-dimensional maximum probability atlas of the human brain, with particular reference to the temporal lobe. Hum. Brain Mapp. 19 (4), 224–247.

Hammers, A., Chen, C.H., Lemieux, L., Allom, R., Vossos, S., Free, S.L., Myers, R., Brooks, D.J., Duncan, J.S., Koepp, M.J., 2007. Statistical neuroanatomy of the human inferior frontal gyrus and probabilistic atlas in a standard stereotaxic space. Hum. Brain Mapp. 28 (1), 34–48.

Han, X., Hoogeman, M.S., Levendag, P.C., Hibbard, L.S., Teguh, D.N., Voet, P., Cowen, A.C., Wolf, T.K., 2008. Atlas-based auto-segmentation of head and neck CT images. In: Medical Image Computing and Computer-Assisted Intervention—MICCAI 2008, Lecture Notes in Computer Science, vol. 5242, pp. 434–441.

Heckemann, R.A., Hajnal, J.V., Aljabar, P., Rueckert, D., Hammers, A., 2006. Automatic anatomical brain MRI segmentation combining label propagation and decision fusion. NeuroImage 33 (1), 115–126.

Heckemann, R.A., Keihaninejad, S., Aljabar, P., Rueckert, D., Hajnal, J.V., Hammers, A., 2010. Improving intersubject image registration using tissue-class information benefits robustness and accuracy of multi-atlas based anatomical segmentation. NeuroImage 51 (1), 221–227.

Heckemann, R.A., Keihaninejad, S., Aljabar, P., Gray, K.R., Nielsen, C., Rueckert, D., Hajnal, J.V., Hammers, A., The AD Neuroimaging Initiative, 2011. Automatic morphometry in Alzheimer's disease and mild cognitive impairment. NeuroImage 56 (4), 2024–2037.

Heckemann, R.A., Ledig, C., Gray, K.R., Aljabar, P., Rueckert, D., Hajnal, J.V., Hammers, A., 2015. Brain extraction using label propagation and group agreement: Pincram. PLoS ONE 10 (7), e0129211.

Holmes, C.J., Hoge, R., Collins, L., Woods, R., Toga, A.W., Evans, A.C., 1998. Enhancement of MR images using registration for signal averaging. J. Comput. Assist. Tomogr. 22 (2), 324–333.

Kass, M., Witkin, A., Terzopoulos, D., 1988. Snakes: active contour models. Int. J. Comput. Vis. 1 (4), 32–31.

Katkovnik, V., Foi, A., Egiazarian, K., Astola, J., 2010. From local kernel to nonlocal multiple-model image denoising. Int. J. Comput. Vis. 86 (1), 1–32.

Kittler, J., Hatef, M., Duin, R.P.W., Matas, J., 1998. On combining classifiers. IEEE Trans. Pattern Anal. Mach. Intell. 20 (3), 226–239.

Klein, A., Andersson, J., Ardekani, B.A., Ashburner, J., Avants, B., Chiang, M.C., Christensen, G.E., Collins, D.L., Gee, J., Hellier, P., Song, J.H., Jenkinson, M., Lepage, C., Rueckert, D., Thompson, P., Vercauteren, T., Woods, R.P., Mann, J.J., Parsey, R.V., 2009. Evaluation of 14 nonlinear deformation algorithms applied to human brain MRI registration. NeuroImage 46 (3), 786–802.

Klein, A., Tourville, J., 2012. 101 Labeled brain images and a consistent human cortical labeling protocol. Front. Neurosci. 6 (171), 1–12.

Klein, S., van der Heide, U.A., Raaymakers, B.W., Kotte, A.N.T.J., Staring, M., Pluim, J.P.W., 2007. Segmentation of the prostate in MR images by atlas matching. In: IEEE International Symposium on Biomedical Imaging: From Nano to Macro (ISBI), pp. 1300–1303.

Kuncheva, L.I., 2004. Combining Pattern Classifiers: Methods and Algorithms. John Wiley & Sons, Inc, Hoboken, New Jersey, USA.

Landman, B., Warfield, S.K., 2012. MICCAI 2012 Grand Challenge and Workshop on Multi-Atlas Labeling, URL https://masi.vuse.vanderbilt.edu/workshop2012/index.php/Main_Page.

Landman, B.A., Asman, A.J., Scoggins, A.G., Bogovic, J.A., Xing, F., Prince, J.L., 2012. Robust statistical fusion of image labels. IEEE Trans. Med. Imaging 31 (2), 512–522.

Ledig, C., Heckemann, R.A., Makropoulos, A., Hammers, A., Lötjönen, J., Menon, D., Rueckert, D., 2015. Robust whole-brain segmentation: application to traumatic brain injury. Med. Image Anal. 21 (1), 40–58.

Leung, K.K., Barnes, J., Modat, M., Ridgway, G.R., Bartlett, J.W., Fox, N.C., Ourselin, S., 2011. Brain MAPS: an automated, accurate and robust brain extraction technique using a template library. NeuroImage 55 (3), 1091–1108.

Lötjönen, J.M.P., Wolz, R., Koikkalainen, J.R., Thurfjell, L., Waldemar, G., Soininen, H., Rueckert, D., 2010. Fast and robust multi-atlas segmentation of brain magnetic resonance images. NeuroImage 49 (3), 2352–2365.

Manjón, J.V., Eskildsen, S.F., Coupé, P., Romero, J.E., Collins, D.L., 2014. Nonlocal intracranial cavity extraction. Int. J. Biomed. Imaging 2014 (Article ID: 820205), 11 pages.

Marcus, D.S., Wang, T.H., Parker, J., Csernansky, J.G., Morris, J.C., Buckner, R.L., 2007. Open Access Series of Imaging Studies (OASIS): cross-sectional MRI data in young, middle aged, nondemented, and demented older adults. J. Cogn. Neurosci. 19 (9), 1498–1507.

Mazziotta, J.C., Toga, A.W., Evans, A., Fox, P., Lancaster, J., 1995. A probabilistic atlas of the human brain: theory and rationale for its development: The International Consortium for Brain Mapping (ICBM). NeuroImage 2 (Part A), 89–101.

Modat, M., Ridgway, G.R., Taylor, Z.A., Lehmann, M., Barnes, J., Hawkes, D.J., Fox, N.C., Ourselin, S., 2010. Fast free-form deformation using graphics processing units. Comput. Meth. Prog. Biomed. 98 (3), 278–284.

Roche, A., Malandain, G., Ayache, N., 1999. Unifying maximum likelihood approaches in medical image registration. RR-3741.

Rohlfing, T., Brandt, R., Menzel, R., Maurer Jr., C.R., 2004. Evaluation of atlas selection strategies for atlas-based image segmentation with application to confocal microscopy images of bee brains. NeuroImage 21 (4), 1428–1442.

Rousseau, F., Habas, P.A., Studholme, C., 2011. A supervised patch-based approach for human brain labeling. IEEE Trans. Med. Imaging 30 (10), 1852–1862.

Rueckert, D., Sonoda, L.I., Hayes, C., Hill, D.L.G., Leach, M.O., Hawkes, D.J., 1999. Nonrigid registration using free-form deformations: application to breast MR images. IEEE Trans. Med. Imaging 18 (8), 712–721.

Sabuncu, M.R., Yeo, B.T.T., Van Leemput, K., Fischl, B., Golland, P., 2010. A generative model for image segmentation based on label fusion. IEEE Trans. Med. Imaging 29 (10), 1714–1729.

Sandor, S., Leahy, R., 1997. Surface-based labeling of cortical anatomy using a deformable atlas. IEEE Trans. Med. Imaging 16 (1), 41–54.

Ségonne, F., Dale, A.M., Busa, E., Glessner, M., Salat, D., Hahn, H.K., Fischl, B., 2004. A hybrid approach to the skull stripping problem in MRI. NeuroImage 22 (3), 1060–1075.

Shattuck, D.W., Mirza, M., Adisetiyo, V., Hojatkashani, C., Salamon, G., Narr, K.L., Poldrack, R.A., Bilder, R.M., Toga, A.W., 2008. Construction of a 3D probabilistic atlas of human cortical structures. NeuroImage 39 (3), 1064–1080.

Shi, W., Lombaert, H., Bai, W., Ledig, C., Zhuang, X., Marvao, A., Dawes, T., O'Regan, D., Rueckert, D., 2014. Multi-atlas spectral PatchMatch: application to cardiac image segmentation. Accepted at MICCAI.

Smith, S.M., 2002. Fast robust automated brain extraction. Hum. Brain Mapp. 17 (3), 143–155.

Song, Z., Tustison, N., Avants, B., Gee, J.C., 2006. Integrated graph cuts for brain MRI segmentation. In: Medical Image Computing and Computer-Assisted Intervention (MICCAI) 2006, vol. 4191. Lecture Notes in Computer Science, pp. 831–838.

Sotiras, A., Davatzikos, C., Paragios, N., 2013. Deformable medical image registration: a survey. IEEE Trans. Med. Imaging 32 (7), 1153–1190.

Studholme, C., Hill, D.L.G., Hawkes, D.J., 1999. An overlap invariant entropy measure of 3D medical image alignment. Pattern Recogn. 32 (1), 71–86.

Ta, V.T., Giraud, R., Collins, D.L., Coupé, P., 2014. Optimized PatchMatch for near real time and accurate label fusion. In: Medical Image Computing and Computer-Assisted Intervention (MICCAI 2014), Lecture Notes in Computer Science, vol. 8675, pp. 398–406.

Thirion, J.P., 1998. Image matching as a diffusion process: an analogy with Maxwell's demons. Med. Image Anal. 2 (3), 24 60.

Tong, T., Wolz, R., Coupé, P., Hajnal, J.V., Rueckert, D., 2013. Segmentation of MR images via discriminative dictionary learning and sparse coding: application to hippocampus labeling. NeuroImage 76, 11–23.

Tzourio-Mazoyer, N., Landeau, B., Papathanassiou, D., Crivello, F., Etard, O., Delcroix, N., Mazoyer, B., Joliot, M., 2002. Automated anatomical labeling of activations in SPM using a macroscopic anatomical parcellation of the MNI MRI single-subject brain. NeuroImage 15 (1), 273–289.

van der Lijn, F., den Heijer, T., Breteler, M.M.B., Niessen, W.J., 2008. Hippocampus segmentation in MR images using atlas registration, voxel classification, and graph cuts. NeuroImage 43 (4), 708–720.

Van Leemput, K., Maes, F., Vandermeulen, D., Suetens, P., 1999. Automated model-based tissue classification of MR images of the brain. IEEE Trans. Med. Imaging 18 (10), 897–908.

Vercauteren, T., Pennec, X., Perchant, A., Ayache, N., 2009. Diffeomorphic demons: efficient non-parametric image registration. NeuroImage 45 (Suppl. 1), S61–S72.

Viola, P., Wells III, W.M., 1997. Alignment by maximization of mutual information. Int. J. Comput. Vis. 24 (2), 137–154.

Vovk, U., Pernuš, F., Likar, B., 2007. A review of methods for correction of intensity inhomogeneity in MRI. IEEE Trans. Med. Imaging 26 (3), 405–421.

Wang, H., Das, S.R., Suh, J.W., Altinay, M., Pluta, J., Craige, C., Avants, B.B., Yushkevich, P.A., 2011. A learning-based wrapper method to correct systematic errors in automatic image segmentation: consistently improved performance in hippocampus, cortex and brain. NeuroImage 55 (3), 968–985.

Wang, H., Suh, J.W., Das, S.R., Pluta, J., Craige, C., Yushkevich, P.A., 2013. Multi-atlas segmentation with joint label fusion. IEEE Trans. Pattern Anal. Mach. Intell. 35 (3), 611–623.

Warfield, S.K., Zou, K.H., Wells, W.M., 2004. Simultaneous truth and performance level estimation (STAPLE): an algorithm for the validation of image segmentation. IEEE Trans. Med. Imaging 23 (7), 903–921.

Wells III, W.M., Grimson, W.E.L., Kikinis, R., Jolesz, F.A., 1996. Adaptive segmentation of MRI data. IEEE Trans. Med. Imaging 15 (4), 429–442.

Wolz, R., Aljabar, P., Rueckert, D., Heckemann, R.A., Hammers, A., 2009. Segmentation of subcortical structures and the hippocampus in brain MRI using graph-cuts and subject-specific a-priori information. In: IEEE International Symposium on Biomedical Imaging: From Nano to Macro, pp. 470–473.

Wolz, R., Aljabar, P., Hajnal, J.V., Hammers, A., Rueckert, D., 2010a. LEAP: learning embeddings for atlas propagation. NeuroImage 49 (2), 1316–1325.

Wolz, R., Heckemann, R.A., Aljabar, P., Hajnal, J.V., Hammers, A., Lötjönen, J., Rueckert, D., 2010b. Measurement of hippocampal atrophy using 4D graph-cut segmentation: application to ADNI. NeuroImage 52 (1), 109–118.

Worth, A., Tourville, J., 2013. An ever-improving model of the structure of the living human. In: Proceedings of 10th Annual World Congress of Society for Brain Mapping and Therapeutics (SBMT), p. 20, URL http://www.worldbrainmapping.org/docs/2013-Oral%20Poster%20Abstracts.pdf.

Wu, M., Rosano, C., Lopez-Garcia, P., Carter, C.S., Aizenstein, H.J., 2007. Optimum template selection for atlas-based segmentation. NeuroImage 34 (4), 1612–1618.

Xu, L., Krzyzak, A., Suen, C.Y., 1992. Methods of combining multiple classifiers and their applications to handwriting recognition. IEEE Trans. Syst. Man Cybern. 22 (3), 418–435.

Zhang, J., 1992. The mean field theory in EM procedures for Markov random fields. IEEE Trans. Signal Process. 40 (10), 2570–2583.

Zhang, Y., Brady, M., Smith, S., 2001. Segmentation of brain MR images through a hidden Markov random field model and the expectation maximization algorithm. IEEE Trans. Med. Imaging 20 (1), 45–57.

Zitová, B., Flusser, J., 2003. Image registration methods: a survey. Image Vis. Comput. 21 (11), 977–1000.

# PARSING OF THE LUNGS AND AIRWAYS

# 15

## A.P. Kiraly, B.L. Odry and C.L. Novak

*Siemens Corporate Technology, Princeton, NJ, USA*

## CHAPTER OUTLINE

S. Kevin Zhou (Ed): Medical Image Recognition, Segmentation and Parsing. http://dx.doi.org/10.1016/B978-0-12-802581-9.00015-9

## 15.1 INTRODUCTION

This chapter presents methods and applications for the parsing of the lungs and airways in volumetric images. The airways and lungs are the core respiratory system for the human body, with the airways forming a continually branching tree structure within the lung. Human lungs are normally divided by thin fissures into two lobes in the left lung and three in the right. However, due to the variety of different anatomies, anomalies, and diseases, it is difficult to create a detailed lung, lobe, and airway model that will apply to all patients.

Computed tomography (CT) is the most frequently used imaging modality for volumetric assessment of the lungs and airways, due to its fast acquisition and superior imaging of air and surrounding structures. Magnetic resonance (MR) imaging of the lungs is also possible, but requires longer breath holds and special acquisition requirements. Taking this into consideration, we focus on parsing CT chest images, but review applications for MR lung imaging in the final section.

Chest CT images are crucial for diagnosis, therapy planning, and treatment of a wide variety of lung conditions, including lung cancer and chronic obstructive pulmonary disease (COPD). As COPD has become the third leading cause of death in the United States (Murphy et al., 2013), lung imaging is becoming more common for its treatment and evaluation. CT imaging can be used to phenotype COPD, allowing physicians to distinguish airway-predominant disease from emphysema-predominant disease, thereby allowing for more effective treatment plans (Pistolesi et al., 2008; Bafadhel et al., 2011). As lung cancer screening with CT has gained acceptance (Aberle et al., 2011; Wood et al., 2012; Jaklitsch et al., 2012; Wender et al., 2013), there is increasing demand for software to detect and analyze lung lesions in CT images.

A single CT volume typically consists of over 400 individual slices. Thorough manual analysis of the lungs is clinically impractical, and therefore more qualitative evaluation is commonly done. Proposed methods such as Sheehan et al. (2002) for performing a quantitative evaluation of the lungs based on visual inspection have never been clinically adopted, due to the time-consuming nature of manually collecting such measurements. Evaluation of chest CT is often focused on a particular diagnostic question, with corollary findings dependent on the attention of the radiologist. Automation has the potential to reduce operator variability and error, locate findings extraneous to the original purpose of acquisition, and allow for more rapid evaluations.

The parsing of lungs and its components in volumetric datasets is a critical basis for several automated lung analysis tasks. In the following sections, we review reliable methods for airway and lung parsing, including the detection of lobar boundaries, fissures, and parenchyma. In the final section, we review the applications that depend on the successful parsing of the lungs as a basis for further analysis.

## 15.2 OVERVIEW

We introduce the notation and objectives used throughout the rest of the chapter. Figure 15.1 illustrates the flow of steps as well as the general notation.

The core elements involved in parsing the airways and lungs are the following:

1. Delineation of the lungs, vessels, and individual lobes.
2. Delineation and modeling of the airway tree hierarchy.
3. Quantification of the airway tree (i.e., lumen dimensions, wall thickness, etc.).

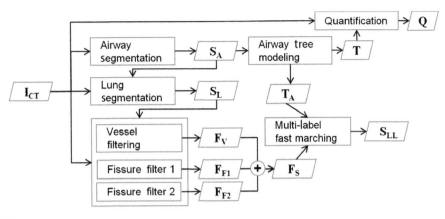

**FIGURE 15.1**

Overview of the described methods for airway and lung parsing: The airway segmentation $S_A$ and lung segmentation $S_L$ form the basis for all following steps. The airway segmentation is used to obtain a model of the airway tree partitioned into lobes $T_A$, and is also used to quantify the airway dimensions $Q$. The lung segmentation, coupled with the original image $I_{CT}$ and the seeds obtained from the partitioned airway tree contribute to the lobar segmentation. The methods are detailed in the text.

We refer to the original CT volume as $I_{CT}$ with the parsing resulting in a segmentation of the lungs $S_L$, further subdivided into lobes $S_{LL}$. The method also computes a segmentation of the airway tree $S_A$, and the airway tree hierarchy $T$. Further details of the components in $T$ are described in Section 15.4 and notation for intermediate results and steps are introduced as necessary.

## 15.3 LUNG AND AIRWAY SEGMENTATION

The lungs are frequently imaged with CT due to the possibility of acquisition within a single breath-hold as well as good delineation of air-filled structures. They appear as nondense structures surrounded by the denser chest wall (Kazerooni, 2001). As a result, there are many successful fully automatic methods for detecting and segmenting the lungs from CT (Beichel et al., 2011).

We describe methods to obtain the lung mask $S_L$ and airway tree segmentation $S_A$ that provide a robust basis for further parsing.

### 15.3.1 AIRWAY SEGMENTATION

A variety of approaches exist to achieve a good extraction of the bronchial tree (Brown et al., 2009). Typically there will be trade-offs between accuracy and speed in order to avoid lengthy preprocessing steps. Trachea detection is usually the first step in parsing the lungs and airways in those approaches that must satisfy performance criteria. It allows for a fast region extraction from an initial seed in the trachea.

One approach for trachea detection is to select a slice from the volume, typically located at 20% of the volume depth, and together with a small number of adjacent slices, look for regions of specific intensity matching air. For each found region, the centroid is compared to an estimated center of the chest, shifted toward the anterior in order not to be mistaken for the esophagus. The trachea is selected as the cluster located closest to the estimated anterior center. Additional criteria, such as the size of the region and distance to the chest boundaries, are taken into account to select the correct region candidate. If no region is found, the process is started again, at a lower depth in the volume, toward the feet.

Once the trachea is detected, the bronchial tree extraction process begins. An adaptive thresholding approach is applied as follows:

1. *Initial extraction*: The center of the region candidate $M_{centroid}$ serves as a seed point to grow the airway tree. First, a layered or adaptive threshold segmentation, constrained both in the number of layers $n_{layers}$ and the overall volume of the tree $V_{tree}$, is run from the seed point $M_{centroid}$, with an initial threshold $t_{init}$.
2. *Layering*: From this initial segmentation $V_{tree}(t_{init})$, a controlled iterative segmentation is performed, increasing the intensity threshold $t_i$ by 1 at each iteration $i$, and therefore adding voxels to the initial volume estimate. At iteration $(i + 1)$, the size of the segmentation is compared to that of iteration $i$ to assess whether the volume increase is legitimate or if it is the result of leakage into the parenchyma. Volume increases are checked against threshold $t_{MaxVolIncrease}$, monitored at each iteration, and recorded when the volume threshold check fails. When this volume threshold verification fails twice in a row (iterations $(i + 1)$ and $(i + 2)$), the segmentation is stopped and rolled back to the volume that was obtained at iteration $i$. Otherwise, the large increase is accepted and the process continues similarly.
3. *Processing*: Average or median filtering can be applied along with the layering process to handle noise generated by low-dose acquisitions and sharp reconstruction kernels.

Once a segmentation is obtained from this method, it can be extended by finding additional branches. Terminal branches are computed based on locally maximal distance values from the trachea seed. From the set of terminal branches, we are now able to apply additional processing to detect new branches.

The first approach is to use local layering, increasing the optimal threshold found by the global approach. This will ensure that parenchyma leaks at low threshold values in one part of the lungs will not prevent segmentation of valid airways elsewhere in the lung. This step is applied at each terminal site to ensure that all airways are grown as much as possible. The same logic of volume control is applied to prevent leakage.

Another method of lengthening the tree is an approach described in Fetita et al. (2004), where axial and radial propagation potentials are used to control the growth of lower-order airways. Our experience has shown that the adaptive method works better with sharp reconstruction kernel data, while the propagation potential approach is more effective with soft reconstruction kernel data. The decision to lengthen the tree can be based on the performance requirements as mentioned earlier. Branch lengthening can add substantial processing time, depending on the number of terminal branches.

Once the tree is obtained, the original seed point $M_{centroid}$ is moved up, to the first slice the trachea is actually detected on. This assists with the tree modeling process.

## 15.3.2 LUNG SEGMENTATION

Lung segmentation is a fundamental step in lung parsing. The lungs are two well-defined regions, so a region-growing approach is appropriate. Seeds are placed in both left and right lungs, and with care taken throughout to ensure that the lungs are not merged into one.

To do so, we employ an iterative process to control the growth and prevent leakages between the left and right lungs. The seed points $S_1 \ldots S_n$ derived from the airway segmentation are directly used to initiate region growing within the left and right lungs. They are derived from the points in the airway tree that fall furthest to the left or right. A fast threshold $t_{fast}$ (we have used $-524$ HU) is utilized to quickly define a surface within a $5 \times 5 \times 5$ cube around the seed points. From these initial surfaces, both lungs are grown simultaneously, for a number $N_1$ of iterations. A second slower growth process is then run with a lower threshold $t_{slow}$ for a number $N_2$ of iterations, with $N_2 < N_1$. The concept is to use a slower growth and thus prevent leakage from one lung to the other. In case of connected lungs, the slow growth process is done again, lowering the slow threshold by 20 HU. Lungs are finally filled to close gaps created by vessels and airways to result in the lung mask $S_L$.

From there, depending on the application, additional processing is done. For instance, for the task of detecting lung nodules, the lung surface can be smoothed out to recover nodules attached to the chest wall. This can be done by morphological operations or by rolling ball processing on the lung surface as in Fan et al. (2002) and Shen et al. (2004). In cases of fibrosis, a thresholding technique will not succeed in segmenting areas of damaged tissue. In these situations, a lung model, using initial elements of the shape obtained by thresholding, can be applied, as in Birbeck et al. (2014).

## 15.4 AIRWAY TREE PARSING

Various approaches exist for obtaining an airway tree model. A common step-wise approach is segmentation, obtaining a skeleton, followed by refinement (Kiraly et al., 2004a). In some methods, both the modeling and segmentation are done simultaneously (Tschirren et al., 2005). We prefer a stepwise approach to allow for a structured implementation. The following describes a skeletonization-based method for obtaining an airway tree hierarchy that is generically applicable to the segmentation of any branching tubular structure.

Figure 15.2 outlines the approach to obtain a hierarchical airway tree model $\mathbf{T}$ from the airway tree segmentation $\mathbf{S_A}$, and a preselected *root site* denoting the approximate starting location of the tree. The computed description of the tree's hierarchy is suitable for further parsing or direct use. The hierarchical tree structure $\mathbf{T} = (\mathbf{V}, \mathbf{B}, \mathbf{P})$ is composed of a set of *L sites* $\mathbf{V} = \{\mathbf{v}_1, \ldots, \mathbf{v}_L\}$, *M branches* $\mathbf{B} = \{\mathbf{b}_1, \ldots, \mathbf{b}_M\}$, and *N paths* starting from the root site $\mathbf{P} = \{\mathbf{p}_1, \ldots, \mathbf{p}_N\}$.

A site $\mathbf{v} = (\mathbf{x}, \mathbf{d})$ specifies a location and direction within the tree, where $\mathbf{x}$ is the *3D location* $(x, y, z)$ within $\mathbf{S_A}$ and $\mathbf{d}$ is a *direction* represented by a quaternion vector $(X, Y, Z, W)$. A quaternion implicitly contains the *direction* and also an up vector to specify a complete camera orientation (Shoemake, 1985; Morrison, 1992). The direction is later used to obtain airway measurements as described in Section 15.6.

A set of sites $\mathbf{v}_a, \mathbf{v}_b, \ldots \mathbf{v}_l \in \mathbf{V}$ define a branch $\mathbf{b} = \{\mathbf{v}_a \ldots \mathbf{v}_l\}$. The final site $\mathbf{v}_l$ of $\mathbf{b}$, or $l_\mathbf{b}$, is either a branching point to the next branch or an end point to the tree. The first site $\mathbf{v}_a$ of $\mathbf{b}$, or $f_\mathbf{b}$, is either the start of a particular branch or the start of the entire tree as is the case for the root branch.

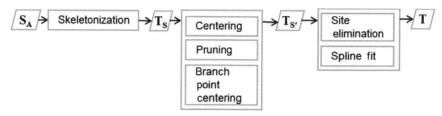

**FIGURE 15.2**

Overview of the steps in computing the hierarchical airway tree structure **T** from the airway segmentation image **S$_A$**. The skeletonization process computes a rough structure **T$_S$** which is later refined into the final result.

Finally, for $\mathbf{p} \in \mathbf{P}$, a path is a complete traversal through the tree from the root to a terminal branch. $\mathbf{p} = \{\mathbf{b}_1 \ldots \mathbf{b}_m\}$ consists of a subset of connected branches $\mathbf{b}_1, \ldots, \mathbf{b}_m \in \mathbf{B}$. All paths $\mathbf{p}$ must start with the root branch $\mathbf{b}_1$ and end with a terminal branch.

The method described for computing the tree model consists of three separate stages, as shown in Figure 15.2. Like many skeletonization approaches, the raw skeleton is computed from a binary image and progressively refined. The first stage computes a 3D skeleton **T$_S$** from the presegmented airway image **S$_A$**, where **S$_A$** is computed using the approach described in Section 15.3. **T$_S$** gives an initial estimate of the tree structure **T** as a 26-connected binary skeleton.

The subsequent two stages refine **T$_S$** to compute the final tree **T**. Stage 2 consists of three operations that center and prune the tree. Stage 3 results in the final smooth subvoxel-interpolated tree description. Section 15.4.1 describes the skeletonization method while the two refinement stages are presented in Section 15.4.2. Figure 15.3 shows an example of the results at each stage.

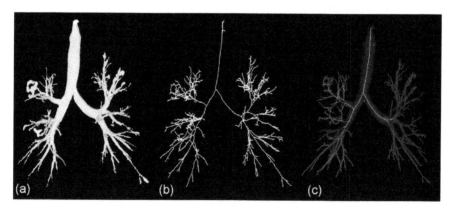

**FIGURE 15.3**

Examples of the tree modeling process. (a) The segmentation of the airway tree; (b) the result of the skeletonization process to produce a tree with rough branches as well as some false branches; and (c) the final result after the refinement stage. The branches are colored according to their classification into the different lobar regions.

## 15.4.1 TREE SKELETON COMPUTATION

The initial 3D skeleton $\mathbf{T_S}$ is produced by selectively removing foreground voxels (belonging to the segmentation) until a thin 26-connected structure of the original segmented image $\mathbf{S_A}$ remains. In general, the selective removal of voxels must preserve the homotopy of the original structure while attempting to retain as much of its original geometry as possible. Various skeletonization approaches exist that are tailored to meshes (Au et al., 2008; Cao et al., 2010), volume surfaces (Saha et al., 1994, 1997), or tubular structures (Wan et al., 2002; Tschirren et al., 2003; Yu et al., 2003; Kiraly et al., 2004a).

The method described here is similar to Kiraly et al. (2004a) but improves the skeletonization by more accurate distance transforms and reduces the type of refinements. In Saha et al. (1994, 1997), a *simple point* is defined as a voxel in a binary image for which its removal does not change the homotopy of the object. The skeletonization proceeds by removing simple points in a particular order while preserving special marked points:

- Compute distance transform of $\mathbf{S_A}$ from the given root site, yielding $\mathbf{S_R}$.
- Mark locally maximum distance values as special points.
- Compute distance transform of $\mathbf{S_A}$ from the surface, to yield $\mathbf{S_D}$.
- Remove simple points in order of distance values (low to high).

The distance transform used in these steps is computed using an efficient implementation of the multi-pass scanning method to compute a true Euclidean distance (Bailey, 2004). Next, locally maximum distance values are used to mark special points that are not deleted. This is similar to the approach used in Zhou and Toga (1999) but with a different distance transform.

The second distance transform image, $\mathbf{S_D}$, is used to queue the simple points that are iteratively deleted. The result is a voxel-level discrete skeleton that exhibits local deviations and false branches from the ideal central axis as shown in Figure 15.3(b). The second distance transform is used for the refinement stages as well.

In order to proceed to the next stages, the discrete binary tree is converted to the tree structure $\mathbf{T}$. Each voxel is converted into a site $\mathbf{v}$ by a recursive process. The conversion of the skeleton to $\mathbf{T}$ begins at the voxel closest to the root site and follows its 26-connected neighbors to define the root branch $\mathbf{b_1}$. When an encountered voxel has only two neighbors, it is stored as a site in $\mathbf{V}$ and added to branch $\mathbf{b_1}$. Otherwise, with three or more neighbors, a branch point is identified and (two or more) new branches begin, $\mathbf{b_2}$ and $\mathbf{b_3}$. This process continues recursively for new branches until the entire skeleton has been processed. Once in this data structure, subsequent processing to delete or move sites will not change the tree's basic homotopy, only its geometry.

## 15.4.2 TREE REFINEMENT

The main purpose of Stages 2 and 3 is to eliminate false branches typically contained in the initial skeleton and to create a subvoxel centered tree structure. The steps of Stage 2 consist of the following operations:

- voxel-level centering
- branch pruning
- branch point centering

During each step, the tree **T** is updated. Note that changes to site positions do not impact the tree homotopy since they are stored in an ordered basis at the branch level. At this point further changes only impact the geometry of the tree. Intuitively, a false branch is one that is not a true airway branch and merely an artifact of the skeletonization process.

Voxel-level centering iteratively moves each site $v \in$ **T**, aside from those specially marked initially, toward maximally local values in the distance image $S_D$. In other words, sites are iteratively moved until they reach the locally maximal distance from the segmentation boundary. For each site **v**, its 3D location **x** is shifted in space to 3D location **y** when

$$S_D(\mathbf{y}) > S_D(\mathbf{x}) \quad \text{and} \quad \mathbf{y} \in N_{26}(\mathbf{x}) \tag{15.1}$$

where $N_{26}(\mathbf{x})$ represents the 26-connected neighbors of **x** and $S_D(\cdot)$ gives the distance from the surface that was previously computed. This operation is continued until the following condition holds:

$$\forall \mathbf{z} \in N_{26}(\mathbf{x}), \quad S_D(\mathbf{z}) \leq S_D(\mathbf{x})$$

Once a local maxima is achieved, the distance value is temporarily associated with each site **v** and referred to as $S_D(\mathbf{v})$.

Next, branches are eliminated (pruned) based on a distance ratio with parent branches. Relatively short terminal branches that are unlikely to be true branches are eliminated. In essence, a terminal branch is eliminated if it does not extend a sufficient length beyond a sphere inscribed about its parent branch point. The following is used to identify such branches:

$$\frac{L_\mathbf{b} - S_D(l_{\mathbf{b_P}})}{S_D(l_{\mathbf{b_P}})} < 1 \tag{15.2}$$

where $L_\mathbf{b}$ is the length of a branch **b**, measured as the sum of the distances between consecutive branch sites, $\mathbf{b_P}$ represents the parent branch of **b**, and $l_{\mathbf{b_P}}$ is the last site of $\mathbf{b_P}$. Criterion (Eq. 15.2) deletes a branch that does not extend at least one radius beyond its parent's branch-point region. This eliminates a branch that is short relative to its parent's branch-point region of support. The final step in Stage 2 focuses on the final site of each nonterminal branch. The location of the first site of each child branch is averaged with last site of the parent branch to provide a definitive location for the bifurcation site.

The third and final stage concerns the creation of subvoxel smooth sites with viewing directions assigned to the quaternions. A cubic uniform (third-order) open B-spline is fit to the locations forming each branch, and interpolates a new set of equally spaced 3D locations along each branch fit. Before this spline can be smoothly fit, redundant information is first eliminated by removing near-by sites along each branch. This is accomplished by eliminating sites within the maximally inscribable sphere at the beginning and end of each branch, followed by the intermediate sites.

These eliminated sites are chosen so that they do not alter the tree geometry, shorten tree branches, or result in a subsequently fitted spline to reach outside of the segmentation $S_A$. The tree's branch points, which define the tree's branch hierarchy, and the individual branches themselves are retained. Given the branches ordered by generation and subordered by length, the following operations are applied to each branch $\mathbf{b} \in \mathbf{B}$. For each site $v \in \mathbf{b}$, starting with $l_\mathbf{b}$ and considered in reverse order, eliminate any site $\mathbf{v} \in \mathbf{V}$ if

$$\mathbf{v} \in S_D(\nu) \quad \text{and} \quad \mathbf{v} \neq \nu \tag{15.3}$$

where $\mathbf{S_D}(\cdot)$ was defined as in Eq. (15.1). This process preserves and favors branch points ($l_b$ for branches $\mathbf{b} \in \mathbf{B}$). The result is a tree with sparse branches for which the spline fitting can be applied smoothly.

Once again, a cubic uniform (third-order) open B-spline is fit to the remaining 3D locations and interpolated into a new set of equally spaced 3D locations along each branch fit (Swift et al., 2002). The sites are interpolated at a resolution equal to the minimum of the $x$, $y$, and $z$ sampling intervals of the original image. It is also possible to perform spline fitting directly on the integer-valued viewing sites available after Stage 2. While the resulting splines would be smooth, they would have numerous erroneous undulations.

The 3D locations $\mathbf{x}$ for the set of sites need no further change, but the viewing directions $\mathbf{d}$ still are needed. The direction obtained from the B-spline can be directly set as the viewing direction $\mathbf{d}$ for each site. For the case of obtaining measurements, this approach is sufficient, but for a smooth visualization proceeding though the sites, the camera up orientation must be preserved. This can be accomplished using the method described in Paik et al. (1998). To do this, we leave the up vector for the first viewing site $\mathbf{b}(1)$ unchanged. Next, for $\mathbf{b}(2)$, we project $\mathbf{b}(1)$'s up vector onto the plane perpendicular to $\mathbf{b}(2) = (\mathbf{x}(2), \mathbf{d}(2))$. This projected up vector is used as the new up vector of $\mathbf{d}(2)$, and performed recursively throughout the tree.

The result is a tree structure with smooth paths for a complete hierarchical description of the airway tree or any other hierarchical tree structure given in a segmented form.

## 15.5 LOBAR SEGMENTATION

The lungs are subdivided into lobes separated by very thin fissures. Recognition of the lobar boundaries is important for the diagnosis and treatment of many diseases of the lungs, and radiologists routinely report lung abnormalities according to the lobe(s) in which they fall. In normal human anatomy, there are three lobes on the right and two on the left.

Due to the extent of the fissures, manual delineation of the lobar boundaries is infeasible in most clinical settings. Thus, an automatic method is highly desirable. However, the fissures defining the lobar divisions are often difficult to visualize even in high resolution CT. Furthermore, a substantial fraction of patients have incomplete or missing fissures. In addition, many disease conditions can cause additional difficulties in detecting the fissures. Figure 15.4 shows examples of fissure appearances.

Fully automatic approaches to lung lobe segmentation can be broadly divided into boundary-based or region-based methods. Among boundary-based approaches that directly target the detection of fissures, Pu et al. (2009) proposed a threshold on the lungs to identify patches of fissures. Zhang et al. used an atlas to initialize fissure locations; these were refined by a ridgeness operator and the method achieved an average root mean square error of less than 2 mm on normal datasets. Van Rikxoort et al. (2010) made use of a multi-atlas approach that performed well on low-dose data but had a running time of 2 h. An atlas-based approach for lobe location followed by multi-label graph cuts was proposed by Nimura et al. (2012).

Region-based methods are based around a core method to define lobar regions. Wiemker et al. (2005) introduced a segmentation framework based upon competitive region growing, and proposed Hessian-based filters for the enhancement of fissures, from which distance maps were computed. Hessian-based fissure filtering has become the basis for fissure filtering in later methods including the

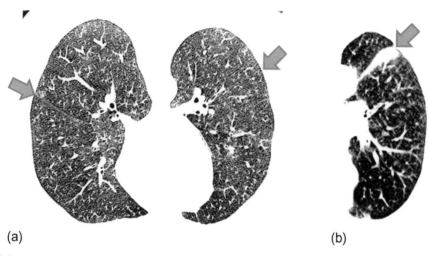

(a)            (b)

**FIGURE 15.4**

Examples of fissures from axial CT slices. (a) The arrow on the left shows a typical visible fissure. Note that vessels are rarely near fissure locations. The arrow on the right of (a) shows a region where the fissure is barely visible. (b) An extremely thick fissure (indicated by the arrow).

method described below. Kuhnigk et al. (2005) introduced a framework for lobar segmentation based on the watershed transform. Recently, Lassen et al. (2013) extended this framework with the use of airways, fissures, and vessels and evaluated the method on thin-slice normal dose data to achieve an average error on the order of 1 mm.

As previously illustrated in Figure 15.1 the lobe segmentation method described here is composed of several steps, detailed in the next sections. An example result from the method is shown in Figure 15.5.

### 15.5.1 AIRWAY TREE MODELING AND SEED GENERATION

The segmented airway tree provides the basis for the localization of the lobar seeds. We determine an airway segmentation and path structure using the method in Section 15.4. Again, the result is a series of three-dimensional (3D) locations that form a hierarchy of branches. Each terminal branch, that is, the last branch on a given path, is classified into one of the five lobar regions.

Path divergence is used to classify the terminal branches. This process is started by determining the point of divergence between paths to the left and right lungs to localize the carina. Next, general anatomical directions (left/right, anterior/posterior) based upon patient orientation are used to determine further path divergences and obtain the divisions into upper, middle, and lower lobes. The result is five sets of seed points for the final processing into a segmentation for each lobe $S_1 \ldots S_5$.

### 15.5.2 FISSURE AND VESSEL LOCALIZATION

Lung segmentation is first performed to isolate the region for vessel and fissure localization, as described in Section 15.3. Given the computed lung mask $\mathbf{S}_L$, vessel segmentation and fissure filter

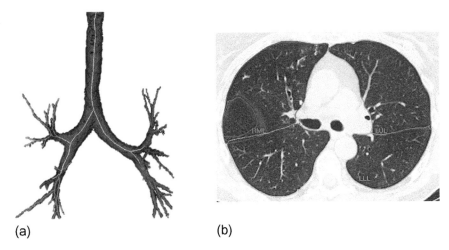

(a)                              (b)

**FIGURE 15.5**

An example of a segmented airway with branches classified according to lobe shown in (a). The end points of each branch are used as seeds for a multi-label fast marching. The axial CT slice in (b) shows the regions of the lung divided by the fissures, resulting in two lobes in the left lung and three in the right lung.

operations are performed within its confines. The Hessian matrix $\mathbf{H}$ is computed on the image to obtained the sorted eigenvalues $|\lambda_1| \leq |\lambda_2| \leq |\lambda_3|$. Plate or tube like structures are characterized based upon the ratio of values. All operators are computed at locations within the lung mask $\mathbf{S_L}$ on the original image $\mathbf{I_{CT}}$ and utilize specific threshold ranges for fissures and vessels. Only a single scale $\sigma$ of the in-plane voxel spacing is used since fissures tend to be thin structures, and only thin vessels (which are near fissure boundaries) are of interest. These operations result in the first fissure image $\mathbf{F_{F1}}$ and the vessel segmentation image $\mathbf{F_V}$.

Additionally, we make use of a second fissure filter based on first-order derivative approximation of the Gaussian function. A directional Gaussian is computed in 3D to obtain plate-like features. Those above a set threshold are kept, and a gradient vector-based connected component labeling is used to keep components with more than 100 voxels for both fissure filtered images. This results in $\mathbf{F_{F2}}$.

### 15.5.3 MULTI-LABEL FAST MARCHING

The fissure likelihood image $\mathbf{F_S}$ is computed from the vessel and fissure filter images, $\mathbf{F_V}$, $\mathbf{F_{F1}}$, and $\mathbf{F_{F2}}$. The union of the fissure filter images is taken and a distance transform is applied within a region of 12 mm. The same is done for the vessel image $\mathbf{F_V}$. The vessel image is then inverted such that the vessel locations contain the greatest distance value. The sum of the two images is taken. The end result is a speed image that allows fronts to propagate quickly through vessels and slowly near any fissure locations.

A multi-label fast marching approach is described in Sifakis and Tziritas (2001). We take this approach in 3D to perform a fast marching to solve the following:

$$\|\nabla T(\mathbf{x})\| = \frac{1}{\mathbf{F_S(x)}'} \tag{15.4}$$

where $\mathbf{x} = (x, y, z)$ is a 3D location in the image, $T(\mathbf{x})$ is the volume of crossing times, and $\mathbf{F_S(x)}$ determines the propagation speed.

First, the seeds $S_1 \ldots S_5$ are set to distance value 0. The propagation speed image $\mathbf{F_S}$ modulates the speed of the front. Instead of using a standard fast marching approach, the labels are also propagated to define regions simultaneously.

Once the fast marching is completed, the labels are also propagated and the image is labeled with the lobe regions. Each lung is computed independently to take advantage of multi-threading. The fissure locations are then identified as the crossing between two different labels.

## 15.6 QUANTIFICATION OF AIRWAY DIMENSIONS

Abnormal airways have been known for several years to be a contributing factor to reduced airflow in diseases such as chronic obstructive pulmonary diseases (COPDs) and asthma. The quantification of airway dimensions, that is, lumen diameter and wall thickness, are critical in assessing extent and severity of related diseases. There has been a renewed focus on methodologies to accurately measure airway characteristics with more objective means than the visual assessment routinely used clinically.

Since the full-width-half-maximum (FWHM) approach was proposed in 1993 (Amirav et al., 1993) as the first to give accurate measurements of airway characteristics, new techniques have been developed to improve upon it. In Kiraly et al. (2005), FWHM is extended with a segmentation-limited option that uses thresholding for estimation of the lumen. Another FWHM improvement in Wiemker et al. (2004) focuses on an unsupervised computation of bronchial lumen and wall thickness using radial derivatives along a sphere radius. In Saba et al. (2003), measurements are based upon the scanner point spread function (PSF) to provide a better estimate of the error and thereby provide additional accuracy.

Morphological filtering-based methods have also been developed, as in Preteux et al. (1997), where connection cost-based marking and conditional watershed techniques are utilized. Additional examples are provided by Kiraly et al. (2007) and Tschirren et al. (2005) where minimum-cost functions based on first- and second-order derivatives to estimate inner and outer airway contours are used. Measurements are computed on radially resampled cross-sections with the need for calibration of weights to compensate for over- and under-segmentation caused by derivatives.

FMWH is commonly considered as a reference for airway quantification, as none of the newer methods has truly emerged as a standard. We will therefore try to address the robustness aspect of FWHM, by integrating checks to the original approach, and by including additional analysis to improve overall accuracy and robustness of the measurements.

### 15.6.1 FWHM IMPROVEMENTS

The FWHM method uses the profiles from rays cast in all directions around the center of an airway in order to determine the positions of airway walls. There is no specific connection or relationship between the computed wall positions from one ray profile to the next. In the usual case where there

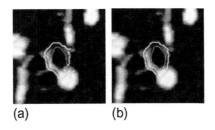

(a)                    (b)

**FIGURE 15.6**

FWHM result (a) and modified FWHM result (b). Lumen contour does not leak into the airway wall, and outer contour is brought back in, limiting leaks into the accompanying artery.

are partial volume effects around the airway, this can lead to irregular contours, as well as over- or under-segmentation of the lumen and/or wall.

We first focus on providing a robust center for the ray-casting process, by locally computing the center of the lumen airway from the 2D airway cross-section. Using a first pass of the FWHM, we determine a luminal area and define the center as the center of mass of this area. The airway wall's inner and outer contours, expressed as distances from this center point, are smoothed to prevent large distances between consecutive contour points and to address the lack of continuity between consecutive measurements. A gradient is applied throughout the contours, and sections of the contours exhibiting large differences are detected. Those sections correspond to under- or over-segmentation of the luminal and wall areas. Contours are recovered using a linear transformation from the beginning to end of the section (Odry et al., 2012). Figure 15.6 shows an example airway before and after the improvement process.

## 15.6.2 ACTIVE CONTOUR

The FWHM method provides an initial estimation of airway dimensions. We use the context of the image to improve this estimation with the help of an active contour (AC). As we unravel the cross section perpendicular to the airway, the inner and outer boundary segmentations should ideally correspond to a line as shown in Figure 15.7. This makes it easier to deal with partial volume effects and to prevent leakage into the parenchyma. The airway segmentation is performed in two steps, one for each boundary. Outer wall estimation is computed after the final inner boundary segmentation so that it can make use of the inner wall information.

### 15.6.2.1 Inner contour estimation

We define an initial contour $C$ as a horizontal line across the luminal area. Here, to simplify the process, we consider $C$ as a polygon instead of the implicit active contour. The number of points of the polygon is stable during the curve evolution process, since it depends on the resolution of the unraveled image. Each point $p_i$ on the polygon is issued from ray $i$ at angle $\theta_i$, with a radius $r(\theta_i)$ from the image center. The connection of all the neighboring points represents the polygon. Each polygon point is expressed as:

(a)                    (b)

**FIGURE 15.7**

Cross section (a) and corresponding unraveled image (b). The lumen area is shown at the bottom of the unraveled image.

$$p_i = p(i) = \begin{pmatrix} \theta_i \\ r(\theta_i) \end{pmatrix}$$

(15.5)

The inner wall estimation consists of finding a partial differential equation (PDE) that updates $r(\theta_i)$ such that the energy is minimized. Considering the uniformity of the luminal area, we choose to use a region-based segmentation to separate it from the rest of the image. To preserve the circularity of the boundary, we also add a smoothness constraint between the points along the curve. The active contour energy equation that we use can be expressed as follows:

$$E(C) = \lambda_1 \int_{\Omega_{in}} ((I(p_i) - \mu_{in}))^2 \, d\Omega_{in} + \lambda_2 \int_{\Omega_{out}} ((I(p_i) - \mu_{out}))^2 \, d\Omega_{out} + \alpha \cdot \text{Length}(C)$$

(15.6)

where $I(p_i)$ is the value of the image at $p_i$. $\Omega_{in}$ and $\Omega_{out}$ represent the areas below (lumen) and above (parenchyma) the contour. Here, the area term is not utilized. $\mu_{in}$ and $\mu_{out}$ are the means inside and outside the contour, or here, the regions below and above the contour. $\alpha$ is a term that weights the curvature term relative to the data term, while $\lambda_1$ and $\lambda_2$ are fixed parameters determined empirically.

The length of the contour "Length(C)" is expressed via the curvature "alpha", as expressed in the speed term definition. More specifically in our case, the speed term $\frac{\partial r}{\partial t} = F \cdot N$ where $F$ is the force term that deforms the contour and $N$ is the normal to the polygonal point $p_i$.

$$\frac{\partial r}{\partial t} = (\lambda_1(I(p_i) - \mu_{in})^2 + \lambda_2(I(p_i) - \mu_{out})^2) + \alpha \cdot K \cdot N \bullet \begin{pmatrix} 0 \\ 1 \end{pmatrix}$$

(15.7)

$K$ is the curvature of the curve at $p_i$. The update vector is oriented along the curve normal. The last dot product $\bullet$ projects the vector onto the y-axis of the transformed image along which $r(\theta_i)$ is evolved. Since the image is unraveled, the curvature is computed using both ends of the image to create the closed contour.

As described previously, we use the output of the FWHM to initialize the AC. Usually, the contour converges to a minimum after a few iterations. Figure 15.8 shows the inner contour after FWHM initialization and after convergence. The AC helps reduce over-segmentation by the FWHM.

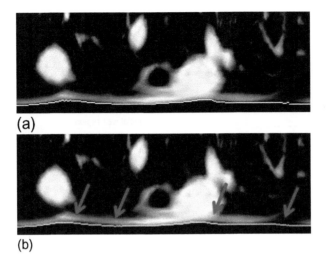

(a)

(b)

**FIGURE 15.8**

Inner contour segmentation (a) initial FWHM measurement (b) active contour adjustment, converging after 11 iterations. The red arrows point to the slight differences with the FWHM results.

### 15.6.2.2 Outer wall estimation

Similarly, the outer contour from the FWHM is used as an initialization of the outer active contour (see Figure 15.6). We base the approach for computing the outer wall boundary on the method from Odry et al. (2008b) and adjust the equation based on the fact that the initial estimate of the contour has already been calculated from FWHM.

The outer contour minimization is defined as follows:

$$\frac{\partial r}{\partial t} = \begin{pmatrix} \lambda_1(I(p_{outer}(i)) - \upsilon_{wall}(d_i))^2 + \lambda_2(I(p_{outer}(i)) - \upsilon_{par}(d_i))^2 \\ +\alpha \cdot K \\ -(d_i - \overline{d}) \cdot H(I(p_{outer}(i)) - \omega \cdot \mu_{wall}) \end{pmatrix} \cdot N \bullet \begin{pmatrix} 0 \\ 1 \end{pmatrix} \qquad (15.8)$$

with $\upsilon_{wall}$ being the intensity average between inner and outer contour points $p_{inner}(i)$ and $p_{outer}(i)$ at location $\theta_i$. $\upsilon_{par}$ is the intensity average between $p_{outer}(i)$ and $p_{par}(i)$. $p_{inner}(i)$ is the symmetrical point with respect to $p_{outer}(i)$, located in the parenchyma, as shown in Figure 15.9. $H$ represents the Heaviside function $H(x)$. The goal is to prevent growth into bright nonwall structures such as adjacent vessels. The intensity at $p_{outer}(i)$ is compared to the average intensity of the whole wall, $\mu_{wall}$. A higher intensity value at $p_{outer}(i)$ aims to decrease the wall size at this location; $d_i$ and $\overline{d}$ represent the wall size at $\theta_i$ and the average wall thickness, respectively, and $\omega$ is set to 1.0.

In our case, since the initial contour is estimated thanks to the FWHM process, the equation needs to be adjusted. To avoid a long convergence time and getting stuck in a local minima (possibly causing a completely erroneous segmentation), we add an additional curvature feature in the equation $K_{large}$, based on a larger scale. In Eq. (15.8), the curvature was computed from the immediate neighbors of $p_{outer}(i)$. This term will now become $K_{small}$, while the larger scale curvature feature is computed based

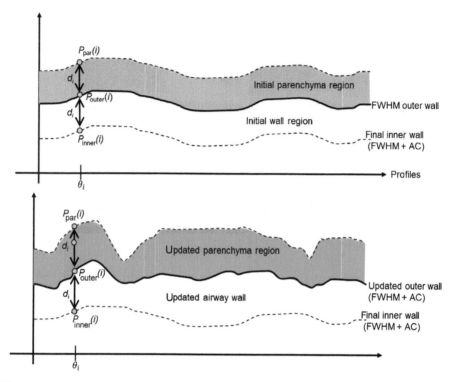

**FIGURE 15.9**

Update of outer contour, based on a local region-based process. The top graph depicts the initial estimation of the outer wall from the final inner wall segmentation using the combined full width half maximum (FWHM) and active contour (AC) methods. The distance $d_i$ between polygon points $p_{inner}(i)$ and $p_{outer}(i)$ is equal along the contour. In tan is the targeted region within $d_i$ distance of the outer wall. On the bottom graph, the outer wall evolves as the distance between $p_{inner}(i)$ and $p_{outer}(i)$ does. Region-based segmentation is done using the targeted density region in tan defined by $p_{par}(i)$ and the region in white between outer and inner wall estimates.

on distant neighbors—five voxels apart—on each side. This allows for a quicker straightening of the curve, with the focus here being on compensating for discontinuities.

Additionally, now that some of the contour points can be far outside the wall, landing in the parenchyma, we extend the use of the Heaviside function $H(x)$. It will also exclude from the wall those voxels with intensities outside of 75% and 115% of the wall mean, instead of just excluding bright areas. The complete speed term becomes:

$$\frac{\partial r}{\partial t} = \begin{pmatrix} \lambda_1(I(p_{outer}(i)) - v_{wall}(d_i))^2 + \lambda_2(I(p_{outer}(i)) - v_{par}(d_i))^2 \\ +\alpha_1 \cdot K_{small} + \alpha_2 \cdot K_{large} \\ -(d_i - \bar{d}) \cdot H(I(p_{outer}(i)) - \omega_1 \cdot \mu_{wall}) - (d_i - \bar{d}) \cdot H(\omega_2 \cdot \mu_{wall} - I(p_{outer}(i))) \end{pmatrix} \cdot N \bullet \begin{pmatrix} 0 \\ 1 \end{pmatrix}$$

$$(15.9)$$

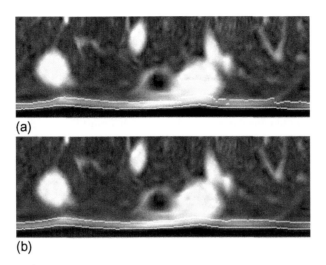

**FIGURE 15.10**

Outer wall segmentation. On top, initialization from FWHM computation. We can see discontinuities in the FWHM that the active contour should correct. On the bottom, active contour after convergence, with the adjacent artery excluded.

$\omega_1 = 1.15$ and $\omega_2 = 0.75$. Those values can be adjusted depending upon the application this method is used for. Figure 15.10 shows the result of the active contour iterations.

### 15.6.2.3 Convergence

At each AC evolution, a convergence value is computed by summing the displacement of the curve along its length. The active contour is evolved for about 500 iterations. The curve representing those displacements (in mm) is generated. From the convergence graph, multiple local minima are selected and the contour iteration that shows the lowest average density is selected as the final step of the evolution of the active contour.

The result is a method that combines two existing measurement methods, whereby the first is used as an initialization for the second approach. Specifically the FWHM approach is used as an initialization for the AC approach. The advantage of combining both methods is a more robust outcome for determining the contours that delineate the lumen and wall extent.

Given the final contours to define the extent of the lumen and wall, it is straightforward to determine the lumen diameter, lumen area, wall thickness, and wall area. These measurements may be used to detect and quantify diseased airways as described in the applications section.

## 15.7 APPLICATIONS

There are a wide variety of clinical applications that require or benefit from a parsing of the lungs. The following outlines how different parsing capabilities are used in a variety of diagnostic tasks.

## 15.7.1 LUNG SEGMENTATION

The segmentation of a thoracic scan to produce a lung mask that distinguishes lung from nonlung areas is a common first step in many automatic algorithms for detecting disease, including lung nodule detection (e.g., Goo et al., 2003; Ge et al., 2005) and pulmonary embolism (PE) detection (e.g., Zhou et al., 2007; Wittenberg et al., 2010). Automatic detection of the lungs allows subsequent processing to limit operations to relevant areas, reducing possible false positives in nonlung areas, and increasing the speed of the algorithm by reducing the areas of the image that must be considered. Automatic detection of the lung area also allows quantification of the lung volume for applications such as evaluating the severity of emphysema (Gierada et al., 2010; Dijkstra et al., 2013) and for planning surgery (Morimura et al., 2013; Lee et al., 2014).

## 15.7.2 LUNG LOBE SEGMENTATION

Similarly the automatic division of the lungs into the lobes is also highly useful for evaluating emphysema, as physicians typically want to measure the severity of emphysema in each lobe. Although the lobes can be challenging to segment accurately due to the difficulty of detecting the fissures and the prevalence of incomplete fissures, the distribution of disease by lobe is a key indicator used to plan treatments for emphysema. Treatments that depend on knowledge of the lobe boundaries include living-donor lobar lung transplantation (Starnes et al., 2004), surgical removal of diseased lobes (Washko et al., 2008), and nonsurgical alternatives such as one-valve placement to collapse diseased lobes (Fiorelli et al., 2014) or thermal ablation of diseased lobes (Herth et al., 2012).

Another common use for lobe segmentation is for automated reporting of findings. When radiologists report detected abnormalities, they typically indicate in which lobe the finding is located. Automated lobe segmentation can speed up the workflow by automatically assigning a finding to the correct lobe and including that information in the report. The lobar location of findings is also used in planning interventions such as biopsy or radiotherapy.

## 15.7.3 AIRWAY SEGMENTATION

Automatic detection and segmentation of the bronchial tree is a common preprocessing step in several applications, including automatic detection of the lobar boundaries. Since the fissures are typically not well visualized in scans, and since many patients have missing or incomplete fissures, a segmentation of the bronchial tree is frequently used to help delineate the location and extent of each lobe (e.g., Ross et al., 2009; Lassen et al., 2013).

Airway segmentation is also used in planning interventions such as bronchoscopic evaluation of the lungs, as a model of the pathways through the lungs may be used to plan the best approach to an area that will be biopsied (Kiraly et al., 2004b; Mori et al., 2005). The airway tree model may also be useful for planning other interventions such as one-way valve placement for emphysema treatment (Fiorelli et al., 2014) or bronchial thermoplasty for asthma treatment (Dombret et al., 2014), in order to determine where treatment should take place and to estimate the amount of lung that will be affected.

Segmentation of the airway tree, followed by measurement of the dimensions of the branches is utilized in evaluation of diseases of the airways, including chronic obstructive pulmonary disorder (COPD), cystic fibrosis (CF), and asthma (Robinson, 2007; Mets et al., 2013; Asker et al., 2014). Measurements of the lumen diameter (or area), wall diameter (or area), and ratios of airway dimensions can be used to diagnose airway diseases and monitor therapy. These measurements have the potential to be used to personalize therapy to individual patients according to who is and is not responding to a given treatment, and may be used in clinical trials to evaluate new therapies.

### 15.7.4 PULMONARY VESSEL SEGMENTATION

In addition to the pulmonary airway tree, the lungs contain branching trees of both pulmonary arteries and pulmonary veins. The automatic detection and segmentation of these vessels may be used as a first step in localizing possible locations of pulmonary emboli (Zhou et al., 2007; Bouma et al., 2009). Localization of vessels is also used in many automatic lung lobe segmentation algorithms (Ross et al., 2009; Lassen et al., 2013). It has been frequently observed that pulmonary vessels seldom cross fissure boundaries, so their absence is a key feature that can be used in localizing lobar boundaries.

In healthy lungs, bronchial segments are generally paralleled by a pulmonary artery of similar size. This observation has allowed radiologists to use the relative sizes of an airway branch and its adjacent artery to diagnose abnormally dilated airways. In a healthy airway, the ratio of the bronchial lumen to the adjacent artery should be approximately 1.0. The "signet ring sign," where the lumen is much larger than the adjacent artery, is an indicator of bronchiectasis (Algin et al., 2011). It is also possible for computer algorithms to automatically locate the accompanying artery, compute the lumen-to-artery ratio, and report this measurement (Odry et al., 2008a).

### 15.7.5 THORACIC LANDMARK DETECTION

In addition to the boundaries of the lungs, lobes, airways, and pulmonary vessels, additional landmarks near the lungs may by automatically identified and used to aid in the performance of a clinical application. One such task is the automatic classification of lymph nodes into stations (Kongkuo et al., 2008). The assignment of lymph nodes to the correct region of the body, or station, is used in lung cancer staging. The stations are defined by key landmarks including the trachea, carina, and aortic arch. Automatic localization of these landmarks can be used in automating the reporting of involved lymph nodes for greater speed and reliability.

### 15.7.6 PARENCHYMAL SEGMENTATION AND EVALUATION

Given the overall lung volume, the regions of the lungs corresponding to the parenchyma may be identified by subtracting the airways and vessels. Given a mask of the parenchyma, it is straightforward to calculate the percentage of the lungs that are below a threshold to yield the emphysema index (Heussel et al., 2009). Additional quantitative measurements of emphysema may be obtained, including percentiles, slope, and relative size of bullae (Blechschmidt et al., 2001; Madani et al., 2006; Chae et al., 2010). There has also been research on automatic differentiation between centrilobular emphysema and other types (Kim et al., 2009).

The lung parenchyma may be evaluated following contrast administration to detect perfusion deficits caused by pulmonary embolism or other conditions. Automatic detection of the parenchymal region is used to exclude irrelevant areas from the visualization of the result, in order to ease interpretation.

Patterns or textures within the parenchyma may also be indicative of diseases such as interstitial lung disease (ILD), and techniques have been developed to automatically detect and classify regions of the lung parenchyma according to disease type (Iwasawa et al., 2009; Park et al., 2009).

### 15.7.7 EXPIRATION IMAGING

Although most research on lung parsing assumes that the lungs are imaged at full inspiration, it is becoming increasingly common to acquire a scan at expiration as well. This allows physicians to look for areas of air trapping where the patient is not effectively exhaling from some regions of the lungs, and to detect bronchomalacia, where the patient's bronchi collapse during expiration. Automated technology to detect air trapping or malacia are still in the earliest stages (Goris et al., 2003; Bogoni and Valadez, 2012), but methods to parse both inspiration and expiration images of a patient, and then match them to each other, would be a welcome tool for pulmonary evaluation.

### 15.7.8 MR IMAGING

Although the algorithms described in Sections 15.2 through 15.6 assume that the lungs are imaged with CT, there are some promising new research techniques for imaging the lungs with MR (e.g., Woodhouse et al., 2005; de Lange et al., 2007; Mugler et al., 2010; Revel et al., 2012; Wielpuetz et al., 2014). The appearance of the lungs in MR is quite different from that in CT, and varies greatly according to the specific pulse sequence. Thus, current algorithms based on CT acquisition may have to be extensively modified for use in MR. As MR lung imaging technology becomes used clinically, we may expect to see the development of new algorithms created or adapted for parsing the lungs from MR images.

### 15.8 CONCLUSION

The lungs and airways exhibit substantial variations in appearance between individuals due to natural variations in anatomy, respiration, and cardiac motion, as well as the effects of pulmonary diseases. At the same time, the lung appearance in CT is also very well delineated between air and soft tissue, allowing the use of low dose acquisition techniques for many applications. Machine learning techniques hold promise as more labeled data becomes available. To date, these techniques have been applied only to the detection of a single type of abnormality, such as lung nodules or pulmonary emboli, and proposed for the detection of structures such as the lung fissures. A complete analysis of the type performed by radiologists, who are tasked with detecting all types of abnormalities, remains many years in the future. Recently, deep neural networks with unsupervised learning have shown remarkable results in a wide variety of topics, including image processing (Bengio, 2009; Le, 2013). Given enough data, sparse autoencoders that can automatically derive features are useful to classify and segment structures such as airways. An early example of results with a sparse autoencoder applied to regions of the lungs is shown in Figure 15.11. Unlike previous approaches of applying machine learning techniques for lung imaging, this approach does not require a list of features but derives the features automatically. We anticipate that such techniques will play a key role in providing the segmentation of fine structures of the lungs and airways in the future.

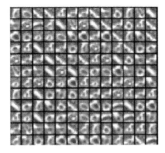

**FIGURE 15.11**

Initial learned filters from deep learning methods applied to detect airways and fissures. A visualization of the resulting filters derived from a convolutional sparse encoding of lung regions within a CT volume is shown.

The segmentation, classification, and quantification of the lungs, lobes, vasculature, and the airway tree from images of the chest serve as the core foundation for many important medical applications. These range from diagnosis and surgical planning, to assisting in research on new treatments. As medical imaging devices acquire ever more detailed images of the lungs, both in terms of spatial and temporal resolution, manual image interpretation will become increasingly impractical. Thus, automated parsing methods will play an increasingly critical role in both clinical and research settings.

# REFERENCES

Aberle, D.R., Adams, A.M., Berg, C.D., Black, W.C., Clapp, J.D., Fagerstrom, R.M., Gareen, I.F., Gatsonis, C., Marcus, P.M., Sicks, J., 2011. Reduced lung-cancer mortality with low-dose computed tomographic screening. N. Engl. J. Med. 365 (5), 395–409.

Algin, O., Gokalp, G., Topal, U., 2011. Signs in chest imaging. Diagn. Interv. Radiol. 17 (1), 18–29.

Amirav, I., Kramer, S.S., Grunstein, M.M., Hoffman, E.A., 1993. Assessment of methacholine-induced airway constriction by high resolution cine computed tomography (HRCCT). J. Appl. Phys. 75 (5), 2239–2250.

Asker, S., Asker, M., Ozbay, B., 2014. Evaluation of airway wall thickness via high-resolution computed tomography in mild intermittent asthma. Respir. Care 59 (4), 550–556.

Au, O.K.-C., Tai, C.-L., Chu, H.-K., Cohen-Or, D., Lee, T.-Y. 2008. Skeleton extraction by mesh contraction. ACM Trans. Graph. 27 (3), 44: 1–44:10.

Bafadhel, M., Umar, I., Gupta, S., Raj, J.V., Vara, D.D., Entwisle, J.J., Pavord, I.D., Brightling, C.E., Siddiqui, S., 2011. The role of CT scanning in multidimensional phenotyping of COPD. Chest J. 140 (3), 634–642.

Bailey, D.G., 2004. An efficient Euclidean distance transform. In: Combinatorial Image Analysis, IWCIA 2004, pp. 394–408.

Beichel, R., Kiraly, A., Kuhnigk, J., McClelland, J., Mori, K., van Rikxoort, E., Rit, S., de Bruijne, M., van Ginneken, B., Kabus, S., 2011. Fourth International Workshop on Pulmonary Image Analysis. CreateSpace.

Bengio, Y., 2009. Learning deep architectures for AI. Found. Trends Mach. Learn. 2 (1), 1–127.

Birbeck, N., Kohlberger, T., Zhang, J., Sofka, M., Kaftan, J., Comaniciu, D., Zhou, S.K., 2014. Lung segmentation from CT with severe pathologies using anatomical constraints. Med. Image Comput. Comput. Assist. Interv. 17 (Pt 1), 804–811.

Blechschmidt, R.A., Werthschutzky, R., Lorcher, U., 2001. Automated CT image evaluation of the lung: a morphology-based concept. IEEE Trans. Med. Imaging 20 (5), 434–442.

Bogoni, L., Valadez, G., 2012. System and method for automatic detection and measurement of malacia in the airways. U.S. Patent 8,195,269.

Bouma, H., Sonnemans, J.J., Vilanova, A., Gerritsen, F.A., 2009. Automatic detection of pulmonary embolism in CTA images. IEEE Trans. Med. Imaging 28 (8), 1223–1230.

Brown, M., de Bruijne, M., van Ginneken, B., Kiraly, A., Kuhnigk, J.M., Lorenz, C., McClelland, J.R., Mori, K., Reeves, A., Reinhardt, J.M., 2009. The Second International Workshop on Pulmonary Image Analysis. CreateSpace. ISBN 1448680891.

Cao, J., Tagliasacchi, A., Olson, M., Zhang, H., Su, Z., 2010. Point cloud skeletons via Laplacian-based contraction. In: Proceedings of IEEE Conference on Shape Modeling and Applications, pp. 187–197.

Chae, E.J., Seo, J.B., Song, J.W., Kim, N., Park, B.W., Lee, Y.K., Oh, Y.M., Lee, S.D., Lim, S.Y., 2010. Slope of emphysema index: an objective descriptor of regional heterogeneity of emphysema and an independent determinant of pulmonary function. AJR Am. J. Roentgenol. 194 (3), W248–W255.

de Lange, E.E., Altes, T.A., Patrie, J.T., Parmar, J., Brookeman, J.R., Mugler, J.P., Platts-Mills, T.A., 2007. The variability of regional airflow obstruction within the lungs of patients with asthma: assessment with hyperpolarized helium-3 magnetic resonance imaging. J. Allergy Clin. Immunol. 119 (5), 1072–1078.

Dijkstra, A.E., Postma, D.S., ten Hacken, N., Vonk, J.M., Oudkerk, M., van Ooijen, P.M., Zanen, P., Mohamed Hoesein, F.A., van Ginneken, B., Schmidt, M., Groen, H.J., 2013. Low-dose CT measurements of airway dimensions and emphysema associated with airflow limitation in heavy smokers: a cross sectional study. Respir. Res. 14, 11.

Dombret, M.C., Alagha, K., Philippe Boulet, L., Yves Brillet, P., Joos, G., Laviolette, M., Louis, R., Rochat, T., Soccal, P., Aubier, M., Chanez, P., 2014. Bronchial thermoplasty: a new therapeutic option for the treatment of severe, uncontrolled asthma in adults. Eur. Respir. Rev. 23 (134), 510–518.

Fan, L., Qian, J.Z., Odry, B.L., Shen, H., Naidich, D.P., Kohl, G., Klotz, E., 2002. Automatic segmentation of pulmonary nodules by using dynamic 3D cross-correlation of interactive CAD systems. In: Sonka, M., Fitzpatrick, J.M. (Eds.), SPIE Medical Imaging 2002: Image Processing, vol. 1362.

Fetita, C.I., Prêteux, F., Beigelman-Aubry, C., Grenier, P., 2004. Pulmonary airways: 3-D reconstruction from multislice CT and clinical investigation. IEEE Trans. Med. Imaging 23 (11), 1353–1364.

Fiorelli, A., Petrillo, M., Vicidomini, G., Di Crescenzo, V.G., Frongillo, E., De Felice, A., Rotondo, A., Santini, M., 2014. Quantitative assessment of emphysematous parenchyma using multidetector-row computed tomography in patients scheduled for endobronchial treatment with one-way valves. Interact. Cardiovasc. Thorac. Surg. 19 (2), 246–255.

Ge, Z., Sahiner, B., Chan, H.P., Hadjiiski, L.M., Cascade, P.N., Bogot, N., Kazerooni, E.A., Wei, J., Zhou, C., 2005. Computer-aided detection of lung nodules: false positive reduction using a 3D gradient field method and 3D ellipsoid fitting. Med. Phys. 32 (8), 2443–2454.

Gierada, D.S., Bierhals, A.J., Choong, C.K., Bartel, S.T., Ritter, J.H., Das, N.A., Hong, C., Pilgram, T.K., Bae, K.T., Whiting, B.R., Woods, J.C., Hogg, J.C., Lutey, B.A., Battafarano, R.J., Cooper, J.D., Meyers, B.F., Patterson, G.A., 2010. Effects of CT section thickness and reconstruction kernel on emphysema quantification relationship to the magnitude of the CT emphysema index. Acad. Radiol. 17 (2), 146–156.

Goo, J.M., Lee, J.W., Lee, H.J., Kim, S., Kim, J.H., Im, J.G., 2003. Automated lung nodule detection at low-dose CT: preliminary experience. Korean J. Radiol. 4 (4), 211–216.

Goris, M.L., Zhu, H.J., Blankenberg, F., Chan, F., Robinson, T.E., 2003. An automated approach to quantitative air trapping measurements in mild cystic fibrosis. Chest 123 (5), 1655–1663.

Herth, F.J., Ernst, A., Baker, K.M., Egan, J.J., Gotfried, M.H., Hopkins, P., Stanzel, F., Valipour, A., Wagner, M., Witt, C., Kesten, S., Snell, G., 2012. Characterization of outcomes 1 year after endoscopic thermal vapor ablation for patients with heterogeneous emphysema. Int. J. Chron. Obstruct. Pulmon. Dis. 7, 397–405.

Heussel, C.P., Herth, F.J., Kappes, J., Hantusch, R., Hartlieb, S., Weinheimer, O., Kauczor, H.U., Eberhardt, R., 2009. Fully automatic quantitative assessment of emphysema in computed tomography: comparison with pulmonary function testing and normal values. Eur. Radiol. 19 (10), 2391–2402.

Iwasawa, T., Asakura, A., Sakai, F., Kanauchi, T., Gotoh, T., Ogura, T., Yazawa, T., Nishimura, J., Inoue, T., 2009. Assessment of prognosis of patients with idiopathic pulmonary fibrosis by computer-aided analysis of CT images. J. Thorac. Imaging 24 (3), 216–222.

Jaklitsch, M.T., Jacobson, F.L., Austin, J.H., Field, J.K., Jett, J.R., Keshavjee, S., MacMahon, H., Mulshine, J.L., Munden, R.F., Salgia, R., et al., 2012. The American Association for Thoracic Surgery guidelines for lung cancer screening using low-dose computed tomography scans for lung cancer survivors and other high-risk groups. J. Thorac. Cardiovasc. Surg. 144 (1), 33–38.

Kazerooni, E.A., 2001. High resolution CT of the lungs. Am. J. Roentgenol. 177 (3), 501–519.

Kim, N., Seo, J.B., Lee, Y., Lee, J.G., Kim, S.S., Kang, S.H., 2009. Development of an automatic classification system for differentiation of obstructive lung disease using HRCT. J. Digit. Imaging 22 (2), 136–148.

Kiraly, A., Helferty, J., Hoffman, E., McLennan, G., Higgins, W., 2004a. Three-dimensional path planning for virtual bronchoscopy. IEEE Trans. Med. Imaging 23 (11), 1365–1379.

Kiraly, A.P., Helferty, J.P., Hoffman, E.A., McLennan, G., Higgins, W.E., 2004b. Three-dimensional path planning for virtual bronchoscopy. IEEE Trans. Med. Imaging 23 (11), 1365–1379.

Kiraly, A.P., Reinhardt, J.M., Hoffman, E.A., McLennan, G., Higgins, W.E., 2005. Virtual bronchoscopy for quantitative airway analysis. In: Amini, A.A., Manduca, A. (Eds.), SPIE Medical Imaging 2005: Physiology, Function, and Structure from Medical Images, vol. 5746, pp. 369–383.

Kiraly, A., Odry, B., Novak, C., Naidich, D., 2007. Boundary-specific cost functions for quantitative airway analysis. Proceedings of MICCAI 4791, 784–791.

Kongkuo, L., Merritt, S.A., Higgins, W.E., 2008. Extraction and visualization of the central chest lymph-node stations. In: Giger, M.L., Karssemeijer, N. (Eds.), SPIE Medical Imaging 2008: Computer-Aided Diagnosis, vol. 6915.

Kuhnigk, J., Dicken, V., Zidowitz, S., Bornemann, L., Kuemmerlen, B., Krass, S., Peitgen, H., Yuval, S., Jend, H., Rau, W.S., Achenbach, T., 2005. Informatics in radiology (infoRAD): new tools for computer assistance in thoracic CT. Part 1. Functional analysis of lungs, lung lobes, and bronchopulmonary segments. Radiographics 25 (2), 525–536.

Lassen, B., van Rikxoort, E.M., Schmidt, M., Kerkstra, S., van Ginneken, B., Kuhnigk, J.M., 2013. Automatic segmentation of the pulmonary lobes from chest CT scans based on fissures, vessels, and bronchi. IEEE Trans. Med. Imaging 32 (2), 210–222.

Le, Q.V., 2013. Building high-level features using large scale unsupervised learning. In: 2013 IEEE International Conference on Acoustics, Speech and Signal Processing (ICASSP), pp. 859–598.

Lee, D.K., Chun, E.M., Suh, S.W., Yang, J.H., Shim, S.S., 2014. Evaluation of postoperative change in lung volume in adolescent idiopathic scoliosis: measured by computed tomography. Indian J. Orthop. 48 (4), 360–365.

Madani, A., Zanen, J., de Maertelaer, V., Gevenois, P.A., 2006. Pulmonary emphysema: objective quantification at multi-detector row CT-comparison with macroscopic and microscopic morphometry. Radiology 238 (3), 1036–1043.

Mets, O.M., Schmidt, M., Buckens, C.F., Gondrie, M.J., Isgum, I., Oudkerk, M., Vliegenthart, R., de Koning, H.J., van der Aalst, C.M., Prokop, M., Lammers, J.W., Zanen, P., Mohamed Hoesein, F.A., Mali, W.P., van Ginneken, B., van Rikxoort, E.M., de Jong, P.A., 2013. Diagnosis of chronic obstructive pulmonary disease in lung cancer screening computed tomography scans: independent contribution of emphysema, air trapping and bronchial wall thickening. Respir. Res. 14, 59.

Mori, K., Ema, S., Kitasaka, T., Mekada, Y., Ide, I., Murase, H., Suenaga, Y., Takabatake, H., Mori, M., Natori, H., 2005. Automated nomenclature of bronchial branches extracted from CT images and its application to biopsy path planning in virtual bronchoscopy. Med. Image Comput. Comput. Assist. Interv. 8 (Pt 2), 854–861.

Morimura, Y., Chen, F., Sonobe, M., Date, H., 2013. Inspiratory and expiratory computed tomographic volumetry for lung volume reduction surgery. Interact. Cardiovasc. Thorac. Surg. 16 (6), 926–928.

Morrison, J., 1992. Quaternion interpolation with extra spins. In: Graphics Gems, vol. III. Academic Press, Inc., Boston, MA, pp. 96–97.

Mugler, J.P., Altes, T.A., Ruset, I.C., Dregely, I.M., Mata, J.F., Miller, G.W., Ketel, S., Ketel, J., Hersman, F.W., Ruppert, K., 2010. Simultaneous magnetic resonance imaging of ventilation distribution and gas uptake in the human lung using hyperpolarized xenon-129. Proc. Natl Acad. Sci. 107 (50), 21707–21712.

Murphy, S.L., Xu, J., Kochanek, K.D., 2013. National Center for Health Statistics. National Vital Statistics Report. Deaths: Final Data for 2010, vol. 61, 4. Centers for Disease Control and Prevention.

Nimura, Y., Kitasaka, T., Honma, H., Takabatake, H., Mori, M., Natori, H., Mori, K., 2012. Lung lobe segmentation based on statistical atlas and graph cuts. In: van Ginneken, B., Novak, C.L. (Eds.), SPIE Medical Imaging 2012: Computer-Aided Diagnosis, vol. 8315.

Odry, B.L., Kiraly, A.P., Novak, C.L., Naidich, D.P., Lerallut, J.F., 2008a, An evaluation of automated broncho-arterial ratios for reliable assessment of bronchiectasis. In: Giger, M.L., Karssemeijer, N. (Eds.), SPIE Medical Imaging 2008: Computer-Aided Diagnosis, vol. 6915, pp. 69152M-1-69152M-9.

Odry, B.L., Kiraly, A.P., Slabaugh, G.G., Novak, C.L., Naidich, D.P., Lerallut, J.F., 2008b, Active contour approach for accurate quantitative airway analysis. In: Hu, X.P., Clough, A.V. (Eds.), SPIE Medical Imaging 2008: Physiology, Function, and Structure from Medical Images, vol. 6916.

Odry, B.L., Kiraly, A.P., Novak, C.L., Naidich, D.P., 2012. Comparison of analysis methods for airway quantification. In: van Ginneken, B., Novak, C.L. (Eds.), SPIE Medical Imaging 2012: Computer-Aided Diagnosis, vol. 8315.

Paik, D.S., Beaulieu, C.F., Jeffrey, R.B., Rubin, G.D., Napel, S., 1998. Automated flight path planning for virtual endoscopy. Med. Phys. 25 (5), 629–637.

Park, S.O., Seo, J.B., Kim, N., Park, S.H., Lee, Y.K., Park, B.W., Sung, Y.S., Lee, Y., Lee, J., Kang, S.H., 2009. Feasibility of automated quantification of regional disease patterns depicted on high-resolution computed tomography in patients with various diffuse lung diseases. Korean J. Radiol. 10 (5), 455–463.

Pistolesi, M., Camiciottoli, G., Paoletti, M., Marmai, C., Lavorini, F., Meoni, E., Marchesi, C., Giuntini, C., 2008. Identification of a predominant COPD phenotype in clinical practice. Respir. Med. 102 (3), 367–376.

Preteux, F.J., Fetita, C.I., Grenier, P., 1997. Modeling, segmentation, and caliber estimation of bronchi in high-resolution computerized tomography. In: Preteux, F.J., Davidson, J.L., Dougherty, E.R. (Eds.), Proceedings of SPIE, Statistical and Stochastic Methods in Image Processing II, vol. 3167, pp. 58–69.

Pu, J., Zheng, B., Leader, J., Fuhrman, C., Knollmann, F., Klym, A., Gur, D., 2009. Pulmonary lobe segmentation in CT examinations using implicit surface fitting. IEEE Trans. Med. Imaging 28 (12), 1986–1996.

Revel, M., Sanchez, O., Couchon, S., Planquette, B., Hernigou, A., Niarra, R., Meyer, G., Chatellier, G., 2012. Diagnostic accuracy of magnetic resonance imaging for an acute pulmonary embolism: results of the IRM-EP study. J. Thromb. Haemost. 10 (5), 743–750.

Robinson, T.E., 2007. Computed tomography scanning techniques for the evaluation of cystic fibrosis lung disease. Proc. Am. Thorac. Soc. 4 (4), 310–315.

Ross, J.C., Estepar, R.S., Diaz, A., Westin, C.F., Kikinis, R., Silverman, E.K., Washko, G.R., 2009. Lung extraction, lobe segmentation and hierarchical region assessment for quantitative analysis on high resolution computed tomography images. Med. Image Comput. Comput. Assist. Interv. 12 (Pt 2), 690–698.

Saba, O.I., Hoffman, E.A., Reinhardt, J.M., 2003. Maximizing quantitative accuracy of lung airway lumen and wall measures obtained from X-ray CT imaging. J. Appl. Physiol. 95, 1063–1075.

Saha, P.K., Chaudhuri, B.B., Majumder, D.D., 1994. Topology preservation in 3D digital space. Pattern Recognit. 27 (2), 295–300.

Saha, P.K., Chaudhuri, B.B., Majumder, D.D., 1997. A new shape preserving parallel thinning algorithm for 3D digital images. Pattern Recognit. 30 (12), 1939–1955.

Sheehan, R.E., Wells, A.U., Copley, S.J., Desai, S.R., Howling, S.J., Cole, P.J., Wilson, R., Hansell, D.M., 2002. A comparison of serial computed tomography and functional change in bronchiectasis. Eur. Respir. J. 20 (3), 581–587.

Shen, H., Goebel, B., Odry, B.L., 2004. A new algorithm for local surface smoothing with application to chest wall nodule segmentation in lung CT data. In: Fitzpatrick, J.M., Sonka, M. (Eds.), SPIE Medical Imaging 2004: Image Processing, vol. 1519.

Shoemake, K., 1985. Animating rotation with quaternion curves. ACM SIGGRAPH 19 (3), 245–254.

Sifakis, E., Tziritas, G., 2001. Moving object localisation using a multi-label fast marching algorithm. Signal Process. Image Commun. 16 (10), 963–976.

Starnes, V.A., Bowdish, M.E., Woo, M.S., Barbers, R.G., Schenkel, F.A., Horn, M.V., Pessotto, R., Sievers, E.M., Baker, C.J., Cohen, R.G., Bremner, R.M., Wells, W.J., Barr, M.L., 2004. A decade of living lobar lung transplantation: recipient outcomes. J. Thorac. Cardiovasc. Surg. 127 (1), 114–122.

Swift, R., Kiraly, A., Sherbondy, A., Austin, A.L., Hoffman, E.A., McLennan, G., Higgins, W.E., 2002. Automatic axes-generation for virtual bronchoscopic assessment of major airway obstructions. Comput. Med. Imaging Graph. 26 (2), 103–118.

Tschirren, J., Hoffman, E.A., McLennan, G., Sonka, M., 2003. Branchpoint labeling and matching in human airway trees. In: Clough, A., Amini, A. (Eds.), SPIE Medical Imaging 2003: Physiology and Function—Methods, Systems, and Applications, vol. 5031.

Tschirren, J., Hoffman, E.A., McLennan, G., Sonka, M., 2005. Intrathoracic airway trees: segmentation and airway morphology analysis from low-dose CT scans. IEEE Trans. Med. Imaging 24 (12), 1529–1539.

Van Rikxoort, E., Prokop, M., de Hoop, B., Viergever, M., Pluim, J., van Ginneken, B., 2010. Automatic segmentation of pulmonary lobes robust against incomplete fissures. IEEE Trans. Med. Imaging 29 (6), 1286–1296.

Wan, S., Ritman, E., Higgins, W., 2002. Multi-generational analysis and visualization of the vascular tree in 3D micro-CT images. Comput. Biol. Med. 32 (2), 55–71.

Washko, G.R., Hoffman, E., Reilly, J.J., 2008. Radiographic evaluation of the potential lung volume reduction surgery candidate. Proc. Am. Thorac. Soc. 5 (4), 421–426.

Wender, R., Fontham, E.T., Barrera, E., Colditz, G.A., Church, T.R., Ettinger, D.S., Etzioni, R., Flowers, C.R., Scott Gazelle, G., Kelsey, D.K., et al., 2013. American Cancer Society lung cancer screening guidelines. Cancer J. Clin. 63 (2), 106–117.

Wielpuetz, M.O., Puderbach, M., Kopp-Schneider, A., Stahl, M., Fritzsching, E., Sommerburg, O., Ley, S., Sumkauskaite, M., Biederer, J., Kauczor, H.U., et al., 2014. Magnetic resonance imaging detects changes in structure and perfusion, and response to therapy in early cystic fibrosis lung disease. Am. J. Respir. Crit. Care Med. 189 (8), 956–965.

Wiemker, R., Blaffert, T., Buelow, T., Renisch, S., Lorenz, C., 2004. Automated assessment of bronchial lumen, wall thickness and bronchioarterial diameter ratio of the tracheobronchonchial tree using high-resolution CT. Proc. CARS 1268, 967–972.

Wiemker, R., Buelow, T., Blaffert, T., 2005. Unsupervised extraction of the pulmonary interlobar fissures from high resolution thoracic CT data. Int. Congr. Ser. 1281, 1121–1126. ISSN 0531-5131.

Wittenberg, R., Peters, J.F., Sonnemans, J.J., Prokop, M., Schaefer-Prokop, C.M., 2010. Computer-assisted detection of pulmonary embolism: evaluation of pulmonary CT angiograms performed in an on-call setting. Eur. Radiol. 20 (4), 801–806.

Wood, D.E., Eapen, G.A., Ettinger, D.S., Hou, L., Jackman, D., Kazerooni, E., Klippenstein, D., Lackner, R.P., Leard, L., Leung, A.N., et al., 2012. Lung cancer screening. J. Natl Compr. Cancer Netw. 10 (2), 240–265.

Woodhouse, N., Wild, J.M., Paley, M.N., Fichele, S., Said, Z., Swift, A.J., van Beek, E.J., 2005. Combined helium-3/proton magnetic resonance imaging measurement of ventilated lung volumes in smokers compared to never-smokers. J. Magn. Resonan. Imaging 21 (4), 365–369.

Yu, K.C., Ritman, E.L., Kiraly, A.P., Wan, S.W., Zamir, M., Higgins, W.E., 2003. Toward reliable multi-generational analysis of anatomical trees. In: Clough, A., Amini, A. (Eds.), SPIE Medical Imaging 2003: Physiology and Function—Methods, Systems, and Applications, vol. 5031, pp. 178–186.

Zhou, Y., Toga, A.W., 1999. Efficient skeletonization of volumetric objects. IEEE Trans. Vis. Comp. Graph. 5 (3), 196–209.

Zhou, C., Chan, H.P., Sahiner, B., Hadjiiski, L.M., Chughtai, A., Patel, S., Wei, J., Ge, J., Cascade, P.N., Kazerooni, E.A., 2007. Automatic multiscale enhancement and segmentation of pulmonary vessels in CT pulmonary angiography images for CAD applications. Med. Phys. 34 (12), 4567–4577.

# AORTIC AND MITRAL VALVE MODELING FROM MULTI-MODAL IMAGE DATA

# 16

**S. Grbic[1], I. Voigt[1], T. Mansi[1], B. Georgescu[1], R. Ionasec[2] and D. Comaniciu[1]**

*Imaging and Computer Vision, Siemens Corporate Technology, Princeton, NJ, USA[1]*

*Siemens Healthcare, Forchheim, Germany[2]*

## 16.1 INTRODUCTION

The valves are essential anatomical structures regulating the heart chamber hemodynamics and the blood flow between the heart and the systemic and pulmonary circulations. Valvular heart disease (VHD) is the most prevalent subgroup of cardiovascular disease (CVD), which affects 2.5% of the global population and requires yearly over 100,000 surgeries in the United States alone. Yet, heart valve operations are the most expensive and riskiest cardiac procedures, with an average cost of $141,120 and 4.9% in-hospital death rate (Lloyd-Jones et al., 2009).

S. Kevin Zhou (Ed): Medical Image Recognition, Segmentation and Parsing. http://dx.doi.org/10.1016/B978-0-12-802581-9.00016-0

Due to the strong anatomical, functional, and hemodynamic interdependency of the heart valves, VHDs do not affect only a single valve, but rather several valves are impaired. Recent studies demonstrate strong influence of aortic valve replacement on mitral valve function (Tzikas et al., 2010; Harling et al., 2011). Especially in the context of minimally invasive valve replacement procedures such as transcatheter aortic valve implantation (TAVI) longer implants such as the Medtronic CoreValve® can cause direct impairment of mitral valve function leading to heart failure (Giordana et al., 2013). Thus, there is a clinical need for morphological and functional assessment of the combined aortic and mitral valve apparatus for decision making during diagnosis and severity assessment as well as treatment selection and planning.

Decisions in valvular disease management increasingly rely on noninvasive imaging. Techniques like transesophageal echocardiography (TEE) and cardiac computed tomography (CT) imaging, enable dynamic 4D scanning of the beating heart over the whole cardiac cycle. Precise morphological and functional knowledge about the valvular apparatus is considered a prerequisite for the clinical workflow including diagnosis, therapy-planning, surgery, or percutaneous intervention as well as patient monitoring and follow-up. Nevertheless, most noninvasive investigations to date are based on 2D images, user-dependent processing and manually performed, potentially inaccurate measurements (Bonow et al., 2006).

The progress in medical imaging is matched by important advances in surgical techniques, bioprosthetic valves, robotic surgery, and percutaneous interventions, which have led to a twofold increase in the number of valve procedures performed in the United States since 1985 (Jablokow, 2009). There has been a major trend in cardiac therapy toward minimally invasive transcatheter procedures as they offer the potential to reduce procedural morbidity, mortality, and costs of valve treatment when compared to classical surgery. However, without direct access and view to the affected anatomy those interventions are usually performed in so-called hybrid ORs, equipped with advanced imaging technology. Thus, procedures such as the transcatheter aortic valve implantation (TAVI) are guided via real-time intra-operative images provided by X-ray fluoroscopy and transesophageal echocardiography systems (Agarwal and Triggs, 2004). Powerful computer-aided tools for extensive noninvasive assessment, planning and guidance are mandatory to continuously decrease the level of invasiveness and maximize effectiveness of valve therapy.

Until recently, cardiac modeling was almost exclusively focused on the left ventricle (LV) (Park et al., 1996; Staib and Duncan, 1996). Rueckert and Burger (1997) and Fritz et al. (2006) achieved a combined model of the two ventricles, LV and right ventricle (RV). A few methods in the literature also consider the left and right atria (Lorenz and von Berg, 2006; Huang et al., 2007; Ecabert et al., 2008; Zheng et al., 2008; Zhuang et al., 2010a,b), but none explicitly handle the heart valves. The majority of existent valve models presented in the literature are generic and rough approximations of the true valvular anatomy. Their primary application is the analysis of the blood-tissue interaction during the cardiac cycle as well as mechanical and functional behavior of the valvular apparatus. The first cardiac model to include the heart valves was proposed by Peskin and McQueen (1996). De Hart et al. (2002) introduced a refined computational model of the aortic valve while Soncini et al. (2009) presented a realistic finite element model of the physiological aortic root from medical imaging data. Kunzelman et al. (2007) introduced the first 3D finite element model of the mitral valve. Votta et al. (2008) presented an extended mitral valve model based on *in vivo* data. Watanabe et al. (2005) introduced a geometrical model of the mitral valve, obtained from real-time 3D TEE. The study by Veronesi et al. (2009) also considers the aortic valve to investigate the functional dependency between the two left-side valves. Schievano et al. (2007) proposed an analysis protocol of the pulmonary trunk based on rapid prototyping systems. Recently introduced models of the aortic valve (Ionasec et al., 2008; Waechter and et al., 2010), the mitral valve (Conti et al., 2010; Schneider et al., 2010) aortic-mitral coupling (Ionasec et al., 2009b; Veronesi et al., 2009; Ionasec et al., 2010) address important aspects of data-driven valve models.

In this chapter, we present a patient-specific model of the aortic and mitral valve model estimated from multi-modal cardiac images. Section 16.2 describes a morphological and functional representation of the aortic and mitral valves. The patient-specific parameters of the cardiac models are estimated from 4D cardiac images using learning-based methods. Section 16.3 describes algorithms for object detection and rigid motion estimation, nonrigid motion estimation, and surface boundary estimation from 4D data (CT and echocardiography). Part of this work has been reported in our previous publications (Ionasec et al., 2009b,c, 2010; Vitanovski et al., 2009, 2010; Grbić et al., 2012, 2014; Swee and Grbić, 2014).

## 16.2 PHYSIOLOGICAL MODEL OF THE HEART VALVES

In this section, we introduce the aortic and mitral valve models, which are capable of capturing their morphological, functional, and pathological variations. To reduce anatomical complexity and facilitate effective estimation, the heart valve model is represented on three abstraction layers (Grbić et al., 2010a,b, 2012, 2013a,b; Swee and Grbić, 2014):

- *Global motion model*: which represents the global location and motion of each valve.
- *Anatomical landmark model*: representing the motion of the corresponding anatomic landmarks.
- *Complete valve model*: which parameterizes the full anatomy and dynamics of the valves using dense surface meshes.

### 16.2.1 GLOBAL MOTION MODEL

The global dynamic variation of each valve is parameterized through a similarity transformation in the Euclidean 3D space, which includes nine parameters.

$$\boldsymbol{B}_t = \left\{ \left(c_x, c_y, c_z\right), \left(\alpha_x, \alpha_y, \alpha_z\right), \left(s_x, s_y, s_z\right) \right\} \quad t \in \{1 \ldots n\} \tag{16.1}$$

where $(c_x, c_y, c_z)$ is the translation, $(\alpha_x, \alpha_y, \alpha_z)$ the Euler angle representation of the rotation, $(s_1, s_2, s_3)$ the similarity transformation scaling factors, and the time variable $t$ captures the temporal variation during the cardiac cycle.

### 16.2.2 ANATOMICAL LANDMARK MODEL

A set of 20 anatomical landmarks, described in the next paragraph, are used to parameterize the complex and synchronized motion pattern, which explains the nonlinearities of the hemodynamic movements. Thereby, each landmark is described by a time-step trajectory $t$ in a 3D space, normalized by the temporal dependent similarity transformation $\boldsymbol{B}$:

$$\boldsymbol{L}_t^j(\boldsymbol{B}) = \{x, y, z\} \quad j \in \{1 \ldots 20\} \ t \in \{1 \ldots n\} \quad \boldsymbol{L}_t^j \in \mathbb{R}^3 \tag{16.2}$$

## 16.2.3 COMPLETE VALVE MODEL

The final valve model is completed with a set of six dense surface meshes (four AV and two MV). Each mesh is sampled along anatomical grids of vertices defined by the landmarks:

$$M_t^q (L, B) = \{\vec{v}_1, \vec{v}_2, \ldots, \vec{v}_K\} \quad t \in \{1 \ldots n\} \quad q \in \{1 \ldots 6\} \quad \vec{v}_i \in \mathbb{R}^3 \tag{16.3}$$

where $\vec{v}_i$ are the vertices, and $K$ is the total number of vertices of mesh $q$. Each anatomical landmark has a fixed correspondence on the parameterized surface mesh.

### 16.2.3.1 Aortic valve

Four surface structures represent the aortic valve: aortic root, left coronary leaflet, right coronary leaflet, and noncoronary leaflet. The aortic root connects the ascending aorta to the left ventricle outflow tract and is represented through a tubular grid (see Figure 16.1). This is aligned with the aortic circumferential $u$ and ascending directions $v$ including $36 \times 20$ vertices and 1368 faces. The root is constrained by six anatomical landmarks, that is, three commissures and three hinges, with a fixed correspondence on the grid. The three aortic leaflets, the $L$-, $R$-, and $N$-leaflet, are modeled as paraboloids on a grid of $11 \times 7$ vertices and 120 faces (see Figure 16.3). They are stitched to the root on a crown-like attachment ring, which defines the parametric $u$ direction at the borders. The vertex correspondence between the root and leaflets along the merging curve is symmetric and kept fixed. The leaflets are constrained by the corresponding hinges, commissures, and tip landmarks, where the $v$ direction is the ascending vector from the hinge to the tip.

### 16.2.3.2 Mitral valve

The mitral valve is composed of seven landmarks including three trigons, two commissures, two leaflet tips, and two papillary muscle tips (see Figure 16.2). The leaflets separate the left atrium and left ventricle hemodynamically and are connected to the endocardial wall by the saddle-shaped mitral annulus. Both are modeled as paraboloids and their upper margins implicitly define the annulus. Their grids are aligned with the circumferential annulus direction $u$ and the orthogonal direction $v$ pointing from the annulus toward leaflet tips and commissures (see Figure 16.3). The anterior leaflet is constructed from $18 \times 9$ vertices and 272 faces while the posterior leaflet is represented with $24 \times 9$ vertices and 368 faces. Both leaflets are fixed by the mitral commissures and their corresponding leaflet tips. The left/right trigons and the postero-annular midpoint further confine the anterior and posterior leaflets, respectively. The papillary muscle tips (anterolateral and posteromedial) represent the main incision points of the mitral valve chordae tendineae at the left ventricle.

## 16.3 PATIENT-SPECIFIC MODEL PARAMETER ESTIMATION

A hierarchical estimation approach is utilized to deduce model parameters, introduced in the previous section from 4D cardiac CT and TEE images. Robust machine learning techniques are applied to estimate the global valves, anatomic landmarks, and complete valve surface model parameters.

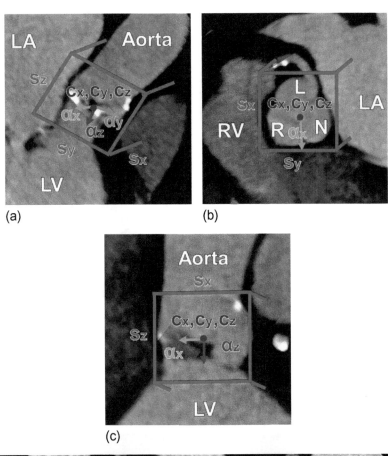

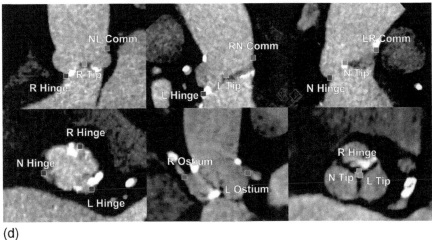

**FIGURE 16.1**

Global motion and anatomical landmark model of the aortic valve. The similarity transform is represented as a bounding box around the aortic valve estimated from 4D cardiac CT. (a) Perspective view; (b) long axis; (c) short axis; and (d) landmarks relative to the anatomical location illustrated in long and short axis from an example CT study.

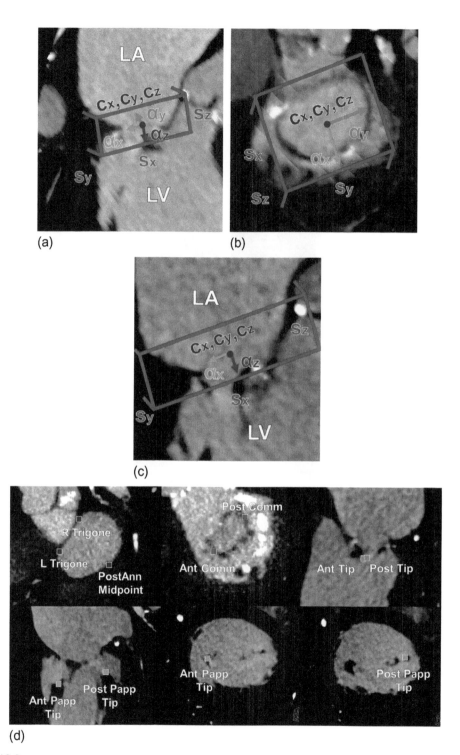

**FIGURE 16.2**

Global motion and anatomical landmark model of the mitral valve. The similarity transform is represented as a bounding box around the mitral valve estimated from 4D cardiac CT. (a) Perspective view; (b) long axis; (c) short axis; and (d) landmarks relative to the anatomical location illustrated in long and short axis from an example CT study.

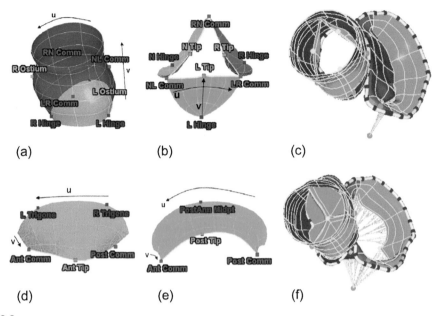

**FIGURE 16.3**

Isolated surface components of the aortic and mitral models with parametric directions and spatial relations to anatomical landmarks: (a) aortic root, (b) aortic leaflets, (c) aortic-mitral in end-systole, (d) anterior mitral leaflet, (e) posterior mitral leaflet, and (f) aortic-mitral in end-diastole.

## 16.3.1 OBJECT DETECTION AND RIGID MOTION ESTIMATION

To determine the location of each valve from multimodal cardiac images we estimate the parameters $B_t$, defined in Section 16.2.1 from a sequence of volumes $I$:

$$\arg\max_{B_t} p(B_t|I_t) = \arg\max_{B_t} p(B_0, \dots, B_{n-1}|I_0, \dots, I_{n-1}) \tag{16.4}$$

### Location estimation

We solve Eq. (16.4), by rephrasing the object localization as a classification problem and estimate $B_t$ for each time step $t$. The probability $p(B_t|I_t)$ can be modeled by a classifier $D$, which evaluates and scores a large number of hypotheses for $B_t$. To perform the search of the nine parameters efficiently we utilize the marginal space learning (MSL) framework (Zheng et al., 2008) and subdivide the original parameter search space into a subset of marginal spaces:

$$\Sigma_1 \subset \Sigma_2 \subset \cdots \subset \Sigma_n = \Sigma$$

The nine-dimensional location space described by the similarity transform in a 3D Euclidean space is decomposed as follows:

$$\Sigma_1 = (c_x, c_y, c_z)$$
$$\Sigma_2 = (c_x, c_y, c_z, \vec{\alpha}_x, \vec{\alpha}_y, \vec{\alpha}_z)$$
$$\Sigma_3 = (c_x, c_y, c_z, \vec{\alpha}_x, \vec{\alpha}_y, \vec{\alpha}_z, s_x, s_y, s_z)$$

where $\Sigma_1$ represents the position marginal space, $\Sigma_2$ the position and the orientation marginal space, and $\Sigma_3$ the position, orientation, and scale marginal space, which coincides with the original domain. The optimal arrangement for the order of marginal spaces is based on the parameter variation in each subspace. Due to the CT and TEE acquisition protocols and physiological variations of the heart, the highest variance comes from translation followed by orientation and scale.

From the marginalization of the search domain, the target posterior probability can be expressed as:

$$p(\boldsymbol{B}_t|I_t) = p(c_x, c_y, c_z|I_t)$$
$$p(\vec{\alpha}_x, \vec{\alpha}_y, \vec{\alpha}_z|c_x, c_y, c_z, I_t)$$
$$p(s_x, s_y, s_z|\vec{\alpha}_x, \vec{\alpha}_y, \vec{\alpha}_z, c_x, c_y, c_z, I_t)$$

Instead of using a single classifier $D$, we train classifiers for each marginal spaces $D_1$, $D_2$, and $D_3$, and estimate $\boldsymbol{B}_t$ by gradually increasing the dimensionality. Classifiers are trained using the probabilistic boosting tree (Tu, 2005) with Haar and steerable features (Zheng et al., 2008). After each stage a limited number of candidates, sorted by their posterior probability, are kept: 100 candidates are retained in $\Sigma_1$, 50 in $\Sigma_2$, and 25 in $\Sigma_3$. This method significantly reduces the search space.

### Motion aggregation

To obtain a temporally consistent global motion $\boldsymbol{B}_t$ for each valve model, a RANSAC estimator is employed. We assume a constant model for the cardiac motion, which drives the global movement of each valve. From randomly sampled candidates, the one yielding the maximum number of inliers is picked as the final motion. Inliers are considered within a distance of $\sigma = 7$ mm from the current candidate and extracted at each time step $t$. The distance measure $d(\boldsymbol{B}_t^1, \boldsymbol{B}_t^2)$ is given by the maximum $L1$ norm of the standard unit axis deformed by the parameters $\boldsymbol{B}_t^1$ and $\boldsymbol{B}_t^2$, respectively:

$$L1(\vec{a}_1, \vec{a}_2) = \max\{|x1 - x2|, |y1 - y2|, |z1 - z2|\}$$
$$d(\boldsymbol{B}_t^1, \boldsymbol{B}_t^2) = \frac{1}{4}(L1(\vec{c}_1, \vec{c}_2) + L1(\vec{X}_1 s_{x1}, \vec{X}_2 s_{x2}) + L1(\vec{Y}_1 s_{y1}, \vec{Y}_2 s_{y2}) \tag{16.5}$$
$$+ L1(\vec{Z}_1 s_{z1}, \vec{Z}_2 s_{z2}))$$

where $X$, $Y$, and $Z$ are the unit axes obtained from the Euler angles $(\vec{\alpha}_x, \vec{\alpha}_y, \vec{\alpha}_z)$, $\vec{c}$ the position vectors, and $s_x, s_y, s_z$ scale parameters.

## 16.3.2 TRAJECTORY SPECTRUM LEARNING FOR NONRIGID MOTION ESTIMATION

Based on the determined global location and rigid motion, in this section, we introduce a trajectory spectrum learning algorithm to estimate nonlinear landmark movements from volumetric sequences (Ionasec et al., 2009a). Considering the representation in Section 16.2.2, Eq. (16.2), the objective is to find for each landmark $j$ its trajectory $\vec{L}_t^j$, with the maximum posterior probability from a series of volumes $I_t$, given the rigid motion $\boldsymbol{B}_t$:

$$\arg\max_{\vec{L}_t^j} p(\vec{L}_t^j|I_t, \boldsymbol{B}_t) = \arg\max_{\vec{L}_t^j} p(\vec{L}_0^j, \dots, \vec{L}_{n-1}^j| \tag{16.6}$$
$$I_0, \dots, I_{n-1}, \boldsymbol{B}_0, \dots, \boldsymbol{B}_{n-1})$$

It is difficult to solve Eq. (16.6) directly; thus various assumptions, such as the Markovian property of the motion (Yang et al., 2008), have been proposed to the posterior distribution over $\vec{L}_t^j$ given images up to time $t$. However, results are often not guaranteed to be smooth and may diverge over time, due to error accumulation. These fundamental issues can be addressed effectively if both temporal and spatial appearance information is considered over the whole sequence at once. A trajectory can be uniquely represented by the concatenation of its discrete Fourier transform (DFT) coefficients,

$$\vec{s}^j = [\vec{s}^j(0), \vec{s}^j(1), \dots, \vec{s}^j(n-1)] \tag{16.7}$$

where $\vec{s}^j(f) \in \mathcal{C}^3$ is the frequency spectrum of the $x$, $y$, and $z$ components of the trajectory $\vec{L}_t^j$, and $f = 0, 1, \dots, n-1$. The magnitude of $s_f^j$ is used to describe the shift-invariant motion according to the shift theorem of DFT, while the phase information is used to handle temporal misalignment. Equation (16.6) can be reformulated as finding the DFT spectrum $s_f^j$, with the maximal posterior probability:

$$\arg\max_{s_f^j} p(s_f^j | I_t, \boldsymbol{B}_t) = \arg\max_{s_t^j} p(\vec{s}_0^j, \dots, \vec{s}_{n-1}^j | \\ I_0, \dots, I_{n-1}, \boldsymbol{B}_0, \dots, \boldsymbol{B}_{n-1}) \tag{16.8}$$

Instead of estimating the motion trajectory directly, we apply discriminative learning to detect the spectrum $s_f^j$ in the frequency domain by optimizing Eq. (16.8).

### Search space marginalization

Inspired by the MSL, we efficiently perform trajectory spectrum learning and detection in DFT subspaces with gradually increased dimensionality. The intuition is to perform a spectral coarse-to-fine motion estimation, where the detection of coarse level motion (low frequency) is incrementally refined with high-frequency components representing fine deformations.

As described earlier, the motion trajectory is parameterized by the DFT spectrum components $\vec{s}_f^j, f = 0, \dots, n-1$. We differentiate between two types of subspaces, individual component subspaces $\Sigma^{(k)}$ and marginalized subspaces $\Sigma_k$ defined as:

$$\Sigma^{(k)} = \{\vec{s}(k)\} \tag{16.9}$$

$$\Sigma_k = \Sigma_{k-1} \times \Sigma^{(k)} \tag{16.10}$$

$$\Sigma_0 \subset \Sigma_1 \subset \cdots \subset \Sigma_{r-1}, \quad r = |\zeta| \tag{16.11}$$

The subspaces $\Sigma^{(k)}$ are efficiently represented by a set of corresponding hypotheses $\mathcal{H}^{(k)}$ obtained from the training set. The pruned search space enables efficient learning and optimization:

$$\Sigma_{r-1} = \mathcal{H}^{(0)} \times \mathcal{H}^{(1)} \times \cdots \times \mathcal{H}^{(r-1)}, \quad r = |\zeta|$$

### Learning in marginal trajectory spaces

The algorithm starts by learning the posterior probability distribution in the DC marginal space $\Sigma_0$. Subsequently, the learned detector $D_0$ is applied to identify high probable candidates $\mathcal{C}_0$ from the hypotheses $\mathcal{H}^{(0)}$. In the following step, the dimensionality of the space is increased by adding the next spectrum component (in this case the fundamental frequency, $\Sigma^{(1)}$). Learning is performed in the restricted space defined by the extracted high probability regions and hypotheses set $\mathcal{C}_0 \times \mathcal{H}^{(1)}$. The same operation is repeated until reaching the genuine search space $\Sigma_{r-1}$.

For each marginal space $\Sigma_k$, corresponding discriminative classifiers $D_k$ are trained on sets of positives $\text{Pos}_k$ and negatives $\text{Neg}_k$. We analyze samples constructed from high probability candidates $\mathcal{C}_{k-1}$ and hypotheses $\mathcal{H}^{(k)}$. The sample set $\mathcal{C}_{k-1} \times \mathcal{H}^{(k)}$ is separated into positive and negative examples by comparing the corresponding trajectories to the ground truth in the spatial domain using the following distance measure:

$$d(\vec{U}_1, \vec{U}_2) = \max_t \|\vec{U}_1(t) - \vec{U}_2(t)\| \tag{16.12}$$

where $\vec{U}_1$ and $\vec{U}_2$ denote two trajectories for the $j$th landmark. Positives are in a certain distance $\text{dist}_{pos}$ (e.g., 1.5 mm) to the ground truth over the whole trajectories. Negatives, however, are selected individually for each time step, if the tested position in space and time is larger than $\text{dist}_{neg}$ (e.g., 3.5 mm). The probabilistic boosting tree (PBT) is applied to train a strong classifier $D_k$.

### Motion trajectory estimation

The local nonrigid motion is parameterized by both magnitude and phase of the trajectory spectrum $\vec{s}_f^j$. The parameter estimation is conducted in the marginalized search spaces $\Sigma_0, \ldots, \Sigma_{r-1}$ using the trained spectrum detectors $D_0, \ldots, D_{r-1}$ as shown in Figure 16.4. Starting from an initial zero-spectrum, we incrementally estimate the magnitude and phase of each frequency component $\vec{s}(k)$. At the stage $k$, the corresponding robust classifier $D_k$ is exhaustively scanned over the potential candidates $\mathcal{C}_{k-1} \times \mathcal{H}^{(k)}$. The probability of a candidate $\vec{C}_k \in \mathcal{C}_{k-1} \times \mathcal{H}^{(k)}$ is computed by the following objective function:

$$p(\vec{C}_k) = \prod_{t=0}^{n-1} D_k(\text{IDFT}(\vec{C}_k), I, t) \tag{16.13}$$

where $t = 0, \ldots, n-1$ is the time instance (frame index). After each step $k$, the top 50 trajectory candidates $\mathcal{C}_k$ with high probability values are preserved for the next step $k+1$. The procedure is repeated until a final set of trajectory candidates $\mathcal{C}_{r-1}$, defined in the full space $\Sigma_{r-1}$, is computed.

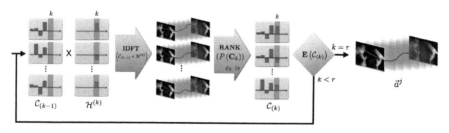

**FIGURE 16.4**

Diagram depicting the estimation of nonrigid landmark motion using trajectory spectrum learning.

### 16.3.3 COMPLETE VALVE MODEL ESTIMATION

The final stage in our hierarchical model estimation algorithm is the delineation of the full morphology and dynamics of the anatomies depicted as surface models:

$$\arg\max_{M_t^q} p(M_t^q | L_n, B_t, I_t) = \arg\max_{M_t^q} p(M_0^q, \ldots, M_{n-1}^q |$$
$$I(0), \ldots, I(n-1), B_0, \ldots, B_{n-1}, L_0, \ldots, L_{n-1}) \tag{16.14}$$

The shape model is first estimated in the end-diastole (ED) and end-systole (ES) phases of the cardiac cycle and then the nonrigid deformation is propagated to the remaining phases using a learned motion prior.

#### Shape space modeling with ShapeForest

While the classical Statistical Shape Model (or global SSM/*gSSM*) is typically represented as a Gaussian parametric model constructed by computing the principal component analysis (PCA) on the covariance matrix of all aligned ground truth shapes $S$, such an approach is unable to accurately model the complex morphological and pathological variation found in the heart valve's morphology. We instead employ a constrained form (the constrained SSM/*cSSM*) wherein the classical SSM is constructed out of $\bar{S}$, the subset of $S$ containing the most representative shapes for each particular instance. We obtain $\bar{S}$ using the *ShapeForest*.

The ShapeForest infers $\bar{S}$ by learning the shape-manifold based on geometric features defined by the sparse landmark model $L$. Two simple geometric features are utilized: *distance* features and *random plane* features. Distance features ($f_{\text{dist}}$) are generated for each unique landmark pair $(p, q)$ in $L$ as the Euclidean distance between landmarks:

$$f_{\text{dist}}(p, q) = \sqrt{\sum_{i \in \{x,y,z\}} (p^i - q^i)^2} \tag{16.15}$$

By comparison, random plane features ($f_{\text{rp}}$) are generated for each landmark $p$ in $L$ as the shortest distance between $p$ and a randomly generated plane:

$$f_{\text{rp}}(p) = \frac{ap^x + bp^y + cp^z + d}{\sqrt{a^2 + b^2 + c^2}} \quad ax + by + cz + d = 0 \tag{16.16}$$

The ShapeForest itself is constructed as a forest of un-pruned decision trees, similar to Breiman's random forest ensemble classifier (Breiman, 2001). At each tree, each nonleaf node contains a feature $f_\theta \in \{f_{\text{dist}} \cup f_{\text{rp}}\}$ and threshold value $\tau$, with both leaf and nonleaf nodes further containing a subset of shapes $S_t \in S$. Using this construction, the ShapeForest is able to learn the distance function between the geometric features and the shape variance, clustering shape instances with similar shape characteristics in the leaf nodes.

#### Training with ShapeForest

A subset of ground truth shapes $S_t = \{M_1, M_2, \ldots, M_v\} \in S$ is randomly sampled at each tree. Using the corresponding set of sparse landmarks $LM_t = \{L_1, L_2, \ldots, L_v\}$, geometric features are computed, and $S_t$ and $LM_t$ are placed at root nodes in their respective trees. The following training algorithm is executed for every tree in the ShapeForest:

1. For each feature type $f_\theta \in \{f_{\mathrm{dist}} \cup f_{\mathrm{rp}}\}$, construct a set of splitting candidates $\phi = (f_\theta, \tau)$, where each $\tau$ represents one of a number of threshold values, equally spaced between $\min(f_\theta(LM_t))$ and $\max(f_\theta(LM_t))$.

2. For each $\phi$, partition the set of shapes at the current node $S_t$ into left and right subsets:

$$S_l(\phi) = \{s_v | s_v \in S_t \wedge f_\theta(L_v) \leq \tau\} \tag{16.17}$$
$$S_r(\phi) = \{s_v | s_v \in S_t \wedge f_\theta(L_v) > \tau\} \tag{16.18}$$

Using generalized procrustes analysis (GPA), align shapes within subsets $S_t$, $S_l(\phi)$, and $S_r(\phi)$ to produce aligned sets $S_t^a$, $S_l^a(\phi)$, and $S_r^a(\phi)$.

3. For each $\phi$, compute the information gain $I(S_t, \phi)$ achieved from splitting $S_t$ into $S_l(\phi)$ and $S_r(\phi)$ as:

$$I(S_t, \phi) = \sum_{s \in S_t^a} \log(\delta(s)) - \sum_{i \in \{l,r\}} \left( \sum_{s \in S_i^a(\phi)} \log(\delta(s)) \right) \tag{16.19}$$

where $\delta(s) = s - \bar{s}$ is the deviation of aligned shape $s$ from mean shape $\bar{s}$, calculated from the set $s$ belonging to $(S_t^a, S_l^a(\phi)$, or $S_r^a(\phi))$, similar to Cootes et al. (1995).

4. Find $\phi^*$, the splitting candidate that produces the largest information gain:

$$\phi^* = \underset{\phi}{\mathrm{argmax}} \; I(S_t, \phi) \tag{16.20}$$

5. If $I(S_t, \phi^*)$ is greater or equal to a minimum splitting criteria and the tree is not at maximum depth, split the node into children, letting $S_t = S_l(\phi^*)$ at the left node and $S_t = S_r(\phi^*)$ at the right node. Update $LM_t$ at each child node accordingly. Finally, save at current node $S_t$, $f_\theta$, and $\tau$ from $\phi^*$, and $\bar{L}$ as the GPA-aligned mean of landmarks that are associated with each shape in $S_t$.

6. Repeat steps 1-5 of the algorithm at each child node until each tree is fully grown.

## Model estimation in key cardiac phases

Using the previously estimated model parameters, a precomputed shape of the valvular model is placed into the volumes $I(t_{\mathrm{ED}})$ and $I(t_{\mathrm{ES}})$. When given the sparse landmark model $L_t^j$ obtained from a CT image as described earlier in Section 16.3.2, the ShapeForest computes the feature values for $L_t^j$, $f_\theta(L) \in \{f_{\mathrm{dist}}(L_t^j) \cup f_{\mathrm{rp}}(L_t^j)\}$. Each individual decision tree is then traversed from their root node through the evaluation of $f_\theta(L)$ against $\tau$ at each node, branching left or right based on the outcome of this comparison, until a leaf node is reached. The set of shapes $S_t$ at each traversed leaf node are finally aggregated in a shape-frequency histogram, with the most frequently occurring shapes found across all trees used to construct an instance specific constrained SSM. Using $L_t^j$ and the constrained SSM inferred by ShapeForest, an initial shape model $(M_t^q)$ is generated and fitted to the image data. The Powell optimization is then used consecutively to estimate the coefficients for the first five largest eigenvectors. Starting with the largest eigenvector the best value is found to accurately match $L_t^j$ in the images. The initial estimate is then deformed to fit the true valvular anatomy using learned object boundary detectors, regularized by cSSM (see Figure 16.5).

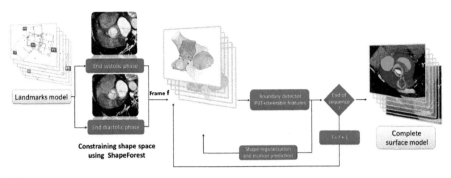

**FIGURE 16.5**

Diagram depicting the estimation of the comprehensive valve model. Estimation in the full cardiac cycle.

Learning-based methods provide robust results (Zheng et al., 2008; Yang et al., 2008) by utilizing both gradients and image intensities at different image resolutions and by incorporating the local context. Hence, the nonrigid deformation is guided by a boundary detector $D_b$ learned using the probabilistic boosting tree and steerable features (Zheng et al., 2008). After initialization, $D_b$ evaluates hypotheses for each discrete boundary point along its corresponding normal direction. The new boundary points are set to the hypotheses with maximal probability. To guarantee physiologically compliant results, the final model is obtained after projecting the estimated points to the cSSM learned using the ShapeForest (Ionasec et al., 2010; Swee and Grbić, 2014).

## Motion estimation

Starting from the detection results in the ED and ES phases, the model deformations are propagated in both forward and backward directions using learned motion priors similar to Yang et al. (2008) (see Figure 16.5). The motion prior is estimated at the training stage using motion manifold learning and hierarchical $K$-means clustering, from a preannotated database of sequences containing one cardiac cycle each. First, the temporal deformations are aligned by 4D generalized Procrustes analysis. Next, a low-dimensional embedding is computed from the aligned training sequences using the ISOMAP algorithm (Tenenbaum et al., 2000), to represent the highly nonlinear motion of the heart valves. Finally, in order to extract the modes of motion $\vec{X}_m$, the motion sequences are clustered with hierarchical $K$-means based on the Euclidean distance in the lower dimensional manifold.

One-step forward prediction is used to select the correct motion mode for predicting time step $T$. Therefore, the previous shapes $M_t^q$ from time steps $t = 1 \dots T - 1$ and the corresponding time steps in each of the motion modes $\vec{X}_m$ are subsampled by a constant factor $k$ and the thin plate spline (TPS) transformation $T_{\text{TPS}}$ computed. The mean error between the warped shape and the corresponding shape on each motion mode is computed, and the motion mode with minimum distance is selected for prediction:

$$E_{\text{TPS}}\left(\overline{\overline{X}}_m(t), M_t\right) = \frac{k}{N} \sum_{j=1}^{N/k} \left\|\overline{\overline{X}}_m^{\,j}(t) - T_{\text{TPS}}(M_t^j)\right\| \tag{16.21}$$

$$\overline{\overline{X}}(T) = \arg\min_m \frac{1}{T-1} \sum_{t=1}^{T-1} E_{\text{TPS}}\left(\overline{\overline{X}}_m(t), M_t\right) \tag{16.22}$$

where $N$ denotes the number of points in $M_t$, $\overline{\overline{X}}_m^{\,j}$ and $M_t^j$ are shape vertices, and $\overline{\overline{X}}(T)$ the selected motion mode. The shape prediction $M_T'$ for the following frame $T$ is then computed by inverse TPS mapping $M_T' = T_{\text{TPS}}^{-1}(\overline{\overline{X}}(T))$ and the boundary detector $D_b$ deforms the initialization to make it fit the data in the update step. To ensure temporal consistency and smooth motion and to avoid drifting and outliers, two collaborative trackers, an optical flow tracker, and a boundary detection tracker $D_b$, are used in our method. The results are then fused into a single estimate by averaging the computed deformations and the procedure is repeated until the full 4D model is estimated for the complete sequence.

## 16.4 EXPERIMENTAL RESULTS

In this section, we demonstrate the performance of the proposed patient-specific parameter estimation framework from multi-modal images. Experiments are performed on a large and heterogeneous data set acquired using CT and TEE from 476 patients affected by a large spectrum of cardiovascular and valvular heart diseases: regurgitation, stenosis, prolapse, aortic root dilation, and bicuspid aortic valve. The imaging data set includes 613 cardiac CT, 5061 TEE collected from medical centers around the world.

Each volume in our data set is associated with an annotation obtained through an expert-guided process that includes the manual placing of anatomical landmarks and delineation of anatomical surfaces. The obtained models are consider, as ground truth and were used for training and testing of the proposed algorithms. Threefold cross validation was performed for all experiments and reported results reflect performance on unseen test data.

### 16.4.1 PERFORMANCE OF THE OBJECT LOCALIZATION AND RIGID MOTION ESTIMATION

The performance of the global location and rigid motion estimation, $\theta$, described in Section 16.3.1 is quantified at the box corners of the detected time-dependent valve bounding box. The average Euclidean distance between the eight bounding box points, defined by the similarity transformation parameters $\{(c_x, c_y, c_z), (\vec{\alpha}_x, \vec{\alpha}_y, \vec{\alpha}_z), (s_x, s_y, s_z)\}$ and the ground-truth box is reported. Table 16.1 illustrates the mean errors and corresponding standard deviations distributed over the aortic and mitral valve and employed image modalities. The average accuracy of the individual detection stages is $3.09 \pm 3.02$ mm for position, $9.72 \pm 5.98°$ for orientation, and $6.50 \pm 4.19$ mm for scale.

**Table 16.1  Accuracy of the Global Location and Rigid Motion Estimation, Quantified From the Box Corners and Reported Using the Mean Error and Standard Deviation Distribution Over Each Valve and Employed Modality**

| Mean/STD (mm) | Aortic Valve | Mitral Valve |
| --- | --- | --- |
| Cardiac CT | $4.40 \pm 1.98$ | $6.94 \pm 2.19$ |
| TEE | $4.78 \pm 3.26$ | $5.00 \pm 2.02$ |

**Table 16.2  Accuracy of the Nonrigid Landmark Motion Estimation, Quantified by the Euclidean Distance and Reported Using the Mean Error and Standard Deviation Distribution Over the Aortic and Mitral Valve and Employed Modality**

| Mean/STD (mm) | Aortic Valve | Mitral Valve |
| --- | --- | --- |
| Cardiac CT | $2.72 \pm 1.52$ | $2.79 \pm 1.20$ |
| TEE | $2.79 \pm 1.26$ | $3.60 \pm 1.56$ |

## 16.4.2 PERFORMANCE OF THE NONRIGID-LANDMARK MOTION ESTIMATION

The accuracy of the trajectory spectrum learning algorithm (see Section 16.3.2), which estimates the nonrigid landmark motion model, $L$, is measured using the Euclidean distance between detected and corresponding ground truth landmark trajectories. Table 16.2 demonstrates the precision expressed in mean errors and standard deviations, distributed over the two valves and two data sources. Note that reported values are obtained by averaging the performance of individual landmarks with respect to the corresponding valve.

## 16.4.3 PERFORMANCE OF THE COMPREHENSIVE VALVE MODEL ESTIMATION

The accuracy of the comprehensive valvular model estimation, $M$ (see Section 16.3.3), is evaluated by utilizing the point-to-mesh distance. For each point on a surface $\vec{p}$, we search for the closest distance (computed based on the triangulated mesh model) on the other surface to calculate the Euclidean distance. To guarantee a symmetric measurement, the point-to-mesh distance is calculated in two directions, from detected to ground truth surfaces and vice versa. Table 16.3 contains the mean error and standard deviation distributed over the two valves and image types. Examples of estimation results are given in Figure 16.6.

**Table 16.3 Accuracy of the Valve Model Estimation, Quantified by the Point-to-Mesh Distance and Reported Using the Mean Error and Standard Deviation Distribution Over the Aortic and Mitral Valve and Employed Modality**

| Mean/STD (mm) | Aortic Valve | Mitral Valve |
|---|---|---|
| Cardiac CT | 0.69 ± 0.19 | 2.02 ± 0.57 |
| TEE | 1.35 ± 0.54 | 2.29 ± 0.64 |

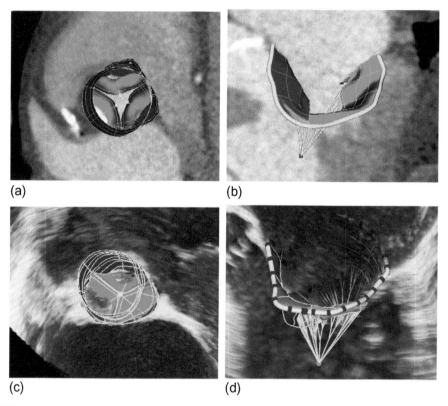

**FIGURE 16.6**

Examples of complete valves model estimation: (a) aortic valve in cardiac CT, (b) mitral valve in cardiac CT, (c) aortic valve in TEE, and (d) mitral valve in TEE.

On a standard PC with a six-core 2.8 GHz processor and 8.0 GB memory, the total computation time for all three estimation stages is 4.8 s per volume (approximately 120 s for average length volume sequences), from which the global location and rigid motion estimation requires 15% of the computation time (approximately 0.7 s), nonrigid landmark motion 54% (approximately 2.6 s), and complete valve model estimation 31% (approximately 1.5 s).

## 16.5 CONCLUSIONS

In this chapter, we propose a personalized model for quantitative and qualitative evaluation of the left heart valvular apparatus from multi-modal cardiac image data. It is capable of delineating the full anatomy and dynamics needed to depict a large variation of valve pathologies, especially diseases affecting several valves. Its hierarchical approach using state-of-the-art machine learning algorithms enables patient specific model estimation within 4 s per volume.

The method described in this chapter has the potential to advance the current patient management of valvular heart disease by reducing the associated morbidity, mortality, and treatment costs. This is especially valid with the recent increase of minimally invasive techniques which are replacing regular open-heart valve repair and replacement procedures.

## REFERENCES

Agarwal, A., Triggs, B., 2004. Tracking articulated motion using a mixture of autoregressive models. In: Proceedings of the European Conference on Computer Vision III, pp. 54–65.

Bonow, R.O., Carabello, B.A., Chatterjee, K., de Leon Jr., A.C., Faxon, D.P., Freed, M.D., Gaasch, W.H., Lytle, B.W., Nishimura, R.A., O'Gara, P.T., O'Rourke, R.A., Otto, C.M., Shah, P.M., Shanewise, J.S., 2006. ACC/AHA 2006 guidelines for the management of patients with valvular heart disease: a report of the American College of Cardiology/American Heart Association Task Force on Practice Guidelines (writing Committee to Develop Guidelines for the Management of Patients With Valvular Heart Disease). Circulation 114 (5), 84–231.

Breiman, L., 2001. Random forests. In: Machine Learning, pp. 5–32.

Conti, C., Stevanella, M., Maffessanti, F., Trunfio, S., Votta, E., Roghi, A., Parodi, O., Caiani, E., Redaelli, A., 2010. Mitral valve modelling in ischemic patients: finite element analysis from cardiac magnetic resonance imaging. In: Computing in Cardiology, pp. 1059–1062.

Cootes, T.F., Taylor, C.J., Cooper, D.H., Graham, J., 1995. Active shape models—their training and application. Comput. Vis. Image Underst. 61 (1), 38–59.

De Hart, J., Peters, G., Schreurs, P., Baaijens, F., 2002. A three-dimensional computational analysis of fluid-structure interaction in the aortic valve. J. Biomech. 36 (1), 103–110.

Ecabert, O., Peters, J., Schramm, H., Lorenz, C., von Berg, J., Walker, M.J., Vembar, M., Olszewski, M.E., Subramanyan, K., Lavi, G., Weese, J., 2008. Automatic model-based segmentation of the heart in CT images. IEEE Trans. Med. Imaging 27 (9), 1189–1201.

Fritz, D., Rinck, D., Dillmann, R., Scheuring, M., 2006. Segmentation of the left and right cardiac ventricle using a combined bi-temporal statistical model. In: SPIE Medical Imaging, pp. 605–614.

Giordana, F., Capriolo, M., Frea, S., Marra, W.G., Giorgi, M., Bergamasco, L., Omedè, P.L., Sheiban, I., D'Amico, M., Bovolo, V., et al., 2013. Impact of TAVI on mitral regurgitation: a prospective echocardiographic study. Echocardiography 30 (3), 250–257.

Grbić, S., Ionasec, R., Vitanovski, D., Voigt, I., Wang, Y., Georgescu, B., Navab, N., Comaniciu, D., 2010a, Complete valvular heart apparatus model from 4D cardiac CT. In: International Conference on Medical Image Computing and Computer-Assisted Intervention Medical Image Computing and Computer-Assisted Intervention: MICCAI, vol. 13, pp. 218–226.

Grbić, S., Ionasec, R.I., Zäuner, D., Zheng, Y., Georgescu, B., Comaniciu, D., 2010b, Aortic valve and ascending aortic root modeling from 3D and 3D+t CT. In: Wong, K.H., Miga, M.I. (Eds.), SPIE Medical Imaging, pp. 76250H-76250H-8.

Grbić, S., Ionasec, R., Vitanovski, D., Voigt, I., Wang, Y., Georgescu, B., Navab, N., Comaniciu, D., 2012. Complete valvular heart apparatus model from 4D cardiac CT. Med. Image Anal. 16 (5), 1003–1014. http://dx.doi.org/10.1016/j.media.2012.02.003.

Grbić, S., Ionasec, R., Mansi, T., Georgescu, B., Vega-Higuera, F., Navab, N., Comaniciu, D., 2013a, Advanced intervention planning for transcatheter aortic valve implantation (TAVI) from CT using volumetric models. In: 2013 IEEE International Symposium on Biomedical Imaging: From Nano to Macro.

Grbić, S., Mansi, T., Ionasec, R., Georgescu, B., Schoebinger, M., Navab, N., Comaniciu, D., 2013b, Image-based computational models for TAVI planning: from CT images to implant deployment. In: International Conference on Medical Image Computing and Computer-Assisted Intervention.

Grbić, S., Swee, J.K., Ionasec, R., 2014. ShapeForest: Building constrained statistical shape models with decision trees. In: Fleet, D., Pajdla, T., Schiele, B., Tuytelaars, T. (Eds.), Computer Vision—ECCV 2014, Lecture Notes in Computer Science, vol. 8691. Springer International Publishing, pp. 597–612.

Harling, L., Saso, S., Jarral, O.A., Kourliouros, A., Kidher, E., Athanasiou, T., 2011. Aortic valve replacement for aortic stenosis in patients with concomitant mitral regurgitation: should the mitral valve be dealt with? Eur. J. Cardiothorac. Surg. 40 (5), 1087–1096.

Huang, J., Huang, X., Metaxas, D., Axel, L., 2007. Dynamic texture based heart localization and segmentation in 4-D cardiac images. In: ISBI 2007 4th IEEE International Symposium on Biomedical Imaging From Nano to Macro 2007. IEEE, pp. 852–855.

Ionasec, R.I., Georgescu, B., Gassner, E., Vogt, S., Kutter, O., Scheuering, M., Navab, N., Comaniciu, D., 2008. Dynamic model-driven quantification and visual evaluation of the aortic valve from 4D CT. In: ICCAI, pp. 686–694.

Ionasec, R.I., et al., 2009a. Robust motion estimation using trajectory spectrum learning: application to aortic and mitral valve modeling from 4D TEE. In: Proceedings of the International Conference on Computer Vision.

Ionasec, R.I., Voigt, I., Georgescu, B., Houle, H., Hornegger, J., Navab, N., Comaniciu, D., 2009b, Personalized modeling and assessment of the aortic-mitral coupling from 4D TEE and CT. In: MICCAI, Heidelberg, pp. 767–775.

Ionasec, R.I., Wang, Y., Georgescu, B., Voigt, I., Navab, N., Comaniciu, D., 2009c, Robust motion estimation using trajectory spectrum learning: application to aortic and mitral valve modeling from 4D TEE. In: Proceedings of the Twelfth International Conference on Computer Vision (ICCV). IEEE, Kyoto, Japan.

Ionasec, R.I., Voigt, I., Georgescu, B., Wang, Y., Houle, H., Vega-Higuera, F., Navab, N., Comaniciu, D., 2010. Patient-specific modeling and quantification of the aortic and mitral valves from 4-D cardiac CT and TEE. IEEE Trans. Med. Imaging 29 (9), 1636–1651. http://dx.doi.org/10.1109/TMI.2010.2048756.

Jablokow, A., 2009. National Center for Health Statistics: National Hospital Discharge Survey: Annual summaries with detailed diagnosis and procedure data. In: Data on Health Resources Utilization, vol. 13.

Kunzelman, K., Einstein, D., Cochran, R., 2007. Fluid-structure interaction models of the mitral valve: function in normal and pathological states. Philos. Trans. R. Soc. Lond. B, Biol. Sci. 362 (1484), 1393–1406.

Lloyd-Jones, D., Adams, R., Carnethon, M., De Simone, G., Ferguson, T.B., Flegal, K., Ford, E., Furie, K., Go, A., Greenlund, K., Haase, N., Hailpern, S., Ho, M., Howard, V., Kissela, B., Kittner, S., Lackland, D., Lisabeth, L., Marelli, A., McDermott, M., Meigs, J., Mozaffarian, D., Nichol, G., O'Donnell, C., Roger, V., Rosamond, W., Sacco, R., Sorlie, P., Stafford, R., Steinberger, J., Thom, T., Wasserthiel-Smoller, S., Wong, N., Wylie-Rosett, J., Hong, Y., American Heart Association Statistics Committee and Stroke Statistics Subcommittee, 2009. Heart disease and stroke statistics—2009 update: a report from the American Heart Association Statistics Committee and Stroke Statistics Subcommittee. Circulation 119 (3), e21-e181.

Lorenz, C., von Berg, J., 2006. A comprehensive shape model of the heart. Med. Image Anal. 10 (4), 657–670.

Park, J., Metaxas, D., Young, A., Axel, L., 1996. Deformable models with parameter functions for cardiac motion analysis from tagged MRI data. IEEE Trans. Med. Imaging 15 (3), 278–289.

Peskin, C.S., McQueen, D.M., 1996. Case Studies in Mathematical Modeling: Ecology, Physiology, and Cell Biology. Prentice-Hall, Englewood Cliffs, NJ, USA. 309–337 .

Rueckert, D., Burger, P., 1997. Geometrically deformable templates for shape-based segmentation and tracking in cardiac MR images. In: EMMCVPR '97: Proceedings of the First International Workshop on Energy Minimization Methods in Computer Vision and Pattern Recognition. Springer-Verlag, London, UK, pp. 83–98.

Schievano, S., Migliavacca, F., Coats, S., Khambadkone, L., Carminati, M., Wilson, N., Deanfield, J., Bonhoeffer, P., Taylor, A., 2007. Percutaneous pulmonary valve implantation based on rapid prototyping of right ventricular outflow tract and pulmonary trunk from MR data. Radiology 242 (2), 490–449.

Schneider, R.J., Perrin, D.P., Vasilyev, N.V., Marx, G.R., Del Nido, P.J., Howe, R.D., 2010. Mitral annulus segmentation from 3D ultrasound using graph cuts. IEEE Trans. Med. Imaging 29 (9), 1676–1687.

Soncini, M., Votta, E., Zinicchino, S., Burrone, V., Mangini, A., Lemma, M., Antona, C., Redaelli, A., 2009. Aortic root performance after valve sparing procedure: a comparative finite element analysis. Med. Eng. Phys. 31 (2), 234–243.

Staib, L.H., Duncan, J.S., 1996. Model-based deformable surface finding for medical images. IEEE Trans. Med. Imaging 15 (5), 720–731.

Swee, J.K., Grbić, S., 2014. Advanced transcatheter aortic valve implantation (TAVI) planning from CT with ShapeForest. In: Golland, P., Hata, N., Barillot, C., Hornegger, J., Howe, R., Medical Image Computing and Computer-Assisted Intervention—MICCAI 2014, vol. 8674. Lecture Notes in Computer Science, pp. 17–24. Springer International Publishing.

Tenenbaum, J.B., de Silva, V., Langford, J.C., 2000. A global geometric framework for nonlinear dimensionality reduction. Science 290 (5500), 2319–2323.

Tu, Z., 2005. Probabilistic boosting-tree: learning discriminative methods for classification, recognition, and clustering. In: ICCV 2005, vol. 2, pp. 1589–1596.

Tzikas, A., Piazza, N., van Dalen, B.M., Schultz, C., Geleijnse, M.L., van Geuns, R.J., Galema, T.W., Nuis, R.J., Otten, A., Gutierrez-Chico, J.L., et al., 2010. Changes in mitral regurgitation after transcatheter aortic valve implantation. Catheter. Cardiovasc. Interv. 75 (1), 43–49.

Veronesi, F., Corsi, C., Sugeng, L., Mor-Avi, V., Caiani, E., Weinert, L., Lamberti, C., Land, R., 2009. A study of functional anatomy of aortic-mitral valve coupling using 3D matrix transesophageal echocardiography. Circ. Cardiovasc. Imaging 2 (1), 24–31.

Vitanovski, D., Ionasec, R.I., Georgescu, B., Huber, M., Taylor, A., Hornegger, J., Comaniciu, D., 2009. Personalized pulmonary trunk modeling for intervention planning and valve assessment estimated from CT data. In: International Conference on Medical Image Computing and Computer-Assisted Intervention, London, USA, pp. 17–25.

Vitanovski, D., Tsymbal, A., Ionasec, R., Georgescu, B., Huber, M., Hornegger, J., Comaniciu, D., 2010. Cross-modality assessment and planning for pulmonary trunk treatment using CT and MRI imaging. In: International Conference on Medical Image Computing and Computer-Assisted Intervention (MICCAI), Beijing, China.

Votta, E., Caiani, E., Veronesi, F., Soncini, M., Montevecchi, F., Redaelli, A., 2008. Mitral valve finite-element modelling from ultrasound data: a pilot study for a new approach to understand mitral function and clinical scenarios. Philos. Transact. A Math. Phys. Eng. Sci. 366 (1879), 3411–3434.

Waechter, I., et al., 2010. Patient specific models for planning and guidance of minimally invasive aortic valve implantation. In: MICCAI 2010, Lecture Notes in Computer Science. Springer.

Watanabe, N., Ogasawara, Y., Yamaura, Y., Kawamoto, T., Toyota, E., Akasaka, T., Yoshida, K., 2005. Quantitation of mitral valve tenting in ischemic mitral regurgitation by transthoracic real-time three-dimensional echocardiography. J. Am. Coll. Cardiol. 45 (5), 763–769.

Yang, L., Georgescu, B., Zheng, Y., Meer, P., Comaniciu, D., 2008. 3D ultrasound tracking of the left ventricle using one-step forward prediction and data fusion of collaborative trackers. In: IEEE Conference on Computer Vision and Pattern Recognition.

Zheng, Y., Barbu, A., Georgescu, B., Scheuering, M., Comaniciu, D., 2008. Four-chamber heart modeling and automatic segmentation for 3D cardiac CT volumes using marginal space learning and steerable features. IEEE TMI 27 (11), 1668–1681.

Zhuang, X., Rhode, K.S., Razavi, R.S., Hawkes, D.J., Ourselin, S., 2010a. A registration-based propagation framework for automatic whole heart segmentation of cardiac MRI. IEEE Trans. Med. Imaging 29 (9), 1612–1625.

Zhuang, X., Yao, C., Ma, Y., Hawkes, D., Penney, G., Ourselin, S., 2010b, Registration-based propagation for whole heart segmentation from compounded 3D echocardiography. In: IEEE International Symposium on Biomedical Imaging From Nano to Macro 2010. IEEE, pp. 1093–1096.

# MODEL-BASED 3D CARDIAC IMAGE SEGMENTATION WITH MARGINAL SPACE LEARNING

# 17

**Y. Zheng**

*Imaging and Computer Vision, Siemens Corporate Technology, Princeton, NJ, USA*

## CHAPTER OUTLINE

## 17.1 INTRODUCTION

Cardiovascular disease is the number one cause of death in the developed countries and it claims more lives each year than the next seven leading causes of death combined (Lloyd-Jones et al., 2009). The costs for addressing cardiovascular disease in the United States will triple by 2030, from 273 billion to 818 billion (in 2008 dollars) (Heidenreich et al., 2011). With the capability of generating images of a patient's inside body noninvasively, medical imaging is ubiquitously present in the current clinical practice. Various imaging modalities, such as computed tomography (CT), magnetic resonance imaging (MRI), ultrasound, and nuclear imaging, are widely available in clinical practice to generate images of the heart. And, different imaging modalities meet different clinical requirements. For example, ultrasound is most widely used for cardiac function analysis (i.e., the pumping of a cardiac chamber) due to its low cost and free-of-radiation dose; nuclear imaging and MRI are used for myocardial perfusion imaging to measure viability of the myocardium; while CT reveals the most detailed cardiac anatomical structures and is routinely used for coronary artery imaging.

S. Kevin Zhou (Ed): Medical Image Recognition, Segmentation and Parsing. http://dx.doi.org/10.1016/B978-0-12-802581-9.00017-2

Physicians review these images to determine the health of the heart and to diagnose disease. Due to the large amount of information captured by the images, it is time consuming for physicians to identify the target anatomy and to perform measurements and quantification. For example, many 3D measurements (such as the volume of a heart chamber, the heart ejection fraction, the thickness and the thickening of the myocardium, or the strain and torsion of the myocardium) are very tedious to calculate without the help of an intelligent postprocessing software system. Various automatic or semi-automatic cardiac imaging analysis systems have been developed and demonstrated to reduce the exam time (thereby increase the patient throughput), increase consistency and reproducibility of the exam, and boost diagnosis accuracy of a radiologist.

Automatic segmentation (including automatic localization) of the target anatomical structure is often a prerequisite for disease diagnosis and quantification. Many generic nonmodel-based image segmentation methods (from simple thresholding and region growing to more advanced approaches, e.g., active contours, level sets, graph cuts, random walker) can be applied. There are a few limitations of these approaches in the application to cardiac image segmentation. First, since no or little prior shape information is exploited, such approaches often lack robustness under imaging artifacts. Second, no anatomical information is explicitly provided after segmentation. However, in the medical domain, the anatomical information is important for disease diagnosis and quantification (e.g., to measure the size of the aortic root, we need to know the location of the aortic root in the segmented aorta mask).

A model-based segmentation approach is preferred in cardiac image segmentation. The prior model information can be represented in different formats, that is, voxel labels in an atlas or a geometric surface mesh in an active shape model (ASM) (Cootes et al., 1995). An atlas-based method tries to transfer the voxel labels from a presegmented atlas to an input volume through volume registration. However, volume registration is often computationally expensive, especially for nonrigid volume registration. In this chapter, we review our previous work on model-based cardiac image segmentation with marginal space learning (MSL) (Zheng and Comaniciu, 2014). We developed a comprehensive anatomical cardiac model including four chambers, aorta, pulmonary arteries, pulmonary veins, and coronary arteries. The segmentation of a cardiac anatomy is normally composed of two steps: automatic object pose estimation, followed by detailed delineation of the object boundary. To accurately localize a 3D object, we need to estimate nine pose parameters (three for position, three for orientation, and three for anisotropic scaling). In our approach, MSL is applied to efficiently estimate the object pose. After that, a mean shape (an average shape calculated from a training set) is aligned to the estimated pose to provide an initial segmentation. The segmentation is further refined using a discriminative ASM (i.e., an ASM with a machine learning-based boundary detector).

This general approach can be applied to segment different anatomical structures in various imaging modalities, including all four cardiac chambers. The heart is connected to other body parts via five great vessels (namely, aorta, pulmonary arteries, pulmonary veins, superior vena cava, and inferior vena cava). Due to the limited field-of-view, the great vessels are only partially present in many volumes. Furthermore, some great vessels (e.g., pulmonary veins) exhibit large anatomical variations (Zheng et al., 2014). Therefore, we cannot directly apply the MSL-based segmentation framework to detect and segment the great vessels. Here, we present part-based segmentation approaches. A holistic object can often be naturally split into several parts and each part is simpler and more consistent, thereby facilitating the model-based segmentation.

Coronary artery disease is the most common cardiac disease. However, segmentation of the coronary arteries is a challenging problem due to their large anatomical variations and small caliber.

Even though the whole coronary tree exhibits large variations, the relative position of the major coronary arteries, namely left anterior descending artery (LAD), left circumflex artery (LCX), and right coronary artery (RCA), with respect to the cardiac chambers is quite consistent. We can predict the initial centerline path of a major coronary artery using the segmented cardiac chambers (Zheng et al., 2013). After extracting the major coronary artery centerlines, the side branches can be extracted using a data-driven approach (Tek et al., 2008).

The remainder of this chapter is organized as follows. First, we briefly review the MSL-based anatomical structure segmentation framework in Section 17.2. After that, we present approaches to segmenting cardiac chambers in Section 17.3, great vessels in Section 17.4, and coronary arteries in Section 17.5. In Section 17.6, we quantitatively evaluate the segmentation accuracy of cardiac chambers and coronary artery centerlines on cardiac CT data. This chapter is concluded in Section 17.7.

## 17.2 MARGINAL SPACE LEARNING FOR 3D OBJECT SEGMENTATION

Previously, we proposed MSL (Zheng et al., 2007, 2008) as an efficient and robust method for 3D anatomical structure detection and segmentation in medical images. Here, we give a brief overview of MSL and interested readers are referred to Zheng and Comaniciu (2014) for more details. Our technique is based on recent advances in learning discriminative models to exploit rich information embedded in a large expert-annotated database. We formulate the segmentation as a two-step learning problem: anatomical structure localization and boundary delineation as shown in Figure 17.1.

Object localization (or detection) is a prerequisite for an automatic segmentation system and discriminative learning-based approaches have proved to be efficient and robust for solving 2D object detection problems (Viola and Jones, 2001). In these methods, object detection is formulated as a classification problem: whether an image block contains the target object or not. The object pose parameter space is quantized into a large set of discrete hypotheses and an exhaustive search is used to pick the best hypothesis. To be specific, each hypothesis is tested by the trained classifier to get a detection score and the hypothesis with the largest score can be taken as the final detection result.

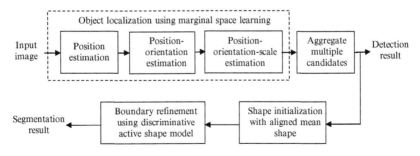

**FIGURE 17.1**

Diagram of MSL-based nonrigid object detection and segmentation.

To accurately localize a 3D object, nine pose parameters need to be estimated (three for translation, three for orientation, and three for anisotropic scaling). With the exponential increase of potential pose parameter combinations, exhaustive search is not practical for 3D object detection. The idea of MSL is not to learn a classifier directly in the full similarity transformation space but to incrementally learn classifiers on marginal spaces. In our case, we split the estimation into three steps: position estimation, position-orientation estimation, and position-orientation-scale estimation. After each step, we only keep a small number of promising hypotheses; therefore, the pose parameter space is pruned significantly to increase the detection efficiency.

After detection, we get the position, orientation, and scale of the object. The mean shape is aligned to the estimated transformation to get a rough estimate of the object shape. We then deform the shape to fit the object boundary. Active shape models (ASM) (Cootes et al., 1995) are widely used to deform an initial estimate of a nonrigid shape under the guidance of image evidences and shape prior. The nonlearning-based generic boundary detector in the original ASM (Cootes et al., 1995) is not robust under complex background or weak edges. Learning-based methods have been demonstrated to have better performance on boundary detection in 2D images (Martin et al., 2004; Dollár et al., 2006) since they can exploit more image evidence than a handcrafted boundary detector. In the previous work (Martin et al., 2004; Dollár et al., 2006), a detector was trained to detect the boundary with a specific orientation (e.g., horizontal boundary). In order to detect a boundary with different orientations, we need to perform detection on a set of rotated images. In this work, we use discriminative ASM by extending learning-based methods to 3D and completely avoiding time-consuming volume rotation using efficient steerable features.

MSL provides a generic framework for automatic object detection and segmentation. Its efficiency can be further boosted by exploiting the prior constraints among the pose parameters in the marginal spaces (Zheng et al., 2009a), resulting in detection speed of a fraction of a second for most applications. MSL has been successfully applied to many 3D anatomical structure detection and segmentation problems in all major medical imaging modalities. Please refer to Zheng and Comaniciu (2014) for a comprehensive list of exemplar applications of MSL in medical imaging.

## 17.3 CARDIAC CHAMBER SEGMENTATION

In this section, we apply the MSL framework to detect/segment all four cardiac chambers, namely, left ventricle (LV), right ventricle (RV), left atrium (LA), and right atrium (RA). For the LV, we segment both the endocardium and epicardium surfaces; while for the other chambers, we only segment the endocardium since the myocardium of those chambers is too thin for us to reliably distinguish epicardium from endocardium. Important landmarks (e.g., valves and ventricular septum cusps) are explicitly represented in our model as control points. Please note, in some applications (e.g., 3D visualization of coronary arteries or radiotherapy planning to treat lung nodules), it is desirable to separate the whole heart from surrounding tissues (a.k.a. heart isolation), which requires an accurate segmentation of the pericardium (the outermost surface of the heart). The same technology presented in this section can also be applied for pericardium segmentation. Due to the page limit, we will omit it and interested readers are referred to Zheng et al. (2010) for more details.

The MSL framework presented in Section 17.2 can be applied directly for cardiac chamber segmentation. However, control points in our mesh representation have different image characteristics

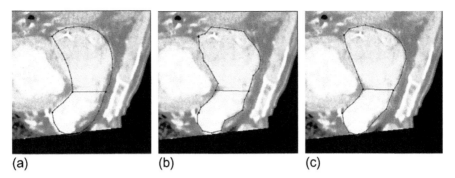

(a)          (b)          (c)

**FIGURE 17.2**

Nonrigid deformation estimation for control points (the tricuspid lateral and the right ventricular outflow tract lateral) on the right ventricle divergence plane. (a) Detected mean shape. (b) After boundary adjustment. (c) Final result after projecting the adjusted shape onto a shape subspace (25 dimensions).

and should be treated specially. As shown in Ecabert et al. (2006), without special processing, the connection of different chambers around the mitral or tricuspid valve cannot be delineated well. Our nonrigid boundary delineation process has three steps. We first estimate the deformation of control points. The thin-plate-spline (TPS) model (Bookstein, 1989) is then used to warp the initial mesh toward the refined control points for better alignment. Last, the normal mesh points are deformed to fit the image boundary. Note that, in the last step, the control points are kept unchanged.

In what follows, we illustrate the refinement of the control points on the RV divergence plane, which splits the RV into three parts (namely, RV main body, inflow tract, and outflow tract). All other control points are refined in a similar way. First, MSL is used to detect the pose of the divergence plane. After that, we get an aligned mean shape for the control points. Figure 17.2(a) shows the aligned mean shape under the estimated pose. The boundary detectors are then used to move each control point along the normal direction to the optimal position, where the score from the boundary detector is the highest. After adjustment, the control points fit the boundary well, but the contour is not smooth (Figure 17.2(b)). Finally, we project the deformed shape onto a shape subspace (Cootes et al., 1995). In all our experiments, to determine the dimension of a shape subspace, we demand it to capture 98% of shape variations. As shown in Figure 17.2(c), the statistical shape model is very effective to enforce the prior shape constraint.

The refined control points can be used to warp a mesh to make it fit the image better. Figure 17.3(a) shows the mean shape aligned with the detected RV pose. Figure 17.3(b) shows the refinement of the control points, which fit the data more accurately, but inconsistent with the mesh. Using the original and refined control points as the anchor points, we can estimate the nonrigid deformation of the TPS model and use it to warp the mesh points. As shown in Figure 17.3(c), the mesh points and the control points are consistent again after warping. Since the control points are clustered around the aortic and mitral valves for the LV, we add the point farthest from the mitral valve (which is the LV apex) as an anchor point in the TPS model to warp the LV. A similar treatment is applied to warp both atria.

Due to the large variation introduced by cardiac motion, each chamber is processed separately since the variation of a chamber is smaller than that of a whole heart. After chamber pose estimation, the

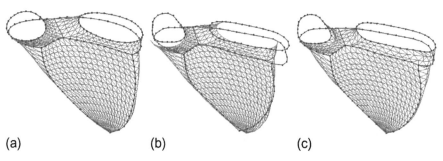

(a)          (b)          (c)

**FIGURE 17.3**

Right ventricle (RV) mesh warping using control points. Blue dots indicate control points (which are connected by red contours for visualization) and brown shows the RV mesh. (a) Mean shape using the estimated RV pose. (b) After control point refinement, the mesh is not consistent. (c) Warped mesh, where the control points and the mesh are consistent again.

initial mesh of atria and ventricles may have conflict around the mitral and tricuspid valves. Using the control points around the valves as anchor points in TPS warping, we can resolve such mesh conflict. After the whole segmentation procedure, further mesh conflict can be resolved through a postprocessing step.

After TPS warping, the mesh points are closer to the chamber boundary. To further reduce the error, we again train a boundary detector for each mesh surface. The boundary detectors are then used to adjust each point (the control points are kept unchanged in this step). Figure 17.4(a) shows the aligned LV in a cardiac CT volume. Figure 17.4(b) shows the adjusted shape. The shape constraint is enforced by projecting the adjusted shape onto a shape subspace to get the final result, as shown in Figure 17.4(c). These steps can be iterated a few times.

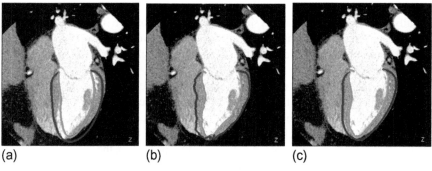

(a)          (b)          (c)

**FIGURE 17.4**

Nonrigid deformation estimation for the left ventricle with green for the endocardium and magenta for the epicardium. (a) Mean shape. (b) After boundary adjustment. (c) Final result after projecting the adjusted shape onto a shape subspace (50 dimensions).

## 17.4 GREAT VESSEL SEGMENTATION

The heart is connected to other body parts via five great vessels, namely, aorta, pulmonary arteries, pulmonary veins (PV), superior vena cava, and inferior vena cava. Great vessels exhibit large variations due to either a limited imaging field-of-view or an anatomical variation. Direct application of MSL may not work well. In this section, we review our part-based approaches for segmenting great vessels, focusing on the aorta and PVs. The proposed methods can also be extended to segment other great vessels, for example, pulmonary arteries (Zhong et al., 2012).

### 17.4.1 PART-BASED AORTA SEGMENTATION

In this work, we present a part-based aorta model (as shown in Figure 17.5(a)) by splitting the whole aorta into four parts: aortic root, ascending aorta, aortic arch, and descending aorta. Located at the center of the heart, the aortic root is always present in a cardiac scan; therefore, it is detected and segmented as the first step (Figure 17.5(b)) using MSL. If no aortic root is detected, the input volume

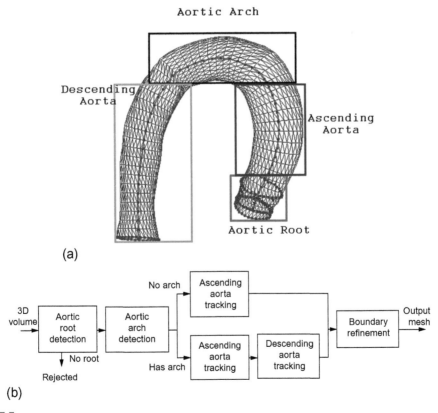

**FIGURE 17.5**

Automatic aorta segmentation with (a) the part-based aorta model and (b) automatic segmentation workflow.

is rejected. Otherwise, we move on to detect the aortic arch. Similarly, MSL is exploited to train a separate detector for the aortic arch. For about half of the volumes in our cardiac CT dataset, the aortic arch may be out of the field-of-view. If no aortic arch is present, normally the descending aorta is also missing; therefore, we skip the descending aorta segmentation step, as shown in Figure 17.5(b). The length of the ascending and descending aorta parts captured in a volume varies significantly. It is difficult to detect them as whole objects. We use a tracking technique to deal with this variation. Since the intersection of the ascending and descending aorta parts with an image slice is close to a circle, we train a 2D circle detector using Haar wavelet features and the probabilistic boosting-tree (Tu, 2005) to detect aortic circles as primitive structures for tracking. Starting from the aortic root, we detect an aortic circle on the next slice (toward the patient's head). The detector normally outputs multiple circle candidates around the true position. We pick the one closest to the circle on the current slice. If the aortic arch is detected in the volume, the tracking procedure stops on the slice touching the aortic arch. Otherwise, it stops when no aortic circle is detected or it reaches the top volume border. Tracking of the descending aorta is similar except that it starts from the aortic arch and moves toward the patient's toe. It stops on the slice with no aortic circle detected.

Assembling all the aortic parts together (the tracked aortic circles, aortic root, and aortic arch if it is present), we get an initial surface mesh of the aorta. The initialization is close to the true aorta boundary. However, a circle does not fit the boundary exactly. A learning-based boundary detector is applied for final boundary delineation. Specifically, a two-step iterative approach is used. (1) Use the learning-based boundary detector to adjust each mesh point along the surface normal to the optimal position where the response of the boundary detector is the largest. (2) Apply generic mesh smoothing (Taubin, 1996) to get a smooth surface. We repeat the above two steps a few iterations to improve the boundary delineation accuracy.

MSL can efficiently detect an object as a whole. However, as a model-based approach, it cannot deal with structural variations. Almost all previous work uses bottom-up approaches (Rueckert et al., 1997; de Bruijne et al., 2003; Zhao et al., 2006) to track the aorta centerline to handle the variations. They are neither automatic nor robust on noisy images. In comparison, we use MSL to detect the aortic root and arch, and use bottom-up tracking to detect ascending/descending aorta parts that have large variations in length. Our system is a carefully balanced combination of both approaches.

## 17.4.2 PULMONARY VEIN SEGMENTATION

Automatic segmentation of pulmonary veins (PV) has important applications for planning and visual guidance of the catheter-based ablation of atrial fibrillation (AF), the most common cardiac arrhythmia. The PVs exhibit large structural changes not just from limited field-of-view, but also from intrinsic anatomical variations in the PV drainage patterns (Marom et al., 2004). The majority of the population have two separate PVs on each side of the LA chamber, namely the left inferior PV (LIPV) and left superior PV (LSPV) on the left side, and the right inferior PV (RIPV) and right superior PV (RSPV) on the right side. A significant proportion (about 20-30%) of the population have anatomical variations and the most common variations are extra right PVs (where, besides the RIPV and RSPV, one or more extra PVs emerge separately from the right side of the LA chamber) and the left common PV (where the LIPV and LSPV merge into one before joining the chamber).

Similar to aorta segmentation, we developed a part-based approach to segmenting the PVs. As shown in Figure 17.6(a), our part-based LA model includes the LA chamber body, appendage, and four

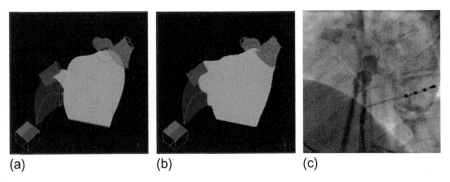

(a)                               (b)                               (c)

**FIGURE 17.6**

Part-based left atrium (LA) mesh model. (a) Meshes for the separate LA parts. (b) Final consolidated mesh model. (c) Overlay of the model onto fluoroscopic images to provide visual guidance during surgery. Note: Cyan for the LA chamber, dark red for the appendage, green for the left inferior pulmonary vein (PV), magenta for the left superior PV, orange for the right inferior PV, and blue for the right superior PV.

major PVs. The shape of the appendage is close to a tilted cone and the PVs have a tubular structure. For AF ablation, physicians only care about a proximal PV trunk; therefore, we only detect a trunk of 20 mm in length, originating from its ostium. Each part is a much simpler anatomical structure compared to the holistic one and therefore can be detected and segmented using a model-based approach (i.e., MSL in this case). After detecting and segmenting all parts, we merge them into a consolidated mesh (see Figure 17.6(b)).

Compared to the holistic approach (Manzke et al., 2010), the part-based approach can handle large structural variations. The MSL-based detection/segmentation works well for the LA chamber. However, independent detection of other parts is not as robust, either due to the low contrast (appendage) or the small object size (PVs). In C-arm CT, the appendage is particularly difficult to detect since the appendage is a pouch without outlet and the blood flow is slow inside the appendage, preventing the complete filling of contrast agent. In many datasets, the appendage is only barely visible. The MSL detector may pick the neighboring left superior PV, which often touches the appendage and has higher contrast. However, the relative position of the appendage to the LA chamber is quite consistent. The best performance is achieved by treating the appendage and chamber as a consolidated object. One MSL-based pose detector is trained to detect the combined object (see Figure 17.7).

Through comparison experiments, we found neither a holistic approach nor independent detection worked for the PVs. In this work, we propose to enforce a statistical shape constraint (Cootes et al., 1995) in PV detection. The point distribution model (PDM) is often used to enforce the statistical shape constraint among a set of landmarks. The shape variation is decomposed into orthogonal deformation modes through principal component analysis (PCA). A deformed shape is projected onto a low-dimensional deformation subspace to enforce a statistical shape constraint. For each PV, an MSL detector can estimate nine pose parameters, that is, three position parameters $(T_x, T_y, T_z)$, three orientation Euler angles $(O_x, O_y, O_z)$, and three anisotropic scaling parameters $(S_x, S_y, S_z)$. Different from the conventional PDM, we also want to enforce the constraint among the estimated orientation and size of PVs. One solution is to stack all PV pose parameters into a big vector to perform PCA.

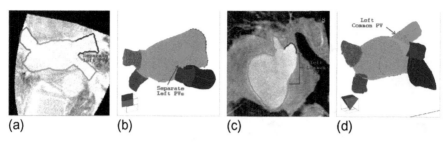

(a)                    (b)                    (c)                    (d)

**FIGURE 17.7**

Pulmonary vein (PV) segmentation results on two datasets. (a, b) A patient with separate left inferior (green) and superior (magenta) PVs. (c, d) A patient with a left common PV.

However, the position and orientation parameters are measured in different units. If not weighted properly, the extracted deformation modes may be dominated by one category of transformation. Furthermore, the Euler angles (for 3D orientation representation) are periodic (with a period of $2\pi$), which prevents the application of PCA. Boisvert et al. (2006) proposed to build a shape model on a Riemannian manifold on which we have an intrinsic measurement of the orientation distance. However, they still need to heuristically assign a proper weight to the distance in translation w.r.t. the distance in orientation.

In this work, we use a new presentation of the pose parameters to avoid the above problems. Alternative to the Euler angles, the object orientation can be represented as a rotation matrix $R = (R_x, R_y, R_z)$ and each column of $R$ defines an axis. The object pose parameters can be fully represented by a four-point set $(T, V_x, V_y, V_z)$, where $T$ is the object center and

$$V_x = T + S_x R_x, \quad V_y = T + S_y R_y, \quad V_z = T + S_z R_z \qquad (17.1)$$

The pose of each PV is represented as four points. Besides the constraint among the PVs, we also add the already detected LA chamber center and appendage center to stabilize the detection. In total, we get a set of 18 points.

In our experiments, after detecting the position, orientation, and size of the PVs, we project their poses onto a subspace with eight dimensions (which explains about 75% of the total variation) to enforce a statistical shape constraint. After enforcing a statistical shape constraint, the PV center is given by point $\hat{T}$. We can recover the orientation ($\hat{R}$) and scale ($\hat{S}$) by simple inversion of Eq. (17.1). However, the estimate $\hat{R}$ is generally not a true rotation matrix ($\hat{R}^T\hat{R} \neq I$). We want to find the nearest rotation matrix $R_o$ to minimize the sum of squares of elements in the difference matrix $R_o - \hat{R}$, which is equivalent to

$$R_o = \arg\min_R \text{Trace}((R - \hat{R})^T(R - \hat{R})) \qquad (17.2)$$

subject to $R_o^T R_o = I$. Here, Trace(.) is the sum of the diagonal elements. The optimal solution is given by Horn (1987)

$$R_o = \hat{R}(\hat{R}^T\hat{R})^{-1/2} \qquad (17.3)$$

After constrained detection and segmentation, we get six separate meshes (the LA chamber, appendage, and four PVs), as shown in Figure 17.6(a). There may be gaps and/or intersections among different meshes. However, physicians prefer a consolidated mesh with different anatomical structures labeled with different colors. To generate such a consolidated mesh, we first project the proximal rim of a PV or appendage along the centerline onto the LA chamber to eliminate the gaps among different mesh parts. Now, the part meshes are fully connected. However, the mesh intersections may still be present since a piece of the PV mesh may lie inside the chamber. It is complicated to work directly on the meshes. Instead, we convert the meshes to a volume mask, and generate a new mesh from the volume mask using the marching cubes algorithm (Lorensen and Cline, 1987). Since PV/appendage meshes are connected to the LA chamber in a pure geometric operation, the region around the ostia is not segmented accurately. After converting the meshes to a volume mask, we perform constrained region growing a few layers to improve the segmentation accuracy around the ostia of the appendage and PVs.

## 17.5 CORONARY ARTERY SEGMENTATION

Coronary artery disease is the most common heart disease in the United States (Lloyd-Jones et al., 2009). Computed tomography angiography (CTA) is a widely used noninvasive imaging modality for diagnosis of coronary artery disease. However, automatic segmentation of a coronary artery in CTA is a challenging problem due to the large anatomical variation and small caliber of an artery. Almost all previous approaches are data driven (Lesage et al., 2009; Schaap et al., 2009), which try to trace a centerline from an automatically detected or manually specified coronary ostium. No or little high-level prior information is used; therefore, the centerline tracing procedure may terminate too early at a severe occlusion or an anatomically inconsistent centerline course may be generated. Though the connectivity of coronary arteries exhibits large variations, the position of the major coronary arteries, namely LAD, LCX, and RCA, relative to the heart chambers is quite stable. In this work, we exploit the automatically segmented chambers to (1) predict the initial position of the major coronary centerlines and (2) define a vessel-specific region-of-interest (ROI) to constrain the following centerline refinement.

The prior knowledge of coronary arteries is embedded in a mean shape model composed of four heart chambers and three major coronary arteries. The visible length of a major coronary artery can vary greatly either due to anatomical variations (especially in the distal segment) or insufficient contrast agent inside the vessel. To handle such a variation, we present a novel two-step approach to generating a mean coronary centerline. We first align all centerlines in the training set to the same coordinate system by warping them onto the space of the mean heart chamber shape, which is generated using a method presented in Zheng et al. (2008). Here, we use again the nonrigid transformation defined by the TPS model (Bookstein, 1989). The deformation field is estimated using the heart chamber mesh points as anchor points and it is then used to warp the annotated coronary centerlines. Figure 17.8(a) shows the aligned LAD centerline points. We then pick a centerline that best represents the whole shape population. That means the average Euclidean distance from other centerlines to this optimal centerline (one-way distance) is the smallest. Suppose two centerlines $A$ and $B$ are given and they are represented as a set of equidistant points $A_0, A_1, \ldots, A_{m-1}$ and $B_0, B_1, \ldots, B_{n-1}$, respectively. For each point $A_i$

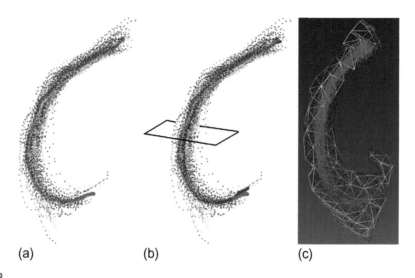

(a) (b) (c)

**FIGURE 17.8**

Generating the centerline mean shape and region-of-interest mesh for the LAD from a set of aligned training centerlines. (a) Aligned centerline point cloud and the coarse mean centerline (red line). (b) The refined mean centerline (blue line). (c) Region-of-interest mesh enclosing the whole point cloud.

on centerline $A$, we calculate the minimum distance to centerline $B$ as $d(A_i, B)$. The one-way average Euclidean distance from $A$ to $B$, $D(A, B)$ is defined as

$$D(A, B) = \frac{1}{m} \sum_{i=0}^{m-1} d(A_i, B) \qquad (17.4)$$

Given a set of aligned centerlines $C^0, C^1, \dots, C^{k-1}$, the coarse mean centerline $M^c$ is picked as the one with the minimum one-way distance from the other centerlines to it,

$$M^c = \underset{C^i}{\operatorname{argmax}} \sum_{j=0}^{k-1} D(C^j, C^i) \qquad (17.5)$$

We use the one-way distance to bias toward a longer centerline to model the full length of a coronary artery. The mean centerline picked by the algorithm is always one of the longest, which is shown as the red thick line in Figure 17.8(a). It has a realistic shape since it is just one exemplar training centerline. Furthermore, it is located roughly at the center of the point cloud of the aligned centerlines.

We further refine the mean centerline by moving it even closer to the center of the point cloud. At each point on the coarse mean centerline, we generate a cutting plane perpendicular to the tangent direction at that point, as shown in Figure 17.8(b). The intersections of all centerlines with the cutting plane are calculated and the mean centerline point is then adjusted to the mean position of intersections. After adjustment, the refined mean centerline (the blue thick line in Figure 17.8(b)) is closer to the point cloud center.

Using the mean shape model composed of the heart chambers and major coronaries, an initial centerline can be generated and is then further refined. However, without proper constraints in the refinement procedure, the extracted centerline may be traced to a noncoronary structure. Sometimes, a distal side branch may be picked as the main trunk, for example, a long-diagonal branch is picked as the LAD. In this work, we present a vessel-specific coronary mask to constrain the search of each major coronary centerline. Besides reducing centerline tracing leakage and branch labeling errors, the coronary ROI mask can also speed up the computation since irrelevant voxels are excluded. Starting from the aligned point cloud of the training centerlines (Figure 17.8(a)), we generate a surface mesh tightly enclosing all aligned centerlines (Figure 17.8(c)). Since such a surface mesh defines a region-of-interest (ROI) for each major coronary during centerline refinement, we call it an ROI mesh. The ball-pivoting algorithm (Bernardini et al., 1999) is used to generate the ROI mesh. Given a ball with a certain size, we roll it around the point cloud. The surface mesh (which may have multiple pieces) is defined by the outer surface of the region that the ball cannot roll into. To generate a single-piece surface mesh, we set the ball size to a relatively large value (10% of the maximum distance of any point pairs in the cloud). The generated ROI mesh is tight and it is then expanded a bit (5%) to provide a safety margin. The vessel-specific ROI mesh can be combined with the pericardium-based coronary mask (Zheng et al., 2011a) to further constrain the search of a major coronary centerline. The proposed method can be extended to define an ROI mesh for the whole left or right coronary tree (including all side branches). In Shahzad et al. (2010), a similar ROI is exploited for automatic calcium scoring. However, their ROI is generated using multi-atlas-based registration, which is far more time consuming than our approach.

Given an input volume, the heart chambers are segmented (Zheng et al., 2008) and coronary ostia are detected (Zheng et al., 2011b) automatically, and they are then used to predict the initial position of the coronary arteries. Since the heart chambers and coronary ostia are available in both the mean shape and the input volume, we use them to estimate a TPS deformation field (Bookstein, 1989). The pretrained mean shape centerline is then transformed to the input volume, using the estimated deformation field, to provide an initial estimate of the centerline. A dynamic programming-based optimization is then applied to refine the initial centerline path. The initial centerline is represented as a set of evenly sampled points $P_i$, for $i = 0, 1, \ldots, n - 1$. For each point $P_i$, we uniformly sample $41 \times 41$ candidate positions $P_i^j$ on a plane perpendicular to the centerline path at this point. The candidates $P_i^j$ are sampled on a regular grid of $20 \times 20$ mm$^2$ (with grid spacing of 0.5 mm) centered at the initial centerline point. Now, the problem is how to select the best position for each point $P_i$. It can be formulated as a shortest path computation problem,

$$\bar{P}_0^{J(0)}, \bar{P}_1^{J(1)}, \ldots, \bar{P}_{n-1}^{J(n-1)} = \arg\min_{P_i^{J(i)}} \sum_{i=0}^{n-1} C(P_i^{J(i)}) + w \sum_{i=0}^{n-2} \left\| P_i^{J(i)} - P_{i+1}^{J(i+1)} \right\| \tag{17.6}$$

The first term is the cost for a single node, measuring how likely this point is at the center of the vessel. Here, a machine learning-based vesselness (Zheng et al., 2011a) is used as the node cost. The second term is the total length of the path by summing the Euclidean distance between two neighboring points on the path. Free parameter $w$, which is used to balance the two terms, is heuristically tuned on a few datasets and then fixed throughout the experiments. The optimal path can be calculated efficiently using dynamic programming. For patients with short discernible coronaries, the centerline extracted by this model-driven step may be too long; therefore, the distal centerline may be traced into a noncoronary structure. We shrink the centerline from the end point, one by one, if its vesselness score is less than a threshold. The centerline is then extended to the distal end to extract the full length of the coronary. After the verification-and-extension process, errors in the distal centerline are corrected.

After extracting centerlines of the three major coronary arteries, the algorithm starts to trace side branches. First, the bifurcation of a side branch is detected on a major centerline using region growing-based lumen segmentation. Starting from a centerline point, bright voxels connected to the current point are added iteratively. The growing front (composed of the added voxels in the latest iteration) is monitored. If a side branch presents, the region growing procedure will go into it. A side branch is detected when we find a front with a distance to the existing major centerline larger than a threshold. At each detected bifurcation point, a data-driven centerline tracing process is initialized. Please refer to Tek et al. (2008) for more details for the tracing of a coronary subtree from a given starting point.

Though in general the extracted centerline is located at or close to the lumen center, sometimes it may take a shortcut at a tortuous segment or be attracted to calcifications. Further postprocessing is applied to move the centerline to the lumen center. After centerline extraction, various coronary analysis tasks can be performed, for example, coronary lumen segmentation (Lugauer et al., 2014), coronary lesion detection (Kelm et al., 2011), or coronary calcium scoring (Kelm and Zheng, 2014).

## 17.6 EXPERIMENTS

In this section, we quantitatively evaluate the accuracy of automatic four-chamber segmentation and coronary artery centerline extraction on cardiac CT data. We want to emphasize that the proposed methods are generic and they can be retrained for different image modalities. For example, the MSL-based chamber segmentation method can be extended to 3D ultrasound (Yang et al., 2011) and MRI (Lu et al., 2011). Due to the space limit, we omit the evaluation on great vessel segmentation, even though our part-based approaches also work well on these tasks. Please refer to Zheng et al. (2012) for more details of aorta segmentation and Zheng et al. (2014) for pulmonary vein segmentation, respectively.

### 17.6.1 EVALUATION OF CARDIAC CHAMBER SEGMENTATION

In this experiment, we quantitatively evaluate our cardiac chamber segmentation approach. As a widely used criterion, the symmetric point-to-mesh distance, $E_{p2m}$, is used to measure the surface segmentation accuracy. For each point on a mesh, we search for the closest point (not necessarily mesh triangle vertices) on the other mesh to calculate the minimum Euclidean distance. We calculate the point-to-mesh distance from the detected mesh to the ground truth and vice versa to make the measurement symmetric.

In our experiments, we estimate the pose of each chamber separately. Therefore, we use $4 \times 9 = 36$ pose parameters to align the mean shapes. As shown in the second column of Table 17.1, the mean $E_{p2m}$ error after heart localization is 3.17 mm for the LV endocardium, 2.51 mm for the LV epicardium, 2.78 mm for the LA, 2.93 mm for the RV, and 3.09 mm for the RA. Alternatively, we can treat the whole

**Table 17.1 Mean and Standard Deviation (in Parentheses) of the Point-to-Mesh Error (in Millimeters) for the Segmentation of Heart Chambers Based on Cross Validation**

|  | After Rigid Localization | After Control Point Refinement | Final Segmentation |
|---|---|---|---|
| Left ventricle endocardium | 3.17 (1.10) | 3.00 (1.11) | 0.84 (0.47) |
| Left ventricle epicardium | 2.51 (0.78) | 2.35 (0.73) | 1.21 (0.41) |
| Left atrium | 2.78 (0.98) | 2.67 (1.01) | 1.32 (0.42) |
| Right ventricle | 2.93 (0.75) | 2.40 (0.82) | 1.55 (0.38) |
| Right atrium | 3.09 (0.86) | 2.90 (0.92) | 1.57 (0.48) |

heart as one object in heart localization, then we use only nine pose parameters. In this way, the mean $E_{p2m}$ error achieved is 3.52 mm for the LV endocardium, 3.07 mm for the LV epicardium, 3.95 mm for LA, 3.94 mm for the RV, and 4.64 mm for the RA. Obviously, treating each chamber separately, we can obtain a better initialization.

In our nonrigid deformation estimation, control points and normal mesh points are treated differently. We first estimate the deformation of control points and then use TPS warping to make the mesh and control points consistent. As shown in the third column of Table 17.1, after control point-based alignment, we slightly reduce the error for the LV, LA, and RA by 5% and significantly reduce the error by 17% for the RV since the control points are more uniformly distributed on the RV mesh. After deformation estimation of all mesh points, the final segmentation error ranges from 0.84 to 1.57 mm for different chambers. (Please note, the 0.84 mm error in LV endocardium segmentation is achieved after further postprocessing (Zheng et al., 2009b).) The LV and LA have smaller errors than the RV and RA due to the use of contrast agent in the left heart (as shown in Figure 17.9).

Figure 17.9 shows several examples for heart chamber segmentation using the proposed approach. It performs well even under severe streak artifacts (as shown in the second example). Since our system is trained on volumes from all phases from a cardiac cycle, we can process volumes from the end-systolic phase (which has a significantly smaller blood pool for the LV) without any difficulty, as shown in the last example in Figure 17.9.

With moderate code optimization, we achieved an average speed of 4.0 s for the automatic segmentation of four chambers on a computer with a dual-core 3.2 GHz processor and 3 GB memory. The computation time is roughly equally split on the MSL-based similarity transformation estimation and the nonrigid deformation estimation.

## 17.6.2 EVALUATION OF CORONARY ARTERY CENTERLINE EXTRACTION

Our coronary centerline extraction algorithm was trained on a proprietary dataset (108 volumes) and evaluated on the public Rotterdam coronary CTA database (Schaap et al., 2009). The Rotterdam database contains a training set (8 datasets) and a test set (24 datasets), and each dataset has four manually annotated coronary artery centerlines, namely the RCA, LAD, LCX, and a randomly picked large side branch. An algorithm is evaluated with the overlap and accuracy inside (AI) metrics. The

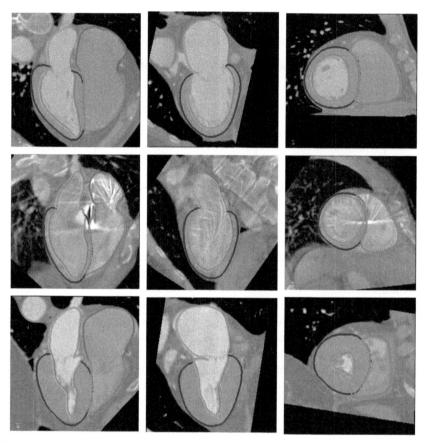

**FIGURE 17.9**

Examples of heart chamber segmentation in 3D CT volumes with green for the LV endocardium, magenta for the LV epicardium, cyan for the LA, brown for the RV, and blue for the RA. Each row represents three orthogonal cuts of a volume.

overlap metric is further broken down into three individual measurements, including overlap (OV), overlap until first error (OF), and overlap with the clinically relevant trunk of the vessel (OT). All measurements are based on point-to-point correspondence between the detected centerline and the ground truth. A centerline point is claimed to be detected correctly if its distance to the corresponding ground truth point is no more than the radius of the annotated lumen at that point. The AI metric measures the distance between the extracted centerline and the ground truth for the correctly detected centerline part. A score is further assigned based on the inter-observer variability (score 100 for a perfect result and score 50 for an error matching the inter-observer variability). The algorithms are

**Table 17.2 Comparison With Other Automatic Centerline Extraction Methods on the Rotterdam Coronary CTA Test Set (24 Datasets) Using the Overlap Metrics**

| Method | Overall Rank | OV | | | OF | | | OT | | |
| | | % | Score | Rank | % | Score | Rank | % | Score | Rank |
|---|---|---|---|---|---|---|---|---|---|---|
| Proposed method | 8.91 | 93.5 | 53.4 | 10.98 | 76.5 | 54.9 | 8.22 | 95.6 | 70.0 | 7.54 |
| GFVCoronary Extractor | 9.02 | 93.7 | 55.9 | 10.73 | 74.2 | 52.9 | 9.09 | 95.9 | 68.5 | 7.24 |
| GVFTube'n'Linkage | 10.52 | 92.7 | 52.3 | 12.31 | 71.9 | 51.4 | 10.35 | 95.3 | 67.0 | 8.91 |
| SupervisedExtraction | 11.28 | 90.6 | 53.8 | 12.75 | 70.9 | 49.0 | 10.52 | 92.5 | 61.2 | 10.56 |
| DepthFirstModelFit | 11.86 | 84.7 | 48.6 | 14.26 | 65.3 | 49.2 | 10.19 | 87.0 | 60.1 | 11.14 |
| COR Analyzer | 12.92 | 87.7 | 50.3 | 14.53 | 71.7 | 47.8 | 12.00 | 89.8 | 59.5 | 12.22 |
| AutoCoronaryTree | 15.07 | 84.7 | 46.5 | 15.88 | 59.5 | 36.1 | 14.23 | 86.2 | 50.3 | 15.11 |
| CocomoBeach | 16.23 | 78.8 | 42.5 | 17.66 | 64.4 | 40.0 | 14.19 | 81.2 | 46.9 | 16.83 |
| VirtualContrast | 16.44 | 75.6 | 39.2 | 18.26 | 56.1 | 34.5 | 14.80 | 78.7 | 45.6 | 16.27 |

Notes: *The semi-automatic methods participated in the ranking, but are removed in the table due to the page limit. Available at http:// coronary.bigr.nl/centerlines/results/results.php (last checked on April 27, 2015).*

ranked on each vessel and the average ranking is reported. Please refer to Schaap et al. (2009) for more details about the datasets and evaluation metrics.

On the training set, our method outperforms the other automatic methods on all overlap metrics (OV, OF, and OT). On the test set, as shown in Table 17.2, our method has the best average ranking (ranking first on OF, and second on OV and OT) among all automatic methods (nine submissions in total). Regarding the accuracy measurement (AI), the proposed method clearly outperforms all other 22 algorithms (including both automatic and semi-automatic methods) on both the training and test sets. Table 17.3 shows the ranking of all algorithms on the test set using the AI metric. With an average score of 51.6, we achieve an accuracy comparable to inter-observer variability. Please refer to http:// coronary.bigr.nl/centerlines/results/results.php for more details. Figure 17.10 shows a few examples of extracted centerlines using the proposed method.

## 17.7 CONCLUSIONS AND FUTURE WORK

In this chapter, we reviewed our previous work on automatic cardiac image segmentation, including the segmentation of cardiac chambers, great vessels, and coronary arteries. Our approaches are built upon the general MSL-based object detection/segmentation framework, which has been successfully applied to segment cardiac chambers efficiently. Various approaches have been presented to handle anatomical variations of great vessels and coronary arteries. State-of-the-art performance achieved by our algorithms can be attributed to (1) a model-based approach exploiting shape priors and (2) discriminative learning on a large annotated training set. However, pathologies are still a big challenge

**Table 17.3 Comparison With Other Centerline Extraction Methods on the Rotterdam Coronary CTA Test Set (24 Datasets) Using the Accuracy Inside (AI) Metric**

| Method | Automatic | AI mm | AI Score | AI Rank |
|---|---|---|---|---|
| Proposed method | Y | **0.20** | **51.6** | **2.48** |
| ShapeRegression | N | 0.23 | 49.6 | 3.10 |
| MHT | N | 0.23 | 47.9 | 3.86 |
| SupervisedExtraction | Y | 0.25 | 47.3 | 4.28 |
| Tracer | N | 0.26 | 44.4 | 6.17 |
| COR Analyzer | Y | 0.25 | 44.8 | 6.78 |
| VirtualContrast2b | N | 0.27 | 41.6 | 7.56 |
| DepthFirstModelFit | Y | 0.28 | 41.9 | 7.63 |
| BayesianMaxPaths | N | 0.29 | 37.0 | 10.41 |
| GFVCoronaryExtractor | Y | 0.30 | 37.1 | 10.41 |
| CocomoBeach | Y | 0.29 | 37.7 | 10.71 |
| AutoCoronaryTree | Y | 0.34 | 35.3 | 11.32 |
| VesselTractography | N | 0.36 | 30.7 | 14.99 |
| VirtualContrast | Y | 0.39 | 30.6 | 15.01 |
| GVFTube'n'Linkage | Y | 0.37 | 29.8 | 15.79 |
| KnowledgeBasedMinPath | N | 0.39 | 29.2 | 16.22 |
| ElasticModel | N | 0.40 | 29.3 | 16.22 |
| TwoPointMinCost | N | 0.46 | 28.0 | 16.94 |
| AxialSymmetry | N | 0.46 | 26.4 | 18.07 |
| StatisticalTracking | N | 0.51 | 25.1 | 18.22 |
| TubSurfGradFlow | N | 0.47 | 24.8 | 19.14 |
| 3DInteractiveTrack | N | 0.51 | 24.2 | 19.84 |
| CoronaryTreeMorphoRec | N | 0.59 | 20.7 | 20.75 |

Note: *Available at http://coronary.bigr.nl/centerlines/results/results.php (last checked on April 27, 2015).*

to all automatic segmentation methods. For example, for a patient with congenital heart disease, the left and right chambers may be mirrored and the learned shape priors from a normal population cannot be applied anymore. At Siemens, we are lucky to have access to a large real patient dataset collected all over the world. However, for some rare pathologies, only a handful of data are available. Under all these scenarios, a user interaction is mandated. How to leverage more information from one or a few user mouse clicks to maximally improve the segmentation accuracy is one of our future research topics.

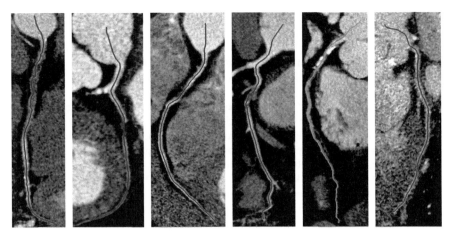

**FIGURE 17.10**

Examples of the extracted coronary centerlines on the Rotterdam database. The first five patients have occlusions and the last one has low image quality.

## ACKNOWLEDGMENTS

The author would like to thank Fernando Vega-Higuera, Michael Scheuering, and Matthias John for providing data and coordinating clinical evaluation of our automatic cardiac segmentation algorithms. The author also wants to thank Jianhua Shen for implementing part of the model-driven coronary centerline extraction algorithm and Huseyin Tek for integrating his data-driven coronary side branch tracing algorithm. Many colleagues at Siemens Corporate Technology provided constructive comments and suggestions during the development of the methods.

## REFERENCES

Bernardini, F., Mittleman, J., Rushmeier, H., Silva, C., Taubin, G., 1999. The ball-pivoting algorithm for surface reconstruction. IEEE Trans. Visual. Comput. Graph. (5(4)), 349–359.

Boisvert, J., Pennec, X., Labelle, H., Cheriet, F., Ayache, N., 2006. Principal spine shape deformation modes using Riemannian geometry and articulated models. In: Proceedings of the Conference on Articulated Motion and Deformable Objects, pp. 346–355.

Bookstein, F., 1989. Principal warps: thin-plate splines and the decomposition of deformations. IEEE Trans. Pattern Anal. Machine Intell. 11 (6), 567–585.

Cootes, T.F., Taylor, C.J., Cooper, D.H., Graham, J., 1995. Active shape models—their training and application. Comput. Vis. Image Underst. 61 (1), 38–59.

de Bruijne, M., van Ginneken, B., Viergever, M.A., Niessen, W.J., 2003. Adapting active shape models for 3D segmentation of tubular structures in medical images. In: Proceedings of the Information Processing in Medical Imaging, pp. 136–147.

Dollár, P., Tu, Z., Belongie, S., 2006. Supervised learning of edges and object boundaries. In: Proceedings of the IEEE Conference on Computer Vision and Pattern Recognition, pp. 1964–1971.

Ecabert, O., Peters, J., Weese, J., 2006. Modeling shape variability for full heart segmentation in cardiac computed-tomography images. In: Proceedings of SPIE Medical Imaging, pp. 1199–1210.

Heidenreich, P.A., Trogdon, J.G., Khavjou, O.A., et al., 2011. Forecasting the future of cardiovascular disease in the United States: a policy statement from the American Heart Association. Circulation 123, 933–944.

Horn, B.K.P., 1987. Closed form solution of absolute orientation using unit quaternions. J. Opt. Soc. A 4 (4), 629–642.

Kelm, B.M., Zheng, Y., 2014. Automatic coronary calcium scoring using native and contrasted CT acquisitions. In: MICCAI Challenge on Automatic Coronary Calcium Scoring, pp. 1–8.

Kelm, M., Mittal, S., Zheng, Y., Funka-Lea, G., Bernhardt, D., Vega-Higuera, F., Comaniciu, D., 2011. Detection, grading and classification of coronary stenoses in computed tomography angiography. In: Proceedings of the International Conference on Medical Image Computing and Computer Assisted Intervention, vol. 3, pp. 25–32.

Lesage, D., Angelini, E.D., Bloch, I., Funka-Lea, G., 2009. A review of 3D vessel lumen segmentation techniques: models, features and extraction schemes. Med. Image Anal. 13 (6), 819–845.

Lloyd-Jones, D., Adams, R., Carnethon, M., et al., 2009. Heart disease and stroke statistics—2009 update. Circulation 119 (3), 21–181.

Lorensen, W.E., Cline, H.E., 1987. Marching cubes: a high resolution 3D surface construction algorithm. Comput. Graph. 21 (4), 163–169.

Lu, X., Wang, Y., Georgescu, B., Littmann, A., Comaniciu, D., 2011. Automatic delineation of left and right ventricles in cardiac MRI sequences using a joint ventricular model. In: Proceedings of the Functional Imaging and Modeling of the Heart, pp. 250–258.

Lugauer, F., Zheng, Y., Hornegger, J., Kelm, B.K., 2014. Precise lumen segmentation in coronary computed tomography angiography. In: MICCAI Workshop on Medical Computer Vision, pp. 137–147.

Manzke, R., Meyer, C., Ecabert, O., Peters, J., Noordhoek, N.J., Thiagalingam, A., Reddy, V.Y., Chan, R.C., Weese, J., 2010. Automatic segmentation of rotational X-ray images for anatomic intra-procedural surface generation in atrial fibrillation ablation procedures. IEEE Trans. Med. Imaging 29 (2), 260–272.

Marom, E.M., Herndon, J.E., Kim, Y.K., McAdams, H.P., 2004. Variations in pulmonary venous drainage to the left atrium: Implications for radiofrequency ablation. Radiology 230, 824–829.

Martin, D., Fowlkes, C., Malik, J., 2004. Learning to detect natural image boundaries using local brightness, color and texture cues. IEEE Trans. Pattern Anal. Machine Intell. 26 (5), 530–549.

Rueckert, D., Burger, P., Forbat, S.M., Mohiaddin, R.D., Yang, G.Z., 1997. Automatic tracking of the aorta in cardiovascular MR images using deformable models. IEEE Trans. Med. Imaging 16 (5), 581–590.

Schaap, M., Metz, C.T., van Walsum, T., et al., 2009. Standardized evaluation methodology and reference database for evaluating coronary artery centerline extraction algorithms. Med. Image Anal. 13, 701–714.

Shahzad, R.K., Schaap, M., van Walsum, T., Klein, S., Weustink, A.C., van Vliet, L.J., Niessen, W.J., 2010. A patient-specific coronary density estimate. In: Proceedings of the IEEE International Symposium on Biomedical Imaging, pp. 9–12.

Taubin, G., 1996. Optimal surface smoothing as filter design. In: Proceedings of the European Conference on Computer Vision, pp. 283–292.

Tek, H., Gulsun, M.A., Laguitton, S., Grady, L., Lesage, D., Funka-Lea, G., 2008. Automatic coronary tree modeling. In: Proc. MICCAI Grand Challenge Coronary Artery Tracking, 1–8.

Tu, Z., 2005. Probabilistic boosting-tree: learning discriminative methods for classification, recognition, and clustering. In: Proceedings of the International Conference on Computer Vision, pp. 1589–1596.

Viola, P., Jones, M., 2001. Rapid object detection using a boosted cascade of simple features. In: Proceedings of the IEEE Conference on Computer Vision and Pattern Recognition, pp. 511–518.

Yang, L., Georgescu, B., Zheng, Y., Wang, Y., Meer, P., Comaniciu, D., 2011. Prediction based collaborative trackers (PCT): a robust and accurate approach toward 3D medical object tracking. IEEE Trans. Med. Imaging 30 (11), 1921–1932.

Zhao, F., Zhang, H., Wahle, A., Scholz, T.D., Sonka, M., 2006. Automated 4D segmentation of aortic magnetic resonance images. In: Proceedings of the British Machine Vision Conference, pp. 247–256.

Zheng, Y., Barbu, A., Georgescu, B., Scheuering, M., Comaniciu, D., 2007. Fast automatic heart chamber segmentation from 3D CT data using marginal space learning and steerable features. In: Proceedings of the International Conference on Computer Vision, pp. 1–8.

Zheng, Y., Barbu, A., Georgescu, B., Scheuering, M., Comaniciu, D., 2008. Four-chamber heart modeling and automatic segmentation for 3D cardiac CT volumes using marginal space learning and steerable features. IEEE Trans. Med. Imaging 27 (11), 1668–1681.

Zheng, Y., Comaniciu, D., 2014. Marginal Space Learning for Medical Image Analysis—Efficient Detection and Segmentation of Anatomical Structures. Springer, Berlin.

Zheng, Y., Georgescu, B., Comaniciu, D., 2009a, Marginal space learning for efficient detection of 2D/3D anatomical structures in medical images. In: Proceedings of the Information Processing in Medical Imaging, pp. 411–422.

Zheng, Y., Georgescu, B., Vega-Higuera, F., Comaniciu, D., 2009b, Left ventricle endocardium segmentation for cardiac CT volumes using an optimal smooth surface. In: Proceedings of SPIE Medical Imaging, vol. 7259, pp. 1–11.

Zheng, Y., Georgescu, B., Vega-Higuera, F., Zhou, S.K., Comaniciu, D., 2010. Fast and automatic heart isolation in 3D CT volumes: optimal shape initialization. In: Proceedings of the MICCAI Workshop Machine Learning in Medical Imaging, pp. 84–91.

Zheng, Y., John, M., Liao, R., Nottling, A., Boese, J., Kempfert, J., Walther, T., Brockmann, G., Comaniciu, D., 2012. Automatic aorta segmentation and valve landmark detection in C-arm CT for transcatheter aortic valve implantation. IEEE Trans. Med. Imaging 31 (12), 2307–2321.

Zheng, Y., Loziczonek, M., Georgescu, B., Zhou, S.K., Vega-Higuera, F., Comaniciu, D., 2011a, Machine learning based vesselness measurement for coronary artery segmentation in cardiac CT volumes. In: Proceedings of SPIE Medical Imaging, pp. 1–12.

Zheng, Y., Tek, H., Funka-Lea, G., 2013. Robust and accurate coronary artery centerline extraction in CTA by combining model-driven and data-driven approaches. In: Proceedings of the International Conference on Medical Image Computing and Computer Assisted Intervention, pp. 74–81.

Zheng, Y., Tek, H., Funka-Lea, G., Zhou, S.K., Vega-Higuera, F., Comaniciu, D., 2011b, Efficient detection of native and bypass coronary ostia in cardiac CT volumes: anatomical vs. pathological structures. In: Proceedings of the International Conference on Medical Image Computing and Computer Assisted Intervention, vol. 3, pp. 403–410.

Zheng, Y., Yang, D., John, M., Comaniciu, D., 2014. Multi-part modeling and segmentation of left atrium in C-arm CT for image-guided ablation of atrial fibrillation. IEEE Trans. Med. Imaging 33 (2), 318–331.

Zhong, H., Zheng, Y., Funka-Lea, G., Vega-Higuera, F., 2012. Segmentation and removal of pulmonary arteries, veins and left atrial appendage for visualizing coronary and bypass arteries. In: Proceedings of the Workshop on Medical Computer Vision (in conjunction with CVPR), pp. 24–30.

# SPINE DISK AND RIB CENTERLINE PARSING

# 18

**S. Kevin Zhou[1], A. Wimmer[2] and B.M. Kelm[2]**

*Medical Imaging Technologies, Siemens Healthcare Technology Center, Princeton, NJ, USA[1]*
*Siemens Healthcare GmbH, Forchheim/Erlangen, Germany[2]*

## CHAPTER OUTLINE

## 18.1 INTRODUCTION

Spine and ribs are central parts of the human skeletal system. Usually, the human vertebral column consists of 24 articulated vertebrae (Figure 18.1(a)) connected through 23 spinal disks and 8-10 vertebrae fused to build the sacrum (S1) and the coccyx. Among the 24 articulated vertebrae, usually 7 are cervical (C1, ..., C7), 12 are thoracic (T1, ..., T12), and 5 are lumbar vertebrae (L1, ..., L5), which are uniquely identified by noting that only the thoracic vertebrae have articulated joints with 2 rib bones, respectively. A typical human rib cage (Figure 18.1(b)) has 24 ribs that are attached posteriorly to the thoracic vertebrae and form 12 pairs. Each rib (Figure 18.1(c)) consists of a head, neck, and a shaft with the head of the rib being the end part closest to the spine and the neck of the rib being the flattened part that extends laterally from the head.

S. Kevin Zhou (Ed): Medical Image Recognition, Segmentation and Parsing. http://dx.doi.org/10.1016/B978-0-12-802581-9.00018-4

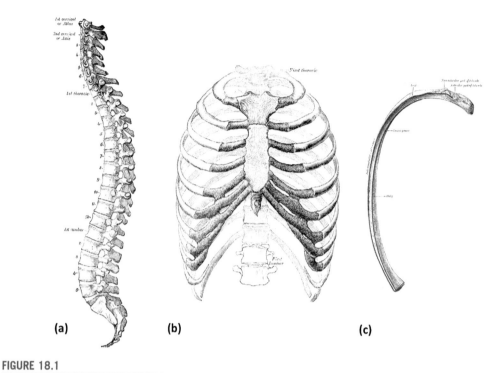

(a)       (b)                              (c)

**FIGURE 18.1**

(a) Spine. (b) Rib cage. (c) A rib is curved and twisted in 3D. All images are from Wikipedia.

Spinal cord and brain together make up the central nervous system and thus diseases associated with the spine are very often critical, if not life-threatening. This includes neurological, oncological, and orthopedic diseases that may affect various parts of the spine, including the vertebrae, spinal disks, and the spinal cord. For ribs, oncological lesions, traumatic fractures, etc. are the main findings.

An automatic system for localizing the spinal disks can be part of a computer-aided diagnosis system for analyzing pathologies of the spine, the spinal disks, or the vertebrae (Wels et al., 2012; Hammon et al., 2013). Furthermore, approaches for modeling biomechanical behavior of the spinal column could benefit from such a system and allow for patient-specific analyses to guide therapeutic decisions (Seifert and Dillmann, 2007; Tschirhart et al., 2007; Adams and Dolan, 2011). Beyond being a primary target of medical diagnosis, the vertebral column often serves as a reference system in medical reporting. For this purpose, physicians are interested in an automatic vertebra labeling that avoids error-prone manual counting. Such a labeling may further support systems for semantic body parsing (Seifert et al., 2009, 2010; Mirzaalian et al., 2013) and semantic annotation in automatically generating semantic descriptions of anatomical locations as frequently used by physicians (Klinder et al., 2009; Seifert et al., 2010). Also, during the acquisition of medical images such as CT and MR, the vertebrae are often employed to align the acquisition and/or reconstruction geometries with the orientation of the vertebrae to achieve a standardized region of interest. As manual alignment is both tedious and operator-dependent, it is desirable to employ a robust and fully automatic system.

Finding rib metastases and fractures in chest CT scans typically involves reading hundreds of axial CT slices to visually track changes in rib cross-section area. However, manual reading is rather time consuming and rib anomalies are frequently missed in practice due to human error (Galanski, 2003). Automatic extraction of rib anatomical centerlines can be used to enhance the visualization of the unfolded rib cage, which will make routine bone reading tasks more efficient and effective for the radiologists (Ramakrishnan et al., 2011). The extracted and labeled rib centerlines can also serve as the reference to localize organs (Wang et al., 2006), register pathologies (Shen and Shao, 2003), and guide correspondence between serial thoracic CT scans for interval change analysis (Mohr et al., 2007). In addition, the derived rib geometry can assist with rib cage fracture fixation surgeries (Helzel et al., 2009).

An automatic procedure for detecting and segmenting the spinal column and ribs faces various challenges, however. Varying contrasts, partial field of views, image artifacts, and pathologies can compromise the detection of spinal disks and ribs based on local image features. Thus, global models for spine and ribs are required for robustness. Such models must also cope with missed detections and pathological deformations in ribs and spine (e.g., various forms of scoliosis, kyphosis, and lordosis). But global model fitting is often slow due to too many degrees of freedom. In this chapter, we present methods for parsing spine disks and rib centerlines, built on top of hierarchical representation and machine learning methods for improved robustness, accuracy, and speed.

## 18.2 RELATED WORK

Several approaches for the automatic detection and segmentation of the vertebral column have been proposed in the past. Many of the recent algorithms are learning-based and follow a part-based methodology which combines appearance models with geometric information about the relation between the vertebrae.

One of the first works that followed this approach was presented by (Schmidt et al., 2007). They propose a trainable approach based on extremely randomized trees in combination with a complete graphical model which they efficiently solve using a novel A*-search-based inference algorithm for exact maximum a posteriori (MAP) estimation. Huang et al. (2008, 2009) propose a three-step approach comprising a vertebra detector based on AdaBoost, spinal column fitting using the random sample consensus (RANSAC) algorithm and a final segmentation step using an iterative normalized-cut algorithm. Corso et al. (2008) and Alomari et al. (2011) argue that a two-level probabilistic model is required to separate pixel-level properties from object-level geometric and contextual properties. They propose a generative graphical model with latent disk variables, which they solve by generalized expectation maximization (EM).

Jäger et al. (2009) rely on an iterative spinal cord segmentation method based on Markov random fields for assessing spinal geometry in terms of computed planes through the vertebral bodies. In order to pay respect to, in particular, scoliotically deformed spinal columns, their method does not depend on any prior information about the shape of the spine nor on the shape of the vertebral bodies. A comprehensive system for spine segmentation was proposed by Klinder et al. (2009). The approach starts with the tracking of the spinal canal which is subsequently used for a curved planar reformation (CPR) of the CT volume. The detection of vertebra candidates employs the generalized Hough transform on that CPR volume. Vertebrae are then identified and labeled using an appearance model learned from annotated data. Finally, the vertebrae are segmented using a vertebra-specific point distribution model.

A quite different learning-based approach is presented by Glocker et al. (2012). The authors propose an approach based on random forest regression which can even predict the position of vertebrae that are not within the imaged field of view. While the localization accuracy somewhat suffers, the approach is very fast and works on CT acquisitions with arbitrary field-of-view. Major et al. (2013) propose a system for automated landmarking and labeling of fully and partially scanned spinal columns in CT volumes. Their approach starts with the detection of the spinal canal, similar to Klinder et al. (2009). Different from Klinder et al. (2009) and similar to Kelm et al. (2010), Major et al. employ generic learning-based detectors to generate disk candidates. Instead of using a global probabilistic model for the spinal column, such as proposed by Schmidt et al. (2007) and Kelm et al. (2010), Major et al. introduce a local "three-disk model" that is used to identify matching disk candidates. For labeling, Major et al. rely on the detection of three specialized transition detectors that are trained to detect the transitions between cervical, thoracic, lumbar, and sacral vertebrae, respectively.

Finally, Zhan et al. (2015) present a learning-based approach that is shown to work on CT as well as MR. A global probabilistic model is proposed which is then optimized in a hierarchical fashion. Zhan et al. (2015) also employ contextual information extracted with specialized detectors to support an accurate labeling of the spinal column, which also works in image volumes covering only parts of the spine. The principle of redundancy (Zhou et al., 2010) leads to a very robust approach that even works in the presence of severe imaging artifacts and abnormal anatomies.

Despite its clinical importance, automatic detection and labeling of ribs in CT scans has not been extensively studied before and remains a challenging task. Most of the prior works model the ribs as elongated tubular structures and employ Hessian or structure tensor eigensystem analysis for ridge voxel detection (Aylward and Bullitt, 2002; Shen et al., 2004; Staal et al., 2007); however, these algorithms are usually computationally expensive and, moreover, the rib marrow is typically less denser than its boundary so the rib center points are not exactly ridge voxels. To construct the rib centerline, tracking-based methods such as Kalman filter are usually used to trace detected rib center points from one slice to the next (Kim et al., 2002; Shen et al., 2004; Kiraly et al., 2006; Ramakrishnan et al., 2011); however, some of them require manual initial seed points and, more critically, these point to point tracking methods are highly sensitive to local ambiguities or discontinuities posed by rib pathologies like fractures and bone metastases, which are nevertheless of the most interest to radiologists. For all of these algorithms, each rib is individually detected and traced, hence rib labeling requires a separate heuristic method (Staal et al., 2007; Ramakrishnan and Alvino, 2011).

## 18.3 SPINE DISK PARSING

We propose a hierarchical, part-based model that can be trained for both MR and CT. To this end, we first describe our probabilistic model that combines the individual parts, that is, the spinal disks, and then proceed with the description of our disk detectors.

### 18.3.1 PROBABILISTIC SPINE MODEL

The spinal column is modeled by a probabilistic graphical model which is depicted as a factor graph in Figure 18.2. Each of the random variables $b_s$ ($s \in \{1, \ldots, N\}$) represents the pose of a certain spinal

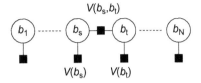

**FIGURE 18.2**

Factor graph modeling the relation between the spinal disks.

disk, which is defined by its position $\boldsymbol{p}_s = [x_s, y_s, z_s]^T$, its scale $\boldsymbol{s}_s = [s_s^x, s_s^y, s_s^z]^T$ and its orientation $\boldsymbol{q}_s$ in the form of a unit quaternion (Karney, 2007). A distribution over disk poses is then defined by the Gibbs distribution:

$$\log \Pr(\boldsymbol{b}_1, \ldots, \boldsymbol{b}_N | \boldsymbol{\Theta}, X) = \sum_s V_s(\boldsymbol{b}_s | \boldsymbol{\theta}_s, X) + \sum_{s \sim t} V_{st}(\boldsymbol{b}_s, \boldsymbol{b}_t | \boldsymbol{\theta}_{st}) - A(\boldsymbol{\Theta}) \tag{18.1}$$

where $A(\boldsymbol{\Theta})$ is the log partition function, $X = (x_i)_{i=1,\ldots,M}$ represents the image data and $\boldsymbol{\Theta} = \{\boldsymbol{\theta}_s, \boldsymbol{\theta}_{st}\}$ subsumes all model parameters which are detailed in the following.

The pair potential between two neighboring disks $\boldsymbol{b}_s$ and $\boldsymbol{b}_t$ combines relative position, relative scale, and relative orientation terms

$$V_{st}(\boldsymbol{b}_s, \boldsymbol{b}_t | \boldsymbol{\theta}_{st}) = V_{\text{pos},st} + V_{\text{sca},st} + V_{\text{rot},st} \tag{18.2}$$

Relative position is modeled by a Gaussian pair potential

$$V_{\text{pos},st}(\boldsymbol{b}_s, \boldsymbol{b}_t) = -\frac{1}{2} \boldsymbol{d}_{\text{pos}}^T(\boldsymbol{b}_s, \boldsymbol{b}_t) \boldsymbol{\Sigma}_{\text{pos},st}^{-1} \boldsymbol{d}_{\text{pos}}(\boldsymbol{b}_s, \boldsymbol{b}_t) \tag{18.3}$$

where the displacement vector $\boldsymbol{d}_{\text{pos}}(\boldsymbol{b}_s, \boldsymbol{b}_t) = \mathbf{R}_s^{-1}(\boldsymbol{p}_t - \boldsymbol{p}_s) - \boldsymbol{\mu}_{\text{pos},st}$ is computed relative to the orientation of disk candidate $\boldsymbol{b}_s$. Thus, the position term is invariant with respect to translations and rotations applied to both disk candidates $\boldsymbol{b}_s$ and $\boldsymbol{b}_t$.

The parameters of the position term are the mean displacement vector $\boldsymbol{\mu}_{\text{pos},st}$ and the covariance matrix $\boldsymbol{\Sigma}_{\text{pos},st}$ which is assumed to be diagonal here. Mean and covariance of the displacement vector are estimated from the annotated training data for each pair potential of the spinal chain model independently.

Prior terms on relative orientation and scale are obtained as

$$V_{\text{sca},st}(\boldsymbol{b}_s, \boldsymbol{b}_t) = -\frac{1}{2} \boldsymbol{d}_{\text{sca}}^T(\boldsymbol{b}_s, \boldsymbol{b}_t) \boldsymbol{\Sigma}_{\text{sca},st}^{-1} \boldsymbol{d}_{\text{sca}}(\boldsymbol{b}_s, \boldsymbol{b}_t) \quad \text{and} \tag{18.4}$$

$$V_{\text{rot},st}(\boldsymbol{b}_s, \boldsymbol{b}_t) = -\frac{\alpha(\boldsymbol{q}_t \boldsymbol{q}_s^{-1} \boldsymbol{\mu}_{\text{rot},st}^{-1})^2}{2\sigma_{\text{rot},st}^2} \tag{18.5}$$

Here, the scale difference is $\boldsymbol{d}_{\text{sca}}(\boldsymbol{b}_s, \boldsymbol{b}_t) = \boldsymbol{s}_t - \boldsymbol{s}_s - \boldsymbol{\mu}_{\text{sca},st}$ and the quaternions $\boldsymbol{q}_s$ and $\boldsymbol{q}_t$ are associated with the rotation matrices $\mathbf{R}_s$ and $\mathbf{R}_t$. The rotation angle $\alpha(\boldsymbol{q}) = \alpha([q_0 q_1 q_2 q_3])$ is computed from the quaternion as $2\arccos(q_0)$.

All parameters are again estimated from the training data. For the scale term, $\boldsymbol{\mu}_{\text{sca},st}$ is just the mean scale difference and $\boldsymbol{\Sigma}_{\text{sca},st}$ the corresponding (diagonal) covariance matrix. The orientation term defines the variance parameter $\sigma_{\mathrm{rot},st}$ and the quaternion mean parameter $\boldsymbol{\mu}_{\mathrm{rot},st}$, which is determined as the Fréchet mean (Boisvert et al., 2008). Collecting all instances of a certain disk pair $(\boldsymbol{b}_s, \boldsymbol{b}_t)$ into the training sample $\mathcal{P}_{st}$, the Fréchet mean for the corresponding orientation term is determined as

$$\boldsymbol{\mu}_{\mathrm{rot},st} = \underset{|\boldsymbol{q}|=1}{\mathrm{argmin}} \sum_{(\boldsymbol{b}_s,\boldsymbol{b}_t)\in\mathcal{P}_{st}} \alpha(\boldsymbol{q}_t\boldsymbol{q}_s^{-1}\boldsymbol{q}^{-1})^2 \tag{18.6}$$

It can be efficiently computed using the eigen-decomposition proposed by Karney (2007). The Gaussian variance is estimated with

$$\sigma_{\mathrm{rot},st}^2 = \frac{1}{|\mathcal{P}_{st}|-1} \sum_{(\boldsymbol{b}_s,\boldsymbol{b}_t)\in\mathcal{P}_{st}} \alpha(\boldsymbol{q}_t\boldsymbol{q}_s^{-1}\boldsymbol{\mu}_{\mathrm{rot},st}^{-1})^2 \tag{18.7}$$

Finally, the single site is defined by a probabilistic disk detector as

$$V_s(\boldsymbol{b}_s|\boldsymbol{\theta}_s, \boldsymbol{X}) = \log(\mathrm{Pr}(\boldsymbol{b}_s|\boldsymbol{\theta}_s, \boldsymbol{X})) \tag{18.8}$$

Note that the probability $\mathrm{Pr}(\boldsymbol{b}_s|\boldsymbol{\theta}_s, \boldsymbol{X})$ of disk $s$ being in pose $\boldsymbol{b}_s$ is over a nine-dimensional parameter space and has to be defined for every possible position, orientation, and scale in the image volume. An exhaustive evaluation of the single site as well as the pair potentials on the uniformly discretized nine-dimensional parameter space would quickly become computationally infeasible. Therefore, we adopt the marginal space learning (MSL) paradigm of Zheng et al. (2008).

## 18.3.2 SPINAL DISK DETECTION

Instead of searching the whole nine-dimensional parameter space for possible objects, MSL employs three estimation steps in which the dimensionality of the search space is incrementally enlarged (cf. Figure 18.3). In each step, MSL only considers the most promising partial candidate solutions in a fashion similar to beam search (Koller and Friedman, 2009, p. 1156).

Originally, MSL has been designed to detect a single, specific object such as a particular organ or landmark (Zheng et al., 2008). For the detection of multiple objects of the same class, Kelm et al. (2010) introduced an iterative extension of MSL, iterated marginal space learning (iMSL). By means of a repeated analysis of candidate clusters iMSL ensures that even less salient entities of the sought object

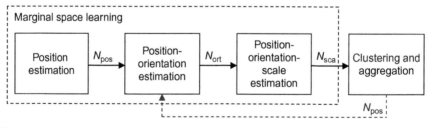

**FIGURE 18.3**

Graphical overview of marginal space learning and its iterative extension (blue).

are detected while preserving the computational advantages of MSL. This approach is particularly well-suited for the detection of spinal disks.

A schematic overview of *i*MSL is depicted in Figure 18.3. In the first step, the position detector, a machine learning classifier based on Haar-like features, is evaluated on each voxel of the region of interest. The $N_0$ most likely candidates are collected in the set of initial position candidates $\mathcal{P}_0$. Then, the best $N_{\text{pos}}$ ($N_{\text{pos}} \ll N_0$) candidates from $\mathcal{P}_0$ are evaluated using the orientation detector whose top candidates are evaluated using the scale detector. The resulting set $\mathcal{D}_{\text{sca}}$ contains disk candidate detections with all estimated parameters. Using pairwise average-linkage clustering (Hastie et al., 2001) with Euclidean distance, clusters of candidate disks are obtained. The number of clusters is determined by the cut in the dendrogram for which the distance of the merged clusters first exceeds twice a specified radius $R$. The most likely $N_A$ box candidates of each resulting cluster are averaged and added to the set of detected disk candidates $\mathcal{D}$. After removing all position candidates from $\mathcal{P}_0$ that are closer than the cluster radius $R$ to any of the detections in $\mathcal{D}$, orientation and scale detection are repeated on the remaining position candidates until no position candidates are left or no new disk candidates are detected.

After the first iteration *i*MSL produces the same results as standard MSL with equivalent parameters. Formally, the number of candidate evaluations that are necessary for *i*MSL is $N = H_{\text{pos}} + N_{\text{iter}}(N_{\text{pos}}H_{\text{ort}} + N_{\text{ort}}H_{\text{sca}})$ where $N_{\text{iter}}$ is the number of executed iterations. Since the number of positions examined with the position classifier $H_{\text{pos}}$ is the same for both, *i*MSL and MSL, and since it dominates the number of evaluations $N$ for sufficiently small $N_{\text{pos}}$ and $N_{\text{ort}}$, *i*MSL does not require significantly more computation time than MSL with the same candidate numbers $N_{\text{pos}}$ and $N_{\text{ort}}$ ($\Delta N = (N_{\text{iter}} - 1)(N_{\text{pos}}H_{\text{ort}} + N_{\text{ort}}H_{\text{sca}})$). Starting with the second iteration, however, *i*MSL examines less likely partial solution candidates obtained with the position detector and thus increases the detection rate, that is, the sensitivity of the detector.

### 18.3.3 INFERENCE

The probabilistic spine model described in the previous section is discretized using the disk candidates detected with *i*MSL. Each random variable $b_s$ is transformed into a discrete random variable where each state represents one of the detected disk candidates. In order to allow for missed detections, an extra "missing" state is introduced. Note that *i*MSL detects disk candidates with high sensitivity which usually results in more disk candidates than actual disks. The MAP estimate, that is, the maximum of Eq. (18.1), provides the optimum assignment of a disk candidate to one of the disk variables according to the probabilistic spine model. Thus, only those disk candidates that form a valid spine are selected and are implicitly assigned a suitable label. The MAP is efficiently computed by belief propagation where, due to the tree structure of the factor graph (cf. Figure 18.2), a single forward-backward pass yields the exact solution (Kschischang et al., 2001).

### 18.3.4 EVALUATION

Datasets

Experiments have been conducted based on 42 MR and 30 CT volumes. The $T_1$-weighted MR volumes (FL3D-VIBE sequence) were obtained from 42 healthy volunteers. About one-half of the volumes has been acquired on two 1.5 T scanner models (MAGNETOM Avanto and MAGNETOM Espree, Siemens

AG, Erlangen) with TR $= 5/4$ ms, TE $= 2$ ms and a flip angle of 10°. The other half has been obtained from two 3 T scanner models (MAGNETOM Trio, MAGNETOM Verio, Siemens AG, Erlangen) with TR $= 4/3$ ms, TE $= 1$ ms and again a flip angle of 10°. Each of the volumes was recorded in a two-station scan and subsequently combined to a volume covering the whole spine (approximately 860 mm $\times$ 350 mm $\times$ 190 mm). Susceptibility artifacts and intensity variations due to magnetic field inhomogeneities were present in the data. No bias field correction was performed.

CT data covering the thoracic and lumbar spine was acquired from 30 patients with bone lesions. It was reconstructed in sagittal slices, most at about 3 mm distance (three volumes with 2 mm and one with 1.2 mm), using various medium to hard convolution kernels (B50f, B60f, B70f). The in-plane resolution was between 0.48 mm and 1.70 mm. Various hyperdense disease patterns were present in the data stemming from osteoblastic bone lesions and diffuse sclerotic areas within the vertebral bodies. In some patients, metallic spinal fixators yielded severe streaking artifacts that contributed to the challenge of this data set.

Both, CT and MR volumes were resampled to an isotropic resolution of 2.1 mm for spinal disk detection and to an isotropic resolution of 6 mm for spine part localization.

Each spinal disk has been manually annotated with four defined landmarks. From these, ground truth boxes have been derived for the spinal disks as well as for the lumbar, thoracic, and cervical spine regions.

For spine part detection, standard MSL was run using $N_{pos} = 500$ position, $N_{ort} = 50$ orientation, and $N_{sca} = N_A = 20$ scale candidates. For hypothesis generation we used position hypotheses at the volume resolution of (6 mm), orientation hypotheses at a resolution of 3.3° and scale hypotheses at 6 mm resolution.

For disk detection, $i$MSL was employed with a cluster radius of $R = 6$ mm, $N_0 = 3000$ initial position candidates and 500 detection candidates for the remaining detection estimation steps ($N_{pos} = 500$, $N_{ort} = 500$, $N_{sca} = 500$). In each cluster, the top $N_A = 20$ candidates were then averaged to obtain a disk candidate. Hypotheses were again generated at volume resolution (2.1 mm), orientation hypotheses again at 3.3° and scale hypotheses at 4.0 mm resolution.

Note that the choice of hyperparameters is not critical for the performance of $i$MSL as long as they are within a reasonable range. The cluster radius $R$, for example, determines the minimum distance that can be obtained between any two detections. For the cervical disks we measured a distance of $18 \pm 2$ mm in our training data, which means that the cluster radius $R$ should certainly be smaller than 9 mm to avoid merging candidates from neighboring disks. The number of initial position candidates $N_0$, for example, should exceed a certain minimum number. It can be estimated from a few examples by examining the minimum number of candidates required to cover all disks after position detection, which we did on some MR volumes. Detailed results from an experimental analysis of the influence of the hyperparameters are found in Kelm et al. (2012).

## Results

All evaluation results have been obtained using 10-fold cross validation, ensuring that training and testing data never originated from the same subject. Every ground truth annotation for which no disk within a distance of 10 mm was detected was counted as a missed detection.

In MR, spinal disks were detected with a sensitivity of 98.64% and only 0.0731 false positives per volume, yielding a positive predictive value of 99.68%. The overall processing time on a 2.2 GHz dual core laptop computer was between 9.9 s and 13.0 s, and 11.5 s on average where most of the time

**Table 18.1  Disk Detection Results Using Tenfold Cross Validation Based on 42 $T_1$-Weighted MR Volumes and 30 CT Volumes**

|  |  | Position Error (mm) | | | | Angular Error (°) | | | |
|---|---|---|---|---|---|---|---|---|---|
|  |  | Cerv. | Thor. | Lumb. | Avg. | Cerv. | Thor. | Lumb. | Avg. |
| MR | Mean | 2.09 | 2.41 | 2.86 | 2.42 | 4.86 | 3.38 | 3.80 | 3.85 |
|  | Stdev | 1.06 | 1.33 | 1.30 | 1.28 | 3.34 | 2.11 | 2.40 | 2.62 |
|  | Median | 1.84 | 2.18 | 2.68 | 2.19 | 3.89 | 2.90 | 3.37 | 3.17 |
| CT | Mean | – | 3.40 | 2.80 | 3.22 | – | 4.77 | 3.72 | 4.47 |
|  | Stdev | – | 1.78 | 1.59 | 1.75 | – | 3.07 | 2.57 | 2.97 |
|  | Median | – | 3.11 | 2.54 | 2.94 | – | 4.32 | 3.21 | 3.97 |

Notes: *Left: position error. Right: angular error between normals.*

was spent on disk candidate detection. In CT, a sensitivity of 98.04% was achieved while 0.267 false positives per volume were obtained, yielding a positive predictive value of 98.43%.

The accuracy of the detected spinal disks has been evaluated by the position distance and the angle between the disk plane normals of the detected spinal disks and the ground truth annotation (cf. Table 18.1). On average, a position error of 2.42 mm (about 1 voxel) and an angular error of 3.85° was obtained for the MR data. For the CT data, the position error of 3.22 mm and the angular error of 4.47° was slightly worse, which can be attributed to both the smaller data set available for training and the presence of pathologies and artifacts (cf. Figure 18.5).

Four examples from the MR data set are shown in Figure 18.4. The rightmost example shows a case where the volunteer has been instructed to lie down twisted in order to obtain a spine recording with unusual pose. Still the proposed approach could locate and label all spinal disks reliably.

Figure 18.5 shows four examples from the CT data set. The examples exhibit various spinal pathologies and age-related degenerations. Nevertheless, our method could locate and label the spinal disks with high reliability. The rightmost example shows that, even in the presence of severe metal artifacts, our spinal disk detector is sensitive and robust enough to detect the spinal disks that are hardly visible. However, this example also shows a failure to detect the last spinal disk between L5 and the sacrum, resulting in a mislabeling of all other disks. A detailed analysis of this case revealed that the L5/S1 disk was detected with *i*MSL but not selected with the global prior model.

Our results provide evidence that the presented approach also works in the presence of pathological deformations of the spinal column (e.g., scoliosis, kyphosis, lordosis, etc.) and pathologies that result in unusual appearance of individual disks (e.g., degeneration, herniation, desiccation, etc.) and vertebral bodies (e.g., compression fractures, hemivertebrae, diffuse sclerosis, etc.). In this as well as other applications, we have observed that MSL is very robust to imaging artifacts and unusual appearances of the sought object. Using *i*MSL increases sensitivity and helps detect disks with very unusual appearance. The CT examples in Figure 18.5 show cases in which disks within diseased vertebrae and disks in the presence of severe artifacts can reliably be detected. Furthermore, since the global spine model is restricted to candidates provided by the disk detector, abnormalities such as scoliosis, kyphosis, lordosis, compression fractures, and hemivertebrae can be robustly handled. The volunteer with the unusual pose in Figure 18.4 provides evidence toward this. Simple retraining of

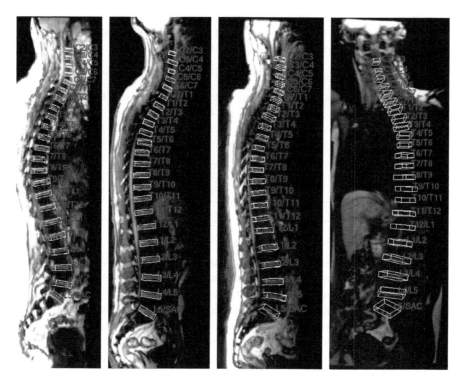

**FIGURE 18.4**

Four examples from the MR data with detection results. Although the volunteer in the rightmost example lay down in an unusual pose, all spinal disks were detected and labeled correctly.

our system, with more abnormal cases added, enables the detectors as well as the prior model to handle pathologies and degenerations even more reliably.

## 18.4 RIB CENTERLINE PARSING

Below, we first introduce a rough-to-exact representation for ribs and then present the inference algorithms. We then discuss the clinical concept of rib unfolding that speeds up rib reading and finally present the experimental results.

### 18.4.1 ROUGH-TO-EXACT REPRESENTATION

Each rib $\mathbf{R}_m$ ($m = 1 : M; M = 24$) can be exactly represented by, say, a binary mask or a 3D mesh. Since direct inference of high-dimensional objects is challenging, we resort to a *rough-to-exact* representation. We associate each rib with its centerline $\mathbf{C}_m$ represented by a set of points $\mathbf{C}_m = \{\mathbf{x}_{mn}; n = 1 : N_m\}$, where $N_m$ is proportional to the length of rib $\mathbf{R}_m$. We then divide each rib into

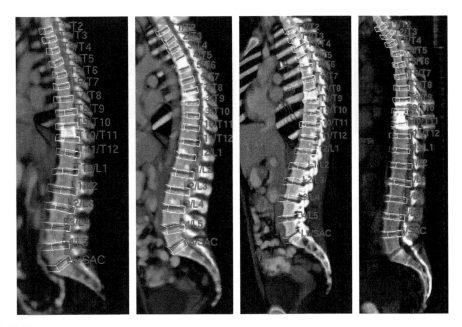

**FIGURE 18.5**

Four examples from the CT data set with detection results. The hyperdense areas within some of the vertebral bodies are either well-defined osteoblastic bone lesions or diffuse sclerotic areas. The rightmost example shows that our method can also cope with severe artifacts, here stemming from a spinal fixation. Note, however, that in this example the last spinal disk was missed and the labeling was erroneously shifted by one.

several short rib centerline segments $\mathbf{C}_{mk}$ ($k = 1 : K$) and further constrain each rib segment to follow a rigid transformation $\mathcal{T}(\hat{\mathbf{C}}_{mk} | \mathbf{t}_{mk}, \mathbf{r}_{mk}, \mathbf{s}_{mk})$ of a template $\hat{\mathbf{C}}_{mk}$, where $\mathbf{t}$, $\mathbf{r}$, and $\mathbf{s}$ denote translation, rotation, and scale parameters, respectively. In other words, a rib centerline undergoes *piecewise rigid* transformation and is *piecewise smooth* at the roughest representation level.

Hierarchical inference is then employed in a rough-to-exact fashion to progressively approximate the truth as the inference of low-dimensional objects tends to be more robust and less likely to be stuck in local minima. Specifically, we infer first the set of rigid transformations $\{(\mathbf{t}_{mk}, \mathbf{r}_{mk}, \mathbf{s}_{mk}); m = 1 : M; k = 1 : K\}$ for all rib centerline segments, then the rib centerlines $\{\mathbf{C}_m; m = 1 : M\}$, and finally the rib masks $\{\mathbf{R}_m; m = 1 : M\}$. Following, we discuss the inference module.

## 18.4.2 RIB CENTERLINE CAGE EXTRACTION

Figure 18.6 illustrates the algorithmic pipeline for extracting a rib centerline cage. We first train a probabilistic boosting tree (Tu, 2005) to robustly highlight the rib centerline voxels while suppressing the rest of the background voxels. Given an unseen volume, we perform an exhaustive scanning to obtain a bottom-up probability map $\mathcal{P}$. We now fit a rib centerline cage to maximize the sum of detected responses, allowing each rib belonging to the cage to undergo a piecewise rigid transformation. All

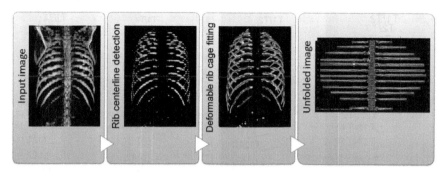

**FIGURE 18.6**

A graphical illustration of key steps of the rib centerline extraction and rib unfolding pipeline.

ribs are matched simultaneously so that shape constraints can be imposed on neighboring ribs during matching to overcome the distractions from adjacent bone structures such as clavicle or adjacent ribs, and all ribs are automatically labeled after matching.

In the template, the rib centerline segment $\hat{\mathbf{C}}_{mk}$ contains a set of points $\hat{\mathbf{C}}_{mk} = \{\mathbf{x}_n; n = 1 : N_{mk}\}$. For each rib centerline segment $\mathcal{C}_{mk}$, we define the response fitting energy as

$$E^{mk}_{\text{unary}} = \sum_{n=1}^{N_{mk}} \mathcal{P}(\mathcal{T}_{mk}(\mathbf{x}_n|\mathbf{t}_{mk}, \mathbf{r}_{mk}, \mathbf{s}_{mk})) \tag{18.9}$$

and find the top candidates of $\{\mathbf{t}_{mk}, \mathbf{r}_{mk}, \mathbf{s}_{mk}\}$ that maximize it.

Instead of exhaustively searching the original nine-dimensional parameter space of $(t_x, t_y, t_z, r_x, r_y, r_z, s_x, s_y, s_z)$, which is slow, we follow the principle of marginal space learning (MSL) (Zheng et al., 2008) for efficiency. To be specific, the transform estimation is split into three steps: position estimation, position-orientation estimation, and position-orientation-scale estimation. First, the positional marginal space is searched exhaustively and a small portion of the best position hypothesis is preserved. Second, the orientation marginal space is exhaustively searched for each position candidate and a limited number of best position-orientation candidates are kept after this step. Finally, the scale parameters are searched in the constrained space in a similar way. It is shown that this marginal space searching effectively reduces the number of testing hypotheses by six orders of magnitudes, compared with exhaustive full space search (Zheng et al., 2008).

Till now, each rib segment is searched individually and therefore likely matched to a wrong rib due to the similarity between adjacent ribs. To avoid this problem, we impose the pairwise smoothness constraints on the transform parameters of neighboring rib segments in a Markov random field (MRF) model:

$$E^k_{\text{MRF}} = \sum_{m=1}^{M} E^{mk}_{\text{unary}}(\mathcal{T}_{mk}) - \lambda \sum_{(i,j) \in N_{\text{rib}}} E^{ij,k}_{\text{pair}}(\mathcal{T}_{ik}, \mathcal{T}_{jk}) \tag{18.10}$$

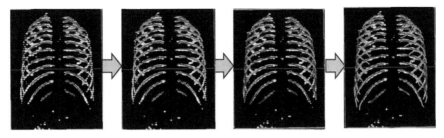

**FIGURE 18.7**

Rib centerline cage fitting. Each rib centerline is split into four segments and the registration is performed on a total of 12 pairs of rib segments together starting from the segments connected to the central vertebrae.

where $\lambda$ is the regularization parameter, $N_{\text{rib}}$ is the set of neighboring rib pairs $(i, j)$, and $E_{\text{pair}}^{ij,k}$ measures the mean Euclidean distance between two neighboring rib centerline segments $\mathbf{C}_{ik}$ and $\mathbf{C}_{jk}$ transformed by $\mathcal{T}_{ik}$ and $\mathcal{T}_{jk}$, respectively.

$$E_{\text{pair}}^{ij,k}(\mathcal{T}_{ik}, \mathcal{T}_{jk}) = \sum_{n=1}^{N_{ik}} \frac{1}{N_{ik}} \|\mathcal{T}_{ik}(\mathbf{x}_n) - \mathcal{T}_{jk}(\mathbf{x}_n)\|^2 + \sum_{n=1}^{N_{jk}} \frac{1}{N_{jk}} \|\mathcal{T}_{ik}(\mathbf{x}_n) - \mathcal{T}_{jk}(\mathbf{x}_n)\|^2 \tag{18.11}$$

To improve fitting robustness, we further split each rib centerline equally into four segments ($K = 4$). Starting from the first rib centerline segment ($k = 1$) connected to the central vertebrae, we search for the optimal rigid transformation parameters $\{\mathbf{T}_{mk}; m = 1 : M\}$ simultaneously by maximizing Eq. (18.10). The results are then used to initialize the pose of the next rib segment ($k = k + 1$) and repeat the optimization until all rib segments are matched ($k = K$). Figure 18.7 illustrates this process.

The optimization of MRF energy function Eq. (18.10) is generally NP-hard. To simplify the problem, we relax the neighborhood $N_{\text{rib}}$ by only considering *all* vertical pairs of neighboring ribs from the same side (e.g., the first and second rib on the left or right) and *one* horizontal pair of neighboring ribs from both sides (we chose the sixth ribs on the left and right side). The resulting H-shaped graph contains no loops of cliques and thus can be efficiently solved via dynamic programming. First, the transformation parameter $\mathcal{T}_{i,k}$ is searched separately that maximizes Eq. (18.9) in the manner of marginal space learning and a number of top candidates are kept for each rib centerline segment; then the optimal transformations for all rib centerline segments can be found by adding smoothness constraints in Eq. (18.10).

Because each rib segment is transformed rigidly, the overall rib centerline estimated so far is piecewise smooth and subject to small deviation due to slight deformation of each rib segment as well as limited resolution of the discrete transformation parameter search space. We employ the active contour model (Kass et al., 1988) to further refine the centerline so that it is globally smooth.

## 18.4.3 RIB SEGMENTATION VIA GRAPH CUT

After estimating the rib centerline, we then set up a graph cut problem (Boykov and Funka-Lea, 2006) to obtain the segmentation of each rib. We denote the graph by $(\mathcal{V}, \mathcal{E})$, where $\mathcal{V}$ contains all nodes in the graph (or all voxels in consideration) and $\mathcal{V}$ describes all edges in the graph (or all pairs of neighboring voxels). We first compute a function $\mathcal{M}(p)$ for $p \in \mathcal{V}$, which measures the shortest distance of a voxel $p$ to the centerline. This function can be viewed as a prior.

The segmentation is achieved by minimizing the following energy function:

$$E(L) = \sum_{p \in \mathcal{V}} D_p(L_p) + \sum_{(p,q) \in \mathcal{E}} V_{p,q}(L_p, L_q) \tag{18.12}$$

where $L = \{L_p \mid p \in \mathcal{V}\}$ is the binary labeling ($L_p \in \{0, 1\}$) of all nodes $\mathcal{V}$. The unary data term $D_p$, which encourages the voxel to stay close to the prior information, is defined as

$$D_p(L_p) = L_p(1 - g(\mathcal{M}(p))) + (1 - L_p)g(\mathcal{M}(p)) \tag{18.13}$$

where $g(x) = \frac{1}{1+e^{-x/\tau}}$ with $\tau$ controlling the influence of the prior. The pairwise interaction term $V_{p,q}$, which encourages the neighboring voxels with similar intensities to share the same label, is defined as

$$V_{p,q} = \lambda\, e^{-\frac{(I_p - I_q)^2}{2\sigma^2}} \delta(L_p \neq L_q) \tag{18.14}$$

where $\delta(.)$ is the delta function, that is $\delta(x) = 1$ if $x$ is true and is 0 otherwise, and $\lambda$ and $\sigma$ are the regularization parameter and contrast coefficient, respectively. After segmentation, the rib centerlines are updated.

## 18.4.4 RIB UNFOLDING VIA GEOMETRIC TRANSFORMATION

Rib assessment using traditional visualization demands significant time from radiologists as a rib has a complex shape with a diagonal course across numerous CT sections and a twist along its longitudinal axis. During reading based on standard multi-planar reformats (MPRs), the radiologists must look for bone lesions or fractures in a large number of CT images rib-by-rib and side-by-side and trace these anomalies across numerous slices and manually adjusted views. This process is tedious and time-consuming. Furthermore, fractures or lesions can be variable and inconspicuous, especially if no dislocation is present or if the fracture orientation is parallel to the orientation of the section that is used for detection.

We overcome these limitations of the conventional solutions by following a novel approach of virtually unfolding the rib cage into a single image using automatically generated curved planar reformats (CPRs) of the ribs. This technology saves reading time by bypassing the need for manual foraging while still maintaining or going beyond the accurate and comprehensive diagnostic requirements that come with traditional bone assessment.

First, based on the extracted centerline, a cross-section orthogonal to the rib centerline is formed at each rib centerline point. In this cross-section image, a rib is typically elliptically shaped. From the obtained rib segmentation result, we obtain this "ellipse" and then compute its long axis as the so-called up-vector.

Since ribs are curved and twisted in 3D, rib unfolding then generates a 2D image from a 3D CT volume by simultaneously "uncurving" and "untwisting" the ribs purely geometrically. The "uncurving" operation extends a curved rib centerline to a straight line. The second "untwisting" operation follows the up-vector for each rib centerline point while "uncurving" the rib along its centerline. Figure 18.8 shows a variety of rib unfolding results with different pathological conditions.

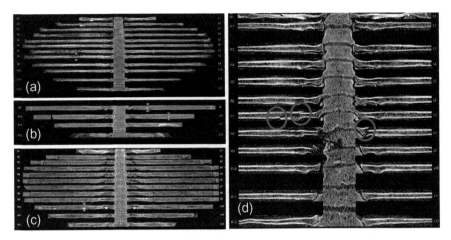

**FIGURE 18.8**

Rib unfolding results with different pathological conditions. (a) Extensive osteolysis of ribs. (b) Small rib lesions and partial rib cage. (c) Tiny lesion. (d) Multiple bone fractures (in red circles) from a trauma patient.

The 2D unfolded view provides a quick glance at all ribs. When a user finds a suspicious rib finding in the 2D view, the user can interactively click it and move the mouse around it along the rib and the system can synchronously display, based on the derived geometric transformation, the corresponding sagittal, transverse, and coronal MPRs and a cross-section view perpendicular to the rib of interest for a detailed 3D review. This feature greatly accelerates the reading process. The radiologists can also compare the left and right side of the unfolded rib cage and spot anomalies as differences between both halves, which also speeds up the reading process.

### 18.4.5 SYSTEM PERFORMANCE

#### Quantitative benchmarking

We quantitatively benchmarked the performance of our rib centerline extraction on a database of 112 thoracic CT scans from different subjects and hospitals, exhibiting significant variations in the size, shape, and pathologies of the rib cages, with slice distances up to 5 mm. In particular, we compared it with the tracing-based method in Ramakrishnan et al. (2011) and Ramakrishnan and Alvino (2011) and the nonrigid robust point matching method (RPM) in Chui and Rangarajan (2003). Our method does not miss, falsely detect, or mislabel a single rib while the tracing-based method misses 8%, falsely detects 3.2%, and mislabels 40% of all ribs. Using a modified Hausdorff distance, we showed that our method outperforms RPM by one order of magnitude (1.7 mm vs 12.3 mm). Figure 18.9 shows some challenging cases where the proposed method still yields reasonably good results. Refer to Wu et al. (2012) for more experimental details.

#### Qualitative assessment of rib unfolding

It is difficult to quantify the unfolding quality. Instead, we requested two clinical experts to visually inspect the unfolding images of 326 datasets with 119 standard cases (thoracic CT scans but not from trauma patients) and 207 trauma cases and then score the quality in consensus. These scans

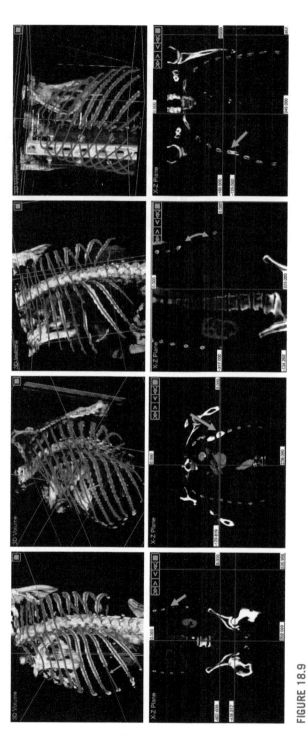

**FIGURE 18.9**

Difficult cases: (first column) missing rib segments, (second column) rib metastases, (third column) unusually large rib spacing, and (fourth column) connected ribs. The top row shows 3D volume rendering images, whereas the bottom row shows 2D coronal planes.

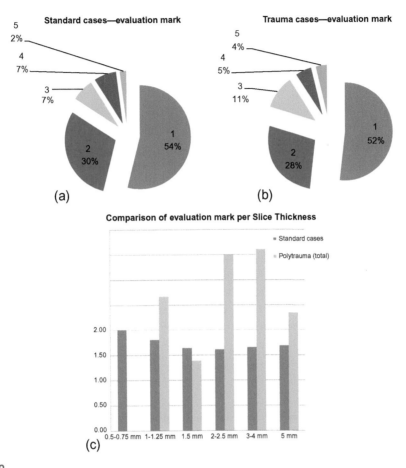

**FIGURE 18.10**

Qualitative assessment of rib unfolding quality for (a) standard cases, (b) trauma cases, and (c) difference ranges of slice thickness.

acquired by scanners manufactured by different vendors at different sites are of different slice thickness (up to 5 mm resolution) and different CT reconstruction kernels (sharp or smooth). Radiologists are interested in finding bone fracture(s) for a trauma case and bone lesion(s) for a standard case.

We used a five-scale scheme to rate the rib unfolding quality: "1" means perfect quality with no or minor corrections necessary; "2" good quality with moderate corrections necessary, "3" acceptable quality with involved corrections necessary provided that the user has time, "4" bad quality with serious problems such as rib centerlines crossing over each other, and "5" no unfolding computed, which actually means that no ribs are detected.

From Figure 18.10(a) and (b), it is clear that the system is able to produce acceptable or better rib unfolding results for 91% of standard and trauma cases! In general, trauma cases are a bit more difficult to handle as there are 2% more failures and 4% more acceptable results than standard cases. Figure 18.10(c) shows that the unfolding quality in general is robust to slice thickness for standard cases.

For trauma cases, it seems that the unfolding quality degrades as slice thickness increases. We also found that the reconstruction kernel, whether smooth or sharp, does not affect the unfolding quality.

In a separate clinical evaluation (Ringl et al., 2015), it is shown that on average rib unfolding shortens bone reading speed by 50% and improves diagnostic sensitivity of recognizing bone fractures by 10%.

## 18.5 CONCLUSIONS

We have presented automatic systems for detecting spine disks and segmenting all ribs present in the image. For spine disk detection, the approach uses an iterative extension of MSL for disk candidate detection along with an anatomical network that incorporates spatial context in the form of a prior on the nine-dimensional disk poses. Since the entire approach is learning-based, it can be trained for CT and MR alike. Our results based on 42 MR and 30 CT volume data sets have superior sensitivity and localization accuracy. For rib centerline extraction, we have used a rough-to-exact rib representation and accordingly broken a highly complex rib inference problem into a series of less complex tasks, thereby improving the robustness and efficiency of the solution. The proposed algorithm achieves superior results when tested on hundreds of datasets. After the rib centerlines are extracted, we have generated a novel image by unfolding 3D ribs into a 2D plane, with quality rated as accepted or beyond for over 90% of unseen cases. Clinical study has shown that rib unfolding shortens the rib assessment time and increases diagnostic sensitivity.

## REFERENCES

Adams, M.A., Dolan, P., 2011. Biomechanics of vertebral compression fractures and clinical application. Arch. Orthop. Trauma Surg. 131 (12), 1703–1710.

Alomari, R.S., Corso, J.J., Chaudhary, V., 2011. Labeling of lumbar discs using both pixel- and object-level features with a two-level probabilistic model. IEEE Trans. Med. Imaging 30 (1), 1–10.

Aylward, S.R., Bullitt, E., 2002. Initialization, noise, singularities, and scale in height ridge traversal for tubular object centerline extraction. IEEE Trans. Med. Imaging 21 (2), 61–75.

Boisvert, J., Cheriet, F., Pennec, X., Labelle, H., Ayache, N., 2008. Geometric variability of the scoliotic spine using statistics on articulated shape models. IEEE Trans. Med. Imaging 27 (4), 557–568. ISSN 0278–0062. http://dx.doi.org/10.1109/TMI.2007.911474.

Boykov, Y., Funka-Lea, G., 2006. Graph cuts and efficient ND image segmentation. Int. J. Comput. Vis. 70 (2), 109–131.

Chui, H., Rangarajan, A., 2003. A new point matching algorithm for non-rigid registration. Comput. Vis. Image Underst. 89 (2), 114–141.

Corso, J.J., Alomari, R.S., Chaudhary, V., 2008. Lumbar disc localization and labeling with a probabilistic model on both pixel and object features. In: Proceedings of the MICCAI, pp. 202–210.

Galanski, M., 2003. Spiral and Multislice Computed Tomography of the Body. Thieme, Stuttgart.

Glocker, B., Feulner, J., Criminisi, A., Haynor, D.R., Konukoglu, E., 2012. Automatic localization and identification of vertebrae in arbitrary field-of-view CT scans. In: Proceedings of the MICCAI, pp. 590–598.

Hammon, M., Dankerl, P., Tsymbal, A., Wels, M., Kelm, M., May, M., Suehling, M., Uder, M., Cavallaro, A., 2013. Automatic detection of lytic and blastic thoracolumbar spine metastases on computed tomography. Eur. Radiol. 23 (7), 1862–1870.

Hastie, T., Tibshirani, R., Friedman, J., 2001. The Elements of Statistical Learning, Springer Series in Statistics. Springer, New York.

Helzel, I., Long, W., Fitzpatrick, D., Madey, S., Bottlang, M., 2009. Evaluation of intramedullary rib splints for less-invasive stabilisation of rib fractures. Injury 40 (10), 1104–1110.

Huang, S.H., Lai, S.H., Novak, C., 2008. A statistical learning approach to vertebra detection and segmentation from spinal MRI. In: Proceedings of the ISBI, pp. 125–128.

Huang, S.H., Chu, Y.H., Lai, S.H., Novak, C.L., 2009. Learning-based vertebra detection and iterative normalized-cut segmentation for spinal MRI. IEEE Trans. Med. Imaging 28 (10), 1595–1605.

Jäger, F., Hornegger, J., Schwab, S., Janka, R., 2009. Computer-aided assessment of anomalies in the scoliotic spine in 3-D MRI images. In: Proceedings of the MICCAI, pp. 819–826.

Karney, C.F., 2007. Quaternions in molecular modeling. J. Molec. Graph. Modell. 25, 595–604.

Kass, M., Witkin, A., Terzopoulos, D., 1988. Snakes: active contour models. Int. J. Comput. Vis. 1 (4), 321–331.

Kelm, B.M., Zhou, S.K., Suehling, M., Zheng, Y., Wels, M., Comaniciu, D., 2010. Detection of 3D spinal geometry using Iterated Marginal Space Learning. In: Proceedings of the 2010 MICCAI Workshop on Medical Computer Vision, LNCS, 6533. Springer-Verlag, Berlin, Heidelberg, pp. 96–05.

Kelm, B.M., Wels, M., Zhou, S.K., Seifert, S., Suehling, M., Zheng, Y., Comaniciu, D., 2012. Spine detection in CT and MR using iterated marginal space learning. Med. Image Anal. 17 (8), 1283–1292.

Kim, D., Kim, H., Kang, H.S., 2002. Object-tracking segmentation method: vertebra and rib segmentation in CT images. In: Medical Imaging 2002, pp. 1662–1671.

Kiraly, A.P., Qing, S., Shen, H., 2006. A novel visualization method for the ribs within chest volume data. In: Medical Imaging, p. 614108.

Klinder, T., Ostermann, J., Ehm, M., Franz, A., Kneser, R., Lorenz, C., 2009. Automated model-based vertebra detection, identification, and segmentation in CT images. Med. Image Anal. 13 (3), 471–482.

Koller, D., Friedman, N., 2009. Probabilistic Graphical Models, Principles and Techniques, Adaptive Computation and Machine Learning. The MIT Press, Cambridge, MA.

Kschischang, F.R., Frey, B.J., Loeliger, H.A., 2001. Factor graphs and the sum-product algorithm. IEEE J IT 47 (2), 498–519.

Major, D., Hladuvka, J., Schulze, F., Bühler, K., 2013. Automated landmarking and labeling of fully and partially scanned spinal columns in CT images. Med. Image Anal. 17 (8), 1151–1163.

Mirzaalian, H., Wels, M., Heimann, T., Kelm, B.M., Suehling, M., 2013. Fast and robust 3D vertebra segmentation using statistical shape models. In: Proceedings of the IEEE EMBC, pp. 3379–3382.

Mohr, M., Abrams, E., Engel, C., Long, W.B., Bottlang, M., 2007. Geometry of human ribs pertinent to orthopedic chest-wall reconstruction. J. Biomech. 40 (6), 1310–1317.

Ramakrishnan, S., Alvino, C., 2011. An automatic method for rib ordering and pairing in 3D medical images. In: 2011 IEEE International Symposium on Biomedical Imaging: From Nano to Macro, pp. 1201–1204.

Ramakrishnan, S., Alvino, C., Grady, L., Kiraly, A., 2011. Automatic three-dimensional rib centerline extraction from CT scans for enhanced visualization and anatomical context. In: SPIE Medical Imaging, p. 79622X.

Ringl, H., Lazar, M., Töpker, M., Woitek, R., Prosch, H., Asenbaum, U., Balassy, C., Toth, D., Weber, M., Hajdu, S., et al., 2015. The ribs unfolded—a CT visualization algorithm for fast detection of rib fractures: effect on sensitivity and specificity in trauma patients. Eur. Radiol. 25, 1865–1874.

Schmidt, S., Kappes, J., Bergtholdt, M., Pekar, V., Dries, S., Bystrov, D., Schnörr, C., 2007. Spine detection and labeling using a parts-based graphical model. In: Proceedings of the IPMI, pp. 122–133.

Seifert, S., Dillmann, R., 2007. Biomechanical modeling of the cervical spine on the basis of tomographic data. Biomed. Tech. 52 (5), 337–345. http://dx.doi.org/10.1515/BMT.2007.056.

Seifert, S., Barbu, A., Zhou, S.K., Liu, D., Feulner, J., Huber, M., Sühling, M., Cavallaro, A., Comaniciu, D., 2009. Hierarchical parsing and semantic navigation of full body CT data. In: Proceedings of the SPIE Medical Imaging, pp. 725–732.

Seifert, S., Kelm, M., Möller, M., Mukherjee, S., Cavallaro, A., Huber, M., Comaniciu, D., 2010. Semantic annotation of medical images. In: Proceedings of the SPIE Medical Imaging.

Shen, H., Shao, M., 2003. A thoracic cage coordinate system for recording pathologies in lung CT volume data. In: 2003 IEEE Nuclear Science Symposium Conference Record, vol. 5, pp. 3029–3031.

Shen, H., Liang, L., Shao, M., Qing, S., 2004. Tracing based segmentation for the labeling of individual rib structures in chest CT volume data. In: Medical Image Computing and Computer-Assisted Intervention—MICCAI 2004. Springer, pp. 967–974.

Staal, J., van Ginneken, B., Viergever, M.A., 2007. Automatic rib segmentation and labeling in computed tomography scans using a general framework for detection, recognition and segmentation of objects in volumetric data. Med. Image Anal. 11 (1), 35–46.

Tschirhart, C.E., Finkelstein, J.A., Whyne, C.M., 2007. Biomechanics of vertebral level, geometry, and transcortical tumors in the metastatic spine. J. Biomech. 40 (1), 46–54.

Tu, Z., 2005. Probabilistic boosting-tree: learning discriminative methods for classification, recognition, and clustering. In: Proceedings of the ICCV, vol. 2, pp. 1589–1596.

Wang, H., Bai, J., Zhang, Y., 2006. A relative thoracic cage coordinate system for localizing the thoracic organs in chest CT volume data. In: 27th Annual International Conference of the Engineering in Medicine and Biology Society, 2005. IEEE-EMBS 2005, pp. 3257–3260.

Wels, M., Kelm, B.M., Tsymbal, A., Hammon, M., Soza, G., Sühling, M., Cavallaro, A., Comaniciu, D., 2012. Multi-stage osteolytic spinal bone lesion detection from CT data with internal sensitivity control. In: van Ginneken, B., Novak, C.L. (Eds.), Proceedings of the SPIE Medical Imaging, vol. 8315.

Wu, D., Liu, D., Puskas, Z., Lu, C., Wimmer, A., Tietjen, C., Soza, G., Zhou, S.K., 2012. A learning based deformable template matching method for automatic rib centerline extraction and labeling in CT images. In: 2012 IEEE Conference on Computer Vision and Pattern Recognition (CVPR), pp. 980–987.

Zhan, Y., Jian, B., Maneesh, D., Zhou, X., 2015. Cross-modality vertebrae localization and labeling using learning-based approaches. In: Li, S., Yao, J. (Eds.), Spinal Imaging and Image Analysis, Lecture Notes in Computational Vision and Biomechanics, vol. 18. Springer International Publishing, pp. 301–322.

Zheng, Y., Barbu, A., Georgescu, B., Scheuering, M., Comaniciu, D., 2008. Four-chamber heart modeling and automatic segmentation for 3D cardiac CT volumes using marginal space learning and steerable features. IEEE Trans. Med. Imaging 27 (11), 1668–1681.

Zhou, X.S., Peng, Z., Zhan, Y., Dewan, M., Jian, B., Krishnan, A., Tao, Y., Harder, M., Grosskopf, S., Feuerlein, U., 2010. Redundancy, redundancy, redundancy: the three keys to highly robust anatomical parsing in medical images. In: Proceedings of the International Conference on Multimedia Information Retrieval. ACM, pp. 175–184.

# DATA-DRIVEN DETECTION AND SEGMENTATION OF LYMPH NODES

# 19

**J. Feulner[1] and A. Barbu[2]**

*Giesecke & Devrient GmbH, Munich, Germany[1]*
*Department of Statistics, Florida State University, Tallahassee, FL, USA[2]*

## CHAPTER OUTLINE

S. Kevin Zhou (Ed): Medical Image Recognition, Segmentation and Parsing. http://dx.doi.org/10.1016/B978-0-12-802581-9.00019-6

## 19.1 INTRODUCTION

Lymph nodes (LNs) are highly relevant in clinical practice and routinely examined. LNs can become enlarged due to cancer in nearby regions or cancer in the lymphatic system itself, which is called lymphoma. Detecting enlarged LNs and tracking their number and size over time is a common task for diagnosis and monitoring the effectiveness of the treatment. It is commonly carried out on 3D computed tomography (CT) images. Manual analysis is not only tedious; the results of different readers, and even the results of the same reader, can also differ considerably. Segmenting all LNs by hand is in practice typically too time consuming to be done, although the added clinical value would be high. A system for automatic LN detection and segmentation is therefore desirable. Automatic detection is, however, challenging because LNs can easily be confused with muscles and vessels that are *a priori* more likely and have a similar X-ray attenuation coefficient. Examples of LNs can be seen in Figures 19.12 and 19.14.

In this chapter, we present learning-based techniques for LN detection and segmentation in CT data, and their application to detecting axillary, pelvic, abdominal, and mediastinal LNs. We thereby focus on LNs of at least 10 mm in size, because smaller ones are clinically less relevant and hard to measure and detect (Therasse et al., 2000). While the LNs themselves look similar in all regions, detection is more difficult in the abdominal and the mediastinal regions where they are often hard to distinguish from neighboring structures. Detection is easier in the less cluttered axillary and pelvic regions.

An overview of our proposed method is shown in Figure 19.1. Given a CT volume image that typically shows a larger part of the body, regions of interest are automatically detected and extracted from the volume. This step helps to reduce the amount of data that needs to be handled and can also improve the detection accuracy as it reduces false alarms and simplifies the learning problem. Next, a cascade of binary classifiers is trained to detect LN center candidates in the regions of interest using Haar-like and gradient-aligned features. Then, a segmentation algorithm is initialized with each detected center. Finally, another binary classifier verifies the detections based on features extracted from the segmentations. Thus, detection and segmentation mutually influence each other. These segmentation-based features and also to some extent the gradient-aligned features are problem-specific

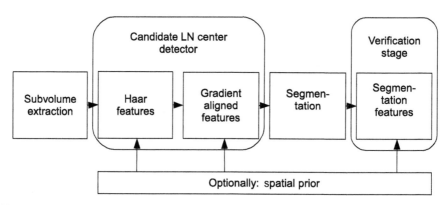

**FIGURE 19.1**

Overview of the different steps of the proposed detection system.

and able to extract information that is difficult to capture with "off-the-shelf" features. A considerable improvement of the detection performance can be achieved in regions where LNs are typically distributed nonhomogeneously by using a spatial prior, or probabilistic atlas, that can be generated in the training phase.

This chapter is based on our prior work on axillary and pelvic (Barbu et al., 2012) as well as mediastinal (Feulner et al., 2013) LN detection.

## 19.2 RELATED WORK

Early approaches on LN detection in CT data were nonlearning based. In Kitasaka et al. (2007), two cascaded special filters that act as a blob detector are proposed to detect abdominal LNs. In Feuerstein et al. (2009), a similar approach is used to detect mediastinal LNs. Here, the first filter is replaced with a Hessian-based blob detector. Both Kitasaka et al. (2007) and Feuerstein et al. (2009) produce a high number of false alarms. In Dornheim et al. (2006), a mass spring model was proposed to segment LNs. Later it was also used for detecting neck LNs (Dornheim and Dornheim, 2008).

In more recent publications on the topic, at least at some point machine learning techniques are employed. In Nimura et al. (2014), a first-order gradients-based blob detector that is called a radial structure tensor is used to generate abdominal LN candidates that are verified by a support vector machine (SVM). A detection rate of 82.0% with 21.6 false alarms per case is reported, which outperforms (Kitasaka et al., 2007). In Roth et al. (2014), the deep convolutional neural network architecture of Krizhevsky et al. (2012) was used to verify mediastinal and abdominal LN candidates generated using the methods of Cherry et al. (2014) and Liu et al. (2014). Promising results are reported, but all ground-truth LNs were passed into the verification stage for evaluation so that mainly the neural network and not the whole system was evaluated, which limits the comparability of the results.

Almost all published methods use a cascade of detectors in order to filter out easy negatives at an early stage.

The idea of coupling segmentation with detection has been proposed earlier in Leibe et al. (2008) and was applied to detect possibly partially occluded pedestrians. There, image patches are classified into visual codebook elements that vote for the object center. A fuzzy segmentation is generated from votes of codebook elements that contribute to a detection, and a model is fitted to the segmentation in order to verify it. The approach followed in this chapter differs from Leibe et al. (2008) in the following ways:

- The segmentation has a sharp boundary instead of being fuzzy and is generated differently. We evaluated both fitting a triangulated mesh by optimizing a Gaussian Markov random field (MRF) using gradient descent and a graph cuts-based method.
- Features are extracted from the segmentation and used to train a classifier that either accepts or rejects the segmentation.

Spatial priors of the different expected tissue classes are often used for segmentation-by-registration in the brain. Due to the rigid skull, multiple 3D brain scans of the same patient are typically similar, and differences between multiple patients are still relatively low compared to other body regions. The priors are usually used to model the normal brain and not pathologies such as tumors (see, for instance, Moon et al., 2002; Van Leemput et al., 1999a,b; Prastawa et al., 2003; Gooya et al., 2011; Bauer et al.,

2010; Wang et al., 2013. Priors of pathologic tissue are less valuable for segmentation-by-registration, but they can considerably improve the performance of pathology detectors, in particular LN detectors.

## 19.3 LN CENTER CANDIDATE DETECTION

Although we are eventually interested in segmenting LNs, the segmentation methods need to be initialized with a point close to the LN center. We therefore start with generating a set of possible LN center candidates. This is done using a cascade of binary classifiers trained on two different large feature sets: 3D Haar features and self-aligning features. Both AdaBoost and trees of AdaBoost classifiers have proven to work well for these feature sets as they automatically select and weight relevant features.

### 19.3.1 HAAR FEATURES

The first stage of the processing pipeline should reject obvious negatives and retain a sensitivity close to 100%. It also needs to be efficient, because a larger area is exhaustively scanned. These requirements make cascades of classifiers trained on 3D Haar features a suitable and popular choice.

Each classifier of the cascade is trained to learn the probability

$$p(m = 1 | H(t)) \tag{19.1}$$

of whether there is an LN model instance at a given position $t = (x, y, z)$. Here, $H$ denotes the Haar feature vector extracted at position $t$. Given the output of the $i$th classifier of the cascade, a set of position candidates $C_{Hi} = \{t_1, \ldots, t_{|C_{Hi}|}\}$ is generated and passed to classifier $i + 1$.

### 19.3.2 SELF-ALIGNING FEATURES

The second stage of the detection pipeline uses a set of features that are self-aligned to high gradients. The self-alignment ensures that the feature values will be consistent for different LNs independent of their size and shape. These features are computed based on rays cast in 14 directions in 3D space from each candidate location. These 14 directions are $(\pm 1, 0, 0), (0, \pm 1, 0), (0, 0, \pm 1)$, and $(\pm 1, \pm 1, \pm 1)$. Of the 14 directions, 10 are shown in Figure 19.2 for clarity.

**FIGURE 19.2**

Self-aligning features are computed along 14 directions relative to the candidate's position.

**FIGURE 19.3**

In each direction, local gradient maxima above different thresholds $\tau_j$ are found. The solid black dot at the lower left indicates the center of the LN candidate.

In each direction $d_i, 1 \le i \le 14$, local maxima of the gradient above each of 10 thresholds $\tau_j = 10j, 1 \le j \le 10$ (see Figure 19.3), are found at three scales $s_k = 1/2^k, 1 \le k \le 3$. Some of the features are based on the 24-point features that were described in Zheng et al. (2008). These 24 features are computed at a point $t$ based on a given direction $d = (d_x, d_y, d_z)$ and are

- Intensity features $I^k(t), k \in \{1/3, 1/2, 1, 2, 3\}$ and $\ln I(t)$, where $I(t)$ is the intensity value
- The three components of the intensity gradient $g = (g_x(t), g_y(t), g_z(t))$
- The norm $\|g\|$ of the intensity gradient
- The dot products $g \cdot d$, $\ln |g \cdot d|$, and $|g \cdot d|^k, k \in \{1/3, 1/2, 1, 2, 3\}$
- The quantity $\sqrt{\|g\|^2 - (g \cdot d)^2|}$
- The angle $\theta = \cos^{-1} \frac{g \cdot d}{\|g\|}$ as well as $|\theta|^k, k \in \{1/3, 1/2, 1, 2, 3\}$ and $\ln|\theta|$

The self-aligning gradient features are

- Each of the 24-point features described previously is computed at each of the first three local maxima for each direction $d_i$, threshold $\tau_j$, and scale $s_k$.
- Each of the 24 feature types described previously is computed halfway between the candidate location and each of the first three local maxima, for each $d_i$, $\tau_j$, and $s_k$.
- The distance to each of the first three local maxima for each $d_i$, $\tau_j$, and $s_k$.
- The differences between distances to the corresponding first three local maxima in any combination of two different directions $d_i, d_j$ for each $\tau_k, s_l$.

About 64,000 features are obtained from the 14 directions, 3 local maxima in each direction, 3 scales and the feature types described above. Some of these features are based on appearance while others are based on the shape of the iso-gradients around the LN candidate. These features were constructed to serve as a step away from the rigid Haar features, which are always computed at the same location relative to the window of interest, toward segmentation-based features that are computed relative to the LN segmentation. In these features, we are not committing to any segmentation yet but are taking into consideration multiple segmentation alternatives in each direction through the three local maxima of the gradient.

Now, a cascade of AdaBoost classifiers is trained to learn the probability $p(m = 1|A(t))$ of whether there is a true LN ($m = 1$) given the vector $A$ of gradient aligned features extracted at position $t$. Each of these classifiers further filters the candidate set of the previous one by rejecting suspected false alarms and generates a new set $C_{Ai}$. The set of the last classifier is passed to the next stage for verification, which is described in the next section.

## 19.4 SEGMENTATION-BASED VERIFICATION

While standard features such as Haar features work well for a broad range of applications, better performance can be achieved using features that are designed for a particular problem. The previous steps give us a set of LN center candidates that are now used to initialize automatic segmentation. The idea is now that the resulting segmentations will be different depending on whether the underlying detection was a true LN or a false alarm, which allows us to verify LN detections using their segmentations. The final classifier of the detection pipeline again outputs a probability estimate that the examined candidate is a true positive instead of a false positive, and this probability is used as a final detection score. This classifier is trained on features extracted from the automatic segmentation result.

We used two different segmentation methods: a deformable triangulated model and a graph-cuts-based approach.

### 19.4.1 DEFORMABLE MODEL

The deformable model is well suited for detecting and segmenting LNs that have a blob-like shape, as the clinically most relevant solid LNs usually have. Such LNs can be described by using a radial function $r : S^2 \to \mathbb{R}$ defined on the sphere in 3D, representing the distance from the LN center to its boundary in all directions.

We use a triangulated sphere with 162 vertices, 480 edges, and 320 triangles that has been generated by recursively subdividing the 20 triangular faces of an icosahedron twice (Figure 19.4). The number of faces quadruples with each subdivision.

The edges of this triangulation induce a neighborhood structure between the vertices. Two vertices are considered neighbors if there is a triangulation edge connecting them.

This shape representation can accurately describe blob-like shapes even when they are not convex. It has some difficulty representing the extremities of very elongated shapes (with aspect ratio at least 4:1). However, out of the more than 900 solid LNs that have been manually segmented using this representation, we encountered such difficulties with 26 LN (2.8% of all solid LN).

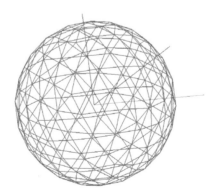

**FIGURE 19.4**

Sphere triangulation with 162 vertices and 320 triangles.

Given a candidate LN center $t$ obtained from the previous step of the detection pipeline, a segmentation using this location is fully determined by the radii $r_i, i = 1, \ldots, N$ for all directions $d_i$, where $N = 162$ in our case. These radii form a vector $r = (r_1, \ldots, r_N)$.

An LN shape model must be flexible enough to handle the great shape variability, and at the same time it has to cope with the lack of particular commonalities. Popular generative models such as PCA do not suit these requirements well because they are too rigid. Instead, we use a Gaussian MRF as a shape prior and combine it with a data term.

To find the segmentation vector $r$ we propose an approach similar to the active shape models (Cootes et al., 1995) but using a robust data cost, gradient optimization and a Gaussian MRF shape prior.

Given the candidate location $t$, the most likely LN boundary location $y_i$ is found in each direction $d_i, i = 1, \ldots, N = 162$ as the first location where the intensity difference from the candidate center is larger than a threshold $D_{max}$, as illustrated in Figure 19.5:

$$y_i = \operatorname*{argmin}_{r \in (0, R_{max})} |I(t) - I(t + rd_i)| > D_{max} \tag{19.2}$$

From the measurement vector $y = (y_1, \ldots, y_N)$, the segmentation $r$ is obtained by minimizing the following energy function

$$E(r) = \alpha \sum_{i=1}^{N} \rho(r_i - y_i) + \sum_{i=1}^{N} \frac{1}{2|\partial i|} \sum_{j \in \partial i} (r_i - r_j)^2 \tag{19.3}$$

where $\rho(x) = \ln(1 + x^2/2)$ is a robust function and for each $i$, $\partial i$ are the neighbors of $i$ on the sphere triangulation. Remember that two vertices are neighbors if there is an edge of the sphere triangulation connecting them.

The first term in Eq. (19.3) is a robust data term, while the second term is the Gaussian MRF prior that encourages the neighboring vertices to have similar radii.

The robust data term ensures that the segmentation is robust to any sporadic outliers in the measurements $y_i$, as illustrated in Figure 19.6. If a measurement $y_i$ does not exist, its corresponding term is removed from the first sum of Eq. (19.3).

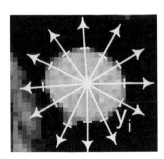

**FIGURE 19.5**

Measurements $y_i$ are found for each direction $d_i$ as the most probable boundary location.

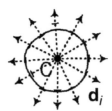

**FIGURE 19.6**

The robust data term and Gaussian MRF obtain a smooth segmentation that ignores outliers in the measurements $y_i$ taken at directions $\mathbf{d}_i$.

Minimization of the energy from Eq. (19.3) is done by gradient descent, starting with $\mathbf{r} = \mathbf{y}$ as initialization. The energy gradient can be computed analytically, obtaining the following update iteration:

$$r_i \leftarrow r_i - \eta \left( \alpha \frac{r_i - y_i}{1 + (r_i - y_i)^2/2} + \sum_{j \in \partial i} \left( \frac{1}{|\partial i|} + \frac{1}{|\partial j|} \right) (r_i - r_j) \right) \tag{19.4}$$

In practice, we use $\eta = 0.1$ and 1000 gradient update iterations, while $D_{\max} = 50, \alpha = 1.6$. These parameters were chosen by cross-validation. We found that the dependence of the detection performance on $D_{\max}$ and $\alpha$ is quite smooth, meaning that the performance only slowly changes if these values are modified.

## 19.4.2 DEFORMABLE MODEL-BASED FEATURES

Once the deformable model has been fitted to the image, it is used to compute a special set of features:

- Each of the 24-point features described in Section 19.3.2 is computed at the 162 segmentation vertices using the directions from the LN center. For each feature, the 162 values are sorted in decreasing order.
- For each of the 24-point features, the 81 sums of feature values at the pairs of opposite vertices are computed and sorted in decreasing order. Two vertices are opposite if the line connecting them passes through the LN center, as illustrated in Figure 19.7. The sphere mesh is constructed to be symmetrical relative to the center, so every vertex has exactly one opposite vertex.

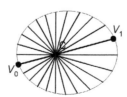

**FIGURE 19.7**

Mesh vertices $V_0$ and $V_1$ are opposite if the line connecting them passes through the LN center C.

- The 81 diameters (distances between opposite vertices relative to the segmentation center) are sorted in decreasing order. For each diameter the following features are computed:

  1. The size of each diameter
  2. Asymmetry of each diameter, that is, the ratio of the larger radius over the smaller radius
  3. The ratio of the $i$th sorted diameter and the $j$th diameter for all $1 \leq i < j \leq 81$
  4. For each of the 24 feature types, the max or min of the feature values at the two diameter ends
  5. For each of the 24 feature types, the max or min of the feature values halfway to the diameter ends

In total, there are about 17,000 features based on the shape and appearance of the segmentation result.

## 19.4.3 GRAPH-CUTS

Alternatively to fitting a triangulated model, we use a segmentation method that is based on graph cuts. While the triangulated model is faster and works very well for approximately spherical LNs, graph cuts are a bit less restrictive and have advantages with LNs that have a more complicated shape. They convert the image into a graph representation. Voxels correspond to vertices and are connected according to a neighborhood criterion that is either a 6-neighborhood or a 26-neighborhood in this work. Graph cuts are a popular segmentation method because they can be used to noniteratively optimize cost functions of the form

$$\hat{x} = \underset{x}{\operatorname{argmax}} \sum_i \lambda_i x_i - \sum_{ij} \beta_{ij} x_i (1 - x_j) \tag{19.5}$$

where $x_i \in \{0, 1\}$ is a random variable associated with voxel $i$ that is either 1 for "foreground" or 0 for "background," $\lambda_i$ is the so-called unary weight of voxel $i$, and $\beta_{ij}$ is the so-called binary weight of the edge from voxel $i$ to voxel $j$. The cost function (19.5) is optimized by adding two special vertices to the graph, a source $s$ and a sink $t$, that are directly connected to all voxel nodes. If $\lambda_i > 0$, then there is an edge with a capacity $\lambda_i$ from the source to voxel node $i$. If $\lambda_i < 0$, then there is an edge from voxel node $i$ to the sink with capacity $-\lambda_i$. When the minimum cut (or the maximum flow) is computed that separates the source $s$ from the sink $t$, and $x_i$ is set to 1 if voxel $i$ is on the source side of the cut and to 0 otherwise, then the result will equal $\hat{x}$ (Greig et al., 1989).

The range of the attenuation coefficients of LNs is restricted, which can be exploited by setting the weight $\lambda_i$ depending on the probability $p(x_i = 1|I_i)$ that voxel $i$ is foreground given its intensity $I_i$, and $\beta_{ij}$ depending on the probability $p(x_i = 1, x_j = 0|I_i, I_j)$ that voxel $i$ is foreground and voxel $j$ is background given their intensities. Here, we set the unary capacity $\lambda_i$ to

$$\lambda_i = \log \frac{p^u(x_i = 1|I_i)}{1 - p^u(x_i = 1|I_i)} \tag{19.6}$$

the logarithm of the odds that voxel $i$ is foreground given its intensity value $I_i$. The probability $p(x_i = 1|I_i)$ is estimated nonparametrically using a histogram; $u$ is a normalizing constant that is used to balance the influence of the unary and binary capacities. It was set to 0.13 in the experiments because it led to the best segmentation results. Then, $\lambda_i$ approaches $-\infty$ as $p(x_i = 1|I_i)$ approaches zero. The effect is that it is infinitely expensive to label voxel $i$ as foreground if it is for sure a background voxel. Similarly, $\lambda_i$ approaches $\infty$ as $p(x_i = 1|I_i)$ approaches 1, meaning that labeling voxel $i$ as foreground if it belongs for sure to the foreground leads to an infinite gain of the cost function (19.5).

Since we do already have the position $t$ of the LN center candidate, we only consider a cubic subvolume centered at $t$ for segmentation. The cube has a fixed size of $4 \times 4 \times 4$ cm³, which is relatively large and ensures that almost all LNs fit into this region. We place a foreground seed point at $t$ by setting the unary weights $\lambda_{t_i}$ of the corresponding voxel and their direct neighbors to $\infty$, and we place background seeds with $\lambda_i = -\infty$ on all boundary voxels of the cubic region.

Graph cuts can suffer from the so-called small cut problem that can especially arise if some or all seeds have a small surface, like our foreground seed. For instance, if we set all unary capacities $\lambda_i$ except the seeds to 0 and all of the binary capacities $\beta_{ij}$ to a positive constant, then the cost of a cut would grow linearly with its surface, meaning that the cheapest cut simply separates the foreground seeds from their nonseed neighbors. In our setting, simply adding a radial correction factor $\frac{1}{r_{ij}^2}$ to the binary capacities $\beta_{ij}$ solves the problem, where $r_{ij}$ denotes the radius, that is, the distance of the center point of the edge from voxel $i$ to voxel $j$ to the central foreground seed at $t$. Using the correction factor directly as binary capacity $\beta_{ij} = \frac{1}{r_{ij}^2}$ will give all concentric spherical cuts centered at $t$ approximately the same cost, which removes the bias toward a small cut. Spherical cuts are still preferred over nonspherical ones due to the smaller surface, which is desirable for segmenting LNs that mostly have a blob-like shape.

In addition to the voxel intensities at the start and end vertices $i$ and $j$ and to the distance to the center point $t$, we let the capacity $\beta_{ij}$ also depend on the *direction* of the corresponding edge. We set the capacity to

$$\beta_{ij} = -\frac{1}{r_{ij}^2} \cdot \frac{1}{d_{ij}} \log \left[ p(\text{out}_{ij}) p(x_i = 1, x_j = 0 | I_i, I_j) \right] \tag{19.7}$$

where

$$p(\text{out}_{ij}) = \frac{\cos \alpha_{ij} + 1}{2} \tag{19.8}$$

is an estimate of the probability that the edge pointing from voxel $i$ to $j$ is directed outward. $p(\text{out}_{ij})$ is a geometric term that does not depend on image intensities, but only on the angle $\alpha_{ij}$ between the vector from voxel $i$ to $j$ and the vector from the central positive seed to the midpoint of the line segment connecting voxels $i$ and $j$. If the edge from $i$ to $j$ is pointing straight away from the center, then $\cos \alpha_{ij} = 1$, and if it points toward it, then $\cos \alpha_{ij} = -1$. In Eq. (19.7), $d_{ij}$ is the Euclidean distance of the voxels $i$ and $j$. It is irrelevant in a 6-neighborhood system where all distances between direct neighbors are the same.

Making $\beta_{ij}$ directed enables incorporating additional knowledge about the object boundary. If we move away from the center, we rather expect to leave the LN and not to enter it. For an inward pointing edge from $i$ to $j$, $p(\text{out}_{ij}) = 0$ and $\beta_{ij} = \infty$, making it infinitely expensive to cut this edge. For an outward pointing edge with $p(\text{out}_{ij}) = 1$ with adjacent voxel intensities such that $p(x_i = 1, x_j = 0 | I_i, I_j) = 1$, the binary capacity will be $\beta_{ij} = 0$ such that cutting this edge comes at no costs.

In Eq. (19.7), $p(x_i = 1, x_j = 0 | I_i, I_j)$ can be expressed as

$$p(x_i = 1, x_j = 0 | I_i, I_j) = \frac{p(x_i = 1, x_j = 0, I_i, I_j)}{p(I_i, I_j)} \tag{19.9}$$

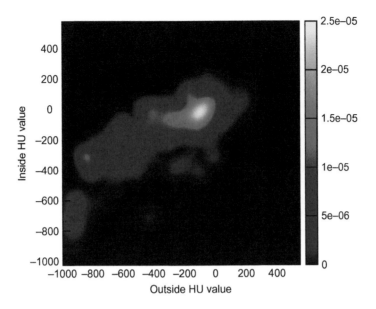

**FIGURE 19.8**

Estimate of the probability $p(x_i=1, x_j=0|I_i, I_j)$. It is asymmetric because the interior of an LN usually has a higher attenuation coefficient than its surroundings.

Both $p(x_i = 1, x_j = 0, I_i, I_j)$ and $p(I_i, I_j)$ are estimated nonparametrically using joint intensity histograms. $p(I_i, I_j)$ is set to the number of neighboring voxels with intensities $I_i$ and $I_j$ divided by the number of neighboring voxels. $p(x_i = 1, x_j = 0, I_i, I_j)$ is computed by first counting the number of neighboring voxels with the properties that voxel $i$ is inside an LN and has an intensity of $I_i$, and voxel $j$ is outside any LN and has an intensity of $I_j$, and then dividing this number by the number of neighboring voxels. However, $p(x_i = 1, x_j = 0, I_i, I_j)$ is sparse because of a limited number of training examples of points on the boundary of LNs. Therefore, $p(x_i = 1, x_j = 0|I_i, I_j)$ is smoothed with a Gaussian filter with $\sigma = 40$ Hounsfield units (HU), which is effectively a Parzen estimation. Figure 19.8 shows the estimated probability $p(x_i = 1, x_j = 0|I_i, I_j)$. All histograms have 400 equally spaced bins in each dimension, where the lowest bin corresponds to $-1024$ HU and each bin is 4 HU wide. Voxels with an intensity outside this range are dropped and not added to the histogram. During test, $p(x_i = 1, x_j = 0|I_i, I_j)$ is set to 0 if either $I_i$ or $I_j$ is outside the range. The implied error is tolerable because LNs and directly adjacent structures are, with very few exceptions, inside this relatively wide range.

### 19.4.4 GRAPH-CUTS-BASED FEATURES

Similar to the description in Section 19.4.2, a set of features is extracted from the segmentation result. Due to the two different representations of a segmentation, we do not use precisely the same set of features.

All features are computed on volume images with a voxel spacing of $1 \times 1 \times 1$ mm$^3$. All volumes are resampled to this resolution if necessary. The first kind of features is histogram based: Given a binary segmentation mask image, a hierarchy of normalized histograms of the intensity values *inside* the segmentation is computed. The histogram at the first level has 256 bins. Each bin is 1 HU wide, and the first bin corresponds to $-128$ HU. LNs typically fall into this range of HU values. At the next level, the number of bins is halved, and the width of each bin is doubled. In total, seven levels are used. The entry of each bin of each pyramid level is a scalar feature.

The second kind of features are again based on a hierarchy of histograms, but the histograms are now computed from the 3 mm wide *neighborhood* of the segmentation. The neighborhood is determined using morphological operations. Additionally, we use the second, third, and fourth central moments of the histograms both inside and outside the segmentation.

Next, 100 points are, with equal probability, randomly sampled with replacement from the surface voxels of the segmentation. As in Section 19.4.2, the gradient is computed at each point, and the points are sorted by their gradient magnitude. The sorting is necessary to enumerate the points. At each point, the normal to the surface is computed, and the normal is sampled at seven positions with a spacing of 1 mm between the samples. At each sample, again the 24-point features explained in Section 19.3.2 are computed. All scalar features at all samples at all normals at all points are added to the feature pool.

Furthermore, features are used to capture the relative position of the LN center $t$ within the tight axes-aligned bounding box of the segmentation. A relative position $t'$ of $t$ inside this box is computed that is normalized to lie in $[-0.5, 0.5]$ for each dimension. A value of 0 indicates that $t'$ is centered, and values of $-0.5$ and $0.5$ indicate that $t'$ lies on the bounding box wall in this dimension, meaning that the width of the box is used as unit length in each dimension. The minimum relative distance to any wall of the box, the difference of the maximum and the minimum distance to any wall, and the relative distance averaged over the three dimensions are used as features.

Finally, the volume, the surface, the sphericity, the maximum flow value, and the maximum flow divided by the surface are used. In total, the feature pool contains 51,436 features.

## 19.5 SPATIAL PRIOR

Due to clutter and the great variety of shapes and sizes, detecting LNs only from their local appearance is very difficult, and as much prior knowledge as possible should be incorporated for best detection results. This is especially true for the mediastinum that is especially cluttered. In particular, we know that

- LNs do not appear just anywhere. In the mediastinum, they always lie in fat tissue, so space inside any organ can be excluded.
- LNs are not uniformly distributed in fat tissue. Instead, in the mediastinum, it is much more likely to observe LNs below the aortic arch and close to the trachea.

It turns out that exploiting this prior knowledge can help to greatly reduce the number of false detections and thus improve the overall detection performance.

We model this knowledge using a spatial prior probability $p(m = 1|t)$ of observing an LN at a given location $t$. Three increasingly complex priors are proposed and compared against each other. Although we employ such a spatial prior currently only in the region of the mediastinum, the principle is also applicable in other body regions.

### 19.5.1 AUTOMATIC LANDMARK DETECTION AND ORGAN SEGMENTATION

While variant 1 is a trivial prior, the variants 2 and 3 depend on anatomical structures that first need to be detected in a CT volume image. We automatically find a set of 20 salient anatomical landmarks that lie mostly but not exclusively in the chest area and can be detected robustly. The detection method used here is described in Seifert et al. (2009) and Liu et al. (2010). Examples of landmarks are the bifurcation of the trachea, the bottom tip of the shoulder blade left and right, the topmost point of the aortic arch, and the topmost point of the lung left and right.

Besides the landmarks, a number of different organs are segmented. The lungs and the trachea are detected using simple thresholding followed by a morphological opening operation. The four heart chambers are segmented as described in Zheng et al. (2007). The esophagus is segmented using the approach of Feulner et al. (2009). The latter two methods both combine discriminative learning with model fitting. The esophagus is of special interest as it is often surrounded by LNs but at the same time can be confused with lymphatic tissue. All segmentation methods do not require user interaction.

### 19.5.2 VARIANT 1: CONSTANT PRIOR

In variant 1, the probability $p(m = 1|t)$ is simply modeled to be constant

$$p_1(m = 1|t) = \text{const.} \tag{19.10}$$

which means that no prior knowledge is used. This serves as a baseline for the remaining two variants.

### 19.5.3 VARIANT 2: BINARY MASK

In the second variant, the spatial prior is modeled to be proportional to a binary mask $B(t)$:

$$p_2(m = 1|t) \propto B(t) = \begin{cases} 0 & \text{if } t \text{ is inside an organ} \\ 1 & \text{otherwise} \end{cases} \tag{19.11}$$

that labels regions that cannot contain LNs with 0 and other regions with 1. The lungs, the trachea, the esophagus, and the heart are excluded, that is, labeled with 0 in the mask.

### 19.5.4 VARIANT 3: SOFT PRIOR

The third variant consists of the binary mask $B(t)$ and a probabilistic atlas

$$G(t) \in [0, 1] \tag{19.12}$$

which is learned in the space of a reference patient. Nonrigid inter-subject registration is used to map segmented LNs from a set of test patients to the reference patient, where they are averaged. The segmentations are binary masks, and thus $G(t)$ is the spatial probability of lymphatic tissue. The learned probabilistic atlas is blurred with a Gaussian filter with a standard deviation of 12 mm, or 12 voxels with our 1 mm voxel spacing, which is necessary because of limited training data. This can also be considered as a Parzen estimation.

The registration is based on the set of 20 landmarks. If a landmark is not detected, for example, because it is not visible in the image, it is omitted. A thin-plate spline (TPS) transformation (Bookstein, 1989) is created from the detected landmarks and the reference landmarks and used for the warping.

During training, the transformation maps from the reference space to the current image, and for the testing phase, it maps into the other direction.

The prior is then modeled to be

$$p_3(m = 1|t) \propto B(t)G(t) \tag{19.13}$$

proportional to the product of the binary mask and the probabilistic atlas.

Figure 19.9 shows examples of the different prior types along with the original volume image they were computed from. Each image in a column shows the same slice of the volume, and the slices are parallel to the coordinate planes. Figure 19.9(a) shows the original volume. The binary prior $p_2(m = 1|t)$ shown in Figure 19.9(b) excludes already considerable portions of the volume. The "soft" prior $p_3(m = 1|t)$ shown in Figure 19.9(c) puts special focus on relatively small regions of the volume.

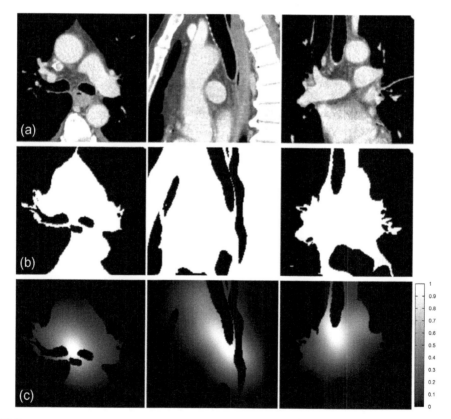

**FIGURE 19.9**

Examples of different spatial priors computed for a test volume. The three columns show axis-aligned orthogonal slices of the volume. (a) The input volume. (b) The binary prior $p_2(m=1|t)$ (see Eq. 19.11) that excludes air and organs. (c) The "soft" prior $p_3(m=1|t)$ (see Eq. 19.13). As the absolute values of the prior do not matter in our model, the prior can have an arbitrary positive scaling factor.

## 19.6 EXPERIMENTS
### 19.6.1 EXPERIMENTAL SETUP

In our experiments, we focus on solid LNs and ignore those that have a fatty core, because these are typically benign and less relevant. We furthermore concentrate on LNs larger than 10 mm in accordance with the RECIST guidelines (Therasse et al., 2000), since smaller LNs are not considered as measurable.

In the testing phase, a large solid LN is considered as detected if the center $t$ of a detection is inside the tight axis-aligned bounding box of the LN. An LN is considered as a false negative (FN) if its size is at least 10 mm and it is not detected. A detection is considered a false positive (FP) if it is not inside the bounding box of any LN (large or small, solid or not). Thus, a detection on a small or nonsolid LN is not a false positive.

The way positive and negative training samples are generated considerably affects the detection performance. The problem with positive training examples is that the manual LN segmentations are often not convex. The main reason is that it is often not decidable where one LN ends and another one begins because there is no visible boundary. The straightforward approach would be to take the point of gravity or the center of the bounding box as a positive example. However, this point is often close to the LN's boundary or even outside the actual node. As a solution, a depth map is computed for each ground truth LN. The map contains the shortest distance to the surface for each voxel. Local maxima of the depth map that have a minimum distance of 2 mm from the surface are selected as positive training samples. Only LNs with a minimum size of 10 mm are used for training.

The negative training samples of the first stage are generated by randomly sampling the training images, but no candidates are generated inside ground truth LNs and in regions of the mediastinum where the spatial prior has a value of 0 because these regions are not considered during test. This avoids confusing the detector with data it will never see in the testing phase. In later stages, the negative training examples always come from the false positive detections of the previous stage. Thus, the classifiers get specialized on the difficult examples.

To avoid overfitting, all training datasets are mirrored by all three coordinate planes, resulting in $2^3 = 8$ times as much training data, but only the original data were used for testing.

### 19.6.2 AXILLARY AND ABDOMINAL/PELVIC REGION

The axillary region contains the most clearly visible LNs and it is easiest to detect and segment. The pelvic region contains some abdominal LNs and is more challenging.

#### 19.6.2.1 System description

The system for detecting axillary and pelvic LNs follows the architecture from Figure 19.1. We used a cascade of five classifiers without any spatial prior to detect the axillary and pelvic LNs. The first two stages use Haar features, the third and fourth stage use self-aligning features, and the fifth stage uses features extracted from a deformable model-based candidate segmentation as described in Section 19.4.1. In each of the stages, we use AdaBoost to train the classifiers. Table 19.1 shows the parameter settings and the feature types of the classifiers in the detection pipeline that were used in this section.

**Table 19.1 Features and Parameter Settings of the Classifiers of the Detection Pipeline for Axillary and Abdominal/Pelvic LNs: The Number of Weak Classifiers of Each Stage and the Number of Detection Candidates Generated at Each Stage**

| Classifier | Features | # Weak Classifiers Axillary/Pelvic | Candidates |
|---|---|---|---|
| Stage 1 | Haar | 22/25 | Not fixed |
| Stage 2 | Haar | 67/75 | Not fixed |
| Stage 3 | Gradient aligned | 40/60 | Not fixed |
| Stage 4 | Gradient aligned | 120/180 | 1500/3000 |
| Stage 5 | Segmentation based | 26/32 | 100 |

Note: *Each stage is an AdaBoost classifier.*

For our experiments, we used two CT datasets, one of 131 CT scans from 84 patients for the axillary region and one of 54 scans of 45 patients for the pelvic region. The data were obtained from routine scans of cancer patients from the United States, China, and Germany. Patients were administered intravenous contrast bolus. Typical soft tissue kernels (B20-B41) were used in the reconstruction. The CT volumes were rescaled to a resolution of $1.5 \times 1.5 \times 1.5$ mm$^3$. Expert-reviewed segmentations of the axillary and pelvic LNs were available. Of the 917 axillary LNs, 371 were large ($>10$ mm) and solid and 546 were either small ($<10$ mm) or nonsolid. Of the 1029 pelvic LNs, 569 were large and solid, and 460 were small or nonsolid.

We used sixfold cross-validation for evaluation. For each fold, the classifiers were trained on the training data and evaluated on the test data.

Occasionally, two or more detections are close together. In order to reduce the number of such double detections, the detected centers are subjected to a nonmaximal suppression step that keeps the largest score detection and removes any other detections with center inside its bounding box, and so on.

### 19.6.2.2 Result

Examples of detected candidates for an axillary and a pelvic region are shown in Figure 19.10, and examples of detected and segmented LNs can be seen in Figures 19.11 and 19.12.

The results are summarized in Table 19.2 and in Figure 19.13. Table 19.2 shows results of our own implementation of the method from Feuerstein et al. (2009) that is based on the Min-DD filter (Kitasaka et al., 2007). This implementation is evaluated on the same axillary and pelvic datasets as our own method for easy comparison.

Figure 19.13 shows the results of replacing the AdaBoost verification classifier with a random forest of 100 trees trained on the same set of segmentation-based features. To emphasize the importance of the segmentation-based features, another comparison is made with a classifier trained on resized LNs that searches through 890 scale combinations of width-height-depth for each LN candidate and returns the largest score. This classifier is named "AdaBoost scale" and performs much worse than the one using

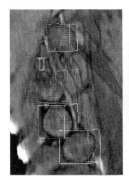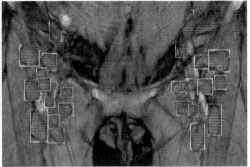

**FIGURE 19.10**

Detected LN candidates in an axillary and a pelvic region. The red crosses indicate the candidate locations. The ground truth bounding boxes of solid (yellow) and nonsolid (cyan) LNs are shown as well.

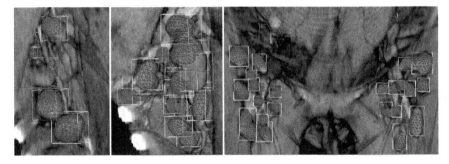

**FIGURE 19.11**

Examples of detected and segmented LNs (red meshes) along with the ground truth bounding boxes of solid (yellow) and nonsolid (cyan) LN.

segmentation-based features and feature selection. Finally, the LN detector without the verification stage is also evaluated, shown under the name "LN candidates."

Examples of missed detections and false positives are shown in Figure 19.14.

### 19.6.3 MEDIASTINAL REGION

Apart from the axillary and the abdominal/pelvic regions, the techniques explained in this chapter were also applied to detect LNs in the mediastinal region. Regarding LN detection, the mediastinal region differs from the axillary and the pelvic regions in that there is less fat tissue, less space where LNs can possibly occur, and more clutter such as blood vessels. While the clutter makes the detection problem more difficult, we can make use of the fact that large regions are unlikely or even impossible to contain LNs, and some relatively small regions are very likely to contain multiple LNs.

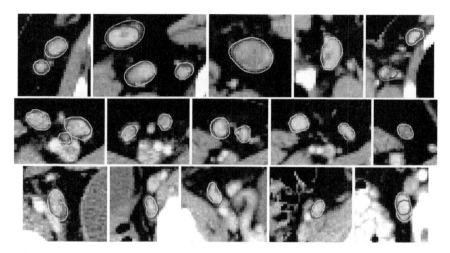

**FIGURE 19.12**

Examples of detected LNs (red). Solid LN ground truth segmentations are shown in yellow and nonsolid in cyan.

**Table 19.2 Detection Results and Comparison with Other Methods**

| Method | Target Area | # Cases | LN Size (mm) | # LN | # TP | # FP | TP Rate (%) | FP /Vol | Time /Vol |
|---|---|---|---|---|---|---|---|---|---|
| Ours | Axillary | 131 | >10 | 371 | 308 | 134 | 83.0 | 1.0 | 20 s |
| Feuerstein et al. (2009)[a] | Axillary | 131 | >10 | 371 | 308 | 4346 | 83.0 | 33.2 | 5 min |
| Ours | Pelvic + abdom. | 54 | >10 | 569 | 455 | 172 | 80.0 | 3.2 | 30 s |
| Feuerstein et al. (2009)[a] | Pelvic + abdom. | 54 | >10 | 569 | 424 | 5741 | 74.5 | 106.3 | 10 min |
| Kitasaka et al. (2007) | Abdomen | 5 | >5 | 221 | 126 | 290 | 57.0 | 58 | 2-3 h |
| Feuerstein et al. (2009) | Mediastinum | 5 | >1.5 | 106 | 87 | 567 | 82.1 | 113.4 | 5 min |
| Ours | Mediastinum | 54 | >10 | 289 | 176 | 332 | 60.9 | 6.1 | 1-2 min |
| Feuerstein et al. (2009)[a] | Mediastinum | 54 | >10 | 289 | 53 | 2099 | 18.3 | 38.9 | 20 min |
| Feuerstein et al. (2009)[b] | Mediastinum | 54 | >10 | 289 | 148 | 326 | 51.2 | 6.0 | 20 min |

[a] Our own implementation.
[b] Our own implementation that includes our "soft" prior.

A suitable way of representing and using this knowledge is a spatial prior as described in Section 19.5. Here, we use and compare the different mentioned variants.

### 19.6.3.1 System description
We use a cascade of four classifiers that are supported by a spatial prior to detect mediastinal LNs. The first two stages use Haar features, the third stage uses self-aligning features, and the fourth stage uses features extracted from a graph cuts candidate segmentation as explained in Section 19.4.4. In each of

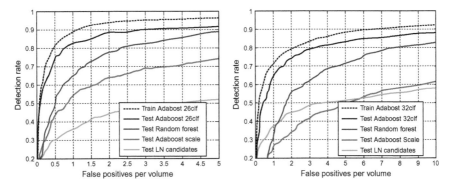

**FIGURE 19.13**

LN detection results with sixfold cross-validation. Left: Axillary LN evaluation on 131 volumes containing 371 LNs. Right: Pelvic and abdominal LN evaluation on 54 volumes containing 569 LNs.

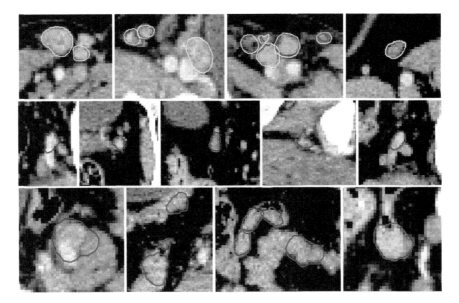

**FIGURE 19.14**

Examples of missed detections and false positives. The automatic segmentations are shown in red and the ground truth in yellow.

the first two stages, we use a probabilistic boosting tree (PBT) classifier, and in the last two stages, we use AdaBoost directly, which is equivalent to a PBT with a single level. Table 19.3 lists the parameter settings and the feature types of the classifiers in the detection pipeline that were used in this section.

For our experiments, we use 54 CT datasets with a resolution of $1 \times 1 \times 1$ mm$^3$ showing the chest area that were all taken from patients with lymphoma. Expert-reviewed segmentations of the mediastinal LNs, in total 1086, are available.

**Table 19.3 Features and Parameter Settings of the Classifiers of the Detection Pipeline for Mediastinal LNs: The Number of Levels in the PBT Classifier, the Number of Weak Classifier per AdaBoost Node, and the Number of Detection Candidates Generated at Each Stage**

| Classifier | Features | Tree Levels | Weak Class. | Candidates |
|---|---|---|---|---|
| Stage 1 | Haar | 2 | 20 | Not fixed |
| Stage 2 | Haar | 2 | 20 | 2000 |
| Stage 3 | Gradient aligned | 1 | 270 | 200 |
| Stage 4 | Segmentation based | 1 | 270 | 100 |

Note: *In stages 3 and 4, only a single AdaBoost classifier is used.*

We use threefold cross-validation for evaluation. For each fold, the spatial prior, the classifiers, and the graph cuts weights for the segmentation are trained on the training data and evaluated on the test data. Six extremely large LNs larger than 5 cm are not used for training (but for testing) in order not to distract the classifiers with rare extreme cases; 289 LNs are used for training.

Instead of nonmaximal suppression, we spatially cluster and merge detections here to avoid double detections. Two detections are merged if their distance is below a distance threshold $\theta_d = 6$ mm. The confidence value of the merged detection is set to the sum of the original ones.

### 19.6.3.2 Result

Figure 19.15(a–e) shows the detection performance of different methods and different parameter settings as free-response receiver operating characteristic (FROC) curves. Some statistics are shown in the bottom three lines of Table 19.2.

#### Influence of the graph neighborhood size

We evaluated the detection performance for a 6- and a 26-neighborhood system of the graph (Figure 19.15(a)). The two results are very similar, indicating that the computationally less expensive 6-neighborhood is sufficient. A larger neighborhood leads to a smoother segmentation, though.

#### Most useful segmentation-based features

As AdaBoost ranks the weak classifiers by their classification error, we can easily identify the most powerful segmentation-based features of stage 4, where 270 features are selected out of a pool consisting of 51,436 scalar features. For a 6-neighborhood, the single feature with the lowest classification error in each cross-validation fold is the ratio of the surface of the segmentation and the cost of the minimum cut. Also useful are central moments of the intensity histogram of voxels outside but in the direct vicinity of the segmentation: The third moment is among the top 11 features in all folds, and the fourth moment was among the selected features in two of the three folds.

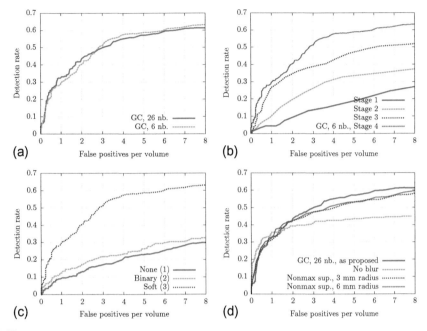

**FIGURE 19.15**

Detection performance of different methods and different parameter settings. (a) Influence of the neighborhood size. (b) Performance at different stages of the cascade. (c) Effect of using different prior types. (d) Effect of blurring the probability map and of using nonmaximal-suppression instead of clustering. See text for further details.

## Performance at different pipeline stages

Figure 19.15(b) shows the detection performance at different levels of the cascade (see Table 19.3). At four false positives per volume image, the true positive rates at stages 1–4 are 0.15, 0.31, 0.43, and 0.57, respectively. The performance improves considerably from stage to stage.

## Influence of the spatial prior

Figure 19.15(c) shows a comparison of the three increasingly complex priors explained in Section 19.5. Not using a spatial prior (red curve) leads to a poor performance due to many false positive detections. The performance is slightly better when the binary prior (see Eq. 19.11) is used, even though the improvement is not significant ($p = 0.831$). The "soft" prior (see Eq. 19.13), which is the product of the binary prior and a probabilistic atlas, greatly improves the performance (blue curve). At a false positive rate of 4 per volume, the true positive rate increases from 0.21 when no prior is used to 0.57, which is significant on a 99% confidence level ($p = 0.996$). This shows how helpful it is to include prior anatomical knowledge.

### Comparing clustering with nonmaximal suppression

Clustering and nonmaximal suppression are conceptually similar techniques to avoid multiple detections for a single LN. While nonmaximal suppression rejects weaker detections next to a stronger one, clustering merges close detections and adds their scores. Figure 19.15(d) shows a comparison. On our data, clustering performs slightly better, but the differences are small and not significant.

### Comparing alternative methods on our data

Figure 19.16(a) shows a comparison with the system of Feulner et al. (2010), where the last two stages of the detection pipeline are replaced with a bounding box detector. The method of this chapter performs significantly (90% confidence level, $P = 0.947$) better, which shows the benefit of combining detection and segmentation.

Figure 19.16(b) shows a comparison with the reimplemented version of the method of Feuerstein et al. (2009) (red curve). It produces a high number of false positives. The performance does, however, improve remarkably if the method is combined with our "soft" prior (blue curve). The "extended 3D Min-DD" filter output $f(t)$ of Feuerstein et al. (2009) serves as the detection score, which is a central difference of HU values around the point $t$. Since this can be positive or negative, it is not possible to directly multiply the prior with the filter output. Instead, the filter output is first transformed by a sigmoid function and then multiplied with the prior $p_3(m = 1|t)$ to get the new detection score $q(t)$:

$$q(t) = p_3(m = 1|t) \frac{1}{1 + \exp\left(-\frac{f(t) - \gamma}{\eta}\right)} \tag{19.14}$$

We empirically tuned the parameters $\gamma = 500$ HU and $\eta = 100$ HU of the sigmoid function. The resulting performance is much better than before but still below our systems' performance. It also takes much longer to process a volume image (about 20 min). All processing time measurements can be found in the rightmost column of Table 19.2.

Example detections and segmentations of our method can be seen in Figure 19.17, second column. The small colored boxes indicate the detection results, which can also lie in other slices and are

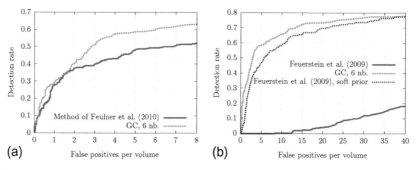

**FIGURE 19.16**

Comparison with prior work. (a) Comparison of the proposed graph cuts-based segmentation method and a 6-neighborhood with the method of Feulner et al. (2010). (b) The method of Feuerstein et al. (2009), either as it is or extended with our "soft" prior, compared to our graph cuts-based method with a 26-neighborhood. Note that the range of the horizontal axis differs from the other plots.

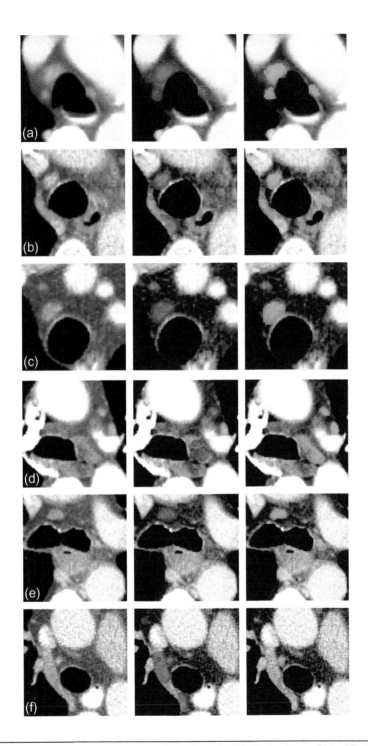

**FIGURE 19.17**

Detection and segmentation examples on unseen data shown in 2D. First column: Plain CT slices. Second column: Detections (small colored boxes) and resulting segmentations (red) of the proposed graph cuts-based method with a 26-neighborhood. The detection score is color coded in HSV color space. Violet means lowest, and red means highest score. The detection center is sometimes not near enough to the current slice and therefore invisible. Third column: Manual ground truth segmentations (green).

therefore not always visible. The third column shows the manual segmentations. Rows (a–e) are good examples, and row (f) shows some false positive detections that often lie on vessels.

In order to assess the quality of the manual annotations and to enable a comparison with the quality of the automatic detections, we measured the intra-human observer variability by having 10 of the CT volumes annotated a second time by the same person a few months later. We treated the first segmentations as ground truth, and the second ones like automatic detections to measure TPR and FP. The resulting TPR was 54.8% with 0.8 false positives per volume on average, meaning that the annotator redetected surprisingly few LNs but also hardly found additional ones. It demonstrates that consistently finding LNs is not easy even for a human.

## 19.7 CONCLUSION

Automatically detecting and segmenting LNs is challenging because of limited contrast, and because of the similarity to other structures like muscles and vessels that are *a priori* more likely. We identified a set of techniques that have proven to work well.

Cascaded detection approaches keep the computational requirements tractable as they allow rejecting the majority of the negatives at an early stage. The first stage of the cascade should quickly decide if it is worth considering a candidate more closely or not. Later stages can be more computationally demanding.

Problem-specific feature sets that adapt to the underlying image data, such as gradient-aligned and segmentation-based features, help. Coupling segmentation with detection can improve the detection performance.

Augmenting training examples of LNs with mirrored versions help to reduce overfitting. Other geometric transformations, such as rotations, might also help.

Incorporating anatomical knowledge by estimating and using a spatial prior probability of lymphatic tissue considerably improves the performance of the discriminative detectors. It enables rejecting detections that are anatomically unlikely or even impossible.

Most of these techniques can also be used independently from the remaining system, so using a subset in another detection framework will in most cases be straightforward.

## REFERENCES

Barbu, A., Sühling, M., Xu, X., Liu, D., Zhou, S.K., Comaniciu, D., 2012. Automatic detection and segmentation of lymph nodes from CT data. IEEE Trans. Med. Imaging 31 (2), 240–250.

Bauer, S., Seiler, C., Bardyn, T., Buechler, P., Reyes, M., 2010. Atlas-based segmentation of brain tumor images using a Markov Random Field-based tumor growth model and non-rigid registration. In: 2010 Annual International Conference of the IEEE Engineering in Medicine and Biology Society (EMBC), pp. 4080–4083.

Bookstein, F., 1989. Principal warps: thin-plate splines and the decomposition of deformations. IEEE Trans. Pattern Anal. Mach. Intell. 11 (6), 567–585.

Cherry, K.M., Wang, S., Turkbey, E.B., Summers, R.M., 2014. Abdominal lymphadenopathy detection using random forest. In: Proc. SPIE 9035, Medical Imaging 2014: Computer-Aided Diagnosis.

Cootes, T., Taylor, C., Cooper, D., Graham, J., et al., 1995. Active shape models-their training and application. CVIU 61 (1), 38–59.

Dornheim, L., Dornheim, J., 2008. Automatische detektion von lymphknoten in CT-datensätzen des halses. In: Bildverarbeitung für die Medizin, Informatik aktuell. Springer, Berlin, Germany, pp. 308–312.

Dornheim, J., Seim, H., Preim, B., Hertel, I., Strauß, G., 2006. Segmentation of neck lymph nodes in CT datasets with stable 3D mass-spring models. In: MICCAI (2), Copenhagen, Denmark, Lecture Notes in Computer Science, vol. 4191, Springer, Berlin, pp. 904–911.

Feuerstein, M., Deguchi, D., Kitasaka, T., Iwano, S., Imaizumi, K., Hasegawa, Y., Suenaga, Y., Mori, K., 2009. Automatic mediastinal lymph node detection in chest CT. In: SPIE Medical Imaging, Orlando, FL, USA, pp. 72600V.

Feulner, J., Zhou, S.K., Cavallaro, A., Seifert, S., Hornegger, J., Comaniciu, D., 2009. Fast automatic segmentation of the esophagus from 3D CT data using a probabilistic model. In: MICCAI (1), London, UK, Lecture Notes in Computer Science, vol. 5761, Springer, Berlin, pp. 255–262.

Feulner, J., Zhou, S.K., Huber, M., Hornegger, J., Comaniciu, D., Cavallaro, A., 2010. Lymph node detection in 3-D chest CT using a spatial prior probability. In: IEEE Conference on Computer Vision and Pattern Recognition (CVPR), San Francisco, CA, USA, pp. 2926–2932.

Feulner, J., Zhou, S.K., Hammon, M., Hornegger, J., Comaniciu, D., 2013. Lymph node detection and segmentation in chest CT data using discriminative learning and a spatial prior. Med. Image Anal. 17 (2), 254–270.

Gooya, A., Pohl, K., Bilello, M., Biros, G., Davatzikos, C., 2011. Joint segmentation and deformable registration of brain scans guided by a tumor growth model. In: Fichtinger, G., Martel, A., Peters, T. (Eds.), Medical Image Computing and Computer-Assisted Intervention—MICCAI 2011, Lecture Notes in Computer Science, vol. 6892. Springer, Berlin/Heidelberg, pp. 532–540.

Greig, D.M., Porteous, B.T., Seheult, A.H., 1989. Exact maximum a posteriori estimation for binary images. J. R. Stat. Soc. Ser. B (Methodol.) 51 (2), 271–279.

Kitasaka, T., Tsujimura, Y., Nakamura, Y., Mori, K., Suenaga, Y., Ito, M., Nawano, S., 2007. Automated extraction of lymph nodes from 3-D abdominal CT images using 3-D minimum directional difference filter. In: MICCAI (2), Brisbane, Australia, Lecture Notes in Computer Science, vol. 4792, Springer, Heidelberg, pp. 336–343.

Krizhevsky, A., Sutskever, I., Hinton, G.E. 2012, ImageNet classification with deep convolutional neural networks. In: Advances in Neural Information Processing Systems.

Leibe, B., Leonardis, A., Schiele, B., 2008. Robust object detection with interleaved categorization and segmentation. Int. J. Comput. Vis. 77 (1-3), 259–289.

Liu, D., Zhou, K., Bernhardt, D., Comaniciu, D., 2010. Search strategies for multiple landmark detection by submodular maximization. In: 2010 IEEE Conference on Computer Vision and Pattern Recognition (CVPR), pp. 2831–2838.

Liu, J., Zhao, J., Hoffman, J., Yao, J., Zhang, W., Turkbey, E.B., Wang, S., Kim, C., Summers, R.M., 2014. Mediastinal lymph node detection on thoracic CT scans using spatial prior from multi-atlas label fusion. In: Proc. SPIE 9035, Medical Imaging 2014: Computer-Aided Diagnosis.

Moon, N., Bullitt, E., van Leemput, K., Gerig, G., 2002. Model-based brain and tumor segmentation. In: Proceedings of 16th International Conference on Pattern Recognition, 2002, vol. 1, pp. 528–531.

Nimura, Y., Hayashi, Y., Kitasaka, T., Furukawa, K., Misawa, K., 2014. Automated abdominal lymph node segmentation based on RST analysis and SVM. In: Proc. SPIE 9035, Medical Imaging 2014: Computer-Aided Diagnosis.

Prastawa, M., Bullitt, E., Moon, N., Van Leemput, K., Gerig, G., 2003. Automatic brain tumor segmentation by subject specific modification of atlas priors. Acad. Radiol. 10 (12), 1341–1348.

Roth, H.R., Lu, L., Seff, A., Cherry, K.M., Hoffman, J., Wang, S., Liu, J., Turkbey, E., Summers, R.M., 2014. A new 2.5D representation for lymph node detection using random sets of deep convolutional neural network observations. MICCAI, Boston, MA, USA, Lecture Notes in Computer Science, vol. 8673, Springer, Switzerland, pp. 520–527.

Seifert, S., Barbu, A., Zhou, S.K., Liu, D., Feulner, J., Huber, M., Suehling, M., Cavallaro, A., Comaniciu, D., 2009. Hierarchical parsing and semantic navigation of full body CT data. In: SPIE Medical Imaging, vol. 7259, 1, Orlando, FL, USA, p. 725902.

Therasse, P., Arbuck, S., Eisenhauer, E., Wanders, J., Kaplan, R., Rubinstein, L., Verweij, J., Van Glabbeke, M., Van Oosterom, A., Christian, M., et al., 2000. New guidelines to evaluate the response to treatment in solid tumors. J. Natl Cancer Inst. 92 (3), 205.

Van Leemput, K., Maes, F., Vandermeulen, D., Suetens, P., 1999a. Automated model-based tissue classification of MR images of the brain. IEEE Trans. Med. Imaging 18 (10), 897–908.

Van Leemput, K., Maes, F., Vandermeulen, D., Suetens, P., 1999b. Automated model-based tissue classification of MR images of the brain. IEEE Trans. Med. Imaging 18 (10), 897–908.

Wang, H., Suh, J., Das, S., Pluta, J., Craige, C., Yushkevich, P., 2013. Multi-atlas segmentation with joint label fusion. IEEE Trans. Pattern Anal. Mach. Intell. 35 (3), 611–623.

Zheng, Y., Barbu, A., Georgescu, B., Scheuering, M., Comaniciu, D., 2007. Fast automatic heart chamber segmentation from 3D CT data using marginal space learning and steerable features. In: IEEE International Conference on Computer Vision (ICCV), Rio de Janeiro, Brazil, pp. 1–8.

Zheng, Y., Barbu, A., Georgescu, B., Scheuering, M., Comaniciu, D., 2008. Four-chamber heart modeling and automatic segmentation for 3D cardiac CT volumes using marginal space learning and steerable features. IEEE Trans. Med. Imaging 27 (11), 1668–1681.

# POLYP SEGMENTATION ON CT COLONOGRAPHY

# 20

**J. Yao and R.M. Summers**

*Imaging Biomarkers and Computer-Aided Diagnosis Laboratory and Clinical Image Processing Service, Radiology and Imaging Sciences Department, Clinical Center, National Institutes of Health, Bethesda, MD, USA*

## CHAPTER OUTLINE

S. Kevin Zhou (Ed): Medical Image Recognition, Segmentation and Parsing. http://dx.doi.org/10.1016/B978-0-12-802581-9.00020-2

## 20.1 COLONIC POLYP AND COLON CANCER

Colon cancer is a cancer from uncontrolled cell growth in the colon. Colon cancer is the third most commonly diagnosed cancer in the world, but it is more common in developed countries. Around 60% of cases were diagnosed in the developed world. Colon cancer is the second leading cause of death from cancer in the United States. It is estimated that in 2014, 71,830 men and 65,000 women will be diagnosed with colorectal cancer and 26,270 men and 24,040 women will die of the disease in the United States (Siegel et al., 2014).

Colon cancer is thought to arise from polyps, fleshy overgrowths that occur on the inside wall of the large intestine (also known as the colon). Colonic polyps are extremely common, and occur more frequently as individuals grow older (Cunningham et al., 2010). It is estimated that 50% of people over the age of 60 will have at least one colonic polyp. When certain types of colonic polyps grow large enough, they could become cancerous. The risk of a colonic polyp becoming cancerous increases as the size of the polyp increases (Winawer et al., 2003). Therefore, screening for colonic polyps and removing them before they become cancerous should markedly reduce the incidence of colon cancer (Qaseem et al., 2012). Evidence from clinical trials supports this hypothesis (citation to FOBT literature).

The American Cancer Society recommends a number of tests for screening healthy subjects with an average risk for developing colon cancer (Stein et al., 2011). For example, colonoscopy is recommended beginning at the age of 50 and thereafter every 7-10 years if no colonic polyps or cancers are found. Unfortunately, many patients do not undergo screening due to the perceived inconvenience and discomfort of existing screening tests. CT colonography (CTC), a CT scan-based imaging method, has been under study for the past 20 years and shows promise as a method of colorectal cancer screening that may be acceptable to many patients (Gluecker et al., 2003; van Gelder et al., 2004). Figure 20.1 illustrates colon anatomy and a colonic polyp shown in the optical colonoscopy (OC) and CTC.

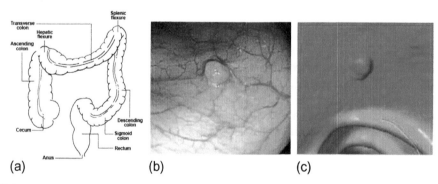

(a)     (b)     (c)

**FIGURE 20.1**

Colon and colonic polyps: (a) illustration of colon anatomy. (b) Optical and (c) three-dimensional virtual colonoscopy images of a 0.8-cm polyp in the sigmoid colon of a 60-year-old man.

## 20.2 CT COLONOGRAPHY

The use of CT imaging for the detection and staging of colon cancer was first proposed in 1980 (Ellert and Kreel, 1980; Husband et al., 1980). In 1983, Coin et al. (1983) demonstrated that CT had potential as a mass screening method for colorectal polyps. The terms "virtual colonoscopy" and "CT colonography" were formally introduced in 1994 by Vining et al. (1994). Since then, several clinical studies have been carried out and technologies were gradually improved because of the advance of both hardware and software. Investigations have been conducted to improve the scanning parameters, the stool and fluid tagging techniques, and the colon preparation techniques (Pickhardt et al., 2003; Frentz and Summers, 2006). To test the effectiveness of CTC in a clinical setting, OC was used as the reference standard (Hara et al., 1996).

A standard preparation for a CTC study is as follows. One to two days before the procedure, patients undergo a standard 24-h clear-liquid diet colonic preparation. On the day of the procedure, patients are orally administered laxatives: 45 mL of sodium phosphate (Fleet 1 preparation; Fleet Pharmaceuticals, Lynchburg, VA). Patients also consume oral contrast agents in divided doses; a total of 250 mL of barium sulfate (Scan C, Lafayette Pharmaceuticals, Lafayette, IN; 2.1% by weight) is administered for solid fecal tagging and a total of 60-mL solution of diatrizoate meglumine and diatrizoate sodium (Gastrografin; Bracco Diagnostics, Princeton, NJ) is administered to opacify any luminal fluid (Macari et al., 2001; Pickhardt, 2007).

Adequate distention of the colon, like proper bowel cleansing, is critical to technical success. During the CTC procedure, a small flexible rectal catheter is inserted into the rectum to allow the medical staff and the patient to self-insufflate the colon immediately before the CT scanning. Insufflating the colon with room air or carbon dioxide ($CO_2$) allows for polyps to be viewable on a CT scan because of the large contrast between air and soft tissue. The use of $CO_2$ has been shown to decrease pain compared to those who receive room air (Holemans et al., 1998).

Currently, CTC is performed with the patient in both the supine position and the prone position. The protocol requires only one breathhold per scanning position. Although increasing radiation exposure, adding a prone scan in addition to a supine scan has been shown to increase the sensitivity of detecting polyps by 13-15% with little effect on the specificity (Fletcher et al., 2000). The optimal settings for CTC aim to decrease scanning time, decrease radiation exposure, and increase image quality. Several parameters can be adjusted according to protocol. A high pitch value decreases the scanning time, a lower tube current reduces the radiation exposure, and a smaller slice thickness improves image quality. Typical CT scanning parameters include a 1.25-2.50 mm collimation, a table speed of 15 mm/s, a reconstruction interval of 1 mm, and tube current of 100 mAs and 120 kVp (Taylor et al., 2003). Figure 20.1 shows an example of 2D slices of CTC and 3D colon reconstruction generated from CTC.

CTC is a less invasive technique compared to OC. CTC can be used to detect both precancerous polyps and colon cancers. The accuracy of CTC is reported by some investigators to be close to that of traditional OC (Pickhardt et al., 2003). Since the technique is mainly diagnostic, polyps found at CTC must be removed at a subsequent colonoscopy procedure. This separation of diagnostic and treatment phases presents an opportunity to reduce the number of unnecessary invasive OC procedures for screening purposes. CTC images provide means to characterize the polyp in terms of both size and density heterogeneity, which can then be employed to evaluate whether a sequential OC is necessary. Figure 20.2 shows examples of colonic polyps on CTC.

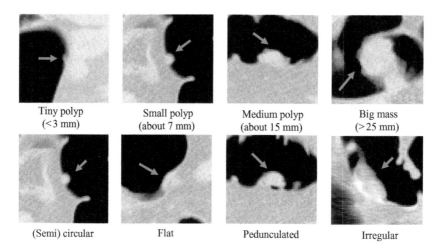

| | | | |
|---|---|---|---|
| Tiny polyp (<3 mm) | Small polyp (about 7 mm) | Medium polyp (about 15 mm) | Big mass (>25 mm) |
| (Semi) circular | Flat | Pedunculated | Irregular |

**FIGURE 20.2**

Examples of polyps on CTC.

Consequently, the ability to distinguish high-risk polyps from benign polyps is crucial to optimizing the value of CTC as a primary screening method. One characteristic used to predict the malignancy risk of a polyp is its size. Polyp size is usually determined by making a linear measurement during OC. In CTC, when a polyp is segmented from the image, its linear diameter and 3D volume can be reliably derived (Yeshwant et al., 2006). Polyp size measurement has been the subject of extensive investigation (Summers, 2010).

Radiologists read CTC studies in two main ways. One is 2D image interpretation, where radiologists scan through the 2D slices and form 3D pictures in their brain. Another is 3D fly-through image interpretation, where computer graphics techniques are employed to reconstruct the 3D inner surface of the colon from the CT data and the radiologist navigates through the colon along its centerline. One investigation suggested that radiologists can achieve higher diagnostic accuracy using 3D rather than 2D image interpretation (Pickhardt et al., 2003). Figure 20.1 shows a 2D and 3D view of a colon.

The traditional way to navigate the colon along the centerline is not efficient due to the limited view angle and the lengthy navigation. A more efficient way is to unfold and flatten the colon and view the entire surface from above. In this way, the entire colon can be viewed in one glance. This is not possible in OC, but it can be implemented in CTC via computer graphics techniques.

Many techniques have been proposed to unfold the colon. The most common techniques were based on raycasting. Vilanova et al.'s (2004) method first unfolded the colon locally using a local projection and then globally unfolded the colon using a suitable parameterization. Wang et al. (1998) proposed a technique using the electrical field of a charged centerline to transform the colon into a straight cylinder-like shape and uniformly sample the planar cross sections orthogonal to the centerline. Sudarsky et al. (2008) presented an efficient method based on skeletal subspace deformation and uniform raycasting along the central path. Another category of approaches is based on conformal-mapping. Haker et al. (2000) used angle-preserving conformal mapping to map the entire colon surface onto a flat plane. Hong et al. (2006) proposed a conformal mapping based on minimizing harmonic energy to achieve angle preserving and minimum distortion. The conformal mapping techniques have to deal with texture distortion and surface parameterization. Furthermore, they often require high-quality surfaces and are computationally expensive. Another type of approach is based on local projection. Paik et al. (2000) proposed various map projection techniques including cylindrical and planar projections for the 3D fly-through. Vos et al. (2001) projected six orthogonal images onto an unfolded cube to render the complete field of view.

A reversible colon unfolding technique is proposed in Yao et al. (2010). Given a CTC data set, the 3D colon surface is first segmented using thresholding, region growing, and level sets (Franaszek et al., 2006). Then the centerline of the colon is extracted based on fast marching level set and topographical thinning (Van Uitert and Summers, 2007). After that, rotation-minimizing frames (RMFs) are established along the centerline. Then, a recursive ring set technique is applied to map vertices on the colon surface to their corresponding centerline points. Next, mesh skinning is employed to straighten the colon. Next, cylindrical projection is applied to flatten the colon. Finally, reverse transformation is computed for every vertex. Mesh skinning is a skeleton-driven deformation technique widely used in computer animation. This technique can be applied to straighten the colon using its centerline as the skeleton of the colon. The result of the colon unfolding is shown in Figure 20.3 (Yao et al., 2010).

## 20.3 COMPUTER-AIDED DETECTION AND DIAGNOSIS ON CTC

CTC is a promising diagnostic tool for detecting colorectal polyps; however, CTC requires a trained radiologist to do a lengthy interpretation of the CT images, which is both costly and prone to human error (Summers et al., 2005). Challenges associated with CTC include a lack of consistency in results between radiologists and difficulty in detecting smaller polyps (6-9 mm). Proposed solutions to these obstacles include double readings or a computer-aided detection (CADe) and computer-aided diagnosis (CADx) system. CAD systems have the potential to decrease the time needed to complete an interpretation and increase the accuracy of the diagnosis.

The objective of a CADe system is to identify and mark suspicious lesions on the CTC scan. Radiologists can use the results from the CAD system along with 3D or 2D CT images to make a final diagnosis. Computer vision and computer graphics techniques, such as colon and polyp segmentation, supine-prone registration, novel unfolded view, and virtual fly-through, can also help radiologists dictate the cases. A typical CADe pipeline is shown in Figure 20.4.

The objective of a CADx system is to characterize a potential lesion. The system suggests whether an abnormality is a lesion or not, whether a lesion is benign or malignant. Clinicians can then develop appropriate treatment plans accordingly. Figure 20.5 shows the pipeline of a typical CADx system.

In either, a CADe system or a CADx system, polyp segmentation is an essential component. In order to compute the features and characterization of a lesion, an accurate segmentation is necessary.

## 20.4 POLYP SEGMENTATION

Polyp segmentation is defined as delineating the polyp boundary from the colon wall. Polyp segmentation provides the entire voxel set of a polyp, which can be used to quantify the characteristics of a polyp. Several comprehensive volumetric features and statistical analysis, such as the density distribution

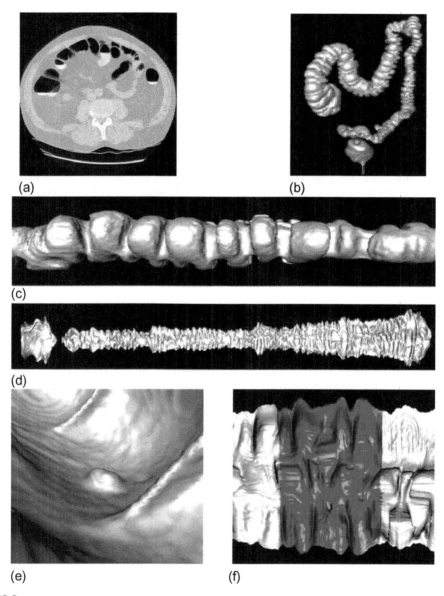

**FIGURE 20.3**

CTC reading and colon unfolding. (a) 2D axial slice; (b) 3D colon surface; (c) straightened colon; (d) unfolded colon; (e) endoluminal view of polyps; and (f) unfolded view of the same polyp in (e).

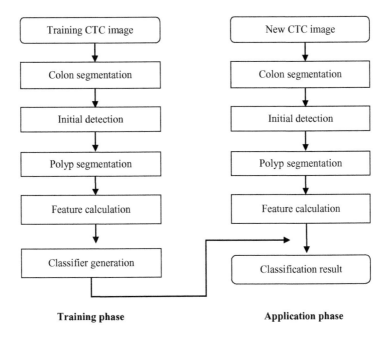

**FIGURE 20.4**

Block diagram of computer-aided detection (CADx).

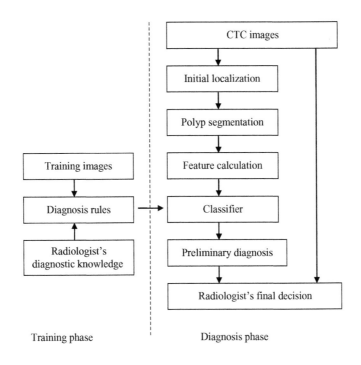

**FIGURE 20.5**

Block diagram of computer-aided detection (CADx).

within the polyp, the volume and dimension of the polyp, and its relationship with surrounding tissues, can be obtained (Yao et al., 2004). Furthermore, polyp segmentation is also essential in creating a ground truth database for training, improving, testing, and validating CAD systems.

### 20.4.1 CHALLENGE

Colonic polyp segmentation is a challenging task for several reasons. First, polyp shapes are irregular. Polyps can be categorized in different shape categories: sessile, pedunculated, or flat, and 3D shape/appearance variation is big even within the same category. Second, polyp sizes vary greatly. The size ranges from 5 mm to over 50 mm. Third, the surrounding regions are complex. The colon could be underdistended. There could be residual stool and fluid in the surrounding region. Haustral folds and other structures can complicate the segmentation task. Methods utilizing both shape and densitometry information are necessary for a successful segmentation. Figure 20.2 shows a variety of polyps that show different shape, appearance, and surrounding environment.

### 20.4.2 STATE-OF-THE-ART POLYP SEGMENTATION TECHNIQUES

Investigation on polyp segmentation techniques on CTC have been carried out in the past two decades. The methods can be classified as model-based methods or learning-based methods.

In model-based methods, both 2D and 3D models were developed. When a 2D model is used, the segmentation was conducted on each 2D slice and then stacked together to form a 3D shape. Chen et al. (2006) proposed a method using bias-corrected fuzzy *c*-means and a 2D gradient vector flow deformable model for colonic polyp segmentation. Jerebko et al. (2002) used Canny edge operators to locate potential polyp-lumen boundaries, and the Radon transformation to connect the boundaries and identify round structures. Their method was primary 2D and only worked well on round polyps. Dijkers et al. (2005) proposed a method to segment polyps using the colon surface. After a seed was placed, the patch grew over the surface based on surface normal criteria and several stopping conditions according to the polyp shape. The method relied on the surface normal and was sensitive to image noise. The segmentation cannot be automated since several key parameters need to be manually set according to the character of a polyp.

In learning-based methods, image pixels are classified as polyp or nonpolyp according to its attributes. Learning-based methods often need a postprocessing step to generate a smooth and continuous boundary. Lu et al. (2008) proposed a three-stage probabilistic binary classification approach for automatically segmenting polyp voxels from their surrounding tissues in CT. The system integrated multi-level information for discriminative learning to align the 3D colon surface around a detected polyp. The supervised learning system offered a principled means of encoding semantic clinical expert annotations of colonic polyp tissue identification and segmentation. The learning generality to unseen data was bounded by boosting and stacked generality. van Wijk et al. (2010) proposed a method that measures the amount of protrudedness of a polyp in a scale adaptive fashion. A supervised pattern recognition technique was applied to correct polyp segmentation using a logistic classifier. Ye et al. (2010) designed a five-dimensional feature vector for each voxel, then applied nonparametric mean shift clustering, superpixel, and graph cut algorithms to segment the polyp.

### 20.4.3 DEFORMABLE MODEL-BASED POLYP SEGMENTATION

In this section, one advanced polyp segmentation technique based on a 3D deformable model is elaborated. The segmentation consists of two stages: polyp border enhancement and a 3D deformable model. The location of a polyp is first provided either through an automatic detection algorithm or by manual placement. In the enhancement stage, a 50 mm × 50 mm × 50 mm subvolume centered at the polyp centroid is first cropped from the entire image volume. Confining the segmentation in a subvolume can speed up the computational process and reduce impact from unrelated tissues (e.g., liver, bones). Then, a 3D knowledge-guided intensity adjustment strategy based on spherical ray casting is performed to enhance potential polyp regions. After that, a fuzzy clustering is applied to the enhanced image, and membership values of "lumen," "polyp tissue," and "nonpolyp tissue" classes are computed. In the deformable model stage, an initial surface is first placed at the seed point. The deformable model is then driven by image forces derived from the membership map computed in the enhancement stage, together with external forces and intrinsic model forces. The haustral fold region is marked based on criteria of dual distance to the colon wall, and a counter-force is applied to control the surface evolution. Weights for the forces are adaptively updated, and the model resolution and topology are also adaptively maintained during the model evolution.

#### 20.4.3.1 3D knowledge-guided intensity adjustment

The voxel intensity of polyp tissue is similar to that of soft tissue of the colon wall. While the border between polyp and lumen inside the colon is prominent, there is often no distinct border between polyp and nonpolyp soft tissues on the colon wall. When human experts delineate a polyp, they have to estimate the boundary based on knowledge of typical polyp shapes and continuity of the polyp boundary to fabricate an artificial border between the polyp region and the colon wall. Inspired by this observation, a 3D knowledge-guided intensity adjustment strategy is designed to enhance potential polyp regions. Three pieces of knowledge are exploited in this method:

1. Colonic polyps abut colon lumen.
2. Polyp-lumen boundaries tend to have convex curvatures.
3. Polyp boundaries are smooth and continuous.

To utilize the knowledge, the boun between lumen and colon wall are first identified using an iso-value of $-700$ HU. Then shape index (SI) and curvedness (CV) at the boundary are computed (Weisstein, 1999) to characterize the boundary shape. SI and CV as proposed by Koenderink and van Doorn (1992) are functions of the principle curvature ($\kappa_1$, $\kappa_2$), and can be written as,

$$SI = \frac{2}{\pi} \arctan\left(\frac{\kappa_2 + \kappa_1}{\kappa_2 - \kappa_1}\right)$$

$$CV = \frac{\sqrt{\kappa_2^2 + \kappa_1^2}}{2}, \qquad \kappa_2 \geq \kappa_1 \tag{20.1}$$

SI indicates the type of a shape, and CV measures the degree of curvature. SI is in the range of $[-1, 1]$, and CV in the range of $[0 \ldots 1]$. Six boundary types can be defined (Koenderink and van Doorn, 1992) according to the value of SI and CV.

$$S(v) = \begin{cases} \text{flat, if} & \text{CV}(v) <= 0.03 \\ \text{cap, if} & \text{CV}(v) > 0.03, 1 >= \text{SI}(v) >= 5/8 \\ \text{ridge, if} & \text{CV}(v) > 0.03, 5/8 > \text{SI}(v) >= 3/8 \\ \text{saddle, if} & \text{CV}(v) > 0.03, 3/8 > \text{SI}(v) >= -3/8 \\ \text{rut, if} & \text{CV}(v) > 0.03, -3/8 > \text{SI}(v) >= -5/8 \\ \text{cup, if} & \text{CV}(v) > 0.03, -5/8 > \text{SI}(v) >= -1 \end{cases} \tag{20.2}$$

where $S(v)$ is the local shape at the vertex $v$. By definition, a "cap" has convex curvatures in both principal directions, while a "cup" has concave curvatures in both principal directions. Other shapes are intermediate states between "cap" and "cup." The polyp should resemble more like a "cap" than a "cup." Figure 20.6(b) shows the boundary type using a color scheme (Yao and Summers, 2007).

A ray casting approach is employed to explore the relationship between a voxel and its surrounding boundary. For each voxel $v$ inside the subvolume, a bundle of evenly spaced rays are shot in different directions $d_k$, as shown in Figure 20.6(c). A spiral-point technique explained in Saff and Kuijlaars (1997) is adopted to generate uniformly distributed points on a sphere and it uses the spherical coordinates $(\theta, \varphi)$, $0 \leq \theta \leq \pi$, $0 \leq \varphi \leq 2\pi$, to compute the directions of the out-shooting rays. $\theta$ and $\varphi$ are defined according to

$$h_k = -1 + \frac{2(k-1)}{(N-1)}$$

$$\theta_k = \arccos(h_k)$$

$$\varphi_k = \left( \varphi_{k-1} + \frac{3.6}{\sqrt{N(1 - h_k^2)}} \right) \mod 2\pi$$

$$d_k = (\sin\theta_k \cos\varphi_k, \sin\theta_k \sin\varphi_k, \cos\theta_k) \tag{20.3}$$

where $N$ is the total number of rays ($N = 50$ in the method), $1 \leq k \leq N$, and $d_k$ is the shooting direction of ray $k$. Figure 20.6(c) illustrates the shooting rays in the image plane of $\theta = \pi/2$. A shooting ray stops when it hits the lumen or reaches the end of the shooting range, and a score is assigned according

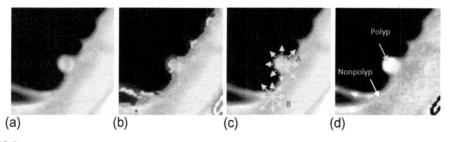

(a)          (b)          (c)          (d)

**FIGURE 20.6**

3D Knowledge-guided intensity adjustment. (a) Original image of a 7 mm polyp; (b) boundary type map (red: cap, green: cup, yellow: ridge, cyan: rut, and blue: flat); (c) spherical shooting rays, red dots are hitting points; (d) enhanced image.

to the hitting point. The score for a voxel is the summation of the scores of all its out-shooting rays. The scoring scheme is designed empirically as follows based on the local shape at the hitting point:

$$\text{score}(v) = \sum_{k=1}^{N} E(v, d_k, v_k)$$

$$E(v, d_k, v_k) = \begin{cases} 1 & \text{if} \quad S(v_k) = \text{cap} \\ 0.25 & \text{if} \quad S(v_k) = \text{ridge} \\ 0 & \text{if} \quad S(v_k) = \text{saddle} \\ -0.25 & \text{if} \quad S(v_k) = \text{rut} \\ -1 & \text{if} \quad S(v_k) = \text{cup} \\ 0.1 & \text{if} \quad S(v_k) = \text{flat} \\ -0.1 & \text{if} \quad v_k \text{ is out of range} \end{cases} \tag{20.4}$$

where $E$ is the score of a shooting ray, $N$ is the total number of ray directions, $d_k$ is the shooting direction, and $v_k$ is the hitting point at direction $d_k$. Under this scoring scheme, a voxel will be awarded a high score if it is close to boundaries with convex curvatures (cap or ridge), and will be penalized if it is not. For instance, in Figure 20.6(c), voxel $A$ in the potential polyp region is given a high score since half of its out-shooting rays hit "cap" boundaries; whereas voxel $B$ in the nonpolyp region is given a low score (a negative score in this case) since all its out-shooting rays hit either a "cup" boundary or no boundaries. The intensity of a voxel is then adjusted based on its score

$$\text{Adjustment}(v) = \text{score } (v)/N \tag{20.5}$$

Voxels with positive adjustment are members of the enhanced region; remaining voxels are members of the nonenhanced region. The enhanced intensity is then denoted as

$$I'(v) = I(v) + \text{Adjustment } (v) \tag{20.6}$$

here $I(v)$ is the image intensity, $I'(v)$ is the enhanced intensity. The 3D knowledge-guided intensity adjustment process is shown in Figure 20.6.

### 20.4.3.2 Fuzzy c-means clustering
After the knowledge-guided intensity adjustment, a fuzzy clustering is conducted on the enhanced image to classify the pixels into different tissue types. Fuzzy c-means (FCM) clustering Pham and Prince (1998) is a technique used in nonsupervised image segmentation for voxel classification. In FCM, a set of tissue classes is first determined. Each pixel is then classified by its membership values of the tissue classes according to its attributes. Membership value for a certain class indicates the likelihood of the pixel belonging to that class. Each tissue class has a centroid. The objective of FCM is to compute membership values to minimize the within-cluster distances and maximize the between-cluster distances. Details of the FCM technique can be found in Pham and Prince (1998). Three tissue classes are defined in the polyp segmentation problem: lumen, polyp tissue, and nonpolyp tissue, where a membership value is assigned to each class for each voxel. The adjusted pixel intensity is used as the

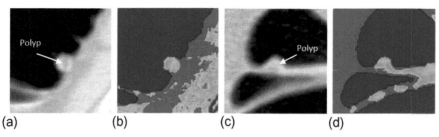

(a)    (b)    (c)    (d)

**FIGURE 20.7**

Fuzzy $c$-means clustering. (a) Image for a 7 mm polyp not on haustral fold; (b) fuzzy membership map (green: polyp tissues, red: nonpolyp tissues, blue: lumen air); (c) image of a 10 mm polyp on haustral fold; (d) fuzzy membership map.

feature for FCM clustering. The initial estimate of the class centroid is derived from prior knowledge about the CT attenuation of tissues. The initial value for "lumen" class is a low value ($-900$ HU). Since opacified fluid is presented in most of our studies, a fluid removal process (Franaszek et al., 2006) is conducted to convert the high intensity fluid voxels to air voxels. The initial intensity of "polyp tissue" class is given as the average intensity of the enhanced region, and that of "nonpolyp tissue" class is the average intensity of the nonenhanced region. The enhanced and nonenhanced regions were defined in Section 20.4.3.1. The result of FCM is a membership map for each tissue class. The membership value ranges from 0 to 1, with higher values indicating that a voxel more likely belongs to a particular class. FCM has an advantage over the hard segmentation technique such as thresholding in the way that it can handle the partial volume effect more effectively. Furthermore, the process is unsupervised so it can be applied to images with different intensity distributions, without the need to set any arbitrary hard thresholds. Figure 20.7 shows two examples of fuzzy clustering, one for a polyp not on a haustral fold and one for a polyp on a haustral fold (Yao and Summers, 2007).

### 20.4.3.3 Haustral fold detection

Using the FCM method in Section 20.4.3.2, pixels on a haustral fold could be categorized as polyp tissues according to their intensity. To handle this problem, a dual-distance algorithm is developed to determine whether a voxel is on a haustral fold. This algorithm utilizes the knowledge that a haustral fold is a thin structure and both sides of its surface about the colon lumen, that is, for any voxel on the fold, its distances to the lumen in the direction perpendicular to the fold surface and the opposite direction (dual-distance) should be smaller than the thickness of a typical fold. The algorithm is described as follows: for a voxel $v$ on the colon wall, shoot a ray in every direction and locate the first point ($p_1$) hitting the lumen, then shoot a ray in the opposite direction of $\vec{vp_1}$ and locate the point ($p_2$) hitting the lumen on the other side (Figure 20.8(a)). The ray shooting algorithm was described in Eq. (20.2). Then both distance of $d_1 = |\vec{vp_1}|$ and $d_2 = |\vec{vp_2}|$ are computed. If $p_1$ or $p_2$ cannot be located, $d_1$ or $d_2$ will be assigned a maximum value. The ray with smallest $d_1 + d_2$ is defined as the piercing ray. The distance of two hitting points on the piercing ray is called the dual-distance.

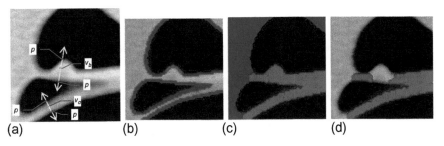

**FIGURE 20.8**

Haustral fold detection: (a) dual distance algorithm; (b) mean curvature map (red: convex, blue: flat or concave); (c) distance map (red: passes distance criteria); (d) detected haustral fold (red: fold region).

Furthermore, curvature property is employed to differentiate voxels of polyps on folds and voxels on folds. The following rules are used to determine whether a voxel $v$ belongs to a fold but not on a polyp.

$$\varsigma(v) = \begin{cases} 1 & \text{if } d_1(v) + d_2(v) < \text{Th}_\text{fold} \quad \text{and} \\ & \text{Curv}(p_1) < \text{Th}_\text{convex}, \text{Curv}(p_2) < \text{Th}_\text{convex} \\ 0 & \text{otherwise} \end{cases} \tag{20.7}$$

here $\varsigma(v)$ indicates whether a voxel belongs to the fold, $\text{Th}_\text{fold}$ is the threshold for maximum fold thickness (10 mm in current method), $\text{Curv}(p)$ is the mean curvature at voxel $p$, $\text{Th}_\text{convex}$ is a threshold to test if a curvature is convex ($-0.1$ in current method). If the dual-distance of a voxel is smaller than the fold thickness threshold and its hitting points ($p_1, p_2$) on the piercing ray do not have convex curvature, then the voxel belongs to a fold but not on a polyp. Figure 20.8(a) illustrates the dual-distance algorithm, Figure 20.8(b) shows the mean curvature map, Figure 20.8(c) shows the regions that passed the dual distance criteria, and Figure 20.8(d) shows a color map of the detected fold region.

### 20.4.3.4 Adaptive deformable models

After the image is enhanced and potential fold regions are marked, an adaptive deformable model is applied on the membership map to locate the polyp boundaries. Deformable models have been widely used in medical image segmentation (McInerney and Terzopoulos, 1996). The active contour model is the most commonly used model in 2D image segmentation, which was first introduced by Kass et al. (1988). Cohen (1991) proposed a balloon force that significantly increases the capture range. The active contour model was later extended to 3D images (Cohen and Cohen, 1993; Xu et al., 2000). Here, in this method, the traditional deformable model is enhanced by introducing a counter-force to control the model evolution on the haustral fold and by adaptively maintaining the model resolution during the evolution.

An initial model of the polyp is first placed at the seed location and the initial parameters are set. Then an iterative process is started. During each iteration, deformation forces are computed, and the model is updated according to the forces. Then the force weights and other control parameters are adaptively updated. The model resolution and topology is also adaptively maintained. The iterative process is repeated until all forces reach a balance (the model remains unchanged during two iterations) or a maximum number of iterations (currently 100, which exceeds the maximum polyp size) are executed.

The deformable model is represented as triangular meshes. The mesh data structure consists of a list of triangles and a list of vertices. Each vertex stores its 3D coordinate and a set of reference pointers to incident triangles. Each triangle stores reference pointers to its vertices and reference pointers to adjacent triangles sharing common edges. The so-called winged data structure was first introduced in Baumgart (1975), which allows efficient retrieval of vertex neighbors and triangle neighbors.

The initial model is a $2 \times 2 \times 2$ cube at the seed point. The deformable model is driven by the combination of internal force, image force, external force, and a counter-force in the fold region. The internal forces intend to maintain the smoothness and continuity of the model. They are computed as

$$F_{\text{internal}}(v) = \alpha \nabla^2 s(v) - \beta \nabla^2 (\nabla^2 s(v)) \tag{20.8}$$

where $s$ is the surface model and $v$ is a vertex on the model. The first term on the right-hand side is the first-order partial derivative which makes the model continuous and acts like an elastic membrane. The second term is the second-order derivative which makes the model smooth and acts like a rigid thin plate. By adjusting the weights $\alpha$ and $\beta$, the relative importance of the membrane term and the thin-plate term is balanced. $\alpha = 1$ and $\beta = 1$ are used in the method. $v$ is the 3D coordinate of a vertex. $\nabla^2$ is the partial derivatives which are computed using a Laplacian operator and finite difference on the triangular mesh.

Polyp boundaries tend to have larger gradients than other regions on the membership map. Therefore, the gradient of the edge map can be used as the image forces to attract the model, that is

$$F_{\text{image}}(v) = \nabla \left( G_\sigma \left( |\nabla G_\sigma (\mu(v))|^2 \right) \right) \tag{20.9}$$

where $\mu(v)$ is the membership map of "polyp tissue" class, $\nabla$ is the gradient operator, and $G_\sigma$ is the Gaussian operator, which is used to smooth the image and increase the capture range. $|\nabla G_\sigma (\mu(v))|^2$ computes the gradient magnitude of the membership map, which represents an edge map.

An expansion force is exerted to inflate the model from its initial state and prevent it from collapsing. The expansion force at a vertex $v$ is

$$F_{\text{expansion}}(v) = \vec{N}(v) \tag{20.10}$$

where $N(v)$ is the surface normal at vertex $v$. The expansion force points outward in the direction of surface normal.

Polyps on haustral folds need special treatment since the deformable model often leaks into the fold region. Figure 20.10(f) shows an over-segmented polyp on the fold. In order to address this problem, one more force is introduced in the deformable model to offset the expansion force at the fold region. The so-called counter-force is written as

$$F_{\text{counter}} = -F_{\text{expansion}} \tag{20.11}$$

After adding the counter-force, the force equation in the deformable model becomes:

$$F(v) = w_{internal}F_{internal}(v) + w_{image}F_{image}(v)$$
$$+ w_{expansion}F_{expansion}(v) + \varsigma(v)w_{counter}F_{counter}(v) \qquad (20.12)$$

where $w_{counter} = w_{expansion}$. $w_{expansion} = 5$, $w_{internal} = 2$, and $w_{image} = 5$ are set empirically in the current method. $\varsigma(v)$ is the normal direction at $v$. The location of a vertex $v$ on the model is updated at each iteration using Eq. (20.12),

$$v^{(t)} = v^{(t-1)} + \tau F(v^{(t-1)}) \qquad (20.13)$$

where $t$ is the evolution time, $\tau$ is the step size, and $F$ is the deformation force.

The model resolution is measured by the distance between adjacent vertices (i.e., the edge length). It is desirable to maintain the resolution during the model evolution. If the resolution is too high (vertices are too close), too many vertices need to be updated during each iteration which therefore slows down the converging process. On the other hand, if the resolution is too low (vertices are too sparse), there might not be a sufficient number of vertices to accurately snap the boundary. Furthermore, uneven vertex distribution will cause uneven internal and expansion forces, which may result in incorrect model deformation. Therefore, evenly distributed vertices are also desirable, that is, the resolution should be consistent throughout the model.

Two edge-based operations are carried out to adaptively maintain the model resolution: (1) if one edge is too short, it will be collapsed into one vertex; (2) if one edge is too long, it will be split into two edges by inserting one vertex in the middle. After each operation, the neighborhood will be retiled to form a valid triangular mesh. Figure 20.9 illustrates the adaptive mesh maintenance operations. In Figure 20.9(a), edge $v_1 - v_2$ is collapsed into one vertex $v'$ and its neighborhood is retriangulated. In Figure 20.9(b), edge $v_1 - v_2$ is split into two edges by inserting a vertex $v'$, and the two triangles incident to the edge are also split into four triangles. The edge length is maintained at the length of 1-4 voxel size in the current method.

Figure 20.10 shows the visual results of some segmented polyps with and without the counter-force. The examples include a medium-sized sessile polyp (Figure 20.10(a)), a polyp under fluid (Figure 20.10(b)), two lobulated masses (Figure 20.10(c) and (d)), and polyps on haustral folds (Figure 20.10(e) and (f)) (Yao and Summers, 2007). The visual results showed that the deformable model produced generally accurate polyp-lumen border and a fairly good estimate for the polyp-colon borders. The segmentation running time is less than 3 s for most polyps.

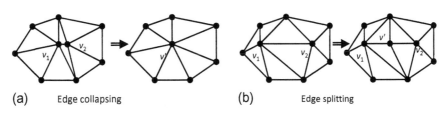

(a)     Edge collapsing          (b)     Edge splitting

**FIGURE 20.9**

Adaptive model maintenance operations.

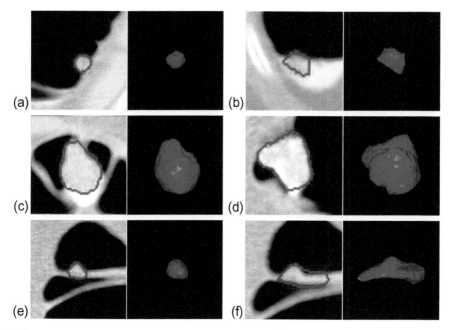

**FIGURE 20.10**

Segmentation results: left of each pair is 2D axial images superimposed with segmentation result; right of each pair is 3D surface reconstruction of the segmentation. (a) 7 mm sessile polyp; (b) 11 mm polyp under fluid; (c) 20 mm lobulated mass; (d) 20 mm lobulated mass; (e) segmentation of a 10 mm polyp on-fold with counter-forces; (f) segmentation of same polyp without counter-forces.

## 20.5 POLYP MEASUREMENT AND CHARACTERIZATION

After the polyp region is segmented out from the rest of the image, characteristic properties of the polyp can be derived. Among the properties, size is the most important for making clinical decisions.

### 20.5.1 POLYP SIZE MEASUREMENT

Taylor et al. (2007) investigated the relative accuracy and reproducibility of manual and automated polyp size measurements. They discovered that the automatic measurement differences are within the expected limits of inter- and intraobserver agreement for all measurement techniques. Automated and manual 3D polyp measurements are more accurate than manual 2D measurements. Wijk et al. (2008) developed an automatic method to measure the polyp size by evaluating the degree of protrusion. The evaluation was conducted on both phantom and real patient data.

In OC, clinicians measure the longest diameter of a polyp using either a calibrated guide wire or by comparing the polyp with an instrument of known size. In CTC, radiologists are interested in not only the linear size of a polyp but also its volume. Both the linear and volumetric measurements of a polyp can be easily obtained from its segmentation. To estimate the longest diameter axis, a principal component analysis (PCA) is applied (Jolliffe, 1986) to compute the principal axes of a polyp, and then the polyp surface is projected to the principal axes. The PCA method can be written as

$$\overline{Y} = \frac{1}{n} \sum_{i=1}^{n} Y_i$$

$$C = \frac{1}{n-1} \sum_{i=1}^{n} (Y_i - \overline{Y})(Y_i - \overline{Y})^T \tag{20.14}$$

where $Y_i$ is a vertex on the polyp surface, $n$ is the total number of vertices, $\overline{Y}$ is the centroid of the surface, and $C$ is the covariance matrix. The eigenvectors $\Phi = \{\phi_1, \phi_2, \phi_3\}$ of $C$ form the principal axes of the polyp. The linear measurement is then computed as

$$L_k = \left| \underset{i=1}{\overset{n}{\text{Max}}} \left( \Psi_{\phi_k}(Y_i) \right) - \underset{i=1}{\overset{n}{\text{Min}}} \left( \Psi_{\phi_k}(Y_i) \right) \right|, \quad k = 1, \ldots, 3 \tag{20.15}$$

where $\Psi_{\phi_k}(Y_i)$ is a function to project $Y_i$ to axis $\phi_k$, and Max and Min are functions to find the two extreme points of the projections. $L_1$ is the longest linear measurement of the polyp.

The volumetric measurement (polyp volume) is simply the summation of all voxels inside the segmented region.

$$V_A = \sum_i P(v_i) \tag{20.16}$$

where $V_A$ is the segmented volume, and $P(v_i)$ is the volume of a voxel $v_i$ inside the segmented region.

## 20.5.2 POLYP HEIGHT MEASUREMENT AND CHARACTERIZATION

Colonic polyps are abnormal growths protruding outward from the colon wall, and are characteristically round in shape. In contrast, haustral folds and other normal colonic structures tend to be circumferential and ridge-shaped. The colon surface can be viewed as a terrain and polyps as mountains (bumps) on the terrain. The unique topographic features of mountains (bumps) can assist us in distinguishing polyps from the rest of the colon surface. To characterize the height pattern, height maps can be computed from the CTC data, which are also called as digital elevation models (Taylor et al., 2003) in geographic information systems (GISs).

### 20.5.2.1 Height map generation
The approach to generate a height map is illustrated in Figure 20.11 (Yao et al., 2009). The method is based on a ray-casting technique. To detect a polyp, a projection plane is placed over it. The projection plane is determined by its normal, its distance to the colon surface and the location of the detection, and is represented as

$$\mathbf{P}(\vec{n}, v, s) : \vec{n} \circ (x - (v + \vec{n} \cdot s)) = 0 \tag{20.17}$$

here $\mathbf{P}$ is the projection plane, $\vec{n}$ is the unit normal of the plane, $v$ is the detection location, $s$ is the distance from the plane to the detection, $x$ is any point on the plane, $\circ$ is the dot product of two 3D

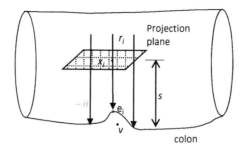

**FIGURE 20.11**

Height map generation based on ray casting.

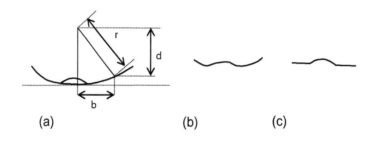

**FIGURE 20.12**

Local colon flattening: (a) local colon flattening, (b) height profile before flattening, (c) height profile.

vectors. Orthogonal projection is used to avoid the projection distortion associated with perspective projection. For every point $x_i$ on the projection plane, a ray $r_i$ is cast onto the colon surface. The point that ray $r_i$ encounters the colon surface is $e_i$. The equation for the projection ray is

$$e_i = x_i - \vec{n} \cdot d_i \qquad (20.18)$$

where $d_i$ is the distance between $x_i$ and $e_i$, which is recorded at $x_i$, and $\vec{n}$ is the unit normal of the plane. An implicit iso-surface associated with the colon surface in the 3D image is used to locate point $e_i$. The iso-value in use is $-700$ HU.

Since the colon is a curved tubular structure and orthogonal projection is used, the height values for pixels off the center of the map are artificially higher than they actually are (Figure 20.12). The colon needs to be flattened to get more precise height measurement. The flattening is implemented by compensating the height distance measurement according to the distance to the center of the map. The process is illustrated in Figure 20.12 and Eq. (20.19),

$$\Delta d = r - \sqrt{r^2 - b^2}$$
$$d' = d + \Delta d \qquad (20.19)$$

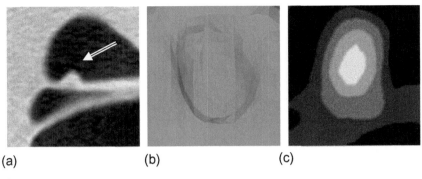

(a)                    (b)                    (c)

**FIGURE 20.13**

Colonic polyp and height map: (a) 2D CT slice of a 10 mm polyp, (b) 3D endoluminal view, and (c) height map.

where $r$ is the radius of the colon tube, $b$ is the distance to the center of the map, $d$ is the measured height distance, and $d'$ is the adjusted height distance. The radius of the colon section can be computed from the center line to the colon surface. Figure 20.12(a) shows the local colon flattening. Figure 20.12(b) is the height profile before the flattening. It shows that the height contrast between the polyp and its surrounding region is smaller than the real value. This effect can be significant especially for flat polyps. Figure 20.15(c) is the height profile after the flattening.

After the distance map to the projection plane is computed and compensated, it is normalized and converted to a digitized height map using the following equation,

$$h_i = d_c' - d_i' + \max D \qquad (20.20)$$

where $d_i'$ and $h_i$ are the height distance and height value at pixel $i$, max $D$ is the maximum distance in the distance map, and $d_c$ is the distance in the center of the map. In this way, the height map is normalized to a banded range around the center of the height map, which is the height value for the candidate location. The height map is converted to a raster image where the image intensity indicates the height. The brighter the pixel is, the higher the height is. The physical size of the height map is 25 mm × 25 mm, and it is sampled in a 128 × 128 image grid. A typical height map is shown in Figure 20.13(c).

### 20.5.2.2 Topographic features

The height differential and directional slopes in the height map reveal the topographic features of a terrain surface. In the case of a polyp with ideal semi-spherical shape, the slope from its apex to the base should be homogeneous and steep in every direction. In the case of haustral fold, the slopes are steep in the directions perpendicular to the ridge and low in the directions parallel to the ridge. In the normal flat colon surface, the slopes are generally low in all directions. Figure 20.14 demonstrates the height map and 3D endoluminal view of polyp, haustral fold, and normal colon surface. It is noted that the height map for a polyp presents a concentric pattern, while the other two do not.

The height map is centered at the location of the detection, that is, the height of the center of the map is the height of the point passing through the casting ray at the detection point ($v$ in Figure 20.11).

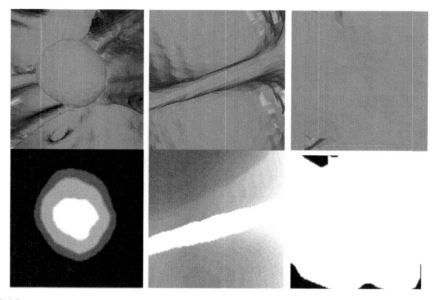

**FIGURE 20.14**

Height map of structures in CTC. First row: 3D endoluminal view; second row: height map; first column: a 14-mm polyp; second column: haustral fold; third column: flat colon surface.

Therefore, the search for the apex is conducted around the center of the height map. In the case where there is a plateau, the center of the plateau is used. From the peak, the directional slope is computed for every direction defined by angle $\theta$ (Figure 20.15). The computation is done by accumulating the height difference along the direction $\theta$,

$$d(\theta) = \sum_{t=1...n} (H(\theta,t) - H(\theta,t+1)) = H(\theta,0) - H(\theta,n)$$
$$H(\theta,t) = h(A + r(\theta)^* t)$$
$$r(\theta) = (\cos\theta, \sin\theta) \tag{20.21}$$

where $d(\theta)$ is the accumulative directional slope at angle $\theta$, $A = (A_x, A_y)$ is the coordinate of the apex, $t$ is the time step, $h(.)$ is the height value retrieved from the height map through linear interpolation, $H(\theta, t)$ is the height value represented by angle and step. $\theta$ goes from $0°$ to $360°$. $n$ is the number of steps to accumulate the height difference, which is determined by a sliding transition window technique; $18°$ intervals are evaluated. Figure 20.15 illustrates how the directional slopes are computed. Several topographic features can be derived from the directional slopes. The mean $M(d)$ and standard deviation $STD(d)$ of directional accumulative slopes in all directions are among the most useful ones.

To further explore the characteristics of slope changes in all directions, the directional accumulative slopes are transformed into a contour in a polar coordinate system centered at the apex, named as slope contour. The angular coordinate is the slope direction (angle) and the radial coordinate is the accumulative slope (Figure 20.16). The slope contour summarizes the characteristics of the slope

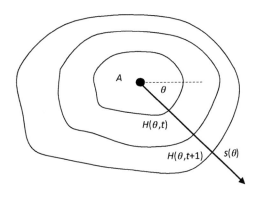

**FIGURE 20.15**

Directional slope computation. *A* is the apex.

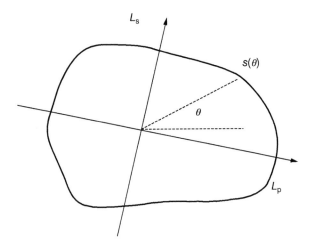

**FIGURE 20.16**

Slope contour.

distribution. A PCA (Lay, 2000) is conducted on the slope contour to compute the principal and secondary axes of the contour. The lengths of the principal and secondary axes ($L_p$, $L_s$) and the slope aspect ratio AS $= L_p/L_s$ are computed as topographic features. Compactness $= 4\pi$ (area)/(perimeter)$^2$ is also derived as an additional feature. These features are translation, rotation, and scale invariant.

### 20.5.2.3 Concentric index and projection direction optimization

In the ray casting method, different projection directions could produce very different height maps. Figure 20.17 shows height maps of the same polyp in Figure 20.13 from different projection directions.

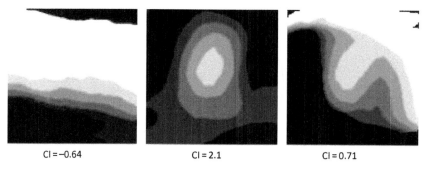

CI = −0.64        CI = 2.1        CI = 0.71

**FIGURE 20.17**

Height maps of the same polyp in Figure 20.13 from different projection directions.

The middle one is the optimal projection where the projection plane is placed right over the polyp. It demonstrates a concentric pattern. A concentric index is designed to gauge this pattern,

$$CI = M(d) - STD(d) \qquad (20.22)$$

where CI is the concentric index, $M(d)$ and $STD(d)$ are the mean and standard deviation of accumulative directional slopes. A height map with bigger and more homogeneous directional slopes in all directions tends to have a higher concentric index. Figure 20.17 marks the CI values from different projection directions.

The projection direction is optimized by maximizing the concentric index. The projection plane is determined by its normal (projection direction) and its distance to the colon surface. Since orthogonal projection is used, the distance does not affect the height map generation. However, if the plane is too far from the detection, it may be behind the opposite colon wall and the polyp may be occluded; on the other hand, if the plane is too close to the detection, it may cut across the polyp and thus the height map is not complete. The plane is initially placed 10 mm from the detection, and will be moved closer if it is behind the opposite wall. The optimization process can be written as

$$\underset{\vec{n}}{\arg\max} \, (CI \, (P(\vec{n}), v, s)) \qquad (20.23)$$

here, CI is the concentric index of the height map generated from the projection plane $P$, $\vec{n}$ is the normal of the plane, $v$ is the detection location, and $s$ is the distance from plane to detection. Since $v$ and $s$ are known, the only variable to optimize is $\vec{n}$. All possible projection directions are sampled to select the optimal direction. One way to generate the set of all directions in 3D space is the spiral-point technique (Saff and Kuijlaars, 1997), which produces uniformly distributed points on a sphere. The number of directions $N$ is determined by the angle interval between adjacent directions, which is approximately $N = \left(\frac{218.4}{\alpha}\right)^2$ ($\alpha$ is the angle interval). For instance, the method generates 1908 directions at a 5° angle interval. Each direction requires one height map generation and evaluation, which takes about 0.03 s in our system. Therefore, it takes about $1908 \times 0.03 = 57$ s to exhaustively search all directions at 5° intervals. The CAD system typically generates about 50 detections per data set at this stage. It will take 3000 s (about 50 min) for just the projection optimization alone, which makes the exhaustive search not practical. In order to improve the time efficiency, a multi-scale spherical search scheme is adopted. In this scheme, the search starts with a big angle interval and decreases the angle interval in following iterations. A full range search $(0 \leq \theta \leq \pi, 0 \leq \phi \leq 2\pi)$ is conducted at the coarsest scale. After that, a local search is conducted in the neighborhood of the direction obtained from the previous scale. The range of neighborhood is twice of the angle interval in the previous scale. A three-scale searching scheme is designed, with 30°, 10°, and 5° intervals at each scale. The first scale takes $(218.4/30)^2 = 53$ evaluations, the second scale of refinement at 10° intervals takes $(30/10 \times 2 + 1)^2 = 49$ evaluations, and the third scale of refinement at 5° intervals takes $(10/5 \times 2 + 1)^2 = 25$ evaluations. Altogether it takes at most $53 + 49 + 25 = 127$ height map evaluations for this scheme. To further limit the search, if a projection plane is out of the lumen which indicates projecting from the back of the polyp, it should be excluded from further consideration. The multi-scale searching technique is robust. The interval for the first scale is 30°, and a 30° margin is added on both sides in the second scale. It then covers $3 \times 30 = 90°$ for any chosen projection angle, which is 1/4 of the angle span. Furthermore, polyps usually have one side against the colon wall, which makes almost half of the projection angles invalid.

### 20.5.2.4 Polyp height and width measurement

Height and width are two important characteristics of a polyp. Their measurement is not trivial since the polyp orientation and the boundary between polyp and normal colon are hard to determine. The height map can be used to address this problem. To conduct the measurement, the tip and base of a polyp need to be located in the height map. The highest point in the center of the height map is used as the tip of the polyp. The interface between the polyp surface and its surrounding colon region is the polyp neck. The neck can be detected by examining the directional height profile. Starting from the highest point in the center of the height map (the polyp tip), the height value is sampled along a specified direction to plot the height profile. The neck location occurs in two scenarios in the height profile (Figure 20.18). In the first case (Figure 20.18(a)), the neck is located at where the changes of the height values are smaller than a height threshold ($t_h$) for a certain distance (distance threshold, $t_d$). In the second case (Figure 20.18(b)), the neck location lies at where the height value starts to increase. The first case indicates that the portion of the polyp rests on a flat colon region, while the second case implies that the portion of the polyp touches other structures such as haustral folds. A transition window is assigned to identify

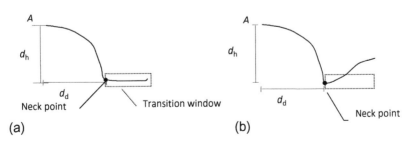

(a)                                             (b)

**FIGURE 20.18**

Directional height profile and transition window. (a) Scenario 1: polyp connects to normal colon surface; (b) scenario 2: polyp next to other structures or the arch of colon is highly curved. A is apex of the height map.

the two scenarios in the height profile. The height of the transition window is the height threshold ($t_h$) and the width is the distance threshold ($t_d$). The transition window is slid along the height profile and stops in the following two scenarios when it reaches the neck point: (1) the heights of all points in the window are within a range,

$$|h_i - h_j| < t_h, \quad \forall i \in W, \ \forall j \in W \tag{20.24}$$

where $W$ is the transition window, $i$ and $j$ are points in the window, and $h_i$ and $h_j$ are heights of points $i$ and $j$ in the height profile; or (2) the heights of all points in the window are bigger than that of the first point in the window,

$$h_j \geq h_k, \quad \forall j \in W \tag{20.25}$$

where $W$ is the transition window, $k$ is the first point in the window, and $j$ is any other point in the window. The size of the transition window is currently set as $t_h = 1$ mm and $t_d = 4$ mm. The window size can handle polyps with plateaus as large as 8 mm without triggering the termination of the sliding transition window.

Figure 20.19(d) shows the polyp tip and neck points in two height maps. For each neck point, its relative height to the tip ($d_h$) and its span distance along the profile ($d_d$) from the tip are computed. The polyp height is the average height difference between polyp tip and polyp neck points, and the polyp width is the average of span distances. They are computed as

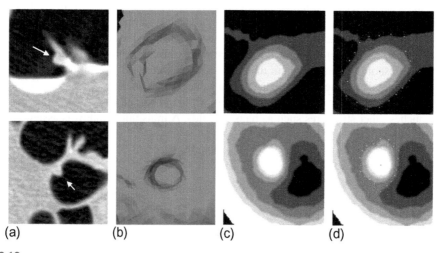

**FIGURE 20.19**

Examples of polyp height map. (a) 2D transverse slice; (b) 3D surface rendering; (c) height map; (d) height map with tip and neck locations (dark dot is the tip, bright dots are the neck locations). First row: a 10 mm adenoma polyp; manual measurement: height = 5.9 mm, width = 8.6 mm; height map measurement: height = 3.67 mm, width = 9.02 mm. Second row: a 6 mm hyperplastic polyp; manual measurement: height = 3.0 mm, width = 4.7 mm; height map measurement: height = 3.22 mm, width = 5.98 mm.

$$PH = \underset{i=1...N}{\text{AVG}} (d_h^i)$$

$$PW = \underset{\substack{i=1...N/2 \\ j=i+N/2}}{\text{AVG}} (d_d^i + d_d^j) \qquad (20.26)$$

here PH is the polyp height, PW is the polyp width, $N$ is the total number of directions in the evaluation, $d_h^i$ are $d_d^i$ are the height and distance of $i$th neck point; 20 directions at $18°$ angle intervals are used. Considering artifacts and outliers, the top 10% and bottom 10% of $d_h$ and $d_d$ values are excluded in the evaluation of height and width. Essentially, the height measurement is the depth of protrusion from the colon wall and width measurement is the projected 2D spread. Figure 20.19 shows two examples of polyp height maps and their measurements.

## 20.6 DATA ACQUISITION AND VALIDATION EXPERIMENT

The CTC data were acquired as follows. Patients underwent a 24-h colonic preparation that consisted of oral administration of a cathartic barium and iodine contrast agents. Each patient was scanned in supine and prone positions using a four-channel or eight-channel CT scanner (GE LightSpeed or LightSpeed Ultra). CT scanning parameters included 1.25- to 2.5-mm section collimation, 15 mm/s table speed, 1-mm reconstruction interval, 100 mAs, and 120 kVp. The patient also underwent OC on the same day of the CTC. The colonoscopists used a calibrated guide wire to measure the polyp size and recorded the polyp location and a subjective assessment of the polyp shape (sessile, pedunculated, or flat). After the CTC data were transferred to a workstation, the manual segmentation was performed by a consensus panel consisting of a research trainee and an experienced radiologist to delineate the border of every polyp in an axial view of the CTC. The manual segmentation and OC measurements were used as the reference standard.

The segmentation accuracy is evaluated by Dice coefficient between the automatic segmentation and the manual segmentation,

$$DC = \frac{2|S_A \cap S_M|}{|S_A| + |S_M|} \qquad (20.27)$$

where DC is the Dice coefficient, $S_A$ is the segmented region of the automatic method, and $S_M$ is the manually segmented region by an expert. $S_A \cap S_M$ are the voxels common to both $S_A$ and $S_M$.

Manual measurements were made with a measurement tool in the Viatronix V3D software (research version 1.3.0.0; Viatronix, Stony Brook, NY) for the polyp height and width. Minimum and maximum widths were measured for each polyp in the 3D view in Viatronix. An ellipse was used to model each polyp from a birds-eye view. The minor axis of the ellipse corresponds to the minimum width and the major axis corresponds to the maximum width. The height of the polyps from the colonic wall was measured in the 2D cross-sectional view in Viatronix. The cross-sectional plane was chosen so that it was perpendicular to the polyp base. The height was measured as the length from the peak to the neck of the polyp. The manual measurement was conducted twice by the same operator in a 2-week time interval and the mean of two measurements was used. The correlation and agreement of height map and manual measurements were evaluated using regression and Bland-Altman analysis (Bland and Altman, 1986).

## 20.7 RESULTS

### 20.7.1 DATA SETS

The patient population consisted of 395 asymptomatic adults between 40 and 79 years of age at three medical institutions (Pickhardt et al., 2003; Summers et al., 2005). Eighty-three polyps were identified in the database. Table 20.1 lists the distribution of CTC studies and polyps. Among these polyps, 43 polyps are categorized as on haustral folds by a radiologist. The criteria are either the base of the polyp is on a fold or over 50% of the polyp surface touches the fold.

**Table 20.1  Lists the Study Distribution Among All Three Institutes**

|  | Total Patients | Total Polyps | Polyps On-Fold |
|---|---|---|---|
| Institute 1 | 123 | 17 | 10 |
| Institute 2 | 149 | 32 | 12 |
| Institute 3 | 123 | 34 | 21 |
| Total | 395 | 83 | 43 |

### 20.7.2 SEGMENTATION VALIDATION

The linear measurement $L_1$ is validated against the linear measurement obtained from the OC $L_o$. Figure 20.20 is the scatter plot of largest linear measurement from segmentation ($L_1$) and linear OC measurement ($L_o$), the $R^2$ value is 0.6081. Paired $t$-test shows that $P(T \leq t) < 10^{-5}$ for the hypothesis of the mean difference = 0.

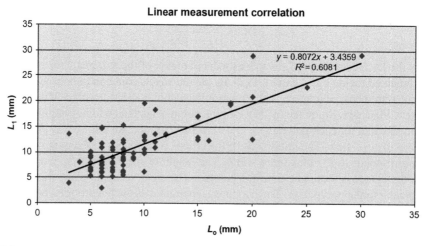

**FIGURE 20.20**

Correlation between linear measurement from computer segmentation and linear OC measurement.

The volumetric measurement is validated against the manual segmentation from CTC by comparing their overlap Dice coefficient and volumetric measurements. Figure 20.21(a) shows an example of the manual and automatic segmentation superimposed in one view. Figure 20.21(b) shows the histogram of Dice coefficient of $D$; the mean value is 0.752, the standard deviation is 0.154, the maximum value is 0.918, and the minimum value is 0.217. Figure 20.21(c) is the scatter plot of the volume of the automatic ($V_A$) versus that of manual segmentation ($V_M$), $R^2$ value is 0.9824. Paired $t$-test also shows that $P(T \leq t) = 0.37$ for the hypothesis of the mean difference $= 0$, which means no significant difference. Since the linear regression analysis in Figure 20.21(c) is dominated by the five largest polyps, another correlation test using only a partial list of polyps having $V_M < 1000\,mm^3$ was performed. The result is shown in Figure 20.21(d). The $R^2$ value is 0.6824, and $P(T \leq t) = 0.06$ for the hypothesis of the mean difference $= 0$.

To evaluate the role of the counter-force on the segmentation of polyps on haustral folds, manual and automated measurement of polyps on haustral folds (on-fold) and not on haustral folds (not-on-fold) are compared, with and without the counter-force (Table 20.2). The results showed better agreement for polyps not-on-fold than polyps on-fold. The counter-force greatly improved the performance for polyps on-fold, with agreement increase for all measures. For polyps not-on-fold, the segmentation achieved similar performance with and without the counter-forces.

### 20.7.3 HEIGHT AND WIDTH MEASUREMENTS

Fifty polyps were randomly selected and their height and width were manually measured (Summers et al., 2009). Those polyps are varied in size, histology, shape, and location. The height and width were validated against the categorized OC size measurement. Figure 20.22 shows the box-whisker plots of the correlation. The regression trend line of the mean of each category is also displayed. It indicates that heightmap measurements correlate better with OC size than the manual measurements.

The correlations of height map and manual measurements are shown in Figure 20.23. The paired $t$-test for the height measurement shows that the Pearson correlation is 0.74, $P(T \leq t)$ is 0.11. The paired $t$-test for the width measurement shows that Pearson correlation is 0.75, $P(T \leq t)$ is 0.17. The regression analysis shows fairly good correlations between polyp height and width measurements. However, the correlation is not statistically significant. One possible reason is that the height map measurements and manual measurements do not exactly measure the same property. The manual measurement requires a subjectively chosen perpendicular cross plane, while the height map method automatically optimizes the best plane for measurement.

A Bland-Altman analysis was conducted to evaluate the agreement of the two measurements and the repeatability of two manual measurements. Figure 20.24 shows the Bland-Altman plot of height and width measurement between the height map technique and the manual technique. Figure 20.25 shows the Bland-Altman plot of the two repeated manual height and width measurements. Table 20.3 lists the agreement of the Bland-Altman analysis in Figures 20.24 and 20.25. The results indicate the agreement between the two methods is relatively low. Since high correlations are achieved in paired $t$-tests, this means that there is a systematic difference between these two techniques. The agreement of width measurement is better than that of height measurement. These observations may be explained by the way the manual measurements are conducted. For the height measurement, a perpendicular plane needs to be chosen, which is not a trivial manual task. Another observation is that the agreement of height measurement from the manual and height map method is comparable to the repeatability agreement of two manual height measurements. This further indicates that manual height measurement is subjective.

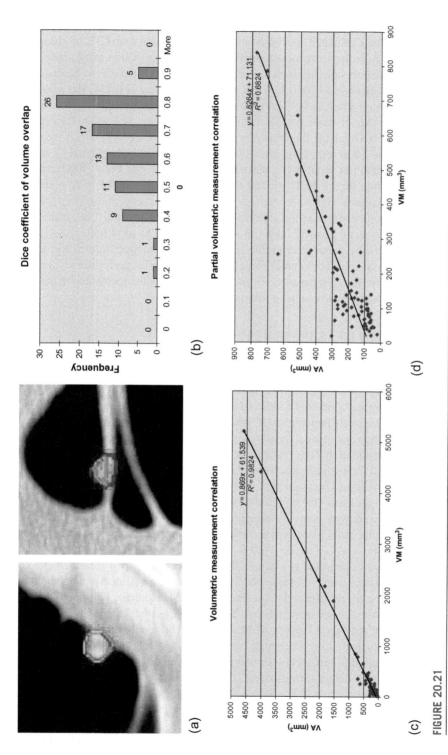

**FIGURE 20.21**

Validation of volumetric measurement against manual segmentation on CTC. (a) Superimposition of manual and automatic segmentation; (b) histogram of Dice coefficients of volume overlap (mean 0.752, standard deviation 0.154); (c) correlation of volumetric measurement between automatic segmentation ($V_A$) and manual segmentation ($V_M$), $R^2 = 0.9824$, paired $t$-test showed $P(T \leq t) = 0.37$ for hypothesis of the mean difference = 0; (d) partial correlation of volumetric measurement for polyps < 1000 mm$^3$, $R^2 = 0.6824$, $P(T \leq t) = 0.06$ for the hypothesis of mean difference = 0.

**Table 20.2  Comparison of Manual and Automated Measurement for Polyps On-Fold and Not-On-Fold, With and Without Counter-Forces**

| Agreement | Force | All Polyps | Polyps On-Fold | Polyps Not-On-Fold |
|---|---|---|---|---|
| Linear measurement correlation ($R^2$) | W/o counter-force | 0.3163 | 0.1553 | 0.5343 |
|  | With counter-force | 0.6081 | 0.5099 | 0.5404 |
| Volumetric measurement correlation ($R^2$) | W/o counter-force | 0.8629 | 0.8032 | 0.9741 |
|  | With counter-force | 0.9824 | 0.9732 | 0.9870 |
| Dice coefficient (mean, standard deviation) | W/o counter-force | $0.701 \pm 0.176$ | $0.622 \pm 0.238$ | $0.792 \pm 0.128$ |
|  | With counter-force | $0.752 \pm 0.154$ | $0.715 \pm 0.192$ | $0.795 \pm 0.125$ |

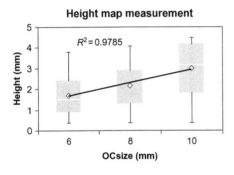

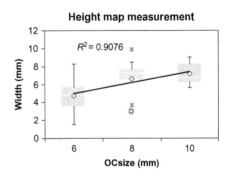

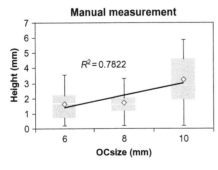

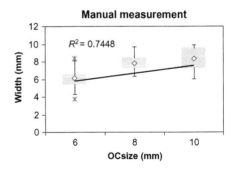

**FIGURE 20.22**

Box-whisker plots show correlation of polyp size measured in OC and height measurement using height map (upper left), width measurement using height map (upper right), manual height measurement (lower left), and manual width measurement (lower right).

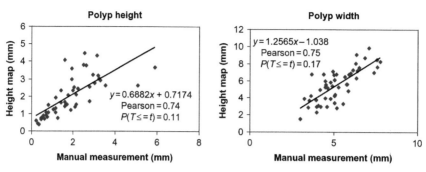

**FIGURE 20.23**

Correlation and paired *t*-test between manual and height map measurements.

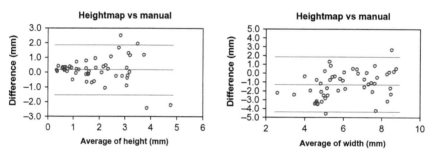

**FIGURE 20.24**

Bland-Altman plots of inter-method agreement of height and width measurements.

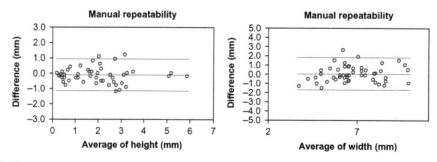

**FIGURE 20.25**

Bland-Altman plots of repeatability agreement of manual height and width measurements.

**Table 20.3 Bland-Altman Analysis of Inter-Method Agreement and Repeatability of Manual Measurements**

| Measurement | Mean Difference (mm) | 95% Bland-Altman Limits of Agreement (mm) | r Value |
|---|---|---|---|
| *Inter-method* | | | |
| Height | 0.1 | −1.5, 1.8 | 0.09 |
| Width | −1.3 | −4.3, 1.7 | 0.43 |
| *Repeatability* | | | |
| Height | −0.1 | −1.1, 0.9 | 0.04 |
| Width | 0.0 | −1.7, 1.8 | 0.15 |

# 20.8 DISCUSSION

Colonic polyp segmentation is not an easy task due to the irregular polyp shape and complex surrounding regions. The deformable model overcomes some of the difficulties by ensuring smoothness and continuity of the polyp boundaries. Knowledge-based enhancement and fuzzy clustering try to mimic the manual segmentation by generating an artificial border between the polyp and its surrounding colon wall. Currently the segmentation requires a seed point to start. The seeds can be manually placed close to the center of the polyp, or be obtained from an automated detection program, for example, a CAD system. In the latter case, no user intervention is required.

The segmentation algorithm is applicable to a wide range of polyps and had been tested on data from three different institutions. The colon preparation and CT scanning protocol were slightly different among the institutions. The sizes of polyps ranged from 3 to 50 mm. The shape, location, and surrounding vicinity of polyps also varied greatly.

The segmentation of polyps on haustral folds presents more challenges since the deformable model often leaks into the fold region. Criteria based on dual-distance to the fold boundary can be applied to detect the fold region and impose a counter-force to prevent the deformable model from overexpansion. The counter-force is very effective in improving the segmentation for polyps on haustral folds. In the meantime, it does not affect the segmentation for those not on haustral folds.

One characteristic used to predict the malignancy risk of a polyp is its size and growth rate. Currently, polyp size is usually determined by the linear measurement estimated during OC. However, linear measurement is not consistent since it does not account for 3D geometry of the polyp (Yeshwant et al., 2006). Clinicians may not be able to measure the longest axis of a polyp due to the angle limitation of the scope. In addition, OC measurements are often estimated crudely by comparison with an open forceps. Volumetric measurement is considered a more reliable way to characterize the polyp size. Accurate 3D polyp segmentation is essential in providing the volumetric measurements. Tracking polyp size change over time is important for surveillance of medium-sized polyps since growth may indicate the presence of advanced neoplasia. An evolving clinical concept is that medium sized polyps, if left unresected in the colon, should be monitored during subsequent CTC examinations to determine their growth rate and malignancy potential. However, inter-observer and intra-observer variability make it unreliable to compare two measurements at different times (Yao et al., 2004).

Computer segmentation provides consistent measurements since it is based on the same set of rules. The segmentation was validated against the linear measurement from the OC and manual segmentation from the CTC. Another purpose of polyp segmentation is to compute quantitative features for the CAD system. The segmentation produces both the polyp boundary and its interior voxels, which can be used to compute 3D shape and density distribution.

In summary, the polyp segmentation method based on 3D adaptive deformable models is robust. The method had been applied to CTC studies using different protocols and from different institutes. The method provides consistent and accurate measurement for the linear and volumetric size of the polyps.

## ACKNOWLEDGMENTS

This work was supported by the National Institutes of Health Clinical Center. We thank Perry Pickhardt and Richard Choi for providing CT colonography data and Viatronix for providing the V3D research software.

## REFERENCES

Baumgart, B., 1975. A polyhedron representation for computer vision. In: National Computer Conference and Exposition, New York, NY, USA.

Bland, J.M., Altman, D.G., 1986. Statistical methods for assessing agreement between two methods of clinical measurement. Lancet 1, 307–310.

Chen, D., Hassouna, M.S., Farag, A.A., Falk, R., 2006. An improved 2D colonic polyp segmentation framework based on gradient vector flow deformable model, MIAR, LNCS 4091, pp. 372–379.

Cohen, L., 1991. On active contour models and balloons. Comput. Vis. Graph. Image Process. Image Underst. 53 (2), 211–218.

Cohen, L.D., Cohen, I., 1993. Finite element methods for active contour model and ballons for 2D and 3D images. IEEE Trans. Pattern Anal. Mach. Intell. 15, pp. 1131–1147.

Coin, C., Wollett, F., Coin, J., 1983. Computerized radiology of the colon: a potential screening technique. Comput. Radiol. 7, 215–221.

Cunningham, D., Atkin, W., Lenz, H., Lynch, H., Minsky, B., Nordlinger, B., Starling, N., 2010. Colorectal cancer. Lancet 375 (9719), 1030–1047.

Dijkers, J.J., van Wijk, C., Vos, F.M., Florie, J., Nio, Y.C., Venema, H.W., Truyen, R., van Vliet, L.J., 2005. Segmentation and size measurement of polyps in CT colonography, Med Image Comput Comput Assist Interv. 2005;8(Pt 1):712–9.

Ellert, J., Kreel, L., 1980. The value of CT in malignancy colonic tumors. J. Comput. Tomogr. 4, 225–240.

Fletcher, J., Johnson, C., Welch, T., 2000. Optimization of CT colonography technique: prospective trial in 180 patients. Radiology 216, 704–711.

Franaszek, M., Summers, R.M., Pickhardt, P.J., Choi, J.R., 2006. Hybrid segmentation of colon filled with air and opacified fluid for CT colonography. IEEE Trans. Med. Imaging 25 (3), 358–368.

Frentz, S.M., Summers, R.M., 2006. Current status of CT colonography. Acad. Radiol. 13 (12), 1517–1531.

Gluecker, T., Johnson, C., Harmsen, W., Offord, K., Harris, A., Wilson, L., Ahlquist, D., 2003. Colorectal cancer screening with CT colonography, colonoscopy, and double-contrast barium enema examination: prospective assessment of patient perceptions and preferences. Radiology 227 (2), 378–384.

Haker, S., Angenent, S., Tannenbaurn, A., Kikinis, R., 2000. Nondistorting flattening maps and the 3-D visualization of colon CT images. IEEE Trans. Med. Imaging 19 (7), 665–670.

Hara, A., Johnson, C., Reed, J., 1996. Detection of colorectal polyps by computed tomographic colonography: feasibility of a novel technique. Gastroenterology 110, 284–290.

Holemans, J., Matson, M., Hughes, J., Seed, P., Rankin, S., 1998. A comparison of air, $CO_2$ and air/$CO_2$ mixture as insufflation agents for double contrast barium enema. Eur. Radiol. 8, 274–276.

Hong, W., Gu, X., Qiu, F., Jin, M., Kaufman, A., 2006. Conformal virtual colon flattening, Proceedings of the 2006 ACM symposium on Solid and physical modeling, pp. 85–93.

Husband, J., Hodsun, N., Parsons, C., 1980. The use of computed tomography in recurrent rectal tumors. Radiology 134, 677–682.

Jerebko, A., Franaszek, M., Summers, R., 2002. Radon transform based polyp segmentation method for CT colonography computer aided diagnosis. In: RSNA.

Jolliffe, I., 1986. Principal Component Analysis. Springer Verlag, Berlin.

Kass, M., Witkin, A., Terzopoulos, D., 1988. Snakes: active contour models. Int. J. Comput. Vis. 1, 321–331.

Koenderink, J.J., van Doorn, A.J., 1992. Surface shape and curvature scales. Image Vis. Comput. 10 (8), 557–565.

Lay, D., 2000. Linear Algebra and It's Applications. Addison-Wesley, New York, NY.

Lu, L., Barbu, A., Wolf, M., Liang, J., Salganicoff, M., Comaniciu, D., 2008. Accurate polyp segmentation for 3D CT colongraphy using multi-staged probabilistic binary learning and compositional model. In: IEEE Conference on Computer Vision and Pattern Recognition.

Macari, M., Lavelle, M., Pedrosa, I., 2001. Effect of different bowel preparations on residual fluid at CT colonography. Radiology 218, 274–277.

McInerney, T., Terzopoulos, D., 1996. Deformable models in medical image analysis: a survey. Med. Image Anal. 1 (2), 91–108.

Paik, D.S., Beaulieu, C., Jeffrey, R.B., Karadi, C., Napel, S., 2000. Visualization modes for CT colonography using cylindrical and planar map projections. J. Comput. Assist. Tomogr. 24 (2), 179–188.

Pham, D.L., Prince, J., 1998. An adaptive fuzzy c-means algorithm for image segmentation in the presence of intensity inhomogeneities. Pattern Recogn. Lett. 20, 57–68.

Pickhardt, P.J., 2007. Screening, CT colonography: how I do it. Am. J. Roentgenol. 189, 290–298.

Pickhardt, P.J., Choi, J.R., Hwang, I., Butler, J.A., Puckett, M.L., Hildebrandt, H.A., Wong, R.K., Nugent, P.A., Mysliwiec, P.A., Schindler, W.R., 2003. Computed tomographic virtual colonoscopy to screen for colorectal neoplasia in asymptomatic adults. N. Engl. J. Med. 349 (23), 2191–2200.

Qaseem, A., Denberg, T., Hopkins, R.J., 2012. Screening for colorectal cancer: a guidance statement from the American College of Physicians. Ann. Intern. Med. 156 (5), 378–386.

Saff, E.B., Kuijlaars, A.B.J., 1997. Distributing many points on a sphere. Math. Intell. 19 (1), 5–11.

Siegel, R., Desantis, C., Jemal, A., 2014. Colorectal cancer statistics, 2014. CA Cancer J. Clin. 64 (2), 104–117.

Stein, A., Atanackovic, D., Bokemeyer, C., 2011. Current standards and new trends in the primary treatment of colorectal cancer. Eur. J. Cancer 47 (Suppl. 3), 312–314.

Sudarsky, S., Geiger, B., Chefd'hotel, C., Guendel, L., 2008. Colon Unfolding Via Skeletal Subspace Deformation in MICCAI. Springer-Verlag, Berlin, New York, NY.

Summers, R.M., 2010. Polyp size measurement at CT colonography: what do we know and what do we need to known? Radiology 255 (3), 707–720.

Summers, R.M., Yao, J., Pickhardt, P.J., Franaszek, M., Bitter, I., Brickman, D., Krishna, V., Choi, J.R., 2005. Computed tomographic virtual colonoscopy computer-aided polyp detection in a screening population. Gastroenterology 129, 1832–1844.

Summers, R.M., Frentz, S.M., Liu, J., Yao, J., Brown, L., Louie, A., Barlow, D.S., Jensen, D.W., Dwyer, A.J., Pickhardt, P.J., Petrick, N., 2009. Conspicuity of colorectal polyps at CT colonography: visual assessment, CAD performance, and the important role of polyp height. Acad. Radiol. 16 (1), 4–14.

Taylor, S., Halligan, S., Bartram, C., 2003. Multi-detector row CT colonography: effect of collimation, pitch, and orientation on polyp detection in a human colectomy specimen. Radiology 229, 109–118.

Taylor, S.A., Slater, A., Halligan, S., Honeyfield, L., Roddie, M.E., Demeshski, J., Amin, H., Burling, D., 2007. CT colonography: automated measurement of colonic polyps compared with manual techniques—human in vitro study. Radiology 242 (1), 120–128.

van Gelder, R., Birnie, E., Florie, J., Schutter, M., Bartelsman, J., Snel, P., Laméris, J., Bonsel, G., Stoker, J., 2004. CT colonography and colonoscopy: assessment of patient preference in a 5-week follow-up study. Radiology 233 (2), 328–337.

Van Uitert, R., Summers, R.M., 2007. Automatic correction of level set based subvoxel precise centerlines for virtual colonoscopy using the colon outer wall. IEEE Trans. Med. Imaging 26, 1069–1078.

van Wijk, C., van Ravesteijn, V.F., Vos, F.M., van Vliet, L.J., 2010. Detection and segmentation of colonic polyps on implicit isosurfaces by second principal curvature flow. IEEE Trans. Med. Imaging 29 (3), 688–698.

Vilanova, A., Groller, E., 2004. Geometric modeling for virtual colon unfolding. In: Brunnett, G., et al. (Eds.), Geometric Modeling for Scientific Visualization. Birkhauser, Berlin, p. 488.

Vining, D., Shifrin, R., Grishaw, E., Liu, K., Gelfand, D., 1994. Virtual colonoscopy. Radiology 193, 446.

Vos, F.M., Serlie, I., van Gelder, R., Post, F.H., Truyen, R., Gerritsen, F.A., Stoker, J., Vossepoel, A., 2001. A new visualization method for virtual colonoscopy. In: MICCAI. Springer, Heidelberg.

Wang, G., McFarland, G., Brown, B.P., Vannier, M.W., 1998. GI tract unraveling with curved cross sections. IEEE Trans. Med. Imaging 17 (2), 318–322.

Weisstein, E.W., 1999. CRC Concise Encyclopedia of Mathematics, second ed. Chapman and Hall/CRC, Boca Raton, FL.

Wijk, C.V., Florie, J., Nio, C.Y., Dekker, E., de Vries, A.H., Venema, H.W., van Vliet, L.J., Stoker, J., Vos, F.M., 2008. Protrusion method for automated estimation of polyp size on CT colonography. Am. J. Roentgenol. 190 (5), 1279–1285.

Winawer, S., Fletcher, R., Rex, D., Bond, J., Burt, R., Ferrucci, J., Ganiats, T., Levin, T., Woolf, S., Johnson, D., Kirk, L., Litin, S., Simmang, C., Gastrointestinal Consortium Panel, 2003. Colorectal cancer screening and surveillance: clinical guidelines and rationale-update based on new evidence. Gastroenterology 124 (2), 544–560.

Xu, C., Pham, D., Prince, J., 2000. Medical image segmentation using deformable models. In: Sonka, M., Fitzpatrick, J. (Eds.), Handbook of Medical Imaging, vol. 2. Medical Image Processing and Analysis. SPIE, pp. 129–174.

Yao, J., Summers, R., 2007. Adaptive deformable model for colonic polyp segmentation and measurement on CT colonography. Med. Phys. 34 (5), 1655–1664.

Yao, J., Miller, M., Franaszek, M., Summers, R.M., 2004. Colonic polyp segmentation in CT colonography based on fuzzy clustering and deformable models. IEEE Trans. Med. Imaging 23 (11), 1344–1352.

Yao, J., Li, J., Summers, R.M., 2009. Colonic polyp detection and measurement using topographical height map. Pattern Recogn. 42 (6), 1029–1040.

Yao, J., Chowdhury, A.S., Aman, J., Summers, R.M., 2010. Reversible projection technique for colon unfolding. IEEE Trans. Biomed. Eng. 57 (12), 2861–2869.

Ye, X., Beddoe, G., Slabaugh, G., 2010. Automatic graph cut segmentation of lesions in CT using mean shift superpixels. J. Biomed. Imaging 19, pp. 1–14.

Yeshwant, S., Summers, R.M., Yao, J., Brickman, D., Choi, J.R., Pickhardt, P.J., 2006. Polyps: linear and volumetric measurement at CT colonography. Radiology 241, 802–811.

# DETECT CELLS AND CELLULAR BEHAVIORS IN PHASE CONTRAST MICROSCOPY IMAGES

# 21

## M. Chen[1] and T. Kanade[2]

*Computer Engineering Department, State University of New York, Albany, NY, USA[1]*
*Robotics Institute, Carnegie Mellon University, Pittsburgh, PA, USA[2]*

## CHAPTER OUTLINE

S. Kevin Zhou (Ed): Medical Image Recognition, Segmentation and Parsing. http://dx.doi.org/10.1016/B978-0-12-802581-9.00021-4

## 21.1 INTRODUCTION

Modern technology has enabled monitoring of large populations of live cells over extended time periods in experimental settings. Live imaging of cell populations growing in a culture vessel has been widely adopted in biomedical experiments. Such experiments create large numbers of time-lapse images, and the information embedded in these images holds tremendous promise for scientific discovery. The growing amount of such data calls for automated or semi-automated computer vision tools to detect and analyze the dynamic cellular processes, and to extract the information necessary for biomedical study.

Live cells are often of low contrast with little natural pigmentation; therefore, they usually need to be stained or fixed in order to be visible under bright field microscopy or fluorescence microscopy. However, fixing or staining may destroy the cells or introduce artifacts. Label-free imaging, in particular phase contrast microscopy, is highly desirable for live cell imaging because it allows cells to be examined in their natural state, and therefore enables live cell imaging over extended time periods. We focus in this chapter on analyzing time-lapse images from phase contrast microscopy.

While there is benefit in studying cellular behavior at the single cell level, we focus in this chapter on computer vision analysis of cellular dynamics in large cell populations. In particular, we are interested in data where the cell populations are dense, and there is considerable touching and occlusion among neighboring cells. Figure 21.1 is an example of such image data.

In studying cell populations in time-lapse imaging, manual analysis is not only tedious, the results from different people, and even the results from the same person, can also differ considerably. Moreover, it becomes impractical to manually analyze the behavior of each individual cell in a large population throughout an experiment over an extended time span. Much of the current practice in biomedical study is to manually examine a small subset of the entire cell population, and research conclusions are often drawn based on such manual analysis of a subset of the data. This is suboptimal; it could be misguided when the subset is not representative of the entire cell population. Therefore, automating the process for analyzing each individual cell and its behavior in large populations in time

**FIGURE 21.1**

Example image of dense cell population in phase contrast microscopy.

lapse label-free images is not only interesting and challenging computer vision research, it also has the potential of transforming how studies concerning cell population dynamics are done, and what they may discover.

## 21.2  COMPUTER VISION TASKS IN ANALYZING CELL POPULATIONS

The computer vision tasks necessary for understanding cellular dynamics include cell segmentation and cell behavior understanding, involving cell migration tracking, cell division detection, cell death detection, and cell differentiation detection. Dense cell population data present a set of challenges for each of the tasks. For instance, the cells may be touching or occluding each other, which makes it difficult to segment cells from one another, and the level of difficulty only increases as live cells proliferate and further increase the population density; detecting cell migration and division are also made more difficult when neighboring cells introduce ambiguity. Throughout the recent decade, much progress has been made toward automated analysis of cell populations in time-lapse label-free images; however, the technology is not yet ready to be deployed for biomedical researchers to use. In this chapter, we discuss the problem definition, the state of the art, and promising future directions for each of the computer vision tasks, with the intent to inspire and accelerate research on this important topic.

## 21.3  CELL SEGMENTATION

Segmenting individual cell regions from the background and neighboring cells is often the first step in the automated image analysis process. Before we discuss the computer vision approaches for cell segmentation, it is useful to briefly introduce how a phase contrast microscope works.

### 21.3.1  PHASE CONTRAST MICROSCOPY

We adopted the following description of phase contrast microscopy from Murphy (2001), Rost and Oldfield (2000), and Davidson and Keller (2001). Phase contrast microscopy is a contrast-enhancing optical technique that is often employed to produce high-contrast images of transparent specimens, such as live cells in culture. Its optical mechanism translates minute variations in phase into corresponding changes in amplitude, which can be visualized as differences in image intensity.

Figure 21.2 illustrates the optical mechanism of a phase contrast microscope. An incident wavefront in an illuminating light beam is divided into two components upon passing through a specimen. The primary component is an undeviated or undiffracted planar wavefront, referred to as the surround (S) wave, which passes through and around the specimen, but does not interact with the specimen. The other component is a deviated or diffracted spherical wavefront (D) wave, which is scattered in many directions that passes through the full aperture of the objective lens. The concept key to the design of a phase contrast microscope is the segregation of the surround and diffracted wavefronts emerging from the specimen, which are projected onto different locations in the objective rear focal plane. Moreover, the amplitude of the surround wave must be reduced and the phase advanced or retarded (by a quarter wavelength) in order to maximize the intensity differences between the specimen and the background in the image plane.

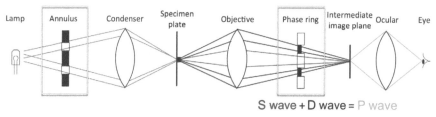

**FIGURE 21.2**

The optical mechanism of a phase contrast microscope. The red rays correspond to the S wave, the blue rays correspond to the D wave, the green rays correspond to the resulting particle P wave.

Two common effects in images produced by phase contrast microscopy are the halo and shade-off contrast patterns in which the observed intensity does not directly correspond to the optical path differences between the specimen and the surrounding medium in the culture vessel. These effects are generally referred to as *phase artifacts*. For instance, in positive phase contrast microscopy, the specimen typically appears darker than the surrounding medium when the refractive index of the specimen exceeds that of the medium. Therefore, bright halos usually appear along the boundaries between the specimen and the medium. However, if the phase retardation introduced by the specimen is large enough (e.g., a phase shift of the diffracted wave by approximately a half wavelength, instead of a quarter wavelength), interference between the diffracted waves and the surround waves can become constructive, making these specimens appear brighter than the surrounding medium. The presence of such artifacts, in addition to the ambiguity in defining boundaries when the cells are touching, occluding each other, or approaching confluence, makes automated segmentation in phase contrast microscopy images challenging.

## 21.3.2 AUTOMATED CELL SEGMENTATION

As observed in Murphy (2001), the imaging mechanisms of microscopy and natural images are different. Beside the phase artifacts as described here, as effective as phase contrast technique is at enhancing contrast between the specimen and the surrounding medium, the resultant images are still of low contrast. Segmentation techniques that operate directly on image intensity, such as thresholding, morphological operations, or edge detection (Wu et al., 1995; Li et al., 2008a; House et al., 2009), are not adequate when the intensity contrast is low. Algorithms that operate on image gradient, such as level sets or marker-controlled watershed (Yang et al., 2005; Xiong et al., 2006; Li et al., 2008a; Padfield et al., 2009b; Ambuhl et al., 2012), are more effective under low contrast, but are sensitive to initializations. Techniques that more explicitly detect the cells regions, such as Laplacian of Gaussian filters for cell blob detection (Smith et al., 2008) or active contour for obtaining cell boundaries (Grimm et al., 2003; Li et al., 2009), are unreliable when the cell boundaries are irregular or ambiguous. Algorithms adopting the graph cut framework suffer from oversegmentation due to regional minima (Ta et al., 2009; Lesko et al., 2010). To the best of our knowledge, cell segmentation algorithms that treat phase contrast microscopy images the same as natural images have not produced robust results on challenging data.

The most promising line of attack to date takes a *domain-specific* approach, mathematically models the imaging mechanism of phase contrast microscopy, and restores the *artifact-free* image by computing the phase retardation features. Yin et al. (2012) designed a linear imaging model to approximate the image formation process of phase contrast microscopy. Through a reconstruction approach, phase artifacts are removed based on this imaging model, the artifact free image is obtained, and cells can be segmented using plain thresholding.

The advance made by Yin et al. (2012) is significant because it represents a qualitative leap from previous developments that treat phase contrast microcopy images the same as general natural images. However, the proposed linear imaging model fails to segment bright cells in phase contrast microscopy images, such as cells that are undergoing division or death. This is because the linear imaging model assumes that the phase retardation caused by cells is small, which does not hold true when cells become thick during the proliferating or dying process and thus appear bright in phase contrast microscopy. In particular, Yin et al. (2012) models the surround S wave $l_S$ and the diffracted D wave $l_D$ as:

$$l_S = i\zeta_p A\, e^{i\beta}$$
$$l_D = \zeta_c A\, e^{i(\beta+\theta(x))} + (i\zeta_p - 1)\zeta_c A\, e^{i(\beta+\theta(x))} \cdot \text{airy}(r) \tag{21.1}$$

where $A$ and $\beta$ are the amplitude and phase of the incident light, respectively; $\zeta_c$ and $\zeta_p$ are the amplitude attenuation factors caused by cells and the phase ring, respectively; $\theta(x)$ is the phase retardation caused by the specimen at location $x$; and $\text{airy}(r)$ is an obscured Airy pattern (diffraction pattern with a bright region in the center surrounded by a series of concentric dark and bright rings (Yin et al., 2012)). The resulting particle wave $l_P$ is calculated as $l_P = l_S + l_D$.

During the imaging model derivation in Yin et al. (2012), the exponential terms in Eq. (21.1) are approximated using $e^{i\theta(x)} \approx 1 + i\theta(x)$. This approximation is valid only when the phase retardation $\theta(x)$ is close to 0. The assumption is not applicable to general cases because $\theta(x)$ is a function of the refractive indices and the thickness of cells, and varies depending on cell types and cellular stages such as proliferation or death.

Su et al. (2012) advanced this model further and proposed a phase contrast image restoration method based on the dictionary representation of diffraction patterns. The dictionary corresponds to different phase retardations caused by specimens during different cellular stages including proliferation and death.

We adopted the following derivation from Su et al. (2012). Let $\lambda$ denote the wavelength of the incident light; $t$ be the thickness of the cell; and $n_1$ and $n_2$ denote the refractive indices of the cell and the surrounding medium, respectively. The phase retardation $\theta$ can be calculated as:

$$\theta = \frac{2\pi}{\lambda}(n_1 - n_2)t$$

Different from the approach in Yin et al. (2012), instead of assuming that phase retardation $\theta$ is close to 0, the term $e^{i\theta(x)}$ in Eq. (21.1) is approximated using a linear combination of $\{e^{i\theta_m}\}_{m=0}^{M-1}$:

$$e^{i\theta(x)} = \sum_{m=0}^{M-1} \psi_m(x)\, e^{i\theta m}, \quad \text{s.t. } \psi_m(x) \geq 0$$

where $\{\theta_m\} = \{0, \frac{2\pi}{M}, \ldots, \frac{2m\pi}{M}, \ldots, \frac{2(M-1)\pi}{M}\}$.

**Table 21.1 Cell Segmentation Performance Comparison Between Approaches in Su et al. (2012) and Yin et al. (2012)**

| | Seq. 1 | | Seq. 2 | | Seq. 3 | |
|---|---|---|---|---|---|---|
| | Su et al. (2012) | Yin et al. (2012) | Su et al. (2012) | Yin et al. (2012) | Su et al. (2012) | Yin et al. (2012) |
| Average precision | 94.3% | 87.8% | 96.7% | 34.8% | 96.3% | 31.4% |
| Average recall | 92.1% | 85.8% | 94.2% | 15.7% | 93.2% | 34.7% |
| Average *Fscore* | 0.9319 | 0.8676 | 0.9543 | 0.1749 | 0.9472 | 0.3212 |

Now each pixel at position $x$ has a feature vector $\Psi(x) = \{\psi_0(x), \ldots, \psi_m(x), \ldots, \psi_{M-1}(x)\}$ that corresponds to diffraction patterns to describe it. Su et al. (2012) constructs the dictionary $\{H_m\}_{m=0}^{M-1}$, where $H_m$ is a basis of diffraction patterns with phase retardation $\theta_m$, and represent the observed image $g$ as:

$$g = \sum_{m=0}^{M-1} H_m \Psi_m, \quad \text{s.t. } \Psi_m \geq 0$$

Segmentation in Su et al. (2012) is achieved through clustering the feature vectors $\Psi(x)$. Table 21.1 (obtained from Su et al., 2012) compares the performance of the algorithms in Yin et al. (2012) and Su et al. (2012) on the same data. Performance measures produced by Su et al. (2012) are consistently superior, and the improvement is substantial when the data contains considerable cell division (Seq. 2) or cell death (Seq. 3). The method in Su et al. (2012) reliably detected bright cells where Yin et al. (2012) missed. By using a dictionary representation of different phase retardations that correspond to different cell types or cellular stages, Su et al. (2012) further strengthened the category of approach proposed by Yin et al. (2012) and made it robust.

Since the restored feature vectors $\Psi(x)$ correspond to phase retardation information, cells can be classified further into different cellular stages. Su et al. (2012) employed a combination of different phase retardations to detect cells of various cellular stages.

The progress made by Yin et al. (2012) and Su et al. (2012) has inspired a number of developments because the derived imaging model effectively maps a phase contrast microscopy image to a phase feature space. Nketia et al. (2014) and Su et al. (2013) investigated cell segmentation by clustering neighboring pixels' phase retardation feature vectors. Aggregating pixels eliminates the local redundancy of an image and reduces computational cost by decreasing the number of elements for clustering. Nketia et al. (2014) performs an oversegmentation of the phase contrast microscopy image using simple linear iterative clustering superpixels (Achanta et al., 2010). Each superpixel is initially characterized by the mean and covariance of the multidimensional pixel phase retardation feature vector within it, which is augmented by an adjacency graph to incorporate neighborhood information. Su et al. (2013) partitions a microscopy image into *atoms* by clustering neighboring pixels based on pairwise similarity of phase retardation features. Phase retardation is statistically homogeneous within an atom, and the atoms are used as elements for segmentation. Compared to a superpixel-based approach, the atoms are better able to preserve local structure of cell images, most importantly, cell regions and halos are aggregated into separate atoms.

The above algorithms estimating and utilizing optics-related features represent the state of the art in segmenting phase contrast microscopy images. As presented in Kaakinen et al. (2014), the image restoration process can drastically boost the segmentation performance of Watershed, active contours, or Otsu thresholding. However, parameters critical to the success of the algorithms need to be determined via a learning procedure for each type of cell under each particular microscope, and the process is compute intensive. As an alternative, Huh (2013) proposes diffraction pattern filtering, which shares a similar idea as the restoration methods in Yin et al. (2012) and Su et al. (2012), but is orders of magnitude more efficient. Given a phase contrast microscopy image, it first locates the foreground area by dilating the edge map of the image since the background generally has uniform texture without edges. It then computes the median pixel value of the background area, which is the inverse of the foreground area, and subtracts it from the entire image for flat-field correction. Finally, it filters a phase contrast microscopy image with the basis diffraction patterns $\{H_m\}_{m=0}^{M-1}$, as introduced by the phase contrast image formation model. Huh (2013) suggests that this method is more economical in terms of memory usage and compute time, and the result is more stable in that it uses each of the $M$ bases once and the order of filtering does not affect the results. On the other hand, the restoration-based method does not show such stability since it often selects different sets of bases in a different order (with repetition) for different images when they do not show similar levels of cell density. Moreover, the restoration method converges to local optima, so the results can vary depending on the optimization schemes used.

The convergence of these investigations suggests that the domain-specific approach of restoring artifact-free images is a propitious direction toward robust cell segmentation. The imaging model as expressed in Eq. (21.1) is evidently sufficient to capture the imaging mechanism of the phase contrast microscope; how to solve it efficiently and effectively for image restoration deserves more investigation.

## 21.3.3 INTERACTIVE CELL SEGMENTATION

As discussed in Section 21.3.2, the state-of-the-art automated cell segmentation algorithms need proper parameter setting to work, and there are still errors due to the complexity of the data. It is therefore useful to explore semi-automated approaches such as interactive cell segmentation. Both Nketia et al. (2014) and Su et al. (2013) investigated semi-supervised learning for cell segmentation: after clustering pixels into *elements* such as superpixels or atoms based on phase retardation feature vectors, semi-supervised classification is adopted by annotating a few *elements*; then identities of unlabeled *elements* are determined by propagating the labels from the annotated *elements*. Such user interaction is not straightforward for the user to determine what intervention would be the most effective such that human annotation can be minimized while the system performance is maximized. When the user has to bear the burden to make an analysis tool work, the usability of the tool is often compromised, and so is the usefulness of it.

Su et al. (2014) improved the interactive cell segmentation approach by proposing a framework for active semi-supervised learning. There are two interesting ideas in this framework. One is active sample selection for initial annotation by minimizing the expected prediction error bound. The particular tool used is transductive Rademacher complexity (El-Yaniv and Pechyony, 2007). This step helps pick the most informative samples for humans to annotate, which not only optimizes human intervention but also potentially improves the segmentation performance. The other interesting idea is active correction propagation. The uncertainty of the predicted label on each unlabeled sample is measured using entropy, and the most uncertain samples are corrected or verified by human. Such human corrections are propagated to other unlabeled data via an affinity graph, where similar errors are corrected based on the given human intervention. A straightforward implementation for such correction propagation would be to modify the affinity matrix and redo the label propagation; however, that would be too inefficient for an interactive application. Instead Su et al. (2014) proposed a correction propagation scheme by augmenting the affinity graph with auxiliary nodes called virtual supervisors, which was shown to converge quickly. It would be useful to evaluate this framework extensively on more data and more diverse data. If the premise of the framework holds, this may lead to an analysis tool that is practical enough to be used by biomedical researchers.

The developments made in theory and in systems toward cell segmentation in phase contrast microscopy images have been exciting and promising. As the first step in many cell image analysis tasks, robust and efficient cell segmentation would lay the foundation for the next steps toward cell behavior understanding.

## 21.4 CELLULAR BEHAVIOR UNDERSTANDING

The behavior of individual cells and how they interact with other cells can be observed *in vitro*. It is fundamental to biomedical researchers to study dynamic changes in cellular behavior. We discuss the state-of-the-art computer vision techniques for detecting and analyzing four types of cell behavior, as well as potential directions for further investigation.

### 21.4.1 CELL DIVISION

We obtained the following biology background information from (Alberts et al., 2002). Cell division is the separation of a cell into two daughter cells. In *eukaryotic* cells, that is, cells contain a nucleus and other organelles enclosed within membranes, cell division entails division of the nucleus closely followed by division of the *cytoplasm*, that is, contents that are outside the nucleus. More specifically, *mitosis* is the division of the nucleus of a eukaryotic cell, involving condensation of the DNA into chromosomes, and separation of the duplicated chromosomes to form two identical sets; *cytokinesis* is the division of the cytoplasm into two. In a typical cell, cytokinesis accompanies every mitosis event.

According to Alberts et al. (2002), the first visible sign of cytokinesis in an animal cell is the appearance of a pucker, or *cleavage furrow*, on the cell surface. The furrow deepens and spreads around the cell until it completely divides the cell in two. The central problem for a cell undergoing cytokinesis is to ensure that it occurs at the right time and in the right place. Cytokinesis must not occur too early, or it will disrupt the path of the separating chromosomes. It must also occur at the right place to separate the two segregating sets of chromosomes properly so that each daughter cell receives a complete set. Therefore, detecting the timing of cytokinesis is of significance to biomedical research.

In computer vision literature, the detection of cell division is often referred to as mitosis detection. We follow this convention for consistency. However, as described above, the meaning of cell division and mitosis are not identical in biology. There is work on mitosis detection in regions extracted from whole-slide images, including the mitosis detection contests at the International Conference on Pattern Recognition (ICPR) in 2012 and 2014. We are primarily interested in behaviors of live cells in a large

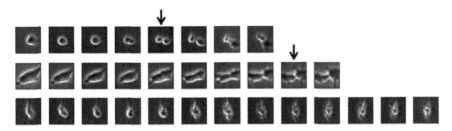

**FIGURE 21.3**

Positive (top two) and negative (bottom) examples of cell mitosis. Note that the mitosis process can vary in temporal lengths. Cytokinesis, the puckering of the cell membrane to split a cell into two, typically displays a figure eight shape as in the first sequence; however, a figure eight shape is often not clearly observed, as in the second sequence. The last sequence contains cell death, which exhibits similar visual characteristics to mitosis at the beginning of the process.

population over extended time periods, hence we focus this section on mitosis detection in live cell populations in time-lapse images from phase contrast microscopy.

Figure 21.3 shows a few examples of mitosis in time-lapse phase contrast microscopy images. Although there are variations among the examples, there appears to be a sequence of changes that can be observed during mitosis: the cell becomes brighter, more circular, and smaller, then exhibits a *figure-eight* shape before splitting into two cells. From the perspective of computer vision research, mitosis is an event, or an observable behavior, that happens over a number of temporally consecutive images. There is a spatiotemporal visual pattern to this event, but there are also considerable variations in this pattern to make automated detection difficult.

Since mitotic cells exhibit visual changes over time, one could formulate mitosis detection as a tracking problem. Such a scheme largely depends on the accuracy of cell tracking, which is a challenging problem by itself, particularly when analyzing large cell populations over extended time periods. We have observed more robust performance from approaches that formulate mitosis detection as an event detection/behavior understanding problem, and search for spatiotemporal patterns that match the sequence of appearance changes that typically accompany mitosis. Li et al. (2008b) extracted volumetric Haar-like features from spatiotemporal patches over the entire image space, and employed a fast cascade learning framework for classification. Due to the search over the entire image space, it is inefficient and sometimes ineffective. Debeir et al. (2008) reduced the search space by first detecting candidate mitotic cell regions based on brightness changes and linking the candidate regions in consecutive frames into candidate linkages. Each candidate linkage was then validated based on its length. This is more efficient than Li et al. (2008b) because of the reduced search space; however, validating candidate linkages based on their lengths is not a robust criterion for detecting mitosis. In recent years, a number of algorithms utilizing conditional random fields (CRF) have yielded strong performance. We discuss a few state-of-the-art techniques.

### 21.4.1.1 Detecting mitosis and birth event

As explained previously, for a cell undergoing cytokinesis, it is critical to ensure that it occurs at the right time and right place. It is important for biomedical researchers to know the timing and location of each *birth event*, that is, in which frame of the time-lapse image sequence and at what image coordinates that a mother cell separates into two daughter cells. Although the timing of birth events could be determined after a mitotic event has been identified, as in a *two-pass* approach, Huh et al. (2011) and Huh and Chen (2011) have demonstrated that simultaneously determining both the occurrence of mitosis and the timing of the birth event achieves better performance.

While Huh and Chen (2011) is a significant improvement over Huh et al. (2011) at handling data under high cell confluence, that is, when a high percentage of the space in a tissue culture vessel is occupied by cells, their underlying strategy is consistent. Since candidate detection can reduce the search space and improve efficiency, as demonstrated in Debeir et al. (2008), the first step in the analysis is to employ image processing techniques to locate candidate patches in the images, and form candidate patch sequences in the time-lapse image sequence. Then a classifier is designed to simultaneously determine if there is a mitosis event in a candidate patch sequence, and if so, in which particular image frame the birth event occurred. CRF is a good fit for this task because it is capable of predicting a sequence of labels for a sequence of samples while taking into account the context of samples, such as the neighboring samples.

In Huh et al. (2011), the proposed classifier is termed event detection conditional random field (EDCRF), the structure of which is shown in Figure 21.4. The main idea of EDCRF as introduced in Huh et al. (2011) is: if there is a mitotic event, visual changes before and after the mitotic event are separately modeled; otherwise, the entire visual transition is modeled together. This strategy is useful when an event shows a different pattern of visual change before and after the event. In the case of mitosis, before a birth event, a mitotic cell becomes brighter, rounder, and smaller; while after the birth event, two newborn cells become darker and more stretched. Therefore, by separately modeling mitotic and postmitotic stages, not only are the disparate visual changes more precisely modeled, but also the timing of a birth event is explicitly modeled. We show the formulation of EDCRF in Huh et al. (2011): suppose that $n$ candidate patch sequence and label pairs $\{(x_1, y_1), (x_2, y_2), \ldots, (x_n, y_n)\}$ are given, and each label $y_i$ is defined as

$$y_i = \begin{cases} p, & \text{if the } p\text{th patch of } x_i \text{ contains a birth event} \\ 0, & \text{if there exists no birth event in } x_i \end{cases}$$

Each sequence $x = (x_1, x_2, \ldots, x_m)$ consists of $m$ candidate patches where $x_j$ denotes the $j$th patch ($m$ can be different for different sequences, i.e., candidate sequences can have different lengths).

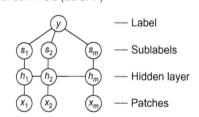

Event Detection Conditional
Random Field (EDCRF)

**FIGURE 21.4**

Graphical representation of event detection conditional random field (EDCRF).

We assume hidden variables $h = (h_1, h_2, \ldots, h_m)$, and sublabels $s = (s_1, s_2, \ldots, s_m)$, where $h_j$ and $s_j$ correspond to $x_j$. When a sequence label $y$ is given, the sublabels $s_1, s_2, \ldots, s_m$ are defined as

$$
S_j = \begin{cases}
N & \text{if } y = 0 \\
B & \text{if } y > 0 \text{ and } j < y \\
A & \text{if } y > 0 \text{ and } j \geq y
\end{cases}
$$

where labels $N, B$, and $A$ represent *No birth event*, *Before the birth event*, and *After the birth event (including the birth event)*, respectively. As a result, if there exists a birth event in a given candidate sequence, the sublabels before the event are set to be $B$ and the other sublabels are set to be $A$. Otherwise, all the sublabels are set to be $N$. Under these definitions, a latent conditional model for each sequence becomes:

$$
P(y|x, \theta) = P(s|x, \theta) = \sum_h P(s|h, x, \theta) P(h|x, \theta)
$$

where $\theta$ is a set of parameters of the model.

The latent dynamic conditional random field (LDCRF) scheme proposed by Morency et al. (2007) was adopted to make the modeling efficient. It restricts that each subclass label is associated only with hidden states in a disjoint set $\mathcal{H}_s$, such that

$$
P(s|\mathbf{h}, \mathbf{x}, \theta) = \begin{cases}
1, & \text{if } \forall h_j \in \mathcal{H}_{s_j} \\
0, & \text{otherwise}
\end{cases}
$$

The proposed model is thus simplified as

$$
P(y|x, \theta) = \sum_{h : \forall h_j \in \mathcal{H}_{S_j}} P(h|x, \theta)
$$

Now $P(h|x, \theta)$ can be defined using the typical CRF formulation as

$$
P(h|x, \theta) = \frac{1}{Z} \exp \left( \sum_{j=1}^m f^{(s)}(h_j, x, j) \cdot \theta^{(s)}(h_j) + \sum_{j=2}^m f^{(t)}(h_{j-1}, h_j, x, j) \theta^{(t)}(h_{j-1}, h_j) \right)
$$

where $Z$ is a partition function. $f^{(s)}(h_j, x, j)$ and $f^{(t)}(h_{j-1}, h_j, x, j)$ are a state and a transition function, respectively. $\theta^{(s)}$ and $\theta^{(t)}$ are the parameters of state and transition functions, respectively, and $\theta = \{\theta^{(s)}, \theta^{(t)}\}$. Sublevel transitions are restricted to be $\{N, N\}$, $\{B, B\}$, $\{B, A\}$, or $\{A, A\}$, which represent *no event*, *before the event*, *during the event*, and *after the event*, in the order given. No other transitions are allowed besides these four.

The learning stage obtains the optimal $\theta^*$. To test a new sequence $x$, the probabilities of the conditional model with all possible $y$ and $\theta^*$ are computed as follows:

$$
P(y = 0|x, \theta^*) = P(s_1 = N, \ldots, s_m = N|x, \theta^*)
$$
$$
= P(s_1 = N|x, \theta^*) = \sum_{h_1 \in H_N} P(h_1|x, \theta^*)
$$

Note that $s_1 = N$ leads to $s_2, \ldots, s_m = N$, under the aforementioned restricted transition rule. Similarly

$$P(y = 1|x, \theta^*) = P(s_1 = A, \ldots, s_m = A|x, \theta^*)$$
$$= P(s_1 = A|x, \theta^*) = \sum_{h_1 \in H_A} P(h_1|x, \theta^*)$$

and for $j = 2, \ldots, m$

$$P(y = j|x, \theta^*) = P(s_1 = B, \ldots, s_{j-1} = B, s_j = A, \ldots, s_m = A|x, \theta^*)$$
$$= P(s_{j-1} = B, s_j = A|x, \theta^*)$$
$$= P(s_{j-1} = B|x, \theta^*) - P(s_{j-1} = B, s_j = B|x, \theta^*)$$
$$= P(s_{j-1} = B|x, \theta^*) - P(s_j = B|x, \theta^*)$$
$$= \sum_{h_{j-1} \in H_B} P(h_{j-1}|x_r \theta^*) - \sum_{h_j \in H_B} P(h_j|x_r \theta^*)$$

To detect mitosis occurrence in each candidate patch sequence, compare $P(y = 0|x, \theta^*)$ and $1 - P(y = 0|x, \theta^*)$. If the former is greater, EDCRF determines that there is no mitotic event in the sequence. Otherwise, the temporal localization of the birth event is established by comparing $P(y = 1|x, \theta^*), \ldots,$ and $P(y = m|x, \theta^*)$. More formally,

$$y^* = \begin{cases} 0, & \text{if } P\left(y = 0|x, \theta^*\right) > 0.5 \\ \arg\max_{y=1,\ldots,m} P(y|x, \theta^*), & \text{otherwise} \end{cases}$$

Huh et al. (2011) compared the performance of EDCRF for mitosis occurrence detection to that of a previous work for mitosis occurrence detection using hidden conditional random field (HCRF) (Liu et al., 2010). EDCRF demonstrated superior performance in terms of precision, recall, $F$-measure, and the AUC of the PR-curve. A Student's paired $t$-test on the $F$-measures shows that the performance improvement is statistically significant at the significance level 0.01 ($p = 0.0008$). The intuition is that the information on birth event timing can complement mitosis occurrence detection. The design of EDCRF simultaneously models the existence of a mitosis event and the timing of a birth event, whereas HCRF cannot utilize the information on birth event timing due to its limited expression power.

Huh et al. (2011) also compared the performance for birth event identification between EDCRF and two different two-pass approaches. In these two-pass approaches, the detection of mitosis occurrence and the temporal localization of birth events are sequentially performed. HCRF as employed in Liu et al. (2010) was applied for mitosis occurrence detection, then one approach adopts support vector machines (SVM) to identify birth events, while another utilizes CRF to identify birth events. As reported in Huh et al. (2011), EDCRF consistently outperforms the two-pass approaches in terms of precision, recall, $F$-measure, and AUC of the PR-curve regardless of cell type. Student's paired $t$-tests on the $F$-measures show that the performance improvements are statistically significant at the significance level 0.01. These two-pass approaches suffer from the fact that SVM is not capable of modeling temporal dynamics and CRF does not capture the hidden state structures in candidate patch sequences. Therefore, when mitosis occurrence detection is wrong, the identification of a birth event is not meaningful.

### 21.4.1.2 Detecting mitosis and birth event under high confluence

The advances achieved by Huh et al. (2011) were significant compared to previous work; however, if cell confluence increases beyond a certain level this approach is no longer effective at extracting mitosis candidates and validating them. The reason mitosis detection is more challenging in high confluence cell populations under time-lapse phase contrast microscopy is twofold. One reason is that the search space is significantly larger. Since crowds of deformable cells are moving, touching, occluding each other, and bright halos appear and disappear among the cells, candidate regions would need to be more carefully selected. The other reason is that the previously distinctive visual properties of birth events are no longer reliable. Under high confluence, the appearances of cells are determined both by the external stimuli from neighboring cells and the internal states of the cells, thereby exhibiting a high degree of variation. To resolve such ambiguity, the change of a mitotic cell's visual properties over time must be more closely examined.

Huh and Chen (2011) tackled this problem by directly extracting and validating birth event candidates, instead of mitosis candidates as was done in Huh et al. (2011). It determines when (in which image frame in the time-lapse sequence) and where (at which $x$ and $y$ image coordinates) birth events occur through three steps: detection of birth event candidates, incorporation of temporal information, and validation of the candidates. It first applies cascade filtering to detect image patches that exhibit visual properties of birth events, thereby reducing the search space. Secondly, it creates candidate patch sequences by linking patches in the neighboring image frames that precede and succeed the patches that contain birth event candidates. For candidate validation, similar to Huh et al. (2011), Huh and Chen (2011) designed a graphical probabilistic model to simultaneously capture the most probable timing of a birth event and the appearance changes of the candidate mother and daughter cells over time. Huh and Chen (2011) named the model two-labeled hidden conditional random field (TL-HCRF), as shown in Figure 21.5.

If EDCRF is what enabled (Huh et al., 2011) to outperform competing techniques, Huh and Chen (2011) achieves strong performance owing to both TL-HCRF and robust birth event candidate sequence detection prior to validation.

Figure 21.6 displays the appearance model of a birth event as proposed in Huh and Chen (2011). It employs a combination of two small circles, one large circle, and one ellipse, to explicitly represent the two daughter cell regions, the halo region, and the contacting region of the two daughter cells,

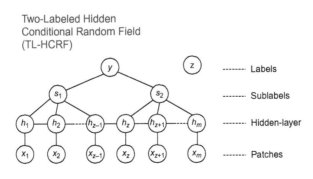

**FIGURE 21.5**

Graphical representation of two-labeled hidden conditional random field (TL-HCRF).

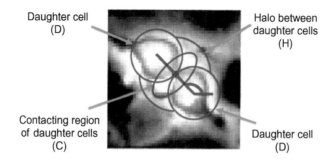

Daughter cell (D)

Halo between daughter cells (H)

Contacting region of daughter cells (C)

Daughter cell (D)

**FIGURE 21.6**

The appearance model of a birth event as proposed in Huh and Chen (2011).

respectively. Based on this model, four features were computed for each image patch: brightness, brightness change, brightness of the contacting region of two daughter cells, and asymmetry. These four features were chosen based on domain knowledge, and were proven effective at eliminating image background and most nonmitotic cells from the search space. This step is important both for efficiency and for the validation procedure to be effective.

The main idea of TL-HCRF as presented in Huh and Chen (2011) is as follows. Given a sequence $X$, TL-HCRF has two label variables $y$ and $z$; $y$ indicates whether $X$ contains an event, and $z$ indicates which patch is the most likely to contain the event. More formally, during training,

$$y = \begin{cases} 1, & \text{if } X \text{ contains a birth event} \\ 0, & \text{otherwise} \end{cases}$$

$$z = \begin{cases} p, & \text{if the } p\text{th patch of } X \text{ contains a birth event} \\ q, & \text{if there is no birth event in } X \end{cases}$$

During testing, $y$ is not observed; rather, it is an unknown that needs to be inferred. On the other hand, $z$ is given as the timing of the birth event candidate, that is:

$$z = q$$

Hence, if a birth event exists in a candidate patch sequence and the information is known via annotation (as it is during the training phase), $z$ is known as its timing; if there is no birth event or the information is not known, $z$ is set as the timing of the birth event candidate in the candidate patch sequence. Note that in Huh and Chen (2011) the candidate patch sequence is that of a birth event, not a mitotic event as defined in Huh et al. (2011).

Suppose that observation $X$ consists of $m$ patches, $X = (x_1, x_2, \ldots, x_m)$, where $x_j$ denotes the $j$th patch. $H$ is a set of hidden states, $H = (h_1, h_2, \ldots, h_m)$, where $h_j$ corresponds to $x_j$ for $j = 1, \ldots, m$; $s_1$ and $s_2$ are two sublabels, as shown in Figure 21.5. For a given $z$, $s_1$ is connected with $h_1, h_2, \ldots, h_{z-1}$, while $s_2$ is connected with $h_z, h_{z+1}, \ldots, h_m$. The values of $s_1$ and $s_2$ depend on the label of $y$:

$$\begin{cases} s_1 = N, & s_2 = N & \text{if } y = 0 \\ s_1 = B, & s_2 = A & \text{if } y = 1 \end{cases}$$

Similar to the definition in EDCRF, labels $N$, $B$, and $A$ correspond to *No event, Before the event*, and *After the event (including the event)*, respectively. Therefore, if there exists a birth event in a candidate patch sequence, the patches and hidden variables whose timing precedes the event are associated with sublabel $B$, while those who succeed the event (including the event) are associated with sublabel $A$; if there is no birth event in a candidate patch sequence, all the patches and hidden variables are associated with sublabel $N$.

During testing, label $z$ is set as the timing of the birth event candidate, so the event timing is fixed rather than being inferred. Inference is performed on $y$ only to determine if a birth event occurred in the image frame where the birth event candidate is. Under these definitions, Huh and Chen (2011) developed a latent conditional model:

$$P(y|X, z; \theta) = P(s_1, s_2|X, z; \theta) = \sum_h P(h, s_1, s_2|X, z; \theta)$$

where $\theta$ is a set of parameters of the model, $\theta = \{\theta^{(s)}, \theta^{(t)}, \theta^{(1)}\}$. $\theta^{(s)}$ and $\theta^{(t)}$ are parameters of the state and transition functions, respectively; while $\theta^{(1)}$ is the parameter associated with the sublabels. As derived in Huh and Chen (2011), the optimal parameter $\theta^*$ can be obtained during the training phase using belief propagation.

To validate each birth event candidate patch sequence extracted from test images, TL-HCRF computes the probability that the birth event candidate in the candidate patch sequence is indeed a birth event. Let the candidate patch sequence be $X = (x_1, x_2, \ldots, x_m)$ where $x_j$ denotes the $j$th patch. $z$ is set as the timing of the birth event candidate, that is, the $z$th patch in the candidate patch sequence contains the birth event candidate. The conditional probability $P(y = 1|x, z; \theta^*)$ is computed to infer $y$, the variable indicating birth event occurrence, where $\theta^*$ is the optimal model parameter obtained during training. Based on the conditional probability, the label $y$ is determined to be:

$$y^* = \begin{cases} 1, & \text{if } P(y = 1|x, z; \theta^*) > 0.5 \\ 0, & \text{otherwise} \end{cases}$$

As shown above, if the conditional probability is less than or equal to 0.5, the candidate birth event is determined to be a nonbirth event. In the case where there is a birth event, there could be multiple spatiotemporally adjacent candidate patch sequences with conditional probabilities greater than 0.5. To avoid duplicate detection of the same birth event, Huh and Chen (2011) constructed a graph in which each node represents a birth event candidate. An edge is added between two nodes if the candidates are closely located in the spatiotemporal volume. In each connected component in the graph, only the birth event candidate associated with the greatest conditional probability is labeled a birth event; the others are considered duplicate detections and labeled as nonbirth events.

Compared to previous probabilistic models including EDCRF, TL-HCRF achieves superior performance by explicitly representing the timing of a birth event, whether it is given by annotation or as the timing of a birth event candidate. EDCRF can model birth event timing, but it assumes that a birth event can occur in any patch in a candidate patch sequence and does not make use of the information on the timing of birth event candidates. Moreover, in order to make the inference of all sublabels tractable, EDCRF restricts each sublabel to be associated only with a disjoint set of hidden states, which may further compromise its performance.

Huh and Chen (2011) demonstrated that TL-HCRF not only achieves higher $F$-measure and AUC of PR-curve than EDCRF, it is also more compute efficient. The advantage is more significant for cell image data under high confluence. At high cell confluence, bright halos are often observed along the boundaries of cells in contact with one another, and bright cells are sometimes touching as well. In such cases, the method proposed in Huh et al. (2011) often fails at precisely locating birth event candidates. This is because it computes the center of a birth event candidate as the center of a bright patch, which under high confluence may contain halos or a part of another cell in addition to the cell of interest. Moreover, without domain knowledge-based birth event detection, the method in Huh et al. (2011) often treats halos between cells as birth event candidates. When more spurious birth event candidates are included, the performance suffers. Besides, since the orientation of birth events is not taken into account in Huh et al. (2011), it is not effective at classifying ambiguous cases, which are more prevalent under high confluence. On the other hand, the approach proposed in Huh and Chen (2011) detects birth event candidates not only using brightness cue but also via cascaded filtering, taking into account the orientation of birth events, thereby obtaining fewer number but higher quality birth event candidates.

It is worth noting that Huh and Chen (2011) report comparable strong performance on different cell types, even though birth events of different cell types exhibit different visual characteristics. This indicates that the algorithm may be applicable to various cell types as long as manual annotation is available. As the amount of reagent varies causing the culture condition to change, the algorithm demonstrates stable performance, which suggests that it is robust to small variations in appearances.

### 21.4.1.3 Detecting mitosis without temporal inference

In Sections 21.4.1.1 and 21.4.1.2, we discussed state-of-the-art approaches that treat mitosis detection as an event detection/behavior understanding problem, and employ probability models suitable for temporal sequence analysis to detect and localize the events. Those approaches are powerful yet can be compute intensive. In this section, we introduce recent work that detects mitotic cells without temporal inference (Liu et al., 2013).

Analogues to the techniques in Huh et al. (2011) and Huh and Chen (2011), only in the spatial domain, Liu et al. (2013) first extracts candidate mitotic cell regions to reduce the search space. In particular, it employs a cell segmentation scheme similar to that of Yin et al. (2012) and Su et al. (2012), except that the restored artifact-free image is the *inverted* phase contrast microscopy image, because mitotic cells in the inverted phase contrast microscopy image exhibit the same visual characteristics as normal nonmitotic cells in positive phase contrast microscopy. For each candidate region, a set of image features $X$ is computed and represented as a linear combination of bases $\Phi^*$ with coefficient $\omega$. As described in Liu et al. (2013), $\Phi^*$ is a dictionary of bases where each basis characterizes a certain visual pattern of mitotic cell region or nonmitotic cell region such that an image can be sparsely reconstructed using this dictionary. $\omega$ reflects the correlation between image feature set $X$ and the bases $\Phi^*$; therefore, it is utilized as the feature representation of each candidate mitotic cell region. The optimal bases $\Phi^*$ and reconstruction coefficients $\varpi = \{\omega_i^*\}_{i=1}^N$ are computed from the training samples by optimizing a convex objective function (Liu et al., 2013). An SVM classifier is trained with $\varpi = \{\omega_i^*\}_{i=1}^N$, and applied to classify each candidate region, represented by its coefficient $\omega$, as being a mitotic cell or not.

Experiments reported in Liu et al. (2013) demonstrate that using raw pixel intensity to form the image feature set $X$ yielded better performance than computed feature descriptors including SIFT, GIST, and HoG. This suggests that the representation using $\Phi^*$ and $\omega$ can potentially avoid the nontrivial task of feature extraction for deformable object recognition. The performance on mitosis detection is close to that of EDCRF (Huh et al., 2011), although the timing of a birth event cannot be determined using this approach alone.

The progress made toward automated mitosis detection in phase contrast microscopy images has been steady and exciting. State-of-the-art algorithms can typically achieve around 90% precision and recall on challenging datasets. A common theme among the state-of-the-art algorithms is to detect candidates to reduce the search space and remove spurious detection, compute feature descriptors that capture the visual characteristics, and then employ a classifier for candidate validation. To make further improvement, a few critical issues need to be investigated: (1) how to represent mitoses of different cell types with different appearances and which may exhibit different visual changes throughout the process; (2) the random fields-based methods cannot take into account nonlinearity among features and could therefore compromise the performance of sequence classification; (3) feature representation and model learning have been separately treated in existing approaches. It could be useful to examine what visual feature to extract and what feature representation to adopt that could maximally benefit the learning of the object model.

Robust and efficient detection of mitosis is not only important for monitoring cell proliferation, but it is also critical to accurate tracking of cell migration in a large population over extended time periods. We will witness the interplay of these two analysis tasks in later sections of this chapter.

## 21.4.2 CELL MIGRATION

Cell migration is a cellular process by which cells translate from one location to another. It is associated with important biological phenomenon including wound healing and immune responses. Traditionally cell migration is evaluated in time-lapse images, involving a manual procedure to track one or more cells throughout the image sequence. Automated or semi-automated tracking of cell migration alleviates manual labor, allows for high-throughput data analysis, and potentially enables the study and engineering of an individual cell's fate in a population. We examine state-of-the-art computer vision techniques that track large populations of cells in time-lapse phase contrast microscopy images.

Tracking multiple moving objects over extended time periods is difficult, automatically or interactively, let alone tracking hundreds to thousands of cells in a population where cells are touching, overlapping, proliferating, and moving in and out of the field of view. Before diving into individual algorithms, it is important to define proper metrics for evaluating cell migration tracking performance.

Most current literature reports trajectory-level evaluations, that is, how well human annotated ground-truth cells are followed by computer-generated trajectories. This is useful for evaluating the correctness of spatial correspondence between cells in successive image frames; however, it does not capture the *developmental correctness* such as the mother-daughter relationship, as encapsulated in the cell *lineage tree*. Figure 21.7 is an example of a cell lineage tree with its vertices representing cells and its branches encoding mother-daughter relations, where each branching is caused by a cell mitotic event. Cell tracking performance evaluation metrics that take into account cell lineage would be more rigorous than simple trajectory-level assessment. However, due to the extra dimension of intercell relationship, it is also more challenging to achieve high accuracy using such metrics

We introduce a set of lineage-level evaluation criteria as proposed in Bise et al. (2011), namely *target effectiveness*, *track purity*, and *mitosis branching correctness*. To compute *target effectiveness*, first associate each human annotated target cell with a computer-generated track that contains the most

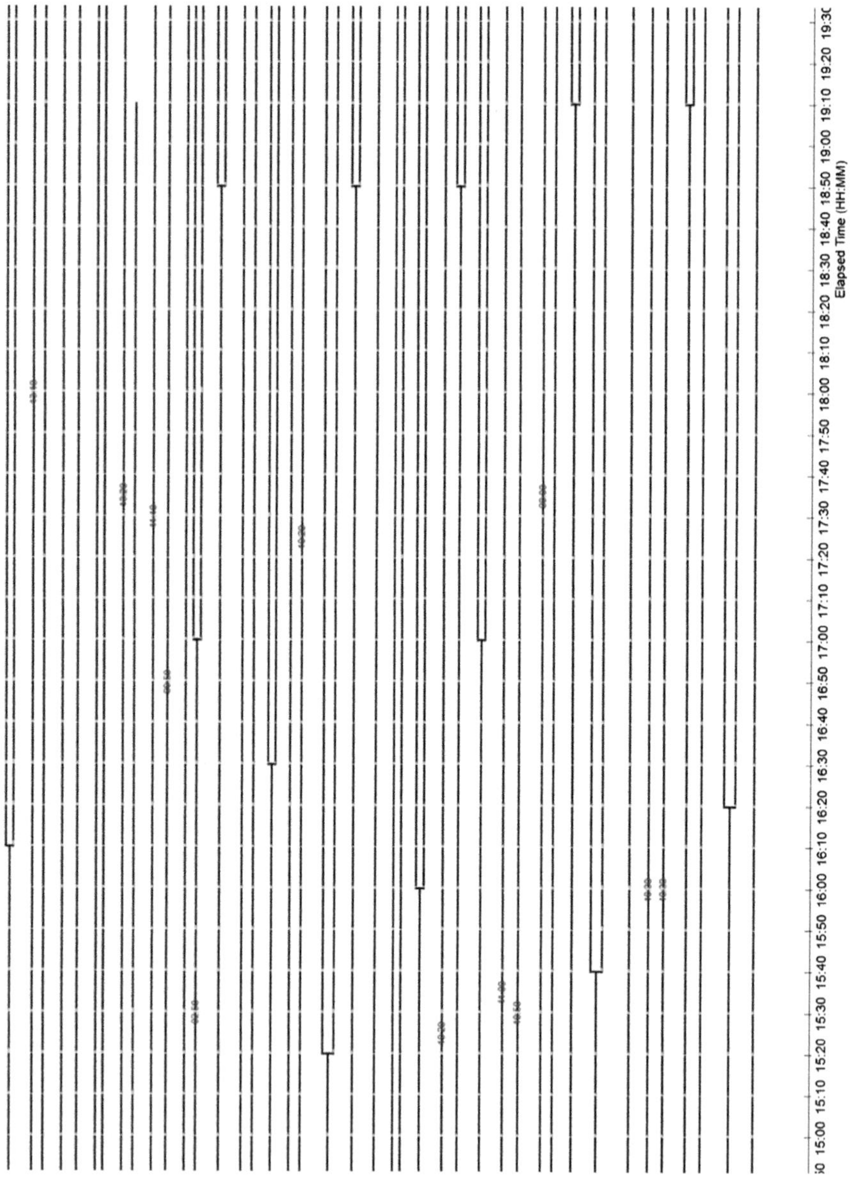

**FIGURE 21.7**

Example of a cell lineage tree.

observations of that target cell. Then target effectiveness is computed as the number of observations of the target cell in the associated track divided by the total number of image frames that contain the annotated target. It indicates how many frames that contain the target are followed by computer-generated tracks, analogues to the concept of *recall*. *Track purity* is defined in Bise et al. (2011) in the same manner to reflect how well computer-generated tracks are followed by human annotated targets, analogues to the concept of *precision*. Note that track purity can only be measured when all cells in a time-lapse image sequence have been manually annotated and tracked. These two metrics evaluate the trajectory-level performance.

To assess lineage-level performance, in particular, the accuracy of mother-daughter relationships between branches in the lineage tree, Bise et al. (2011) defined *mitotic branching correctness* as illustrated in Figure 21.8. A mitosis branching is considered correctly detected if the time distance between the human annotated birth event and the computer detected birth event is below a preset threshold. Then *mitotic branching correctness* is computed as the number of the correctly detected mitosis branching divided by the total number of mitotic events in the human annotated ground truth. This metric evaluates the lineage-level performance.

The research problem of computer vision tracking of cell populations in time-lapse images has attracted much effort over the years, and much progress has been made. However, unlike the cases for cell segmentation or cell mitosis detection, the performance of tracking individual cells in a large population typically degrades over time even at the trajectory-level, and there has not emerged a line of attack that achieves robust performance at the lineage-level. The magnitude of the challenge is nontrivial: errors typically exist in cell detection/segmentation, cells are deformable so the appearances can change drastically, cells in a population may touch or occlude each other, cells may divide or merge, and cells may leave or enter the field of view at random. Besides being a tantalizing research problem, there is real need in understanding individual cell behavior in a population over time for biomedical study, and manual tracking of thousands of cells over thousands of images is not scalable; therefore, automated tracking, albeit elusive, is a worthy pursuit. We discuss several schools of approach and their strengths and weaknesses in the following sections.

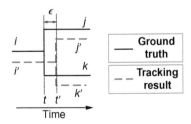

**FIGURE 21.8**

The mitotic branching correctness measures the accuracy of mother-daughter relationships between tree branches. Black lines indicate ground truth trajectory, and red dotted lines indicate tracking results. In the ground truth, there is a birth event at time $t$ in which cell $i$ divides into cell $j$ and $k$. If the automatic tracking results include a birth event of the cell $i'$ that corresponds to cell $i$, and children $j'$, $k'$ of the cell $i'$ also correspond to cell $j$ and $k$, and the time distance between the two birth events, $\epsilon = //t - t'//$, is close enough (i.e., $\epsilon < \theta\epsilon$), it is considered as a correctly detected mitosis branching. The correctness of mitotic branching is the number of the correctly detected mitosis branching divided by the total number of the mitotic events as annotated by human.

### 21.4.2.1 Cell tracking by predictive filtering

Kalman filtering (Roweis and Ghahramani, 1999) and particle filtering (Arulampalam et al., 2002) are commonly employed for multi-target tracking tasks. Variations of them have been applied to cell tracking with respectable performance (Li et al., 2006; Shen et al., 2006; Smal et al., 2008). Since tracking is achieved by estimating the most probable current state from the posterior probability distribution computed based on a predefined model of the object motion, filtering-based methods have difficulty when the motion model is undefined or highly variable for the cell type.

### 21.4.2.2 Cell tracking by model-based contour evolution

Model-based tracking is achieved by constructing a model of the object and updating the model in the successive image frames. Within the context of cell tracking, model-based methods include those using active contours (Dormann et al., 2002.; Mukherjee et al., 2004; Dufour et al., 2005; Padfield et al., 2009b; Dzyubachyk et al., 2010), and those using mean-shift (Debeir et al., 2005). Mean-shift-based cell tracking obtains good performance when the cell shape can be well defined and cell migration speed is not fast; otherwise, it is not effective. Active contour-based tracking is more powerful at modeling cells whose shape is highly deformable. It performs tracking by defining an energy function associated with a cell contour in the previous image frame, and minimizing the energy function to locate the same cell's contour in the current image frame. The weakness of active contour-based methods is that they are prone to be stuck in local minima, which is not uncommon in the presence of phase artifacts. Methods that help escape from local minima include simulated annealing (Press et al., 2007), but they also incur considerable computational cost. Although model-based contour evolution approaches are robust to certain topology changes, they are not equipped to handle cells undergoing mitosis or cells leaving/entering the field of view.

### 21.4.2.3 Cell tracking by frame-to-frame association

Segmentation-based frame-to-frame association is the most efficient approach for tracking if cells can be reliably detected. After detecting cell regions, linear programming with multiple hypotheses (Al-Kofahi et al., 2006; Li et al., 2008a) and minimum-cost flow framework (Padfield et al., 2009a) have been investigated to resolve data association across image frames. Although frame-to-frame association methods have demonstrated reasonable tracking performance using the trajectory-based evaluation metric, they are not effective at dealing with cells touching or dividing; hence, their performance suffers under the lineage-based evaluation metric.

### 21.4.2.4 Cell tracking by global association

Bise et al. (2011) proposed a global spatio-temporal data association algorithm to obtain cell trajectories and lineage trees. It first employs the method developed in Yin et al. (2012) to segment cell regions, and applies the method proposed in Huh et al. (2011) to detect cell mitosis and birth events. Then it constructs *tracklets*, that is, short trajectories, by linking cell segmentation results using frame-to-frame association. Tracklets are considered reliable if cell regions in successive image frames are sufficiently close in spatial location, and there are no extra ambiguous detections near the cell regions. The set of reliable tracklets is denoted as $X = \{X_i\}$. Let $T = \{T_k\}$ be a hypothesis set of cell lineage trees over the entire time-lapse image sequence. Each tree $T_k$ corresponds to a cell progeny from the ancestor to all of its descendants, and is formed by associated tracklets. Given the observation tracklet set $X$, the posteriori probability is maximized to solve for the best hypothesis $T^*$:

$$T^* = \arg\max_T P(T|X)$$

$$= \arg\max_T P(X|T)P(T)$$

$$= \arg\max_T \prod_{x_i \in X} P(x_i|T) \prod_{T_k \in T} P_{\text{Tree}}(T_k)$$

where likelihoods of input tracklets are conditionally independent given $T$, and $T_k \in T$ cannot overlap with each other, that is, $T_k \cap T_l = \emptyset, \forall\, k \neq l$. Bise et al. (2011) solves this maximum-a-posteriori problem using linear programming.

Evaluated on the same data as used in Li et al. (2008a), the global association method (Bise et al., 2011) obtains on average 19% improvement in terms of target effectiveness, and 27% improvement in terms of mitosis branching correctness. The intuition is that if there is a false positive segmentation near a mitotic cell, the frame-to-frame association method may incur a mother-daughter relationship error. Since the global association method observes the cell for several frames after the apparent birth event, it can recognize that one of the daughter cells is a false positive, assuming false positives typically would disappear, and gains better mitosis branching correctness. Moreover, the global data association framework is able to link tracklets to form not only sequential structures but also tree structures, resulting in both cell migration trajectories and lineage trees.

Although cell migration is likely the most studied cellular behavior, the performance of existing approaches over large cell populations has not reached the same level as cell segmentation or mitosis detection, largely due to the enormity of the challenge. It is unlikely that significant performance improvement can be attained via further motion modeling or object modeling; rather, a holistic approach considering the interplay of relevant cellular behaviors may hold the promise for more robust cell tracking performance at both the trajectory level and the lineage level.

## 21.4.3 CELL DEATH

We obtained the following definition from Kroemer et al. (2015): cell death is the event of the biological cell ceasing to carry out its functions. This may be the result of the natural process of old cells dying and being replaced by new ones, or may result from such factors as disease, localized injury, or the death of the organism to which the cells belong. *Apoptosis* describes a specific morphological aspect of cell death that is accompanied by *rounding-up* of the cell, *retraction* of pseudopodes, *reduction* of cellular volume, chromatin condensation, nuclear *fragmentation*, little or no ultrastructural modifications of cytoplasmic organelles, plasma membrane *blebbing* (but maintenance of its integrity until the final stages of the process), and engulfment by resident phagocytes (*in vivo*). Hence, the term apoptosis should be applied exclusively to cell death events that occur while manifesting several of these morphological features. It is worth noting that it is not correct to assume that "programmed cell death" and "apoptosis" are synonyms because cell death, as it occurs during physiological development, can exhibit nonapoptotic features. It is also becoming clear that mitosis and apoptosis are toggled or correlated in some manner and that the balance achieved depends on signals received from appropriate growth or survival factors (Bowen, 1993).

It is important for biomedical study to detect apoptosis to further understand normal tissue development, disease progression, drug effectiveness, and optimal drug delivery. At present, apoptosis detection typically involves the use of fluorescence assays, stains, or biomarkers. As explained in Section 21.1 of this chapter, such processes are not suitable for studying live cells over extended time periods. Label-free imaging, in particular phase contrast microscopy, is more favorable. At the time of this writing, there is one published work on automated apoptosis detection in phase contrast microscopy images (Huh et al., 2012). We introduce the algorithm and discuss future directions for investigation.

Similar to the flow of analysis as presented in Huh et al. (2011) and Huh and Chen (2011), Huh et al. (2012) first detects image regions that are candidates for apoptotic cells, then applies a classifier to validate if a candidate is indeed an apoptotic cell. In finding candidate image regions for apoptotic cells, it draws on the visually observable morphological aspect of apoptosis, namely the rounding-up of the cell and the reduction of cellular volume. As the apoptotic cell rounds-up, the increased thickness would make it appear brighter in positive phase contrast microscopy, and consecutive frames over time would show expansion of the bright area around the cell. As the apoptotic cell reduces in volume, the previously dark cell area would show shrinkage over successive frames.

Huh et al. (2012) modified the method proposed in Yin et al. (2012) to segment both bright and dark cell areas. Note that the revised method resembles a special case of the approach later proposed in Su et al. (2012). After the cell areas are detected, Huh et al. (2012) incorporates temporal information to determine if the detected bright cell areas are candidates for cells that undergo the beginning of apoptosis. To accomplish this, it examines whether there is increase in the bright area around a cell over consecutive image frames, as well as if there is decrease in the dark area of a cell over these frames. Only when there is sufficient change will that bright cell be considered a candidate for an apoptotic cell. Parameters used include the number of consecutive frames to examine, the radius of the image neighborhood to check, and the threshold for minimum change. These parameters are computed using training data to attain a certain level of high recall and as high a precision measure as possible.

From the candidate cell regions, Huh et al. (2012) form candidate patch sequences using standard correlation tracking. For each patch in the candidate patch sequence, it computes two features to capture the visual characteristics of apoptosis. One feature is a brightness change histogram, computed over each patch and its preceding patch in the sequence, to represent brightness change over time. The other feature is the rotation invariant uniform local binary pattern ($LBP^{riu2}$) (Ojala et al., 2002), as a way to encode the texture in an apoptotic cell as it undergoes the process, such as nuclear *fragmentation* and plasma membrane *blebbing*. As noted in Huh et al. (2012), these features are robust to global illumination variations.

For candidate sequence validation, Huh et al. (2012) employed a linear support vector machine and achieved around 90% average precision and recall on data of high cell density. As the authors pointed out, using more sophisticated classifiers such as those proposed in Huh et al. (2011) and Huh and Chen (2011) did not attain higher performance. The intuition is that the morphological aspect of apoptosis is not as unique as that of mitosis. To further boost performance, a bidirectional tracking approach may help reduce the false positive and false negative detections.

Although some other publications mention cell death detection, they generally determine it as a byproduct of cell tracking, that is, if the trajectory of a cell terminates during cell tracking, the cell is considered dead. However, this simple heuristic often yields poor results because many cell trajectories terminate due to failures in cell tracking as opposed to actual cell death. In addition, this assumes that cell death occurs at the end of a trajectory, which is not necessarily true because dead cells whose appearances are similar to live cells may still be tracked.

### 21.4.4 CELL DIFFERENTIATION

We obtained the following definition from https://stemcellbioethics.wikischolars.columbia.edu/ Module+3+-+Cellular+Differentiation: cellular differentiation is the normal process by which a cell becomes increasingly specialized in form and function. The classic example is the process by which a zygote develops from a single cell into a multicellular embryo that further develops into a more complex fetus. Cellular differentiation is regulated by many processes and substances including cell size, shape, polarity, density, metabolism, and extracellular matrix composition. Under the influence of these external factors, each cell is programmed to differentiate and eventually mature into its specialized cell, such as heart, muscle, skin, and brain cells.

Similar to the case for cell apoptosis detection in biomedical study, current practice for cell differentiation detection involves reagents, stains, antibodies, or fluorescent dyes, which cannot support continuous monitoring of intact live cells over extended time periods. Label-free imaging such as phase contrast microscopy is more advantageous; however, research on automated detection of cell differentiation in phase contrast microscopy is preliminary. We present a published work on detecting muscle myotubes (Huh et al., 2013). During the differentiation of muscle stem cells, muscle myotubes are formed by the fusion of mononucleated progenitor cells known as myoblasts. Given a phase contrast microscopy image containing both myoblasts and myotubes, the goal of muscle myotube detection is to identify the area where myotubes are located, that is, to determine whether or not each pixel of the image belongs to myotubes. This information is useful for measuring how far differentiation has progressed and provides guidance for human intervention. Figure 21.9 shows an example of myotube formation.

Huh et al. (2013) adopts a supervised learning framework for differentiation detection. Given a training set of pairs of phase contrast microscopy images and the corresponding manually labeled image that indicates differentiated cell regions, it learns a statistical model over the training samples, based on which differentiated cell regions are determined for images in the testing dataset.

First, it restores the artifact-free phase contrast microscopy images. It then divides the images into segments, or superpixels, based on pixel intensity similarity. Superpixel segmentation not only lowers the computational cost by reducing the number of samples to be examined, but also enhances the detection accuracy by incorporating neighborhood information. Huh et al. (2013) adopted the entropy

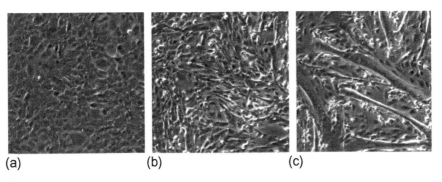

(a)                              (b)                              (c)

**FIGURE 21.9**

Process of myotube formation: (a) single-nucleated myoblasts; (b) nascent myotubes; and (c) mature myotubes formed by the additional fusion of myoblasts with nascent myotubes.

rate superpixel segmentation method (Liu et al., 2011), which can explicitly control the size balance, with the reported parameter setting. The third step is feature extraction. Over each superpixel area, Huh et al. (2013) quantifies the texture pattern using the rotation invariant uniform local binary pattern ($LBP^{riu2}$) (Ojala et al., 2002), and measures the distribution of the pattern labels as a feature vector for each image. The number of features is reduced by applying singular value decomposition. For validation, Huh et al. (2013) utilizes the extracted features to train a linear support vector machine over superpixels. The superpixels that contain more positive pixels than negative ones are used as positive samples and the opposite cases are used as negative samples. Testing is also conducted over superpixels; as a result, the pixels belonging to the same superpixel are determined to have the same label. Huh et al. (2013) reported superior performance compared with that of the method where feature extraction was performed on phase contrast microscopy images rather than the restored artifact free images. Huh et al. (2013) also demonstrated that significant performance gain was achieved by adopting the superpixel scheme.

The proposed supervised learning framework could potentially apply to the detection of other types of differentiation, as long as sample data where differentiated cell regions are annotated is available; temporal information could also be incorporated into the framework to possibly improve the performance for detecting differentiation in an image sequence. Work on automated detection of cell differentiation is still in the early stage. Huh et al. (2013) explored detecting cell regions that contain differentiation and focused on individual images; more investigation is warranted to study the evolution pattern of cell differentiation over time.

## 21.5 SYSTEMS FOR ANALYZING CELL POPULATIONS IN TIME-LAPSE IMAGING

From Sections 21.2 to 21.4, we examined the computer vision tasks necessary for understanding cellular dynamics involving cell segmentation and cell behavior understanding, namely cell migration tracking, cell division detection, cell death detection, and cell differentiation detection. We discussed the problem definition, the state of the art, and promising future directions for each of the computer vision tasks. While no individual task can be considered a mission accomplished and each warrants further investigation, there is a pressing practical need for integrated systems that can automatically analyze time-lapse images of cell populations in phase contrast microscopy.

At the time of this writing, commercially available systems that offer automated analysis of cell images typically perform cell counting without the capability for tracking or other cellular behavior understanding. For instance, Sysmex's CellaVision (https://www.sysmex.com/us/en/Products/Hematology/CellImageAnalysis/Pages/Cell-Image-Analysis.aspx) is designed for cell identification after histological staining for pathology purposes or disease diagnosis; similarly, Medica's EasyCell assistant (http://www.medicacorp.com/products/hematology-imaging-analyzers/) identifies white blood cell types for hematology imaging; and Nexelom's products (http://www.nexcelom.com/Products/) specialize in cell counting in brightfield and multichannel fluorescence microscopy. The systems that appear to offer cell tracking capability all operate within fluorescence microscopy, and time-lapse fluorescence image sequences are generally much shorter than time-lapse phase contrast image sequences because of the issue of light phototoxicity; therefore, the task of automated tracking is not as challenging. Some examples are PerkinElmer's Volocity (http://www.perkinelmer.com/industries/

lifesciencesresearch/cell-imaging/image-analysis.xhtml/), which is primarily an image acquisition tool for confocal fluorescence microscopy with limited tracking capabilities because it is imaging a small area of intracellular components, usually at high resolution; GE Healthcare Life Sciences' IN Cell Analyzer (http://www.gelifesciences.com/webapp/wcs/stores/servlet/catalog/en/GELifeSciences-ca/brands/in-cell-analyzer/) has been advertised to segment and track cells in fluorescence microscopy; outside the commercial domain, CellProfiler (http://www.cellprofiler.org/) is a free open source software primarily designed for fluorescence imaging. To the best of our knowledge, there is no publicly available system, fee-based or free, that offers automated analysis of cellular dynamics in a population in time-lapse phase contrast microscopy images.

Work on integrated systems for automated analysis of cellular dynamics in phase contrast images has so far been limited to academia, likely due to the lack of maturity of existing algorithms, and the nontrivial overhead associated with integrating heterogeneous research codes into a user-facing system where users are biomedical researchers, not computer scientists. Kanade et al. (2011) presents a system that integrates automated cell segmentation, mitosis detection, and cell tracking functionalities, utilizing techniques introduced in Yin et al. (2012), Liu et al. (2010), and Bise et al. (2011), respectively. Figure 21.10 is the schema. On top of the computer vision analysis, the system computes metrics useful for biomedical researchers, and provides a graphical user interface (GUI) that is intuitive for them to check the experiment progress. As soon as a new biology experiment is started and images are captured, uploaded, and processed, all the results (segmentation, mitosis detection, tracking, and cell metrics) can be viewed in the GUI. The GUI also offers an offline mode during an online experiment so that a user can review the results in the previous image frames. Compatible to the GUI, Kanade et al. (2011) additionally offers a web application as a lightweight tool that enables biomedical researchers to monitor their experiments from anywhere with an internet connection.

Ker et al. (2011) details an experiment employing the system developed in Kanade et al. (2011) for automating the decision process for real-time adaptive subculture of stem cells. The decision on subculture has been traditionally based on human operators' visual assessment of cell confluency, which is inherently subjective, prone to intra- and inter-operator variability, and expensive with skilled labor. Applying the system developed in Kanade et al. (2011), confluency measurements are computed based on cell segmentation results, fit to a predictive model (e.g., second-order polynomial), and used to objectively determine the appropriate time to subculture cells. In addition to the local and web GUI where the user can conveniently monitor the experiment, the system alerts the user by email and text

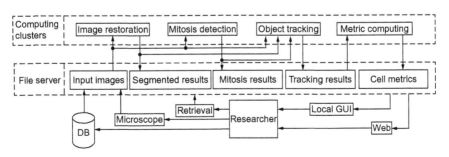

**FIGURE 21.10**

A computer vision system for cell image analysis.

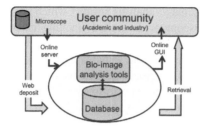

**FIGURE 21.11**

An open bio-image analysis ecosystem.

messaging 4 hours prior to reaching a predefined confluency threshold so that preparations for cell culture can be made, and an additional reminder is sent when the predefined threshold for confluency is reached. Yin et al. (2011) further improves the prediction method in Ker et al. (2011) using a data-driven approach to learn the cell growth model from a training set of cell culture experiments, and to build a linear subspace using principal component analysis. For a new experiment with the same cell culture condition as the training set, it projects the observed confluency data onto the linear subspace to predict future confluency. This data-driven approach achieves more accurate prediction than parametric models often used for data fitting, such as polynomial or exponential models.

We would like to make a point of the vision that was emerging in Kanade et al. (2011), the vision of building an open collaborative research community that shares data, expertise, tools, and resources across the boundaries of institutions and geography, enabled by the internet and web-based technologies. Figure 21.11 further illustrates this vision. Biomedical researchers around the globe can upload images from their database to the shared file server or capture images in real time and upload them online. Once images are uploaded to the shared file server, the shared computing clusters run cell image analysis algorithms to process images, compute relevant metrics, and output results to the file server. Biomedical researchers can retrieve image analysis results to check their experiment progress via a web-based GUI that can be accessed using any internet-ready device (e.g., mobile, wearable), without having to watch over the experiment in their lab for hours. Such an open collaborative ecosystem promises to collectively advance the state of the art because computer vision researchers benefit from more and more diverse data and expertise from biomedical researchers around the globe to develop more robust and powerful analysis tools, which in return benefits the biomedical researchers who contributed the data or expertise and who may not have access to computer vision skills or high-performance computing resources. This vision may sound utopian, but it is within reach if there is collective will.

## 21.6 OPEN SOURCE CELL IMAGE SEQUENCE DATA

Time-lapse images of live cells take special expertise and resources to acquire. In order to invite broader participation to advance the field, it is necessary to have open source data available for research purposes. Open access data also enable meaningful and rigorous performance comparison, when different algorithms are evaluated on the same data.

More and more researchers are making their data (sometimes even computer programs) openly available from their personal websites. We spotlight two relatively more extensive and elaborative open data repositories. http://celltracking.rit.albany.edu/login.php is a website that offers time-lapse phase contrast microscopy image sequences and the corresponding ground truth data and processing results. There are a total of 48 image sequences obtained under four different cell culture conditions, rendering 12 sequences under each culture condition. The images are captured every 5 min and each sequence consists of 1000 images at the resolution of 1392 × 1040 pixels. Using this site, researchers can download either single sequences of images or groups of sequences of images. http://www.codesolorzano.com/celltrackingchallenge/Cell_Tracking_Challenge/Datasets.html is a website that provides 2D and 3D time-lapse video sequences of fluorescently counter-stained nuclei or whole cells moving on top or immersed in a substrate, along with 2D phase contrast and differential interference contrast microscopy videos of cells moving on a flat substrate of varying rigidity. With more cell image analysis contests offered at conferences, we anticipate that there will be more open source data available and more benchmarking of performance.

In this chapter, we examine the computer vision tasks necessary for analyzing cellular dynamics in time-lapse phase contrast microscopy images. We discuss the problem definition, the state of the art, and promising future directions for each of the computer vision tasks. We overview the landscape of existing commercial and open source systems that offer automated cell image analysis, and advocate for building an open bio-image analysis ecosystem to foster broader and deeper collaborations that will catalyze momentous progress in this important field.

# REFERENCES

Achanta, R., Shaji, A., Smith, K., Lucchi, A., Pascal, F., Sabine, S., 2010. Slice superpixels. EPFL Technical Report 149300.

Al-Kofahi, O., Radke, R.J., Goderie, S.K., Shen, Q., Temple, S., Roysam, B., 2006. Automated cell lineage a rapid method to analyze clonal development established with murine neural progenitor cells. Cell Cycle 5 (3), 327–335.

Alberts, B., Johnson, A., Lewis, J., 2002. Molecular Biology of the Cell, fourth ed. Garland Science, New York.

Ambuhl, M., Brepsant, C., Meister, J.J., Verkhovsky, A., Sbalzarini, I.F., 2012. High-resolution cell outline segmentation and tracking from phase-contrast microscopy images. J. Microsc. 245, 161–170.

Arulampalam, M., Maskell, S., Gordon, N., Clapp, T., 2002. A tutorial on particle filters for online nonlinear/non-Gaussian Bayesian tracking. IEEE Trans. Signal Process. 50 (2), 174–188.

Bise, R., Yin, Z., Kanade, T., 2011. Reliable cell tracking by global data association. In: Proceedings of IEEE International. Symposium on Biomedical Imaging.

Bowen, I.D., 1993. Cell Biology International 17. Portland Press, Great Britain, pp. 365–380.

Davidson, L., Keller, R., 2001. Basics of a light microscopy imaging system and its application in biology. In: Periasamy, A. (Ed.), Methods in Cellular Imaging. Oxford University Press, New York, pp. 53–65.

Debeir, O., Van Ham, P., Kiss, R., Decaestecker, C., 2005. Tracking of migrating cells under phase-contrast video microscopy with combined mean-shift processes. IEEE Trans. Med. Imaging 24 (6), 697–711.

Debeir, O., Mégalizzi, V., Warzée, N., Kiss, R., Decaestecker, C., 2008. Videomicroscopic extraction of specific information on cell proliferation and migration *in vitro*. Exp. Cell Res. 314 (16), 2985–2998.

Dormann, D., Libotte, T., Weijer, C., Bretschneider, T., 2002. Simultaneous quantification of cell motility and protein-membrane-association using active contours. Cell Motil. Cytoskel. 52 (4), 221–230.

Dufour, A., Shinin, V., Tajbakhsh, S., Guillen-Aghion, N., Olivo-Marin, J.C., Zimmer, C., 2005. Segmenting and tracking fluorescent cells in dynamic 3-D microscopy with coupled active surfaces. IEEE Trans. Image Process. 14 (9), 1396–1410.

Dzyubachyk, O., van Cappellen, W.A., Essers, J., Niessen, W.J., Meijering, E., 2010. Advanced level-set-based cell tracking in time-lapse fluorescence microscopy. IEEE Trans. Med. Imaging 29 (3), 852–867.

El-Yaniv, R., Pechyony, D., 2007. Transductive rademacher complexity and its applications. In: Proceedings of the 20th Annual Conference on Learning Theory, pp. 157–171.

Grimm, H.P., Verkhovsky, A.B., Mogilner, A., Meister, J.J., 2003. Analysis of actin dynamics at the leading edge of crawling cells: implications for the shape of keratocyte lamellipodia. Eur. Biophys. J. 32, 563–577.

House, D., Walker, M.L., Wu, Z., Wong, J.Y., Betke, M., 2009. Tracking of cell populations to understand their spatio-temporal behavior in response to physical stimuli. In: Proceedings of Workshop on Mathematical Modeling in Biomedical Image Analysis (MMBIA), Miami, FL, USA, pp. 186–193.

Huh, S., 2013. Toward an automated system for the analysis of cell behavior: cellular event detection and cell tracking in time-lapse live cell microscopy (doctoral dissertation). Technical Report, CMU-RI-TR-13-06.

Huh, S., Chen, M., 2011. Detection of mitosis within a stem cell population of high cell confluence in phase-contrast microscopy images. In: Proceedings of IEEE Conference on Computer Vision and Pattern Recognition, pp. 1033–1040.

Huh, S., Ker, D., Bise, R., Chen, M., Kanade, T., 2011. Automated mitosis detection of stem cell populations in phase-contrast microscopy images. IEEE Trans. Med. Imaging 30 (3), 586–596.

Huh, S., Ker, D.F.E., Su, H., Kanade, T., 2012. Apoptosis detection for adherent cell populations in time-lapse phase-contrast microscopy images. In: Proceedings of International Conference on Medical Image Computing and Computer Assisted Intervention, pp. 331–339.

Huh, S., Chen, M., Su, H., Kanade, T., 2013. Efficient phase contrast microscopy restoration applied for muscle myotube detection. In: Proceedings of International Conference on Medical Image Computing and Computer Assisted Intervention.

Kaakinen, M., Huttunen, S., Paavolainen, P., Marjomaki, V., Heikkila, J., Eklund, L., 2014. Automatic detection and analysis of cell motility in phase-contrast time-lapse images using a combination of maximally stable extremal regions and Kalman filter approaches. J. Microsc. 253 (1), 65–78.

Kanade, T., Yin, Z., Bise, R., Huh, S., Eom, S., Sandbothe, M., Chen, M., 2011. Cell image analysis: algorithms, system and applications. In: Proceedings of IEEE Workshop on Applications of Computer Vision, pp. 374–381.

Ker, D.F.E., Weiss, L.E., Junkers, S.N., Chen, M., Yin, Z., Sandboth, M.F., Huh, S., Eom, S., Bise, R., Osuna-Highley, E., Kanade, T., Campbell, P., 2011. An engineered approach to stem cell culture: automating the decision process for real-time adaptive subculture of stem cells. PLoS ONE 6 (11), e27672.

Kroemer, G., et al., 2015. Classification of cell death: recommendations of the nomenclature committee on cell death 2009. Cell Death Different. 16.1 (2009), 3–11. PMC Web.

Lesko, M., Kato, Z., Nagy, A., Gombos, I., Toandro, Z., Viandgh, L., Viandgh, L., 2010. Live cell segmentation in fluorescence microscopy via graph cut. In: 20th International Conference on Pattern Recognition (ICPR), pp. 1485–1488.

Li, K., Miller, E., Weiss, L.E., Campbell, P.G., Kanade, T., 2006. Online tracking of migrating and proliferating cells imaged with phase-contrast microscopy. In: Proceedings of Computer Vision and Pattern Recognition Workshop, pp. 65–72.

Li, K., Miller, E.D., Chen, M., Kanade, T., Weiss, L., Campbell, P.G., 2008a. Cell population tracking and lineage construction with spatiotemporal context. Med. Image Anal. 12 (5), 546–566.

Li, K., Miller, E.D., Chen, M., Kanade, T., Weiss, L.E., Campbell, P.G., 2008b, Computer vision tracking of stemness. In: Proceedings of IEEE International Symposium on Biomedical Imaging, pp. 847–850.

Li, F., Zhou, X., Zhao, H., Wong, S., 2009. Cell segmentation using front vector flow guided active contours. In: 12th International Conference on Medical Image Computing and Computer-Assisted Intervention. Springer-Verlag, pp. 609–616.

Liu, A.A., Li, K., Kanade, T., 2010. Mitosis sequence detection using hidden conditional random fields. In: Proceedings of IEEE International Symposium on Biomedical Imaging.

Liu, M.Y., Tuzel, O., Ramalingam, S., Chellappa, R., 2011. Entropy rate superpixel segmentation. In: Proceedings of IEEE Conference on Computer Vision and Pattern Recognition, pp. 2097–2104.

Liu, A., Hao, T., Gao, Z., Su, Y., Yang, Z., 2013. Nonnegative mixed-norm convex optimization for mitotic cell detection in phase contrast microscopy. Comput. Math. Methods Med, November, 2013, Article ID 176272, 10 pp.

Morency, L.P., Quattoni, A., Darrell, T., 2007. Latent-dynamic discriminative models for continuous gesture recognition. In: Proceedings of IEEE Conference on Computer Vision and Pattern Recognition, pp. 1–8.

Mukherjee, D.P., Ray, N., Acton, S.T., 2004. Level set analysis for leukocyte detection and tracking. IEEE Trans. Image Process. 13 (4), 562–572.

Murphy, D., 2001. Phase Contrast Microscopy. Fundamentals of Light Microscopy and Electronic Imaging. Wiley-Liss, New York, pp. 97–112,

Nketia, T., Rittscher, J., Noble, A., 2014. Utilizing phase retardation features for segmenting cells in phase contrast microscopy images. Medical Image Understanding and Analysis, 2014.

Ojala, T., Inen, M.P., Ma, T., 2002. Multiresolution gray-scale and rotation invariant texture classification with local binary pattern. IEEE Trans. Pattern. Anal. Mach. Intell 24 (7), 971–987.

Padfield, D., Rittscher, J., Roysam, B., 2009a, Coupled minimum-cost flow cell tracking. In: Proceedings of International Conference on Information Processing in Medical Imaging, pp. 374–385.

Padfield, D., Rittscher, J., Thomas, N., Roysam, B., 2009b. Spatio-temporal cell cycle phase analysis using level sets and fast marching methods. Med. Image Anal. 13, 143–155.

Press, W.H., Teukolsky, S.A., Vetterling, W.T., Flannery, B., 2007. Numerical Recipes: The Art of Scientific Computing, third ed. Cambridge, New York.

Rost, F., Oldfield, R., 2000. Phase-Contrast Microscopy. Photography With a Microscope. Cambridge University Press, Cambridge, England, pp. 131–136.

Roweis, S., Ghahramani, Z., 1999. A unifying review of linear Gaussian models. Neural Comput. 11 (2), 305–345.

Shen, H., Nelson, G., Kennedy, S., Nelson, D., Johnson, J., Spiller, D., White, M.R.H., Kell, D.B., 2006. Automatic tracking of biological cells and compartments using particle filters and active contours. Chem. Intell. Lab. Syst. 82 (1-2), 276–282.

Smal, I., Draegestein, K., Galjart, N., Niessen, W., Meijering, E., 2008. Particle filtering for multiple object tracking in dynamic fluorescence microscopy images: application to MI-crotubule growth analysis. IEEE Trans. Med. Imaging 27 (6), 789–804.

Smith, K., Carleton, A., Lepetit, V., 2008. General constraints for batch multiple-target tracking applied to large-scale video microscopy. In: Proceedings of IEEE Conference on Computer Vision and Pattern Recognition (CVPR), Anchorage, AK, USA.

Su, H., Yin, Z., Huh, S., Kanade, T., 2012. September phase contrast image restoration via dictionary representation of diffraction patterns. In: Medical Image Computing and Computer Assisted Intervention—MICCAI.

Su, H., Yin, Z., Huh, S., Kanade, T., 2013. Cell segmentation in phase contrast microscopy images via semi-supervised classification over optics-related features. Med. Image Anal. 17 (7), 745–765.

Su, H., Yin, Z., Kanade, T., Huh, S., 2014. Interactive cell segmentation based on correction propagation. In: IEEE International Symposium on Biomedical Imaging.

Ta, V.T., Lézoray, O., Elmoataz, A., Schüpp, S., 2009. Graph-based tools for microscopic cellular image segmentation. Pattern Recogn. 42, 1113–1125.

Wu, K., Gauthier, D., Levine, M., 1995. Live cell image segmentation. IEEE Trans. Biomed. Eng. 42 (1), 1–12.

Xiong, G., Zhou, X., Ji, L., Bradley, P., Perrimon, N., Wong, S., 2006. Segmentation of drosophila RNAI fluorescence images using level sets. In: IEEE International Conference on Image Processing (ICIP), pp. 73–76.

Yang, F., Mackey, M.A., Ianzini, F., Gallardo, G., Sonka, M., 2005. Cell segmentation, tracking, and mitosis detection using temporal context. In: Proceedings of the 8th International Conference on Medical Image Computing and Computer Assisted Intervention (MICCAI), Palm Springs, CA, USA, pp. 302–309.

Yin, Z., Ker, D.F.E., Junkers, S.N., Kanade, T., Chen, M., Weiss, L.E., Campbell, P.G., 2011. Data-driven prediction of stem cell expansion cultures. In: The 33rd Annual International Conference of the IEEE Engineering in Medicine and Biology Society.

Yin, Z., Kanade, T., Chen, M., 2012. Understanding the phase contrast optics to restore artifact-free microscopy images for segmentation. Med. Image Anal. 16 (5), 1047–1062.

# Index

Note: Page numbers followed by *f* indicate figures and *t* indicate tables.

**515**